Oxford AQA Psychology

A LEVEL YEAR 2

w/D

Simon Green
David Cox
Rob Lewis
Kevin Silber
Julia Willerton

OXFORD
UNIVERSITY PRESS

OXFORD
UNIVERSITY PRESS

Great Clarendon Street, Oxford, OX2 6DP, United Kingdom

Oxford University Press is a department of the University of Oxford. It furthers the University's objective of excellence in research, scholarship, and education by publishing worldwide. Oxford is a registered trade mark of Oxford University Press in the UK and in certain other countries

© Oxford University Press 2016

Authors: David Cox, Simon Green, Rob Lewis, Kevin Silber and Julia Willerton

The moral rights of the authors have been asserted

First published in 2016

British Library Cataloguing in Publication Data available

978-1-40-852739-9

10 9 8 7 6 5 4 3 2 1

Paper used in the production of this book is a natural, recyclable product made from wood grown in sustainable forests.

The manufacturing process conforms to the environmental regulations of the country of origin.

Printed in Great Britain by Bell and Bain Ltd., Glasgow.

Contents

Contents

Introduction

By now, half way through your A Level Psychology course, you are familiar with the nature of psychology, its variety of different topics, and the range of research methods. The second year of the course builds on the foundations from the first year. You will need a deeper knowledge of research methods, so this book will continue the approach of the Year 1 text; besides chapters dedicated to research methods, throughout the remaining chapters the methods used by researchers in psychology will be illustrated and linked back to the research methods section.

A range of compulsory and optional topics will enable you to broaden and deepen your knowledge of psychology. At the end of the course you will be familiar with many core topics in psychology and with some more specialized areas chosen by you and your teacher. If you choose to pursue degree-level study in psychology, you will have had an excellent introduction. If you choose to pursue alternative career paths, you will have acquired a range of what we call transferable skills. Psychology is unusual in combining the skills of the scientist, including statistics and research design, with the ability to think conceptually and to develop skills of oral and written communication. Students successful in A Level Psychology will find they have a number of transferable skills highly valued in today's work environment. This book will help you to develop these skills.

Structure of the book

This book is designed for students who have completed the first year of the AQA Psychology specification. After revisiting and expanding research methods, the chapters that follow cover the specification precisely. Coverage of Issues and debates is compulsory. This is followed by chapters on each of the optional topics; Relationships, Gender, Cognition and development, Schizophrenia, Eating behaviour, Stress, Aggression, Forensic psychology, and Addiction.

Throughout Issues and debates and the options there is discussion of research methods relevant to that chapter, and links to the research methods chapter. The best way to fully understand research methods is to do small-scale studies with your teacher; suggestions for appropriate studies occur in each chapter.

Key features of the book

EXAMPLE EXAM QUESTION

Example exam questions are given throughout the book on the full range of topics.

Exam hint

Exam hints accompany example exam questions, giving you expert guidance on what to look out for.

KEY STUDY

Certain research studies are described in detail. All studies mentioned in the AQA specification are provided as 'key studies'.

THINKING SCIENTIFICALLY

'Thinking scientifically' features contain important information about how to evaluate key studies.

Link

Link boxes appear throughout the book and link to further information on topics.

Research methods link

Link boxes appear throughout the book and link back to the **Research methods** section.

Key term

These are the terms given on the specification that you will need to be able to define and understand.

ACTIVITIES

Short activities for home or the classroom aim to develop your understanding of the subject.

PRACTICAL ACTIVITY

A suggestion for a practical investigation is included at the end of each chapter.

Exam focus

At the end of every chapter there is an example exam question, model student answers, and examiner feedback.

Assessment objectives

These were covered in Book 1, but as the key to good marks is to fulfil the assessment objectives it is worth reminding you what they are.

AO1 – Demonstrate knowledge and understanding of scientific ideas, processes, techniques and procedures

AO2 – Apply knowledge and understanding of scientific ideas, processes, techniques and procedures:

- In a theoretical context
- In a practical context
- When handling qualitative data
- When handling quantitative data

AO3 – Analyse, interpret and evaluate scientific information, ideas and evidence, including in relation to issues, to:

- Make judgements and reach conclusions
- Develop and refine practical design and procedures

You will need to develop the ability to analyse and evaluate psychological theories, concepts, studies, and findings. This may involve what we call methodological evaluation of studies to determine whether they are valid and whether the findings are reliable. In addition, the significance of findings for our understanding of behaviour is a major issue in evaluating studies. Finally, in some questions you will need to be able to apply your knowledge and understanding to unfamiliar situations. For instance, given a particular scenario, can you apply your knowledge of the causes of schizophrenia to explain why someone is experiencing symptoms of the disorder?

Throughout the specification there is an emphasis on research methods and findings, and your understanding of these will be assessed in the examination. You will build on the skills you acquired in the first year. These include relating research findings to theories and models, understanding how to carry out psychological investigations, and the ability to select appropriate methods. Additional skills include evaluation of research methods in terms of, for instance, validity and ethics, and the application of psychological findings to the real world. As you can see, many of these skills relate to the Research methods topic. Others overlap with the analytic and evaluative assessment objectives mentioned earlier. This is why it is important not to worry too much over which assessment objective you are dealing with at any particular time.

The examination is designed so that if you answer the question set you will automatically be satisfying the various assessment objectives, so do not waste time worrying whether a question is AO1, AO2, or AO3. You must read the question carefully and look for the command words – for example, explain, discuss, briefly outline, outline, evaluate – and do what it asks. For instance, if there is a scenario and you are asked to answer the question with reference to the scenario, then you must do this to have a chance of full marks. For more guidance on the exam and how to develop your exam skills, see page 536.

Assessment at A Level

There are three papers at A Level. For Papers 1 and 2 all questions are compulsory, so you will need to have covered all the specification content for these papers. All papers will use a mix of question styles, from multiple-choice and short answers to extended writing. Note that research methods questions may occur in any paper, besides the specific research methods section of Paper 2.

- Paper 1 – Introductory topics in psychology: Social influence, Memory, Attachment, Psychopathology (covered in Book 1)
- Paper 2 – Approaches in psychology, Biopsychology, Research methods (covered in Book 1, extended in Book 2)
- Paper 3 – Issues and debates (compulsory), Option 1 (one from Relationships, Gender, Cognition and development), Option 2 (one from Schizophrenia, Eating behaviour, Stress), Option 3 (one from Aggression, Forensic psychology, Addiction)

After revisiting research methods, the sequence of Paper 3 topics in this book follows the A Level specification.

If all goes well you will complete your A Level in psychology successfully. You probably began the course not really knowing what to expect, but by the end of the course you will have realized what a varied subject psychology can be. Although research methods can be dry, you can now call yourself a budding scientist, familiar with research methods. You will also be aware of how psychology helps us to understand many aspects of human behaviour, from short-term memory to the treatment of offenders. Even if you do not pursue psychology at university, we hope that studying the subject to A Level with this book gives you those transferable skills mentioned earlier, plus fond memories of a fascinating and very relevant subject.

Dave Cox, Simon Green, Rob Lewis, Kevin Silber, and Julia Willerton

Research methods

Introduction

The goal of psychology is to describe behaviour, predict behaviour, and ultimately control or change behaviour. This is not an easy task. Whilst people are naturally drawn to observe the behaviour of others and develop their own theories to explain what they see, humans are, alas, characterized by their biased and faulty thinking. We cannot therefore rely on such observations to be free from things like prejudice and emotional distortion.

Psychological evidence must be gathered as dispassionately as possible, and this is achieved through the use of the scientific method. This emphasizes the use of empirical evidence, i.e. evidence gathered by means of objective observation and measurement. It is an orderly, systematic approach to finding things out, and the knowledge gained through scientific procedures is considered the most dependable. It is the scientific method that has enabled the accumulation of a vast knowledge-base about behaviour. In order to be able to understand its value and appreciate how psychologists come to the conclusions they do, it is essential to know about the research processes that created this knowledge.

In this section we will be looking at some of the most important scientific methods used in psychological research. We will also look at the kinds of data gathered by this research, how this data is analysed, and how conclusions about behaviour are drawn from this data.

What is covered in Research methods?

Research methods and experiment designs

Experimental methods

A great deal of psychological knowledge has been gained by the use of experimental methods. In experiments, psychologists seek to control and manipulate events in order to establish precise cause-and-effect relationships. There are a number of types of experiments: laboratory, field, natural, and quasi-experiments.

Laboratory experiments

A **laboratory experiment**, sometimes referred to as a 'true' experiment, has three key features: direct manipulation of an independent variable, control, and randomization.

Direct manipulation of an independent variable

The **independent variable (IV)** is something that is altered by the researcher to bring about a change in behaviour. This change is measured as the **dependent variable (DV)**. It is important that these variables are **operationalized**. This means that it must be clear what the variables are and how they are measured. For example, if a researcher was interested in looking at the influence of alcohol on memory then he or she would need to be clear about the type and quantity of alcohol, and how exactly its effects on memory are going to be tested. A lack of such clarity can have serious consequences for the findings and conclusions of research.

The logic behind manipulating the IV to see the effect on the DV is returned to frequently elsewhere in this chapter.

Control

Control is achieved when, other than the independent variable, all other variables (known as **extraneous variables**) are held constant, so that changes in the dependent variable can only be due to the manipulation of the independent variable. Control is also accomplished by having a control group and one or more experimental groups. Participants in the experimental group receive the independent variable treatment and participants in the control group do not. The control group then provide a baseline measure. If all other variables are controlled then any difference in outcomes between the control and experimental groups must be due to the independent variable. Control is discussed further on page 15.

Randomization

Participants are randomly allocated to conditions, for example by flipping a coin or using odds and evens with a random numbers table. This is to ensure that any extraneous influence associated with the participant is as likely to affect one group as the other and will therefore have little or no influence on the dependent variable. Other things are randomized too, for example the order in which stimuli are presented to participants, and the order in which participants take part in the experiment. Randomization is discussed further on pages 13–14.

Key terms

Laboratory experiment: an experiment that is carried out in a controlled environment where the independent variable is manipulated and extraneous variables are controlled, and cause-and-effect relationships are established.

Independent variable (IV): the variable that is manipulated in an experiment.

Dependent variable (DV): something that is measured following manipulation of the IV.

Operationalization of variables: how variables are defined and measured.

Extraneous variable: an unwanted variable that adds error to an experiment.

ACTIVITY 1: LABORATORY EXPERIMENTS

Look through the Key Studies in the chapters on Issues and debates in psychology, Relationships, and Gender. Select one laboratory experiment and identify the following features:

(a) The independent variable (IV)

(b) The dependent variable (DV)

(c) Variables that were controlled.

Field experiments

Field experiments are controlled studies that take place in natural settings. Like a laboratory experiment, the independent variable is manipulated in an effort to find a causal relationship. As this method seeks to measure natural behaviour, participants are often unaware that they are involved in research. The dependent variable is the behaviour of the participant.

ACTIVITY 2: FIELD EXPERIMENTS

Look through the Key Studies in the chapters on Social influence, Memory, and Attachment in Book 1. Identify one field experiment and answer the following questions:

(a) What was the independent variable (IV)?

(b) What was the dependent variable (DV)?

(c) What extraneous variables were controlled?

(d) What did the researchers fail to control that might have had an effect on the results?

Key terms

Field experiment: an experiment that takes place outside a laboratory environment, where the independent variable is manipulated and cause-and-effect relationships can be inferred.

Natural experiment: an experiment where naturally occurring changes in independent variables are observed.

Quasi-experiment: an experiment where participants cannot be randomly assigned to experimental and control groups.

Natural experiments

In a **natural experiment** the independent variable is unplanned and has occurred because of a naturally occurring event. Sometimes, practical and ethical reasons dictate that this is often the only experimental method that can be used. Because the event is not planned by researchers, there is no control over variables and no direct manipulation of the independent variable. As a consequence, it is more difficult to pinpoint a cause-and effect relationship due to particular variables.

Quasi-experiments

In many kinds of research participants cannot be randomly assigned to experimental and control groups. In such cases, rather than random assignment to conditions, participants are often matched in some way, for example males may be in one condition and females in another, but they are matched for age, educational background, or other important variables. Strictly speaking, there is no control condition in a **quasi-experiment**, rather there is a comparison condition; for example, if we are comparing males to females in some regard, one is not providing a control (baseline) condition but a point of comparison between the two conditions.

The terms quasi- and natural experiment are often used interchangeably, or the natural experiment is considered a type of quasi-experiment. One key way to identify the difference between a quasi- and a natural experiment is regarding the extent to which there is planned manipulation of the independent variable. It is not possible to do this in natural experiments, but it is possible in quasi-experiments.

Strengths and limitations of experiment types

	Strengths	Limitations
Laboratory experiment	• High levels of control of extraneous variables. • High degree of replicability. • Cause-and-effect relationships can be uncovered.	• Reduced ecological validity. • Increased risk of investigator effects and demand characteristics. • Participants are often required to behave in ways that are artificial.
Field experiment	• Cause-and-effect relationships can be uncovered. • Higher levels of ecological validity than a true experiment. • Reduction in demand characteristics.	• Reduced control over extraneous variables. • Often more time consuming.
Natural and quasi-experiment	• Useful where it would be impractical or impossible to manipulate variables. • High levels of ecological validity.	• Not always possible to clearly identify cause-and-effect relationships.

Table 1 Strengths and limitations of different types of experiment

Experimental design

A basic experiment involves two conditions: one in which the variables are held constant (the control condition) and another in which the independent variable is manipulated (the experimental condition). If all variables other than the independent variable are held constant, then any difference in outcomes between the two conditions must be due to the independent variable. In each condition there are participants, and a decision has to be made when designing an experiment whether participants will take part in one or both conditions.

There are three types of experimental design: independent groups, repeated measures and matched pairs.

Independent groups design

In the **independent groups design**, different participants are used in each of the conditions, i.e. each group of participants is independent of the other. In a true experiment, the condition in which each participant is placed is decided randomly. By random allocation it is hoped that participant variables balance out across conditions, although of course there is always the chance that they will not. The effect of participant variables on results can be reduced by increasing the size of the sample – 'outlier' scores (extreme scores) have less effect when there are more scores.

An example would be when a sample of 20 participants is selected to take part in a study on working memory. They are divided into two groups by the toss of a coin. Ten participants will be in the control condition, where they will silently read through a list of words before being tested for recall. The other ten participants will be in the experimental condition and read through a list of words while repeating the word 'the' out loud. They are then tested for recall. The performance of participants in one group is independent of the performance of participants in the other (see Fig. 1).

Control condition	Experimental condition
Participant 1	Participant 11
Participant 2	Participant 12
Participant 3	Participant 13
Participant 4	Participant 14
Participant 5	Participant 15
Participant 6	Participant 16
Participant 7	Participant 17
Participant 8	Participant 18
Participant 9	Participant 19
Participant 10	Participant 20

Fig. 1 An example of independent groups design

Repeated measures design

In the **repeated measures design**, the same participants are used in each of the conditions of the experiment. So for example, participants in one condition might be required to read through a list of words whilst repeating the word 'the' out loud before being tested on their recall of the list. The same participants would also read through a list of words in silence before being tested for recall (see Fig. 2).

This design avoids the problem of participant variables encountered in independent groups designs. Any difference in scores between the two conditions cannot be because people in one condition just happen to be better at the task than ones in the other condition. There are drawbacks with this design however. For one, two sets of stimulus materials will need to be developed, and these will need to be carefully assessed as being equivalent to one another in all respects. Also, it may be that the scores in the two conditions are different because the same participants were used. For example, they may have improved through practice, or become fatigued. These are order effects, and researchers must take steps to minimize these when using a repeated measures design. There are two principle methods of dealing with order effects: counterbalancing and randomization.

Control condition	Experimental condition
Participant 1	Participant 1
Participant 2	Participant 2
Participant 3	Participant 3
Participant 4	Participant 4
Participant 5	Participant 5
and so on	and so on

Fig. 2 An example of repeated measures design

Key term

Repeated measures design: an experimental design where each participant takes part in all conditions of the experiment.

Key terms

Counterbalancing: a strategy for reducing order effects by ensuring that participant variables occur with equal frequency in all conditions of the experiment.

Randomization: the process of using chance to decide the order in which participants experience the experimental or control condition when using a repeated measures design. It is also used to decide the order of use of stimuli.

Matched pairs design: an experimental design where participants in each condition of the experiment are matched according to important variables.

Confounding variable: an uncontrolled variable that has an effect on the dependent variable.

Counterbalancing

The **counterbalancing** strategy for reducing order effects has half the participants doing one condition first, and the other half of the participants the same condition second. In this way, any order effects are balanced between the two conditions and thus should have no greater effect on the overall scores of one condition than another. For example, if we label the experimental condition 'A' and control condition 'B' then, as can be seen in Figure 3, we can counterbalance so that some participants do A first and some do B first.

Participant 1 – A	Participant 1 – B
Participant 2 – B	Participant 2 – A
Participant 3 – A	Participant 3 – B
Participant 4 – B	Participant 4 – A
Participant 5 – A	Participant 5 – B
Participant 6 – B	Participant 6 – A

Fig. 3 An example of counterbalancing: order effects are balanced between the two conditions

Randomization

This strategy involves **randomizing** the order of trials. Rather than participants alternately experiencing one condition first then the other, researchers randomly assign whether or not participants do one or other condition first. As in other cases where researchers use the mathematical properties of chance, such as in random sampling, this is an example of researchers using chance to control variables.

Matched pairs design

In the **matched pairs design**, participants are matched as closely as possible with another participant. They are then randomly allocated to one condition or the other. For example, if researchers were investigating the effects of watching prosocial films (films that promote social acceptance) on the behaviour of children, they might want to match children on their prior levels of prosocial behaviour. Once two children are matched on this important variable, one child could be randomly assigned to the experimental condition (exposure to prosocial films) and the other to the control condition (no exposure to prosocial films).

In some ways matched pairs could be seen as a design somewhere between independent groups and repeated measures – it allows researchers to use the same stimulus materials for all participants, thus eliminating one potential **confounding variable**. As the pairs are matched on the important variables, it also reduces participant variables and the impact of individual differences. However, these benefits are dependent on the ability of researchers to both identify the key characteristics that need matching and then to effectively match pairs on this variable. This is a complex and indeed often impossible task, leading some researchers to argue that the only true matched pairs design is one using identical twins.

Design	Strengths	Limitations
Independent groups design	• There are no order effects. • As both conditions can be tested simultaneously, there is a potential saving of time and effort. • As participants are involved in one condition only, potential investigator effects and demand characteristics are reduced.	• Participant variables may affect the results. By chance, participants in one group may differ in some crucial way to participants in the other. • Participants are only doing one condition, therefore twice as many participants are needed for this design compared to repeated measures.
Repeated measures design	• Uses fewer participants – get two or more scores per participant, saving time, effort and money. • Participant variables are not a concern.	• There is a risk of order effects and, because of the need to limit these, the design can be a complex one. • The cost of a loss of participants is greater, since data for both conditions is lost compared to one in independent groups design.
Matched pairs design	• Good control of participant variables. • Eliminates order effects.	• Matching participants is very difficult.

Table 2 Strengths and limitations of experimental designs

Variables and control

A defining feature of the laboratory experiment is the manipulation and control of variables. By only having one thing differing between conditions (the independent variable), researchers can conclude that any difference in the measured behaviour of participants (the dependent variable) must be due to this one thing that differs. That researchers can say that the manipulation of the variable caused the difference is the great strength of the experimental method. However, this can only be said to the extent that all other important variables have been controlled, so that researchers can confidently say that only the manipulation of the IV caused the change.

Control is essential to the experimental method. However, the reality is that it is virtually impossible to eliminate interference from unwanted variables. These variables that have unwanted effects are called **extraneous variables**, and an essential part of the design of an experiment is to ensure that extraneous variables have as little influence on the outcome as possible.

Extraneous variables can come from *random error*. A random error is something that cannot be predicted, such as a participant's state of mind during the experiment, or something physical like having a cold (or even being cold!). Because random errors are just that – random – then the only way to deal with them is by randomly allocating participants to experimental and control conditions, so that the effect of errors might be balanced out and therefore have minimal impact. One source of random errors comes from a lack of **standardization**. Standardization means that all participants in a study have exactly the same experience, so that individual experience does not cause some participants to engage with the study differently. Procedures therefore need to be standardized to ensure that all participants have the same experience. For example, the instructions given to participants need to be exactly the same so that if there is an error in interpretation it then affects all participants in all conditions.

Key terms

Extraneous variable: an unwanted variable that adds error to an experiment.

Standardization: a means of ensuring that all participants in an investigation have exactly the same experience.

Extraneous variables can also come from *constant error*. These errors are more serious than random errors because they have more of an effect on one condition of the experiment than the other. A typical source of constant error is when participant characteristics affect one condition more than the other, often a result of failing to counterbalance or randomize. Randomization in this sense is not just used to randomly allocate participants to conditions in a repeated measures design, but also to randomly allocate order or use of stimuli. For example, an extraneous variable might arise from the order of words presented to participants in a memory recall task – perhaps the words at the end of the list are less familiar than those at the start.

A constant error that remains uncontrolled in an experiment becomes a confounding variable. This is something that has an effect on the dependent variable, thus making it is impossible to say that the DV is the result of the IV – it could well be one or more constant errors causing the difference.

ACTIVITY 3: CONTROLS

A psychologist is conducting an experiment to investigate whether time of day influences reaction time. The psychologist invites participants to complete a computer-based game during which coordination errors are recorded. Participants complete this game either at 12 midnight or at 6am.

(a) Identify one likely source of random error.
(b) Identify one likely source of constant error.
(c) Outline three controls that you would use in this experiment to deal with extraneous variables.

Observational techniques

Observational techniques are useful when the researcher wants to study natural behaviour. This might involve, for example, discovering the circumstances under which certain behaviours occur and their frequency. On the face of it, this resembles what we as humans do anyway – 'people-watch'. We are constantly watching the behaviour of others and inferring causes and origins for what we see. Observation as a scientific method, however, involves making objective systematic observations. What is to be recorded from observations is planned in advance, before the observations begin, based on clear and testable hypotheses. This ensures that observations are recorded as objectively as possible.

Types of observation

There are different types of observation, varying in the degree to which they reflect natural behaviour, the extent to which the participants know they are being observed, and the level of involvement of the researcher in the observational context.

Controlled versus naturalistic observation

Laboratory experiments often involve observations of behaviour. For example, a psychologist might investigate the likelihood of a person administering electric shocks to another participant with and without another person present. This would be an example of a **controlled observation**. Alternatively, researchers may want to observe behaviour in entirely natural settings. For example, they may wish to investigate the queuing behaviour of shoppers. There is no control of the setting and people make their own choices about how they behave. This is called **naturalistic observation**.

	Strengths	Limitations
Controlled observation	High level of control. Easier to establish cause-and-effect relationships.	The environment is artificial, therefore you may not get natural behaviour.
Naturalistic observation	High degree of natural behaviour meaning findings can be generalized to everyday life.	No control of variables so difficult to establish cause-and-effect relationships.

Table 3 Strengths and limitations of controlled and naturalistic observations

ACTIVITY 4: CONTROLLED OBSERVATION

Ainsworth's Strange Situation (page 164 in Book 1) is an example of a controlled observation.
(a) State one limitation of this example of a controlled observation.
(b) How might researchers make this controlled observation a naturalistic one? What drawbacks might they face in doing this?

Covert versus overt observation

Psychologists will often choose to observe behaviour without revealing themselves, so that participants are not aware that they are being observed. Observations may take place from hidden viewpoints, from secret cameras, or from behind two-way mirrors. A psychologist might even become a member of a group in order to observe behaviour of individuals, hiding their true intentions and identity. These are known as **covert observations**.

When participants know that their behaviour is being watched and recorded they are taking part in an **overt observation**. With overt observation the psychologists are usually open with the participants about the purpose and scope of the research.

	Strength	Limitation
Covert observation	More valid results from participants because natural behaviour is being observed.	Lack of informed consent means there are ethical issues
Overt observation	Ethically sound as participants know they are being observed and will have given consent.	Participants may not behave naturally if they are aware of being observed.

Table 4 Strengths and limitations of overt and covert observations

Participant versus non-participant observation

Participant observation involves the researchers becoming part of the group or situation that is being observed. For example, if the queuing

Key terms

Controlled observation: observation that takes place in a highly controlled environment such as a laboratory setting.

Naturalistic observation: observing people in their natural environment without control over variables.

Covert observation: observation that takes place without the knowledge or awareness of participants.

Overt observation: observation that takes place with the full knowledge and awareness of participants.

Participant observation: data is gathered by the psychologists whilst being part of the observed group or situation.

behaviour of shoppers is being investigated, then a psychologist might do their observations in the role of a shopper in a queue.

On the other hand, behaviour may be observed at a distance so that the researchers are not involved in what they are observing. In the example of queuing behaviour, the psychologist may pretend to be another shopper at a distance while observing behaviour, or record the behaviour from hidden cameras. This is **non-participant observation**.

	Strengths	Limitations
Participant observation	Greater insights into behaviour are gained by being part of the group/situation, increasing validity of findings.	Objectivity of observations are affected by being part of the group/situation.
Non-participant observation	Lack of direct involvement ensures greater objectivity.	Data lacks richness of that provided by participant observation, e.g. feelings and motivations of participants.

Table 5 Strengths and limitations of participant and non-participant observations

Observational design

To reduce observer bias and ensure that observations really are guided by the hypotheses, it is essential that the 'what' and 'how' of observations are planned in advance. Researchers have to be clear about exactly what behaviour is being observed and exactly how that behaviour is going to be measured and recorded. Without careful consideration of this it is possible that the result will not do what it claims to be doing (i.e. it will lack validity) and that there will be observer bias. Designing observations carefully is essential for reducing observer bias. People in everyday life often interpret the same events differently and it is important that, as far as possible, this tendency is eliminated from psychological research. This is done by making observations systematic and objective through the use of a coding system.

Behavioural categories

It is important to be clear about what the target behaviour actually is. For example, if researchers were interested in observing aggressive behaviour of primary-aged children during school breaks, then at the start researchers would need to decide on what exactly constitutes aggressive behaviour. Aggression can be defined in a number of ways, and many activities in a playground that might look aggressive to a casual observer might not constitute aggression from a psychological perspective. Clarifying what is meant by aggression will involve creating an exhaustive list of all possible behaviours in the playground that would fit the definition of aggression.

This list gives the researchers their **behavioural categories**. The next step would be to develop a coding system so that observations can be made efficiently and objectively. These behavioural categories and codes would be used on an observational checklist, which is used to record the observations. If the researchers want an indication of the degree to which something has occurred, such as a measure of the response to an aggressive behaviour from another child, then they might also include a scale.

Once an observational checklist has been created, a decision has to be made about how the observations will be conducted. For instance, how long the observational period will be and how frequently the observations will be recorded on the checklist.

Event sampling

One option for recording behaviours is to use **event sampling**. This is basically to record on the checklist the number of times a particular thing occurs. For example, researchers might record the number of shoves, kicks and punches observed during the school playtime (see Fig. 4). The chronological order of events is not taken into consideration; this is nothing more than a frequency count.

Slap	III
Kick	I
Push	IIII
Pinch	I
Poke	II

Fig. 4 Example of behavioural categories using event sampling in a study of types of playground aggression

Time sampling

It might be that the order of events is important in the observation. In this case the researchers would record when an event occurs. For example, observations could be taken at predetermined intervals of 30 seconds which are then recorded chronologically (see Fig. 5).

Behaviours	1 (30 secs)	2 (30 secs)	3 (30 secs)	4 (30 secs)	5 (30 secs)	6 (30 secs)	7 (30 secs)
Slap	I		I	I			
Kick				I			
Push	I		I	I		I	
Pinch		I					
Poke					I		I

Fig. 5 Example of behavioural categories using time sampling in a study of types of playground aggression

Although careful design of an observational checklist should maximize the objectivity of observations, in practice it is difficult to be absolutely certain that observations of behaviour will be recorded in the same way by all observers (that is, to ensure that observations are absolutely reliable). There are a number things that researchers can do to ensure a high degree of agreement between observers, and these are discussed in the section on reliability on page 43.

Key terms

Event sampling: a record on an observational checklist of the number of times an event occurs.

Time sampling: a record of an event made on an observational checklist after a standardized interval.

Self-report techniques

As the title suggests, **self-report techniques** require participants to somehow report on themselves. This is typically done by getting participants to answer questions or respond in some way to statements. Two principle methods of doing this are questionnaires and interviews.

Strengths	Limitations
• Allows more detailed access to participant thoughts and feelings. • Enables psychologists to investigate what participants might think, feel, or do in the future.	• They rely on participants being honest, articulate and insightful, which might not always be the case. • Participants may feel they need to give socially desirable answers.

Table 6 Strengths and limitations of self-report techniques

Questionnaires

A **questionnaire** is a list of predetermined questions to which participants must respond. By asking questions the researcher typically seeks to find out what people think and feel about something – in other words, they want to establish the attitudes of people.

There are a number of ways in which a questionnaire can be administered, each having their own advantages and disadvantages depending on such things as the content of the questionnaire, and how important it is that participants do not conspire or are distracted.

- In presence of researcher: questionnaires could be given out to individuals to complete, or to groups of individuals. It may even be conducted over the telephone.
- In absence of researcher: questionnaires could be sent through the post or, as is increasingly the case, via the internet as an email or web page.

Strengths	Limitations
• Can be cost-effective and time-efficient since they can be quickly administered to large numbers of participants. • When completed privately and anonymously they can provide honest data, improving reliability. • The reduced involvement of the researcher lessens the risk of investigator influence on the behaviour of participants.	• Response rates can be poor when administered in absence of the researcher. It can then be difficult to generalize findings. • It may be that only certain people return them, e.g. those who are motivated or who have the time, so that results only represent a certain type of person. • It is difficult to phrase questions in ways that are not open to interpretation by the participants.

Table 7 Strengths and limitations of questionnaires

Questionnaire construction

An effective questionnaire needs a good response rate and needs to be well designed. A poorly designed questionnaire does not become better because lots of people have completed it. There are a number of important considerations when constructing a questionnaire. One is to consider the sequence of questions. For example, it is usually better to start with easy questions that put respondents at ease rather than make them defensive. Some questions might be included that have little relevance to the research aim. These can be useful in obscuring the main purpose of the research so that demand characteristics are reduced (you can read more about demand characteristics on page 36). Another thing to consider is the format of the questions. Questions need to be written in a way that not only makes them clear and not open to interpretation, but also in a way that makes them easy to analyse. There are two basic types of question: open and closed questions.

Closed questions

Closed questions only allow participants to respond in certain kinds of ways. Typically, the questionnaire will provide a fixed number of responses from which the participant selects the one that applies to them. These could be yes/no responses, multiple category choices, or even rating scales where participants are asked to indicate on a scale the extent to which they agree or disagree with something.

'I love Psychology.'	
Yes	☐
No	☐
Don't know	☐

'I find Psychology stimulating.'

|___|___|___|___|___|___|
1   2   3   4   5   6

Not very   Very

A Level Psychology	Excellent	Good	Fair	Poor
Text book				
Class materials				
Classroom				
Topics				

Fig. 6 Some examples of closed questions

Strengths	Limitations
• Good when asking questions with finite, clear-cut answers.	• You need to know the range of answers to the questions.
• Provide control by requiring answers and in a particular way.	• Can frustrate respondents, e.g. when their preferred answer is not available.
• Require minimum effort to answer.	• Can create a lack of engagement.
• Saves time, especially in analysis.	• Longer questionnaires cause fatigue.

Table 8 Strengths and limitations of questionnaires

Open questions

Open questions allow respondents to answer freely without restriction. They allow respondents to answer in more depth, giving opportunities to explain answers and express opinions, providing good qualitative data. Open questions may even contain unexpected content that gives the researchers new lines of enquiry.

What do you feel is the best thing about your Psychology course?

....
....
....
....
....

If you could change one thing about A Level Psychology, what would it be and why would you want the change?

....
....
....
....
....

Fig. 7 Examples of open questions

Strengths	Limitations
Offers flexibility to the respondent in the way he/she responds.	Provide qualitative data which can be difficult to analyse.
Good when you do not know the range of possible answers to put into closed questions.	More time consuming for participants to answer.
Good way of accessing motivations and feelings.	Questions may not be answered in helpful ways, e.g. difficult to interpret.

Table 9 Strengths and limitations of open questions

Interviews

Interviews involve researchers and participants engaging in a face-to-face conversation, so that rather than participants responding to written questions they respond to the verbal questions of the investigator. The way that questions are asked can either be very fixed or can have a considerable degree of flexibility.

Strengths	Limitations
• A well-conducted interview can address sensitive complex issues that other methods are unable to. • Interviews are a good source of **qualitative data**.	• Participant responses can be influenced easily by researchers. • Interviews work best with participants who are confident, honest and articulate. • Interviews are highly dependent on the skills of the interviewer, especially with unstructured interviews.

Table 10 Strengths and limitations of interviews

Structured interviews

Structured interviews involve the use of a set of predetermined questions. The structured interview can appear in many respects like a questionnaire, but the questions are asked rather than written down for the participant to answer themselves. The responses of participants are recorded, either electronically, manually, or a combination of both.

Unstructured interviews

In **unstructured interviews**, the researcher works more to a framework than a set of predetermined questions. There may be questions that are formulated in advance, but the structure of the interview is more likely to be guided by themes than explicit questions. This allows the interviewer to respond to the answers given by the interviewees; for example, to seek clarification or expansion and to pursue new lines of enquiry. It is therefore a much more flexible way of conducting interviews.

Key terms

Structured interviews: an interview that follows a predetermined set of questions.

Unstructured interviews: a flexible interview based around themes rather than fixed questions, allowing interviewers to respond to the answers of interviewees.

	Strengths	Limitations
Structured interviews	Because all participants have the same questions it is possible to compare responses and thus identify trends and patterns.	More time consuming than a questionnaire, often with little obvious additional benefit.
Unstructured interviews	Allows the interviewee to go into more depth and detail than a structured interview.	The information gathered is difficult to analyze objectively. There is an increased risk of investigator bias. Requires considerable skill on the part of the interviewer to be done well.

Table 11 Strengths and limitations of structured and unstructured interviews

Design of interviews

In many respects, the considerations that apply to questionnaire design also apply to the design of interviews.

Interviews can contain open and closed questions, although the latter is less usual. Since the aim is to get as much useful information from participants as possible, it is important to give very careful consideration to the questions being asked. A number of factors will influence this, not least whether the interview is going to be structured or semi-structured. It is important to ensure that the questions being asked are the right questions to get the right kind of information from interviewees with the desired detail. Also, the questions must be worded in such a way so that they cannot be misinterpreted and do not trigger a social desirability response in the interviewee. For example, if a researcher was interviewing a parent about their child-rearing practices, a question such as 'How often do you beat your child?' might not get a very accurate response. It may be that some of the interviewees 'beat their child' but trying to access this information with a question like that is almost certainly going to be unsuccessful.

It is usually good practice to start interviews with basic factual questions and questions of less importance to the research. Interviewees are likely to be most nervous and guarded in their responses at the start of an interview, giving poorer answers to questions. The questions most likely to give the detailed information you want are therefore best left to later in the interview.

Research has shown that the type of interviewer is a factor in interviews, depending on the nature of the interview. For example, the age and gender of the interviewer might influence responses in interviews dealing with sexual matters. Another example is the potential cultural biases that might arise when the interviewer is from a different ethnic group to the interviewee.

Consideration must not only be given to the characteristics of the interviewer but also to interviewing skills. It is not easy to conduct a good interview as it requires well-developed communication skills and lots of practice in interviewing. Often considerable training is needed to ensure that the interviewer has the skill to make the interviewee feel at ease, and that they appear trustworthy so that the interviewee gives full and natural answers.

Correlations

When two or more variables are in some way associated we say they are **correlated**. Correlational studies therefore are ones that look for relationships between variables. The variables being measured are known as **co-variables**. Rather than being a research method as such, correlation is more of a technique used to analyse data. It could be that observational or self-report methods were used to gather data, but correlation techniques are used in the analysis of that data.

Correlational studies only allow researchers to infer relationships between variables, and are particularly useful in situations when it would not be possible to do experimental studies. For example, researchers have found a strong correlation between smoking tobacco and lung disease. It would not be possible to do an experiment to prove that smoking causes lung disease as the practical and ethical difficulties are insurmountable. However, the correlation is so strong, even when important factors like lifestyle are taken into account, that it is generally accepted that the relationship is best explained as a causal one.

A correlational analysis will tell us what kind of relationship exists between the variables. Relationships are positive, negative, curvilinear, or zero correlations.

- A **positive correlation** is when as one variable increases, the other variable increases.

- A **negative correlation** is when one variable increases as the other variable decreases.

- A curvilinear correlation is where there is both a positive and a negative relationship between two variables, for example a relationship may start off being positive but end up being negative (see page 61 for a further discussion of this).

- A zero correlation is when there is no clear relationship between variables.

Key terms

Positive correlation: a relationship between co-variables where one variable increases as another variable increases.

Negative correlation: a relationship between co-variables where one variable increases as another variable decreases.

Correlation	Example
Positive	People of less attractiveness tend to choose less attractive dates.
Negative	The more that people are vaccinated for a specific illness, the less that illness occurs.
Curvilinear	As temperature increases so do levels of aggression, but as temperature continues to increase levels of aggression decrease.
Zero	There is no relationship between intelligence and the amount of ice cream eaten.

Fig. 8 Some examples of correlations

Strengths	Limitations
• Correlations allow researchers to investigate situations that could not be done experimentally. • Correlations do not just indicate a relationship but the strength of that relationship.	• Correlations are seriously affected by sample size – the smaller the sample the less accurate the coefficient (see page 26 for more about coefficients). • Correlations cannot reliably establish cause-and-effect. • Correlations only work for linear relationships; they do not work for curvilinear ones.

Table 12 Strengths and limitations of correlations

Correlation coefficient: a statistical measure of the relationship between two variables, i.e. the degree to which changes to the value of one predict changes to the value of another.

Analysis and interpretation of correlations

Correlational analysis tells us more than just whether the variables are related in some way; it also tells us something about the strength and direction of the relationship. The direction, and to some degree strength, of the relationship can be represented visually on a graph called a scattergram (see page 60 for a description of a scattergram). However, the key way that the strength and direction is indicated is by something called the **correlation coefficient**. This is a numerical representation of the relationships between co-variables, calculated by a statistical test, for instance Spearman's rho. It ranges between +1 and −1, the sign indicating whether the correlation is positive or negative. +1 represents a perfect positive correlation: as one variable increases the other variable will always increase. −1 represents a perfect negative correlation: as one variable increases the other variable will always decrease. In reality, psychological investigations simply do not result in perfect correlations like this. The coefficient sits on a sliding scale somewhere between 0 and +1 or −1. The closer the coefficient is to + or −1, the stronger the correlation is. The correlation grows weaker as it nears 0. At 0, there is absolutely no correlation. The sign in front of the coefficient only indicates the type of correlation, not its strength. For example, +0.6 is exactly the same strength correlation as −0.6, the only difference being that one is a positive correlation and the other is negative.

As a 'rule of thumb', when the calculated coefficient falls below 0.5 (either − or +) then it indicates that the coefficient may not be significant (i.e. large enough for us to be confident that there really is a relationship between two variables). This is not always the case however; for example, coefficients below 0.5 can be significant when larger amounts of data are being analysed. As large coefficients are statistically more likely to occur by chance when the sample size is small, researchers need to be cautious about jumping to conclusions in these circumstances when they find a big and impressive coefficient. (The section on inferential analysis on page 66 will explain the process of how it is decided whether or not findings are significant.)

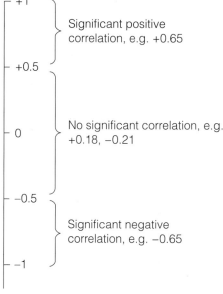

Fig. 9 Correlation scale

The difference between correlations and experiments

The key difference between a correlational study and an experiment is that, unlike experiments, correlations do not reliably point to cause-and-effect relationships. A correlation study gives us an indication of the nature of the relationship between the co-variables, for example if the correlation is positive or negative, but it does not tell us why the co-variables are related. In other words, a correlation does not imply causation.

If, after correlational analysis, a relationship between co-variables is found, the researcher has a decision to make about how the relationship is interpreted. Correlations can occur for a number of reasons, and which reason is selected should be based on a combination of theoretical knowledge and a clear understanding of the data and sample used. For instance, extreme scores (or 'outliers') can distort coefficients considerably, especially with small samples. Also, when a sample is small it is less likely to truly reflect the population it supposedly represents, so conclusions should only be drawn with great caution. As a rule, for statistical reasons, greatest caution should be taken when the sample size is less than 100.

The choices are:

1. **A cause-and-effect explanation.** The researcher could decide that one variable actually caused the other variable to either increase or decrease as the other increased or decreased. However, even though we might elect that a causal relationship is the most likely explanation, the correlation does not prove that this is the case.
2. **A third variable explanation.** Something in the background, other than the measured variables, is creating the apparent relationship between co-variables. For example, there is a relationship between school results and income in later life. School results do not cause increased income, but rather they appear related because of another variable – people who get good grades tend to be harder working.

3. **A chance relationship.** The relationship between co-variables has no meaning beyond chance. Sometimes things appear to be related when in fact they are not – it is just a statistical anomaly, which occasionally happens even with large samples. For example, there is a correlation between teacher salaries and the price of alcohol – as one increases, so does the other. You might look for background economic factors that make these two things look related, but it is almost certainly a chance correlation.

Content analysis

With **content analysis**, behaviour is not directly studied. Rather, it is a process of investigating the content of the medium in which behaviour is recorded. This may be mass media (e.g. TV, film, magazines, etc.), historical documents (e.g. crime records), or any other recorded source. For example, a psychologist might be interested in the different ways in which tabloid newspapers stereotype genders when they describe men and women in their stories. Content analysis is employed when the kind of information sought is either too costly, or not possible or practical to obtain in other ways. It is particularly useful when it is used in conjunction with other methods (known as a 'mixed methods' approach), as the evidence obtained can be used to corroborate data gathered through other methods.

Strengths	Limitations
• It can be relatively straightforward to get access to media that provide rich sources of information.	• There may be a lack of objectivity, since researchers have to make decisions about what behaviour to look for and how to categorize it.
• As the method does not require direct contact with people, investigators cannot influence behaviour.	• It is a description of behaviour rather than an explanation of it.

Table 13 Strengths and limitations of content analysis

Content analysis and coding

Content analysis is basically a statistical process that involves categorizing and quantifying events and aspects of behaviour as they occur in some selected medium. In many respects, the challenges presented by content analysis resemble those in observational studies, the categorizing and coding of events and behaviour. Decisions have to be made very early on about what is being investigated and how this can best be measured. As with other methods, research starts with an operationalized hypothesis, informed by existing theory and research.

As content analysis involves converting content into some kind of objective measure, one of the first considerations is deciding on a coding system relevant to the medium (or 'population') of interest, for example newspaper, film, or web content. Sometimes it is possible to use a pre-existing coding system, validated by previous research. Usually, however, it involves researchers developing their own coding systems. This can be relatively straightforward when dealing with such things as how often a particular word is used, or how many people are involved. Coding is a little trickier when dealing with subjective elements of media, such as interpreting the meaning of what people say or judging emotional responses. Researchers would always need to establish a reliable coding system by repeatedly trialling it, and adjusting it as necessary against samples of material very similar to that which will be used in the eventual study.

As with the observational method, it is important that the reliability of coding is established. This would usually involve at least one independent person using the coding system alongside the researchers, and checking all the coding for close agreement (see page 43 for a description of inter-observer reliability). Following the coding process may be a further thematic analysis of the data, so that the findings are categorized into themes and concepts.

Steps involved in content analysis

Step 1: State the aims and hypotheses. For example, researchers are interested in how mental health is represented in tabloid newspapers and how such reporting might perpetuate negative attitudes towards individuals with mental illness. They hypothesize that tabloid newspapers portray mental health in negative and stereotyped ways.

Step 2: Decide on the sample, that is, the limits of what is going to be analysed. For example, daily tabloids *The Sun* and the *Mirror* published Monday to Friday, over a period of six weeks from the first Monday in May.

Step 3: Decide on units of analysis and develop a coding system. For example, researchers might include the frequency with which mental health issues are reported, the kinds of words used in the reporting, and the emotional content of the reporting.

Step 4: Establish reliability in the coding system. This might be trialled against editions of *The Sun* and the *Mirror* from a period different to that under investigation. Make any adjustments and check for reliability, making further adjustments to the coding system as necessary.

Step 5: Analyse the findings and interpret them in terms of the hypothesis. For example, use qualitative methods (e.g. thematic analysis) and/or quantitative methods (e.g. inferential and descriptive analysis), as appropriate.

Thematic analysis

Thematic analysis is a technique used to identify patterns of meanings and themes within qualitative data. It is used with methods such as case study, content analysis and self-report. Thematic analysis often begins with a process of developing codes with which to label data. The 'data' in this instance are the ideas that you are interested in identifying (i.e. the 'themes'). Having a code which applies to a particular theme makes recording instances of that theme much easier. For example, you may be analysing the content of an interview you have conducted with someone about their childhood school experiences, and this might run to many pages when in text form (called a 'transcript'). Given the context of the research, an example of what you might be looking for could be references to positive feelings about teachers. You might code this 'theme' as 'teacher positive' or 'TP' and note this on the transcript whenever it appears. Negative references to teachers might be coded and recorded as 'NT', and so on (see the discussion of content

> **Key terms**
>
> **Thematic analysis:** a method for analysing qualitative data that focuses on identifying themes and patterns in the data.

analysis on page 28). Researchers will often be already aware of existing theory and research of themes that may emerge from data, and therefore may directly search for themes. Sometimes, however, themes emerge from the analysis which have not been identified in advance.

The data is searched for themes, and similar themes are sorted together. Themes may change as more data is analysed, and new themes emerge. This means that themes are constantly adjusted and data is returned to for further searches of new themes that have emerged. After thorough analysis the themes will be categorized and meaning and patterns within the themes may be identified. When the report is written up, the data within each category provides the evidence for the themes, perhaps presented as, or supported by, direct quotes.

Thematic analysis carries an inherent risk of subjectivity and hence researcher bias. The identification of themes and patterns requires a degree of interpretation, and it is possible that researchers' beliefs may cause differences in how qualitative data is analyzed. While steps should be taken to ensure that subjectivity and its effects are minimized, such as openly identifying possible sources of bias, it is unlikely to be completely eliminated. Such drawbacks, however, are balanced against the richness of data provided by this form of analysis.

Case studies

A **case study** is a detailed investigation of a single individual. It can also be an investigation of an identifiable group of people. Case studies often take place over a period of time, and information is gathered using such methods as observation, interview, psychological tests, and analysis of records (for example, school or medical records). Individuals being studied are often those who are in some way unique or different, such as those displaying the effects of brain damage or consequences of some personal trauma.

Strengths	Limitations
• A great deal of qualitative and **quantitative data** can be gathered, giving a very detailed insight into the person or group. • Allows researchers to study things that they may not be able to any other way.	• A detailed investigation of one person cannot be replicated so it lacks scientific rigour. • The researcher can become too deeply involved with the person or group being studied, affecting objectivity. • The focus on a very small sample means that it is difficult, or sometimes impossible, to generalize the findings.

Table 14 Strengths and limitations of case studies

Scientific processes
Aims and hypotheses

One of the first steps in conducting research is the development of **aims** and hypotheses. An aim is a general statement outlining the purpose of the investigation. It is not invented as such, but derived from a theory. For example, based on what is known about factors that influence human memory, a psychologist might state an aim of research as being 'to investigate the influence of noise on memory'. This is a very general aim. There is nothing wrong with it, but in all likelihood the psychologist will be more informed by existing theory and research, and will have decided what is meant by 'noise' and what 'memory' actually refers to. In this case the aim might be more focused, for example 'to investigate the effects of loud continuous noise on ability to recall random word sequences'.

Having stated the aim the psychologist must now formulate a hypothesis. This is a specific prediction about the outcome of the investigation – a statement that will be tested in the investigation. For example, the psychologist might predict that loud continuous noise will have a negative effect on memory.

However, this is still not a fully written hypothesis. One more thing that must be done is to operationalize the hypothesis. This means that the nature of the variables and how they will be measured must be clear in the hypothesis, and only then will the statement become a testable hypothesis. Having operationalized the variables, the hypothesis might now look something like 'Participants who are exposed to a continuous 100 decibel noise during a task requiring them to learn a random word sequence will have poorer subsequent recall of the word sequence compared to participants who do the task in silence'.

Research hypotheses have different names, depending on the research method. In this case, the hypothesis is predicting that there will be a difference in the performance of participant scores. As this is a hypothesis for an experiment (there is an IV and a DV), it is known as an **experimental hypothesis**. Obviously, hypotheses used with other research methods would not be called 'experimental' hypotheses. When used with correlations, observations, and self-report studies, they are generally referred to as **alternative hypotheses**.

An investigation is carried out to test the hypothesis. It is possible that the results do not support the hypothesis. Does this then mean that the researchers have found nothing? Of course not – in the example of the effects of noise on memory, they will have found that there is no significant difference between the recall of random word sequences in noisy and silent conditions. (The use of the word 'significant' is important here – it is unlikely that there is no difference

> ### Key term
>
> **Aim**: a general statement describing what the study intends to investigate.
>
> **Experimental hypothesis**: a testable statement used in an experiment to predict what will happen in an investigation, i.e. that there will be differences between scores in two or more conditions.
>
> **Alternative hypothesis**: a testable statement used in a non-experimental method to predict what will happen in an investigation.

whatsoever but more likely that the difference was not big enough to be statistically important. This is the idea of statistical significance, which is discussed on pages 66–70.) What the researchers have to do now is reject their experimental hypothesis in favour of something else. This is called the null hypothesis. Inevitably, one hypothesis will be supported and the other will be rejected.

So, whenever researchers formulate hypotheses for their research they will also have constructed appropriate null hypotheses. This is not simply stating the opposite of the experimental or alternative hypothesis – that can just look like another research hypothesis! The null should predict that there is no difference, or relationship, or association, and so on. The null hypothesis is not an afterthought – it is crucial to the scientific method. This is discussed further in the 'Features of science' section on page 46.

Directional and non-directional hypotheses

There are two types of alternative/experimental hypothesis. One type is known as a **directional hypothesis** because it predicts the direction of the results. When hypotheses contain terms like 'greater than' or 'less than' they are being specific about the outcome, and usually indicate that the hypothesis is directional. For example, the following hypothesis is directional because it says that performance in one group of participants will be slower than the other group:

> Reaction time speeds will be slower in participants who have consumed four units of alcohol than in participants who have not consumed alcohol.

A directional hypothesis would be used when previous research indicates that results will go in a particular direction, or when the study is a replication of another which used a directional hypothesis.

Another type of hypothesis is the **non-directional hypothesis**. This is less specific than the directional hypothesis in that it does not predict the direction of the results. When hypotheses contain terms like 'affect' or 'alter' they are not being specific about what the exact outcome will be, and they are usually non-directional hypotheses. For example, the following hypothesis is the previous hypothesis on reaction time but now written as a non-directional hypothesis:

> Drinking four units of alcohol will affect participant reaction time speeds.

Notice that the hypothesis does not predict the particular direction of the effect, only that alcohol will have some kind of effect, maybe speeding it up or maybe slowing it down.

So, when researchers formulate their hypothesis, not only does it have to be written as either an alternative or experimental hypothesis, but it also has to be either directional or non-directional.

Key term

Directional hypothesis: a hypothesis that predicts a very specific direction of outcome of a study, e.g. one thing will be greater than or faster than the other.

Non-directional hypothesis: a hypothesis that does not state a specific direction of outcome of a study, e.g. one thing will affect the other thing.

ACTIVITY 5: HYPOTHESES

Read through each hypothesis and indicate:
(a) Whether it is an experimental/alternative hypothesis or null hypothesis
(b) Whether it is directional or non-directional.

1. People who drive sports cars drive faster than people who drive family saloons.
2. Children exposed to television violence behave more aggressively than children not exposed to television violence.
3. There is a relationship between personality variables measured during childhood and personality variables measured during adolescence.
4. People are more likely to make risky decisions when in a group than when alone.
5. Mood influences the amount of time 10-month-old infants spend looking at complex patterns.
6. As the number of school absences increase exam scores decrease.

Sampling

People who are studied by researchers in order to test theories are known as participants. The selection of participants to take part in research is known as **sampling**. The first step in selecting a sample of participants is to identify the target **population**. The target population is the particular group of people of interest to the research. For example, if you wanted to uncover attitudes to academic work in Year 12 A Level students, then your target population would be Year 12 A Level students. Studying everyone in this population would be impractical – there are many thousands of A Level students in hundreds of schools and colleges. The alternative is to select a number of participants from this population who are representative of everyone else in the population. If the participants in the sample are typical of the people in the population, then the findings can be generalized from the sample to the population. So, if our sample of Year 12 A Level students is representative of the Year 12 A Level student population, whatever we find from our sample could be applied to everyone else in the population who was not part of the study. If the sample is not representative of the target population, then the sample would be biased and we would not be able to apply our findings to anyone other than those who took part in the study. It could be that certain types of people are over- or under-represented. For example, it may be that the sample consists entirely of male students attending a college in a specific area. We could not be sure that the attitude to academic work is either the same or different in schools, in males and females, or even regionally. Our sample is biased, and we have made what is called a sampling error.

To minimize the likelihood of sampling errors we also need to consider the sample size. Generally speaking, the larger the sample the more representative it is of the target population. A large sample however is not always representative. In the above example, our sample could be 500, which appears impressive, but if they are all boys attending private single-sex schools it would be a biased sample. Smaller, more representative samples are better than larger samples that are not representative. Basically, researchers need their sample

Key terms

Sample: the participants selected from a target population to take part in research.

Population: the wider group of people identified as those that findings should apply to.

to be both as large as possible and representative of the population to avoid a biased sample.

Sampling techniques

There are a number of ways of selecting samples in psychological research. Each technique has its strengths and limitations in terms of bias and generalization.

Random sample

In a **random sample**, all members of the target population have an equal chance of being selected to participate in the research. The selection is made according to chance. The logic behind this is that chance selection of participants should mean that no participant characteristic is more likely than another to appear in the sample. This should then reduce (though not eliminate) the likelihood of a biased sample.

There are a couple of ways to create a random sample:

1. **Use computer selection**. For example, all potential participant names or identifying numbers are entered into a program that then selects the required sample size randomly from that data list.

2. **Lottery method.** This is the 'names from a hat' method, where each participant is given a number that is then entered into a lottery. The quantity of numbers selected at random is equivalent to the size of the sample.

Each method has practical implications in terms of how and when they would be used. These can largely be dealt with by common sense. For example, if a population is already recorded as a data set then computer selection would seem logical, and if the population is large then you would have to question how sensible it would be to use the lottery method.

Stratified sample

The **stratified sample** method ensures that the key characteristics of the population are represented in the same proportion in the sample. For example, we might decide that in our study of attitudes to academic work the most vital similarity between the sample and the population is in the proportion of sexes. Now, if the population has 60 per cent female and 40 per cent male, it is essential that our sample also contains 60 per cent female and 40 per cent male participants. We would select the proportions of male and female students by random sampling.

Systematic sample

The **systematic sample** method of selecting participants involves selecting every nth participant from the list of available participants. For example, if the population consists of 200 people and researchers want a sample size of 20, they would divide 200 by 20 giving 10, and every 10th person from the list would be selected to take part. Although participants are selected mathematically, this does not make it a random sample. In the example, every 10th person is selected, but those on the list before the 10th person do not stand a chance of being selected, and the same applies to those lying 11th to 19th, etc.

<aside>

Key terms

Random sample: a sample in which all members of the target population have an equal chance of being selected to participate in research.

Stratified sample: this sampling method aims to ensure that the key characteristics of the population are represented in the same proportion in the sample.

Systematic sample: a mathematical selection of participants, where the population size is divided by the sample size to dictate which participants are selected for the sample.

</aside>

Opportunity sample

The **opportunity sampling** technique simply is that the researchers used whoever was conveniently available. It could be a friend, or someone passing along the corridor at the time.

Volunteer sample

The **volunteer sample** is also called the self-selected sample, which gives a strong hint as to the nature of this sampling technique. Typically, people volunteer themselves as participants in response to adverts in the media, or posters on notice boards. For example, if a psychologist was interested in studying attitudes to weight loss in active dieters, then they might use a notice board in the local health centre where a dieting class is held every week.

> **Key terms**
>
> **Opportunity sample**: a sample that consists of participants who were selected because of their availability.
>
> **Volunteer sample**: a sample where participants self-select.

ACTIVITY 6: SAMPLING

A government report has noted that teachers in England rely less on textbooks than teachers in other countries. Researchers decided to investigate the attitude of Key Stage 5 students in England towards the use of textbooks.

(a) What is the target population in this study?

(b) Identify which sampling technique is most likely to give a representative sample and explain why.

(c) Describe how you would go about gaining a sample of participants using this sampling technique.

Sampling technique	Strengths	Limitations
Random	As the researcher has no control over who is selected, investigator bias is avoided.	Although based on sound laws of mathematical probability that predict that by chance samples should be representative, there is still a possibility that they will not be, thus limiting generalizability.
Systematic	The only input the researcher has is deciding the sample size, therefore it avoids investigator bias.	As with a random sample, there is still a possibility that the sample will not be representative, thus limiting generalizability.
Stratified	By guaranteeing that all key characteristics of the population are present in the sample, it not only avoids investigator bias afterwards, but it is also representative and can be generalized.	If all the key features of the population are not identified then the sample may not be representative, thus limiting generalizability.
Opportunity	Since the selection of participants is very straightforward it is less time-consuming than other techniques.	The researcher may consciously or subconsciously show bias in sample selection, thus limiting generalizability.
Volunteer	Since the selection of participants is very straightforward it is less time-consuming than other techniques.	Sample bias is likely as only certain types of people are motivated to volunteer for research, thus limiting generalizability.

Table 15 Strengths and limitations of sampling techniques in terms of bias and generalization

Pilot studies

Conducting research usually involves a great deal of time, effort and money. It is important therefore that it is right, and that it is not flawed. A key element to this is ensuring that before the researchers conduct their study for real they do a small-scale trial run. By doing this they can check all aspects of their research. For example, as a result of trying out a questionnaire they might discover that certain questions were unclear to participants, or by trialling an experiment they might discover important investigator effects that they should be avoiding. As far as possible, participants who take part in pilot studies should be typical of those expected to take part in the real study. They can offer important insights into their experience of taking part in the study; for example, if boredom had an effect or if they had guessed the purpose of the study and consequently adjusted their behaviour. As a result of the pilot studies, researchers can adjust their design, procedures, and analysis of findings, increasing the reliability and validity of the final research.

Demand characteristics and investigator effects

When taking part in research, participants sometimes try to guess the purpose of the research and change their behaviour accordingly. This change in behaviour is often unconscious, but it can be a deliberate conscious change. The things in the research that give rise to these changes in behaviour (i.e. give hints as to the purpose of the research) are called **demand characteristics**.

There may be a range of motives behind participants altering their behaviour; for example, the participant may be wanting to please the researcher, they may just be nervous, or participants may even be attempting to sabotage proceedings. Whatever the motive, the effect is the same – demand characteristics change what participants do and think, and are confounding variables that can alter the outcome of studies.

It is important that researchers minimize the likelihood of demand characteristics affecting their research. Careful design of a study can often pre-empt demand characteristics and minimize their effects. One way of dealing with them more directly, however, is to use deliberate deception, by telling participants that the study is looking at something other than what it really is. For example, Asch (see Book 1, page 74) did not tell his participants that they were really taking part in an experiment on conformity. There are of course ethical issues with deliberate deception, so it is not something researchers should do without careful consideration.

The more usual solution to demand characteristics in an experiment is to adopt a single blind technique of control. In a true experiment, participants are randomly assigned to a control or experimental condition. Being single blind means that the participant does not know which condition they are in, therefore making it harder to guess what the study is about.

It is also the case that researchers can influence the results of their research. These are called **investigator effects**. It could be that

Key terms

Demand characteristics: subtle clues that make participants aware of what the researcher expects to find or how the participant is supposed to behave.

Investigator effects: the ways that researchers can influence the results of their research, e.g. by unconscious bias.

participants react to something about the investigator, for example their sex or ethnicity, accent or mannerisms. It could even be something subtle in the behaviour of the investigator that, at an unconscious level, biases participants towards the prediction of the study. This latter possibility has been demonstrated many times in psychology. In a classic study by Rosenthal and Lawson (1964), students were given rats that they were told were either 'maze bright' or 'maze dull' and instructed to test their maze-running ability. Those given 'maze bright' rats found that their rats navigated mazes faster than those given 'maze dull' rats, even though the rats were in fact allocated randomly. The students were influenced by what they had been told about the rats beforehand. Rosenthal and Lawson referred to this as 'experimenter expectancy' – the researchers were unconsciously influenced by what they expected to find.

ACTIVITY 7: INVESTIGATOR EFFECTS

A psychologist went into a local school to conduct a study with students. She wanted to know whether gender stereotyping in films had any effect on the attitudes of students towards the opposite sex.

(a) Identify potential investigator effects in this study.

(b) Explain ways in which the study could be designed to minimize these investigator effects.

The most common way to reduce investigator effects is to use a double blind technique of control. This is where neither the participants nor the researchers know the aims and/or conditions of the study. While this still requires an investigator in charge overall, the participants do not come into contact with investigators who can give information or clues about aims, conditions, etc. It has the benefit of not only reducing investigator effects, but, as mentioned previously, demand characteristics too. The double blind technique is a difficult control to set up in a study, but when it is used it is an indicator of good quality research.

Ethical issues

All scientific and professional bodies have codes of conduct governing the behaviour of individuals who operate under their influence. Doctors, for example, are expected to behave in ways that meet the guidance for standards and ethics laid out by the General Medical Council. Chartered Psychologists working in the UK have a *Code of Ethics and Conduct* and a *Code of Human Research Ethics*, produced by the British Psychological Society (BPS). Practioner Psychologists are regulated by the Health and Care Professions Council (HCPC) who have *Standards of Conduct, Performance and Ethics*. It is extremely important that psychologists carefully consider the ethics of their research. Simply put, ethics are moral codes that guide behaviour. As research has the potential to directly or indirectly harm people, researchers have responsibilities to participants to conduct their research in ways that prevent psychological, physical, or cultural harm. Psychologists also need to consider wider issues. For example, some topics of interest to psychologists could be considered to be socially sensitive and findings could have implications far beyond the focus of a particular piece of research.

The BPS *Code of Human Research Ethics* (2010) outlines a set of general ethical principles that apply to all research contexts with human participants. These are a set of four moral principles that are intended to inform the decision-making of researchers, so that the activities of these psychologists reflect the underpinning values of professional psychology. The four principles are outlined in Table 16 below. Each one has a 'value statement', which is further elaborated as a set of standards.

Ethical principle	Value statement
Respect for the Autonomy and Dignity of Persons	'Adherence to the concept of moral rights is an essential component of respect for the dignity of persons. Rights to privacy, self-determination, personal liberty and natural justice are of particular importance to psychologists, and they have a responsibility to protect and promote these rights in their research activities. As such, psychologists have a responsibility to develop and follow procedures for valid consent, confidentiality, anonymity, fair treatment and due process that are consistent with those rights.'
Scientific Value	'Research should be designed, reviewed and conducted in a way that ensures its quality, integrity and contribution to the development of knowledge and understanding. Research that is judged within a research community to be poorly designed or conducted wastes resources and devalues the contribution of the participants. At worst it can lead to misleading information being promulgated and can have the potential to cause harm.'
Social Responsibility	'The discipline of psychology, both as a science and a profession, exists within the context of human society. Accordingly, a shared collective duty for the welfare of human and non-human beings, both within the societies in which psychology researchers live and work, and beyond them, must be acknowledged by those conducting the research.'
Maximising Benefit and Minimising Harm	'In accordance with Ethics Principle 3: Responsibility of the Code of Ethics and Conduct, psychologists should consider all research from the standpoint of the research participants, with the aim of avoiding potential risks to psychological well-being, mental health, personal values, or dignity.'

Table 16 A summary of the four BPS Ethical Principles and their associated 'statement of values'

Each value statement is further elaborated as ethical standards (i.e. the things that psychologists should do in practice to uphold the ethical principles). Some of these are discussed below.

Deception

Deception refers to deliberately withholding information from participants, for example concealing the real purpose of a study; something that the Code says should be avoided. This presents researchers with a conundrum. Presenting participants with all the information about a study may produce demand characteristics that could invalidate the findings, and strict adherence to this standard would mean that a great deal of useful and valuable psychological research would not be done.

In practice, it is accepted that some degree of deception may be necessary in psychological research. For instance, it might be acceptable to withhold information from participants when it is assumed that being deceived would not have affected their willingness to take part. Participants should not be misled if they are likely to object to this when later debriefed. Debriefing occurs after the study and is the process conveying the real purpose of research and ensuring that individuals leave the study unaffected by their participation. If participants do subsequently object then it must be clear to them that they have the right to withdraw from the study at that point and withhold their data.

Consent

This refers to participants agreeing to take part in the study without excessive encouragement or threat. Consent should be sought from participants so that each explicitly agrees to participate knowing the aims and objectives of the research. This is called informed consent. This of course raises similar concerns to those discussed in the context of deception – how exactly do you gain full informed consent without invalidating the research with confounding demand characteristics.

As with deception, this issue is often dealt with by retrospective consent – seeking consent from participants with full disclosure of the aims of the research after they have taken part. Sometimes researchers adopt a policy of prior general consent, where participants agree to take part in a study knowing that it involves some degree of deception. A further option for researchers is to assume presumptive consent, which suggests that if other people have taken part in similar research without a problem then it can be presumed that other participants would have no objection.

The extent to which these are satisfactory solutions to the problems caused by a requirement for consent is debatable and to some extent depends on the aims of the research. For example, it is possible that knowing you are going to be deceived (prior general consent) produces the demand characteristics as much as knowing what the research is about to start with.

Protection of participants

Researchers have a responsibility to ensure that no physical or psychological harm comes to participants taking part in research. In terms of physical harm, participants should not be exposed to risk any greater than they would face in everyday life. For example, if the study is looking at the influence on vitamin supplements on school learning then the risks of taking the vitamins should be no greater when taking part in the study than if supplements were taken outside the research context. Psychological harm is a more vague concept but no less important. This involves preventing participants from embarrassment, stress, or any event that might affect self-esteem.

Basically, participants should leave having taken part in research in the same state as they entered. If psychologists detect at any time during the research that participants are being harmed, or could potentially come to harm, then they must consider terminating the research. This even includes situations where participants say that they are alright or want to continue.

Application of ethical guidelines

Ethical issues in research are not always conveniently black or white. As stated previously, it would be almost impossible to carry out research without some degree of deception. In order to decide whether researchers should be allowed to breach ethical guidelines, a kind of cost–benefit analysis is carried out. This may be by the researchers, an ethics committee that oversees research, or (usually) by both. Essentially, this involves weighing up the likely benefits of a piece of research against the likely costs to the participants. Benefits may include the advantages of such new knowledge and the advancement in understanding offered by it. Costs, on the other hand, might include harm or embarrassment to participants or the social sensitivity of findings. To some extent such analyses always involve an element of opinion and subjectivity, but these are minimized by scrutiny of research proposals by committees rather than individuals, and having very clear rules of conduct of behaviour for researchers.

Most potential ethical issues can be easily predicted and thus dealt with. For example, researchers should seek some form of consent from participants before the study commences. How this is managed depends on the nature of the research. Regardless of how researchers proceed with the issue of consent, it is essential that participants fully understand the implications of giving consent. It should also be stated by researchers that participants have the right to withdraw at any time any data gathered as a result of their participation. Finally, opportunities should also be provided for a full debrief so that any unforeseen negative effects of participation are dealt with. This is especially important when researchers have identified in advance potential risks of physical or psychological harm.

The role of peer review in the scientific process

Having conducted research, psychologists then need to disseminate (spread) it. As many experts as possible should have access to the research so that it is publicly read, evaluated and commented upon by other scientists. This is an integral part of science – the publication and scrutiny of research so that it is validated and added to the body of knowledge.

Once the study is written up as a report by the researchers, it is submitted for publication to a journal. Journals are publications that appear several times a year and contain collections of reports in particular areas of psychology. There are many different journals, and like-minded psychologists all over the world have access to these to keep themselves up to date with current research and thinking.

Reports are not automatically published in journals; they go through a peer review process. Each journal has an editorial board that selects reports for their relevance and quality. These are sent out to other specialists in the field for review. The report is carefully read and is returned by the anonymous reviewers with comments. These comments could suggest it is accepted for publication, or revised before publication. They often recommend that the research is rejected for publication. Many more studies are conducted and written up than are ever published, and this, it is argued, is central to science. Peer review acts as a quality control mechanism, ensuring that only the highest quality scientific research gets put into the scientific and public domains.

Fig. 10 Examples of psychology journals

Peer review is not without its critics, however. Some argue that work that is consistent with existing theory is much more likely to be accepted for publication than research that is 'left field'. Peer review is also subject to bias. A reviewer may have strongly held views at odds with those expressed in the reports. This may influence their views on the quality of the research and thus their recommendations. Finally, there is the 'file drawer' problem. Peer review strongly favours reports that support rather than reject the hypothesis. Therefore, researchers who find that their results support the null are unlikely to try to get their research published. This could lead to misunderstandings, as, for example, one study supporting a theory is published, but a further ten do not ever get seen.

The implications of psychological research for the economy

Other professions have identified their economic value. For example, the Law Society estimates that UK legal services is a market worth over £26 billion, employing over 300,000 people and contributing at least £3 billion to the UK balance of trade. Doing the same for psychology is much more difficult, however. Psychology is more spread out as a profession, and it is almost impossible to judge the economic impact of psychological research that may have been conducted decades earlier – it can contribute in ways difficult to comprehend to the body of knowledge underlying current theory and research. That psychology does indeed make a significant economic impact is indicated by the fact that UK university psychology departments currently receive in excess of £50 million annually in research grants. One criterion for receiving a research grant is the impact that the research has, including its economic impact. However, a great deal of psychological research takes place outside of university, in hospitals, businesses and government departments, and often occurs without contribution from research councils.

The problem is that any economic value placed on psychological research inevitably underestimates its true social value. One could reasonably argue that it is impossible to put a value on improving the quality of life of someone with anxiety, or assisting individuals who cope with constant chronic pain. When such conditions have direct economic impact however, for example because of an inability to work, then it may be possible to calculate an economic benefit. It has been argued that investment in psychotherapy could have considerable positive economic benefits. For example, it is estimated that 40 per cent of people claiming an incapacity benefit are doing so on the grounds of anxiety and depression. The cost of a course of psychotherapy is about equal to one month's lost tax and benefit payment. The clear implication is that investment in psychological services and the research that underpins these services has the potential to make major contributions to the UK economy.

Fig. 11 It is difficult to put an economic value on improving the quality of life

One of the most important goals of psychology is to provide solutions to pressing social problems, such as those associated with violence, drug abuse, senility, or mental health. The economic benefits of such applied research would be much more readily calculable. Most psychological research is not directly applied in this way, however; it is carried out due to curiosity about human nature and animal behaviour. This is not to say that such research has no wider social value and economic value. The value of research outcomes are not always immediately clear, but can have applications and benefits unforeseen at the time of the research. For example, a health worker interested in improving dietary habits might make use of psychological research findings that suggest that restricting access to something actually makes it more attractive. The economic benefits of psychological research in this case are down to the way that psychological knowledge has been applied.

While it is virtually impossible to accurately calculate the economic impact of psychology, its growth in universities, its increased application in business and service industries, and the continuing expansion of psychological services in the health sector suggest that overall psychological research has a positive economic impact.

Reliability

The term **reliability** is used to describe the consistency of a study or some measuring device within a study. If a study can be replicated (repeated with similar results), it is said to be reliable. This idea of replicability is a key feature of science. It should be possible to draw the same conclusions from studies that are repeated time after time, and measuring devices should produce the same results if used in the same way over and over. Without the measuring devices within a study being reliable, the study overall cannot be reliable. If the study was published for other psychologists to read about and comment on, then it would be on the basis that we are confident enough that, if someone else carried out our study exactly the way we did, they would get the same outcomes. If others replicate our study exactly but get different results, then there is a problem with the reliability of our study.

External reliability

When we talk about a test/measure within a study producing similar results if replicated, we are referring to its **external reliability** – the results are consistent. The external reliability of a study is assessed by a method called **test–retest reliability**. This is where a study or a test is repeated several times. For example, if we have devised a way to test very long-term memory for an experiment then we could reasonably assume that if the test were any good we could simply repeat it under similar circumstances and get very similar results. If this were not the case then we could not possibly trust the conclusions of the study – they would be based on very shaky evidence.

To demonstrate test–retest reliability, a correlation between the separate sets of scores could be carried out. Finding a strong positive correlation (so that scores would increase and/or decrease in similar ways) would indicate good reliability and increase confidence in the study and its conclusions. However, there are practical problems with test–retest reliability. For example, results may be influenced by extraneous variables that were not identified and properly controlled either on the first trial or subsequent trials. This might be seen when it is not possible to retest using the same participants, so that significant individual differences influence results.

Ensuring external reliability is important in observational studies. It is vital that an observer is consistent in the way that an observational checklist is used in practice. This can be checked using test–retest reliability methods. For example, an observer could make observations from the same recording on several separate occasions. If there is a strong correlation between the observations then the observer may be observing reliably.

An additional problem arises when there is more than one observer. It is important in these circumstances that observers record events in the same way; to not do so would mean that observations would be inconsistent and therefore lack reliability. This observer reliability can be assessed using **inter-observer reliability**. The observation records of the same event made by all the observers in the study would be

> **Key term**
>
> **Reliability:** refers to consistency of a measure or a study, e.g. if the same results are achieved on another occasion there is said to be reliability.
>
> **External reliability:** the extent to which a study can be replicated.
>
> **Test–retest reliability:** when a test or measure is repeated and gives similar results.
>
> **Inter-observer reliability:** the consistency in the records of two or more observers.

compared. A strong positive correlation in scores would mean that the observations are being made reliably.

Internal reliability

It is important that the measuring instrument used in research has internal consistency; that is, it is constructed in a way that makes it a reliable tool. We can rely on mechanical devices to do what is expected of them, for example stop watches to record time consistently, or a computer program to deliver the same stimuli to all participants. However, a great deal of psychological research relies on such things as questionnaires and tests to measure things like personality or attitude. In these cases it is important that there is consistency within a test so that all items within the test measure the same construct, for example that a measure of some aspect of personality is measuring this throughout the test. One way of ensuring this is the **split-half reliability method**, whereby performance on one half of the test is compared to performance on the other half of the test. For example, if a personality test has 40 items then the score on the first 20 items would be compared to the scores on the second 20 items. A strong positive correlation would indicate **internal reliability** of the test.

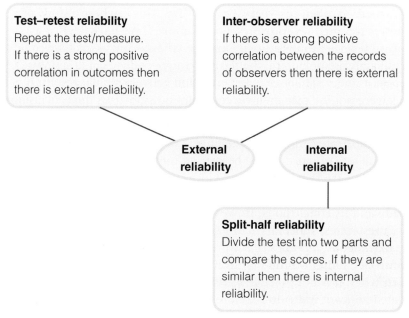

Fig. 12 Ways of assessing reliability

Validity

The term **validity** is used to refer to the extent that something does what it claims to be doing. This could be some tool created to measure something, like a questionnaire to measure personality. The question is, how sure can a researcher be that this questionnaire is truly assessing personality? If there is confidence that it really does do what it says it is doing, then it could be said to be a valid measure of personality. It could also be used to refer to broader concepts, for example whether a study into very long-term memory is really investigating very long-term memory as distinct from long-term memory. If this really is the case, then the study can be said to have validity, in that it really is doing what it says it is doing. Like reliability, validity is an issue that fundamentally affects trust in research – do we trust the data to represent what it claims to, and to what extent can we trust conclusions about behaviour drawn from the study? It is essential therefore that researchers take steps to ensure that their research has validity.

Internal validity

Internal validity refers to tests or measures used in research doing what they claim to do. Internal validity is essential in order to give confidence in the findings and conclusions. For example, if an experiment does not have internal validity then we cannot be sure that the results are only due to the manipulation of the independent variable. It could be that the results are due to something about the test used, demand characteristics, or investigator effects. There must be a sense that the research is doing what it claims to, that it is valid research.

Psychologists use a number of techniques to ensure internal validity. One is to ensure research has **face validity**. A simple and straightforward type of validity, this refers to the extent the research looks (on the face of it) to be doing what it claims to be doing. This might involve one or more expert individuals assessing the design and the measures used in a study to see that they are appropriate to the aims of the study. Of course, this only means that the study or measures in the study *look* as though they are doing what they are intended to – it is not a guarantee that they will, and this is especially the case when the study or measure is of something novel and previously untested.

Another approach to assessing internal validity is to look for **concurrent validity**. This is where the measures in one study (where validity is not known) are compared to measures in another, previously validated study. A strong positive correlation between the two would suggest that the new measure has validity. For example, we may have designed a new and quick way of measuring intelligence. To check for concurrent validity we would compare intelligence test scores on the new test with scores on a well-established intelligence test – if they are very similar then we might argue that our new test has validity. This way of assessing validity is commonly used when psychologists develop new aptitude and ability tests. However, the problem with it is that outcome is only as good as the test to which the new test is compared. If the 'benchmark' test is flawed in some way, then the new test (even if there is a strong positive correlation) would likely contain the same flaws. It can also involve a fair degree of subjective opinion, something that good scientific research always attempts to minimize.

External validity

Research needs to be generalizable beyond the context in which it was carried out. A researcher might be impressed by the results gathered in a tightly controlled laboratory setting on a wet and windy Wednesday evening, but do they apply across people, situations and times? If they do, then they can be said to have external validity.

When research findings can be generalized to settings other than the original research setting, then we say that it has **ecological validity**.

Key terms

Face validity: the extent to which research looks as though it is doing what it claims to.

Concurrent validity: the extent to which a new measure compares to a previously validated measure.

Ecological validity: the extent to which findings can be generalized to other people, situations and times.

This is an important consideration, especially with methods that are highly controlled and less naturalistic, such as laboratory experiments. Researchers do not set out intending that their research will apply only to the sample tested and in the context of the testing. The goal of scientific psychological research after all is to generalize in some way to the population from which the sample was drawn and to give insights into behaviour in general. An example of this in psychology is the series of experiments into obedience to authority carried out by Milgram and his colleagues in the 1960s. When they conducted the experiments in different settings, for example in a university or a rundown office, similar results were found, suggesting ecological validity.

Another way of assessing the external validity of research is to see the extent to which it stands the 'test of time'. If a study is replicated after a period of time and the same or similar results are found then it is said to have **temporal validity**. Whether the period of time between the original study and replication demonstrates temporal validity depends to some degree on the claims of the original study. For example, if it claims something universal about human behaviour (something that is and always will apply), one would reasonably expect to be able to demonstrate this behaviour at any point in the future. The famous Asch studies into conformity could be said to lack temporal validity in that attempts to replicate his original findings have largely failed. It is argued that the high degree of conformity in his study was a reflection of the high rates of social conformity in 1950s USA.

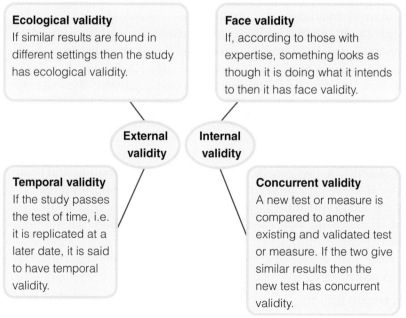

Ecological validity
If similar results are found in different settings then the study has ecological validity.

Face validity
If, according to those with expertise, something looks as though it is doing what it intends to then it has face validity.

External validity

Internal validity

Temporal validity
If the study passes the test of time, i.e. it is replicated at a later date, it is said to have temporal validity.

Concurrent validity
A new test or measure is compared to another existing and validated test or measure. If the two give similar results then the new test has concurrent validity.

Fig. 13 Ways of assessing validity

Features of science

There is no absolutely agreed definition of what psychology is. Some psychologists see it as the study of behaviour, others as the study of human behaviour and mental processes, others still as the study of mental phenomena and processes. What the vast majority of psychologists do agree on, however, is that psychology is a science. As a discipline that attempts to describe, understand, predict, control, and change behaviour, psychology relies heavily on the scientific method.

Objectivity and the empirical method

The scientific approach emphasizes the importance of empirical evidence. This means that evidence is gained through objective observation, experimentation, and measurement of behaviour. Objectivity is the key element here. It means that events are not distorted by emotions and prejudices and are recorded as they actually happen.

Replicability

Replication is essential to scientific research. Findings that cannot be repeated with the same or similar results will not be accepted by the scientific community. Replicability gives confidence that the results are valid and reliable and add to scientific knowledge.

Theory construction and hypothesis testing, and falsifiability

The scientific process begins with an observation of a problem. Maybe this came from academic sources (for example, something seen in published research), it can come from experience (for example, the psychologist has seen something that has piqued their curiosity), or it came from something that needs to be solved (for example, young people starving themselves). This leads to the development of a hypothesis – a testable statement that makes a specific prediction. The next step is to design a study and gather evidence to test this hypothesis. As a result the hypothesis is either accepted or rejected in favour of the null. Further observations are made, and hypotheses proposed and tested. As a result of all of this hypothesis testing, a theory is developed. If data contradicts the theory it will have to be adjusted and further hypotheses will need to be tested. If data continually supports the theory it becomes a law.

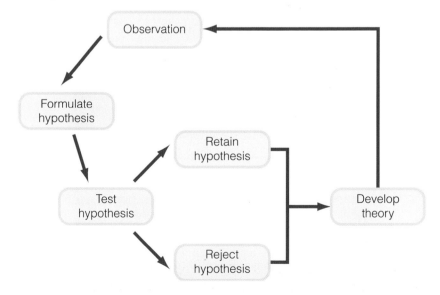

Fig. 14 Hypothesis and theory formation

The philosopher Karl Popper called this process the hypothetico-deductive method. It is based on the idea of **falsifiability** – that a theory has only undergone appropriate scientific scrutiny when researchers have attempted to prove that it is false. By this, he means that research should attempt to falsify the null hypothesis, as we cannot 'prove' the hypothesis. The logic behind this is deceptively simple. Popper used the analogy of the scientist who only ever sees white swans. From this observation he proposes the theory that all swans are white. Observations of any number of white swans will only ever support this theory. We cannot conclusively affirm a hypothesis. However, by seeing just one black swan we can conclusively negate it. So it is with science – no amount of evidence can completely prove that a theory is right, but it takes just one piece of evidence to prove a theory wrong. Thus, for Popper, the scientific method is all about testing the null – it is tested and either accepted, or rejected in favour of an alternative hypothesis. Theories that defy attempts to prove them wrong, over time, become scientific laws. These 'laws' remain in place until there is a 'paradigm shift'.

Paradigms and paradigm shifts

A paradigm is a general theory or law that is accepted by the majority of scientists in that particular field of study. Paradigms are not fixed and unchanging. With time, evidence will accumulate that suggests that the paradigm is less adequate than it was. Eventually, enough evidence will accumulate so that the current paradigm is replaced by another paradigm.

According to the philosopher Thomas Kuhn, science develops through three distinct stages: pre-science, normal science and revolutionary science.

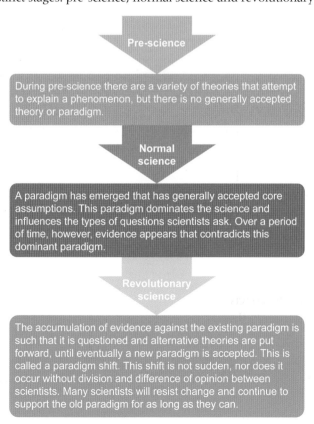

Pre-science

During pre-science there are a variety of theories that attempt to explain a phenomenon, but there is no generally accepted theory or paradigm.

Normal science

A paradigm has emerged that has generally accepted core assumptions. This paradigm dominates the science and influences the types of questions scientists ask. Over a period of time, however, evidence appears that contradicts this dominant paradigm.

Revolutionary science

The accumulation of evidence against the existing paradigm is such that it is questioned and alternative theories are put forward, until eventually a new paradigm is accepted. This is called a paradigm shift. This shift is not sudden, nor does it occur without division and difference of opinion between scientists. Many scientists will resist change and continue to support the old paradigm for as long as they can.

Fig. 15 Kuhn's three distinct stages for the development of science

As a new science, many argue that psychology has no generally accepted paradigm and is still in a period of pre-science, therefore a paradigm has yet to emerge. Others point out that paradigm shifts have already occurred in psychology, for example the shift in the focus of psychology away from behaviourist to cognitive views of behaviour in the 1960s. It has also been suggested that psychology is a discipline fragmented in ways that other disciplines are not, so the likelihood of a paradigm emerging in psychology is remote. For example, a biopsychologist, a humanistic psychologist, and a social psychologist might all be interested in the same behaviour, but their perspectives are so radically different that it is hard to imagine a common paradigm emerging.

Reporting psychological investigations

Having conducted the research the final task for the psychologists is to write it up as a report for publication. Once published, other psychologists will be able to read and comment on the research, and use it to guide their own thinking about the subject matter. It is in this way that findings are communicated and the research contributes to psychology as a science.

While there are some variations, all published research follows the same basic convention in terms of its style and structure. It is usually written in a scientific style and divided up into sections, each of which describes something specific about the research. These are summarized in Table 17 in the order in which they appear in a report.

Section	Purpose
Title	Gives a clear indication of the focus of the study.
Abstract	Provides a brief summary of the theoretical background, aims, method, findings, and conclusions.
Introduction	Presents the relevant background literature and provides a rationale for the current study.
Method	Describes in detail how the study was carried out – the design, selection of participants, materials, and the procedure.
Results	Summarizes the findings, including any descriptive and inferential statistics.
Discussion	Reviews the findings in the light of existing research presented in the introduction.
References	All sources used by the researchers are written strictly according to conventions.

Table 17 A brief summary of report sections

Title
This needs to be concise but still convey the main focus of the study. As a rule of thumb, the title should include the main variables under investigation.

Abstract
Although placed at the start of the report, the abstract is the last thing written. In about 200 words, it includes details of the study aims, methods, design, findings, and conclusions. It provides a short

summary for researchers who, when doing a literature search for their own research interests, might need to look at hundreds of reports. Reading lots of abstracts is much more efficient than reading entire reports, which usually run into thousands of words.

Introduction

This section introduces the background of the study. It provides a context and will contain reviews of past research relevant to the present study. It should be structured in such a way that it leads the reader logically to the aims and hypotheses of the study.

Method

This section includes details of the methodology and describes how the investigation was carried out. It is important that this section has sufficient detail to allow other researchers reading the report to replicate the study. For clarity, the method section is often divided into four sections:

- Design: this is where design decisions are explained, for example if the study is an experiment it would detail the control measure, experimental design, and conditions.
- Participants: key information about participants is described, such as age, gender, etc., and details of the sampling technique.
- Materials: the material and/or apparatus used to carry out the research is detailed. This might include how questionnaires were constructed, or what kind of software was used.
- Procedure: this section describes how the study was carried out. It should include details of instructions and how materials were used.

Results

The findings of the study are reported in this section. This would normally include descriptive statistics, such as measures of central tendency and dispersion displayed in a table, and graphs. It might also include results of inferential analysis, along with a statement of whether or not the hypothesis is supported.

Discussion

This section is where the results are discussed, which includes explanations for the findings in the context of the background research presented in the introduction. It would also include a critical assessment of the study, outlining any shortcomings in the design and conduct of the study – basically, anything that might affect its validity. Any practical or theoretical implications would also be discussed here.

References

All the research cited in the report must be alphabetically listed in this section. This allows psychologists reading the report to find the same sources. A particular convention is used for writing references, usually the Harvard (author-date) system.

Data handling and analysis
The distinction between quantitative and qualitative data

There are two types of data collected in psychological research. One type is called **quantitative data**. This is numerical data, which can be used in inferential analysis. Experimental studies gather quantitative data, as can other methods such as questionnaires and observations. By contrast, qualitative data is not numerical. This might take the form of quotes or themes that reflect thoughts and feelings of participants. Qualitative data is gathered in self-report methods such as interviews and questions. It is also the kind of data typically generated by thematic analysis. Qualitative data can be converted into quantitative data, for example in an interview study responses could be categorized to produce quantitative data.

Quantitative data is generally considered to be more reliable and objective than qualitative data, and it can be analysed statistically to reveal trends, relationships, and differences. However, qualitative data gives much richer detail than numerical data. For example, although it is possible to express as a number the strength of feeling about something by using a scale (giving quantitative data), this tells us little about the origins of those feelings, such as motivation and intent. This is exactly the kind of information qualitative data provides. The issue then is not about which type of data is best, but what is the most appropriate data given the goals of the research.

Primary and secondary data

All psychological research aims to gather information to convert into results that help to support the hypothesis. Depending on the source, this information is classified as either primary or secondary data.

Primary data is data collected from first-hand experience. The advantage of this is that it is data gathered for the purpose of addressing specific research hypotheses. It is collected first-hand and has not been altered in any way by other researchers. This increases its validity. For example, researchers interested in the effects of machine-induced workplace stress can gather primary data specifically related to this issue. While primary data has the advantage of this close focus, it is often time-consuming and expensive to obtain and analyse.

Secondary data is data that has already been published in some form. There are many sources of secondary data, for example government and public sector reports, websites, and books. The key advantage of secondary data is that it is often readily available and inexpensive to obtain. However, because the data is second-hand and has often already undergone some form of interpretation by other researchers, it may have inherent biases.

Whether or not researchers elect to use primary or secondary data depends on many things, including the aims and hypotheses and the resources available, such as budget and expertise.

Key term
Quantitative data: data that is in a numerical form.
Primary data: data collected from first-hand experience.
Secondary data: data collected from already published sources.

Meta-analysis

Meta-analysis is a research method where, rather than conducting new research, the primary data from other studies are re-analysed. That is, it uses secondary data. It enables what may be many studies with relatively small samples to be combined into a single study with a large sample size. The elements of primary data reported as results in published studies are selected and combined, producing quantitative metadata. This metadata can then be analyzed using descriptive and inferential techniques.

Meta-analysis is particularly useful in situations where a topic has been extensively researched. By combining data from as many of these studies as possible, it may be possible to identify common trends that are either not apparent or not convincing in single studies. However, the technique does present some significant challenges. For example, the criteria for including studies have to be very strict, which eliminates many studies. Since it deals with secondary data it relies on the primary research being of good quality, or at least flaws being readily identified so that it can be excluded from the metadata.

Descriptive statistics

As the name suggests, descriptive statistics describe and summarize the data that is collected in a study. There are a number of descriptive statistics used in psychology, including measures of central tendency and measures of dispersion.

Measures of central tendency

The term **measure of central tendency** is used to suggest that one number can be used to represent the general trend of a set of numbers. In other words, it represents the typical number, sometimes referred to as the 'average'. The term 'data set' is often used to describe a group of scores derived from a psychological study. For example, the following is a data set from an experiment on reaction times, and represents the number of times a button was pressed within half a second of being shown an object on a screen:

5 3 6 7 7 4 8 5 4 4 5 3 4 8 17

This data set can be represented by three measures of central tendency, or averages.

Mean

The **mean** is sometimes referred to as the arithmetic average. It is calculated by adding together all the scores in a data set and dividing this number by the total number of scores.

For example, with our data set from the memory experiment we would first add together all the numbers:

$5 + 3 + 6 + 7 + 7 + 4 + 8 + 5 + 4 + 4 + 5 + 3 + 4 + 8 + 17 = 90$

Secondly, we would divide the total (90) by the number of scores (15):

Mean = 90 ÷ 15 = 6

The mean score of the set of data is 6.

Median

The **median** is the middle number of a set of scores after they have been put in numerical order.

So, with the data set from the memory experiment, the first step would be to put the scores in numerical order:

3 3 4 4 4 4 5 5 5 6 7 7 8 8 17

The median is literally the middle number. As this data set has an odd number this is very easy locate – the median score is 5. If there is an even number in the data set then the two middle numbers would be added together and divided by 2 to give the median, for example: 3 3 4 4 4 5 6 7 7 8 8 17. The two middle numbers are 5 and 6. 5 + 6 = 11. 11 ÷ 2 = 5.5. The median of this set of data is 5.5.

Mode

The **mode** is the most frequently occurring number in a data set. It is easier to identify when the numbers are put in numerical order, but with large data sets it is often a good idea to do a frequency count, that is, a tally chart of how often each number appears.

3 3 <u>4 4 4 4</u> 5 5 5 6 7 7 8 8 17

As can be clearly seen, the mode of this data set is 4, as this number occurs more frequently than any other number.

Advantages and disadvantages of measures of central tendency

The data set of memory scores gave us the following measures of central tendency:

Mean = 6

Median = 5

Mode = 4

Here we have three different measures of central tendency from the same set of numbers. The mean is higher because every number is taken into account in its calculation; therefore it is skewed by the one extreme score. Both the median and mode are unaffected by this extreme score. So which measure of central tendency is best? The answer to this is not as clear as it might appear. Some researchers argue that the mean is always the best measure of central tendency to use because it considers every number in a data set. Other researchers suggest that extreme scores create a mean that does not truly represent the data set (and the more extreme the score the more the mean is skewed), and so we should use the median or mode, which are less likely to be affected in this way. An additional problem with the mean is that it is often a decimal fraction, and this can make the mean seem meaningless. For example, the average number of children per family in the UK is 2.6. Can you really have .6 of a child? In practice, measures of central tendency are used in conjunction with a measure of dispersion (described in the next section). As we will see, measures of dispersion are one way of indicating how representative a measure of central tendency is of the data set.

Measure of central tendency	Strengths	Limitations
Mean	• It takes all scores into account so is the most sensitive measure.	• Easily distorted by extreme scores, making it unrepresentative. The median might be more representative in this case. • Can give a peculiar measure that cannot represent reality, e.g. 2.6 children.
Median	• More representative than the mean, especially with small data sets. • Unaffected by extreme scores in one direction, e.g. one extremely high or one extremely low score.	• Less representative when the data set is polarized, i.e. has both one extremely high and one extremely low score.
Mode	• Unaffected by extreme scores. • Most useful with large data sets.	• Unreliable for use with small data sets as small changes to scores can result in it being multimodal, i.e. there being more than one mode.

Table 18 Strengths and limitations of the three measures of central tendency

Measures of dispersion

In addition to knowing the average score, it is usually also useful to know the spread of a set of scores, that is, its variability or dispersion. As was seen in the discussion of measures of central tendency, it is possible to calculate three different scores for the same data set. It would be useful to have a description of data that also includes some indication of how spread out a data set is, as this would tell us something about how representative our measure of central tendency actually is. For example, if we have two sets of scores, each giving us a mean of 24, we would have no idea which is the most representative set, if we did not know how spread out the scores are around the mean. The set that has the lowest spread (more numbers resembling it) would be the most representative (the best) set. There are a number of ways of calculating **measures of dispersion**, but only two will be considered here.

Range

The **range** is normally used when the median is the measure of central tendency of choice. It is a measure of spread calculated by subtracting the lowest score in a data set from the highest score and adding 1. For example:

5 3 6 7 7 4 8 5 4 4 5 3 4 8 17

Key terms

Measures of dispersion: values which give an indication of how spread out a set of scores are.

Range: a measure of dispersion that is the difference between the highest and lowest score in a data set.

The lowest number is 3 and the highest number is 17. To calculate the range:

17 − 3 + 1 = 15. The range of this data set is 15.

It is clear from this that the calculation of the range ignores the other thirteen numbers in the data set, so is a rather coarse figure as it is not considering what is happening in these other numbers.

Standard deviation

The **standard deviation** is a sophisticated measure of dispersion, as it takes into account all numbers in a data set in its calculation. In effect, it is the mean distance of scores from the mean of a set of scores. This means that the larger the calculated standard deviation (or sd), the more spread a set of score are about the mean and therefore the less representative the mean is of this set of scores. The example will help to clarify this.

There is a formula used to calculate the standard deviation. You might sometimes see sd replaced with σ or a single s. It means the same thing.

$$sd = \sqrt{\frac{\Sigma(X - \bar{X})^2}{n - 1}}$$

The standard deviation is much easier to calculate than this formula might suggest.

The mean for the following data set was previously calculated as 6 (note: the mean is often symbolized by an x with a bar above it: $\bar{x}$).

Score (x)	$x - \bar{x}$	$(x - \bar{x})^2$
5	−1	1
3	−3	9
6	0	0
7	1	1
7	1	1
4	−2	9
8	2	4
5	−1	1
4	−2	4
4	−2	4
5	−1	1
3	−3	9
4	−2	4
8	2	4
17	11	121

To explain the process: first we listed our scores (x) as a column. Then we took each score away from the mean, for example for the first number 5 − 6 = −1. Don't worry about minus numbers, because the next step is to square all the subtractions you just calculated, which eliminates the negative sign. So we have 5 − 6 = −1, and −1² = 1; 3 − 6 = −3, and −3² = 9, and so on.

Having completed all these calculations, we then need to use the formula. The first step is to replace the formula under the square root sign with the relevant numbers. This is very straightforward. $\Sigma(x - \bar{x})^2$ simply means to add up all the numbers under the column headed $\Sigma(x - \bar{x})^2$. (Σ simply means 'sum of', or 'add up'.) In our sum this adds up to 173. $n - 1$ is nothing more than the number of scores minus 1. In this case $n - 1 = 14$. We now have all the numbers under the square root, and all that remains is to divide $\Sigma(x - \bar{x})^2$ (which is 173) by $n - 1$ (which is 14). $173 \div 14 = 12.36$. The final step is to calculate the square root of 12.36, which gives us an sd of 3.5.

As long as the data came from a sample drawn at random from the population, the standard deviation can be used to make inferences about the population. $\Sigma(x - \bar{x})^2$ is divided by $n - 1$ in this case, as in the example above. However, if the sample is not drawn at random from the population $\Sigma(x - \bar{x})^2$ it is divided by n.

Measure of dispersion	Strengths	Limitations
Range	• Easy to calculate and give an indication. • Useful when the median is being used as an average, as the range uses the top and bottom of a set and the median is the middle number.	• Easily distorted by extreme scores. • Only uses two numbers no matter how large the data set so is a basic indication of spread at best. • It gives no indication of the spread of scores within a data set.
Standard deviation	• Uses all scores in a data set in its calculation. • It gives a sensitive measure of how all scores are dispersed around the mean. • It is a powerful statistic with applications elsewhere, e.g. in conjunction with normal distributions.	• More difficult to calculate than the range. • As it uses the mean it is distorted by extreme scores.

Table 19 Strengths and limitations of two measures of dispersion

ACTIVITY 8: MEASURES OF CENTRAL TENDENCY AND DISPERSION

The following data sets were gathered in a study looking at driver error and stress:

A: 8, 6, 14, 9, 13, 8, 9, 8, 7, 7, 10

B: 22, 12, 14, 21, 20, 14, 14, 18, 16, 17, 17

(a) Calculate the mean, median and mode of each.
(b) Calculate the standard deviation for each data set. Which mean is most representative of its data set?

Percentages and their calculation

'Per cent' simply means 'per 100'. So, when we say that 20 per cent of students achieved a grade A in a recent test, what we are really saying is that if there were 100 students 20 of them got a grade A. Of course, it is highly unlikely that we will have a nice convenient 100 people in our sample, so we need a way to convert scores to percentages. Let's say that 5 students in a class of 25 get a grade A. What percentage of the class does this represent? We use the following formula:

$$\frac{5}{25} \times 100 = 20$$

So, 20 per cent of the class got a grade A.

Percentages are useful because they enable scores to be compared. For example, it is not possible to tell whether a student who scored 60 out of 70 in their history test did better or worse in her psychology test where she scored 52 out of 60. Converting both scores to percentages allows us to compare them:

$$\frac{60}{70} \times 100 = 85.71\%$$

$$\frac{52}{60} \times 100 = 86.67\%$$

There's not much in it, but she did slightly better in psychology.

Percentages can also be expressed as decimal fractions, something that is quite common in psychology. For example, if 50 per cent of participants answered 'no' to questionnaire item 3, 50 per cent is half, which can also be expressed as 0.5. If 28 per cent of participants answered 'yes' to questionnaire item 4, this can also be expressed as 0.28. Percentages are most often expressed as decimal fractions in psychology when considering probability. You can read more about this on page 69.

Presentation and display of quantitative data

Although statistical analysis is at the core of the scientific method, it is also important to present findings in visually meaningful ways.

Graphs

Graphs help to show patterns in the data; in effect, they are describing the data in a visual way. Histograms, line graphs, and bar charts all show how variables differ in some way. Scattergrams on the other hand give a visual representation of how variables are related.

Histogram

A **histogram** is used to present data that is continuous and occurs as a frequency. For example, the histogram below shows the number of aggressive acts by children at different ages (in months), as observed during school play periods. Notice that the 'number of times' aggressive behaviour is observed is recorded on the vertical (y) axis, and the horizontal (x) axis has a continuous variable count of age in months (each bar representing 6 months).

Key term

Histogram: a graph used to present data that is continuous and occurs as a frequency.

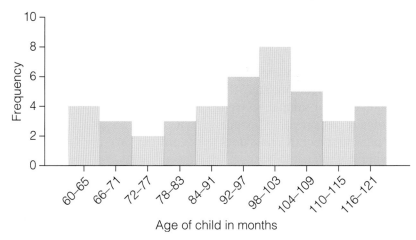

Fig. 16 An example of a histogram showing the number of aggressive acts initiated by children of different ages (in months) during a single period of school break

Line graph

A line graph, as the name suggests, uses lines on a graph to illustrate the results. A line graph can be used as an alternative to a histogram, in which case it would be called a frequency polygon. Instead of bars, a straight line would join the mid-point of each bar. The main advantage of the line graph is that it can give a clear view of how two or more sets of data compare. This is not always easy to see on a histogram.

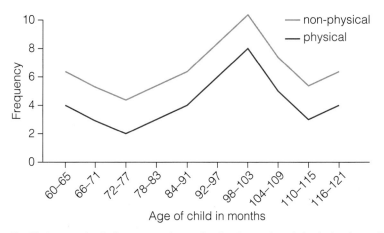

Fig. 17 An example of a frequency polygon showing the number of physical and non-physical acts of aggression initiated by children of different ages (in months) during a single period of school break

A line graph is also often used to illustrate the findings of experiments. It is particularly useful for showing the results of experiments that have more complex designs, for example when there are two or more independent variables. They can give an effective visualization not only of how the results of manipulating several independent variables differ, but also how they might be interacting. See Fig. 18 for an example of a line graph used in the context of an experiment.

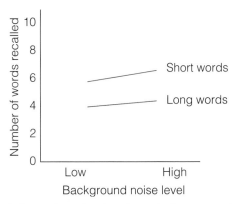

Fig. 18 An example of a line graph used to show the results from an experiment

Bar charts

Bar charts are used when the data is in discrete categories, rather than a continuous variable as with histograms and line graphs. The bars are always of the same width and separated by a gap to show that they are not continuous. A bar chart is useful for displaying two or more sets of data together, as in the example in Fig. 19. A bar chart should be used when the data measured are on an ordinal or nominal scale (see page 64 for more about ordinal and nominal scales).

Note that a bar chart should not be used to plot individual participant scores, that is, each bar representing each participant. Although you might argue that the scores are discrete, the graph is not doing what it should do – summarizing the data. If you want to plot participant scores then it is more appropriate to summarize them as measures of central tendency, for example a mean of scores. While this might give what appears to be a very simple graph, this is not a bad thing. A good graph visualizes and clarifies, so as a rule the simpler the better.

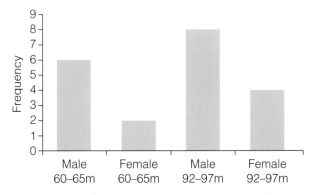

Fig. 19 An example of a bar chart showing the number of aggressive acts initiated by male and female children of ages 60−65 months and 92−97 months

It is usual when using a graph such as a bar chart to illustrate data from an experiment to put the independent variable along the horizontal axis and the dependent variable along the vertical axis.

Draw bar charts representing the distribution of eye colours. First, record as many people's eye colour as possible. Remember to follow ethical guidelines for research. Once you have gathered as much data as possible, plot it on a bar chart. Remember to label the axis properly and to give your graph a title.

(a) Draw a graph showing distribution of eye colours regardless of the sex of the participant.

(b) Draw a graph showing the distribution of eye colour for males and females.

(c) What does each graph show about the distribution of eye colours?

(d) What ethical issues did you identify and how did you deal with these?

Scattergrams

As discussed on the section on correlation (see page 24), scattergrams are used to show relationships between variables. Two scores are used to plot scattergrams: one score will be variable (y) on the vertical axis and the other variable (x) on the horizontal axis. To add plots to a scattergram simply locate the y score on the y-axis and the associated x score on the x-axis. Follow each along its horizontal or vertical path to where the two scores intersect – this is the plot, often indicated with an 'x'.

Once all the pairs of scores have been plotted the scattergram gives some indication of both the direction and strength of the correlation. The scattergram is an illustration of the correlation; however, the correlation itself is determined by the correlation coefficient (see page 24). This is important – while sometimes it gives a clear indication of the nature of the correlation it is often not clear from the scattergram whether the correlation is significant.

When one variable increases or decreases as the other variable increases or decreases, we say we have a positive correlation. A perfect positive correlation (a coefficient of +1) would look like the one in Fig. 20. A slightly less than perfect correlation might look like the one in Fig. 21. Fig. 22 shows another example of a positive correlation, this time with a smaller coefficient.

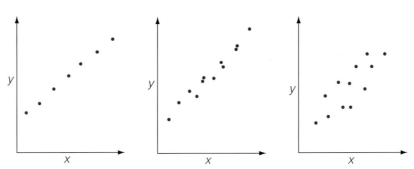

Fig. 20 A perfect positive correlation

Fig. 21 A less than perfect positive correlation

Fig. 22 A positive correlation

When one variable increases as the other variable decreases, we say we have a negative correlation. A perfect negative correlation (a coefficient of −1) would look like the one in Fig. 23. A slightly less than perfect negative correlation might look like the one in Fig. 24. Fig. 25 shows another example of a negative correlation, this time with a smaller coefficient.

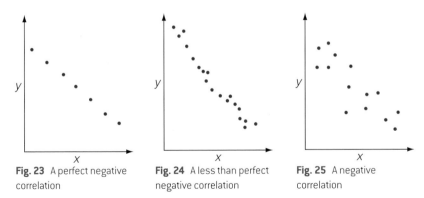

Fig. 23 A perfect negative correlation

Fig. 24 A less than perfect negative correlation

Fig. 25 A negative correlation

It is often the case that no relationship is found between two variables. This is called a zero correlation, and a scattergram might look something like Fig. 26. It is worth remembering, however, that a scattergram can sometimes look like this when the correlation coefficient says there is a significant correlation. Fig. 27 shows what are called curvilinear correlations. A coefficient for a curvilinear correlation might be close to zero, suggesting that there is no correlation between two variables, when there clearly is. A curvilinear correlation shows that two variables are positively correlated up to a point and then become negatively correlated, or vice versa. For example, you might find a positive correlation between performance and anxiety, but after a certain point the anxiety stops having a positive effect and begins having a negative one. Here, the plots on a scattergram may give you a shape something like an inverted U. The coefficient calculated from measures of anxiety and performance on a task would probably suggest zero correlation (the positive relationship being cancelled out by the negative), but there is an important relationship between anxiety and performance being shown by the scattergram. This is why coefficients and scattergrams go together – you do not do one without the other, and vice versa.

ACTIVITY 10: SCATTERGRAMS

Plot the following data sets as scattergrams. Don't forget to label the x and y axes, and draw them to an appropriate scale. Once plotted, decide what kind of correlation each one indicates.

1. y	x		2. y	x		3. y	x		4. y	x
3	2		5	1		7	1		5	5
2	3		2	1		6	2		1	8
6	7		2	5		1	7		3	2
3	5		5	7		4	4		4	6
5	4		7	4		5	3		2	6
8	7		4	3		2	6		5	3
1	1		1	3		4	3		1	1
6	6		8	3		6	1		4	2

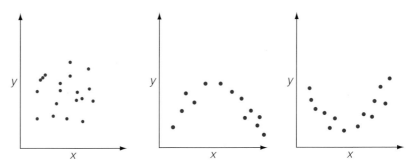

Fig. 26 A zero correlation   **Fig. 27** Curvilinear correlations

Tables

Another way of summarizing data is to use tables. As with graphs, histograms, bar charts, and line graphs, tables should summarize participant scores, not represent them individually. This means that you will need to calculate the appropriate measures of central tendency and dispersion and present these on a clearly labelled table, as in the example in Table 20. Tables should be constructed and labelled in such a way that makes them straightforward to read and gives the data some meaning.

	Experimental condition	
	Control	Experimental
Mean	32	24
Standard deviation	3	4

Table 20 Example of a table showing the mean and standard deviation for the control and experimental conditions of the experiment

Distributions

Sometimes researchers gather data that tells us about how often something occurs. This is known as frequency data. It is this kind of data that would be plotted on a histogram or a bar chart, where the vertical axis is labelled 'Frequency'. The data will form some kind of pattern that may be seen on the graph – this is called its distribution. Others will occur grouped together at the top, bottom or middle. Data can be seen to be distributed in many kinds of ways. For example, some scores or numbers will occur throughout the possible range, from high to low. Others will occur grouped together at the top, bottom or middle of the range of scores. Each distribution has its own name and associated mathematical properties, but the three most important distributions are described below.

Normal distribution

When the mean, median and mode of a distribution are the same (or very similar) you get a very particular shape when it is plotted as a histogram. Most scores would occur around the middle (mean) with fewer being clustered as they occur above and below the mean. If a curved line is drawn through the midpoint of each bar the graph would look something like Fig. 28.

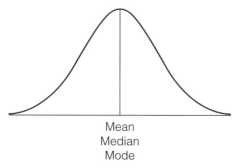

Mean
Median
Mode

Fig. 28 A normal distribution

This distribution is called the normal distribution. Notice that the mean, median and mode lie at the midpoint of the graph and that the graph is symmetrical about these averages. The normal curve, as it is often referred to, has some very important mathematical properties that makes it a very useful distribution to psychologists.

Skewed distributions

Some distributions have most scores falling below the mean. When plotted on a graph this distribution looks something like Fig. 29. This is called a positively skewed distribution.

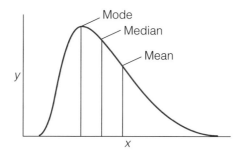

Fig. 29 A positively skewed distribution

Another type of distribution is where scores fall mainly above the mean. This is called a negatively skewed distribution, and data plotted on a graph would look something like Fig. 30.

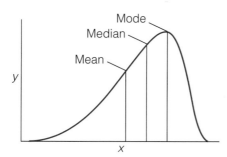

Fig. 30 A negatively skewed distribution

One thing to note with skewed distributions is that they show that the mean is not a very representative score – most scores are either above (i.e. bigger than) or below (i.e. smaller than) the mean. This means that mean should not be used as the sole measure of tendency when distributions are skewed.

Levels of measurement

Numbers can be used in different ways. Sometimes they are used to indicate quantity, such as when we find we have six red socks and five blue socks. Here the numbers contribute to the categorizing of the socks. Another time, numbers might be used to indicate a point on some scale, for example when we feel more strongly about one thing than another or when we compare examination grades. It could also be that we use numbers in more exact ways so that they have very precise properties, for example 20cm is exactly twice as long as 10cm, or a soft-boiled egg takes two minutes less to cook than a hard-boiled egg.

Because numbers can have different meanings depending on how they are used, it is very important to understand what kind of numbers we are gathering from research as data. The way that numbers are used dictates what can be done with them. It will determine to some extent the kind of analysis that can be done on the data and hence the conclusions we can draw from research findings. Each kind of number is said to have a level of measurement. Each level of measurement has a set of characteristics that set rules about the kind of arithmetic that can be done with it.

Nominal level of measurement

Numbers with **nominal level of measurement** are used to classify and categorize things. For example, we could survey the eye colour of 100 students and categorize them accordingly as either blue, brown, green, or other. In doing this we have placed our findings into one of four categories – the data is nominal.

This level of measurement tells us very little about the phenomena it represents. The most meaningful thing it can give information about is quantity. We could, for example, conclude that more people have blues eyes than have green eyes. We have not recorded the degree of blueness so that we can say on a scale that some eyes are bluer than others. We are left with simple comparisons between categories.

Ordinal level of measurement

Rather than simply categorizing data, the **ordinal level of measurement** gives some indication of how data relate to each other. As the name suggests, numbers with an ordinal level of measurement have a position in some kind of rank, ordering, or scale. For example, say we ask participants to indicate on a scale how anxious they feel about a forthcoming exam:

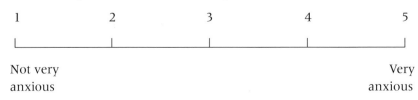

Fig. 31 An example of ordinal level of measurement

A participant who circles 1 is indicating not very much anxiety. We could say that this person is feeling a lot less anxious than another person who indicates 4. This, the ordinal data, is telling us where one piece of data lies in relation to another. Clearly, this tells us more than nominal data does. We could even convert this ordinal data to nominal data by categorizing responses as the number of 1s, number of 2s, etc. However, there are limitations to what ordinal data can tell us and hence what kind of analysis we can do with this kind of data. This can be demonstrated using the anxiety scale. Two participants might circle 1 and another participant might circle 2. We can say that two participants rated themselves the same but we do not know if this rating has the same meaning for each participant – it might mean more or less for one participant than another. Also, one participant indicates a 2 and although this is one higher than the other two participants we cannot say what this represents. What does it mean to rate one higher? If it were a measure on a ruler then we could say absolutely that 3cm is 1cm longer than 2cm. We cannot do the same with ordinal levels of measurement, however, and this is their major limitation. There is no exact distance between points on an ordinal scale. All we can do with ordinal numbers is describe them as bigger than, less than, or equal to. We cannot attribute any further value to them.

Interval level of measurement

Interval data is like ordinal data in that it involves data that can be ordered. Crucially, however, there are equal intervals between points on a scale. Because of this it is possible to carry out meaningful arithmetic. The zero point on interval scales is arbitrary. For example, the Celsius scale of temperature is interval because the distances on the scale are equal (you can take away 30°C from 40°C) and the zero point is not an absolute zero. Someone decided where 0°C should be – it is possible to get colder than 0°C.

Key term

Interval level of measurement: a measurement where the difference between two values is meaningful, e.g. the difference between 5°C and 10°C is the same as that between 15°C and 20°C.

Inferential testing

Key terms

Inferential tests: tests of significance that tell us the probability that the results of the analysis could have occurred by chance.

Significance: when the result of analysis is significant it means that you can say with some degree of confidence that the results are not due to chance.

The ultimate goal of psychological research is to collect data and analyse the results. Statistics are used to describe, summarize, and make sense of the data, such as graphs, percentages, distributions, measures of central tendency, and dispersion. Although these techniques describe data, they do not necessarily permit researchers to draw sound conclusions about the results of the study. For this, researchers need to use statistical tests that will allow them to infer things about what the data mean. Thus, these tests are usually referred to as **inferential tests**.

The data gathered by researchers is generally not complete, in that they only constitute usually a small percentage of all the data available – they came from a sample of the population and not the entire population itself. If the sample is a good one that is, it is truly representative, then inferential tests enable researchers to make generalizations about the population from which it was drawn.

Inferential tests take many forms according to the nature of the study and the type of data gathered. However, they all have in common the notion of **significance**. 'Significant' in the context of inferential analysis simply refers to confidence that the result is not due to chance. When psychologists find a significant result then what they are saying is that they are confident that they do not have chance findings.

The sign test

The idea of significance can be seen most clearly in the context of an experiment. Let's imagine that we have conducted a study because we are interested in finding out whether students who revise in noisy settings (e.g. loud music) are disadvantaged by this (i.e. do worse in exams). After careful consideration and planning we have ended up with a repeated measures design experiment where participants attempt to learn a list of words in silence (the control condition) and then attempt to learn another list of words with background noise (a random hammering sound, the experimental condition). Given what we know of psychological research into this area, our directional hypothesis is that recall of word lists will be greater in the silent condition than in the noise condition. We collect the following data:

Control	Experimental
11	9
8	8
6	8
11	6
10	10
9	7
8	8
10	9
7	8
8	6

Fig. 32

We might look at this data set and from an 'eyeball test' decide that recall is indeed affected by noise. From this we might conclude that revising in noisy surroundings is bad for you and offer this as advice to all revising students. But how sure are you that the difference in performance between the two conditions is sufficiently big that it is significant (i.e. if you repeated the study again in all probability you would get the same or similar outcome)? An inferential test would tell us the probability that the difference in the two sets of scores occurred by chance.

So, we decide to do an inferential test, and choose to do something called a sign test (the section on choosing statistical tests on page 68 will explain how we came to this decision).

Participant	Control	Experimental	Step 1
1	11	9	−
2	8	8	0
3	6	8	+
4	11	6	−
5	10	10	0
6	9	7	−
7	8	8	0
8	10	9	−
9	7	8	+
10	8	6	−

Fig. 33

Step 1: Subtract each participant value in the 'experimental' column from the participant value in the 'control' column, recording its sign. If the two scores are equal, insert a 0.

For example, with Participant 1, $9 - 11$ is -2, so record the minus sign in the Step 1 column; for Participant 2, $8 - 8$ is 0, so insert 0; for Participant 3, $8 - 6$ is $+2$, so insert +.

Step 2: Count the number of times the less frequent sign occurs. This gives us S.

For example, the plus signs are the least frequent sign. They occur twice, so $S = 2$.

Step 3: Count the total number of pluses and minuses. This gives us N. (Do not include 0 in this count).

For example, there are seven signs, so $N = 7$.

Step 4: Decide if the hypothesis is one-tailed or two-tailed (there is no need here to go into the 'what' and 'why' detail of one- and two-tailed tests – just remember that a directional hypothesis is one-tailed and a non-directional hypothesis is two-tailed).

Step 5: You now need to use a table of critical values for the sign test – a section of one is reproduced in Table 21. N means the number of pluses and minus scores (there are 2 pluses and 5 minuses giving an N of 7). Go down the N column until you come to the number 7 and stop. From this point you need to go across to the column headed 0.05 for either a one-tailed or a two-tailed test. In this case, the hypothesis is directional so it is a one-tailed test. The number (or *critical value*) at the intersection of $N = 7$ and 0.05 for a one-tailed test is 0. The rule on the table says that S must be equal to or less than the critical value to be significant. $S = 2$, so it is greater than the critical value of 0, so the result is not significant.

Step 6: State the conclusion. As the result is not significant we cannot reject the null hypothesis – there is no significant difference in recall of words in noisy and silent conditions. Note that if we cannot support the hypothesis (i.e. the result is not significant) then we must retain the null hypothesis.

	Level of significance for one-tailed test				
	0.05	0.025	0.01	0.005	0.0005
	Level of significance for two-tailed test				
N	0.10	0.05	0.02	0.01	0.001
5	0	–	–	–	–
6	0	0	–	–	–
7	0	0	0	–	–
8	1	0	0	0	–
9	1	1	0	0	–
10	1	1	0	0	–
11	2	1	1	0	0
12	2	2	1	1	0
13	3	2	1	1	0
14	3	2	2	1	0
15	3	3	2	2	1
16	4	3	2	2	1
17	4	4	3	2	1
18	5	4	3	3	1
19	5	4	4	3	2
20	5	5	4	3	2

Table 21 Table showing the critical values of S for the sign test. S must be equal to or less than the stated critical value to be significant.

Probability and significance

The end result of all inferential tests is a figure that indicates the probability of the results being due to chance. In the case of this experiment, the figure describes the probability that the difference between the two sets of data is due to chance.

Probability is usually abbreviated p, and is used to indicate that the probability is less than, greater than, or equal to 0.05. A probability of 0.05 is usually used by psychologists as a cut-off point for significance. If there is a less than 0.05 likelihood that the difference occurred by chance, it is assumed that the result did not occur by chance and therefore it represents a significant result. Another way of thinking about this is to imagine doing the same experiment in exactly the same way 100 times. As long as we get the same or similar result at least 95 times then we are satisfied that, in all probability, there is a real difference between the two conditions. The five or fewer times we do not find what we expect is just bad luck – things happen by chance and we have to accept an element of this in psychological research. If we find a significant result we can accept the hypothesis and reject the null hypothesis.

If there is a greater than 0.05 likelihood that the difference occurred by chance then it is assumed that the result is due to chance and therefore is not significant. With a non-significant result we cannot be sure enough that the results did not occur by chance; therefore we must reject the hypothesis and accept the null hypothesis.

Expression	Interpretation	Meaning
$p < 0.05$	The probability that the difference occurred by chance is less than 0.05 (one in twenty, or 5 per cent).	The result is significant.
$p = 0.05$	The probability that the difference occurred by chance is equal to 0.05 (one in twenty, or 5 per cent).	The result is significant.
$p > 0.05$	The probability that the difference occurred by chance is greater than 0.05 (one in twenty, or 5 per cent).	The result is not significant.

Table 22

Sometimes, inferential tests tell us that the null hypothesis can be rejected with greater confidence than 0.05. If analysis indicates that the null can be rejected at the 0.01 level or greater, the result is said to be highly significant. For example, at the 0.01 level we can be 99 per cent confident, and at the 0.001 level we can be 99.9 per cent confident.

ACTIVITY 11: DO A SIGN TEST

A psychologist gave participants a memory test using acoustically similar words (Condition A) and later gave the same participants a memory test using acoustically dissimilar words (Condition B). The data are shown below:

Condition A: 8 9 7 6 6 7 7 8 8 5

Condition B: 6 7 7 5 5 6 6 8 9 5

(a) Write a directional hypothesis for this study.
(b) Use a sign test to analyse the data.
(c) Explain whether the result is significant or not.

Type I and Type II errors

Key term

Type I error: rejecting the null hypothesis and accepting the hypothesis even though findings are due to chance.

Type II error: retaining the null hypothesis even though the hypothesis is correct.

Whilst interpreting the result of a statistical test might seem straightforward, it is possible to make two kinds of error:

- **Type I error**: we reject the null hypothesis and accept the hypothesis, even though findings are due to chance. Also known as a false positive.

- **Type II error**: we might retain the null hypothesis even though the hypothesis is correct. Also known as a false negative.

In effect, a Type I error is caused by making it too easy to support the hypothesis. For example, if we work to a 10 per cent significance level ($p = 0.1$) then we are saying that we only need to be 90 per cent confident in our results for them to be significant. This is a much easier 'target' to hit statistically and therefore we are more likely to accept the hypothesis. Indeed, the likelihood of Type 1 errors can be reduced by making the significance level more stringent. For example, we could make the minimum significance level 1 per cent, which would give us 99 per cent confidence in our results. The risk here, however, is that in making the significance level too stringent we would be increasing the likelihood of a Type II error. A 1 per cent level is a harder 'target' to hit so we are more likely to say the results are due to chance.

The 5 per cent significance level is used by psychologists because it minimizes the likelihood of making both Type I and Type II errors. Five per cent lies nicely between 10 per cent (likely Type I error) and 1 per cent (possible Type II error).

There are times when a psychologist might want a more stringent confidence level, and hence run the risk of a Type II error. For instance, if the result of a study is likely to be controversial in some way researchers might want to make sure that they are not making a Type I error (falsely accepting the hypothesis). It is better to be safe (saying that your results are due to chance) than sorry (making controversial claims that are not really justified).

It is unusual to claim significance with confidence levels below 0.05, for example 0.1. The risk of making a Type I error is too great. In some circumstances a 10 per cent significance level might be acceptable in speculative research as evidence that further research is justified, to try to achieve the minimum 5 per cent level.

Choosing the correct statistical test

Inferential tests are designed to be used for very specific purposes – you can't just randomly select a test that you fancy using. It is important to understand which test to use under which circumstances – using the wrong test will give a statistical outcome which is entirely meaningless. Choosing the right statistical test to use involves asking three questions. You will not be able to select the right test unless you understand (and can correctly answer) these questions, as follows.

1. What kind of data do I have?

Some statistical tests make certain assumptions about data and some statistical tests do not. Tests that do are called parametric tests, whilst tests that make no assumptions about data are called non-parametric tests. These assumptions place restrictions on the use of parametric tests for analysing data. One assumption is that the data comes from a sample drawn from a normally distributed population (see the earlier discussion on normal distribution, page 62). A second assumption is that there is homogeneity of variance in the data. What this means is that the spread of scores in the two data sets is similar (see earlier discussion of measures of dispersion, page 54).

Parametric tests, however, are robust enough to be relatively unaffected by breaking these assumptions. For example, the population might be quite normally distributed, or the spread of scores in the conditions might not be quite equally spread. It might even be that we are not certain about either of these at all, but think that our data might meet these assumptions.

However, the third assumption must be met – the data has to have interval level of measurement. This is because parametric tests involve sophisticated arithmetic operations (addition, subtraction, division, etc.). As explained in the section on levels of measurement (see page 64), nominal and ordinal data are rather crude measurements which do not allow us to do much more than say that one thing is larger than, smaller than, or equal to, something else. What this means, then, is that we can use level of measurement as the key indicator of whether data is parametric. If this particular assumption is met, then we will assume the data is parametric.

It is essential, therefore, that the level of measurement of the data is accurately identified:

- If the data is categorized into groups in some way (such as people with small, medium, or large feet), then the data is nominal.
- If the data is ordered in some way (such as ranks, or points on a scale), then the data is ordinal.
- If the data derives from a measurement of equal intervals (such as the number of test questions answered correctly), then the data is interval.

2. Am I looking for a difference or a relationship between variables?

Some research looks to see if there is a difference between behaviours in two conditions (experiments), and some research seeks to uncover relationships in data (correlations).

3. What is my experimental design?

When the study is an experiment then you must know its design:

- If different participants are used in each condition, it is an independent groups design.

- If the same participants are used in each condition, it is a repeated measures design.
- If different participants are used in each condition, but they are matched in some way, it is a matched pairs design.

Once you have answered these questions correctly you can use the flow chart in Fig. 34 to select the right statistical test to use.

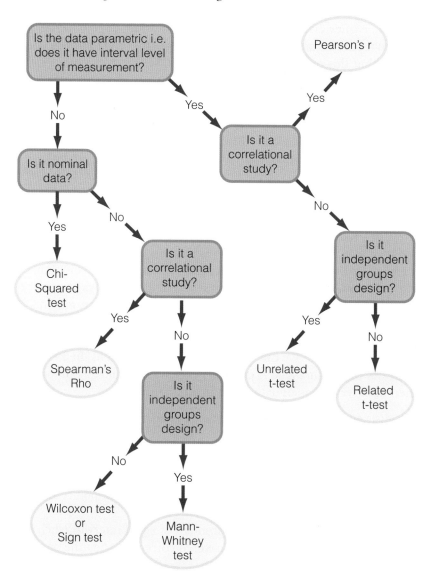

Fig. 34 Flow chart showing the selection of the correct statistical test

EXAMPLE EXAM QUESTION

A psychologist was interested in discovering whether continuously learning and revising throughout an A Level course was a more effective strategy than binge-learning and revising shortly before an exam at the end of an A Level course.

She selected a sample of students from a large sixth form centre. She assessed their learning style with a questionnaire shortly after an A Level examination and, based on their responses, classified them as either 'binge' or 'continuous' learners. She then looked to see if there was a difference in exam marks between the two groups.

(Continuous) Group A	(Binge) Group B
63	48
55	61
61	55
61	60
74	63
73	66
63	45
69	45
68	60
70	48

(a) What kind of experiment did the psychologist conduct? Explain your answer. [3 marks]

(b) Write a hypothesis for this study. State whether your hypothesis is directional or non-directional. [3 marks]

(c) What would be the appropriate statistical test to use in this study? Explain your choice. [4 marks]

(d) Explain how the psychologist might have selected her sample. [3 marks]

Exam hint

You are expected to know about different kinds of experiment, and question (a) tests your understanding by not only asking you to recognize the type of experiment but also to explain your thinking. One way of doing this is by a process of elimination, e.g. does it meet the criteria for a laboratory experiment? If 'yes', you have your answer. If 'no', compare it to the features of a field experiment, and if this does not 'fit', then compare it to a natural experiment, etc. By doing it this way you are also answering the 'explain' part of the question.

Chapter 1: Issues and debates in psychology

Introduction

In this chapter we examine some of the difficult but fascinating debates in which psychologists must engage in order to properly evaluate the research they conduct and the theories they suggest. None of these debates are straightforward and there are no correct answers to the issues being discussed. As you read through the discussions you will need to find your own solutions by weighing up the pros and cons of each argument.

We start by looking at the issue of bias in psychology. These are gender bias and cultural bias, and we will examine how these biases have come about, what impact they have made on psychological theory and how they are now being addressed.

The second topic looks at free will and determinism, and cuts to the very heart of psychology as a science: if there is nothing but the laws of physics then we cannot possess free will, and without free will there are many theories within psychology that can have little meaning. So we ask whether psychology leaves room for free will.

The next topic examines the nature–nurture debate. It is undoubtedly true that most behaviours are the consequence of both nature and nurture, but psychologists have not always believed this to be the case. We look at the evidence and whether it is ever possible to know how much of our behaviour is influenced by nature and how much by nurture.

The fourth topic of the chapter looks at reductionism and holism. Psychology, like other sciences, seeks to explain complex behaviours in terms of its component parts, but not all psychologists believe this to be possible. We will see that theories can fundamentally differ depending on whether you are a reductionist or a holist.

The penultimate topic of the chapter deals with the broad methodological approaches used by psychologists. These fall into two categories, idiopathic and nomothetic. The former is about seeing humans as unique individuals while the latter considers us to have enough similarities for explanations to be generalized to groups.

The final topic of the chapter looks at ethics. We consider what it means to conduct ethical research and examine whether or not psychology has always conducted its research in an ethical manner.

What is covered in Issues and debates?

ISSUES AND DEBATES

Gender and culture in psychology

When psychology first started as a discipline, the world was a very different place to the one in which we now live. In 1879, when Wilhelm Wundt set up the first psychology laboratory, a woman's role in society was secondary to a man's. Similarly, in terms of cultures, the perception of the time would be that white Europeans were superior to other races, particularly black Africans. This situation regarding gender and culture did not change much until the 1970s, despite the suffragette movement of the 1920s that gave women the vote, and a variety of race riots in the early part of the twentieth century (for example, in the USA in 1919 and 1943). It is also important to note at the outset that there have been some interesting controversies regarding gender and culture, and psychology has not always reflected our current thinking about these issues. That is not to say that no women made a success of psychology in the early days. Karen Horney (see Fig. 1.1) was an influential psychologist in the field of psychoanalysis during the 1930s, but it was hard for women to influence the academic world. Furthermore, and probably more importantly, few women were undergraduates of psychology, and the undergraduate population were the people most used for studies in the discipline. It is within these contexts that we must examine how gender and culture have been explored and/or ignored in psychology.

You will most probably have already encountered areas such as conformity and memory. It may not have occurred to you that these areas were first explored in an age when it was assumed that all humans behave in the same way under any given circumstances. There was no suggestion that males might conform differently to females or that the memory of one race might behave differently to that of another. For example, most people are unaware of the bias introduced by the fact that Asch (1951) used only male participants in his original conformity study. Equally, when Keppel and Underwood (1962) undertook their proactive interference study using psychology students at the Northwestern University in Chicago, the ethnic mix of the population of Chicago (according to census data) was 77 per cent white and 23 per cent black. No other ethnicities were recorded as being present in the city, so it is likely that Keppel and Underwood's research sample was almost exclusively white. It is also interesting to note that, at that time, most studies did not even report the gender mix of their participants in the methods section, and none would report the ethnic mix, believing these to be irrelevant to the concepts under investigation. This idea that all humans are the same is called **universality**.

Gender bias

A bias is when you show a prejudice either for or against something, so **gender bias** refers to the idea that psychological data have a bias towards one or other gender. This could be the result of experimenter

Fig. 1.1 Karen Horney, a psychoanalyst who had some alternative theories of neurosis to those of Freud

Key terms

Universality: the belief that all humans are alike, so what is true for one person is true for everyone.

Gender bias: when differences between genders have not been considered properly, leading to a biased or potentially biased conclusion.

biases if all of the experimenters were for, example, male, or it could be a sampling bias if studies tended to be done predominantly on females. You should note at the outset that the bias does not automatically imply that there are gender differences, just that they have not been explored.

It is fair to say that since the 1970s the Western world has grown to show more equality of the sexes in all walks of life. We now have sex discrimination laws (first introduced in the UK in 1975 and as part of the Civil Rights Act of 1964 in the US). We might be tempted, therefore, to believe that psychology would have recognized the importance of gender differences since around this time. Unfortunately, this has largely been untrue. We will explore some early theorists, like Freud, whose work almost exclusively referred to males, but we will also explore more recent studies to see whether or not gender bias is still a problem.

Androcentrism

We have a much more recent history of bias towards males. This bias stems from **androcentrism**: having a male-centred view of the world in which only males matter. Studies are carried out only on males, the results are then considered to be valid for both genders and, where any differences are suspected or noticed, the differences are either ignored or considered to be of no value. For example, Freud's work only ever centred on males. The Oedipus complex is about boys fearing castration by their fathers. The female equivalent of penis envy (the Electra complex) is also centred on the father, as it refers to a girl's desire for her father and the belief that she has already been castrated by her mother. Of course, Freud lived in an extremely male-dominated age so we might reasonably ask if this biased attitude has changed since his time.

> **Key term**
>
> **Androcentrism**: a gender bias that leans particularly in favour of males because the research comes from a male-centred view of the world.

> **Link**
>
> For more on the Oedipus and Electra complexes, see page 219 of Book 1.

> **EXAMPLE EXAM QUESTION**
>
> Briefly outline what is meant by the term androcentrism. (2 marks)

> **Exam hint**
>
> To ensure that you gain both marks, you should provide two separate points that explain what androcentrism is.

Types of gender bias

There are two other ways in which one can introduce bias into theory. The bias can be one that tends to overemphasize differences between the genders or it can be one that minimizes the differences. Hare-Mustin and Marecek (1990) used the terms **alpha bias** and **beta bias** to capture these two alternatives. An alpha bias might exaggerate the difference between males and females when there may not actually be any real differences (for example, women are better at childcare) and a beta bias would minimize or ignore any real differences between the genders (for example, Asch assuming that conformity in women is of no interest).

> **Key terms**
>
> **Alpha bias**: where any differences that might exist between males and females are exaggerated.
>
> **Beta bias**: where any differences that might exist between males and females are ignored or minimized.

Alpha bias

This refers to the exaggeration of differences between males and females. There is no doubting that there are going to be some differences, but research in psychology has sometimes suggested differences that may not actually be there. Freud provides an example here too with his psychosexual theory. He believed women to be less morally mature because their superegos were considered to be less well developed (a consequence of not having castration anxiety). In this way, Freud legitimised the treatment of women as second-class citizens and thereby was guilty of exaggerating the differences between men and women.

ACTIVITY 1.1

Look at the list of behaviours below. Which do you think are ones where there are gender differences and which do you think do not have gender differences? Explore why you hold these views.

Parenting	Long-term memory	Sexual attraction	Sport preference
Reading ability	Cooking	Maths ability	Housework

According to an alpha bias, our common beliefs might be that males are considered to be better at visual and spatial tasks and females are considered to be better at verbal tasks. There are other biases that still seem to be believed by large sections of the general population today. For example, that males are less sensitive and are more physically active; that males are more aggressive and tend to be dominant; that females are more dependent and need social support. If we look at psychological research during the latter half of the twentieth century, we see these ideas being supported by biased research evidence, so it is little wonder why they are generally held to be true. Nevertheless, we must recognize that research bias does not mean that these findings are false, only that they have not been properly investigated.

Evidence of alpha bias Freud's theory of psychosexual development is the most obvious example of alpha bias, as the theory exaggerated the importance of males and assumed that what was true for males was true for females as well. The only concession to females was the inclusion of penis envy for girls to replace castration anxiety in males (see page 219 of Book 1). Another theory that showed alpha bias was Kohlberg's (1958) theory of moral development, which suggested that females have poorer reasoning skills than men and do not achieve the same level of reasoning capacity (see the *Key study*). However, Kohlberg's research was conducted entirely on American boys.

KEY STUDY: **KOHLBERG'S STUDY OF MORAL DEVELOPMENT (1958)**

Kohlberg believed that moral reasoning develops in children in stages. He tested his theory using moral dilemmas in which children had to decide which course of action was morally correct. One such dilemma is reproduced below.

Heinz's wife was dying from a particular type of cancer. Doctors said a new drug might save her. The drug had been discovered by a local chemist and Heinz tried desperately to buy some, but the chemist was charging ten times the money it cost to make the drug, and this was much more than the Heinz could afford. Heinz could only raise half the money, even after help from family and friends. He explained to the chemist that his wife was dying and asked if he could have the drug cheaper or pay the rest of the money later. The chemist refused, saying that he had discovered the drug and was going to make money from it. The husband was desperate to save his wife, so later that night he broke into the chemist's and stole the drug.

The dilemma concerns whether or not Heinz was morally right or wrong to have broken in and stolen the drug. Kohlberg found that the reasons children gave for their reasoning changed as they got older. Children seemed to develop morally in three stages: pre-conventional morality, where the moral code adopted is that of close adults and the motivation is to avoid punishment; conventional morality, where the child begins to internalize the moral standards of significant adults; and post-conventional morality, where morals are now individualized and concern views about justice and the rights of the individual.

On the face of it, this seems like a perfectly acceptable study. However, Kohlberg only used 72 boys as his participants and yet his findings were implicitly being generalized to both males and females. It was assumed that the moral development of boys reflected the moral development of children in general. There was not even a question about whether or not the moral development of girls followed the same pathway. This might well not have been deliberate, but it was a reflection of the thinking of the time (the **zeitgeist**).

> **Key term**
>
> **Zeitgeist**: the 'spirit of the time', in that any period in time has certain social and moral expectations that people will generally adhere to.

THINKING SCIENTIFICALLY: GENERALIZATION

One of the key problems associated with psychological research is the degree to which the results of any study can be generalized to the population. Of course, whether or not generalization is valid might concern who we consider the population to be. Clearly, in the Kohlberg study, there was no justification for generalizing the results to all children, as the data had been gained only from boys. However, even the generalization to boys might be slightly premature as the study used 72 boys who were all from Chicago, so the data may not even reflect boys in general. It is important to recognize that this is not necessarily a fault of the study but an error in the assumptions being made about the meaning of the results. After all, it might have been impractical for the study to include boys from outside of Chicago and, in any case, how wide must the sampling be before the data can be applied to all boys?

The issue of generalization does not apply just to gender, but across all studies and all dimensions. Shortly we will see that it is also a problem for issues concerning cultural bias.

Beta bias

This is shown when a study or theory ignores or minimizes gender differences. Some studies have shown this bias because they have excluded one gender from studies. An example of this is Milgram's (1963) obedience study where the participants used were all male. However, we do have to exercise some caution here: we cannot know the reason for the choice of male participants. Therefore we must consider the alternative possibilities:

1. The behaviour of women does not matter.

2. It would be unfair to put women in this situation.

3. There would not be any differences so there is no need to use both genders.

Alternative possibilities 1 and 2 would imply a strong gender bias but might be as much about the zeitgeist as about wilful bias. Alternative 3 might be justified if a lot of previous research in the area had strongly suggested that men and women do not behave differently on these kinds of task. In Milgram's case this is highly unlikely, but that might not be the case for more recent studies that have used an opportunity sample. Indeed, given that the modern undergraduate psychology population is about 70 per cent female, we might find research that has a gender bias in favour of females simply as a result of opportunity sampling.

Research methods link

For more about opportunity sampling, see page 35.

Evidence of beta bias Alongside Milgram's study stand a huge number of studies from the twentieth century that used only males and then generalized the findings to both genders in terms of a universal theory. For example, the social psychology experiments on conformity by Asch (1951) used males to argue how we all conform. The beta bias here is that either Asch has missed a conformity difference between men and women, or he has assumed that conformity in women is unimportant.

Evaluating gender bias

Our realization of the existence of gender bias has not only had negative consequences. Knowing about alpha bias has heightened our awareness of gender differences and allowed us to question the value of male characteristics within society. Critical analysis of beta bias might have led us to see equality as important in terms of employment and education. However, we must also recognize that gender bias has caused a great deal of harm: alpha bias has enabled prejudice and discrimination through stereotypes, and beta bias ignores the fact that we still inhabit a relatively male-dominated society. Finally, we should remember that gender bias of all types lulls us into believing that all males are one way and all females are another. This ignores individual differences – we will pick up on this theme later in the chapter.

Key terms

Cultural bias: when differences between cultures have not been considered properly, leading to a biased or potentially biased conclusion.

Ethnocentrism: a cultural bias that leans in favour of a particular culture because the research has only been conducted using participants of that culture.

Cultural bias

The issue of **cultural bias** is similar in many ways to the one for gender. Just as with gender, alpha and beta bias are both evident. Here, however, the problem is one whereby most of the research that was carried out in the UK and the US involved only white Caucasians. This leads to **ethnocentrism**, which is where one generalizes the findings from one culture to other cultures. The case for cultural bias is a little different from that for gender bias, as the ability to carry out research on participants from different cultures was, perhaps, not all that easy. The predominance of

UK and European research in psychology has not helped the exploration and evaluation of alternative cultures in the past.

We might consider the problem of cultural bias from a methodological perspective. Research has not only used a very biased sampling method but has also used methodologies that are based on Western views of science. Such methods as the laboratory method have been accused of being **Eurocentric** (Nobles, 1976), in that the approach is not what you might expect from alternative cultures. Added to this problem, there have been few non-white researchers in the history of Western psychology. We might even go further to suggest that much of the Western research conducted before the 1980s might have suffered from a form of racism designed to maintain stereotypes. In some areas of psychology, cultural differences could be extremely important; for example, work by Maheswaran and Shavitt (2000) looked to see if these differences were being recognized in the field of consumer psychology (see the *Key study* on page 82).

Key terms

Eurocentric: a form of ethnocentrism that is particularly focused on the Western world's viewpoint.

Emic: a focus on a single culture to understand it within a local context.

Etic: a focus across multiple cultures in order to understand elements that apply across all cultures.

ISSUES AND DEBATES

ACTIVITY 1.2

Consider whether the methodological issues discussed above in relation to cultural bias are similar to those you might argue for gender bias. What other methodological issues might lead to gender or cultural bias?

Emic and etic approaches

The **emic** approach is one where one culture is studied in order to discover culture-specific behaviours. For example, Bartlett (1932) (pictured in Fig. 1.2) described how Swazi herdsmen could recall the individual characteristics of their cattle. His emic approach allowed him to understand why this capability is important: in Swazi culture cattle are a sign of wealth, and therefore it is important for the herdsmen to know as much about the cattle as they can so that they can properly attend to their needs.

The **etic** approach is one in which research is carried out across cultures in order to discover what elements of a behaviour might be universal. For example, Berry (1969) replicated Asch's conformity study (see Book 1, page 74) to see whether the conformity rates seen in the US were repeated among the Temne people of Sierra Leone or the Inuit of Canada. The Temne had high rates of conformity but the Inuit had low rates; the difference was put down to the alternative styles of living (agricultural community for the Temne and lone hunters for the Inuit). Hence, with the addition of cross-cultural research, we can see that conformity is not a universal behaviour.

Fig. 1.2 Sir Frederick Bartlett. In 1932 he had already realized that there were cultural differences in memory.

Maheswaran and Shavitt (2000) published a review of published research that reflected attempts to consider cultural differences in the field of consumer psychology. Quite simply, this field examines the psychology of buying things. It covers reasons for buying or not buying something, such as cost, advertising, design and social acceptability, to name just a few. The focus of their study was to assess the degree to which the field had considered 'methodological issues that are central to conducting cross-cultural research, including selecting or blending emic and etic research approaches'. In other words, they wanted to see if consumer psychology research recognized that both within and across cultures these issues might influence consumer behaviour in different ways. They found that while progress had been made to consider cultural diversity in consumer behaviour, the research was still concentrated within certain geographical regions, such as the US, Western Europe and the Far East. In particular, they noted that the cross-cultural research that was being undertaken was starting to allow generalizations to be made that could indicate where universality in consumer behaviour was applicable. For example, some methods of persuasion are just as effective in China and Hong Kong as they are in Western countries.

The problems of both gender and cultural bias stem from the more common problem of sampling bias. Much of the research that is conducted in psychology is done by a single researcher or a team that resides in a single locality or within a small region of a single country. It is therefore not surprising that this creates sampling difficulties. Sampling bias in favour of only one gender would be unacceptable in modern research unless there were specific reasons for doing so. Most of the gender-biased research is therefore historical. Sampling bias with respect to culture is more difficult to control for and depends on the researcher having access to multiple cultures. Even then, an ethnic minority in a local region may not behave in the same way as those of the same ethnicity in other parts of the world. Hence, to some degree, sampling bias is inevitable, so the best way to reduce cultural bias is to look at replications of research that have been carried out within different cultures. As it is unreasonable to expect a researcher in one country to also carry out their research in different parts of the world, the ethnic diversity of findings has to wait until studies are naturally replicated elsewhere. However, there is not that much of this research about at present, though the situation is gradually improving. This is, in part, a direct result of globalization and the power of the internet in the sharing of information.

Research methods link

For more on sampling, see pages 31–33.

Evidence for cultural bias

Some of the earliest work showing a cultural bias was done in the field of relationships. Much of the research that was done in the 1960s and 1970s on how relationships form and how they fall apart was carried out using white UK/US participants. This led to a set of theories that were extremely culturally biased. When cross-cultural studies were undertaken, only a few universal behaviours emerged.

Argyle et al. (1986) compared the ways in which friendships develop in Japan and Hong Kong and in Italy and Britain. Japan and Hong Kong are considered to have collectivist cultures where the group is more important than the individual. Italy and Britain have individualist cultures where the reverse is generally true. While Argyle et al. found some universal similarities, for example distinguishing between intimate and non-intimate relationships, they also found numerous differences, such as there being more focus on obedience in the East than in the West. Similarly, Moghaddam (1998) also found cultural differences between the East and the West. He found that in Western non-arranged marriages passion was most important early on, but in the arranged marriages of the East the most important element was commitment.

EXAMPLE EXAM QUESTION

A psychologist carries out a study of logical reasoning using a group of eight-year-old children at an English primary school. The class consists of 90 per cent Asian and 10 per cent white Caucasian pupils. The researcher explains the results in terms of how children reason and makes mention of the cultural differences in the group as part of that explanation.

Explain how the researcher could be guilty of alpha and/or beta bias. (6 marks)

Exam hint

It is probably easiest to answer this question using both alpha and beta bias. For each of them you should explain what is meant by the term and provide an account of how that bias might be evident in the example given. You could also provide an example from the literature to confirm your understanding of the term. If you were to choose only one type of bias you would need to expand on the impact that this bias has on our understanding of psychological processes.

Another field that shows cultural bias is the diagnosis of mental illness. We tend to think that in using the *Diagnostic and Statistical Manual* (DSM) we must have captured what each mental illness is and how to define it. However, even if we take something relatively obvious (to us) like depression, we see that there are important cultural differences. In several countries there is no concept of depression. This is true of China (Tseng and Hsu, 1969), Malaysia (Resner and Hartog, 1970) and Japan (Tanaka-Matsumi and Marsella, 1976), to name just a few. Manson et al. (1985) found that Hopi Indians (a tribe of Native Americans) have five separate illnesses that have an element of what we might recognize as depression, even though they have no recognized illness of depression itself. So we can see that there is a cultural bias in our Western understanding of mental illness.

Cultural relativism

The evidence of cultural bias presented here demonstrates the need to recognize that what any human believes is tied up with that person's own cultural background. For example, you may have been brought up in a religious household or a non-religious one and this will be a part of your own cultural perspective. This is referred to as **cultural relativism**. It is clear that psychology had ignored this aspect of behaviour for a long time but the importance of different perspectives is beginning to be recognized. While we may all be humans, there are probably few universal behaviours, and this is a reflection of our diversity and our success as a species. It is, at last, becoming obvious to us that we have taken our basic evolutionary origins and adapted

Key term

Cultural relativism: a person's own cultural background affects the view they have and the behaviours they display.

them to suit the local environmental conditions across the entire globe. In doing so, we have created different social and cultural norms by which to live our lives. In ignoring such local histories in the past we have created a psychology that is predominantly culturally biased.

KEY POINTS

- Psychologists can have a tendency to believe that all humans are the same – a concept called universality.
- Gender bias occurs when the differences between males and females are not considered properly.
- Alpha and beta bias reflect exaggeration and lessening of differences respectively.
- Some of this bias is the result of a world where men were dominant and this led to an androcentric view of the world.
- Cultural bias occurs when there is a lack of consideration of differences between cultures. This bias leads to ethnocentrism.
- Emic and etic approaches can be used to try to reduce cultural bias and lead to a recognition of cultural relativism.

Free will and determinism

Man is a masterpiece of creation, if only because no amount of determinism can prevent him from believing that he acts as a free being.

Georg Christoph Lichtenberg (1742–1799)

Imagine that you have just been awarded an A* in Psychology at A Level. You would feel that it was right to expect praise because you had worked hard and achieved the highest grade possible. What would you think then, if someone said that none of this achievement had anything to do with you? What if they suggested to you that your achievement was simply the consequence of the Big Bang and all of the physics that has happened since then? This conflict between things happening through choice, on the one hand, and every effect being a consequence of physical causes on the other, is the essence of the free will and determinism debate, which we will discuss in this section. The quote above suggests that our belief in **free will** is an illusion, so let us examine the arguments for and against the possession of free will. Fig. 1.3 illustrates the possible beliefs that one can hold about free will and determinism. It is taken from the work by Roskies (2006), which we will consider later in the chapter.

Key term

Free will: the belief that our behaviour is governed by our choices, and that those choices are only minimally determined by other forces.

Universe is indeterministic		Universe is deterministic
Libertarians	**We have free will**	Compatibilists/ Soft determinists
	No free will	Hard determinists

Fig.1.3 A schematic mapping of the main philosophical positions on freedom of the will

In Fig. 1.3 we see that on one dimension there is whether you believe the universe to be determined (following rules like those of the laws of physics) or to be indeterminate (not following rules or random). On the other dimension is whether or not we have free will. It is then easy to see where the hard determinists, soft determinists and libertarians lie within these two dimensions.

The scientific emphasis on causal explanation

Before we look at the debate in detail, let us just pause a moment to consider why the debate matters. Psychology sees itself as a scientific discipline and, as such, it seeks to explain psychological phenomena by defining their causes. Science dictates that if something has a cause then it must be possible to determine a law that describes that cause. That is, we should be able to provide a **causal explanation** for the phenomenon. For example, the law of gravity explains what causes an object to fall to the floor. Furthermore, I can work out precisely where a ball will hit the floor if I know all there is to know about the physics of the situation. The problem for psychological explanation is that the intervention of free will does not easily allow for causes that lead to predictable outcomes. If I drop a ball next to you, and all of your actions are determined, then I can predict whether or not the ball will land on the floor or if you will have been determined to stick out a hand to catch it. If, however, you have free will that is not determined, I cannot know whether the ball will fall to the floor or end up in your hand. This threatens my ability to derive a causal explanation based on science. Hence, the free will and determinism debate has implications for psychology and for a much wider understanding of nature. Let us then start by examining what it is that we mean by determinism.

Hard and soft determinism

There are a number of different ways in which we can consider what we mean by **determinism**. If we were talking about physics, we might be considering that the universe is made up of atoms, and atoms behave according to the laws of physics (cause and effect). In this context, what every atom does is a consequence of those laws, and as we are just a collection of atoms our actions must also be determined by the laws of physics. This is called physical determinism. If, however, we are considering how our actions are shaped by, for example, our environment and the expectations of society, then we would be talking about a different kind of determinism. This would be environmental determinism. So it is clear that there are different kinds of determinism, and we will explore the most important ones below. However, before we do, we must also consider whether or not every form of determinism excludes the possibility of having any free will. Some forms of determinism do exclude the possibility of free will and they are examples of what we call **hard determinism**. Others suggest that there is room for free will, but that our free will is very constrained by the components that

Key terms

Causal explanation: the ability to explain a phenomenon in terms of the causes that made it happen. Knowing the causes of things allows us to make scientific predictions of what will happen if certain conditions prevail.

Determinism: what happens has to happen and could not have occurred in any way other than the way it did.

Hard determinism:the determinist principle to the letter of the law with no room for the concept of free will.

are deterministic. These views are examples of what we call **soft determinism**. As this soft determinism position incorporates both determinism and free will it is sometimes referred to as compatibilism (a position in which the two different perspectives are compatible). An example of soft determinism would be to consider that the attributes we are born with is the determinism element but the way we choose to live our lives and make decisions is the free will part.

Biological determinism

What if we wanted to argue that we are more than just a collection of atoms? After all, those atoms are put together in such a complex way so as to make intricate organs and tissues. We might, then, want to suggest that we are **biologically determined**. Our biology will dictate some of the things we are able to do. For example, a person might be a good athlete or be tall or slim. The tall person is biologically determined to be able to reach higher up than the short person. However, no human can leap, unaided, over a tall building. In this sense, then, biological determinism refers simply to the things an organism can or cannot do because of their biology. Our brain biology might even determine aspects of our social and cognitive life. Eysenck and Eysenck (1976) believed that our biology was the root of our personality (see the *Key study* on page 87). Underlying these features is our genetic inheritance that has made us athletic, tall or slim. It is this determinism that governs all of our behaviours (even criminal ones, as suggested in Fig. 1.4). We can surmise that these traits and behaviours have been selected as being advantageous in certain circumstances within our evolutionary history. We might, then, consider that we must also be genetically determined.

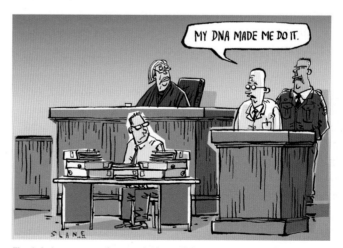

Fig. 1.4 An argument for genetic determinism

Genetic determinism

There are two forms of **genetic determinism**. The first is called genetic fixity – the idea that a child's characteristics are the simple combination of the inherited genes from both parents. We can see this if we consider eye colour (where the dominant gene from either parent will determine the eye colour of the child), and genetic fixity simply extends this principle to all other aspects of behaviour.

The second form of genetic determinism is called innate capacity. This is a less severe form and states that, while our genetics provide us with the limits to our abilities, what happens in the environment dictates whether or not those limits are realized. For example, imagine that your genetics determine that you have the innate capacity to be good, even a genius, at mathematics. If you are brought up in an environment where you can be well educated and are encouraged through home and school to excel then you will achieve that high level of maths capability. However, if you are raised in an environment where education is poor and home and school discourage academic endeavour then this mathematics potential will never be realized. Therefore, innate capacity determines the limits of a person's behaviour, but not whether those limits will definitely be achieved.

This discussion of the difference between genetic fixity and innate capacity highlights another important distinction within determinism: genetic fixity is referred to as hard determinism and innate capacity is referred to as soft determinism. As mentioned earlier, the term hard determinism is used to explain any view where that type of feature (for example, physics, biology, and genetics) is seen to be the only thing driving behaviour. Soft determinism is used to convey that the feature is critical but not the only determinant (for example, genetics modifiable by the environment) and that there is an element of free will guiding the outcome. Note that the modifier can only influence things to a certain degree. So if we return to the example of mathematics, the determinant (your genetic capability to understand maths) can be influenced by a modifier (the environment), but never to the extent that it takes you beyond that determined capacity (the environment can never make you better at maths than your genetics dictate). In this example some degree of free will comes from how the individual uses and/or shapes the environment and makes decisions about potential outcomes.

KEY STUDY:	BIOLOGICAL DETERMINISM OF PERSONALITY – EYSENCK'S THEORY

Many theories of personality started with a belief that personality was a trait, or characteristic. As such, early researchers thought that maybe our personalities are fixed by our genetics and our biology. This would make such theories determinist, and Eysenck's influential theory of personality is one such deterministic theory. Eysenck characterized personality as having three main traits, each trait being a dimension along which we all sit somewhere. The three traits are:

- Extraversion: Eysenck believed that we all sit somewhere along this dimension between being extravert and introvert, with most of us congregating somewhere towards the middle. According to Eysenck, an extravert would be someone who is very outgoing and an introvert would generally be a solitary person.
- Neuroticism: each person would lie somewhere between being totally neurotic and not at all neurotic (referred to as stable). Being neurotic implies that you are emotionally unstable.

- Psychoticism: the degree to which a person shows psychotic tendencies. In this sense of the word, psychotic refers to having aggressive tendencies and being generally hostile to others.

This theory is deterministic because Eysenck believed each of these traits to have an underlying biological cause. Extraversion is suggested to be due to cortical arousal (the degree of natural activation of the cerebral cortex of the brain). If under-aroused you would be an extravert and if over-aroused you would be an introvert. For neuroticism, the suggested relationship was with the threshold of activation of the sympathetic nervous system. This is the system that is activated in the fight-or-flight scenario. Neurotic people exhibit a low threshold, so their system activates even when the potential threat is minimal. Finally, psychoticism was believed to be linked to levels of the hormone testosterone. Having too much testosterone would lead to an aggressive character. Hence we can see how Eysenck's theory is strongly linked to characteristics that are determined by our biology.

THINKING SCIENTIFICALLY: **IS THERE ROOM FOR FREE WILL IN PERSONALITY?**

According to Eysenck's theory, our personality is determined by our brain activation. We can presume that at the level of the brain there is simply a cause and effect chain that leads from one brain state to the next brain state. So Eysenck is proposing that our personality just happens and that we can do nothing to change it. This is not the experience that most of us have about our personality. When we think of the person we are now and the person we were, say, five years ago, most of us would consider that some aspects of our personality have changed and others have remained the same. We would also want to argue that any changes have come about because we have decided to make changes to the way we view and interact in the world. That is, the changes have come about freely through the choices we have made. So the answer to the question in the heading above would seem to be a resounding 'yes'. Unfortunately, there is no definitive answer – it is up to you to weigh up the arguments on either side of the debate and decide which you think has the strongest evidence to support it.

Psychic (psychodynamic) determinism

Link

For more on personality structure and Freud's stages of psychosexual development, see pages 216–217 of Book 1.

Key term

Psychic determinism: behaviour that is determined by psychic (psychodynamic) phenomena.

The psychodynamic approach considers that our behaviour is determined by our unconscious. According to Freud, we are at the mercy of inner forces such as the unconscious, which exerts its influence through the id. Furthermore, the ego's ability to control the id and the superego are determined by the way a person manages their way through the psychosexual stages of development in childhood. Becoming stuck in one stage of development leads to fixation and this will determine the personality traits you display as an adult. So, for example, getting stuck at the oral stage of development will lead to an oral fixation. This in turn will lead to you being orally orientated as an adult (a smoker, a nail-biter, or someone who is quite dependent on others). Freud's beliefs were that these fixations will definitely lead to certain behaviours, which categorizes **psychic determinism** as a form of hard determinism.

Environmental determinism

This form of determinism is best captured by a look at the behaviourist approach. B. F. Skinner believed that our behaviour is governed by reinforcers (rewards and punishments). Every time we actively behave in some way (in other words, a behaviour that is not automatic or a reflex), we are either rewarded for that behaviour or punished for it. These do not have to be physical consequences, like getting a gold star at primary school; they can be psychological consequences, like feeling good about helping a friend through a crisis. Whatever the type of reinforcement, it determines how you behave next time you encounter the same set of circumstances. Now, you may be thinking that not all behaviour is learned because a person received a reward or punishment. Take, for example, Bandura, Ross and Ross's (1961) Bobo doll study. The children learned to behave aggressively even though they themselves had not been rewarded or punished for hitting the Bobo doll – their learning was by observation and imitation. Nevertheless, this would still be an example of **environmental determinism** as, once again, what has happened environmentally (observing the Bobo doll being hit) has determined the outcome of the person's future behaviour.

Key term

Environmental determinism: determinism that happens as a direct result of the influence that our environment has on us.

Link

For more on the behaviourist approach, including the Bobo doll study, see pages 221–225 of Book 1.

EXAMPLE EXAM QUESTION

Outline ONE determinist viewpoint. (4 marks)

Exam hint

As this is a four-mark question, you will need to do more than simply name and describe one form of determinism. You will need to elaborate on the definition by providing an example and should refer to a theory or a piece of research to underline your understanding of the term.

Conclusion

All of these forms of determinism have one thing in common: they reject the notion of free will.

- Physical, biological and genetic determinism argue that we cannot have free will because we are governed by our own internal constitution.

- Psychodynamic determinism argues that we cannot have free will because we are unaware of the unconscious drives that determine our behaviour.

- Environmental determinism argues that we cannot have free will as we simply respond to whether a behaviour (either our own or observed in someone else) has previously been met with good or unpleasant outcomes.

With that in mind, let us next examine the evidence that free will *does* exist.

ACTIVITY 1.3

Let's imagine you have just found out that the universe is determined. Discuss whether that changes anything about your behaviour, your views on things or whether you make 'choices' in the future. You might like to reflect on your behaviour yesterday in what, it turns out, was a deterministic universe then too.

Free will

The idea that we have free will feels like it is at the very heart of what it is to be human. Not only is it something that many religions consider has been handed down by a god, but we also internally feel that every aspect of our daily choices has come about as the result of us making a choice. So free will can be defined as the ability to make a choice (as depicted in Fig. 1.5) – it gives our existence a purpose and denies that our behaviour is determined, either by internal or external forces. Humanist, cognitive and developmental approaches to psychology all require the presence of free will, albeit to a greater or lesser extent. We will also see that free will is an essential component of concepts like responsibility, reward and morality.

Fig. 1.5 Having the ability to make a choice. The man depicted here must decide which path to go down. We might ask how we can know that the choice is real and does not just feel like a real choice.

Humanist free will

The humanistic approach argues that humans have 'personal agency' – that is, they have personal control over the choices they make, the directions in life that they take, and the consequences those choices lead to. Two humanistic psychologists who argued for free will were Maslow and Rogers. Maslow's (1943) model of human motivation allows for determinism with regard to the drive to satisfy our basic needs (hunger, thirst, etc.) but suggests that the higher levels of the hierarchy (for example, self-actualization) require us to have the ability to choose our actions. In other words, Maslow is happy to agree that things like hunger and thirst can be considered from a deterministic perspective as they are merely physical characteristics. It is the choices we make further up the hierarchy that decide whether or not we achieve self-actualization. Similarly, Rogers' (1951) client-centred therapy involves

Link

For more on Maslow's hierarchy of needs, see page 240 of Book 1.

helping the client to decide on their own best course of action by reflecting on the possibilities and their consequences. If there were no free will, there would be no choices to decide between.

Cognition and free will

For cognitive psychologists, the possession of free will is essential. One important component of cognition is decision-making. Information that comes in through our senses is processed by attention, memory and the like, but ultimately all of this information processing leads to a decision being made. This decision could be about the meaning of the object in front of you, about the relationship between different concepts, or about the behavioural actions you should engage in. In any case, these are decisions and the very concept of making a decision requires that you exercise your free will. Another aspect of cognition also requires there to be an element of free will. As humans, we have the ability to reflect on things we have said and done. These reflections serve the purpose of helping us to make the correct decisions in the future. If free will did not exist then there would be no decisions to make and this capability would be pointless. From a deterministic perspective, why would this capacity have evolved, if not to provide us with free will?

KEY STUDY: NEUROSCIENCE, FREE WILL AND RESPONSIBILITY

In 2006, Roskies examined the threat to free will and moral responsibility posed by advances in neuroscience. The threat to free will is that if neuroscience reveals fully the workings of the brain then it will allow us to perfectly predict behaviour due to a certainty of what the brain will do under any environmental circumstance. In other words, it would confirm that we are simply machines and nothing more. However, Roskies suggests that neuroscience is not showing this to be the case. She argues that neuroscience shows that the firing of a neuron or the release of a neurotransmitter substance is probabilistic (not set in stone), and so we can never be certain whether or not a particular neuroscience event will happen. Enter free will and the inability for neuroscience to predict how our choices will influence whether or not particular neurons do, or do not, fire. Not only is this a way of arguing for free will but, as a consequence, it also safeguards a belief in moral responsibility. Roskies goes on to suggest that we, as humans, are really all libertarians (see Fig. 1.3 on page 84), in that we believe ourselves to have free will and do not believe that our inner world, at least, is determined.

THINKING SCIENTIFICALLY: DOES WHAT YOU CANNOT DEMONSTRATE REALLY EXIST?

The debate around free will and determinism is an excellent illustration of two key problems in science. The first is suggested by the title of this box and the second is its mirror image – can you demonstrate that something does not exist? Let us examine these one by one. Demonstrating that free will really does exist seems to be an impossibility because it requires that we could go back in time to a starting point and make a different choice. Without a time machine, this is clearly not going to be possible. So if we cannot absolutely demonstrate the existence of free will then we have to at least question whether or not it exists. The problem of demonstrating that something does not exist is even harder. Imagine that you want to demonstrate that there are no purple unicorns in existence. Every time you hunt for a purple unicorn you do not find one. At what point can you absolutely say that, scientifically, purple unicorns do not exist? This is the problem faced by those who wish to scientifically show that we do not have free will. The debate has gone on since the beginnings of human reasoning and will, no doubt, continue for some time to come.

The development of free will

Many theories about child development incorporate the concept of the development of free will. Despite the psychodynamic approach being seen as deterministic, the concept of the superego, the morality principle, requires that a child develops an ability to recognize right from wrong and is able to make choices between them. Similar principles apply to Kohlberg's (1958) theory of moral development that we discussed earlier in the chapter. What would be the point of developing a system of morals if all of our actions were determined for us by external or internal forces that we have no control over? The same is true regarding the debates between Piaget and Vygotsky about how children learn and develop. There is little point in learning anything unless it helps to inform the future choices we make.

Link

For more on Piaget and Vygotsky see Chapter 4, Cognition and development.

Free will and responsibility

At the beginning of this section it was suggested that you would want to receive praise if you achieved an A* in your A Level Psychology. The reason for having this expectation is that you have free will and are therefore responsible for that great achievement. By the same token, if you had thrown a ball too hard while out in the garden and it had broken a window, you would also feel responsible as you had chosen to throw the ball. You might not have broken the window deliberately but you would still be responsible. Otherwise, your actions would simply be a product of your biology and Roskies (2006) has argued that our increasing neuroscience knowledge does not deny a place for free will and responsibility (see the *Key study* on page 91).

As well as responsibility for actions, psychologists have had things to say about moral responsibility, especially its development in children. Kohlberg's (1958) theory of moral development uses the Heinz story (see page 78) to construct a moral dilemma. Our interest in this dilemma here concerns the following: if we assume that we have free will then there is clearly a moral decision to be made. If, however, we believe in determinism, then Heinz is not in control of his actions and so cannot be held morally responsible for them. So it is clear then that if we want to argue for human responsibility and morality we have to do so from the assumption that humans have free will.

Strengths and limitations of determinism and free will

As with many situations where the alternative positions seem to be two sides of the same coin, arguments in favour of one side are, necessarily, arguments against the other. The strengths of a belief in free will are that we are able to choose between courses of action and can see a purpose to our existence. It also permits us to talk about reward and punishment and to justify the existence of prisons and the judicial process. On the negative side, theories that concern free will are difficult to test and so the existence of free will becomes more about belief than about evidence. In the case of determinism, the theoretical basis is scientific and adheres to the principle of cause and effect. By this account, then, free will is an illusion. However, it reduces humans and other animals to the level of automatic machines and seems not to incorporate the many facets of what it is to be human.

Fig. 1.6 If you had thrown a ball too hard while out in the garden and it had broken a window, you would feel responsible as you had chosen to throw the ball

ISSUES AND DEBATES

ACTIVITY 1.4

Imagine there is a supernatural being looking down on planet Earth. There in his study sits Benjamin, and he is trying to decide whether or not he should go on a train to London tomorrow to visit the Freud Museum. The view of Earth that this supernatural being has allows it to see the future as well as the present. This being knows that Benjamin will indeed go to London tomorrow, as only one timeline exists for him. Consider why Benjamin's future behaviour is seen as determined by the being but might be seen as involving free will by Benjamin. How would Benjamin's behaviour be explained, if at all, by a biological psychologist, a behaviourist, a psychodynamic psychologist or a humanist?

EXAMPLE EXAM QUESTION

Jack has run a 100m finals race representing his school. He finished second in the race. Provide ONE explanation for this result from a determinist's perspective and ONE explanation from a belief in free will. (6 marks)

Exam hint

This question requires that you explain what both of the terms mean and then relate these terms to the example given. You are not required to name a particular form of determinism or free will but to do so might help you to focus your explanation.

KEY POINTS

- The free will and determinism debate has important implications for psychology.
- The search for causal explanation leads us towards a path of determinism.
- For some, there is no room for free will – a position referred to as hard determinism.
- For others, free will and determinism are compatible – a position called soft determinism.
- There are many different forms of determinism, including biological, psychic and environmental determinism.
- Free will is the position whereby we are able to make choices.

- There are different perspectives on free will, including humanist, cognitive and developmental aspects of free will.
- Free will permits us to hold individuals responsible for their actions and this allows both praise for good actions and punishment for bad actions.
- Free will is difficult to test but a lack of free will leaves humans as no different from automatic machines.

The nature–nurture debate

The nature–nurture debate is one of the oldest debates in psychology. It involves the degree to which our behaviour is a consequence of **heredity** (innate) and the degree to which it is a consequence of what happens to us in our **environment** (learned). There is no doubting that we are made up of biological processes and that our genetic constitution greatly influences what we are capable of (**nature**). However, we also want to believe that the environment has an influence on the decisions we make (**nurture**). We will explore some of the historic perspectives on the issue as well as current thinking. First, though, let us define what we mean by nature and nurture.

Nature

Nature refers to the importance of the characteristics that we inherit from our parents. When we say that a behaviour is 'in our nature' we are referring to the fact that we cannot help but be that way because that behaviour has been inherited rather than learned. This idea extends to every aspect of psychology, in that we can always ask the question 'is that an innate characteristic?' If a **nativist** (a person who believes everything comes from nature) asks that question then the answer will be 'yes'.

The nature position is also deterministic (see the previous topic) as it suggests that our genetic inheritance determines absolutely the way we are. According to this view, our genes control every aspect of our behaviour in the same way that they control every aspect of our physical being (for example, height or eye colour). It is important to note that this view implies that every behaviour we are capable of displaying was coded for in our DNA at the time of conception. This, therefore, is a view that supports genetic determinism, a view we have considered earlier in this chapter (see page 86).

There have been many heated nature–nurture debates within psychology. One interesting domain has been the acquisition of language. If we ask why humans are able to construct a sophisticated language then it is hard to get away from the idea that it must be in our nature. While the learning of a particular language will be due to the environment we are brought up in, the capacity to learn a language seems to be innate. Chomsky (1965) was one of the main proponents of this idea, and he suggested that humans have an innate mental capacity called the language acquisition device, which enables us to learn a language. More recently, the innate nature of language has been explored in deaf children. Goldin-Meadow and Mylander (1998) (see the *Key study*) have shown that deaf children naturally use gestures to indicate words and sentences.

Key terms

Heredity: the transfer of genetic characteristics from parents to their offspring.

Environment: the social and cultural forces that shape a person's behaviour.

Nature: the idea that a behaviour is a consequence of heredity.

Nurture: the idea that a behaviour is a consequence of the environment. This includes experience and learning, but also factors such as stress and diet.

Nativist: someone who believes that a behaviour is the consequence of nature rather than nurture.

KEY STUDY: GOLDIN-MEADOW AND MYLANDER (1998)

Goldin-Meadow and Mylander (1998) were interested in the question of whether the capacity for language is innate or learned. Their research was looking at the gestures made by deaf children, specifically by American and Chinese children. The children in the study had hearing parents – while the parents would use gestures as part of speaking, the children were found to introduce their own gestures into their communications. To be counted as a gesture, certain criteria had to be met. For example, the gesture had to be directed at someone and had to include direct eye contact with that person. Reliability of recording gestures was established by having two independent coders. Despite the child-rearing practices being different in the two cultures, similarities were found in structure and patterns of the signs being made by all the children. These similarities suggest that there is an underlying innate feature of language that is shared by all humans.

THINKING SCIENTIFICALLY: IS NATURE AND NURTURE A FALSE DICHOTOMY?

The nature–nurture debate is often presented as one in which we expect to be able to answer the question one way or another. However, it is likely that most behaviours are the result of some innate elements that are then refined as a consequence of interaction with the environment. From a scientific perspective, we must be careful not to fall into the trap of trying to find evidence of one at the expense of the other. This is probably a criticism that can be made of much of the early research, as there were good reasons for researchers to align themselves with one camp or the other. In a modern context, those divisions are less obvious and most researchers now recognize that the most likely explanation of behaviour will include both nature and nurture elements.

There are lots of examples of studies that have pointed to nature as the explanation for behaviour, and they have come from very different areas of psychology. For example, Piaget (1952) suggested that children's development occurs in fixed stages (see page 000). According to Piaget, every child passes through four stages (sensorimotor, pre-operational, operational and formal operational) and must pass through them in this precise order. In other words, there is no possibility for the outside world to change the order or to create the circumstances where a child misses out a stage. Therefore, not only is this theory deterministic, it also claims that it is in our very nature to go through these stages.

ACTIVITY 1.5

Construct a list of twenty common behaviours. For each behaviour, try to determine whether it is innate or learned. If you think the answer might be a combination of both, examine which parts of the behaviour are innate and which are learned.

Another area in which research has been used to suggest that nature holds the key is in that of mental illnesses, such as schizophrenia. Here the question is whether you are born to have schizophrenia or if it is the environment that creates schizophrenia. A typical approach to research in this domain is the study of twins. Twin studies provide a good way to explore the genetic nature of a behaviour. Twins can be identical (both twins develop from the same zygote – egg plus sperm) or non-identical (both twins develop in the same womb but from different zygotes). Identical twins (called monozygotic or MZ twins) will completely share their DNA, and so anything that develops in one twin ought to develop in the other if the behaviour is genetically determined. However, non-identical twins (called dizygotic or DZ twins) will, on average, share 50 per cent of their DNA, so we would expect that if one twin expresses a behaviour, the other twin has a 50 per cent chance of also expressing that behaviour. Furthermore, if the twins are brought up in different environments because one twin is adopted, then we can also explore the influence of the environment on the development of the behaviour. In other words, if the behaviour is purely genetic then MZ twins would both develop it despite their having been brought up in different environments.

Gottesman and Shields (1976) reviewed a number of studies that had explored the development of schizophrenia in MZ and DZ twins. They looked at twin studies (where the twins are brought up in the same environment) and adoption studies (where the twins are brought up in separate environments). A more detailed description and analysis of this study can be found in the chapter on schizophrenia (see page 254). For our purposes here it is important to note that their findings showed a higher concordance rate (the likelihood of one twin developing schizophrenia if the other twin has it) of schizophrenia in MZ twins (58 per cent) than in DZ twins (12 per cent). They also found a greater likelihood of an adopted twin developing schizophrenia if one of their parents also had the illness, and a lower likelihood of a 'normal' twin developing schizophrenia if they were brought up in a family with at least one schizophrenic parent. These results all point towards schizophrenia being a genetically inherited mental illness. We will return to this study later in this topic to consider whether we would want to modify that statement but first we should look at the nurture side of the debate.

Exam hint

All that is required here is for you to define nature and provide one example of a nature explanation. For example, you could refer to any behaviour that is considered to be innate.

EXAMPLE EXAM QUESTION

What is meant by the term nature? (2 marks)

Key term

Nurturist: someone who believes that a behaviour is the consequence of nurture rather than nature.

Nurture

Nurture refers to the importance of the characteristics that we learn from our environment. One of the original **nurturists** was the philosopher John Locke (1632–1704). He claimed that we are born a tabula rasa, a Latin term meaning 'blank slate'. For Locke, the only innate capabilities we are born with are physical, and he believed that our mental domain has to be etched into our minds as a consequence of our thinking and our behaviours. It would be simple to believe that if the nature viewpoint is determinist then the nurture viewpoint must support free will. However, you would be wrong – the nurture position is also a deterministic viewpoint as it argues that all behaviour is determined by nurture.

One psychological approach that is entirely about the nurture perspective is behaviourism (see page 105). The principle behind behaviourism is that all behaviours are entirely shaped by the activities that occur in the environment. Indeed, John B. Watson, the founder of behaviourism once said,

Give me a dozen healthy infants, well-formed, and my own specified world to bring them up in and I'll guarantee to take any one at random and train him to become any type of specialist I might select – doctor, lawyer, artist, merchant-chief and, yes, even beggar-man and thief, regardless of his talents, penchants, tendencies, abilities, vocations, and race of his ancestors.

(Watson, 1930)

Watson's most famous study was the Little Albert study that he carried out with Rosalie Raynor in 1920. Little Albert was an 11 month old boy who showed no fear of rats. Watson and Raynor conditioned Albert to develop a fear of rats by pairing the presentation of a white rat with a loud noise that made Albert scared. Albert had not only developed a fear of white rats but this fear had also spread to similar white objects such as a rabbit, a fur coat and even a toy Santa Claus. This experiment demonstrates that by manipulating the environment, behaviour can be changed. This, therefore, supports the nurture point of view.

Link

For more on the Little Albert study, see page 191 of Book 1.

KEY STUDY: HELD AND HEIN (1963)

Another domain in which there has been a lot of nature–nurture debate has been in the area of perceptual development. There were a number of experiments that tried to decide whether our ability to see is innate or learned. When a baby is born it has eyes that function but that does not necessarily mean it can see everything as we see (note that we are discussing seeing and not perceiving) – so, for example, are we able to see vertical and horizontal lines as soon as we are born? This is a question that was investigated by Held and Hein (1963). They raised kittens in the dark and then exposed them to a kitten carousel (see Fig. 1.7).

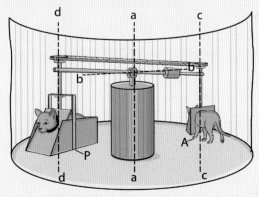

Fig. 1.7 The kitten carousel used by Held and Hein (1963) to explore nature versus nurture in visual perceptual development

The kittens were in pairs such that one kitten (the active kitten) could walk around the environment while the other kitten (the passive kitten) was simply transported without being able to walk. A number of tests were done on the visual capabilities of the kittens, one of which was their performance on the visual cliff (see Fig. 1.8). Here, the kitten is placed on a bridge between two areas. One is shallow when viewed below the glass and the other is deep. The kitten has three choices, to stay still, to move to the deep side or to move to the shallow side. In Held and Hein's experiment, the active kittens moved to the shallow side, whereas the passive kittens showed no discrimination between the deep and shallow sides. This suggests that depth perception requires being active in the environment and so supports a nurture perspective.

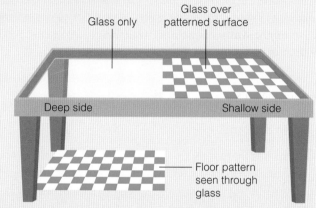

Fig. 1.8 The visual cliff, an apparatus designed to test depth perception

THINKING SCIENTIFICALLY: USING ANIMALS TO MAKE INFERENCES ABOUT HUMANS

Held and Hein's study raises a number of issues. One is the ethical issue of using animals in experiments, especially if the animal is being harmed in some way. We will cover this in more detail later in the chapter so we will not focus on that element here. Instead, we can consider whether the information we get from animal research is applicable to humans. On the plus side, the kitten and the human are both mammals and so there is a commonality there. Likewise, the visual systems of the cat and human are also very similar, so we might expect visual processes to develop in much the same way. However, the cat is a four-legged animal and this might add in a complication. Four-legged animals tend to be more stable, and so when standing at a cliff edge are less likely to suffer from vertigo. By contrast, many humans feel uncomfortable and wary at a cliff edge even if they do not suffer from vertigo. Thus, although the results of the study favour an explanation of learned depth perception, we cannot be sure that the cat's and the human's depth perception develop in exactly the same way.

ACTIVITY 1.6

We have all probably experienced a situation with a relative who does not see us very often remarking that 'you are just like your mother/father'. List five ways in which you think you are like a parent or sibling and five ways in which you think you are different. These can be physical or behavioural traits but the lists should contain a mixture of both. For each item, consider whether you think this is a result of nature or of nurture.

Exam hint

You should explain the genetic differences between monozygotic and dizygotic twins, and then use the figures to explain that monozygotic twins have a higher concordance rate for depression but that the rate is not 100 per cent.

The interactionist approach

You may already be thinking that to argue that a behaviour is purely nature or is purely nurture is a little extreme. Surely both must play some role in most, if not all, behaviours? This is the **interactionist approach** and it is the position that most modern psychologists hold. If we look back at some of the studies we have considered so far in this topic, we might want to conclude that while each points to a role for nature or nurture, none do so in such a way as to exclude a role for the influence of the other.

Let us consider Piaget's (1952) model of child development that you will meet later in the book (see page 210). Each stage that Piaget describes has an age range associated with it and this indicates that there is some overlap of stages. Furthermore, it suggests that not all children follow the stages at the same rate – presumably this is because the different environments of the children lead to different opportunities to move from one stage to the next. Hence, it makes most sense to see these stages as biologically driven but at a rate determined by the environment (nature plus nurture).

An even stronger case can be made for the Gottesman and Shields' (1976) findings. They stated that the concordance rate for MZ twins was 58 per cent. If these twins share 100 per cent of their DNA and schizophrenia is solely controlled by nature (in other words, by DNA), then the concordance rate would be expected to be 100 per cent. We can assume, therefore, that the other 42 per cent chance of both twins having schizophrenia is to do with the environment. Again, then, we have a case where the outcome is a balance between nature and nurture.

If we look at the studies supporting the nurture side of the debate we see there, too, that nature plays a part. In the case of Little Albert, the fear response already existed as part of Albert's repertoire of behaviours, so the conditioning only changed the circumstances in which the fear response was displayed. Likewise, with Held and Hein's study, the basis for depth perception had to be innately wired into the visual system of the kittens (the biology of the eye and brain) or else no amount of environmental activity could lead to its development.

One area of psychology that has embraced the interactionist approach is health psychology. Many health psychology explanations incorporate the idea that our behaviours are the result of biological, psychological and social processes – this interaction is referred to as the biopsychosocial approach. The approach has its origins in an explanation of cardiovascular disease by Engel (1977). He suggested that heart disease is the end point of a large variety of factors,

Key term

Interactionist approach: in the context of nature and nurture, it is one that considers behaviour to be influenced by both nature and nurture.

including genetic vulnerabilities (nature), poverty, diet, smoking, exercise and coping with stress factors (nurture). This approach has been used to explain all manner of health behaviours, including why diets fail to be adhered to or why some people become nicotine addicts or alcoholics.

It is not just in the domain of health that the interactionist approach is important. Maguire et al.'s (2000) study of taxi drivers has shown that the size of brain areas can change if certain environmental conditions are in place. They looked at an area of the brain called the hippocampus. This region of the brain is known to be involved in spatial representation. Since taxi drivers have to internally learn the map of the city in which they work, their hippocampi become larger than in others who are not taxi drivers. This shows that our brain is plastic (in other words, it can change its size and shape according to the environmental activities that we engage in). Clearly, nature creates the brain but the environment has a large say in how it grows and develops.

KEY POINTS

- The nature–nurture debate concerns the degree to which our behaviours are controlled by our heredity and how much they are controlled by our environment.

- The nature view holds that we cannot help the way we are.

- The nurture view holds that we can change the way we are.

- There are many areas of psychology that suggest our behaviour is significantly influenced by our biology. These include the fields of developmental psychology and clinical psychology.

- A purely nurturist view suggests that our entire behavioural repertoire is the result of social and environmental influences. It too has a lot of supporting evidence from numerous fields of psychology.

- No research, however, has demonstrated that a behaviour is purely due to nature or purely due to nurture.

- The interactionist position argues that behaviours have both nature and nurture components and that neither one provides a complete explanation on its own.

Reductionism and holism

In this topic we are going to look at what we might consider to be an adequate explanation for behaviour. This is not as simple as it sounds and we will see that different kinds of psychologists have differing ideas as to what kind of data are required for a complete explanation of a psychological phenomenon. We will start by looking at what we mean by the different kinds of explanation and then consider how psychologists argue that a particular kind is a complete explanation. Of course, there are also those who believe that no single kind provides a complete explanation and we will look at this position at the end of the topic.

Levels of explanation in psychology

Before we delve into the details of reductionism and holism, it is useful to consider the concept of **levels of explanation**. This term refers to the kind of explanation being provided. The lowest level of explanation of relevance to psychology would be biochemical reduction, where all behaviours can be explained at the biochemical level (in terms of the chemical substances in the brain). The next level up would be the physiological level, where the explanation would be in terms of the way in which the brain works (in terms of neurons firing and the structure of the brain). At the top of this hierarchy probably lies the sociocultural level of explanation (explanation in terms of the interactions between the social environment and cultural influences). Going back the other way is referred to as **reductionism** (for example, reducing the psychological level to the physiological level). Reduction is possible if everything about the explanation at a higher level can be fully replicated at the next level down. For example, if you believe that everything we understand about love can be fully explained by talking about neurons firing in the brain then we can say that love can be reduced to brain processes. So what separates out different kinds of reductionists is the lowest level to which they believe reduction works. For the behaviourist, social and environmental factors (that lie above this level) can be explained fully by looking directly at behaviour (for example, in terms of conditioning). For the biochemist, even behaviour can be reduced to chemical interactions in the brain.

If we adopt any single one of the above levels of explanation then we are being some form of reductionist. So where does this leave holism? The holist argues that there may well be different levels of explanation but that behaviour cannot be perfectly reduced to any single one of them. Reducing a higher level to a lower level gives a partial explanation; however, it leaves something out that can only be explained at that higher level.

Level of explanation	Description	Example research evidence
Biological	All can be explained in terms of the working of the brain.	Shinkareva et al. (2010)
Evolutionary	All can be explained by reference to the evolutionary adaptations that lead to a behaviour.	Dawkins (1989)
Behavioural	All can be explained with reference to learning processes.	Tarbox et al. (2006)
Cognitive	All can be explained by understanding the information processing that happens.	Atkinson and Shiffrin (1968)
Social/Environmental	All can be explained by understanding the things that happen in the social environment.	Deregowski (1972)

Table 1.1 Levels of explanation

Reductionism

People often confuse reductionism and determinism (see earlier in this chapter). Reductionism is when we can replace an explanation of a phenomenon at one level with an explanation of that phenomenon at a lower level without losing any of the quality of the explanation. For example, imagine you are trying to explain what water is to someone. Water is a molecule. That is one level of explanation of water. However, water is also composed of two atoms of hydrogen and one atom of oxygen so water can also be explained at a lower level as H_2O. The question we need to ask ourselves is, does the explanation of water lose something if we try to explain it as H_2O? The answer, in this case, is no, so we can say that water can be reduced to H_2O. In other words, explaining hydrogen, oxygen, their relative quantities, and other physical features such as the bonds between the atoms fully explains water – it leaves nothing out.

So how are reductionism and determinism related to each other such that it causes some confusion? Fig. 1.9 shows that reductionism works at a single moment, whereas determinism works across moments.

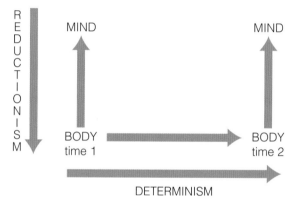

Fig. 1.9 The distinction between reductionism and determinism. Reductionism is about cause and effect at one moment in time and determinism is about cause and effect across time.

In the context of psychology, reductionism is about trying to explain complex systems using the component parts that make them up. So, for example, if you are in love, we can ask whether that mental state can be fully explained by looking at what is going on in the brain. Or maybe we could explain love by reducing it down to its adaptive features that have been passed on through evolution. We could even reduce it to a series of stimulus–response relationships as a behaviourist might do. Critics of reductionism often suggest that this position underestimates the complexity of human behaviour, but reductionism is more about trying to find simple explanations for complex phenomena. Let us explore these alternative kinds of reduction in a little more detail.

Biological reductionism

Biological reductionism is probably the most obvious form of reductionism. With the advances being made in neuroscience it is ever more the case that we can find links between what happens in the brain and what happens psychologically. Take, for example, our current ability to perform brain imaging while a person is engaging in a task. In a recent study by Shinkareva et al. (2010) fMRI was used while participants were viewing different words and pictures. The stimuli were either tools or dwellings. By studying the areas of the brain that became active and the patterns of that activity, participants were able to match patterns of words and pictures to the categories of stimulus. It was then possible for experienced neuroscientists to identify which category had been presented when they had not been present during the experiment.

This gives very strong evidence that we can reduce certain kinds of psychological process (in this case, categorization of simple words or images) to particular types of brain activity. However, we must be cautious not to take this finding too far. The stimuli being used in the study were simple and confined to discrete cognitive categories. This is a long way from being able to understand what a person is thinking on an everyday basis in terms of that thought's cognitive, social and emotional content.

Another study that looked at brain activation was one in which the effect of childhood poverty and chronic stress (Chapter 7 looks at stress in more detail) were investigated as a cause of long-term changes to responses to emotion. Kim et al. (2013) showed that things that happen to you in early life can have a lasting effect on your brain physiology and that these effects can last into later life. This study illustrates how a behavioural response like the stress response might be reducible to a set of activities in certain parts of the brain.

> **Key term**
>
> **Biological reductionism**: all behaviour can be reduced to, and explained by, the biology of the organism at that moment in time.

KEY STUDY: KIM ET AL. (2013)

In a longitudinal study by Kim et al. (2013), 49 participants who lived in childhood poverty at age nine were examined using fMRI at age 24. The imaging was used to look at the brain responses to their ability to regulate their emotions. Participants were asked to experience a negative emotion (through the use of negative images) and then either to maintain that emotion or to try to reduce it using a cognitive technique (i.e. thinking less negatively). Kim et al. found that childhood poverty had reduced activity in parts of the frontal cortex and increased activity in the amygdala (so it affected emotional regulation). These areas of the brain are involved in the regulation of emotions. From a reductionist viewpoint, we can conclude that a lack of emotional regulation can be reduced to activity in certain regions of the brain.

The evidence provided by Kim et al. (2013) would seem to indicate strongly that our ability to regulate our emotions can be fully understood at the level of brain anatomy and physiology. However, what Kim et al. have provided might be said to be a correlation between things that happen in the brain and behaviours that we experience. This kind of research only records what is going on, but to be sure that the relationship is causal we would have to induce a predicted emotional state by externally activating the relevant part of the brain. This, of course, is an unethical thing to do (see the topic on ethics later in this chapter) and so it remains that the relationship is only correlational. While it is possible to do the necessary experiment using animals, we would still be having to make the leap from animal brains to human brains. It is clear, then, that we could strongly argue the case for biological processes playing a role in behaviour, but we can be less certain that a complete reduction to biology is warranted.

Evolutionary reductionism

This form of reductionism tries to explain phenomena as a result of evolutionary adaptation – in other words, a behaviour can be explained by its adaptive value alone. According to Dawkins (1989), our biology only exists as a machine to serve the succession of our genes. Of course, genes themselves cannot act or behave, so they dictate and control the behaviour of the organism through gene expression (referred to as the phenotype). Those expressions that lead to survival of the organism have a chance of being passed on to the offspring. Those that also increase the likelihood of finding a mate have a higher chance of being passed on through successfully having those offspring. This seems a very mechanistic view of our existence as human beings.

Link

For more on phenotypes, see page 236 of Book 1.

Behavioural reductionism

People who subscribe to behavioural reductionism believe that all behaviour can be explained by past learning. A main proponent of this position was Skinner, who developed theories around operant conditioning to explain how previous experiences dictate actions in the present (Skinner, 1938). In simple terms, we will repeat any behaviours that led to a pleasant outcome and not repeat those that led to an unpleasant outcome. For example, imagine that you are learning to drive. If we take the example of steering correctly, the reward (pleasant outcome) might be that you didn't hit the parked car you drove past, so you will steer that way again in the future. However, if the driving instructor had to grab the wheel to stop you hitting the parked car, this will be unpleasant and you will try different behaviours in future until you find one that results in a pleasant outcome. Thinking in terms of behavioural reduction has been shown to have some benefits in the world of autism. The use of token economies can help autistic children to develop positive behaviours – this is where the reward is in the form of a token that can later be used to 'pay' for a reward. Tarbox et al. (2006) used a token economy to reward an autistic boy for attending his therapy sessions. The tokens then could be used for treats. In this way we could suggest that the boy's behaviour could be reduced to the rewards obtained.

Cognitive reductionism

Cognitive psychology is another reductionist approach to psychology. The principle behind cognitive psychology is that behaviour can be defined by information processing. The informational processes are such things as attention, memory and thinking. As these processes can all be replicated in a computer, they can, presumably, be explained in such terms. Hence, the argument is that behaviours can be fully reduced to our cognitions. If we take a simple model of memory like the modal model (Atkinson and Shiffrin, 1968), we can see how this attempted to fully explain how short-term memory gets transferred to long-term memory. In doing so, it claimed that memory was reducible to a cognitive, information-processing model.

> **ACTIVITY 1.7**
>
> Memory is a complex behaviour. Consider how you might construct an explanation of memory by reducing it to the cognitive, behavioural, evolutionary or biological levels of explanation. Do any of these levels leave something important out that could only be accounted for by a holistic approach?

Environmental reductionism

Environmental reductionism is an attempt to explain all behaviour in terms of environmental interactions, especially learning. The most extreme form of this reductionism is behaviourism. The behaviourists believed that all behaviour can be explained completely by the environmental interactions that preceded it. These interactions are what we refer to as conditioning (in its broadest sense). So, for example, a child doing their homework could be reduced to the positive reinforcement received for completing homework on past occasions. Given that the environment is constantly providing feedback to us, it might not be possible to identify all of the environmental consequences that lead to every behaviour. However, the behaviourist would argue that there are enough laboratory-controlled examples to support the basic principle of environmental reduction.

Deregowski (1972) also suggested that the learning achieved through interaction with the environment was enough alone to explain behaviour. He reviewed studies in which people were shown the picture in Fig. 1.10. When this was shown to Western participants, the perception was that the hunter was throwing his spear at the antelope. When it was shown to some non-Western tribal participants, they were unclear as to whether the hunter was trying to spear the antelope or the elephant. The only explanation for that confusion would be a lack of depth perception, and as depth perception requires learning, Deregowski concluded that no learning had taken place. The conclusion would be that depth perception can be reduced to a feature of the environment, namely, learning.

> **Key term**
>
> **Environmental reductionism:** all behaviour can be reduced to and explained by the environmental circumstances impacting on the organism at that moment in time.

Fig. 1.10 An image that requires depth perception to decide whether the elephant or the antelope is being targeted. Failure to resolve this potential ambiguity means that depth perception must be learned.

Exam hint

You will need to name two types of reductionism and then give a brief account of the principle idea that it refers to. It would be useful to provide an example of each type.

Key term

Holism: the idea that complex behaviours cannot be fully explained by reducing them to explanations at lower levels, but must be explained at the highest, holistic level.

EXAMPLE EXAM QUESTION

Briefly outline TWO types of reductionism. (4 marks)

Holism

Holism is the idea that humans are complex individuals whose actions are not explicable from just one point of view. In other words, every time you reduce one level to a lower level, something gets left out of the explanation. A couple of examples might help to explain this. Suppose you and another person are in love with each other. We could explain your behaviour in terms of the social and environmental circumstances that allowed you to meet, the things you have in common, and so on. We could also describe the reasons for the physical attraction in terms of biological features and we could describe the parts of the brain that are active when you have a loving emotion. However, you might find it hard to accept that all of these aspects (the social, the cognitive and the emotional) are just chemicals interacting inside your brain or are just learned behaviours, or just aspects of evolutionary adaptation. You might not consider that any one of those explanations is a complete explanation of being in love. If so, you are a holist.

A second example returns us to the water we considered at the beginning of the topic. There, we decided that we might fully explain water by explaining its constituent parts, namely H_2O. Philosophers have an interesting question following on from such reductionism that you might like to ponder. We know that a body of water is wet. We also know that a body of water is composed of lots and lots of molecules of H_2O. The question is, 'Is a single molecule of H_2O wet?' In other words, does knowing everything there is to know about H_2O tell you about the wetness of water? Depending on whether you are a reductionist or a holist, you will come up with a different solution to the question.

Holism has been used by the humanist approach to psychology. One proponent of this approach was Abraham Maslow. He suggested that the entire human is more than just the collection of biology or cognitions or learned behaviours, as those things do not capture the emotional aspects of our existence, nor do they capture our individuality. This thinking incorporates free will and subjectivity and both of these are things that reductionism has difficulty explaining. The humanist approach gave rise to Maslow's 'hierarchy of needs' theory, which suggests that in order to become a complete individual we must satisfy lower, physical needs but also higher order growth needs. The pinnacle of this is self-actualization – this goes beyond that which can be reduced to the lower levels of the hierarchy (see Fig. 1.11).

Fig. 1.11 Maslow's hierarchy of needs model

Another consequence of holistic thinking was Rogers' (1951) approach to psychotherapy. He used a client-centred approach (called person-centred therapy), in which the client was asked to reflect on their current, subjective understanding of their problem. It therefore viewed the person as a whole being and not as the sum of some component parts. Rogers, therefore, rejected the reductionist and deterministic nature of both behaviourist and psychodynamic therapies.

KEY STUDY:	ROGERS' APPROACH TO THERAPY

Rogers was a humanist who believed that the most appropriate way to provide psychological therapy was to treat the client as an entire human and not as being made up of separate parts like cognitions, emotions and so on. He was, therefore, a holist, and his research centred on trying to understand a person as a whole. His research with clients led him to believe that we all have a real self and an ideal self. The real self is about how I am and how others perceive me. The ideal self is about how I would like to be. For Rogers, psychological anxiety stems from the real and ideal selves being too far apart from each other. This reasoning allowed him to produce seven characteristics that he believed were true of a fully functioning person (Rogers, 1961). These include attributes such as openness to experience, creativity and leading a rich, full life.

Rogers' approach to therapy was person-centred. This means that instead of the therapist making suggestions about what the client should do, the therapist enables the client to come to their own conclusions about the best way forward. This can only come about because the therapist treats the client as a whole, unique individual.

THINKING SCIENTIFICALLY: THE CASE FOR THE CASE STUDY

Many holistic psychologists such as Rogers (1961), prefer to use methodologies with which they can learn what makes the individual the person they are. The case study is not itself a methodology, but uses a collection of methods, such as observations and interviews, to build up a holistic picture of that individual. Thus it is necessarily idiographic (see the next topic). The data, once collected, can be analysed using a number of different qualitative methods that are designed to extract certain kinds of information from the available data. For example, a thematic analysis might be used to pick out the themes that emerged during the course of an interview.

The strength of the case study is that it provides richer and more detailed data than can be achieved through other methods. As well as being holistic, they can be used to provide some initial findings that indicate which direction future research should take. However, they have their limitations in that they do not provide the means for generalization and they can be difficult to replicate.

Exam hint

This requires that you provide a definition of holism and use one example to illustrate the term.

EXAMPLE EXAM QUESTION

What is meant by the term holism? (2 marks)

Evaluating reductionism and holism

There are good and bad points to both reductionism and holism and, in some ways, support for one is a lack of support for the other. The appeal of something like biological reductionism is that it tries to offer a complete explanation of behaviour. However, it fails to acknowledge that the environment has any role to play. Similarly, all forms of reductionist approach feel like they leave something important out and so do not provide a complete explanation. One reason for this feeling might be that to reduce all behaviour to one kind of causal influence oversimplifies the human condition and appears to minimize the importance of complexity.

The main strength of holism is that it argues for all aspects of existence (biological, psychological and social) having an important part to play in explaining behaviour. However, there is not much evidence to support this point of view.

ACTIVITY 1.8

Fill in the table below to make sure you fully understand the different positions covered in this topic.

	Explanation	Example	Strength	Limitation
Biological reduction				
Cognitive reduction				
Environmental reduction				
Behavioural reduction				
Holism				

KEY POINTS

- Psychological explanations can be provided at different levels. Supporters of these different levels of explanation all claim that their level provides a complete explanation of behaviour.

- The levels of explanation can be seen as a hierarchy, with explanation at each higher level being potentially reduced to explanations at lower levels.

- The lowest level of reduction is the physical level, but the lowest useful level for a psychological explanation is probably the biological level.

- Influencing the biological level are the genetic and evolutionary levels that determine our biology.

- Higher levels of reduction are the behavioural and cognitive levels of reduction.

- The highest level of reduction is the environmental level.

- In opposition to reductionism is holism, the position that claims that psychological phenomena cannot be reduced to lower levels of explanation.

- Holism is supported most strongly by the humanist approach in psychology.

Idiographic and nomothetic approaches

One of the many debates in psychology is whether it is better to get lots of data from lots of participants or lots of data from one or two individuals. In this topic we look at the advantages and disadvantages of conducting research on individuals (the **idiographic approach**) or on groups (the **nomothetic approach**). These terms were first introduced into psychology by Gordon Allport in 1937. We will see that the principles behind each approach are different and lead to different kinds of methodology being employed.

Key terms

Idiographic approach: how individuals behave and how they differ.

Nomothetic approach: using group data in order to create theories and laws about people's behaviour in general.

The idiographic approach

The principle behind this approach is that every individual is unique and so it makes sense to only study individuals. The term derives from the ancient Greek work *idios*, which means 'private'. The term embraces well the desire to capture the subjective experience of participants. In order to gather this type of data, a qualitative approach is usually employed. This involves getting in-depth information from each individual (often from an interview, but see the other methods below) and then analysing the data to extract the subjective elements. For example, one such method used for analysing interviews is a thematic analysis. Here the transcript of the interview is scrutinised for any reference to particular themes that are of interest. The themes being looked for can either have been determined before the study began, or can be any that emerge as a consequence of the questions that were asked.

Idiographic methods

Given that the idiographic approach is to collect data from individuals, the most obvious method for the idiographic researcher is the interview. Interviewing was the method of choice of Freud and other psychodynamic researchers. In the modern era, interviews are seen as a major method in social psychology and health psychology, as both of these domains seek to find out the personal stories concerning the topic under investigation. Indeed, interviews are seen as a methodology in almost all fields of psychology.

Alongside interviews, the idiographic researcher might use case studies, self-reports and autobiographies. These will often occur as one-off events where the researcher takes a snapshot of the individual at a moment in time, but they can also be part of a longitudinal approach in which the individual is asked for their account at different, significant time points. This can be a valuable technique in order to discover how individual thoughts and feelings change over time.

In the field of personality research, two important idiographic techniques emerged. The first was Kelly's (1955) repertory grid technique. Kelly was a clinical psychologist and the method was developed to help understand how his patients viewed certain roles, such as mother or father. The method combined a structured interview (see page 23) with a complicated statistical method called factor analysis to construct a personality profile for an individual. The method is designed to tease out how a person views and interprets their own past experiences. Another methodology is called the Q-sort. It was developed by Stephenson (1953) but was adopted by Rogers to investigate personality within his person-centred therapy. The Q-sort consists of 100 cards with statements on them. For a measure of personality, the cards might have things like 'very outgoing' or 'low self-esteem'. The participant/client must place each card on a nine-point scale that ranges from 'not at all like me' to 'extremely like me'. Having done this, the person then distributes the cards in the same fashion again but this time focusing on their ideal self rather than their actual self. The two sorts are compared and this allows the researcher/therapist to understand where a person is at present and what aspects of their personality they would like to change.

In some cases, it is not the methodology itself that is necessarily idiographic but how that methodology is used. An example of this is the observational technique. While observations are usually undertaken on many individuals, the detailed information from each individual being observed is a source of idiographic data. By paying attention to such detail, the researcher can distinguish between what is generally the case and what is displayed by fewer individuals.

Research using an idiographic approach

Piaget famously investigated the way in which children develop. He used only a few children to investigate whether there were universal elements of child development. Indeed, he also carried out a detailed set of observations of his own children's development. This source of rich information not only provided details about the developmental aspects under scrutiny (perceptual development, cognitive development, etc.) but also provided an intimate knowledge of the environmental circumstances under which these developmental changes took place.

Link

See more about Piaget's research in Chapter 4, Cognition and development.

The use of the idiographic approach in psychology has not been confined to humans. Gardner and Gardner (1969) used this approach to study a chimpanzee called Washoe. Their interest was in whether or not a chimpanzee could use language. They tried to teach Washoe American Sign Language, recognizing that the chimpanzee did not have the vocal capacity for real speech. They made detailed observations of Washoe's successes and failures and found that she could learn 350 words. This is similar to the normal vocabulary of a two- to three-year-old human child. Another similar chimp study was conducted by Terrace et al. (1979) in which the chimp Nim Chimpsky was successfully taught 125 signs.

ACTIVITY 1.9

Imagine you are interested in autobiographical memory (i.e. memory for your own personal history). Consider which idiographic methodology you might employ and what, if anything, you might be able to say about how autobiographical memories are stored.

EXAMPLE EXAM QUESTION

Identify TWO features of the idiographic approach. [2 marks]

Exam hint

This is a simple question for which you will get one mark for each correctly identified feature.

In the 1970s, Terrace and his colleagues became interested in whether or not it was possible to teach a chimpanzee human language. His interest came about as a result of three separate strands of the debate. Firstly, Skinner had claimed that there was no reason why an intelligent chimpanzee should not be able to learn language via conditioning. Secondly, Noam Chomsky, a well-known linguist at the time, claimed that only humans could use language. Thirdly, there was anecdotal evidence of Washoe from the Gardner and Gardner study having been taught to sign 350 words. Terrace and his colleagues tried to teach Nim Chimpsky (a play on Noam Chomsky) (see Fig. 1.12) language in a more sophisticated way and by having the chimp live among humans. This was to try to embed him into human culture as Terrace thought this would improve the chimp's chances. Terrace got all of the humans who were interacting with Nim to record every sign he made. Terrace was about to publish that Nim could sign 125 words when he noticed that Nim only ever signed as a response to a human signing. He was not able to use signs spontaneously for anything other than a simple 'gimme' command. He did not use the signs he knew to make conversation as a human would. Terrace concluded that it was not possible to teach sign language to a chimpanzee. At least, it was not possible with this particular chimpanzee.

Fig. 1.12 Nim Chimpsky using American sign language

Strengths and limitations of idiographic research

There are two main strengths of the idiographic approach. The first is that you get a very detailed and often a global understanding of an individual. The second is that idiographic research can lead to new ideas for more general research methodologies. Sometimes, the newest feature of an area to receive attention is the result of a finding from an idiographic study. Another positive aspect of this approach is that the attention to detail in collecting the data makes the participant feel valued.

There are also some limitations to idiographic research. By its very nature of being about the individual, it is difficult to generalize from idiographic data. We are never sure which of the data collected are representative of the larger group, which might be typical of a subgroup, and which are unique to that individual. A second limitation is that the data may be unreliable. Often, the data are an attempt to capture subjective experience. It is possible that the recollection is led by the researcher (experimenter bias) or is subject to demand characteristics. Furthermore, the data will need a degree of interpretation by the researcher and there is room here for subjectivity in that interpretation, especially if the data are emotive in nature (for example, interviews concerning child abuse).

The nomothetic approach

This approach is designed to extract the similarities between people by collecting data from groups and analysing that data on the basis of what the group generally shows. By taking this approach, psychologists attempt to create laws and to underline psychology's claim to be an objective science. The term comes from the ancient Greek word nomos, meaning 'laws', and thetēs, meaning 'one who establishes'; so a nomothete is someone who establishes laws. In order to establish laws, the nomothetic psychologist collects quantitative data, on the basis that only numbers permit statistical calculations and only these calculations allow us to make predictions – the purpose behind having a scientific law.

Just as a physicist can predict where a ball will land when you throw it across a lawn, a psychologist wants to be able to predict, for example, how well a person will do at school if they know the person's IQ. Of course, in the case of the physicist there are a lot of starting conditions that must be known (such as force of the throw, weather conditions, etc.) and the same is true for the psychologist. They must know, for example, the person's schooling opportunities, attention span, and so on. What is clear is that the things the physicist needs to know to make a prediction are far easier to measure than the things the psychologist needs to know. Nevertheless, the nomothetic approach can help us to understand the relative contribution a particular element makes to the overall law about a behaviour. By carrying out a nomothetic study, we might discover that knowing a person's IQ is a big part of our ability to know how that person will do at school. The nomothetic laws that are produced can fall under three categories, shown in Table 1.2.

Classifying people into groups	The purpose of these kinds of laws is to establish how people belong to particular groups and how this knowledge helps us to explain the kinds of behaviour different people will display. One such classification is DSM-5.
Creating principles of behaviour	This is the creation of laws that determine how people or animals will behave in certain situations. For example, Thorndike's 'law of effect' explains how positive reinforcement increases the likelihood that a behaviour will be repeated.
Producing behaviour scales or dimensions	This category establishes dimensions for which a person's position on that dimension can be determined. For example, the personality dimension of introversion and extraversion allows us to establish how introverted or extraverted a person is.

Table 1.2 Categories of the nomothetic approach

Nomothetic methods

The methods used by nomothetic psychologists are scientific and quantitative. These are covered in the Research Methods section at the beginning of this book. The most obvious of these methods is the experiment (pages 10–16). In an experiment, various controls are imposed so that only the variables of interest (there could be only one or many of these) are manipulated. In this way, any changes in the outcome of the behaviour can only be attributed to the manipulations of those variables. However, the experimental method is not the only one used in the nomothetic approach. Correlational designs (pages 24–27) and observations (pages 16–19) have their place here, too, provided they yield quantitative data that can be statistically analysed, as the goal is to be able to provide generalizations from a large set of group data.

It is worth noting that not all nomothetic studies are carried out in laboratories. It is possible to collect valuable data from studies conducted in real-life scenarios where variables are manipulated and as many extraneous variables (pages 15–16) as possible are controlled. These scenarios are referred to as field experiments (pages 9–10) and they can provide greater ecological validity to the objective, scientific method.

Research using the nomothetic method

Most of our psychological knowledge until about the 1980s was derived from nomothetic methods (with a few notable exceptions such as Freud and Piaget). The nomothetic approach was fairly dominant in all areas of psychology. In social psychology Milgram's obedience theory, Sherif's realistic conflict theory concerning prejudice, and Bandura's social learning theory all came from experiments. In cognitive psychology, Atkinson and Shiffrin's modal model of memory, Broadbent's theory of attention, and Johnson-Laird's theories about human reasoning also came from experimental studies. We could construct a similar list for every area of psychology. In addition, areas like personality used correlational designs to test theories about personality dimensions such as extraversion, open-mindedness, neuroticism, and so on.

One of the earliest attempts to demonstrate the existence of nomos within psychology was Thorndike's (1898) law of effect. Thorndike studied learning in cats using a puzzle box (see Fig. 1.13). A cat was placed inside the box and the box had a catch that opened it. Outside of the box was a piece of food to tempt the cat to try to escape the box. The cat would try to escape and would eventually trip the catch by accident. The cat was placed in the box again and again and the time it took for the cat to escape was recorded. Thorndike found that the time taken decreased with each new trial. Thorndike concluded that the food reward provided the drive for the cat to learn and remember how to escape the puzzle box. Hence, Thorndike's law of effect stated that any behaviour that is followed by pleasant consequences is likely to be repeated.

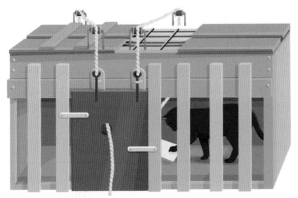

Fig. 1.13 Thorndike's puzzle box

KEY STUDY: SHERIF (1961)

Sherif was interested in how group conflict can lead to prejudice. He conducted a field experiment using 22 boys at a summer camp. The 12-year-old boys all knew each other but were randomly split into two groups. They were picked up from their home town in separate buses and taken to separate areas at the Robbers Cave State Park in Oklahoma. The groups set up separate camps and were unaware that there was a separate group residing a short distance away. The boys were in their own group for a period of time so that they could bond together and create a group identity. They chose names for their group, with one group being the Eagles and the other being the Rattlers.

Once the groups had bonded, Sherif arranged for a competition between the groups that included a tug-of-war, basketball competition and so on to take place over a few days. The winners would receive a trophy. Sherif noticed that an animosity towards the other group had instantly become apparent. When one group was deliberately delayed from getting to one of the events on time, the other group ate their food. What Sherif had created was an in-group, out-group situation whereby a person favours their own group's beliefs and actions and creates a negative stereotype about the outgroup. With very little interference from him, Sherif had created intergroup conflict from which he created his realistic conflict theory.

THINKING SCIENTIFICALLY: THE DANGERS OF GENERALIZATION

Given that Sherif's study was a field experiment, it had high ecological validity and, by using the nomothetic approach, he was able to use his results to construct a theory that he claimed applied to all groups. However, alongside the ethics of the study (see the next topic for more details), he had created artificial groups and was making generalizations from these groups to the general population. In addition, the groups were all boys, were children, and were a biased sample, so we might want to exercise some caution over his interpretation. Had Sherif conducted an idiographic study, he might have discovered that some boys were aggressive in their prejudice, whereas others simply went along with it as they did not want to be seen in a bad light by their own group. If this was the case, then there is a danger of treating all instances of stereotyping and prejudice the same. Undoubtedly, a stereotype emerges as there are a number of the group who do behave in a certain way. However, we must recognize that stereotypes can be misleading and do not tell us whether a particular individual will or will not act according to the stereotype. By assuming the stereotype to be true, and true of all individuals in that group, we create the means for prejudice and discrimination. The nomothetic approach can be guilty of giving scientific credibility to this kind of thinking.

ACTIVITY 1.10

List five research studies that you know and that have used the nomothetic approach. For each study, identify the theory or law that arose from this approach and consider whether any additional information might have been evident had an idiographic approach been utilized alongside the study.

Strengths and limitations of nomothetic research

The main strength of the nomothetic approach is that it is considered to be scientific as it can more easily provide predictions about large numbers of people. It is also considered to be the only approach that can lead to the construction of laws and theories. Furthermore, these laws and theories can be **empirically tested**. Another strength is that this approach tries to combine a number of perspectives, such as biological and social viewpoints.

One limitation of this approach is that the predictions made about groups might not apply to all individuals within the group. It is also the case that when two people within a group behave in an identical way, they may not be doing so for the same reasons. The methodologies used by the nomothetic approach can also be accused of lacking ecological validity, especially when they are laboratory based.

Key term

Empirically tested: testing in a scientific way that allows for a theory to be supported or refuted.

Exam hint

For the strength you could say why it is better than the idiographic approach and for the limitation you could say why it is weaker.

EXAMPLE EXAM QUESTION

Briefly explain ONE strength and ONE limitation of the nomothetic approach. (4 marks)

KEY POINTS

- The idiographic approach is based upon the principle that every individual is unique.
- The main methodology employed in idiographic research is the interview, but other methods, such as case studies, self-reports and autobiographies, can also be used.
- Piaget was a famous user of idiographic methods on humans, but they can also be used in animal research, as in the study of Washoe.

- The idiographic method has the advantage of providing a detailed understanding of the individual, but it is limited in its ability to generalize the results to other people.

- The nomothetic approach is based on the principle that collecting data from groups allows for the construction of theories and laws.

- The methodologies employed by the nomothetic approach are scientific and quantitative, and include experiments as the major method.

- Much of the research in psychology utilizes the nomothetic approach.

- One strength of the nomothetic approach is the ability to empirically test the theories produced, but a limitation is that not all people behave identically to the rest of a group.

Ethics

If you watch reality TV programmes you might ask yourself how the programme makers are allowed to get away with what they ask participants to do. It seems they are not under any requirements to behave in a certain way, nor are they under any obligation to look after the psychological well-being of their participants. Within science, and especially psychology, we must have more concern for the way in which we treat people and the way that what we do to them affects them psychologically. For this reason we have **ethical guidelines** according to which all research must conform. In the UK, Practitioner Psychologists are regulated by the **Health and Care Professions Council** (HCPC) which has *Standards of Performance, Conduct and Ethics* that registered psychologists must adhere to. Chartered Psychologists have a *Code of Ethics* and a *Code of Human Research Ethics* set by the **British Psychological Society** (BPS) that they are guided by. In the US, guidelines are supplied by the American Psychological Association (APA).

Ethics guidelines

Research that is funded by one of the main research councils in the UK must adhere to that research council's ethical framework. Many higher education institutions have their own ethics committee and set their own regulations for research that must be followed by their academic and research staff. However, many institutions and research funding bodies have used the BPS's ethical principles to inform their own policies and practices, in particular the BPS's *Code of Human Research Ethics* (2014).

Some of the more important ethical issues can be seen in Table 1.3.

Key terms

Ethical guidelines: a set of principles that can be used to judge whether or not a piece of research was conducted in an ethical manner.

Health and Care Professions Council (HCPC): a regulator, set up to protect the public against the risk of poor practice. They keep a register of health and care professionals who meet set standards for their training, professional skills, behaviour and health.

British Psychological Society: the professional body and learned society for psychologists in the UK.

Research methods link

See pages 37-42 for more about ethics.

Ethics principle	Description
Informed consent	Every participant should be fully informed about what will happen to them in the study and any psychological consequences that might arise from taking part. They should thereby be able to make an informed choice as to whether or not they wish to take part.
Deception	No participant should be deceived (i.e. lied to) by the researchers concerning the nature of the study or what will happen to them, unless this is absolutely necessary for the success of the study. In cases where deception is deemed necessary, the study must not place the participant in a position where they may encounter physical or psychological harm.
Right to withdraw	All participants must be able to withdraw themselves or their data from the study without having to explain why they wish to do so. Participants must be explicitly informed of the right to withdraw. In order to facilitate withdrawal and maintain anonymity (see confidentiality and anonymity), a participant code must be used to identify the research data.
Confidentiality and anonymity	Personal information about a participant must be kept confidential at all times and data with personal details must be kept in a secure environment. Personal details and other data should be kept separately so that study data are held anonymously. Once data have been analysed and are of no further use, data should be destroyed.
Debriefing	At the end of the study all participants must be debriefed. The debriefing should thank them for their participation, remind them of their right to withdraw their data (up to a defined time limit), remind them about anonymity and confidentiality, inform them further about the purpose of the study, allow them to have any questions answered, ensure that they have not been harmed in any way by taking part in the study, and notify them of who to contact if they should need to talk over their experience at a later date (usually a medical or psychological professional).
Harm to participants	All reasonable measures must be taken to ensure that the participant does not come to any physical or psychological harm whilst taking part in the study or as a result of having taken part.

Table 1.3 Process for ensuring the ethical practice of psychological research in the UK

An abandoned ham sandwich? Or a psychology department experiment? There was no way Fred could tell for sure.

Fig. 1.14 The problems of always providing informed consent

Have psychological studies always been ethical?

It is tempting to launch straight in to a piece on how studies of the past were completely unethical. An obvious choice for consideration is Milgram's (1963) obedience study, in which he successfully persuaded and deceived 63 per cent of participants to deliver a 450-volt shock to another human being. In fact, no real shocks were delivered and the study was done to see if people would obey an authority figure. In the context of Table 1.3, Milgram's study did not provide informed consent, used deception, prevented participants from withdrawing, and was said to have caused the participants considerable psychological harm. However, if we analyse each of these a little more closely, the picture is not that clear. Participants were deceived so they could not have given their informed consent. However, the very nature of the study required that participants did not know the study was about obedience (see Fig. 1.14). Had they known, they would hardly have been obeying. The prevention of participants from withdrawing from the study was also an essential part of the study as obedience requires that you are asked to do something you do not want to be doing. Finally, concerning psychological harm, Milgram (1964) surveyed those who had taken part in his study and found that 83.7 per cent had been glad they had taken part and only 1.3 per cent said that they wished they had not been involved.

What, if anything, was unethical about Milgram's study? The real question may lie in whether there are certain things that just should not be investigated as they pose too much of a risk to the well-being of participants. Here we have the real ethical dilemma. Milgram wanted to understand why ordinary Germans who had become soldiers during the Second World War would murder innocent Jewish civilians, including women and children. He wanted to know if this was a particular German trait or a human tendency to obey. However, we can ask whether the potential harm to participants was too great a price for such understanding. In Milgram's defence, he did not believe that so many participants (63 per cent) would deliver the highest shocks, as those he asked prior to the study believed that few American men would do such a thing.

Unfortunately, Milgram's tangle with ethics is not the only ethical question raised in psychology's chequered research history. Another classic study that raises ethical questions is Zimbardo's prison study. However, some of the most unethical studies are not as well known. Johnson (1939) carried out what has become known as 'The Monster Study'. He wanted to understand why people stutter and believed it to be learned rather than innate. He took 22 orphan children and divided them into two groups, stutterers and non-stutterers. Some in the stutterers group did not initially have stutters. The stutterers group received punishment for normal speech patterns while the non-stutterers group received praise for normal speech. Johnson found that those children in the stutterers group who did not have stutters at the start of the study had stutters by the end of it. Johnson claimed that this showed stuttering to be learned but it was clearly highly unethical to use an experiment to create stutters in non-stuttering children.

KEY STUDY: **ZIMBARDO'S STANFORD PRISON STUDY (1971)**

Zimbardo recruited 24 male students from volunteers, using a variety of psychological tests, to select those who appeared the most stable with no violent or antisocial tendencies. He randomly allocated each student the role of prisoner or guard. Prisoners were arrested at their homes early on Sunday morning, taken to the prison, searched, deloused and dressed in smock uniforms. They were referred to by number instead of by name. The guards were given uniforms, a 'night stick' or truncheon, and dark glasses. They were instructed to keep the prisoners under control but to use no physical violence.

Within a day the prisoners rebelled and ripped off their numbers. The guards responded by locking them in their cells and confiscating their blankets. As the experiment continued, the punishments imposed by the guards escalated. Prisoners were humiliated, deprived of sleep and made to carry out roll call in the night. One, who went on hunger strike in protest at the treatment, was force-fed by the guards and locked in a dark cupboard measuring only around four feet in size. The prisoners rapidly became depressed and passive, with some showing serious stress-related reactions to the experience. The role play, which had been intended to run for two weeks, was called off after just six days.

Zimbardo's interpretation of the findings was that social roles have an extraordinary power over individuals, making even the most well-adjusted capable of extreme brutality towards others. Ordinary, stable individuals can abuse power and behave in violent and antisocial ways if placed in a social role where this is acceptable behaviour. Zimbardo's research has become notorious in social psychology due to the implications of the findings and the ethical debates it provoked. Critics have argued that although Zimbardo asked for consent from his participants, he became too involved to see clearly what was happening and should have called off the study even earlier, as the atmosphere in the prison amounted to a 'living hell'.

The Stanford Prison study has become infamous, not just in social psychology but in popular culture as well, inspiring two feature films and a band, the Stanford Prison Experience. It has also been used to explain real-life atrocities, such as the brutalization of prisoners in Abu Ghraib prison during the Iraq war.

THINKING SCIENTIFICALLY: CAN THE ENDS JUSTIFY THE MEANS?

We can question the ethics of Zimbardo's experiment and there are a number of criticisms we can make, but can it be justified by the information it provided? As mentioned above, Zimbardo became too involved in the study. He played the role of prison warden and so was unable to separate his desire to see what would happen from his need to protect the safety of his participants. Indeed, it is even suggested that he may have encouraged the activities of the guards. It took a graduate student employed to interview participants, Christina Maslach (who later became Zimbardo's wife), to stop the study when she convinced Zimbardo that the experiment was out of hand. If we ask why Zimbardo had not decided to stop the experiment himself, we discover that he, like Milgram, wanted to understand why the Nazi Germans carried out their atrocities on the Jews (he and Milgram were high-school classmates and their fascination may have arisen then). We can list the areas where the study lacked ethical considerations as follows.

• Lack of informed consent as the prisoner participants did not know that they would be arrested in public rather than simply asked to attend the experiment.
• Introduction of psychological harm in that steps were not taken to ensure the psychological safety of the participants. This was the result of experimenter bias on the part of Zimbardo by taking on the role of prison superintendent. Indeed, one prisoner had to leave the study after only 36 hours as he was psychologically disturbed by his experience.

The number of methodological flaws in the study also makes the ethics questionable. The study has been criticized for suffering from sampling bias, experimenter bias, demand characteristics, and a lack of scientific controls.

The question of whether we are better off for Zimbardo having carried out his experiment (the ends justifying the means) is another way in which we might, retrospectively, judge the prison study. Unfortunately, here too the study does not hold up to scrutiny. The brutalization of prisoners in Abu Ghraib clearly shows that the study has not influenced the way in which we behave. All in all, then, we must conclude that Zimbardo's study was highly unethical.

These are just a few examples of unethical research that has been carried out in psychology in the past. However, they were all carried out before the ethical guidelines were in place. Furthermore, they were all carried out as a result of a genuine interest in knowing how humans function psychologically. At the time, this research would probably not have been considered unethical and so we must be careful not to judge too harshly what would have been seen as normal scientific enquiry. Perhaps what is more important is that we can be assured that these kinds of study would not occur in a modern context.

ACTIVITY 1.11

Psychology strives to provide a complete understanding of the human condition. Discuss whether it can achieve this aim if it can only carry out ethical research.

The ethics of using animals in psychological research

As with human research, ethical principles apply equally (or, perhaps, even more so) to animal research. Again, psychology's past has not been shrouded in glory as far as its past use of animals has been concerned. During the twentieth century, animals were used to investigate things it was deemed too cruel to use humans for. Many of these studies involved developmental issues, whether these were to do with environmental aspects of development (see Harlow below), the development of cognitive skills such as perception (Held and Hein – see page 97), or the development of mental illness (see the *Key study* below). As we have seen, the fascination in this era was the nature–nurture debate and using animals provided an easy way to investigate this. We have already encountered Held and Hein's (1963) kitten carousel experiment. There were many other such experiments, but two are worth illustrating as they raise interesting ethical issues.

Harlow (1958) conducted a study using rhesus monkeys to investigate attachment, the process by which an infant bonds with its mother. Baby rhesus monkeys, like human babies, are dependent on their mother for nutrition, comfort, safety and socialization. Attachment theory suggests that a baby will attach most strongly to the provider of food. Harlow tested this by rearing monkeys either in isolation or by providing surrogate mothers. The surrogate mother was either made of wire or of cloth and could be used to provide or not provide food. Harlow discovered that the monkeys would stay with the cloth mother (comfort) even if it did not provide food. They would only venture to the wire food-providing monkey when hungry. From an ethics perspective this was a cruel experiment. The baby monkeys suffered emotional harm from being reared in isolation and could not later socialize with other monkeys. Furthermore, once the female babies became adults they were unable to appropriately look after their own infants.

Link

For more on Harlow's study, see pages 157–158 of Book 1.

Exam hint

For this answer you will need to name three reasons why a piece of research could be called unethical and give an example for each. It is probably easiest to use the BPS *Code of Human Research Ethics* to select the features for this answer.

EXAMPLE EXAM QUESTION

Briefly outline THREE ways in which a piece of research can be considered to be unethical. (6 marks)

Learned helplessness occurs when an animal believes that nothing can be done to alter a bad situation. This belief is the direct result of previous experiences where actions have not made things any better. As a consequence, the animal fails to take measures that are available to avoid a negative outcome due to these prior experiences. Seligman stumbled onto this finding while looking at classical conditioning in dogs using a tone-conditioned stimulus and a shock-unconditioned stimulus. He decided to investigate this further using the following conditions.

Condition 1   Dogs strapped into a harness and then released after a period of time.

Condition 2   Dogs placed in a similar harness and given electric shocks that they could turn off by pressing their nose against a panel.

Condition 3   Dogs placed in a similar harness and given electric shocks that they could not turn off.

After the dogs had been exposed to their condition, they were placed in a shuttle box (see Fig. 1.15). This had two sides separated by a low fence that the dogs could easily jump over. On one side of the box shocks were delivered but on the other side shocks were never delivered. When placed on the shock side, dogs from conditions 1 and 2 quickly learned that jumping over the fence led to safety. However, dogs in condition 3 never learned this and simply lay down in the shuttle box, awaiting the shocks.

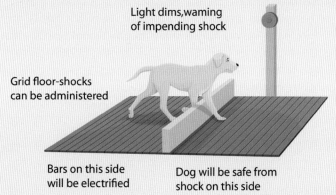

Light dims, waming of impending shock

Grid floor-shocks can be administered

Bars on this side will be electrified

Dog will be safe from shock on this side

Fig. 1.15 Seligman's shuttle box. The dogs were safe from shock on one side of the box but not on the other side.

The decision about whether animal research is ever justified is a difficult one and people are usually on one side or other of the debate. In some ways, we can ask whether the information gained from studies like the one by Seligman help us to better understand human behaviour. The model of why the dogs behaved with learned helplessness has been used to explain some forms of the development of depression in humans. On the other hand, we must ask whether the

ISSUES AND DEBATES

same information could have been gained in a different way. It is unclear what the answer would have been in the case of Seligman's research.

Another consideration often stated is the level of consciousness exhibited by the animal being tested. While this is not easy to ascertain, we generally agree that a dog is more conscious than a pigeon or a rat. On the one hand, it might be more ethical to only use animals that have a low level of consciousness as they are less aware of what is happening to them. However, the risk is that the data obtained are too far removed from the human case to be of any value in determining the behaviour of humans. What is certain is that there are now guidelines that force researchers to thoroughly justify why they need to use animals in their research. Without this justification they will not be permitted to carry out the research. You must decide for yourself where your own personal morality lies with respect to this issue.

ACTIVITY 1.12

Discuss the contribution that animal research has made to psychology. Is there still a role for this kind of research in the future or should we now consider it to be unethical?

Social sensitivity

Socially sensitive research is any research for which the topic area can be regarded as emotionally sensitive (in other words, any research where participants may display an emotional response). A useful definition comes from Sieber and Stanley (1988). They state that such research involves 'studies in which there are potential consequences or implications, either directly for the participants in the research or for the class of individuals represented by the research'.

They identified five areas where social sensitivity is important. These were:

1. The implications of the research.
   For example, research in areas such as cultural differences in IQ could be used to justify discrimination.

2. What will the research be used for?
   Bowlby's work on attachment was criticized for its use in justifying why women should stay at home and look after the children.

3. The effect on public policy.
   Cyril Burt's research on IQ was used to inform government educational policy and led to the introduction of the 11-plus exam.

4. The validity of the research.
   Zimbardo's prison study was invalid as it contained experimenter, methodological and cultural bias.

5. The findings should be freely available
   Open availability of research findings helps to prevent exploitation of the results. We can ask whether the cost of journal articles denies access to research findings.

There are also other issues around socially sensitive research. Privacy refers to not encouraging a participant to reveal more than they intend to. This is especially important in qualitative research that uses interviewing. Equitable treatment is another consideration – the researcher needs to ensure that all participants are treated the same throughout the study. Finally, the ownership of the data can be critically important. The researcher needs to ensure that the data cannot be used for any reason other than that intended by the research.

EXAMPLE EXAM QUESTION

Explain what is meant by the term socially sensitive research. (4 marks)

Exam hint

To answer this question you could use Sieber and Stanley's (1988) definition of socially sensitive research. You should list all five criteria and provide a brief outline of what each one means. By using research examples for a couple of them you will underline to the marker that you truly know what the terms mean.

KEY POINTS

- Psychological research must be conducted in an ethical manner.
- The study that Milgram conducted in 1963 would probably not be considered to be ethical today.
- There are a number of studies that in the past were not required to adhere to the strict guidelines on ethics that we have today.
- There are perhaps even greater ethical issues surrounding the use of animals in psychological research.
- Again, up until the later part of the twentieth century there were few restrictions on what could be done using animals.
- We now have a better idea of how research can be socially sensitive.
- According to Sieber and Stanley (1988) there are five areas where social sensitivity is important.

Example exam questions

1. Which TWO of the following are ethical considerations? **(2 marks)**

   The number of participants   Giving informed consent   Debriefing
   Experimenter bias   The idiographic approach

2. Outline TWO types of determinism. **(4 marks)**

3. Briefly outline what is meant by beta bias in the context of research into gender. **(2 marks)**

4. Briefly explain ONE strength and ONE limitation of a belief in free will. **(4 marks)**

5. Read the item below and answer the questions that follow:

   > A personality researcher used a nomothetic approach to investigate extraversion and introversion in the context of family gatherings. He used a large number of participants and gave them all a questionnaire to fill in. The statements on the questionnaire were all based on how comfortable the person felt when in certain family situations. Answers were provided using a classic 5-point Likert scale along the dimension of 'strongly agree' to 'strongly disagree'.

   a) How might the researcher investigate this using an idiographic approach? **(6 marks)**

   b) Briefly explain the difference between nature and nurture. **(4 marks)**

   c) What is meant by the term cultural bias? **(2 marks)**

Exam focus

Read through the following example exam question, example student answers, and examiner comments. Then, have a go at answering the question yourself!

EXAMPLE EXAM QUESTION, TAKEN FROM PAGE 139

Briefly outline TWO types of reductionism. (4 marks)

Saffy's answer

One type of reductionism is biological reductionism. This is where the researcher claims that a biological explanation provides a complete explanation for the behaviour under consideration. An example of biological reductionism would be research that uses fMRI to show which parts of the brain are involved in a behaviour. This brain activity would be used to explain fully why that behaviour occurred.

A second type of reductionism is environmental reductionism. This is where the researcher claims that an environmental explanation provides a complete explanation for the behaviour under consideration. An example would be where a person was praised for doing their homework and so they behave in a similar way in future. The behaviour can be reduced to the environment in that the positive environment experienced fully explains why the child does the homework.

Examiner comment: This answer receives full marks because for both types of reductionism there is a clear statement of what the term means and this is followed by a good example that illustrates the candidate understands the meaning of the term.

Tim's answer

One type of reductionism is biological reductionism. This is like having an explanation using a part of the brain. For example, it might be saying that a part of the brain causes your arm to move. A second type of reductionism is humanistic reductionism. This is where behaviours can be reduced to our cognitions. An example would be where we reduced memory to its component cognitive parts of sensory memory, short-term memory and long-term memory.

Examiner's comment: For the first part of the answer the candidate has correctly identified a type of reductionism. However, the explanation of what it means is vague and not wholly correct as the use of moving an arm is confused between reductionism and determinism. Hence this part of the answer would get one mark.

The second type is labelled incorrectly as what is described is cognitive reductionism rather than humanistic reductionism (remember that the humanist position is holistic rather than reductionist). However, the explanation of cognitive reductionism is accurate and so this part would also receive one mark.

The overall mark for this answer would be 2 marks.

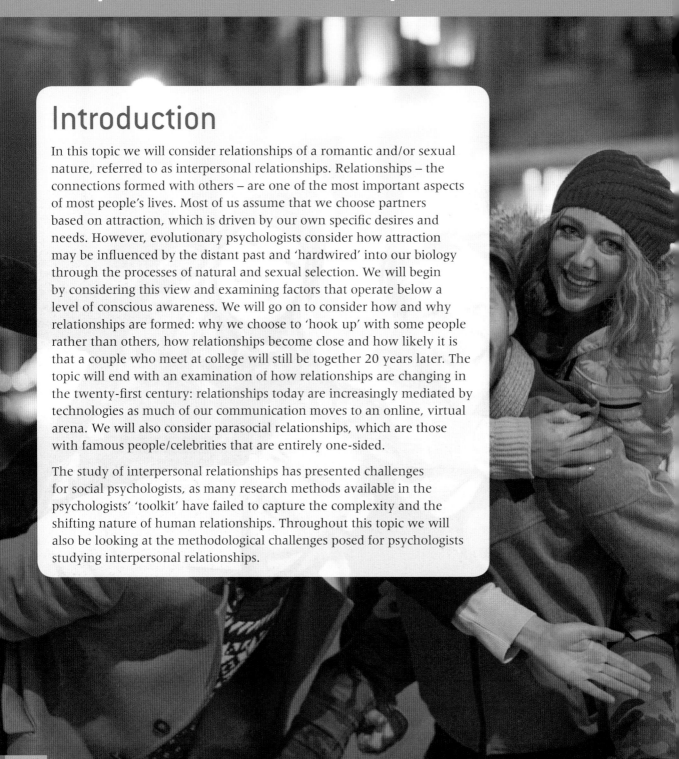

Part 3:
Issues and options in psychology

Chapter 2: Relationships

Introduction

In this topic we will consider relationships of a romantic and/or sexual nature, referred to as interpersonal relationships. Relationships – the connections formed with others – are one of the most important aspects of most people's lives. Most of us assume that we choose partners based on attraction, which is driven by our own specific desires and needs. However, evolutionary psychologists consider how attraction may be influenced by the distant past and 'hardwired' into our biology through the processes of natural and sexual selection. We will begin by considering this view and examining factors that operate below a level of conscious awareness. We will go on to consider how and why relationships are formed: why we choose to 'hook up' with some people rather than others, how relationships become close and how likely it is that a couple who meet at college will still be together 20 years later. The topic will end with an examination of how relationships are changing in the twenty-first century: relationships today are increasingly mediated by technologies as much of our communication moves to an online, virtual arena. We will also consider parasocial relationships, which are those with famous people/celebrities that are entirely one-sided.

The study of interpersonal relationships has presented challenges for social psychologists, as many research methods available in the psychologists' 'toolkit' have failed to capture the complexity and the shifting nature of human relationships. Throughout this topic we will also be looking at the methodological challenges posed for psychologists studying interpersonal relationships.

What is covered in Relationships?

RELATIONSHIPS

Evolutionary explanations for partner preferences

The **evolutionary approach** argues that the behaviours and bodily structures that we see today have their roots in the distant past. For thousands of years, our human ancestors followed a hunter-gatherer existence. They lived in small, close-knit groups, moving around in search of food. Life was harsh. Supplies of food and water were unpredictable, offspring were vulnerable, and many died in the first few years of life. It is hard to imagine how this world, so different from today, could influence our behaviour in relationships. However, in evolutionary terms, only a small amount of time has passed since our ancestors lived a hunter-gatherer existence, and some of the attributes that enabled survival and reproduction in this environment have been passed down to us today, via genes.

Fig. 2.1 An illustration depicting a hunter-gatherer society; activities shown include gathering fruit and roots, and eating dead animals

Sexual selection

According to Charles Darwin, gradual changes in the bodily structures or behaviours of a species occur in response to changes in the environment. Members of any species vary in physical structure (e.g. height, body shape, hair colour), and in behaviour. If a variation of some kind (e.g. long legs) provides a greater chance of survival (faster running speed leading to escape from predators), the individual who possesses this advantage is likely to live longer. They may also leave behind more surviving offspring than those who do not possess the feature. Offspring inherit the characteristic that led to the advantage (e.g. long legs) and, over time, most members of the species come to possess the characteristic. This process is known as **natural selection** – survival of the fittest.

Fig. 2.2 Attracting the girls?

However, some species possess bodily features that do not appear to offer a survival advantage. The male peacock (see Fig. 2.2) has a long and beautiful train (tail), which makes little sense in evolutionary terms as the bird is less able to fly and is therefore more vulnerable to predators. However, female peahens choose males with long and glorious tails as mates. The concept of sexual selection states that bodily features and behaviours that are prized by the opposite sex will lead to increased opportunities for mating. Those who possess the feature are likely to have greater reproductive success and leave behind more offspring. Over time, most members of the species come to possess these attributes. In simple terms, **sexual selection** is survival of the hottest.

The evolutionary approach distinguishes between two types of sexual selection:

- Intrasexual selection takes place when members of one sex (often males) compete for access to the other sex (females). In many species, for example seals and humans, males are larger on average than females (see Fig. 2.3). This implies that males competed for females by fighting in the past, making increased size and weight an advantage for males.

- Intersexual selection takes place when members of one sex (often females) choose from the available pool of mates. The female stickleback fish chooses a male to fertilize her eggs by way of a painstaking 'double audition'. Firstly, she examines the nest built by a prospective male. If she is satisfied with a nest, the male stickleback demonstrates his health and strength by performing a 'zigzag' dance. If the nest and the dance are both satisfactory, the female will choose the male to fertilize her eggs. This process ensures that the female thoroughly 'tests' the male to check his strength and ability to raise the young.

Key term

Sexual selection: a process by which characteristics that lead to reproductive success are passed on to offspring through genes.

Link

You may wish to look back at the concepts of natural and sexual selection in the biological approach topic in Book 1, page 235.

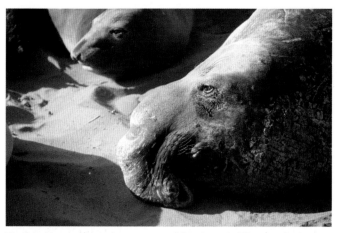

Fig. 2.3 A large male seal next to a small female seal: differences in size between males and females are common in the animal kingdom

Sexual selection and partner preferences

'From a biological perspective, the most significant consequence of attraction is the possibility of making babies. Will attraction lead to sex? And will sex lead to pregnancy?' (Perrett, 2010)

A key principle of evolutionary theory is that those who are most successful at competing for mates will have more surviving offspring than those who are less successful. These offspring will inherit the

---

KEY STUDY: **PARTNER PREFERENCES: PAWLOWSKI AND DUNBAR (1999/2001)**

Pawlowski and Dunbar examined the advertisements placed in The Observer Sunday newspaper's dating column, using a method called content analysis. A sample of advertisements were selected – 445 written by males and 454 written by females – and the researchers counted the references to six categories that were offered and requested by male and female advertisers. The categories were: material resources (e.g. house or car), physical attractiveness, interests, social skills, age, and commitment. They found that:

- Most of the advertisers stated their own age and requested specific age ranges in potential partners. Men requested female partners who were younger than themselves, and women sought older males. Men in their late 30s or 40s sought substantially younger female partners in their twenties.
- Around one quarter of women (24 per cent) sought a man with resources/wealth and over one third of women (35 per cent) referred to the importance of commitment.
- Over half of the female advertisements requested social skills such as a good sense of humour.
- Just under half of male advertisements referred to physical attractiveness, and the same proportion required social skills such as sense of humour.

Research methods link

You can find out more about content analysis by looking at page 26.

attributes that led to their parents' mating success – whether these are bodily features or behaviours – and, over time, most members of the population will come to possess the features that led to successful reproduction. Modern men and women reflect these features, as little time has passed in evolutionary terms for genetic change to take place.

Sexual selection and male preferences

Pawlowski and Dunbar's study (1999/2001) showed that youth is important to males when they are seeking partners. Female fertility is associated with youth and declines rapidly as women grow older. This is consistent with the evolutionary approach: males who preferred young females would leave behind more surviving offspring than those who chose older mates. Waynforth and Dunbar (1995) studied 900 personal advertisements taken from North American newspapers and found that a younger partner was important to nearly half of the men (42 per cent).

Given the link between youth and fertility, the evolutionary approach would predict that males should also be sensitive to physical signs of these in females. In Pawlowski and Dunbar's studies, nearly half of all males requested a physically attractive partner. Cunningham (1986) investigated what types of female faces males find attractive. He systematically varied the size of female facial features including eyes, nose, and mouth, and found that men were most attracted to features usually associated with young children – large eyes, small noses, and small chins. Perrett and Penton-Voak (1997–99) provided computer images of female faces that could be altered by moving the mouse to make them more masculine or feminine (see Fig. 2.4). When instructed to make female faces as attractive as possible, 95 per cent of participants altered the faces by making them more feminine. Cosmetics are used primarily to increase the feminine appearance of female faces: lipstick, for instance, enlarges and reddens the lips, mimicking the effects of the female hormone oestrogen.

The female body shape differs from the male body shape for two reasons: wider hips allow women to give birth, and larger breasts produce milk. This leads to the characteristic 'curve' of the female waist, and generally the curvier the figure, the greater the level of female reproductive hormones such as oestrogen. Singh (1993) investigated male preferences for female body shapes. Across a wide range of cultures he found a preference for a female waist–hip ratio (WHR) of 0.7, which produces a typical 'hourglass' shape. This shape indicates that a female has passed the age of puberty and is unlikely to be pregnant, making it a powerful signal of fertility. The preference for a WHR of 0.7 exists despite cultural differences for curvier or slimmer figures.

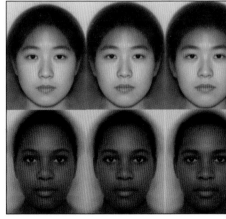

Fig. 2.4 Images from the Perrett and Penton-Voak study. Which face looks more feminine to you? Which do you prefer?

WHAT'S SO SEXY ABOUT THE COLOUR RED? ELLIOT AND NIESTA (2007)

The colour red has long been associated with romance and love, and a single red rose is used to symbolise love on St Valentine's Day in many different cultures. But is there an evolutionary basis to our association of red with sex and love? In many primate species, reddening of the body or face signals that females are fertile, and this acts as a powerful invitation to males. Does the same effect apply in people?

Elliot and Niesta (2007) carried out a series of experiments exploring the effects of red on attraction. In the first of these, 27 male students were shown the same photo of a moderately attractive woman. Fifteen of the students viewed the photo on a red background (experimental condition), and 12 viewed the photo on a white background (control condition). After viewing the photo for five seconds, the students were asked to complete a questionnaire rating the attractiveness of the woman in the picture. The participants who had seen the photo against a red background rated the woman as significantly more attractive than those in the white condition – supporting the claim that red increases attraction. In a second experiment using the same paradigm, male and female students were asked to rate the same photo of a woman on a red or white background. The same effect was found in men, but not in women.

ACTIVITY 2.1

Write the 'design' subsection of the 'Methods' part of a report for Elliot and Niesta's 2007 experiment. You should identify the type of design used, describe the independent and dependent variables, and provide details of the controls that were used. You can find guidelines for report writing in the Research methods chapter on page 49.

Sexual selection and female preferences

Pawlowski and Dunbar found that about a quarter of women (24 per cent) sought a man with resources/wealth, and 35 per cent referred to the importance of commitment. For a female, each child involves a substantial investment of time: nine months of pregnancy. In the past, childbirth was extremely hazardous and each infant would need to be breastfed for a couple of years. Having a male who committed to feeding and protecting the infant and mother would increase the likelihood of the infant surviving. Males with resources would be highly sought after, as would males who could defend the family unit. Reproductive success in females is achieved by ensuring the survival of a small number of offspring.

Buss (1989) carried out a substantial cross-cultural study of partner preferences across 33 countries on five continents. Data was collected from a total of 4601 men and 5446 women aged between 16 and 28 years. Buss found that women valued the financial capacity of potential partners and qualities associated with financial success (ambition and industriousness) more than men did in all of the 33 cultures studied.

We have seen how men seek signs of femininity in potential female partners. Do females seek highly masculine males? Male faces change dramatically at puberty with the surge of testosterone, leading to broader jaws and bigger teeth – useful to our ancestors when fighting for access to females. Perrett and Rowland (1996) found that increasing masculinity in faces made them *less* attractive on average to women, who reported that highly masculine males appeared less kind.

In contrast, women preferred slightly feminine (that is, 'pretty') male faces, which they described as 'more honest, emotional, and warmer' (see Fig. 2.5).

However, there was an important difference in the preference for male faces depending on the female menstrual cycle: at the fertile time of the month, typically around days 9–15 of the cycle, women rated highly masculine men as more attractive (Penton-Voak and Perrett, 1999). The effect wasn't simply restricted to faces: women also preferred a more masculine body shape and deeper voices (Puts, 2005). Highly masculine men would appear to be a mixed blessing for the female of the species!

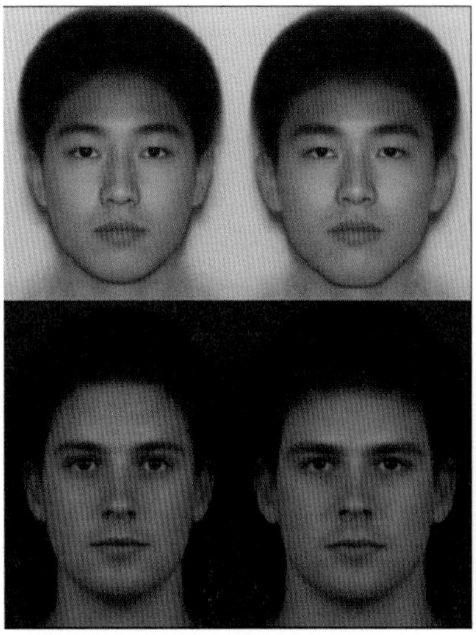

Fig. 2.5 Images from the Perrett and Rowland study. Which face do you prefer?

EXAMPLE EXAM QUESTION

An evolutionary psychologist carried out an analysis of 100 profiles from a dating website. She used a method called content analysis to compare what men and women offered in their profiles.

Explain how the psychologist could have selected an unbiased sample of 100 advertisements and how she could carry out content analysis of the ones she selected. (6 marks)

Exam hint

Start by identifying an appropriate sampling method (e.g. systematic sample), and explain how you would use this approach to select advertisements. Remember that the first stage of content analysis is the identification of categories.

Good looks, good genes?

Some physical features, such as symmetrical faces and long legs, appear to be valued by both females and males. Asymmetry in faces and bodies generally reflects disruptions to prenatal development, such as poor food supply, or exposure to disease or toxins. Symmetrical faces, in contrast, are a reasonable indicator of healthy development, in a similar way to the peacock's tail. Research has shown a surprizing range of advantages associated with symmetrical faces in men, including higher IQ, better dancing (Brown et al., 2005) and faster swimming sperm (Manning et al., 1998). Women with more symmetrical partners also experience more orgasms than women with less symmetrical men (Thornhill, Gangestad, and Comer, 1995).

When faces are adjusted using computer technology to make them more symmetrical (that is, by copying one half of the face), between

60 and 70 per cent of people rate the symmetrical version as more attractive. Using computer-manipulated images, Bruce and Young (1998) found that there is a preference for symmetrical faces in both men and women.

Pawlowski and Sorokowski (2008) asked a sample of 218 males and females to rank the attractiveness of seven pictures of men and seven pictures of women, which were digitally altered for leg length. He found that, in both sexes, five per cent longer legs than average was seen as the most attractive. Long legs signal good nutrition in childhood. Both of these qualities are therefore shortcuts to indicating good health and genes!

Link

You can remind yourself about validity by looking at page 42.

THINKING SCIENTIFICALLY: VALIDITY

Studies on partner preference have made extensive use of personal column advertisements and, in recent years, dating profiles on websites have also been studied. Such material is high in validity: those who have written the advertisements/profiles have done this with the aim of finding a partner, not because they think a psychologist is examining the material. Advertisements are relatively free of demand characteristics, and present few ethical issues, as the material is in the public domain.

There is no guarantee, of course, that advertisments placed on dating sites are accurate. Descriptions are constructed to appeal to others, and profile pictures are chosen carefully to demonstrate the desirability of the advertiser. Some critics have also claimed that personal column advertisements are not representative of the general population of people seeking partners. However, the sheer popularity of dating apps such as Tinder counteracts this criticism – today, everyone seems to be online dating.

Exam hint

This question asks you to focus on what research has shown, so you should construct your answer around findings and conclusions. Keep methodological information to a minimum in your outline.

EXAMPLE EXAM QUESTION

Outline what research has shown about partner preferences in males and females. (6 marks)

Key term

Human reproductive behaviour: sexual behaviours that may lead to reproduction.

Sexual selection and human reproductive behaviour

Human reproductive behaviour refers to sexual behaviours that may lead to reproduction. In 1972, Trivers put forward a parental investment theory that argued that sexual selection is the key factor underpinning reproductive behaviour. He argued that reproductive behaviours originate in the amount of parental investment put into offspring by males and females. For example, the human male's investment in offspring is relatively small. Mating requires little in terms of time and energy, and he does not have to stay close to the offspring and care for them. He has large amounts of sperm and remains fertile throughout his life. The best way for a man to maximize reproductive success is to mate as often as possible with willing fertile females – the more the merrier!

In contrast, the female's investment in each offspring is substantial. The gamete she supplies, the ova, is around one hundred times larger than the sperm, and she has a limited supply, generally producing one ovum per month. A female is physically capable of producing a child – at best – every couple of years. Her reproductive life is short, as fertility declines, limiting the total number of offspring she can produce. Following conception, her prenatal investment is substantial. The best chance of reproductive success for the female is to ensure the survival of a relatively small number of offspring.

As males and females achieve reproductive success in very different ways, parental investment theory predicts that men and women will show different reproductive behaviours designed to maximize their reproductive success.

Concealed ovulation and the formation of pair bonds

A unique aspect of human sexual behaviour is hidden oestrus (ovulation) in the female. Other female primates show their fertility by swelling and reddening of the genitals and face, enabling males to identify easily that the female is ovulating. In human females, ovulation is concealed. Unlike other primates, human females are willing to mate at times other than maximum fertility.

Why do these differences from other primates exist? The most likely explanation is that this unique aspect of female reproductive behaviour has led to the evolution of the 'pair bond', or couple relationship. If human males do not know when a female can get pregnant, they must stay close to her and guard her from other males across her cycle to ensure that any offspring produced are theirs. For the female, the advantage is an increased chance of survival for her offspring when two parents are present.

Parental certainty and sexual jealousy

Another difference between the sexes relates to parental certainty. There were no paternity tests in the hunter-gatherer era, and the only way a male could guarantee offspring were his would be to have sole access to a female. The lack of parental certainty makes males particularly sensitive to the possibility of sexual infidelity – an unfaithful female could lead them to waste valuable resources on infants that were not their own. In contrast, females are certain offspring are theirs as they carry them throughout pregnancy and give birth. Female sexual jealousy tends to be triggered by emotional connections, which could lead the male to remove his support and investment from their family unit.

Buss and Schmitt (1993) asked male and female students to imagine their current boyfriend or girlfriend either having sex with someone else or being in love with someone else. While engaging in these rather dubious fantasies, they were wired up to measure stress responses. The researchers found that men became most distressed at the idea of their partner being sexually unfaithful, whereas women became most distressed at the idea of their partner being in love with someone else. Similar studies have shown these different patterns of jealousy across cultures, from Sweden to China (Geary et al., 1995).

Differences in choosiness

Historically, females have tended to be choosier about who they have sex with than males. This was demonstrated in Clark and Hatfield's studies (1989 and 1990), where a sample of male and female students approached total strangers of the opposite sex on campus and propositioned them with one of three requests, which were:

- to go out with them that night on a date

- to go back to their house with them

- to have sex with them.

Clark and Hatfield found that while 50 per cent of men and women agreed to go out on a date, unsurprisingly none of the women propositioned by an attractive male agreed to sex. However, 75 per cent of the men approached agreed to sex – although only 69 per cent of them agreed to go back to the person's house. Even when Clark modified the experiment in 1990 and assured participants about the trustworthiness of the stranger, the results were still the same – women did not generally agree to casual sex. The general unwillingness to engage in uncommitted sex was also found in lesbians (Buss and Schmitt, 1993).

Why might these differences exist? One-night stands require little investment in terms of time and effort, and would be an opportunity to increase reproductive success for males. In contrast, females need to choose the best available partner with health and strength to pass on to any offspring from the mating. Males with resources and status are particularly attractive. Females are less likely to be attracted to one-night stands, as men do not display a commitment to help to raise any offspring that may result.

Evaluation of sexual selection as an explanation of human reproductive behaviour

It is important to note that evolutionary psychologists do not view these differences in behaviour as conscious or deliberate strategies. Instead, they have been selected simply because they brought reproductive success: sexually opportunistic males left behind more offspring, as did choosy females who chose committed and resourceful mates. Nor does the evolutionary explanation make the assumption that 'natural' differences are desirable. In fact, Buss (2000) argues that acting according to nature's programming – for example, males pursuing casual sexual encounters – can lead to profound unhappiness for both men and women.

Sexual selection provides a plausible explanation of differences in reproductive behaviour between males and females. However, the evolutionary approach is not the only explanation of differences between males and females in reproductive behaviour. Differences in choosiness and readiness to engage in casual sexual encounters can also be explained through cultural practices. In Western society, men could internalize the view that masculinity is characterized by a readiness to have sex whenever the opportunity presents itself, and women could internalize the expectation that 'nice girls' do not have sex with strangers. Dunbar et al. (1999) bring these explanations together, suggesting that evolved behaviours are the basis for cultural patterns – effectively, cultural practices are built on evolution.

The sexual revolution of the 1960s, with the advent of the contraceptive pill, led to changing moral codes. Women in modern, Western societies are much freer to choose their own moral code without serious risk – and many do. Dating apps like Tinder provide the opportunity for short-term casual encounters for both men and women. Today, human reproductive success is no longer the goal for many individuals, particularly in the Western world.

EXAMPLE EXAM QUESTION

Discuss evolutionary explanations of human reproductive behaviour. (16 marks)

KEY POINTS

- Behaviours shown today are thought to have originated in the hunter-gatherer era.
- Sexual selection refers to the selection of features that lead to successful mating.
- Males and females put emphasis on different qualities in potential mates. These differences are thought to relate to reproductive success.
- Males are interested in youth and attractiveness as signs of fertility, whereas females are interested in status and resources in potential mates.
- Both males and females value social skills, such as a sense of humour, in potential mates.
- Human reproductive behaviours include concealed ovulation in females, and differences between the sexes in jealousy and choosiness.
- Sexual selection provides one explanation of reproductive behaviours.
- Cultural factors can also explain the observed differences.

Exam hint

This question requires you to write critically about evolutionary explanations of human reproductive behaviours. You should start by explaining the mechanism of sexual selection, as this is the basis of the evolutionary explanation. You should evaluate the explanation by providing evidence in the form of research studies. Ensure that you do not become sidetracked into evaluating the method used in the studies themselves: keep the focus of evaluation on the explanation!

Attraction and romantic relationships

Boy meets girl, girl meets girl, boy meets boy. What factors will influence whether or not they are attracted to each other and whether initial attraction develops into a longer-term relationship? Until the late 1970s, the study of relationships focused almost exclusively on the processes involved in interpersonal attraction. This research identified a number of factors that were important in the development of personal relationships: physical attraction, similarity of attitudes and social background, and physical proximity, which provided the opportunity to meet. Most of these factors continue to be important today, but physical proximity is less important than in the second half of the last century. We live in a world where technologies – from texting to social media and voice communication programs or apps such as Skype – allow us to develop and maintain relationships with people who do not live close by.

Physical attractiveness and the matching hypothesis

As we have seen in the first section of the chapter, on evolutionary psychology, physical attraction plays an important role in the development of relationships. However, while many people desire a highly attractive partner, in practice there are insufficient beautiful people to go around. Walster and her colleagues put forward a simple theory in 1966, which has become known as the **matching hypothesis**. Walster suggested that rather than seeking the most physically attractive partner, people tend to go for someone who is of a similar level of attractiveness to them – essentially 'in the same league'. This is thought to be because it reduces the chance of rejection.

Early experiments on attraction made use of 'blind date' scenarios where couples were randomly paired up for a date then asked if they planned to meet again. In one such study, Walster et al. (1962) paired male and female students randomly for a dance date but told them they had been matched via a computer. Walster measured which of the couples met for a second date after the dance. In contrast to the claim made in the matching hypothesis, Walster found that girls who were pretty were asked out again by boys, even when the boys were not all that attractive. These findings contradicted the idea of matching on the basis of physical attractiveness.

Fig. 2.6 Celebrity couples: Does matching occur on more than just appearance?

However, studies carried out on couples that have got together outside a blind date scenario provide support for the matching hypothesis. Murstein (1972) collected photos of 99 dating couples and compared these with photos of randomly paired males and females. The real couples were consistently rated as more alike in levels of attractiveness than those who had been randomly paired. Silverman (1971) carried out an observational study and rated couples in bars. He also found that couples tended to be matched in attractiveness. In an extension of the work on matching, McKillip and Riedel (1983) found that pairs of friends were also fairly closely matched in levels of physical attractiveness.

The 1970s and 80s saw a widespread interest in the role of physical appearance and matching, with many studies designed to test the matching hypothesis. Feingold (1988) carried out a meta-analysis of 18 such studies conducted between 1970 and 1987 with a total of 1644 couples, some romantic and others pairs of friends. Feingold found a positive correlation of 0.39 between the romantic couples, which was statistically significant, indicating that matching occurred as the hypothesis predicted. There was more variation in pairs of friends: while male friends tended to be similarly matched for attractiveness, there was no such relationship in pairs of female friends. The same effect occurred in studies that used self-ratings of attractiveness rather than objective ratings by outsiders. People who rated themselves as highly attractive (whether they were or not) tended to seek highly attractive partners. Those with less confidence who rated themselves as pretty ordinary in the dating stakes, tended to seek a partner of that level.

Taylor et al. carried out a study on the matching hypothesis using the Internet dating site Hotornot. They obtained permission to use the site's activity logs to identify who was contacting whom, and how much chat traffic was occurring between different site members.

Sixty heterosexual men and 60 heterosexual women were chosen at random and referred to as 'initiators'. The researchers identified every member of Hotornot who had been contacted by an initiator, referring to these as 'targets'. They collected photos of the targets and the initiators from their profiles, producing a total sample of 996 daters. (To save you doing the maths, this is about eight targets per initiator.) Independent raters were asked to rate all of the photos on a 7-point scale from –3 (very unattractive) to +3 (highly attractive) with a score of zero being average. The raters had no idea who had contacted whom.

What did the researchers find?

- The idea of matching had no bearing on initial contacts. Initiators contacted targets across the spectrum, some of whom were more physically attractive than they were. This was broadly in line with Walster's computer dance finding.
- When it came to responses there was clear evidence of matching. Targets who were of a similar level of attractiveness to the initiator were likely to respond to the contact and start chatting with them. Targets who were more attractive than the initiator were less likely to respond.

THINKING SCIENTIFICALLY: ETHICS

Taylor et al.'s study focuses on a recent version of the personal column advertisement – the dating profile. Because the materials (dating profiles and message traffic) are naturally occurring, they are high in ecological validity. This type of research provides a window into modern dating in the virtual world.

In this study, permission to select profiles and examine chat traffic was gained from the administrators of Hotornot. The actual daters were not asked for their consent for their profiles to be used. However, dating profiles are placed in the public arena and advertisers know that many people will look them at. The BPS *Code of Human Research Ethics* states that research based on observations of public behaviour can be carried out where people reasonably expect that they will be observed by strangers. Hence, this study complies with ethical requirements.

ACTIVITY 2.2A

Before you read the section on filter theory, write down the names of five of your close friends.

Filter theory: social demography, similarity in attitudes and complementarity

Kerckhoff and Davis (1962) argued that relationships develop through three 'filters', with different factors becoming important at different times. They distinguished between the 'field of availables' – the possible people that we could have a relationship with – and the 'field of desirables', a much smaller group who fit our criteria. Kerckhoff and David argued that we 'filter out' unsuitable partners for different reasons at different times. This approach identified three filters in the development of relationships:

- **Filter 1: Social and demographic variables.** Kerckhoff and David noted that most people tend to mix with those who are similar to them– who are roughly the same age, live nearby, and perhaps work or study together. This fairly small group of people makes up the 'field of availables' from which potential partners are chosen. At this stage, people from very different social, economic and educational backgrounds are filtered out. This filter exerts its influence often without people being aware of it.

- **Filter 2: Similarity or having things in common.** Once two people start chatting to each other, similarity of attitudes, values and interests come into play. If two people like the same kinds of things and share attitudes, they are likely to find communication easy and the relationship may progress. However, if two people think differently and share few interests it is likely that the relationship will not progress much further. At this stage people with different attitudes, values and interests are filtered out.

- **Filter 3: Complementarity.** Once a couple have become established in a relationship, the third filter comes into play. This is complementarity of needs between the two people – how well the two people work together as a couple and meet each other's needs.

ACTIVITY 2.2B

Go back to your list of five close friends and compare each person on the list with yourself in relation to age, type of house you live in, and level of education you have achieved. Can you see evidence for demographic similarity between you and your friends? Now, do the same activity in relation to attitudes and interests. Why do you think we tend to select friends and partners from people who are similar in background and attitudes?

Evidence and evaluation

Kerckhoff and Davis (1962) tested their model using a longitudinal study of student couples. Some had been together for less than 18 months and some had been together for more than 18 months. They were asked to complete several questionnaires over a seven-month period in which they reported on similarity of attitudes and personality traits with their partner. It was found that attitude similarity was the most important factor in keeping two people together up to about 18 months into a relationship. After this time, psychological compatibility and the ability to meet each other's needs became important, supporting the claims made by the filter model.

- Filter theory was developed in 1962 when the world was different to the one we live in now. Today we live in an interconnected world, with communication enabled by technologies. We are able to meet and communicate with people who live a long distance away. This, along with ease of travel, means that proximity is a less important demographic variable than in 1962.

- Other demographic factors continue to be important. Sprecher (1998) found that couples matched in physical attractiveness, social background and interests were more likely to develop a long-term relationship. A longitudinal study of couples over 21 years found that those who were similar in educational level and age at the start of their relationship were more likely to stay together. They became more similar in attitudes as time went on (Gruber-Baldini, Schaie and Willis, 1995).

- The filter model is a useful way to think about the factors that are influential in relationship development and when they might come into play. A factor that may be important at one time in a relationship, such as similar attitudes, may assume less relevance later on in the same relationship.

EXAMPLE EXAM QUESTION

Apart from social demography, briefly describe one other filter put forward by the filter theory. (3 marks)

Self-disclosure in romantic relationships

Self-disclosure refers to revealing personal information about oneself to other people and is an important mechanism through which relationships develop. The disclosure of personal information helps to move a relationship onto a more intimate footing. Disclosures generally occur when the discloser believes that the information will not be shared with others outside the pair or couple. As two people get to know each other better, disclosures increase in depth and breadth.

Self-disclosure generally occurs verbally but can also occur via non-verbal behaviour (for example, blushing when someone's name is mentioned in a conversation can be revealing). As a general rule, we disclose more to people we like, and we tend to like people more when they disclose to us. Sprecher et al. investigated this claim experimentally in 2013.

Exam hint

This is a straightforward knowledge question. As only three marks are available, your response should be succinct. You should start by identifying which filter (similarity of attitudes or complementarity) you will consider and explain briefly when the filter operates. You can refer to the findings of research (for example, Kerckhoff and Davis' 1962 study) to illustrate your answer.

Key term

Self-disclosure: revealing personal or private information about oneself to other people.

Sprecher et al. used an experimental method to assess the effects of self-disclosure on how much two people liked each other. The experiment used pairs of students who did not know each other (that is, they were strangers). Each pair of students took part in two interactions in which they were instructed to chat for several minutes:

- In interaction 1, student 'A' (let's call her Amy) was instructed to disclosure a piece of personal information while student B (Beth) listened to this disclosure. Both students were then asked to complete a rating scale in which they recorded how much they liked each other. At this stage, Beth (the listener) reported a higher liking for Amy than vice versa.
- In interaction 2, Beth was asked to disclose personal information to Amy then both were asked for a second time how much they liked each other. At this stage, there was no difference in liking between the students. After both had disclosed, liking had increased so it was equal.

This experimental study shows that disclosing personal information about us generally increases liking in the recipient. Why might this be? The most obvious suggestion is that self-disclosure implies a degree of trust in the listener. This investment of trust leads the listener to like the discloser more.

THINKING SCIENTIFICALLY: EXPERIMENTAL STUDIES

This is an experimental study, which allowed Sprecher et al. a substantial degree of control over the interaction. Sprecher was able to control the length of the interaction and the timing of the disclosure. High levels of control allow the researcher to establish cause and effect – in this case, disclosure (the IV) causes increased liking (the DV). However, experimental studies are often criticised for a lack of ecological validity. In this experiment, the participants were instructed to disclose personal information and would have been aware of the aims and nature of the study. Demand characteristics could therefore have played a part in the outcome of the study, as the participants expected to like the stranger more after they had revealed the personal information.

The participants in this experiment were university students. Students tend to be younger and – arguably – more intelligent than the general population, meaning that the findings cannot be applied beyond the specific population.

Research has indicated that there are differences in self-disclosure based on gender and age. These differences were investigated in a meta-analysis carried out by Dindia and Allen (1992). The researchers selected 205 studies of self-disclosure that had taken place between 1967 and 1990 with a total of 23,702 participants. Dindia and Allen examined the effect of a number of variables including the sex of discloser and listener, the relationship between listener and discloser (for example, a family member, friend, stranger), and how the self-disclosure was recorded (that is, self-report, observation, etc.).

Dindia and Allen found that, on balance, women disclosed more than men, supporting the generally held view that women are more prone to emotional sharing. However, the amount of disclosure was also influenced by the sex of the listener and the relationship between discloser and listener.

- Both males and females disclosed more to a same-sex listener than opposite-sex listener. However, this was also influenced by the relationship with the listener.

- When the listener was a friend or family member, women disclosed substantially more than men. When the listener was a stranger there was no difference in the amount of disclosure between men and women.

Men, it would seem, are more likely to reveal personal information to people they don't know.

Meta-analyses are valuable as they provide much larger samples of data than individual studies. The large sample enables researchers to spot patterns or trends that may not be not visible in smaller samples – a clear advantage. However, in Dindia and Allen's meta-analysis, the sample of studies spans a very long period of time from 1967 to 1990 (23 years) and it is likely that norms about self-disclosure will have changed pretty dramatically during that time period.

KEY POINTS

- The matching hypothesis refers to the tendency to seek partners of a similar level of physical attractiveness to oneself.

- The matching hypothesis is supported by studies of dating couples.

- Filter theory identifies three factors that are important at different stages of relationship development: demographic similarity, shared attitudes and complementarity of needs.

- Proximity plays less of a role in today's connected world than in the past. However, demographic factors such as education continue to be important.

- Self-disclosure involves revealing personal information about oneself to others. It is an important mechanism in the development of close relationships.

- Self-disclosure implies a degree of trust in the listener and increases liking and intimacy (Sprecher, 2013).

- Women generally disclose more than men when the listener is a family member or friend.

- These differences between men and women disappear when the listener is a stranger.

Virtual relationships

So far, we have considered relationships that take place face to face. Perhaps the most notable social change of the last thirty years has been the development of virtual relationships. Since around 2000, the primary use of home computers has been for social interaction. Relationships can start online via dating sites and move to face-to-face format. Many relationships operate simultaneously face-to-face and via social networking sites (SNS), and some relationships, for example

Fig. 2.7 Is the online world equivalent to the 'stranger on a train' phenomenon?

those between online gamers, can take place in a completely virtual world with players never meeting face-to-face. What has research told us about these different kinds of virtual relationships?

In 1975, Rubin noted how highly personal information was often revealed to strangers on a train journey, when people were safe in the knowledge that they were unlikely to meet again. He referred to this as the 'stranger on a train' phenomenon. Research into online relationships initially viewed them in a similar light. Suler (2004) argued that online disclosures had fewer negative repercussions, such as ridicule or rejection, than the sharing of private information face-to-face. Suler referred to this as 'the online disinhibition effect'.

The effects of absence of gating on social relationships

Gating refers to the obstacles (or gates) that get in the way of two people developing a mutually rewarding relationship face-to-face. One of the 'gates' preventing relationship development in the past was the physical distance between two people. This gate has been substantially reduced with the development of communication technologies. Other gates include physical appearance (for example, not attractive or not someone's type), personality characteristics such as shyness, and difficulties with communication such as stuttering. These features are less obvious in chat rooms and on some dating sites, where profile pictures are carefully selected to show daters in the best light.

KEY STUDY: MCKENNA ET AL. (2002)

Are relationships more likely to grow with some of the gates removed? McKenna et al. (2002) carried out an experimental study to investigate the absence of gating. They hypothesized that couples who met first online would like each other more than couples who met first face-to-face. The chat-room environment would remove the gates of physical appearance and shyness, theoretically enabling two people to establish a more intimate connection rapidly.

McKenna et al. selected a group of 31 male and 31 female university students, who were paired randomly and asked to get to know each other in two 20-minute interactions. The independent variable was the presence/absence of gating features. This was manipulated using three conditions, only two of which need concern us here:

1. In the control condition, both 20-minute meetings took place face-to-face
2. In the experimental condition, the students met first in an Internet chat room for 20 minutes and secondly face-to-face.

After each interaction, both members of the pair were asked how much they liked each other using a 14-point scale, which ran from +7 to −7. The researchers found that, in line with their hypothesis, liking was strongest in the experimental condition where the couple met online first.

McKenna's study was carried out well over ten years ago using the environment of an online chat room. Today, there are more ways to interact online than chat rooms. Some sites, such as Reddit, encourage users to use pseudonyms for discussions in communities of common interest. Other online environments – from dating sites such as Tinder to SNS like Facebook – emphasize physical identity and appearance through the use of photos, rather than hiding it. The speed of development of social media means that research studies can be out of date before they are published. The virtual world changes rapidly, with once popular sites such as Friends Reunited, Bebo and MySpace now being distant memories.

EXAMPLE EXAM QUESTION

1. Identify the dependent variable in the McKenna et al. study. How was this operationalized? (1 + 2 marks)
2. Name one statistical test that could be used to assess the results of McKenna et al. for statistical significance. Explain why this test would be appropriate. (1 + 2 marks)

Exam hint

The dependent variable is easy to spot by asking what has been measured as the outcome of an experiment. Test choice depends on experimental design (independent groups or repeated measures) and level of data. Use the flow chart on page 72 to work out which test to use. You should refer to both experimental design and level of data in your justification of your choice of statistical test.

Self-disclosure in virtual relationships

Over the last 20 years there has been an explosion of research into online communication and self-disclosure. Disclosures can take place on SNS such as Facebook and Twitter, and in blogs. These online environments have important differences: on SNS, disclosures are made to members of the social network (friends), whereas blogs are open access and the information disclosed can be read by anyone.

Self-disclosure via the status update

Utz (2015) examined the content and response to status updates on Facebook. Utz asked a sample of Facebook users to judge the content of their own and friend's status updates and to examine the effects of these. He found that the content of status updates was strongly positive and often entertaining. Positive status updates increased feelings of connection and intimacy with Facebook friends in a very similar way to face-to-face self-disclosures.

The online world has been conceptualized as an easier social environment for people who struggle with social relationships face-to-face. Forest and Wood (2012) investigated the disclosures of a group of people with self-identified low self-esteem. While Facebook was seen as a safe place to disclose personal information, Forest and Wood found that disclosures often tended to be negative in nature. Sadly, these negative disclosures were likely to lead to negative or undesirable responses from Facebook friends.

A study of nearly 1100 teenagers found that most online disclosures were thought through (planned) but a small number occurred spontaneously, usually in response to strong emotions (Van Gool et al., 2015).

Self-disclosure on blogs

Blogs are online journals in which individuals reveal their thoughts and feelings. Unlike social networking sites such as Facebook, they are open access, which means that anyone can read them and post a comment in response. Some blogs are written and others are in video format (vlogs). Blogs can focus on specific interests (for example, football, music or politics) or can take the form of a personal diary in which the blogger shares their thoughts on a variety of topics. Blogging is a way of entertaining others, organizing thoughts, expressing creativity and getting feedback (Hollenbaugh and Everett, 2013).

KEY STUDY: HOLLENBAUGH AND EVERETT (2013)

Hollenbaugh and Everett carried out a content analysis of personal journal blogs. They collected their sample using recruitment advertisements on high-traffic sites such as blogger.com and xanga.com. A total of 243 bloggers responded to the advertisements and a sample of 154 met the selection criteria: they were over the age of 18, English-speaking and had posted to their blog at least once a month.

Hollenbaugh and Everett selected the five blogs that were posted immediately before the research study started. Two coders individually carried out a content analysis of each blog, along with the hyperlinks, pictures and videos that were attached. They then compared their results in order to establish inter-rater reliability.

The researchers found that younger bloggers disclosed more personal information in terms of breadth than older bloggers, and female bloggers disclosed more than male bloggers. Unsurprisingly, the most disclosures were from young female bloggers. However, visual anonymity appeared to have an inverse relationship with self-disclosure: bloggers who posted more pictures, videos, etc. identifying themselves disclosed a greater amount of personal information. This finding contradicts the 'online disinhibition effect' put forward by Suler (2004), which suggested that disclosure and anonymity go hand in hand.

THINKING SCIENTIFICALLY: VALIDITY

Hollenbaugh and Everett have selected naturally occurring materials – blog posts – for their analysis. This ensures that the material is higher in validity. The decision to use the five blogs produced before bloggers were asked for consent further ensures the validity of the materials, which were produced naturally without deliberate construction for research purposes. These kinds of written materials are amenable to either quantitative or qualitative analysis.

Social media can also be used to maintain relationships, particularly where a couple is separated by physical distance from each other. Billedo et al. (2015) examined the use of Facebook in distance relationships and compared this with couples who lived close to each other. An online survey of 272 Facebook users who classed themselves as in a relationship indicated that that long-distance couples were more like to use Facebook for 'partner surveillance' than those who lived close to each other. They were also more likely to show higher levels of Facebook-related jealousy.

Link

You can read more about social media in the section on relationship dissolution on page 155.

EXAMPLE EXAM QUESTION

Discuss psychological research into self-disclosure. (16 marks)

Exam hint

This question focuses on self-disclosure but does not specify where the disclosure takes place, so you can include research on face-to-face and/or online disclosures. Aim to cover two or three pieces of research for AO1 and remember to keep your descriptions succinct – there are only six AO1 marks available. You can consider ethics and validity to structure your critical discussion of the research. A good route to AO3 could be a comparison of studies carried out online and face-to-face.

KEY POINTS

- 'Gates' are factors that inhibit the development of a face-to-face relationship. Some gates are absent in some online communications.

- McKenna and Gleeson found that students who first met online liked each other better than those who first met face-to-face.

- Self-disclosure occurs online through social media sites (e.g. in status updates) and in blogs.

- Status updates tend to be positive and to produce positive responses. Negative disclosures are often followed by negative responses.

- Self-disclosure in blogs appears to have a negative relationship with anonymity. Young female bloggers disclose the most information and also identify themselves precisely using pictures and biographical information. This contradicts the 'online disinhibition effect'.

- Social media can be used for partner surveillance in long-distance relationships.

- Social media develop rapidly, hence temporal validity is a challenge for research in this area.

Theories of romantic relationships

The theories covered in this section of the chapter are based on the **economic approach** to relationships. The economic approach works on the assumption that people run relationships in a similar way to a joint bank account – keeping an eye on what they and their partner are putting into and getting out of the relationship. The theories share

Key term

Economic approach: theories that are based on the idea that people run relationships in a similar way to running their finances.

the view that people may choose to move on if someone else offers a better 'deal', in a similar way to a bank offering an incentive to join them. Economic theories help to explain how couples keep their relationship going and the decision to stay or go when relationships get into difficulties. Three economic approaches are social exchange theory, equity theory and Rusbult's investment model.

Fig. 2.8 An economic approach to relationships– what are the partners putting in and taking out?

Social exchange theory

Homans (1961) acknowledged that relationships involve rewards such as social support and sexual gratification, but he also noted that they involve costs. Costs come in different forms: money, time and the incalculable emotional costs produced by loss, betrayal and jealousy. Homans argued that we run our relationships by keeping an eye on the exchange of rewards and costs. Whether or not we are satisfied depends on the ratio between costs and rewards:

• If the rewards in the relationship outweigh the costs, the relationship is said to be in a state of 'profit'.

• If the costs outweigh the rewards, the result is a state of 'loss', which leads to dissatisfaction with the relationship.

Social exchange theory (SET) argues that people are basically selfish, aiming to maximise the rewards they receive and to minimize the costs. This is referred to as the 'mini-max principle'.

Thibaut and Kelley (1959) developed SET further. They viewed relationships as similar to business transactions in which people keep an eye on the 'balance sheet' of their relationship, comparing it with previous relationships and alternatives that may be on offer, just like you might compare the deals offered by different banks. They defined two types of comparison:

• Comparison level (CL) – this involves comparing the current relationship with a general expectation of how rewarding relationships are, an expectation created from your previous experiences. If the current relationship seems more rewarding than those you have experienced previously, you are likely to be satisfied.

- Comparison level for alternatives (CL Alt) – this involves comparing the current relationship with other possible relationships on offer. If the current relationship compares favourably (or there are no alternatives available), you are likely to be satisfied.

Social exchange theory predicts that an individual may decide to leave a relationship if it represents a state of loss. This could occur if the costs outweigh the rewards, if the CL suggests that the relationship is less rewarding than expectations or if the CL Alt offers a viable and attractive alternative.

Evidence and evaluation

KEY STUDY: FLOYD AND WASNER (1994)

Floyd and Wasner tested social exchange theory using a sample of university students (average age of 20). 238 students (65 men and 173 women) were chosen for analysis as they identified themselves as being 'in a relationship' at the time. Each student was asked to complete a 20-item questionnaire that measured:

- satisfaction with the relationship

- commitment to the relationship

- availability of alternative relationships.

Floyd and Wasner then carried out a series of statistical analyses to assess the relationship between the variables. They found that commitment was strongly related to satisfaction with the relationship **and** the availability of alternative relationships, providing some support for SET.

However, Floyd and Wasner's findings showed that satisfaction (CL) and the availability of alternatives (CL Alt) were interconnected rather than separate. In other words, happiness with a current relationship depended to some extent on who was around the corner! Thibaut and Kelley (1959) had originally conceived satisfaction and available alternatives as being separate.

THINKING SCIENTIFICALLY: STUDENT SAMPLES

In common with many studies on relationships, Floyd and Wasner used a sample of students to collect their data. Students provide an easily accessible opportunity sample for researchers to test their ideas. However, the ability to generalize from student samples is limited: students are younger than the general adult population and may be less inclined to settle down. They may also be more intelligent. Studies using student samples are often replicated with larger and more varied samples of adults.

Floyd and Wasner's study also shows how theories are refined in the light of evidence. This is an important aspect of the scientific cycle of enquiry: it is not uncommon in psychology for some elements of a theory to be supported while others are challenged by research.

Social exchange theory views people as self-centred and likely to leave relationships in a state of loss where costs outweigh rewards. Equity theory challenges this view, suggesting that fairness is more important than profit to many people in long-term relationships.

Social exchange theory assumes that people spend a considerable amount of time and effort monitoring their relationships. Argyle (1986) argues that people only really begin to count the costs and monitor relationships *after* they have become dissatisfied with them. Duck (1994) agrees that, in general, people do not keep an eye on other alternatives that are on offer and only start to consider alternatives when they become dissatisfied with their current relationship.

Some people stick with relationships that are extremely unrewarding, for example those suffering personal violence (PV). One reason is the amount that has been put into the relationship in the past. This is the basis of Rusbult's investment model, which you will read about later on.

Equity theory

Equity theory agrees that people weigh up rewards and costs within relationships but argues that people have an expectation that relationships should be fair. According to equity theory, couples keep an eye on what both they and their partner are putting in and getting out. If this is roughly equal they are likely to feel reasonably satisfied with the relationship. However, if this is unequal, with one partner putting in a great deal more effort than the other or getting much more out, the relationship will be experienced as 'inequitable' and this will lead the relationship into problems. This feeling of inequity will lead the 'loser' in the relationship to feel dissatisfied and the 'winner' (perhaps) to feel guilty. If the relationship is of relatively short duration, one partner may simply end it. However, if the couple have been together for a long time they may be motivated to repair the relationship by restoring equity. This could be done by:

- reducing inputs – putting less effort into the relationship

- increasing outputs/rewards – encouraging the other person to put more effort into the relationship.

Evidence and evaluation

KEY STUDY: VAN YPEREN AND BUUNK (1990)

Van Yperen and Buunk carried out a longitudinal study using a sample of 736 people recruited through an advertisement in a local paper. The sample consisted of a mixture of married and cohabiting couples with an average age of 39. Seventy per cent of the couples had children.

The participants were asked to complete an anonymous questionnaire that obtained a score for equity in the relationship using Hatfield's Global Measurement of Satisfaction (Hatfield et al., 1990). At this stage of the study, around two-thirds of men and women felt that their relationship was equitable. About a quarter of men felt that they over-benefited from their relationship (they were getting out more than they were putting in), and about a quarter of women felt that they under-benefited (they were putting in more than they were getting back). One year later the participants were asked about satisfaction in their relationship. The researchers then assessed the correlation between equity at time 1 and satisfaction at time 2.

- The correlation between equity and satisfaction for women was 0.44. This score demonstrates a moderate, positive relationship between the two variables. Greater equity generally went with greater satisfaction, and vice versa for men.
- The correlation between equity and satisfaction for men was 0.20. The relationship between the two variables was still positive, but was much weaker than for women.

THINKING SCIENTIFICALLY: CORRELATION AND CAUSATION

One common criticism of correlational research is the inability to infer causality – although two things go together, it does not mean that one causes the other. In this study, the researchers have incorporated a longitudinal design, with assessment of satisfaction after a period of one year. This shows that there may be a causal link between equity and satisfaction, as equity predicts satisfaction at a later point.

ACTIVITY 2.4

Draw two scattergrams to illustrate the correlations found by Van Yperen and Buunk in the above study. You will need to decide on which axis to place the co-variables (equity and satisfaction) and how to label the scales. You may wish to look at pages 60–62 to remind yourself of how to draw a scattergram.

Equity theory is a more positive approach to relationships than SET. Equity theory emphasises the importance of fairness, whereas SET views people as basically selfish.

Many studies have shown that equity is important in relationship satisfaction and in relationship breakdown. DeMaris (2007) assessed the importance of equity in relation to marital dissatisfaction and later breakdown using a sample of 1500 American couples. He found that a woman's sense of being under-benefited was most important in predicting later disruption. In agreement, Van Yperen and Buunk's study suggests that equity is more important to women than men. Dwyer (2000) argues that lesbians put a considerable value on equity within a relationship.

Link

For more on cultural bias, see pages 80–81 in the *Issues and debates in psychology* chapter.

Some critics argue that truly intimate relationships do not involve counting inputs and outputs. Miell and Croghan (1996) argue that the equity principle reflects the values of Western, individualistic cultures and equity is less important in collectivist cultures. This illustrates the issue of cultural bias – when differences between cultures have not been considered properly, leading to a biased or potentially biased conclusion.

Rusbult's investment model

Key term

Investments: inputs that can't be got back from a relationship, such as time and emotional support.

Rusbult and Van Lange (1996) argue that in order to understand decisions to stay or leave relationships, we must take **investments** into account. Investments are things that have been put into the relationship, and which can't be got back if the relationship ends. Examples of investments are time and emotional support.

The investment model states that the best predictor of whether a couple will stay together is commitment, which is made up of three factors:

- *Satisfaction* with the relationship – a feeling that the relationship provides rewards that are unique.

- A belief that the relationship offers better rewards compared with any alternatives on offer (CL Alt).

- *Investments* in the relationship – which factors act as barriers to dissolution.

- Investment theory can be summarized using the following formula:

$$COM = SAT - ALT + INV$$

(Commitment equals satisfaction minus alternatives plus investments)

Evidence and evaluation

KEY STUDY: **RHATIGAN AND AXSOM (2006)**

Rhatigan and Axsom (2006) studied a group of women who had been victims of intimate partner violence (IPV) and who were housed in women's refuges in North America. Fifty-one women completed Rusbult's investment model scale (Rusbult et al., 1998), which consisted of 29 items measuring the four elements of the model: COM, ALT, INV and SAT.

Rhatigan and Axsom found – unsurprisingly – low levels of satisfaction and commitment in the sample overall. In support of their hypothesis, women who had made fewer investments had lower levels of commitment to their relationship and vice versa.

Rhatigan and Axsom used a sample of women who have suffered violence and sought shelter in a refuge. Hence, there is a limited ability to generalize to other samples. However, the investment model has also been supported by research using different samples, for example Impett, Beals and Peplau (2002) used married couples, and Truman-Schram et al. (2000) used student couples. The use of different samples provides the investment model with a wide base of support.

The difference between the investment model and the two previous theories is the emphasis on past investments (the history of the relationship) rather than a focus on current rewards and costs.

The investment model is particularly helpful in explaining why some people stay in relationships that appear to offer few rewards and high costs. Jerstad (2005) studied men and women and found that investments, notably the amount of time and effort put into the relationship, were the most important predictor of whether or not someone would stay with a violent partner. Those who had experienced the most violence were often the most committed – almost as if their previous experiences were 'investments' that would be rendered worthless if they left.

Research methods link

Research on theories of relationships invariably uses correlational methods, with measurement of variables and relationships between them. You may wish to look back at the advantages and disadvantages of correlational methods on page 25.

RELATIONSHIPS

ACTIVITY 2.5

You have now met all three theories of relationships: social exchange theory, equity theory and the investment model. Construct 6-mark summaries of each theory, emphasizing the differences between them. This will provide a useful means of comparison and evaluation if you have an exam question focused on this topic.

Duck's phase model of relationship breakdown

Duck (1982) developed a stage model of relationship breakdown that focused on how long-term, committed relationships end – that is, the processes involved in splitting up. Duck conceptualized splitting up as consisting of four phases, each with a different focus. The decision to move from one phase to the next was made when one (or indeed both) members of the couple reached a threshold or turning point, which moved the process forwards. In 2006, Rollie and Duck added an additional phase to the end of their model and called this 'resurrection'.

The intra-psychic phase

The start of the break-up process is the unhappiness or dissatisfaction of at least one of the members of the couple. The focus at this point is usually on the partner's behaviour and how they are failing in the relationship. The unhappy party may talk to their friends about the relationship. When they reach the threshold of being unable to stand it, they voice their concerns to their partner and the dyadic phase begins.

Threshold – I can't stand it any more.

The dyadic phase

The unhappiness is now out in the open air. The couple may engage in discussions and talk through possible changes to resolve the difficulties. They may choose to call in intervention teams such as couple counselling – if this is partially successful the relationship may continue. Not all couples address this stage by talking: some enact this by refusing to discuss problems. If the issues are not resolved, the next threshold may be reached.

Threshold – I would be justified in leaving.

The social phase

The relationship problems are now aired publicly as the couple starts to tell their friends and family about the difficulties and the possibility of a split. Rather than being constructed as 'going through a rough patch', the problems are now serious enough to seek the support of friends, who may offer support or take sides. The break-up is becoming inevitable.

Threshold – I mean it.

The grave-dressing phase

This phase takes place after the couple has officially split up. Both parties try to get their side of the story/explanation of the break-up across to people that they want to think well of them. Each partner creates his or her own version of what went wrong and who/what was to blame. These versions are face-saving and are distributed throughout the social network.

Resurrection phase

Resurrection involves focusing on activities that move the individual forward in their new life. This stage involves picking up the pieces and re-establishing oneself as a single person – for example, arranging to go out with friends.

Fig. 2.9 Duck's phase model of relationship breakdown

Exam hint

You cannot be asked a question about the fifth stage of the model, as it is not named on the specification, but you can include it in your discussion of the model.

Evidence and evaluation

Duck's model provides an account of how committed relationships end: the focus is on the process of relationship breakdown, not the causes. In 2006, Rollie and Duck extended their work by identifying gender differences in behaviour during the stages. In the intra-psychic phase, women are particularly concerned with decline in communication whereas men are concerned at the loss of shared activities including sex. In the dyadic phase, some men prefer not to discuss the issues and many women see attempts to avoid talking about the relationship as evasive and further evidence of problems. During the social phase, women tend to be more likely to seek the support of friends and often begin the processes of resurrection earlier than men.

Today, relationship breakdown is not just played out face-to-face but must also be managed in the virtual arena. Lefebvre et al. (2012) have examined the ways in which Facebook is used during the process of relationship breakdown, providing support and extension to Duck and Rollie's 2006 model.

KEY STUDY: LEFEBRVE ET AL. (2012)

Lefebrve et al. studied a sample of 208 college students, chosen because students were among the most frequent users of Facebook (averaging one to two hours per day). Participants were asked to complete an online survey indicating their use of Facebook in the context of a recent relationship break-up. The results were analysed to identify the main types of Facebook use during and after the break-up. Common strategies used during break-ups included:

- Little or no Facebook activity (22 per cent of the sample). This approach was chosen by those who deliberately chose to keep their relationship break up out of Facebook.
- Relational cleansing (22 per cent of the sample). This involved status changes ('it's complicated' or 'single') and removal of signs of the relationship such as wall postings and photos.
- Electronic surveillance (about 10 per cent of the sample). These participants engaged in 'stalking activities', checking where their ex-partner was and what they were doing.

The same three strategies were found after the relationship had ended and other strategies were added. *Withdrawing access* involved blocking or 'un-friending' the ex-partner and their family and friends. Another strategy was *positive impression management*, which involved presenting the self in a positive light, for example posting photos of nights out with friends.

Lefebrve argues that these strategies map onto Duck's model. They demonstrate how people engage in the social, grave-dressing and resurrection phases in their SNS lives. They also show how the phases do not always occur sequentially but are often overlapping.

You can choose any two of the theories covered in this section of the chapter: social exchange theory, equity theory, the investment model and Duck's stage model. Whichever two you choose, keep your description very succinct as only six AO1 marks are available.

A good route to AO3 is examining evidence for and against the theories. Remember that evaluation should be focused on the theory, not on the research that underpins the theory. If you select two similar theories (e.g. SET and equity theory), comparison of the similarities and differences can also be a good route to AO3.

EXAMPLE EXAM QUESTION

Discuss two theories of romantic relationships. (16 marks)

KEY POINTS

- The social exchange theory sees people as selfish, aiming to maximize rewards and minimize costs. The theory states that people compare current relationships with general expectations (CL) and with alternative relationships (CL Alt).

- Research has indicated that satisfaction and availability of alternatives are related to each other rather than separate.

- Equity theory argues that people are motivated by fairness in relationships. Reducing inputs and/or encouraging a partner to put more into the relationship can restore inequity.

- Research shows a positive relationship between equity and satisfaction, supporting the theory. Equity appears more important to women than men.

- Rusbult emphasizes the importance of investments to relationship commitment. Investments, such as time, are things that cannot be reclaimed from the relationship.

- Studies of victims of violence show the importance of investments to relationships.

- Duck's phase model identifies five phases on the dissolution of relationships. This model has received considerable support, including recent studies on SNS.

Parasocial relationships

Parasocial relationship: a one-way relationship formed by a fan towards a famous person who is unaware of their existence.

Parasocial relationships are relationships with famous people; typically pop stars, film stars and athletes. Unlike real relationships, they are entirely one-sided. While the fan is passionately attached to the celebrity, the celebrity does not know them. An element of celebrity worship is viewed as a normal part of teenage development,

Fig. 2.10 Which factors lead fans to form passionate – if one-sided – relationships with celebrities?

when adolescents are engaged in a search for their own identity, but in most people, attachment to celebrities decreases with age. Most parasocial relationships are relatively harmless, but a small number become serious obsessions. There have been examples in which celebrities – the singers Madonna and Joss Stone, and director Steven Spielberg to name a few – have been stalked by obsessed fans.

Levels of parasocial relationships

Parasocial relationships can be measured using questionnaire and scales. The most commonly used scale is the Celebrity Attitude Scale (CAS) devised by McCutcheon in 2002 and revised in 2006. The CAS consists of 23 items, such as 'I like to talk with other fans about XXXX'. Agreement with each statement is measured using a 5-point scale: a score of 5 indicates strong agreement, 3 indicates uncertain or neutral and 1 indicates strong disagreement with the statement.

The CAS is made up of three subscales that measure different elements of parasocial relationships. The subscales are:

- The Entertainment/Social subscale: seven items measure the **social aspects** associated with following the celebrity, such as discussions with friends and shared experiences like attending concerts.

- The Intense Personal subscale: thirteen items measure the **intensity of feelings** towards the celebrity, along with obsessional tendencies.

- The Borderline Pathological subscale: six items measure potentially **harmful** aspects of feelings towards the celebrity.

The remaining eight statements are 'filler items', designed to make respondents think about the questions rather than falling into a pattern of automatic responses (for example, ticking 5 for every statement). The scores are totalled on each of the three subscales to give an overall measurement of attitudes to celebrities.

ACTIVITY 2.6

Read the three statements below and decide which one of the subscales is measured in each item:
- If X asked me to do something illegal as a favour I probably would.
- I consider X to be my soulmate.
- My friends and I like to discuss what X has done.

Now, have a go at devising another item for each of the three subscales. Then complete the CAS on the next page and identify your scores for each of the three subscales. Could you spot the filler items? How honest were your answers?

THE CELEBRITY ATTITUDE SCALE

The purpose of this survey is to identify your views about famous persons. The responses you give are confidential. There are no right or wrong answers, so please answer as openly and thoughtfully as you can. For purposes of the survey we are defining the term "celebrity" as a famous living person (or one who died during your lifetime) that you greatly admire.

Who is your favorite celebrity? _____ (Please choose one famous person, as defined above).

Just in case your favorite celebrity is unknown to us, please circle one or more of the following to describe why your favorite celebrity is famous: Acting Author Artist Medicine Modeling Music News Politics Religion Royalty Radio or TV Talk Show Science Sports Other (please describe) _____

Please use the following scale in response to the items below.
5 = Strongly Agree; 4 = Agree; 3= Uncertain or neutral; 2 = Disagree; 1 = Strongly Disagree

1.	If I were to meet MFC in person, he/she would already somehow know that I am his/her biggest fan.	1	2	3	4	5
2.	One of the main reasons I maintain an interest in MFC is that doing so gives me a temporary escape from life's problems.	1	2	3	4	5
3.	MFC is practically perfect in every way.	1	2	3	4	5
4.	I share with MFC a special bond that cannot be described in words.	1	2	3	4	5
5.	To know MFC is to love him/her.	1	2	3	4	5
6.	When something bad happens to MFC I feel like it happened to me.	1	2	3	4	5
7.	When MFC fails or loses at something I feel like a failure myself.	1	2	3	4	5
8.	The successes of MFC are my successes too.	1	2	3	4	5
9.	I consider MFC to be my soulmate.	1	2	3	4	5
10.	When MFC dies (or died) I will feel (or I felt) like dying too.	1	2	3	4	5
11.	If someone gave me several thousand dollars to do with as I please, I would consider spending it on a personal possession (like a napkin or paper plate) once used by MFC.	1	2	3	4	5
12.	When something good happens to MFC I feel like it happened to me.	1	2	3	4	5
13.	I am obsessed by details of MFC's life.	1	2	3	4	5
14.	I have pictures and/or souvenirs of MFC which I always keep in exactly the same place.	1	2	3	4	5
15.	I love to talk with others who admire MFC.	1	2	3	4	5
16.	Keeping up with news about MFC is an entertaining pastime.	1	2	3	4	5
17.	It is enjoyable just to be with others who like MFC.	1	2	3	4	5
18.	I enjoy watching, reading, or listening to MFC because it means a good time.	1	2	3	4	5
19.	Learning the life story of MFC is a lot of fun.	1	2	3	4	5
20.	I like watching and hearing about MFC when I am with a large group of people.	1	2	3	4	5
21.	My friends and I like to discuss what MFC has done.	1	2	3	4	5
22.	I would gladly die in order to save the life of MFC.	1	2	3	4	5
23.	If I were lucky enough to meet MFC, and he/she asked me to do something illegal as a favor, I would probably do it.	1	2	3	4	5
24.	If I walked through the door of MFC's home without an invitation she or he would be happy to see me.	1	2	3	4	5
25.	I have frequent thoughts about my celebrity, even when I don't want to.	1	2	3	4	5
26.	I often feel compelled to learn the personal habits of MFC.	1	2	3	4	5
27.	MFC would immediately come to my rescue if I needed help.	1	2	3	4	5
28.	MFC and I have our own code so we can communicate with each other secretly (such as over the TV or special words on the radio).	1	2	3	4	5
29.	If MFC was accused of committing a crime that accusation would have to be false.	1	2	3	4	5
30.	If MFC endorsed a legal but possibly unsafe drug designed to make someone feel good, I would try it.	1	2	3	4	5
31.	News about my celebrity is a pleasant break from a harsh world.	1	2	3	4	5
32.	If MFC found me sitting in his/her car, he or she would be upset.	1	2	3	4	5
33.	It would be great if MFC and I were locked in a room for a few days.	1	2	3	4	5
34.	If MFC saw me in a restaurant he/she would ask me to sit down and talk.	1	2	3	4	5

Scoring

Suggested by: Maltby, J., Day, L., McCutcheon, L.E., Houran, J. & Ashe, D. (2006). Extreme celebrity worship, fantasy proneness and dissociation: Developing the measurement and understanding of celebrity worship within a clinical personality context. *Personality and Individual Differences, 40,* 273-283.

Intense personal 1+ 8 + 11 + 2 + 13 + 18 + 24 + 12 + 14 + 16 + 28 + 6 + 3

Entertainment Social 17+ 31 + 23 + 13 + 19 + 29 +5

Borderline Pathological 4 + 22 + 25 + 15 + 20 + 7+ 28

The rest of the items can be considered as filler items.

Fig. 2.11 The Celebrity Attitude Scale

Note: MFC = My Favourite Celebrity.

The CAS identifies three levels of parasocial relationship, from the relatively harmless to the serious. (McCutcheon et al., 2004):

- Level 1: the Entertainment/Social level. This is reflected by high scores on the first subscale but low scores on the second and third scales. The person is attracted to the celebrity because of the entertainment they provide. The celebrity is a source of fun and enjoyment.

- Level 2: the Intense Personal level. This is reflected by high scores on the second scale, showing that the fan has become intensely engaged with their chosen celebrity.

- Level 3: the Borderline Pathological level. A small number of fans score highly on the BP scale. They may make repeated attempts to contact the celebrity and try to find out where they live.

The CAS is viewed as a reliable and valid way of measuring attraction to celebrities. Most studies using the scale have been carried out in the UK and the United States, but recent studies have tested the scale in a variety of cultures. Tengco-Pacquing et al. (2013) compared the scores of a population of Filipinos with Americans, who are often thought to have the most celebrity-obsessed culture. They found – somewhat surprisingly – even higher scores on the second and third scales in Filipinos than in North Americans (see Table 2.1).

	American sample	Filipino sample
Average score on Intense personal scale	14.77 out of 52	23.69 out of 52
Average score on Borderline Pathological scale	7.18 out of 30	10.05 out of 30

Table 2.1 Sample of CAS data from the study by Tengco-Pacquing et al.

THINKING SCIENTIFICALLY: MEASURING PARASOCIAL RELATIONSHIPS USING THE CAS

The CAS uses closed questions with fixed responses (agree, disagree, etc.). Questionnaires are a good way of collecting lots of data relatively quickly. They can be completed easily and, especially when they are posted on the Internet, large samples of data can be collected. The use of fixed responses yields quantitative data (scores) so averages can be calculated and individuals and populations can be easily compared, as Tengco-Pacquing's work indicates.

However, there is no guarantee that the data collected are accurate. The use of fixed-response answers can be frustrating when the preferred answer ('It depends on how I am feeling') is not available. There is also no guarantee that the questionnaire has been completed seriously.

Research methods link

You can refresh your memory about questionnaire design by looking back at pages 18–20 of the research methods chapter.

Explaining parasocial relationships: attachment theory and the absorption-addiction model

The circulation figures of celebrity magazines such as *OK* and *Hello* show that many people have a strong interest in celebrities' lives. But what turns an interest into a fascination and, for some, an intense emotional connection? The first indication of the darker side of parasocial relationships was shown after the death of the actress Marilyn Monroe in 1962. Phillips (1974) found a 12 per cent increase in suicides in North America in the month following her death, which was represented by an additional 303 suicides.

What factors lead individuals to form intense parasocial relationships with celebrities? Attachment theory and the absorption-addiction model share the view that people seek intense parasocial relationships when there are deficiencies, such as loneliness or depression, in their lives. However, there are important differences between these explanations.

Attachment explanations

Attachment explanations are based on attachment theory, which you met in the developmental psychology covered in Year 1. According to Bowlby (1951), each of us develops an internal 'working model' of how relationships work in early childhood, which continues through to adulthood (Waters et al., 2000) if life events do not alter it (Zimmerman et al., 2000). We also develop a characteristic attachment style that can be categorized as secure or insecure (Ainsworth, 1970).

Kienlen (1998) focused on the importance of attachment styles in parasocial relationships. He believed that adults with insecure attachment styles (Type A or C) were more likely to form parasocial relationships than those with secure, Type B attachments. Kienlen believed that parasocial relationships were attractive to insecurely attached people because there was little risk of criticism, disappointment or rejection, which are all part of real relationships.

Evidence and evaluation

KEY STUDY:	MCCUTCHEON ET AL. (2006)

McCutcheon et al. tested the hypothesis that adults who reported an insecure childhood attachment with their parents would form stronger attachments to celebrities than adults who recalled secure attachments as children. A sample of 299 students completed several measurements, including a Celebrity Attitudes Scale (CAS), an unpublished celebrity stalking scale and a relationship questionnaire designed to measure attachment style.

McCutcheon et al. found no relationship between attachment style and attachment to celebrities, contradicting the hypothesis and the attachment explanation. However, insecurely attached adults were more likely to condone stalking-type behaviours towards celebrities.

Link

Have a look back at attachment types in Book 1, page 165.

The absorption–addiction model (McCutcheon, Lange and Houran, 2002)

The absorption–addiction model argues that people pursue parasocial relationships due to deficits in their lives and real relationships. Relationships with celebrities are an attempt to cope with or escape from reality. Absorption in the life of a celebrity can provide a sense of identity and fulfilment. However, parasocial relationships can become addictive, as the individual needs to feel an increasingly stronger sense of involvement with their celebrity.

The absorption–addiction model is closely tied to the three levels of celebrity worship (on page 159). While most fans stay at the fairly harmless Level 1 stage, those who have a weaker sense of personal identity or poorer psychological adjustment may go beyond this and 'absorb' themselves into a celebrity's life to gain a sense of stronger identity. A personal crisis may also lead an individual to move from one stage to the next.

Evidence and evaluation

KEY STUDY: MALTBY ET AL. (2006)

The absorption–addiction model predicts an association between poorer psychological health and scores on the Celebrity Attitude Scale. This was tested by Maltby et al. using a sample of UK students, 126 male and 181 female, living in South Yorkshire. Each student was asked to complete two measurements:

- The 23-item Celebrity Attitude Scale
- A general health questionnaire (GHQ28) devised by Goldberg and Williams (1991), which measures symptoms of depression, anxiety and social dysfunction.

Maltby et al. found that individuals who had reached the first level of celebrity worship, 'entertainment social', had some degree of social dysfunction. They often lacked social relationships in their real life, experienced loneliness, and used the celebrity relationship to 'soothe the empty self'. Those who had reached the second level, 'intense personal', scored highly on anxiety and depression. This study provided support for the pathological view of celebrity worship.

THINKING SCIENTIFICALLY: CORRELATION

This study uses a correlational method; therefore it is important to note that cause cannot be established. While there is an association between poorer mental health and degrees of celebrity worship, it cannot be concluded that one causes the other. In any study that measures aspects of psychological functioning there are potentially serious ethical issues. Although this study uses a non-clinical population (students), researchers would need to ensure that those students who were identified as having some degree of social dysfunction or symptoms such as anxiety/depression were offered appropriate support. Maltby et al. were unable to test the third level, 'borderline pathological', as the GHQ does not include items to measure serious problems with adjustment.

A recent study (McCutcheon, 2014) has begun to tease out the personality factors that play a role in addiction to celebrity worship. Impulsiveness and irresponsibility have been associated with other addictions such as substance abuse and shopping. In McCutcheon's study, 263 students from the US, Jamaica and New Zealand completed the CAS along with scales designed to measure impulsiveness and sensation seeking. McCutcheon found that those who scored highly in impulsiveness were more likely to have strong attachments to celebrities implying that personality factors may underlie celebrity worship.

Exam hint

The term 'research' refers to theories and studies. We have covered two theoretical explanations of celebrity worship here – attachment theory and the absorption-addiction model. Look carefully at the clues in the scenario in order to decide which model would be most applicable.

EXAMPLE EXAM QUESTION

Sammie says she is the number one fan of One Direction. She travels to their gigs if they are in the UK and she checks Twitter several times a day to keep up with tweets from the group members. She collects band souvenirs and her bedroom is like a shrine. Sammie's friend Ruthie likes One Direction too and used to travel around the country following the band with Sammie. Now that she has a Saturday job and a boyfriend, she can't devote her time to going to gigs with Sammie anymore.

How would psychological research explain the experiences of Sammie and Ruthie? Refer to theories and/or studies in your answer. [12 marks]

KEY POINTS

- Parasocial relationships are one-way relationships formed by a fan towards a celebrity.
- The CAS is a reliable and valid way of measuring attraction to celebrities. It consists of 34 statements and three subscales.
- The attachment explanation suggests that celebrity worship is associated with insecure attachments. There is limited evidence to support this claim.
- The absorption-addiction model suggests that celebrity worship is a search for identity. Some evidence supports this claim, with higher scores on the CAS from those who are anxious or depressed.
- Recent research suggests that impulsiveness and sensation seeking may be associated with the addictive elements of celebrity worship.

PRACTICAL ACTIVITY

We have seen that similarity seems to be an important factor in the formation of relationships and friendships. Kandel (1978) found that teenage pairs of close friends were similar in many respects including ethnic background, religion and economic background of parents. Hill, Rubin and Peplau (1976) also found similarities of race, class and religion in dating couples and in pairs of friends. You can investigate this for yourself. First you will need to decide if you intend to look at similarity in pairs of friends or dating couples. You should set a minimum time that they have been friends/known each other, such as six months. You will need a sample of at least ten pairs of friends or ten couples in order to produce sufficient data to carry out statistical analyses.

When you have decided if you are studying friends or couples you will need to consider exactly how you intend to measure similarity. You could focus on attitude, personality or demographic similarity (social background), as all of these have been found to be important. If you decide to focus on attitudes, you will probably be able to find ways of measuring attitudes using internet sources. Personality measurements such as Eysenck's EPI should also be readily available. If you decide to measure demographic similarity you will need to devise a method to 'measure' social background. Your measurements should allow you to produce a score for both members of each pair. You can plot these on a scattergram to see if there is any apparent similarity, and then go on to correlate these using a Spearman's Rank Order test of correlation.

When you have devised your measuring scale, you will need to think through the ethics of this carefully. How do you intend to ask for informed consent from your participants and how will you debrief them afterwards? You will need to keep the results anonymous and confidential.

You can investigate partner preferences by carrying out an analysis of personal advertisements in a similar way to that used by Dunbar and Waynforth (1995). You could choose to focus on comparing heterosexual male and female advertisements in terms of qualities sought and advertised, or you could compare adverts by gay men and women seeking partners.

When you have decided on the focus of your research, you will need to decide where you intend to collect advertisements from. This could include newspapers (free or otherwise), magazines or Internet dating sites. You will also have to consider how many advertisements you intend to study and think about the different ways of choosing them to ensure a fair and unbiased sampling.

Although this material is in the public arena and people clearly intend for their advertisements to be read, you will still need to consider the ethical issues involved in the study. Clearly you cannot contact anonymous advertisers to ask for consent and you cannot debrief them.

When you have made these decisions, you will need to decide exactly how you intend to score the qualities advertised. A pilot study will be helpful at this stage to enable you to see the kinds of qualities referred to. In order to ensure that you have inter-rater reliability, you could devise a recording/scoring scheme with a classmate or partner then score the advertisements separately using your system. Hopefully you should find that the results agree.

Example exam questions

1. Outline Rusbult's investment model. **(3 marks)**

2. Read the item below and answer the questions that follow.

> As part of his A Level psychology work Tom carried out a study to test the matching hypothesis. He collected 20 wedding photos from a local newspaper and cut each photo into two, separating the bride and groom. Tom asked a sample of ten of his classmates to rate each of the 20 photographs, using a scale of 1 to 10 (1 being highly unattractive and 10 being highly attractive). When he had collected the data, Tom added up the scores given to each of the 20 photographs. He decided to carry out a statistical test to see if there was a relationship between the scores given to the members of each couple.

   a) Name an appropriate graph that Tom could use to display the total scores. **(1 mark)**

   b) Identify ONE statistical test that Tom could use to analyse his data. **(1 mark)**

   c) Justify your choice of test with reference to the research study described above. **(2 marks)**

3. Which of the following is NOT one of the phases of Duck's model of relationship breakdown? **(1 mark)**

   Social phase   Grave-dressing phase   Inter-psychic phase   Dyadic phase

4. Discuss evolutionary explanations for partner preferences. **(16 marks)**

Exam focus

Read through the following example exam question, example student answer, and examiner comments. Then, have a go at answering the question yourself!

EXAMPLE EXAM QUESTION

Discuss research into self-disclosure. (16 marks)

Amina's answer

Self-disclosure (SD) refers to the revealing of personal or intimate information about ourselves to others. SD can be done face-to-face or online. There has been a lot of research into face-to-face SD, but less into online SD as it is more recent. SD is an important way for relationships to develop. Disclosing personal information shows that the discloser trusts the listener. When people disclose personal information, they assume that information will not be shared, but this is not always the case.

> **Examiner comment:** Quite a lot of introduction here but not much actual detail on research. This could be shortened!

One study into SD was carried out by Sprecher (2013). Sprecher asked pairs of students to talk to each other and instructed one to self-disclose, then measured how much they liked each other. The student who had listened to the disclosure scored higher on liking. Then the second student was instructed to disclose and liking was measured again — at this point it was equal. Sprecher's study showed that SD increases liking — perhaps because it implies that we like and trust the other person.

> **Examiner comment:** Be precise: state 'experiment'.

This is an experiment and is highly controlled but it lacks validity: in real life, people don't disclose straight after meeting each other.

> **Examiner comment:** Evaluative point could be elaborated by identifying what was controlled (timing of the disclosure).

A meta-analysis by Dindia and Allen (1992) showed that women are more likely to open up than men – especially when the listener is a friend or family member. However, when the listener is a stranger, men are just as likely to open up – this is known as the 'stranger on a train' phenomenon.

Experiments allow for a lot of control about what is disclosed and when, which is a strength. However, they lack validity: in real life self-disclosure is not usually as synchronous. In addition, the experiment used students who may not be representative of the general population. However, the meta-analysis used a large sample, meaning that the findings can be generalized across different populations.

Online SD happens through social networking (status updates) and through blogs. Utz (2015) found that status updates were positive and often increased feelings of connection and intimacy with Facebook friends, which is similar to face-to-face SD. However, one difference is that status updates can be seen by friends and are not just to one person. Another study found that the self-disclosures of people with low self-esteem tended to be negative in nature. Studies of self-disclosure using blogs showed that young female bloggers disclose the most information, which is consistent with face-to-face SD. The studies of SD online use content analysis to analyse the data. The data are naturally occurring, which makes them high in validity. However, there are ethical issues, especially when Facebook posts are analysed without consent.

Examiner comment: Clear summary of research findings without a lot of descriptive detail.

Examiner comment: Again, rather basic statements that could be elaborated on.

Examiner comment: This response squeezes into the bottom of level 3, getting around 9 out of 16 marks. Knowledge of research into self-disclosure is evident. There are occasional inaccuracies. Evaluation is apparent but in several places, it could be more developed, hence the very bottom of the band. The answer is mostly clear and organized. Specialist terminology is mostly used effectively. Lacks focus in places.

Chapter 3: Gender

Introduction

'Men are from Mars and women are from Venus' – so wrote John Gray in 1992 in the book of the same name. This phenomenally successful book was based on an assumption that is taken by many to be a fact. The assumption was this: men and women are biologically different, therefore they are psychologically different. Pick up a newspaper or magazine or watch a film and you will see this view played out: women are emotional, whereas men are rational; men are dominant and women are submissive; women are gentle and men are aggressive. The list of claims goes on and on!

This chapter starts by exploring the meaning of the terms 'sex' and 'gender'. While they are often used interchangeably in daily life, they have different meanings in psychology. Sex refers to the biological state of being male or female, whereas gender refers to differences in behaviour between the sexes and to feeling feminine or masculine. Although gender differences have been overstated, some certainly exist – males are more likely to be aggressive than females, for instance. There has been a great deal of debate about where these gender differences come from, and this chapter explores a number of different approaches, namely the biological, cognitive and psychodynamic approaches and social learning theory.

While these explanations appear to conflict, it is preferable to see them as addressing different questions about gender. Each of the explanations has different implications for change: if gender differences arise largely from biology they are likely to be fixed, but if they arise largely from socialization processes they are more flexible.

Most people experience a clear relationship between biological sex and gender identity: women are biologically female and 'feel' feminine and men 'feel' masculine. But what happens when there is conflict between an individual's biological sex and their sense of gender identity? Transgendered people often report that they feel 'trapped in the wrong body'. What can these experiences tell us about gender?

What is covered in Gender?

GENDER

Sex and gender

Key terms

Sex: the biological fact of being male or female based on genes and hormones.

Gender: the difference between the ways that men and women behave and the concepts of masculinity and femininity.

The terms **sex** and **gender** have different meanings, although they are often (and incorrectly) used interchangeably. Sex refers to the biological fact of being male or female, and to having sex – intercourse. Gender is used rather loosely to refer to differences between the ways that males and females behave, and to the concepts of masculinity and femininity. While it is a relatively simple procedure to determine the sex of a baby at birth, judgements about gender are more subjective. Media sources sometimes judge athletic, well-muscled sportswomen, such as Serena and Venus Williams for example, as 'masculine'. These judgements are – unsurprisingly – met by hostile public reactions.

Fig. 3.1 The toned, athletic and highly competitive Williams sisters – are these qualities usually associated with masculinity?

Hines (2004) identifies three components of psychosexual development:

- **Core gender identity**: an individual's sense of themselves as female or male. This is established in early childhood and is followed by gender role behaviours.
- **Gender role behaviours**: characteristics and behaviours that differ in males and females.
- **Sexual orientation**: erotic/sexual interest in people of the same or opposite sex – or in the case of bisexual people, both sexes. Sexual orientation is generally established during puberty and early adulthood.

In most people, the relationship between sex and gender is relatively straightforward. Biological sex maps onto core gender identity, so that boys feel masculine and girls feel feminine. However, people with **gender dysphoria** (previously called gender identity disorder) experience a mismatch between their biological sex and their core

Key term

Gender dysphoria: a mismatch between biological sex and core gender identity, commonly described as 'feeling trapped in the wrong body'.

gender identity. This is often referred to as feeling trapped in the wrong body. The experience often begins in early childhood, when young children become aware of the distinction between male and female.

Fig. 3.2 Bruce Jenner and Caitlin Jenner: a personal story of gender dysphoria that made international headlines, and in the process helped to raise public consciousness of the issues surrounding the transgender community

Androgyny

There is an assumption that masculinity and femininity are opposite points on a single dimension, with each individual being placed somewhere between the two extremes. Using this approach, an extremely masculine man such as the actor Vin Diesel would be placed at one end, whereas a 'girly' girl such as Kim Kardashian would be placed at the other.

This assumption was challenged by Bem (1971, 1974). She believed that people have both masculine and feminine characteristics in varying proportions and it is the overall balance of these that is important. We will explore this idea by looking at Bem's work.

ACTIVITY 3.1A

Work through the list of personality characteristics below and rate how desirable each characteristic would be for a) a woman and b) a man. If you think the characteristic is very important, give it a score of 5. If you think it is unimportant, give it score of 1.

Affectionate, honest, assertive, kind, helpful, ambitious, warm, athletic, acts like a leader, self-sufficient, competitive, makes decisions easily, easily flattered, likes children, theatrical.

Compare your answers with a couple of other people. How much agreement is there? Working as a group, identify the three most desirable (i.e. top scoring) characteristics for women and for men.

The activity you have just carried out is similar to the method used by Bem to investigate ideas about masculinity and femininity. You can complete part two of this activity (see page 176) after reading about Bem's work.

The Bem Sex-Role Inventory

Bem began by asking 50 male and 50 female students to rate a list of 200 trait (personality) words, such as reliable, honest, gentle and assertive, in relation to how desirable they were for men and women. From the list of 200 items Bem selected 20 traits that were consistently rated as desirable for women. These included affectionate, gentle, understanding, loves children and sensitive. She also selected 20 traits that were consistently rated as desirable for men, including assertive, dominant, forceful, independent and ambitious. These items demonstrate **sex-role stereotypes** – the generalized expectations held about 'typical' masculine and feminine qualities. Finally, Bem selected 20 'neutral' items that were rated as equally desirable for women and men (such as honest, hard-working).

Each of the three sets of 20 items constituted a subscale and the three subscales made up the Sex-Role Inventory (SRI), with 60 items in total. The 60 items were randomly ordered and placed on a self-report questionnaire. Participants were asked to complete the questionnaire by rating themselves on each of the items using a scale of 1 (never or almost never true of me) to 7 (almost always true of me).

Self-reliant						**Aggressive**				
Never	Rarely	Neutral	Often	Always		Never	Rarely	Neutral	Often	Always
○	○	○	○	○		○	○	○	○	○

Warm						**Truthful**				
Never	Rarely	Neutral	Often	Always		Never	Rarely	Neutral	Often	Always
○	○	○	○	○		○	○	○	○	○

Reliable						**Jealous**				
Never	Rarely	Neutral	Often	Always		Never	Rarely	Neutral	Often	Always
○	○	○	○	○		○	○	○	○	○

Gullible						**Yielding**				
Never	Rarely	Neutral	Often	Always		Never	Rarely	Neutral	Often	Always
○	○	○	○	○		○	○	○	○	○

Cheerful						**Friendly**				
Never	Rarely	Neutral	Often	Always		Never	Rarely	Neutral	Often	Always
○	○	○	○	○		○	○	○	○	○

Moody						**Independent**				
Never	Rarely	Neutral	Often	Always		Never	Rarely	Neutral	Often	Always
○	○	○	○	○		○	○	○	○	○

In the next stage of the research, Bem asked a much larger sample of 444 male and 279 female students to complete the SRI by rating themselves on each of the 60 traits. Completion of the SRI produced three scores per person, one for each subscale – masculine, feminine and neutral. These scores were used to classify people into one of four 'gender types':

- Individuals with high scores on masculinity and low scores on femininity were referred to as **masculine**.
- Individuals with high scores on femininity and low scores on masculinity were referred to as **feminine**.

Key term

Sex-role stereotype: a generalized expectation about a typical feminine or masculine quality.

- Individuals with high scores on both masculinity and femininity were referred to as **androgynous**.
- Individuals with low scores on both masculinity and femininity were categorized as **undifferentiated**.

Bem's research confirmed her claim that masculinity and femininity are not opposite poles of a dimension but that individuals possess masculine and feminine traits in varying proportions. Bem referred to people who possess roughly equal amounts of masculine and feminine traits as androgynous. In some people – often men – masculine traits are dominant and in others (generally women) feminine traits are dominant. Bem referred to highly masculine men and highly feminine women as 'sex-typed' individuals. In later work, Bem argued that sex-typed individuals were restricted by gender roles and had poorer psychological health, whereas androgynous individuals had better psychological adjustment.

Key term

Androgynous: possessing a blend of masculine and feminine characteristics in roughly equal proportions.

THINKING SCIENTIFICALLY: TEMPORAL VALIDITY

Bem's research took place over 40 years ago and was carried out with Californian students in the 'hippie' era. It is reasonable to assume that ideas about masculinity and femininity might have changed dramatically since then. However, Holt and Ellis (1998) carried out a partial replication of Bem's work just before the turn of the century and found that 58 of the 60 adjectives from the original SRI still fitted into the three subscales. Therefore, Bem's work demonstrates temporal validity – it continues to be a good measurement of sex-role stereotypes 40 years after it was originally devised.

Although Bem used the term androgyny to refer to personality characteristics (traits), the word is also used in everyday language to refer to people whose physical appearance is sexually ambiguous.

Research methods link

Bem's SRI is an example of a self-report method. You can remind yourself about the strengths and weaknesses of self-report techniques by looking back at pages 19–20.

Fig. 3.3 Two androgynous supermodels

ACTIVITY 3.1B

Locate a copy of Bem's complete SRI on the Internet (you can find this on multiple sites) and complete it to establish your own 'gender type'. Did your familiarity with Bem's work lead you to respond differently than you might have done if you had not read this section of the chapter?

Exam hint

Bem's SRI is the standard method of measuring androgyny. You can focus your answer on the development of the SRI scale or the final constitution of the scale. As only 5 marks are available you will not have space to include both of these in your answer.

EXAMPLE EXAM QUESTION

Explain what is meant by androgyny and outline one method of measuring androgyny. (5 marks)

KEY POINTS

- Sex refers to the biological fact of being male or female and is generally easily identifiable.
- Gender refers to differences in the ways that men and women act and to concepts of masculinity and femininity.
- Bem devised a self-report questionnaire to measure gender called the Sex-Role Inventory (SRI).
- The SRI identifies four gender types: masculine, feminine, androgynous and undifferentiated.
- Androgyny involves possessing both male and female characteristics in roughly equal proportions.
- Sex-typed individuals conform to traditional gender stereotypes.
- Partial replications of Bem's work imply that the scale continues to be relevant.

The role of chromosomes

The sex of a baby is determined at the moment of conception, when ovum and sperm meet to form a zygote (fertilized egg). The ovum and the sperm contribute chromosomes to the zygote: chromosomes contain DNA, which supplies each individual with a unique genetic code. The twenty-third pair of chromosomes determines the sex of the zygote. The female gamete, the ovum, can only supply an X chromosome to the zygote but the male gamete (sperm) can supply an X or a Y chromosome. If the sperm supplies an X chromosome, the zygote will be female with an XX pattern. If the sperm supplies a Y chromosome, the zygote will be male with an XY pattern.

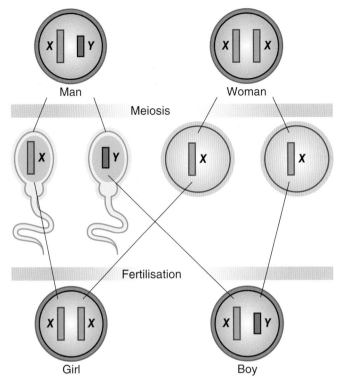

Fig. 3.4 How a baby's sex is determined

For the first six to eight weeks after conception, male and female embryos are identical. Up to this point, male and female embryos have the capacity to generate either a male reproductive system or a female reproductive system. Around eight weeks after conception, the gene on the 23rd chromosome instructs the glands in the embryo to release **hormones**. In the male XY embryo, male hormones called **androgens** stimulate the development of the male reproductive system and simultaneously suppress the development of the female reproductive system, leading to the development of testes and penis. In the female XX embryo, hardly any secretion of hormones takes place, meaning that the 'default' female reproductive system develops with ovaries and a vagina.

One exception to this pattern is androgen insensitivity syndrome (AIS). In AIS, the chromosome pattern is male (XY) but the androgen receptors fail to recognize the circulating male hormones in utero and the male reproductive system does not develop. The baby is identified as a female at birth through the appearance of the genitals, but is genetically (chromosomally) male. AIS is extremely rare, occurring in about one in 20,000 births, and AIS individuals are infertile.

Key terms

Hormones: chemicals released from the endocrine glands. They travel in the bloodstream to target structures.

Androgens: male hormones such as testosterone.

Link

You can refresh your memory about the endocrine system and hormones by looking back at Book 1, pages 259–261.

GENDER

Atypical sex chromosome patterns: Klinefelter's syndrome and Turner's syndrome

A small number of embryos have a different chromosome pattern to the standard XX or XY. Two such conditions are Klinefelter's and Turner's syndromes. These chromosomal patterns occur randomly during the fusion of egg and sperm cells and are not genetic (inherited from parents).

- **Klinefelter's syndrome** results from an XXY chromosome pattern in males. The incidence of Klinefelter's syndrome is around one in 600 males. Males with Klinefelter's syndrome have normal male genitalia but small testes, which do not produce sperm. They are infertile and often have a low sex drive.
- **Turner's syndrome** results from a missing X chromosome in females. The chromosome can be fully missing (Classic Turner's syndrome) or partially missing in some cells (Mosaic Turner's syndrome) and is often described as X0. The condition occurs in around 1 in 2000 females. Girls with Turner's syndrome have normal external genitalia but the ovaries fail to develop, leading to infertility.

Because external genitalia are unaffected, Turner's and Klinefelter's syndromes are often detected around the ages of 13 to 14 when puberty fails to start as expected.

The role of prenatal hormones

The genetic pattern of the embryo, XX or XY, programmes the release of prenatal hormones, the most important of which is **testosterone**. A correlational study by Lutchmaya, Baron–Cohen and Raggatt (2002) measured the amount of foetal testosterone in the amniotic fluid of mothers-to-be, then observed the interaction between these infants – 29 girls and 41 boys – and their parents when the infants were one year old. They found a negative correlation between the amounts of eye contact instigated by the infant and the level of foetal testosterone – the higher the foetal testosterone, the less eye contact. This study shows how infants' interest in social relationships may be related to testosterone levels. Foetal testosterone also correlated negatively with vocabulary size in 18- and 24-month-olds (Lutchmaya et al., 2002). Boys are typically slower to talk than girls and these differences may be underpinned by biology.

As we have seen, underexposure to foetal testosterone in AIS leads to incomplete development of male sex organs, showing the importance of testosterone in the development of biological sex. Overexposure to testosterone also has a range of effects on later behaviour. Most experimental research in this area has been carried out on non-human animals – notably rats and monkeys – but there are also case studies of accidental overexposure to testosterone in human embryos.

Experimental research using animals

KEY STUDY: YOUNG (1964)

Young carried out a series of experimental studies at the University of Kansas to investigate the impact of prenatal sex hormones on behaviour. He chose to study rats, for two reasons: firstly, rats reach sexual maturity quickly, and secondly, male and female rats show distinctly different behaviours when mating. Male rats mount females from behind and females adopt a crouching position, with back arched and head low. Young administered male or female hormones to pregnant rats and observed the behaviours of their offspring. Female rats exposed to prenatal male hormones became dominant and attempted to mount males from behind, whereas male rats exposed to prenatal female hormones adopted the typically female mating position.

Post-mortem studies in the 1970s and 80s indicated that male and female rats showed brain differences in an area called the **hypothalamus**, which regulates sexual behaviour. A brain structure called the sexually dimorphic nucleus of the pre-optic area (SDN-POA) in the hypothalamus was found to be around two times larger in male rats than females. In Young's experiments, it is likely that the administration of prenatal testosterone in female rats acted on the hypothalamus, enlarging the SDN-POA area and masculinising the brain to make it resemble the male rat brain. This was reflected in the masculine mating behaviour shown by the female rats. The administration of female hormones to male embryos would mean that the SDN was not masculinised, leading to the development of female mating behaviour in the male rats.

Young also studied rhesus monkeys. Two pregnant females were injected daily with testosterone between day 40 and day 90 of gestation (the gestation period in rhesus monkeys is around 180 days). The young female monkeys showed a range of behavioural differences to non-exposed monkeys, including increased rough-and-tumble play and masculine attempts at mounting other monkeys.

Key term

Hypothalamus: an area of the forebrain involved in physiological functions such as regulating sexual behaviour.

THINKING SCIENTIFICALLY: ANIMAL EXPERIMENTS

Animal experimentation allows a high degree of control. In these experiments, Young was able to control the amount of hormones the pregnant rats and monkeys were exposed to and the time of exposure. The subsequent environment was controlled and the animals could be carefully observed to see how their behaviour altered compared to a control group of non-exposed animals. The use of rats enabled post-mortems to be carried out to compare the brain structures of exposed and non-exposed rats. None of these would be possible with human research. Today, scanning methods can be used to examine brain structures.

Research methods link

You can refresh your memory for case studies by looking at page 28.

Case studies of human populations

Biological psychologists also make use of naturally occurring case studies of children who have been exposed to unusual levels of sex hormones during prenatal development. Hines carried out a series of case studies examining the development of children who were exposed to high levels of male hormones in utero. This condition is referred to as congenital adrenal hyperplasia (CAH). These studies allow us to see how girls may be affected by prenatal testosterone.

KEY STUDY: **CASE STUDIES OF CAH (HINES ET AL., 1994, 2004, 2014)**

In 1994, Hines examined the amount of rough-and-tumble play shown by CAH girls and boys aged three to eight years old. She compared them with a control group who had been unaffected by excessive prenatal hormone exposure. Hines found that the CAH girls preferred boys as playmates and preferred toys such as cars rather than dolls, in comparison to their non-affected relatives. This study suggests that prenatal testosterone may lead girls to develop more boyish play behaviours.

In 2004, Hines et al. compared a group of 16 adult CAH women and nine CAH men with their unaffected male and female relatives. Both groups were asked to think back and recall their childhood behaviours. They found that women with CAH tended to recall more 'boy-related' play behaviours and less interest in heterosexual relationships. Men with CAH did not differ from their unaffected male relatives.

Hines et al. (2014) studied a sample of 43 CAH girls and 38 CAH boys. The children were compared with a control group made up of 72 of their unaffected relatives (brothers, sisters, etc.) Hines et al. carried out interviews with the children's parents as well as using the DSM diagnostic tool for gender dysphoria to assess the extent to which the children showed cross-gender identification – behaviours characteristic of the opposite sex. They found that the CAH girls were more likely to give cross-gender responses than their unaffected siblings, and around 12 per cent of the female CAH sample showed cross-gender behaviours consistently across both measurements.

Fig. 3.5 Does exposure to prenatal testosterone lead to more 'boyish' rough-and-tumble play in girls?

Case studies provide qualitative data that is rich in detail. Hines' case studies use a variety of methods, including naturalistic observation of play, self-reports, interviews with the children's parents and clinical/diagnostic tools (e.g. DSM-5). This demonstrates the important principle of triangulation – approaching an issue from different angles to allow researchers to cross-check their findings. It is also worth noting that these case studies involve relatively large samples, allowing limited generalizations to be made.

Commentary on the role of prenatal hormones

Lutchmaya et al.'s findings show how foetal testosterone relates to later differences between boys and girls in sociability and language development. Hines' findings imply that overexposure to prenatal testosterone can have a range of effects on behaviour, leading girls to show more traditionally masculine play, and less interest in heterosexual relationships. For a small proportion of females, exposure to prenatal testosterone may be associated with a mismatch between biological sex and core gender identity – the experience of gender dysphoria.

However, while there is a relationship between masculinized behaviour and hormone exposure, the lack of controlled experiments means that we cannot be sure that one causes the other. In addition, corresponding brain differences in the human SDN have been much harder to identify. Brain differences between boys and girls are undetectable until the age of about five or six years. Swaab and Fliers (1985) identified an area corresponding to the SDN called INAH-1, which was around 2.5 times larger in adult males than females. However, subsequent studies (e.g. LeVay, 1991) failed to replicate these findings and identified other possible areas including INAH-3. There is ongoing debate as to whether differences in the SDN might underlie the experience of gender dysphoria, which you can read about later in the chapter. There is also debate about the role played by the SDN in male homosexuality.

As you read the topic on biological psychology, plasticity refers to the ability of the brain to change and adapt throughout life. Maguire et al. (2006) showed how gray matter in the hypothalamus increased in volume as taxi drivers learned to navigate around London. Studies of this nature show how experiences continue to affect brain structures throughout life, and it is very likely that applies to other brain structures.

Hormones in later life

The second major release of hormones occurs during puberty. The pituitary gland releases growth hormones, leading to a growth spurt in both sexes. The pituitary gland also releases follicle stimulating hormone (FSH) and luteinizing hormone (LH). These hormones

Fig. 3.6 Caster Semenya, a South African athlete who was subjected to gender testing at the 2009 World Championships in Athletics to prove that she was female. Because of the existence of different chromosomal patterns such as XO and XXY, genetic testing was abandoned by the International Olympic Committee in 1999 in favour of tests focusing on genes and hormones.

stimulate the testes and ovaries to increase production of androgens and oestrogens, leading to the development of sperm and ova. Both sexes produce both types of sex hormone – for example, the growth of underarm hair and pubic hair is triggered by androgens. The increase in sex hormones leads to an increased appetite to have sex in adolescents.

Oxytocin is a neuropeptide, produced by the hypothalamus and stored in the pituitary gland. It was identified in 1909 by a Greek doctor who discovered its properties in triggering the onset of labour (oxytocin means 'quick birth' in Greek). This led to an interest in the role played by oxytocin in a range of maternal and nurturing behaviours. Oxytocin can be used as a medication to start labour artificially and it is released when mothers breastfeed their infants, promoting mother–infant bonding.

Fig. 3.7 Prairie voles

Originally thought of as a female hormone, oxytocin became a focus of research in the 1970s when it was identified in prairie voles. Prairie voles are unusual animals, as they are one of the few species that form lasting relationships or pair bonds in a similar way to humans.

Since then, interest in oxytocin has gathered speed, with claims that it may underlie a range of sex differences in social behaviours, including face recognition, trust, empathy, and reactions to stress. Oxytocin is sometimes referred to as the cuddle hormone, love hormone or 'social glue' (Zak, 2011). There have even been recent claims that oxytocin may be implicated in causing autism.

Experimental research into the effects of oxytocin has been carried out on animals (usually rodents such as rats and mice). Mice bred to lack an oxytocin receptor gene have shown deficits in social behaviours relating to mating and the nurturing of offspring.

Experimental studies with humans use nasal administration of oxytocin and compare behavioural effects with a control group exposed to a placebo nasal spray. Studies show that oxytocin leads to increased trust in both males and females (Kosfeld et al., 2005). However, in males oxytocin also produces favouritism towards in-group members and discrimination towards members of other social groups (De Dreu et al., 2011).

Oxytocin may also play a role in the responses shown by men and women to stress (Taylor et al., 2000). While the same basic stress hormones and pathways are triggered, women show 'tend or befriend' actions during stressful events, gathering their support network around them. This approach may have been useful to protect offspring in the past. In contrast, men are more likely to show classic 'fight or flight' responses with increased aggression under stress. Taylor argues that oxytocin may play a mediating role in responses to stress. In other words, oxytocin shapes the different ways that men and women react when the fight or flight response is triggered.

EXAMPLE EXAM QUESTION

Discuss research into the role of hormones in sex and gender. (12 marks)

Exam hint

With questions focused on research, it is a good idea to select two or more research methods, as this enables you to compare and contrast the methods as a route to AO3. Animal experimentation and case studies would be the most obvious approach in relation to this question. You should ensure that you cover work on testosterone, but you can also choose to cover some of the work on oxytocin.

Conclusion

The biological approach to gender focuses on how chromosomes, hormones and brain structures influence differences between females and males. There is considerable evidence to suggest that prenatal hormones masculinize brain structures such as the SDN in rats, and these structures are involved in shaping different male and female behaviours, for example during mating. Evidence for brain differences between human females and males is less convincing, and unsurprisingly has produced some of the most intense debates in the history of the discipline. It is likely that biological factors interact with social factors such as modelling and reinforcement in the development of gender.

KEY POINTS

- Sex is determined at conception, with females having an XX and males an XY chromosome pattern.

- Kinefelter's syndrome and Turner's syndrome are rare conditions that occur randomly where chromosomes differ from the typical pattern.

- Hormones are released from glands and travel via the bloodstream to target structures.

- About eight weeks after conception, glands start to release testosterone in male embryos. Experimental studies with rats have shown that exposure to prenatal testosterone enlarges a brain structure called the sexually dimorphic nucleus (SDN).

- Case studies have shown that girls who have been exposed to high levels of prenatal testosterone play more physically than their unaffected sisters and prefer boys as playmates. They also show higher levels of cross-gender identification and gender dysphoria.

- Differences in the size of the SND only appear after about the age of six in girls and boys. The extent and impact of brain differences is debated.

- The second major release of hormones occurs at puberty when follicle stimulating hormone (FSH) and luteinising hormone (LH) lead to the release of androgens and oestrogens.

- Oxytocin is involved in many aspects of maternal behaviours such as labour, breastfeeding and mother–infant bonding.

- Administration of nasal oxytocin increases trust in males and females but also leads to increased in-group favouritism in males.

- Oxytocin may also moderate gender differences in stress responses.

GENDER

Social learning theory applied to gender development

Link

You can refresh your memory for the principles of social learning theory by looking at approaches on page 225 of Book 1.

Bandura and Walters (1963) and Bandura (1977) argued that children learn gender roles in similar ways to behaviour such as aggression. In simple terms, children attend to the behaviour of role models, observe them and then extract what kinds of behaviour are appropriate for girls and boys. This **social learning** is actively transformed into actions, which are shaped through the responses of other people such as parents and peers. Behaviour that conforms to sex-role stereotypes (for example, a girl playing with dolls or a boy playing with cars) is likely to be positively reinforced and non-conformist behaviours discouraged, for example by teasing. In order for a child to imitate the behaviour of a role model, they must pay attention to the behaviour and store a representation of it in their memory. In order to repeat the behaviour, the child should be capable and motivated to reproduce the behaviour.

Observation and modelling

Children are exposed to a variety of role models, including parents, friends, television characters, sporting figures and celebrities. These models demonstrate different ways in which masculinity and femininity are enacted within today's society. Television characters and celebrities are such important role models that research on this topic is considered in detail in the next section of the chapter.

The first role models for young infants are found within the family – parents and siblings – with peers becoming increasingly important as children start nursery and school. If gender roles are learned via observation, then parents who have strongly segregated roles should, theoretically, have children who show stronger gender stereotypes than more egalitarian (equal) families. Fagot et al. (1992) studied the development of children growing up in families with different interpretations of gender roles. The families were divided into traditional (father went out to work and the children were raised by a stay-at-home mother) and egalitarian (both parents worked and shared childcare duties). Fagot et al. interviewed the parents and observed them playing with their toddler at the age of 28 and 48 months. When the children reached the age of four, they were given gender-labelling tasks, for example being shown different kinds of toys and asked if the toy was 'for girls, for boys or for both'. Children in 'traditional' families showed more gender-role stereotyping at age four than those in the egalitarian families, supporting the claim that gender roles are learned from observation of parents.

Reinforcement

According to learning theory, behaviours that are positively reinforced (rewarded) are likely to be repeated, and behaviours that produce negative consequences, such as teasing, are less likely to be repeated. For example, parents might compliment their daughter for wearing a pretty dress but discourage her from climbing trees or playing football. They may compliment their son for a tough tackle on the rugby field and discourage him from crying if he is injured.

Evidence and evaluation

Lytton and Romney carried out a meta-analysis of studies that examined parental treatment and reinforcement of boys and girls. They selected 175 studies with a total of 27,836 participants. Of these studies, 158 were carried out in North America and the remaining 17 in other Western countries. Lytton and Romney examined eight areas of socialization and their main findings were as follows:

- Parents differentially reinforced behaviours for boys and girls, including play activities (for example, climbing trees), toy choice, preference for playmates and style of play. In other words, they encouraged different behaviours in boys and girls and rewarded them for different activities. Fathers provided more differential reinforcement than mothers.
- In the North American studies, girls were more likely to be encouraged to help with housework and boys with outdoor tasks. In Western countries other than the USA, there were also differences in physical punishment – boys were more likely to be smacked than girls.
- There was no evidence of differential treatment of boys and girls in relation to the amount of interaction, communication and warmth. Aggression was discouraged and achievement encouraged in both girls and boys.
- Differential treatment from parents decreased as children got older, so was most noticeable with younger children and less noticeable with older children.

The studies included in Lytton and Romney's meta-analysis were based on parental self-report about how they treated their children. Many parents claim that they treat children in the same way, regardless of whether they are a boy or a girl. A meta-analysis of observational studies (Leaper et al., 1998) found a stronger effect from differential reinforcement by parents than Lytton and Romney did, including some differences in how parents talk to girls and boys during play. This implies that parental self-report may underestimate the extent of differential reinforcement provided by parents. What people do and what they say they do is often rather different!

In addition to Lytton and Romney's meta-analysis, other studies have supported the claim that parents and peers reinforce gender conformity and discourage non-conformity. Fagot and Hagan (1991) found that boys received more positive reinforcement for playing with construction toys such as Lego than girls did when they played with Lego. Siegel (1987) found that fathers were more likely than mothers to respond negatively when their sons carried out 'feminine' play activities. These findings imply that masculinity is reinforced more strongly in boys than femininity in girls.

Peers also shape gender-conformist play. Langlois and Downs (1980) noted that when boys played with girls' toys, they were likely to be ridiculed and teased by their male peers. Archer and Lloyd (1982) found that children as young as three criticized other children who engaged in non-conformist play and were less likely to play with them. Peers are such systematic reinforcers of sex-typed play that Durkin (1995) argues that they play a more important role in gender reinforcement than parents. He suggests that 'the critical variable may not be vertical reinforcement (i.e. parents) so much as horizontal social engagement (i.e. peers)'.

Nature and nurture

In contrast to the biological approach, social learning theory emphasizes the importance of nurture – upbringing and environment – in the development of gender roles. It is likely that biological and social forces work together in the development of gender. A study by Lutchmaya et al. (2004) compared the preferences of babies aged around 24 hours old. The girls showed slight preferences for human faces and the boys preferred a mechanical mobile of the same size and shape. These basic preferences translate into interest in people and social relationships (girls) versus how things work (boys). Therefore, children come into the world with basic preferences for boyish or girlish things set by biology. These preferences then lead them to shape their environments in certain ways or to 'niche pick' (Ridley, 2004). Biological factors such as exposure to prenatal hormones may also affect how responsive children are to parental reinforcement. Ridley refers to the intertwining of the two forces as 'nature via nurture'.

The influence of media on gender roles

From a young age, children in Western cultures are avid watchers of television, and most older children and teenagers have access to online content via smartphones. Some of this content, such as music videos, contains strongly stereotyped images of females and males. In 2002, Bandura extended social learning theory, arguing that children and adults can also learn from symbolic environments, such as media sources, through a process called abstract modelling. In simple terms, abstract modelling involves a person extracting ideas from media images and integrating these into their view of the world.

In the 1970s, content analyses of children's television programmes showed that many contained strong gender stereotypes, especially of girls. It is unsurprising that Morgan (1982) found a positive correlation between the amount of television watched and the strength of gender stereotypes. Children who watched more television held more stereotypical views about the qualities of girls and boys.

Stevens Aubrey and Harrison (2004) carried out a content analysis to examine the kinds of messages children receive about gender in the twenty-first century. Around 200 children aged between six and nine years of age were asked to name their three favourite programmes. The researchers selected the six most frequently chosen programmes (including *Rugrats* and *Arthur*) and recorded five episodes of each programme during May 1999, making a total sample of 30 programmes.

Stevens Aubrey and Harrison analysed the gender portrayals of the characters and found that the programmes contained relatively few gender stereotypes. In fact, many of the characters were gender-neutral or counter-stereotypical. However, there were subtle differences in gender portrayals:

- Male lead characters outnumbered female leads by a ratio of 2:1.
- Boys were more likely to be active than girls, asking questions, directing others, taking orders from others, but also crying.
- Female lead characters were more likely to be good-looking than male leads.
- There were no differences in independence, assertiveness and sensitivity between boys and girls.

Stevens Aubrey and Harrison's work shows how blatant gender stereotypes in children's television have been replaced by more subtle differences in how girls and boys are portrayed. Males are still more likely to take the lead, active roles – a trend that continues in action films. Where females take lead roles, an attractive appearance is important.

Fig. 3.8 Doing gender: what do the characters in *The Big Bang Theory* suggest about being a man or being a woman?

Experimental studies expose children to either gender-stereotypical or counter-stereotypical content and examine their behaviour immediately afterwards. An example of this type of experiment was carried out by Pike and Jennings (2005) to assess the impact of toy advertising on children's perceptions of gender appropriate toys. Children aged five to six years old were randomly allocated to one of three conditions and shown a television advertisement:

- The advertisement showed a gender-neutral toy (Harry Potter Lego or Playmobil airport) being played with by boys.
- The advertisement showed the same gender-neutral toy being played with by girls.
- In the control condition, the advertisement focused on a product that was not a toy (food).

Immediately after viewing the advertisement, the children were asked to sort ten different toys into categories: suitable for boys, suitable for girls, or suitable for both. Children who had watched the second advertisement (girls playing with the toys) placed significantly more of the toys into the 'suitable for both' category.

Fig. 3.9 Playmobil airport: a gender-neutral toy

Pike and Jennings's experiment shows how young children may be influenced by what they have just seen. However, in experiments of this nature, the television content (in this case, the advertisement) is deliberately constructed for the purpose of the experiment rather than naturally occurring. Hence, experimental studies say little about the kinds of programmes children prefer to watch in real life.

EXAMPLE EXAM QUESTION

1. Identify the type of experimental design that was used in Pike and Jennings's experiment. [1 mark]
2. Identify one factor that Pike and Jennings controlled in the above experiment. [1 mark]
3. Name the independent and dependent variables and explain how these have been operationalized. [4 marks]

Exam hint

You can spot the difference between an independent measures and a repeated measures design by asking if the same or different participants were used in the conditions of the experiment. Identifying the experiment design provides a clue to the likely controls: if the design is repeated measures, how were order effects controlled? If the design is independent groups, how were participants allocated to conditions?

Music videos and gender

Music videos are accessible through media platforms including television channels and YouTube. Many of these provide potent messages about gender and sexuality. Hip-hop videos are notable for perpetuating gender stereotypes, with aggressive and dominant men and sexualized images of women wearing few clothes and dancing provocatively. A content analysis of four types of music video (R&B, hip-hop, country and pop) found that females were portrayed as 'a collection of body parts' in hip-hop videos and were more likely than males to show sexually provocative behaviour (Stevens Aubrey and Frisby, 2011).

Kistler and Lee (2010) carried out an experiment to examine the impact of sexualised music videos on male and female college students' attitudes. The students were exposed to either high or low sexual-content videos before completing attitude questionnaires measuring agreement with gender stereotypes, objectification of women, and agreement with the 'rape myth' – the idea that women secretly fantasize about being subjected to sexual violence. Males who had viewed highly sexual content scored significantly higher on all of these than males exposed to low sexual-content videos. There were no differences on the measures between high and low exposure for the female participants, suggesting that exposure to music videos does not alter women's attitudes in the same way.

Fig. 3.10 What messages do music videos such as 'Blurred Lines' or 'Wrecking Ball' convey about males and females?

Alternative explanations of the influence of media on gender roles

Social learning theory (Bandura, 1977) and social cognitive theory (Bandura, 2002) emphasize the importance of observation of role models and extraction of generalized ideas about gender. However, alternative theories also explain the impact of the media on gender roles. Objectification theory (Fredrickson and Roberts, 1997) suggests that the prevalence of sexualized media images of females teaches girls to see themselves from an outside viewpoint, to become continually aware of how they look to others and to view themselves as objects to be evaluated by others. A growing body of research suggests that a tendency to self-objectify may be linked to increasing rates of depression and eating disorders in young women.

Cultivation theory (Signorielli and Morgan, 1990) argues that media shapes perceptions of the world and the more we consume media, the more our views are shaped by it. If television or music videos

GENDER

portray men or women in a particular way, regular exposure to these ideas means that watchers will assume the characteristics apply to people in the real world. This is sometimes referred to as the 'drip, drip, drip effect'. In Morgan's findings (1982), more exposure to television leads to stronger gender stereotypes, supporting cultivation theory. In contrast, the 'drench' hypothesis (Greenberg, 1988) argues that some media figures have more impact than others, particularly those we prefer or choose to watch or listen to.

The influence of culture on gender roles

The term **culture** can be loosely defined as the shared habits of a group of people or community. Triandis (1980) distinguished two aspects of culture:

- Objective aspects such as clothes buildings and foods. These are tangible and can be easily identified.
- Subjective aspects such as values, beliefs and shared ideas. These cannot be seen objectively, but they exert a powerful influence on behaviour.

Margaret Mead, an anthropologist, pointed to the existence of cultural differences in gender roles. Mead carried out a study of three tribes in Papua New Guinea in the 1920s and 30s and found very different gender roles from those in the USA in the 1930s.

- In the Arapesh tribe, both men and women showed typically feminine behaviours and were nurturing, gentle and caring.
- In the Mundugumor tribe, both men and women showed typically masculine behaviours, acting in an aggressive, warlike manner.
- The Tchambuli tribe was most interesting to Mead as the gender roles were reversed from those shown in Western societies – the women were instrumental, robust and practical, whereas the men occupied themselves with flirtation and making themselves attractive via bodily decoration.

Fig. 3.11 Mead 'conducting' Arapesh men playing flutes

Mead's work has since been questioned on a number of grounds, notably that she misunderstood Papua New Guinean customs, but her claim that culture influences gender roles is widely accepted. In simple terms, cultures can be divided into traditional and egalitarian:

- Traditional cultures emphasize different gender roles for women and men. Women operate within the home sphere and take charge of domestic work and childrearing, whereas men operate in the external, economic sphere. Nigeria, Pakistan and India are examples of countries with highly traditional cultures (Williams and Best, 1990).
- Egalitarian cultures minimize differences in gender roles. Men and women can choose to go out to work or stay at home and raise children. Roles are interchangeable and flexible. The Netherlands, Germany and Finland are examples of countries with highly egalitarian cultures (Williams and Best, 1990).

More recent research focuses on two elements: sex-role stereotypes (beliefs about the qualities possessed by women and men) and gender divisions (the activities carried out by women and men in the household and outside world) in different cultures.

Cross-cultural research on gender

Williams and Best (1990) investigated the existence of sex-role stereotypes in students drawn from 27 different countries. Participants were given a list of 300 trait words (for example, hard-working, ambitious) and asked if the characteristic applied to men, to women, or equally to both sexes. Williams and Best found substantial agreement across all 27 countries. They argued that the pancultural existence of male and female gender stereotypes indicates that biological differences between the sexes (for example, women bear children and men are physically stronger) set the stage for the divisions of labour seen across cultures.

KEY STUDY: VAN DE VIJVER (2007)

van de Vijver carried out a substantial study of gender-role stereotypes and division of labour in five cultural groups in the Netherlands: Dutch 'mainstreamers' and the four largest immigrant groups – Turkish, Moroccan, Surinamese and Dutch Antilles (Caribbean) – with first- and second-generation members.

van de Vijver measured sex-role stereotypes using six statements (for example, 'Decisions about important purchases should be made by men') scored using a Likert scale (strongly agree, disagree, etc.). Gender role division was measured using seven activities (for example, shopping, cleaning, cooking) and respondents were asked to indicate if these were carried out by husband, wife or shared.

van de Vijver found that immigrants reported less egalitarian sex-role stereotypes than Dutch mainstreamers, but there were no significant differences in sharing behaviour/division of labour: the sharing of household tasks was similar across all five cultural groups. Second-generation immigrants showed less traditional sex-role stereotypes than their parents but again, there were no differences in the divisions of labour between first- and second-generation immigrants.

THINKING SCIENTIFICALLY: CULTURAL DIFFERENCES

The study of cultural differences poses a series of challenges for the psychologist. Studies provide snapshots that are out of date almost as soon as they are published in a rapidly changing world. The dual processes of Westernization and modernization are leading to the merging of cultures and the emergence of new cultural forms in second-generation immigrants.

GENDER

Explaining the influence of culture

A method of cultural classification was put forward by Hofstede (1980) in an attempt to explain why cultures vary. Hofstede argued that cultures promote different kinds of values – often related to religion and economics – and it is these which influence daily lives. Two dimensions that are relevant to gender are masculinity/femininity and power/distance:

- Masculinity/femininity: masculine cultures value qualities such as independence, competition and achievement (those considered to be masculine attributes), whereas feminine cultures value qualities such as co-operation, caring and interpersonal harmony. The US and Japan are masculine cultures and Sweden, Norway and the Netherlands are feminine cultures.
- Power/distance: this measures the extent to which people in the society accept unequal distribution of power. Power/distance cultures are organized hierarchically and unequal relationships are accepted. Central American countries score highly on power/distance. Cultures with low power/distance scores, such as Denmark, emphasize equality; for example, between parents and their adult offspring.

Hofstede's model has received some support in relation to gender. Best and Williams (1998) carried out a cross-cultural study of gender-role beliefs and found that masculine countries emphasized differences between the sexes, whereas feminine countries minimized differences and showed strong beliefs in gender equality. In support of Hofstede, gender roles were more pronounced in countries that scored higher on power/distance.

Education and religion both play a part in cultural differences. The increased participation of women in higher education and the labour market is also influencing the division of labour and who does what. Some religions emphasize very different roles for men and women whereas others do not. Gender differences are becoming blurred in Western societies, where men are increasingly involved in child rearing and women are increasingly involved in economic activity.

Exam hint

You should approach this type of question by selecting two or three pieces of research evidence and summarizing the key findings of each. Remember that no marks are awarded for methodological information, so stick with findings and resist the temptation to get sidetracked!

EXAMPLE EXAM QUESTION

Outline findings of research into the influence of culture on gender roles. (6 marks)

KEY POINTS

- Social learning theory emphasizes learning through observation and imitation of role models.

- Meta-analyses show how parents provide differential reinforcement for boys and girls in relation to toys and games. Peers also 'police' cross-gender play.

- Media sources such as television and music videos also provide a plentiful source of gender role models.

- Experimental studies show how children's behaviour can be shaped by gender-stereotypical and counter-stereotypical television content.

- Content analyses suggest that gender stereotypes are decreasing in children's television programmes. However, male lead characters still outnumber females and are more likely to take an active role in programmes.

- Many music videos show sexualized images of women. Exposure to highly sexualized content affects men's attitudes on a range of measures.

- Objectification theory argues that young women who view sexualized media images see their bodies as objects to be evaluated by others.

- Gender stereotypes appear to be relatively consistent across cultures.

- In traditional cultures, men and women have strongly stereotyped gender roles, whereas egalitarian cultures allow more flexibility in the roles taken by men and women.

- Studies of first- and second-generation immigrants indicate that behaviours about gender equality change before attitudes and beliefs do.

Cognitive explanations of gender development

Kohlberg's 1966 theory

Kohlberg's theory, published in 1966, is a **cognitive explanation** of gender development. Cognitive explanations focus on how children develop an understanding of gender and how this understanding shapes the development of gender role behaviours.

Kohlberg's theory was based on two premises:

- Children's understanding of the concept of gender develops in three stages, which are loosely linked to age in childhood. These stages are **gender identity**, **gender stability** and **gender constancy** (see Table 3.1 below). In each stage, the child's understanding of gender becomes increasingly complex.

- The development of gender-role behaviours takes place when the child reaches stage three and fully understands that gender is fixed and constant.

> **Key terms**
>
> **Cognitive explanation**: focuses on the child's understanding and active construction of knowledge about gender.
>
> **Gender identity**: the ability to label oneself correctly as a girl or a boy.
>
> **Gender stability**: the understanding that gender is stable across time.
>
> **Gender constancy**: the understanding that gender does not alter despite changes to appearance (clothes, hair, etc.).

Age	Stage	The child understands ...	The child doesn't understand...
2–3½ years old	Gender identity (or gender labelling)	Child can label themselves and others correctly as male or female ('I am a girl and my daddy is a boy').	Child doesn't understand that gender is stable. A boy might say he is going to be a mummy when he grows up.
3½–4½ years old	Gender stability	Child understands that gender is stable across time; for instance, boys know they will become men and girls know they will become women.	Child doesn't understand that physical changes to appearance don't affect gender. When the mother has her hair cut short, the child might say, 'Mummy is a boy now'.
4½–7 years old	Gender constancy (or consistency)	Child understands that gender is constant and is no longer fooled by changes to physical appearance.	

Table 3.1 Kohlberg's stages: gender identity, stability and constancy

Kohlberg argued that once a child reaches the third stage and understands that gender is constant, they become highly motivated to behave in a way that is expected of them as a boy or girl. He argued that between the age of four-and-a-half and seven years, children start to pay attention to same-sex role models and copy them, leading to the development of gender role behaviours.

Evidence and evaluation

Considerable evidence has supported the first premise of Kohlberg's theory – that understanding of gender develops in three stages. Studies have also confirmed that these occur in the order and at pretty much the ages he suggested. Research has also shown that children pay closer attention to same-sex role models once they have reached the stage of gender constancy (after the age of about four and a half). One such study was carried out by Slaby and Frey and is described below.

KEY STUDY: SLABY AND FREY (1975)

Slaby and Frey selected a sample of children aged between two and five. Each child was asked a series of questions to examine which stage of Kohlberg's model they had reached. Children with scores indicating high or low gender constancy were selected and compared.

Each child was shown a silent film in which two adult models – one male and one female – carried out a gender-stereotyped activity (for example, baking a cake, changing a car wheel). The two films were shown simultaneously using a split screen so that children could look at either film. Equipment was used to track their eye movements and direction of gaze to measure the amount of time each child spent looking at both films. This method is referred to as the visual preference technique.

Slaby and Frey found that the children in the high gender constancy group spent more time watching the same-sex model than children in the low gender constancy group. This study supports Kohlberg's claim that children pay greater attention to same-sex models after the stage of constancy has been reached.

THINKING SCIENTIFICALLY: LANGUAGE

One of the difficulties with investigating young children's cognitive development is the use of language-based methods. Children under the age of three have limited understanding of language and more limited speech production. Slaby and Frey have overcome this by using a method based on behaviour – the visual preference technique – which can be used with very young children.

Further evidence was provided by Ruble et al. (1981). They examined the relationship between gender constancy and children's responsiveness to television advertisements for 'girl' and 'boy' toys. Children who had reached gender constancy were sensitive to and picked up the implicit messages in advertisements (for a recent example, an Elsa doll from the film *Frozen* being more suitable for girls than boys). Children who had reached gender constancy were more willing to play with gender-appropriate toys and less willing to play with gender-inappropriate toys.

However, Kohlberg's claim that children only pay attention to same-sex roles after they have reached the stage of gender constancy has been challenged. Bem (1981) and Martin and Halverson (1981) argue that children construct simple gender schemas from about the age of two and, from this point onwards, they are actively engaged in finding out about their own group – boys or girls. This is the basis of gender schema theory.

Gender schema theory (Martin and Halverson, 1981)

Gender schema theory accepts Kohlberg's first premise that young children develop core gender identity (labelling) between the ages of two and three years. However, Martin and Halverson disagree with the second of Kohlberg's claims – that gender roles develop *after* children realize that gender is constant.

According to gender schema theory, children aged between two and three develop a basic gender schema consisting of two groups – boys and girls. The group the child belongs to is the 'in group', whether that is boys or girls, and the other gender is viewed as the 'out group'. This basic division shapes the young child's behaviour as soon as they are aware of it. They actively seek out information about appropriate behaviours and actions for their gender group. Boys pay close attention to boy-related toys, games and activities and focus on finding out about these; they pay minimal attention to toys, games or activities that they perceive as being for girls. Similarly, girls actively find out about girl things and avoid anything that they perceive as being for boys.

As the child develops, their gender schemas become progressively more complex, taking in toys, clothes, sports, academic subjects, musical instruments and even cars. These technically neutral items are categorized as suitable for boys or girls.

Without thinking too much, work quickly through the following list, identifying each item as suitable for boys, girls or either sex.

horse riding	cricket	tennis	sailing	chess
yoga	physics	netball	flute	cooking
maths	violin	sociology	skipping	trumpet
geography	piano	orienteering		psychology
art	history			

Compare your answers with two other people. How much agreement was there? Where do you think your schemas about gender appropriateness have come from?

Evidence and evaluation

KEY STUDY: CAMPBELL ET AL. (2004)

Campbell et al. studied the development of gender schemas in toddlers using a longitudinal design. A sample of 56 children were studied at 27 months of age and again at 39 months. The study took place in the children's homes. The child was seated on their parent's lap, shown an album of pictures and asked to point to:

- the girl or boy (the gender-labelling task)
- the girls' or boys' toy (for example, football, brush and comb set)
- the girls' or boys' game/activity (for example, skipping, football).

After this, the child was given a selection of the toys that they had been shown in the pictures and filmed for 30 minutes as they played with them. Parents were prevented from intervening and influencing the play in any direction, for example encouraging the child to play with the football or toy car.

Correctly completed	27 months	39 months
Gender-labelling task	53%	94%
Stereotyping of toys	20%	51%
Stereotyping of activities	0%	17%

Table 3.2 The results

Campbell found that just over half of the 27-month-olds correctly completed the gender-labelling task, but by 39 months of age, almost all of the sample could correctly identify themselves as boy or girl in line with Kohlberg's theory. Stereotyping of toys was rare in two-year-olds and stereotyping of activities was non-existent. But by 39 months, about half of the sample were labelling toys as suitable for boys or girls and just under a fifth (17 per cent) were identifying activities as suitable for boys or girls.

Fig. 3.12 Testing for gender schemas

This study uses a range of methods to assess children's gender schemas, including observation of free play. The combination of methods provides rich and detailed data. The use of a longitudinal design following the same children as they grow allows the researcher to see how gender understanding develops.

Campbell et al.'s study shows how gender schemas develop rapidly to encompass toys and games between the ages of two and three years of age. Additional evidence for the gender schema theory was provided by Poulin-Dubois et al. (2002) using a sample of 63 Canadian toddlers aged between two and three. The children were asked to choose a doll to carry out a variety of tasks, including shaving (male), vacuuming (female) and sleeping (neutral). Girls aged 24 months chose the gender-appropriate doll for the tasks, implying that girls as young as two had started to incorporate activities into their gender schema. Boys were around 31 months old before they demonstrated similar abilities. This provides support for Martin and Halverson's theory showing how gender schemas develop between the ages of two and three.

Comparing the cognitive theories

Both cognitive theories see the child as active, seeking out information about gender and trying to make sense of the gendered world they live in. In both of these theories, the direction of development goes from cognitive concept (the schema of boy or girl) to information processing (looking at the world through the lens of gender) and then to gender preferences (I am a boy – boys play with cars – I like playing with cars). The difference between Kohlberg's theory and the gender schema theory is the age at which this process takes place. Research studies by Campbell et al. (2004) and Poulin-Dubois et al. (2002) have shown that children pay attention to same-sex role models earlier than Kohlberg thought.

Gender schema theory helps us to explain why children's beliefs and attitudes about gender roles are so resilient. Parents are often baffled by their young children's rigid views. This is explained by the fact that children only pay attention to those things that are consistent with and confirm their schemas. Therefore, if they see someone engaging in behaviour that contradicts their gender schema (for example, a male nursery assistant or female mechanic) they simply fail to notice it. Studies have shown that when young children watch films that depict people contradicting gender-role behaviours, they simply tune them out.

Gender schema theory emphasizes how schemas develop but not where they originate.

ACTIVITY 3.3

Use the above section to write a summary of Kohlberg's theory and gender schema theory, focused on key points of agreement and disagreement.

Exam hint

You have two options to choose from: Kohlberg's theory or the gender schema theory. If you focus your answer on Kohlberg's theory (see page 193), you can use the gender schema theory for critical comparison as AO3. This is fine – but ensure that you keep a critical focus on Kohlberg's theory and don't fall into the trap of simply describing the gender schema theory.

EXAMPLE EXAM QUESTION

Discuss one cognitive explanation of the development of gender. (16 marks)

KEY POINTS

- Cognitive explanations of gender development focus on how children actively construct their understanding of gender as they interact with their environment.
- Kohlberg (1966) argued that children develop an understanding of gender in three stages: identity, stability and constancy. He believed that children start to pay attention to same-sex role models once they have attained constancy.
- Visual preference studies (e.g. Slaby and Frey) show how children in constancy spend more time watching same-sex role models.
- Gender schema theory argues that children start to pay attention to their own gender group as soon as they label themselves as a boy or girl.
- Gender schemas start off simple but rapidly become more detailed and complex, taking in games, toys and school subjects.
- The Campbell et al. (2004) longitudinal study demonstrates the rapid development in schemas between the ages of two and three years.

Psychodynamic explanations of gender development

Freud's psychoanalytic theory

In the early part of the twentieth century, Sigmund Freud put forward an explanation of gender development that is very different from those covered so far. Freud's account attempted to explain how young children move from noticing anatomical differences between boys and girls to developing a gender identity as female or male. Freud's psychodynamic explanation also encompassed sexual orientation/object choice (sexual attraction) in later adolescence and adulthood. The psychodynamic approach stemmed from Freud's clinical work with people undergoing psychological therapy. You may find some of Freud's ideas very odd indeed – it is unsurprising that his views about childhood sexuality, and particularly female development, have led to some of the most heated debates in psychology.

Freud believed that the mind consisted of conscious and unconscious zones. The unconscious was a repository for material that was distressing, painful or embarrassing. Potentially damaging material could be pushed into the unconscious mind through a defence mechanism called repression, which protected the child or adult from anxiety. Once material was in the unconscious, it was no longer accessible but continued to affect behaviour.

Link

You can refresh your memory of the psychodynamic approach by looking back at pages 216–220 of Book 1.

Freud believed that children progress through a series of **psychosexual stages**. In each stage, a different area of the body becomes sensitized as the key source of pleasure for the child. The third, phallic stage was most important for the development of gender. Around the age of three or four, children start to experiment with their bodies and to self-explore via masturbation. It is around this age that they begin to notice the anatomical differences between boys and girls – that is, that boys have a penis and girls do not. This forms the basis for the Oedipus and Electra complexes.

The Oedipus and Electra complexes

At the start of the phallic stage, the mother is still the primary 'love object' for children of both sexes, providing pleasure, comfort and care. Freud believed that young boys experienced an intense sexual attachment to their mother in this stage. This was accompanied by jealousy towards the father and a desire to possess the mother for themselves. The young boy saw his father as a rival for the mother's attention and this resulted in hostility – even hatred – towards the father. Freud believed that these strong emotions, combined with guilt about masturbation, made the boy anxious, and that this anxiety centred on the possibility of castration – the fear that the father would cut off the young boy's penis.

The situation generated so much anxiety in the boy – fear of his father, fear of castration and guilt about his feelings for his mother – that the feelings were repressed into the unconscious mind. Freud argued that boys resolved the Oedipus complex by identifying with their father. This process took place unconsciously and involved the boy taking in various elements of the father to his own psyche (**internalization**) and adopting a masculine identity like the father (**identification**). Freud believed that by copying the father a young boy felt as if he gained access to the mother 'by proxy'.

Far-fetched? Possibly, but Freud's explanation of female gender development was even more incredulous. Freud did not initially propose a separate path for female development – the idea of the Electra complex was put forward later. The first love object for young girls was also the mother. Around the age of three to four, self-exploration led the young girl to realize that she did not have a penis. This led to a sense of loss that Freud called 'penis envy'. (In 1925, Freud argued that the young girl viewed her vagina as a wound that had been caused by castration.) Freud believed that young girls interpreted this lack as a sign that they had already been castrated, and blamed their similarly 'disfigured' mother for the act. These feelings of hostility were threatening and resolved by identification with the mother; her qualities were internalized and the girl adopted a feminine gender role.

Fig. 3.13 Oedipus and Electra – characters from Greek mythology.

Evidence and evaluation

- Freud's account is commendable in that it brings together biology (the anatomical differences between boys and girls) and psychology (the sense/meaning children make of biological differences). However, providing empirical support for Freud's claims is virtually impossible – concepts such as castration anxiety, which are said to be unconscious, are difficult to study with scientific methods.

GENDER

- Freud's theory was developed in the late nineteenth and early twentieth centuries. There was little by way of reliable birth control and heterosexual sex brought the very serious risk of pregnancy. Sex before marriage was frowned on – so much so that unmarried mothers could be incarcerated in mental hospitals and viewed as 'mad'. Marriage was the standard arrangement and divorce was difficult, hence most children grew up with a mother and father. Freud's theory says little about what will happen when children are raised by a single mother or by two fathers or two mothers. For example, what would happen to castration anxiety when there is no father present?
- Freud's theory of female development has met with criticism from feminist psychologists who argue that it is based on male experience and has little to say about female development (Izzard, 2002). Horney (1926) critiqued the concept of penis envy, arguing that men suffer from womb envy – jealousy of women's ability to bear children. Other feminists have argued that penis envy is symbolic – what women have envied about men are the privileges afforded to them in many societies.

Exam hint

It is a good idea to focus your answer on the Oedipus or Electra complex to provide context to your explanation. Remember to refer to both terms – internalization and identification – in your answer.

EXAMPLE EXAM QUESTION

Explain what is meant by internalization and identification in relation to gender. (4 marks)

KEY POINTS

- The psychodynamic approach combines biological differences and children's understanding of these differences.
- The Oedipus and Electra complexes take place during the phallic stage of development.
- Boys wish to possess their mother and develop anger and hostility towards their father. This is resolved by copying the father and adopting a male gender role (identification).
- Girls experience penis envy and are hostile towards their mothers. This is resolved by identification and adoption of a female gender role.
- Freud's ideas were developed around a hundred years ago in a very different world to today's, where many children are brought up by one parent.

Atypical gender development: gender dysphoria (gender identity disorder)

People with gender dysphoria experience a conflict between their biological (assigned) sex and their gender identity. The diagnostic category of gender identity disorder (GID) was included in the *Diagnostic and Statistical Manual of Mental Disorders* (DSM) for the first time in 1980. The category was replaced in DSM-5 with gender dysphoria (GD), removing the word 'disorder' from the label (APA, 2013). The diagnostic criteria were also revised, making it clear that gender non-conformity is NOT a disorder – the critical element for GD is the distress associated with the experience.

The revised diagnostic criteria for gender dysphoria are as follows (APA, 2013):

- A marked difference between the experienced or expressed gender of a person (for example, feeling female) and the gender others would assign them to (male). This is the core symptom and often is referred to as feeling 'trapped in the wrong body'.
- The experience must persist for six months or more.
- The experience is accompanied by distress and impairment in areas of social functioning, for example at work or in social life.
- In children, the experience is verbalized, that is, the child can explain that they feel like a girl or boy. This rules out a diagnosis of GD based on behaviour alone in young children.

Many children show some level of gender dysphoria between the ages of two and four years but in most cases this diminishes during adolescence. Green (1997) studied a group of 44 boys referred in childhood to a clinic for strong feminine behaviours and compared them to a group of 30 control boys matched for age. A follow-up at the age of 18 found that only one of the original 44 remained gender dysphoric and had opted for reassignment surgery. Zucker (2005) obtained similar findings.

Drummond et al. (2008) studied a sample of 30 girls referred to a gender identity clinic between the age of two and three and followed up at seven and 18 years of age. 88 per cent of the girls who had shown strong GD at age seven showed no signs in early adulthood. Around 12 per cent of the original sample continued to show gender dysphoria.

While GD has been a relatively rare condition, the number of people presenting for diagnosis has increased dramatically since the 1970s (Zucker et al., 2008). One notable increase is in the number of adolescents self-referring to clinics over the last ten years.

Psychological explanations of gender dysphoria (GID)

Psychologists have focused on a range of factors that may be associated with the development of GD, including traumatic events, parent–child interactions and family dynamics. The most profitable of these has been the link with childhood trauma. Gehring and Knutson (2005) studied a sample of 42 transsexuals (34 born as men and 8 born as women) and found that 23 (55 per cent) reported some form of unwanted sexual event at an average age of 13. The sexual event generally involved another person satisfying their curiosity about the gender of the sufferer.

Another possible factor in the increase of cases of adolescent GD relates to a link with autism spectrum disorders (de Vries et al., 2010), with many psychologists reporting a co-existence of the two conditions.

However, the search for 'psychological' causes has decreased over the last ten years with an increased understanding of the role played by biological factors in GD.

Biological explanations of gender dysphoria (GID)

Biological explanations for GD focus on exposure to prenatal hormones, genes and sexually dimorphic brain structures (for example, differences in the size and density of the sexually dimorphic nucleus). There is evidence to suggest that exposure to prenatal hormones may play a role in GD, particularly in the female to male direction. Pasterski et al. (2014) found that five out of 39 (12.8 per cent) girls with congenital adrenal hyperplasia (CAH) showed sufficient cross-gender identification to meet the clinical criteria for GD. A recent scanning study (Hoekzema et al., 2015) compared the volume of grey matter in a GD sample with matched controls. The researchers concluded that there were subtle differences in brain architecture, particularly in the sexually dimorphic nucleus, which could underline gender development. However, there is little systematic evidence of how prenatal hormones are involved in male to female gender dysphoria.

There is also some evidence of a genetic component to GD. We can assess the importance of genes to the development of a disorder by comparing the concordance rates shown by identical (MZ) and non-identical (DZ) twins:

- Identical twins develop when one sperm cell meets an egg cell, which divides into two zygotes – hence the term mono (one) zygotic (egg). Identical twins share 100 per cent of their genes.
- Non-identical twins develop when two sperm cells fertilize two eggs, hence di (two) zygotes (eggs). DZ twins are no more genetically alike than siblings, although their shared prenatal environment distinguishes them from non-twin siblings.

KEY STUDY: HEYLENS ET AL. (2012)

If GD involves an inherited component, there should be a higher concordance in MZ than DZ twins. Heylens et al. (2012) carried out a review of case studies that have examined concordance rates between MZ and DZ twins for GD. They identified data from a range of studies via the internet, with a total sample of 23 MZ twin pairs and 21 DZ twin pairs. In all cases one member of the pair had been diagnosed with GD and referred to a gender clinic at a hospital. The data from Heylens' review is shown in Table 3.3.

	MZ (identical) twins	DZ (non-identical) twins
Female twins (n = 13)	Eight pairs of twins: 3 out of 8 concordant 5 out of 8 discordant	Five pairs of twins: All discordant
Male twins (n = 31)	15 pairs of twins: 6 out of 15 concordant 9 out of 15 discordant	16 pairs of twins: All discordant

Table 3.3 Concordance rates for GD in MZ and DZ twins: Heylens et al. (2012)

Heylens' data supports the claim that GD involves a genetic component. In the sets of non-identical twins, none of the co-twins also experienced GD. In the sets of identical twins, between one third and one half of the co-twins also had GD. The effect was slightly stronger for male than female twins.

THINKING SCIENTIFICALLY: TWIN STUDIES

Twin studies are based on the assumption of shared environments – in simple terms, the idea that both members of a twin pair experience the same kind of upbringing. However, MZ twins are often treated more similarly than non-identical twins – for example, being identically dressed. Heylens et al. also note the difficulties in drawing conclusions from a sample identified via an Internet search.

EXAMPLE EXAM QUESTION

1. a Calculate the concordance rates for male and female MD and DZ twins. (4 marks)
   b Draw an appropriate graph to display the data in Table 3.3. (4 marks)

Exam hint

Remember that concordance rates are generally expressed as a percentage rather than a fraction.

KEY POINTS

- Gender dysphoria (GD) was known as gender identity disorder until 2013.
- The core symptom of GD is feeling trapped in the wrong body, accompanied by distress.
- Many children exhibit signs of cross-gender identification but grow out of these during childhood.
- GD has been linked to traumatic events, including unwanted sexual advances during adolescence.
- There is a link between exposure to prenatal testosterone (CAH) and female to male GD in girls.
- MZ twins show higher concordance rates for GD than DZ twins, implying a genetic link.

PRACTICAL ACTIVITY

We have seen that exposure to prenatal hormones such as testosterone may relate to later behaviour. One physiological 'marker' of prenatal testosterone is the relative size of the second and fourth fingers on the hand. This measurement is referred to as 2D:4DR (second digit, 4th digit ratio) and is calculated by measuring the index finger and dividing this measurement by the length of the ring finger. In females, the index finger is generally longer than the ring finger giving a score of more than 1. In males, the ring finger is typically longer than the index finger giving a score of less than one.

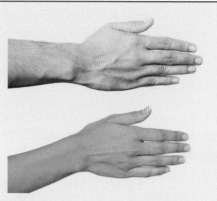

Fig. 3.14 Typical index and ring finger lengths for males and females

In this activity you are going to assess if there is a relationship (correlation) between 2D:4DR score and the handwriting of a sample of male and female students. The method is based on work carried out by Beech and Mackintosh (2005). Beech and Mackintosh collected a sample of handwriting from a set of students and asked other students to rate the writing on a scale of 1 to 5. A score of 1 was used if the rater thought the writer was definitely a boy and a score of 5 if the rater thought the writer was definitely a girl. The scores of 2, 3 and 4 were used for writing that fell between these extremes. Beech and Mackintosh then measured the 2D:4DR of the students who had supplied the handwriting and correlated the two sets of scores. They found a significant correlation between the measures.

You will need to:

1. Devise a method of measuring 2D:4DR. Callipers (often available in the biology department) can be useful here.
2. You will also need to obtain a sample of writing from a group of both male and female participants (suggest around 10–15 in total) who are willing to have their hands measured. You will need to ask for informed consent for both elements of the study.
3. You will need a set of three or four people to rate the handwriting to obtain a score for this measure.

When you have collected your data, you can plot a scattergraph to display your results and, if you wish, carry out a statistical analysis using a Spearman's Rho test of correlation.

Example exam questions

1. Outline one method of measuring androgyny. **(3 marks)**

2. Which of the following is NOT one of Kohlberg's stages of gender development? **(1 mark)**

    Gender constancy   Gender identity
    Gender schema   Gender stability

3. Read the item below and answer the questions that follow.

    > A psychologist carried out a content analysis to examine sex-role stereotypes in children's television programmes. The psychologist recorded a sample of programmes shown between 15:30 and 18:00 on school days and recorded if the lead characters were male or female. The psychologist also recorded if the lead character was physically attractive.
    >
    > The psychologist obtained the following data:
    >
    > | Lead character | Male | Female |
    > | --- | --- | --- |
    > | Attractive | 8 | 7 |
    > | Less attractive | 12 | 3 |
    >
    > The psychologist decided to carry out a statistical test to see if there was a difference in the portrayal of male and female characters in children's television programmes.

    a) Name an appropriate graph the psychologist could use to display the data in the table. **(1 mark)**

    b) Identify ONE statistical test the psychologist could use to analyse the data in the table. **(1 mark)**

    c) Justify your choice of test with reference to the research study described above. **(2 marks)**

4. Discuss biological influences on gender. **(16 marks)**

Exam focus

Read through the following example exam question, example student answer, and examiner comments. Then, have a go at answering the question yourself!

> **EXAMPLE EXAM QUESTION**
>
> Discuss biological and psychological explanations for gender dysphoria.
> (16 marks)

Ryan's answer

Gender dysphoria is diagnosed when there is a discrepancy between someone's biological assigned sex and their gender identity. It is commonly reported as feeling 'trapped in the wrong body'. The experience is accompanied by stress and problems with functioning at work or school. Many children shows signs of cross-gender identification but most grow out of it by their teenage years. However, more teenagers self-refer now to clinics than ever before (Zucker et al., 2008).

Examiner comment: Potentially relevant reference to psychodynamic theory but it isn't followed up after the study (e.g. repression of trauma into the unconscious).

Psychological explanations of GD have focused on different elements of family dynamics, including family trauma and parent–child intersections. Freud's psychodynamic theory predicts that children growing up without two parents might struggle to develop a sense of gender identity. One study of transsexuals found that over half reported some form of unwanted sexual event around the age of puberty. However, this wouldn't account for children showing cross-gender identification at an early age, which many children do.

Examiner comment: Good integration here of methodological critique.

The biological approach focuses on the importance of hormones in the development of gender, including exposure to prenatal testosterone. CAH is one syndrome related to hormone exposure. A study found that GD was much more common in CAH girls with around 12 per cent showing the core symptom of feeling trapped in the wrong body. One difficulty with investigating CAH is that case studies are the key method: case studies are retrospective and they lack scientific vigour as it is almost impossible to establish exactly what happened (e.g. how much testosterone the person was exposed to). Animal studies (e.g. Young, 1964) have shown that rats exposed to high levels of prenatal testosterone go on to show female mating behaviours, but experimental studies cannot be carried out with people for ethical reasons. One suggestion is that prenatal hormones masculinize an area of the brain called the sexually dimorphic nucleus and in future, studies using scanning methods may provide more information on the link between testosterone and GD.

One method of assessing a genetic component is through twin studies, which compare MZ and DZ twins. MZ twins develop when one sperm fertilizes one egg – so the twins are genetically identical. DZ twins share 50 per cent of their genes. Heylens carried out a review of case studies of GD via an Internet search. He found a much higher concordance rate in MZ than DZ twins, with MZ twins showing between 30 and 40 per cent CR. This suggests that genes may play a part but the GD is not wholly genetic – if it were the identical twins they should both experience GD.

> **Examiner comment:** Accurate coverage of twin studies but more commentary could be included on the limits of the sample/ sample size.

It is most likely that biological and psychological factors both play a role in GD, as they both play a role in the development of gender overall. It may be that biological factors set the scene and events such as trauma influence whether GD develops. The more complex an issue is, the more likely it is that both nature and nurture play a part.

> **Examiner comment:** Knowledge of biological and psychological explanations of gender dysphoria is accurate and generally well detailed. Evaluation is thorough and effective. The answer is clear, coherent and focused. Specialist terminology is used effectively. Minor detail and/or expansion of argument sometimes lacking in places. Level four response – 14 out of 16 marks.

Introduction

In this section of the course we are going to look at how children develop the ability to think and reason. Although you were obviously once a small child yourself, you have probably given little thought to how, or indeed what, children think. When we are confronted with the different understanding of a child – for example, when Grace smacks the 'naughty' swing that she has fallen off, or when Sam covers his eyes while playing hide and seek and thinks he can't be seen – we come to realize that children's understanding of the world may be very different to our own.

The chapter starts by exploring two historic and highly influential theories of cognitive development, put forward by Jean Piaget and Lev Vygotsky. These theories emphasize different elements of cognitive development, as we shall see. We move on to consider the much more recent work of Renee Baillargeon, who has built on Piaget's ideas and devised an ingenious method to investigate very young babies' understanding of the physical world and the properties of objects.

The final section of the chapter explores children's understanding of the social world, considering how they learn to take the perspectives of other people and to empathize with them. We end by exploring research into an area of difficulty experienced by children with autism – the difficulty in working out what other people think and feel.

What is covered in Cognition and development?

COGNITION

Piaget's theory of cognitive development

The term **cognitive development** refers to the development of thinking skills. It is broadly agreed there are two questions that need to be answered regarding cognitive development (Goswami, 1998): what develops (how children think and reason at particular ages) and the more complex question of why development takes place.

We start by examining explanations of cognitive development put forward by two psychologists. Jean Piaget's stage theory had a dramatic influence on teaching and education from the 1960s onwards. Lev Vygotsky, a Russian, had rather less impact at the time of writing due to suppression of his ideas under the Stalinist regime, although his theory has recently found favour with developmental psychologists and educationalists. As we shall see, these theorists emphasize quite different elements as playing a key part in cognitive development.

Jean Piaget (1896–1980) was a Swiss-born psychologist whose theory of cognitive development has had a huge influence on our understanding of how children develop the ability to think and reason. Piaget started his scientific life as a biologist, studying snails. He became interested in child development when he worked with Alfred Binet, who was devising some of the first intelligence (IQ) tests for children. Piaget was fascinated by the wrong answers children gave to questions in IQ tests and he became convinced that these revealed important differences between the thinking of adults and children.

Piaget carried out many of his own observations and studies using his three children, Laurent, Lucienne and Jacqueline (see Fig. 4.1). We shall start by examining the building blocks of Piaget's theory before going on to examine his claim that thinking skills develop in stages that are loosely linked to age.

Fig. 4.1 Jean Piaget and his family

The building blocks of Piaget's theory: schemas, assimilation and accommodation

Piaget believed that children and adults construct their understanding of the world through active engagement, trying out actions and seeing what effect they have. Piaget used the idea of the **schema** to refer to knowledge or mental ideas about actions, objects and situations. In young babies, schemas consist of simple action patterns such as grasping objects. Combinations of schemas are known as operations: shaking a rattle, for example, would involve the combination of two schemas, grasping and shaking.

Piaget believed that cognitive abilities developed through two interlinked processes, **assimilation** and **accommodation**. Assimilation involves using an existing schema to deal with a new object or situation. For example, a toddler aged around 15 months has developed a simple action schema of 'posting' a circular shape into a shape sorter. Different-coloured circular shapes given to the toddler are promptly assimilated into this schema and posted into the shape sorter.

Accommodation takes place when an existing schema will not work when faced with a new object or situation: for example, the toddler is given a square that will not fit into the circular hole. The child will need to try the shape in different holes and rotate the shape slightly to make it fit a square-shaped hole. The schema has been updated in the light of experience – accommodation has occurred.

According to Piaget, adult learning proceeds in the same way via assimilation and accommodation. For example, you have been taking driving lessons in your instructor's Nissan Micra but your instructor changes their car to a Renault Clio. As both cars are similar, you are able to apply your driving schemas and 'assimilate' the different car without difficulty. After you have passed your test, you are insured for your parents' automatic car. Your existing driving schemas, which include using a clutch and changing gear, will not work and you must accommodate the schema to fit the new situation.

Equilibration

Piaget likened the young child to a scientist, developing their knowledge through applying schemas and amending these when they do not work. He believed that cognitive development does not take place at a steady rate but occurs in leaps and bounds. Periods of stability are characterized by **equilibrium**: a mental state in which existing schemas can deal with most new information through assimilation. At other times, the child may meet many new objects and experiences that cannot be assimilated, and this state is called **disequilibrium**. The balance between these two states is known as **equilibration**.

Key terms

Schemas: mental ideas about objects, actions and situations.

Assimilation: apply an existing schema to a new object or situation.

Accommodation: changing and updating a schema in the light of experience.

Fig. 4.2 Assimilation and accomodation in action

Key terms

Equilibrium: the mental state that occurs when existing schemas can deal with new information through assimilation.

Disequilibrium: the mental state that occurs when objects and experiences cannot be assimilated.

Equilibration: the balance achieved between using existing schemas to assimilate new information and accommodating (altering) schemas that do not work.

COGNITION

Stages of intellectual development

Piaget theorized that cognitive development took place in stages that are loosely linked to age. In each stage, children show characteristic ways of thinking that change at the end of each stage, with 'cognitive restructuring' taking place. Stages could not be missed out, as each new stage relied on the skills of the previous stage. Cognitive development in Piaget's view is a similar process to learning to walk: the ability unfolds naturally without teaching as the child matures, and the same milestones (for example, rolling over, crawling) occur at pretty much the same age. In Piaget's view, stages are biologically programmed and they unfold as a result of maturation. Development cannot be speeded up or slowed down.

Fig. 4.3 Stages of development

Piaget identified four stages of cognitive development, summarized in Table 4.1, which we will look at in more detail below.

Stage	Age	Characteristics
Sensorimotor	0–2 years	Comprised of six substages. The newborn baby moves from using automatic reflexes to being a toddler who can carry out deliberate actions. **Object permanence** is a key development in this stage.
Pre-operational	2–7 years	The emergence of language allows the toddler to use words as symbols for objects. Thinking is characterized by **egocentrism** and an inability to 'conserve'.
Concrete operations	7–11 years	Egocentricity decreases across this stage. The child develops the ability to perform mental operations such as **conservation** and to reason about physical objects and relationships between them.
Formal operations	11+ years	Formal operations involve the ability for abstract thought and reasoning. Thinking becomes logical.

Table 4.1 Stages of cognitive development

The sensorimotor stage (0–2 years)

The sensorimotor period occurs between birth and the age of around two years. Piaget identified six substages in the period, with thinking becoming gradually more skilled and complex. He noted that very young babies under the age of about six weeks deal with the world by using simple reflexes, such as sucking anything put into their mouth and grasping anything placed in their hand. At around six weeks, these reflexes are no longer automatically triggered but become simple action patterns called 'primary circular reactions', initiated deliberately by the baby; for example, grasping a toy. These are followed by more complex secondary and tertiary reactions and the stage comes to an end at around two years.

An important milestone in the sensorimotor stage is the development of **object permanence**; the understanding that objects and people continue to exist when out of sight. Piaget observed his own children during a simple game in which a toy was hidden by a cloth. Below the age of around nine months, babies appeared to have no interest in the hidden toy and literally acted as if it were 'out of sight and out of mind'. After about nine months old, infants would search for the hidden toy under the cloth. Piaget concluded that object permanence occurs around the age of nine months.

ACTIVITY 4.1

You can try this for yourself if you have any friends or family members with a baby under the age of around a year. Get their interest with a favourite toy then hide it under a cover. How does the baby respond? Do they try to search for the toy? What are the difficulties in observing young infants?

The sensorimotor period ends at around age two, when there is an explosion of language development in toddlers. Language, according to Piaget, provides the basis for 'symbolic thought', in which words are used as symbols to stand for objects. This marks the start of the pre-operational stage.

The pre-operational stage (2–7 years)

Limitation 1: Egocentricity

Piaget focused his description of the pre-operational period on limitations in the child's thinking, identifying a number of mental tasks that children appeared unable to do. Fundamental to these was an inability to see things from other people's viewpoints, which Piaget referred to as **egocentricity**. Egocentricity was demonstrated in a famous study called the 'three mountains task' (Piaget and Inhelder, 1967).

Key term

Egocentricity: the inability to see the world from another person's viewpoint.

KEY STUDY: PIAGET AND INHELDER (1967)

Piaget and Inhelder used a papier mâché model of three mountains placed on a table (see Fig. 4.4). The three

Fig. 4.4 Piaget and Inhelder's three mountains model

mountains were different colours and topped by different features: a cross, a house and snow. Children aged between three and eight years old were encouraged to explore the model and walk around it to see it from all sides. A small boy doll was then placed at different points on the table and the children were asked to carry out several tasks to test their ability to 'see' from the doll's viewpoint.

- The child was given three cardboard shapes of the mountains and asked to arrange them to show what the doll could 'see'.
- The child was given ten pictures and asked to select which one the doll could see.

- The child was asked to choose any picture and then say where the doll needed to stand in order to see that view.

In each of these conditions, children under the age of about seven years old were unable to show the doll's viewpoint. Instead, they tended to choose/create a scene that showed their own view of the mountains, illustrating Piaget's claim that young children are unable to see things from other viewpoints and are therefore egocentric. At the age of around seven, children developed the ability to do the task, decentering and identifying the doll's viewpoint correctly. This ability showed that a child had moved to the next stage, that of concrete operations.

THINKING SCIENTIFICALLY: TASKS THAT MAKE 'HUMAN SENSE'

In 1978, Margaret Donaldson wrote an influential book called *Children's Minds* in which she argued that preschool children were capable of more sophisticated reasoning than Piaget had suggested. Donaldson pointed out that children's understanding is 'embedded' in everyday familiar situations and they make use of context to work out what is meant. Donaldson argued that young children *can* understand another person's viewpoint if they are asked in a way that draws on their knowledge of an everyday situation that makes sense to them, such as a game of hide and seek. We will explore this claim in detail when we evaluate Piaget's theory.

Limitation 2: Class-inclusion tasks

Another limitation identified by Piaget related to class-inclusion tasks, the ability to work out how categories of objects relate to one another. You are aware that the category of 'vehicles' contains examples such as lorries, cars and bicycles. Each of these examples can be further divided; for example, cars can be divided into sports cars, hatchbacks, etc. (see Fig. 4.5).

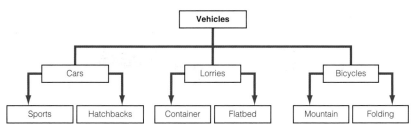

Fig. 4.5 Class inclusion task about vehicles

Piaget used picture cards of animals showing images such as five horses and three pigs. He asked children to count the number of horses, then the number of pigs, and finally all of the animals together. He then asked the children, 'Are there more animals or more horses?' Piaget found young children were unable to answer correctly, leading him to conclude that this level of logic was not available to the child younger than six years old. Even at the age of seven this skill was basic, with children making errors.

Limitation 3: Conservation

A third limitation in the pre-operational child's thinking is the inability to understand that when the shape or appearance of an object changes, the overall quantity remains the same if nothing is added or taken away. Piaget referred to this ability as **conservation**. Piaget studied conservation by giving children two equal amounts of a substance, for example beakers of juice, and asking if they were the same. He then transformed the appearance of one of these by pouring it into a large, tall glass (See Fig. 4.6). Pre-operational children were fooled by the transformation and claimed that the tall beaker had more juice than the shorter beaker.

Piaget argued that pre-operational children fail conservation tasks such as the one above because they focus or centre on one aspect of the change (for example, height) but ignore the other (such as width). In contrast, children around the age of seven are able to focus on both aspects of the situation at once and explain that the level of juice may be higher but the glass is thinner, so one cancels the other out (compensation). They also refer to reversibility ('we could pour it back'). This demonstrates the child's ability to carry out mental operations and marks the start of the concrete operational stage of development.

Fig. 4.6 Conservation

The concrete operational stage (7–11 years)

While the pre-operational stage is defined by the inability to reason, the period of concrete operation reached at about seven years of age is marked by the growing ability to carry out mental operations. Children of seven and above are able to decentre and understand that quantities remain the same even when appearances change. However, their ability to reason is still limited to situations where concrete objects are available – abstract reasoning is beyond their reach.

Piaget demonstrated this using a 'pendulum' task. Children aged 7 to 12 years old were given sets of weights and different lengths of string along with a bar to attach the weights and string to. With this equipment they could make many different simple pendulums. The task set by Piaget was to find out what affected the speed at which the pendulum swung. Children in the concrete operational stage, between 7 and 11, would typically take a trial-and-error approach to the test, randomly varying the length of string or size of the weight. In contrast, children who had reached the age of 11 or 12 solved the problem systematically by varying one factor at a time while keeping others constant. Such factors included the weight of the object attached to the string, the length of string, and how hard the object was pushed.

The formal operational stage (11 years old onwards)

This is the final stage of development, in which Piaget believed that children develop logical reasoning and abstract thought. One of the key features of this stage is said to be deductive reasoning – the ability to generate various hypotheses and test them systematically to find the solution. Piaget believed that by 11 or 12 years old adolescents could now problem solve logically rather than by trial and error. In contrast to concrete-operational children, formal thinkers could consider hypothetical situations and concepts without needing actual objects in front of them.

Exam hint

Explanation questions can be tricky to answer. A good practice for questions like these is to start with an example – for instance, you could explain conservation by referring to a specific substance such as liquid, then move on to the general definition.

EXAMPLE EXAM QUESTION

Explain what is meant by 'conservation'. (3 marks)

Evaluation of Piaget's methods

Piaget used a variety of methods to investigate children's thinking, including careful observations of his three children and devising tasks for children to complete (such as the conservation tasks and the three mountains task). Since Piaget's work was published, many developmental psychologists have tested his ideas and established that children can achieve some mental skills, such as object permanence and conservation, at a younger age than Piaget thought. However, these mental skills will only become apparent when children are tested with sensitive 'child-friendly' tasks.

Bower and Wishart (1972) argued that Piaget's claims about object permanence reflected a lack of motor skills in babies (such as an inability to grasp and move a cloth to reveal a hidden object) rather than a lack of understanding that objects exist when they are out of sight. Bower and Wishart placed a teddy bear in front of four-month-old babies and found that the babies would raise their hands to reach for the toy. When the lights were turned off so the room was dark, babies would still outstretch their arms to the bear, implying that they knew it continued to exist when out of sight. We will examine the debate about object permanence in detail when we consider Baillargeon's work later in this chapter.

A study carried out by Hughes (1975) indicated that pre-operational children can see the world from other viewpoints and are not as egocentric as Piaget thought. Children aged between three and a half and five were shown a 3D model of two intersecting walls (see Fig. 4.7) and a toy policeman was placed at the end of one wall where he could 'see' into two sections of the model. The children were asked to hide a boy doll where the policeman could not see it. Hughes found that 90 per cent of children aged between three and a half and five correctly placed the boy doll in a section of the model where the policeman could not see, suggesting strongly that children can take someone else's perspective if they understand the task. Even when a second policeman was introduced, children could complete the task.

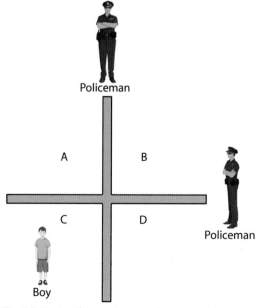

Fig. 4.7 Hughes' 'hide and seek' policeman model

McGarrigle and Donaldson used a sample of 80 pre-operational children aged four to six years old in a conservation of number experiment. Piaget had tested conservation of number by spreading out a line

Fig. 4.8 Conservation of number experiment

of counters or Smarties (see Fig. 4.8) and asking children if they were still the same.

Donaldson argued that the problem with conservation tasks was that they lacked 'human sense'. Asking the same question twice ('Are they still the same?') cues the children to give the answer that something has changed.

McGarrigle and Donaldson used a glove puppet called 'Naughty Teddy' to make the transformation to a row of counters. The independent variable in the experiment was how the transformation occurred:

- In the control condition, the standard Piagetian task was used, with the counters being spread out by the experimenter.
- In the experimental condition, the Naughty Teddy glove puppet emerged from under the table and spread out the row of counters.

In the control condition, 16 per cent of pre-operational children were able to conserve the number. This figure rose to 62 per cent in the experimental condition.

THINKING SCIENTIFICALLY: NAUGHTY TEDDY

The difference between 'Naughty Teddy' and Piaget's task is that the motives and intentions are clear to children: the transformation is accidental and the way in which it happens draws on a familiar situation to children (a naughty action in which something is deliberately messed up), hence they are able to focus on the task and conserve number.

EXAMPLE EXAM QUESTION

1 What type of experimental design was used in McGarrigle and Donaldson's experiment? (1 mark)
2 State the dependent variable and explain how this was operationalized. (2 marks)
3 Write a non-directional experimental hypothesis for McGarrigle and Donaldson's experiment. (2 marks)

Exam hint

You can spot the difference between an independent measures and a repeated measures design by asking if the same or different participants were used in the conditions of the experiment. Remember that a non-directional hypothesis does not make a prediction about the direction of difference.

Evaluation of Piaget's theory

There is fairly universal agreement that Piaget underestimated the ages at which children can achieve mental abilities such as conservation. However, Piaget's claim that children understand and can reason at the level of action (doing) before the level of representation (abstract thinking) is accepted by most developmental psychologists (Goswami, 1998).

A major objection to Piaget's stage theory is the claim that formal operations develop in early adolescence at the age of around 12. According to Keating (1979), around 40 to 60 per cent of college students fail formal operational tasks. Dasen (1994) suggests that only about one third of adults ever reach the formal operations stage. There is general consensus that this stage is not universal as Piaget thought.

Piaget believed that progression from one stage to another was the result of maturation, implying that children cannot progress until they are ready. However, Vygotsky pointed to the importance of social interaction in 'speeding up' or facilitating cognitive development.

Goswami (1998) has argued that Piaget's theory provided precise answers to the important questions of 'what' develops and 'why'. Although his theory is often seen as a domain-general one (implying that cognitive abilities develop together at the same speed), Piaget acknowledged that there would be variations within and between stages.

Exam hint

The key challenge for a question of this nature is getting your description of Piaget's theory sufficiently succinct so that it does not dominate the essay (remember only six AO1 marks are available here). Summarize the key elements, including the building blocks and the idea of stages, and use your discussion of Piaget's methods and evidence as a source for AO3.

EXAMPLE EXAM QUESTION

Describe and evaluate Piaget's theory of cognitive development. (16 marks)

KEY POINTS

- Cognitive development takes place in stages which are loosely linked to age.
- At each stage the child builds knowledge like a scientist, using the processes of assimilation and accommodation.
- Object permanence occurs around nine months of age, in the sensorimotor period.
- Pre-operational children are egocentric and unable to conserve. They are also unable to complete class-inclusion tasks.
- The concrete-operational child can reason but requires concrete (physical) objects.
- Formal operations mark the start of abstract and logical thought.
- Piaget has been criticized for the use of methods that lacked child sense, and led him to underestimate children's reasoning abilities.
- The basic tenet of Piaget's theory that children can reason at the level of action before representation is widely accepted. However, some people do not attain the final stage of formal operations.

Vygotsky's theory of cognitive development

Lev Vygotsky (1896–1934) was a Russian whose ideas and writing were not widely published outside Russia until the 1960s. Because he died young, many of Vygotsky's concepts were relatively underdeveloped and have been reworked by later theorists. However, since his writing was rediscovered in the late twentieth century, his ideas have found favour with many developmental psychologists and educationalists (Light and Oates, 1990). They have also dominated eastern European and Russian child psychology (Durkin, 1995).

The building blocks of Vygotsky's theory: social interaction, language and the zone of proximal development

In contrast to Piaget, Vygotsky did not suggest that children develop the ability to think in age-linked stages. Instead, he emphasized the importance of social interaction, language and cultural context to cognitive development. Vygotsky believed that the ability to think and reason is 'the outcome of a fundamentally social process' (Light and Oates, 1990) in which cognitive skills develop as the child interacts with other people. This takes place in both formal interactions between teachers and pupils at school, and in everyday contexts – at home, with family, siblings and friends. The key to cognitive development is interaction. Interaction enables children to see adults and older children using problem-solving skills and cognitive tools, and to internalize these mental skills to use themselves. In contrast to Piaget's idea of the young child as a scientist is the child as an apprentice, developing thinking skills and mental tools of the trade through interaction with others.

Vygotsky believed that children are born with elementary mental functions such as attention and memory, which develop into higher mental functions or complex thinking skills. The transition from simple to complex thinking is made possible by language. Vygotsky observed that young children talk to themselves, commenting on their actions as they are playing or carrying out difficult tasks. At around seven to eight years of age, speech becomes internalized as an inner voice, which Vygotsky called 'intellectual speech'. This type of inner speech is used to regulate, plan and think and is the basis of higher mental functions. Vygotsky developed this argument to suggest that many mental abilities appear on two 'planes'; first of all socially with other people, then intellectually. This allows a child to move from being able to do things only with the help of others to being capable of doing them alone.

Vygotsky was particularly interested in children's cognitive abilities when they were able to interact with an older or more knowledgeable person. An important concept in Vygotsky's theory was the **zone of proximal development** (ZPD). This was defined as the distance between the child's current developmental level, measured by the tasks they were able to achieve on their own, and their ability when helped by another person – peer or adult – who was more knowledgeable or experienced than themselves. For example, a two-year-old may be able to complete a four-piece jigsaw on their own (current developmental level) but unable to complete a ten-piece jigsaw, despite many attempts. When helped by their older sibling who finds the four corners, the child is able to achieve the harder task.

Fig. 4.9 Lev Vygotsky

COGNITION

Key term

Zone of proximal development: the distance between the tasks the child can do on their own and the tasks they can achieve with the help of a more knowledgeable other.

Scaffolding

While Vygotsky commented on the importance of the ZPD, he did not identify or explain the means by which this support could be delivered. An important development of his theory was the concept of **scaffolding**, proposed by Wood, Bruner and Ross (1976). Scaffolding refers to support or help given to the child by a more knowledgeable other – an adult or peer – while working in the ZPD. Just as physical scaffolding supports a new building, mental scaffolding supports the child in a new task. Both can be removed at a later stage when the building/child can stand alone. Wood and Middleton tested these ideas in an observational study.

KEY STUDY: WOOD AND MIDDLETON (1975)

Twelve mothers were asked to teach their four-year-old children how to put together a tower made of interlocking wooden pieces so that the child could eventually do it on their own. The mother–child teaching sessions were recorded on video and the tapes were played back and analysed. The types of support offered by the mothers were coded and categorized by the researchers. Wood and Middleton identified five types of scaffolding/intervention, which differed in the degree of help offered. These included:

- general suggestions ('Now you build the tower.')
- specific verbal instructions ('Get four blue blocks.')
- indicating materials ('You need to start with that one.')
- preparing for assembly ('Turn it this way round.')
- physical demonstrations ('The wooden peg fits in the small hole.').

Wood and Middleton found that the most successful 'mothers as teachers' were those who adjusted the help that they offered subtly, depending on the child's actions. These mothers would offer more direct help moving 'up' a level when children were struggling, but would back off and move 'down' a level when their child appeared to be managing on their own. Wood and Middleton noted that help was carefully tuned into and contingent or dependent on the child's actions. This demonstrates scaffolding in action.

Fig. 4.10 Scaffolding in action

This study uses observational methods to provide rich, detailed data about the methods naturally used by mothers when playing with their young children. The use of video recording allows the play session to be watched many times by researchers. Although the sample is small, researchers working within this type of framework are less concerned with representative samples and generalizing. Data derived from observations of this nature are qualitative. In order to transform this into quantitative data (numbers), researchers need to code their observations into different categories. This process is a subjective one and is open to interpretation.

Evidence and evaluation

Many studies have supported Vygotsky's claim that cognitive skills are heavily influenced by context and culture. For instance, Nunes (1992) recorded how Brazilian street children who worked as vendors had well-developed mathematical skills, despite having almost no formal schooling. Similarly, Greenfield and Lave (1982) looked at young Mexican girls learning the skill of weaving from older women. They found that the girls started by watching, then worked alongside adults who gave them simple tasks to do and provided help and support to achieve them. Closer to home, Pratt et al. (1992) studied parents helping older children with maths homework and found that some of the variation in children's maths performance was related to how skilfully parents scaffolded them during homework. These studies illustrate how young children internalize a range of mental skills and how scaffolding processes take place in everyday settings and different cultures.

Fig. 4.11 Mexican girls learn the art of weaving from older women

Vygotsky emphasized very different aspects of cognitive development to Piaget. Vygotsky lived in a communist society that valued collective action over the role of the individual, and these ideas are reflected in his theory, which focused on the importance of interaction. Piaget, on the other hand, highlighted the individual nature of the child in cognitive development.

COGNITION

Vygotsky highlighted the importance of culture and context in cognitive development, and his theory can account for the cultural differences seen in cognitive development that we have noted. In contrast, Piaget's theories say little about cultural differences, implying that children go through the same developmental stages regardless of culture.

Another important difference between the two theories relates to their focus. Vygotsky's theory focuses on the processes underlying cognitive development rather than the outcomes. Piaget, in contrast, focused on what children think and believe at different ages. As Vygotsky's work has become better known, empirical support for his theories has started to grow, and since the 1970s his work has been applied in education.

Modern developments in cognitive neuroscience mean that the study of children's cognition is now very similar to that of adult cognition, focusing on processes such as memory development (Goswami, 1998). Few developmental psychologists propose grand theories in the way that Piaget and Vygotsky did.

ACTIVITY 4.2

Spend a few minutes observing a one-to-one interaction between a teacher and learner (for example, a sports coaching session, a parent helping a child with homework or a teacher in a classroom). What kind of scaffolding does the teacher provide when the learner is struggling? Can you identify any of Wood and Middleton's levels of scaffolding?

Exam hint

An example is a great way to illustrate your understanding of concepts. You could refer to Wood and Middleton's research to show how scaffolding extends the child into the ZPD.

EXAMPLE EXAM QUESTION

Explain what is meant by 'zone of proximal development' and 'scaffolding'. (4 marks)

KEY POINTS

- Vygotsky emphasized the importance of social interaction in cognitive development.
- The child is seen as an apprentice, internalizing skills from more knowledgeable others.
- Language is internalized around age eight and becomes intellectual (inner) speech.
- The zone of proximal development (ZPD) refers to the range of tasks that a child can achieve with help.
- Scaffolding is the process used to support a child in the ZPD.
- Many studies have shown how scaffolding occurs in a range of learning environments.
- While Piaget focused on the beliefs of the individual child, Vygotsky focused on different social elements of learning from other people.
- Both theories were shaped by the culture of the theorist.

Baillargeon's work on early infant abilities

In the 1970s and 1980s, researchers questioned Piaget's reliance on 'action' methods to test object permanence. Piaget had used tasks that required infants to use physical skills such as reaching forward and removing a cloth to find a hidden toy. Using this method, he concluded that object permanence develops around eight to nine months of age. Baillargeon devised a different method to assess infants' understanding of the physical world and argued that, contrary to Piaget, infants as young as three and a half months of age understand that objects continue to exist even when they are out of sight.

Violation of expectations research

How can psychologists investigate very young infants' understanding of the physical world? As infants are unable to speak and have a limited behavioural repertoire, researchers have devised subtle measures based on what they *can* do. From birth, infants possess the ability to direct their gaze and look at objects. The visual preference technique involves seating a young infant on a parent's knee and showing the child a series of stimuli such as images or events. Eye-tracking technology is used to measure how much time the infant spends looking at each image or event. If an infant spends more time looking at one thing than another, we can conclude that a) they can tell the difference between them, and b) they prefer or are more interested in the stimuli they look at for longer.

The preferential-looking technique is at the base of **violations of expectation** (VoE) research. A VoE study consists of two stages:

- In stage 1 infants are shown a particular event (for example, a train on a circular track going into a tunnel and emerging) several times. The first stage of the research allows the infants to become familiar with the stimulus and stop responding to it.

- In stage 2, the infants are divided into two groups. Half of the sample are shown an expected event that is compatible with what they have seen before (for example, the train goes into a tunnel and emerges), while the other half are shown an unexpected event (for example, the train fails to emerge from the tunnel or a different object emerges from the tunnel).

The researchers measure the amount of time each group of infants spend looking at the respective events. If the infants look significantly longer at the unexpected event, it is assumed that they have formed an expectation about what should happen and that this expectation has been violated, leading to increased interest. The VoE method has proved extremely valuable in helping us to understand what babies understand and expect about the properties of physical objects.

> **Key term**
>
> **Violation of expectation**: a technique in which an expectancy of a physical event is created then an unexpected event happens.

COGNITION

In 1985 in a classic experiment, Baillargeon, Spelke and Wasserman demonstrated that infants aged five and a half months formed expectations that hidden objects continue to exist, indicating object permanence. In the first stage of the experiment, the infants were seated in front of a 'stage' and shown a 'drawbridge', which started in a flat position, then slowly rotated over 180 degrees to end up in a flat position (see Fig. 4.12). This event was repeated until the infants habituated to the event.

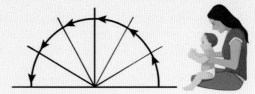

Fig. 4.12 The drawbridge experiment

In the second stage of the experiment, a colourful block of wood was placed in the path of the drawbridge (Fig. 4.13). The drawbridge could raise up to 112 degrees but would then stop and rest, hiding the block of wood.

Fig. 4.13 The expected and unexpected events

The infants were divided randomly into two groups:

- The control group saw an *expected* event (Fig. 4.13a). The drawbridge raised up and then rested on the hidden block of wood at an angle of 112 degrees.
- The experimental group saw an *unexpected* event (Fig. 4.13b). The drawbridge apparently passed through the hidden block of wood as if by magic and returned to a flat position, passing through 180 degrees.

Baillergeon et al. compared the amount of time the infants spent looking at both events and found that this was significantly longer in the unexpected, experimental condition. They concluded that infants' attention was grabbed by the apparently impossible event of a solid object – the drawbridge – moving through the hidden block of wood. Thus Baillergeon et al. concluded that infants remembered that the hidden block existed – demonstrating object permanence – and were surprised when it did not stop the drawbridge in its path.

Critics such as Haith (1998) have suggested that the drawbridge study is based on 'rich interpretation' of infants' abilities. Haith's criticism is based on the scientific idea of parsimony: that is, a scientist should aim for the simplest possible explanation of a phenomenon. Haith argued that the infants may have experienced a lingering visual memory trace (like an afterimage) of the wooden block when it disappeared from view. This is a simpler explanation than Baillargeon's assumption that infants remembered the hidden object.

Rivera et al. (1999) used the same VoE method with a rotating drawbridge and found that infants preferred to look at a complete 180-degree rotation rather than a 112-degree rotation, perhaps because the movement lasted longer. An even simpler explanation was presented by Bogartz et al. (2000), who argued that babies just prefer the more familiar 180-degree rotation to 112 degrees. These are all plausible and simpler explanations for Baillargeon's findings.

Knowledge of the physical world

The first wave of research into infant cognition focused on establishing what young babies know about the physical world and the properties of objects. Using violation of expectation research, Baillargeon established that very young infants possess expectations about different kinds of events, including:

- occlusion events, in which a distant object moves behind a nearer object (train going behind tunnel)

- containment events, in which one object is placed inside another object (teddy put into box)

- covering events, in which a rigid container such as a box is lowered over an object

- support events, in which one object rests upon another.

Baillargeon has carried out a substantial amount of research in this area, and the following study provides a flavour of this kind of work. Baillargeon, Needham and DeVos (1992) set out to establish what babies understand about support phenomenon – a technical term for our knowledge of how objects rest on each other. You and I would understand that Fig. 4.14c below represents an 'impossible' physical relationship between objects, or some trickery!

A sample of 32 babies aged between six and seven months took part in the experiment. The infants were seated on their parent's knee and shown a box resting on a table top (see Fig. 4.14). During the trial, a gloved hand reached out and pushed the box along the supporting surface to different resting positions:

- Fully resting on surface

- 70 per cent on surface

- 15 per cent on surface.

Fig. 4.14 a) Fully resting on surface; b) 70 per cent on surface and c) 15 per cent on surface

COGNITION

Baillargeon used the preferential-looking technique to measure how long infants spent examining each of the different positions. Significantly more time was spent looking at c), the impossible scenario, than a) or b), indicating that infants' expectations about the physical world were violated. In simple terms, the babies expected the box to fall onto the floor and their attention was captured when it did not do this.

Exam hint

This question asks you to show your understanding of VoE research via explanation. You can use one of the studies using VoE to illustrate your explanation. Remember that you must refer to both stages of the VoE studies – habituation and unexpected events.

EXAMPLE EXAM QUESTION

Explain what is meant by violation of expectation research. [4 marks]

Baillargeon's explanation of infant cognitive abilities; innate ideas

The notion of 'innate ideas' was first put forward by Plato, a philosopher in ancient Greece, and developed in the seventeenth century by the French philosopher René Descartes. The notion of innate ideas refers to the belief that infants are born with an inbuilt, instinctive understanding of something. The notion of innate ideas largely fell out of favour in the twentieth century with the impact of behaviourism, which emphasized the importance of learning and environment, but was revived in the 1960s by linguist Noam Chomsky. Chomsky argued persuasively that babies are born with an innate knowledge of the rules of grammar, which enable them to acquire language quickly and easily without being taught. The notion of the innate idea rests on the assumption of biological adaptation; innate knowledge exists because it increased the chance of survival in the past.

Baillargeon (1987) argued that her findings had two possible interpretations: that infants were either born with *innate object knowledge* – a basic, inbuilt understanding of the properties of objects – or that they were born with the ability to quickly and easily acquire object knowledge (*innate fast learning*).

By 2006, Baillargeon had refined and integrated these two ideas to suggest that babies innately possess a concept of persistence – that 'objects persist in time and space' (Baillargeon, 2006) – and build their understanding of objects rapidly and easily from experiences. Basic physical representations of objects become much more complex as they experience the world. For instance, in the case of an object disappearing and reappearing:

- At around four months, babies will notice/react to a reappearing object that is a different size or shape (for example, a train changes to a car in a tunnel)

- By around seven and a half months, babies will notice if the reappearing object is differently patterned (for example, a spotty train becomes a stripy train in the tunnel).

- By 11.5 months, babies will notice if the reappearing object has changed colour.

Thus, infants build a more complex understanding of objects rapidly working from basic innate knowledge.

Evaluating Baillargeon's contribution

Baillargeon has been at the forefront of research on infants' understanding of the physical world. She has provided a clever method, the VoE paradigm, which enables researchers to assess what very young infants understand about objects and the relationships that exist between them. Mareschal and Kaufman (2012) argue that Baillargeon's work has helped us to gradually piece together the 'infant's understanding of the physical support relations that can exist between objects.'

Recent studies have extended Baillargeon's work using brain imaging/scanning methods to identify which structures of the brain are active during tasks, and comparing these to adult brain activity. Kaufman et al. (2003) measured the brain responses of infants in response to a three-scene video in which a toy train disappeared into a tunnel:

- In the expected condition, the train disappeared into the tunnel and re-emerged. The tunnel was lifted up and – unsurprisingly – there was nothing underneath it.

- In the unexpected condition, the second and third scenes were reversed. The train disappeared into the tunnel, which was then picked up to reveal no train. The tunnel was replaced and the train emerged from it. This condition contained the unexpected events of disappearance and reappearance.

Kaufman et al. found that the babies looked longer at the unexpected events (as predicted by Baillargeon) and activity in the right temporal cortex of the brain continued when the train was hidden in both conditions of the experiment, suggesting that the infants were thinking about the hidden object and maintaining a mental representation of the object. This brain activity increased even further in the second condition when the tunnel was lifted up and the train had disappeared. An interpretation of these findings is that brain activity increased as the infants attempted to keep a mental image of the hidden object, with the brain working increasingly hard to do this. The pattern of brain activity was similar in adults, providing further, neural evidence of object permanence.

Baillargeon's work has led to the development of several connectionist models of infant cognition (for example, Mareschal et al., 1999) that use computer simulations of information processing.

However, Baillargeon's work has also generated debate and criticism. As we have seen, Haith and other critics have argued that there are simpler explanations of Baillargeon's findings, based on infants' preferences for familiar scenarios (Rivera et al., 1999).

Exam hint

This question asks you to focus your answer on Baillargeon's explanation of early infant abilities. Ensure that you use the appropriate terminology (for example, the concept of innate object knowledge). You may wish to include an example to illustrate Baillargeon's claim that infants' knowledge of objects develops rapidly, but avoid describing VoE studies in detail.

EXAMPLE EXAM QUESTION

Outline Baillargeon's explanation of early infant abilities. (5 marks)

KEY POINTS

- Baillargeon devised a method to measure infants' knowledge about the world that is known as Violation of Expectation (VoE) research.
- VoE studies suggest that young infants have expectations about occlusion, containment, covering and support events.
- Baillargeon suggests that babies possess basic innate knowledge that is rapidly built on from experience with objects.
- Critics such as Haith argue that there are simpler explanations for Baillargeon's findings, such as a preference for familiarity.

The development of social cognition

So far, we have examined how young children develop an understanding of the physical world. The final topic of this chapter focuses on young children's understanding of the social world, including the beliefs, intentions and actions of other people. Everyday life relies on the ability to predict how people might behave, and this is based partially on the ability to mentally put ourselves in other people's shoes. The section begins by examining Selman's work on 'perspective-taking' before exploring the important concept of theory of mind. Theory of mind underlies much of the research into **social cognition** and provides an influential explanation of the difficulties experienced by children with autism. The topic concludes with a consideration of biological insights into social cognition, with an examination of the role played by mirror neurons.

Key terms

Social cognition: the processing of social information—in simple terms, thinking about and interpreting the actions of other people.

Perspective-taking: the ability to consider situations from other people's points of view.

Selman's levels of perspective-taking

Selman (1976, 1980) argued that the ability to take other people's perspectives into account was important for many social activities, such as group problem-solving and persuading others. Selman investigated children's abilities to see the world from other people's points of view by devising scenarios of social situations. Each scenario involved a number of people, enabling the child to consider the issues from a range of viewpoints. After the child had listened to the scenario, they were asked a series of open-ended questions about how a particular person might respond.

Let's look at an example:

> Emily is ten years old and she loves to ride her BMX bike. One day she almost bumps into a mother with a pushchair when she is crossing the narrow footbridge in the park. Emily's mother sees her and tells her not to cross the bridge on her bike because next time she might run into someone and hurt them.
>
> Later that day, Emily and James are playing in the park on their bikes. James is Emily's 8 year old neighbour. He is pushed to the ground by a group of kids who run off with his bike. Emily sees them go over the narrow footbridge, and realizes that she can catch them up on her bike. But then she remembers what her mother said about not riding her bike on the bridge.
>
> Questions:
>
> 1. Should Emily chase the children?
>
> 2. Do you think Emily's mother will tell her off?
>
> 3. Does Emily think she will be punished?

The scenario involves Emily (the actor), Emily's mother, Emily's friend James (the victim), the kids who took his bike (the perpetrators) and the mother with a pushchair, making it rich in different perspectives. Selman collected qualitative data, recording children's responses and then classifying them into different levels. Selman devised a five-stage model in which children move gradually from egocentric reasoning to an understanding of multiple people's viewpoints and perspectives, along with social conventions (see Table 4.2).

Stage	Age	Characteristics of stage
Stage 0: Egocentric perspective-taking	3–6 years	The child recognizes that people have different thoughts to themselves, but sometimes confuses these. **Do you think Emily's mother would tell her off?** *No, she would be happy that James got his bike back.*
Stage 1: Social informational perspective-taking	5–9 years	The child understands that people have different perspectives based on access to different information. **Do you think Emily's mother would tell her off?** *Emily's mother might tell her off because she doesn't know why Emily went on the footbridge.*
Stage 2: Self-reflexive perspective-taking	7–12 years	The child can now step into another person's shoes and see what the situation would look like from there. **Does Emily think she will be punished?** *No, Emily thinks her mother will understand if she explains why she went on the footbridge.*
Stage 3: Third-party perspective-taking	10–15 years	The adolescent can imagine how the situation might look from the viewpoint of an outsider and can see two peoples' different perspectives. **Does Emily think she will be punished?** *No, because Emily thought she ought to help James. Her mother would only punish her if she thought Emily had gone on the footbridge for fun.*
Stage 4: Societal perspective-taking	14 years to adulthood	The young adult understands that views are influenced and subject to larger societal values, based on religion or civil liberties for example. **Does Emily think she will be punished?** *No, it's important to stand up for other people, especially when they are younger than you are.*

Table 4.2 Selman's stages of perspective-taking

ACTIVITY 4.3

Read the following responses and try to identify which stage of Selman's model each response would fit in. Is your decision clear cut or do responses sometimes combine elements of different stages?

Should Emily chase the children?

Sammy: Emily should chase them; James will be upset that his bike has been nicked and Emily is his friend so she should help.

Do you think Emily's mother will tell her off?

Cara: I think Emily's mother might be a bit cross if she just hears that Emily has been on the bridge but if she knew that Emily was trying to help James, she might not tell her off on this occasion.

Does Emily think she will be punished?

Dan: Yes, she thinks her mother will tell her off because she did something wrong.

Hoffman (1975) has argued that the development of perspective-taking is related to parenting style. Some parents actively encourage their children to take the perspective of the 'victim' when the child has hurt someone with their actions or words (for example, 'How do you think Sophie felt when you left her out of your game?'). A study by Fitzgerald and White (2003) examined the relationship between victim-centred discipline (VCD) and perspective-taking in a sample of 93 North American school children. Each child completed Selman's clinical interview, tailored to their age, and parents completed an interview designed to assess their discipline style. Fitzgerald and White found a significant correlation between VCD parenting and perspective-taking, supporting Hoffman's claim that perspective-taking relates to parenting style. There was also a positive relationship between the child's age and Selman's stages, providing further support for the model.

Evidence and evaluation

Selman has contributed a method to assess perspective-taking that has been widely used by other researchers. The scenario can be tailored towards young children and acted with dolls or used as a straightforward, clinical interview with older children, making this a very flexible method indeed.

Selman has also contributed a model showing how perspective-taking develops over time. A number of studies (for example, Gurucharri, Phelps and Selman, 1984) provide clear support for Selman's stages, emphasizing the developmental nature and increasing complexity and sophistication of perspective-taking abilities. Studies building on Selman's work (such as Fitzgerald and White, 2003) have shown how perspective-taking relates to elements of the social world for example parental style (such as VCD).

Longitudinal studies such as Kurdek (1977) suggest that perspective-taking is a complex social cognitive skill. To understand it fully requires a broader approach than simply describing the stages, such as conducting longitudinal studies. The process of perspective-taking is more complicated than current models suggest.

Today, children's social worlds are more complex and increasingly acted out in an online environment via social networking. Methods of social interaction are not as personal as they used to be. For example, in education, web-based discussions are a common occurrence. Since the dynamics of communication have changed, it is possible that

COGNITION

the development of social cognition, including perspective-taking, have changed as well (Järvelä and Häkkinen, 2003). There is a great need for research to link the different aspects of the children's social worlds together and to understand the role of perspective-taking in parent–child and peer relationships generally (Fitzgerald et al., 2003). Selman's stages of development seem a little outdated given that forms of communication are changing so rapidly.

Exam hint

The specification refers to two methods of analysing qualitative data: coding via content analysis and thematic analysis. You could use either of these approaches here. You can remind yourself about analysing qualitative data by looking at pages 26–28.

EXAMPLE EXAM QUESTION

A researcher carried out a study on perspective-taking. Children aged between five and ten were asked about a scenario in which a young boy rescued a kitten from a tree. He had been told not to climb the tree by his mother. The researcher then asked children to answer the questions 'Should Arjun have climbed the tree?' and 'Do you think his mother will tell him off?'
Explain how the researcher could have analysed the qualitative data they collected from the children. (4 marks)

Theory of mind

Key term

Theory of mind: the understanding that other people have minds and may know or believe very different things to ourselves. Development of ToM is seen as crucial to normal social behaviour.

The term **theory of mind** (ToM) was first used by Premack and Woodruff (1978) in reference to the ability of chimpanzees to deceive their keepers. In simple terms, ToM refers to the ability to mentally put oneself in someone else's place and to guess what they may be thinking or feeling. An everyday example would be your ability to understand that your friend, who is waiting to start their A Level Psychology exam, is feeling nervous – even though you are not.

Testing for theory of mind

False-belief tasks have played an important role in helping us to understand how children develop a theory of mind. One false-belief task was devised by Wimmer and Perner (1983) and referred to as the Maxi test. The children were told a story in which Maxi placed some chocolate into a blue cupboard and then went out to play. While Maxi was out his mother used some of Maxi's chocolate to make a chocolate cake, replacing the leftover chocolate in the green cupboard. Children were asked the question 'Where will Maxi look for the chocolate?'

The test required a young child to distinguish between what they knew (i.e. the actual location of the chocolate in the green cupboard) and what Maxi knew (he had left the chocolate in the blue cupboard). If they were able to do this, they would reason that Maxi would look in the blue (wrong) cupboard where the chocolate was last seen. This would demonstrate ToM, as the child understands that Maxi holds a (false) belief that is different to their own.

Wimmer and Perner found clear differences between children, with the age of four acting as a 'watershed'. Children under four would typically say that Maxi would look in the green cupboard where they knew the chocolate to be. Children over four would typically answer that Maxi would look in the blue cupboard where he had last seen the chocolate.

Another type of false-belief problem is the 'appearance reality' task. A popular example is the Smarties task, devised by Perner, Leekam and Wimmer (1987). Children are shown a Smarties tube and asked to say what they think is in it. Unsurprisingly most reply 'Smarties'. The tube is then opened to reveal a number of crayons. The child is then asked what another child, who is outside of the room, will think is in the tube. In agreement with the Maxi study, children aged around four answer correctly that the other child will think the tube has Smarties in it. Three-year-olds typically give the answer of 'crayons', showing an inability to distinguish what they believe from another person's beliefs. False-belief tests show that children over the age of about four are able to understand that other people believe something different to themselves, showing theory of mind.

Theory of mind as an explanation for autism

Autism was first described by Leo Kanner, working in the US, and Hans Asperger, working in Austria, in the 1940s. Kanner (1943) identified the key symptoms as:

- social withdrawal and problems with communication

- obsession with consistency and 'sameness' and problems in dealing with change

- good at rote learning (for example, lists of words or objects), minimal language skills with objects.

Later research by English psychologists Wing and Gould (1979) systematically divided the symptoms of autism into three areas of impairment, which are known today as 'Wing's triad':

- Social impairment, for example appearing unresponsive, absent or using unusual eye contact

- Impairments to language and communication, for example delayed or impoverished language, unusual or repetitive language

- Impairments to the scope and range of activities and interests, for example fascination with object parts, ritualistic behaviour and heavy dependence on repetitive routines.

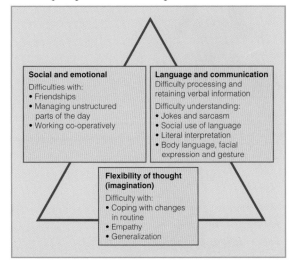

Fig. 4.15 Wing's triad

Autism was originally thought of as a syndrome (that is, a single condition with a set of core symptoms that occur together), but today it is characterized as a spectrum. The term spectrum means that autism is made up of a range of disorders, including Asperger's disorder, with slightly differing patterns of symptoms. The correct term is technically 'autistic spectrum disorders' but it is shorter and easier to refer to it as autism.

There have been many theories about the causes of autism since Kanner and Asperger's first descriptions. Baron-Cohen, Leslie and Frith (1985) have put forward one of the most influential explanations, which proposes that autism arises when theory of mind or 'mentalizing' fails to develop in children. They devised a method that was suitable to use with children with autism to assess their ToM abilities. This method is known as the Sally–Anne test.

The Sally–Anne test

The child is seated at a table with the researcher. There are two dolls and two containers on the table, a basket and a box, both with lids. The following scenes are enacted using the dolls.

This is Sally.   This is Anne.

Sally has a basket.   Anne has a box.

Sally has a marble. She puts her marble in the basket.

Sally goes out for a walk.

Anne takes the marble out of the basket and puts it in the box.

Sally comes back. She wants to play with her marble.

Where will Sally look for her marble?

KEY STUDY: BARON-COHEN, LESLIE AND FRITH (1985)

In 1985, Baron-Cohen, Leslie and Frith carried out a classic study to test their hypothesis that children with autism lack ToM. They used the Sally–Anne test to compare the abilities of three groups of children:

- 20 children with autism aged between 6 and 16 (mean verbal age 5.5 years)
- 14 children with Down's syndrome aged between 6 and 16 (mean verbal age of 3 years)
- 27 typically developing children mean age 4.5 (mean verbal age of 4.5 years)

It is important to note that the children were different chronological (actual) ages but appoximately matched for 'verbal' age – the ability to understand language. Each child was asked three questions; two control questions and the crucial 'belief' question:

- The reality question: 'Where is the marble really?'
- The memory question: 'Where was the marble in the beginning?'
- The belief (crucial) question: 'Where will Sally look for her marble?'

The child was said to have 'failed' the test if they answered the belief question inaccurately by saying that Sally would look for her marble in the box. The 'belief' question was correctly answered by 86 per cent of the Down's syndrome children and 85 per cent of the typically developing children. However, only 20 per cent of the autistic group were able to answer this correctly, supporting Baron-Cohen, Leslie and Frith's hypothesis that autistic children have difficulty in putting themselves in someone else's shoes and taking the perspective of the other.

COGNITION

This was a carefully controlled study in which the researchers selected children with matched mental ages in the three conditions. This was to ensure that any deficits found did not relate to the children's general/verbal intelligence or level of understanding, but to their lack of social understanding.

The Sally–Anne test can only be used on people who have sufficiently developed language skills to understand the story and instructions. This precludes its use with severely autistic people.

Baron-Cohen, Leslie and Frith argued that autistic children fail the 'belief question' because they do not put themselves in Sally's shoes, instead assuming that Sally's understanding is the same as their own. The philosopher Daniel Dennett (1978) argues that if we cannot understand what other people think or want, this would make social interaction very difficult indeed. A child of five who has not developed a theory of mind would struggle with a range of tasks, leading to many of the impairments shown in Wing's triad.

Evidence and evaluation

The Sally–Anne test led to an explosion of research into ToM and autism. By 2012, the paper had been cited (referred to) almost 1500 times in other researchers' work, making it very influential indeed. Subsequent research developed the understanding of the link between ToM and autism. Studies indicated that autistic children make very little use of 'mental state language' (for example, 'I feel' or 'I think') and have great difficulty engaging in deception (such as telling lies). They also struggle to understand irony and metaphor (Roth, 2008).

Coralie Chevallier (2012) identified several criticisms of theory of mind as an explanation of autism. Firstly, she notes that other psychological disorders also include ToM deficits, such as schizophrenia (Sprong et al., 2007) and types of depression (Kerr, Dunbar and Bentall, 2003), indicating that deficits in ToM are not solely implicated in autism. Difficulties with ToM seem to play a role in different kinds of psychological disorders.

More problematically, ToM deficits are not universal in children with autism. Around 20 per cent of children with autism *did* pass the task in Baron-Cohen et al.'s 1985 study. This poses a problem for the idea that autism results from deficits in ToM. Frith (2001) notes that performance in false belief tasks is strongly related to language development in both typically developing children and those with autism, and this relationship has not yet been fully explored.

Finally, while ToM and autism are clearly linked, this approach does not tell us why autistic children fail to develop a theory of mind. One possible biological explanation lies with the mirror neuron system.

Discuss theory of mind as an explanation for autism. [16 marks]

Exam hint

You should start your answer by defining theory of mind *and* autism, then go on to examine evidence for the claim that difficulties with theory of mind underpin autism. Make sure you summarize research evidence (e.g. Baron-Cohen, Leslie and Frith's work) succinctly and, most importantly, show how evidence supports or refutes the explanation.

The role of the mirror neuron system in social cognition

The discovery of **mirror neurons** is one of the most exciting developments in brain research over the last 15 years, especially in relation to social cognition. Neurons are nerve cells that transmit information throughout the brain using electrical impulses. Mirror neurons are a specific type of neuron that 'fires' when an animal (for example, a monkey) performs an action, but also when the animal watches an action performed by someone else.

Key term

Mirror neurons: nerve cells that fire equally when an animal performs an action, or observes (sees/hears) the same action being performed by another animal.

KEY STUDY: **DI PELLEGRINO ET AL. (1992) AND RIZZOLATTI ET AL. (1996)**

In the early 1990s, a research group at the University of Parma was studying the activity of neurons in macaque monkeys. They used a method called single unit recording, which involved implanting thin electrodes into a live monkey's brain to measure the electrical activity of individual neurons. When the monkey reached for a peanut, the F5 neurons in the pre-motor cortex 'fired'. The F5 neurons are part of the brain's system for controlling voluntary movement. In an accidental observation, the researchers noticed that the same F5 neurons fired when the monkey observed another monkey reaching for a peanut while they themselves were inactive. The neurons in the observer's brain seemed to imitate or mirror the activity of the neurons in the active monkey's brain. Because of this, di Pellegrino et al. referred to these neurons as mirror neurons.

The researchers followed up their observation by systematically studying the action of mirror neurons in a series of manipulations. They used electrodes to record the activity of individual F5 neurons while giving actor and observer monkeys a range of different objects to handle. The team established that:

- mirror neurons only fire if there is an interaction between the movement of an effector (hand or mouth) and an object (for example, the monkey reaches for or picks up a banana)
- mirror neurons do not fire in response to random movements by hand or mouth with no target object (for example, the monkey makes a reaching movement with no banana in sight)
- different mirror neurons respond to actions initiated by hands and mouths
- the observer monkey does not have to *see* the movement. Mirror neurons will also fire when an observer monkey hears an actor monkey pick up a peanut and crack the shell open – that is, they respond to the meaning.

COGNITION

Link

For more detail on functional magnetic resonance imaging, see page 282 in Book 1.

THINKING SCIENTIFICALLY: **fMRI**

Systematic single-cell recording involves implanting thin electrodes into the brain so that they contact and measure the activity of individual neurons. This kind of invasive research technique can only be carried out on non-human animals (such as monkeys) rather than on humans. For this reason, studies establishing the existence and action of mirror neurons in humans tend to use neuroimaging techniques such as functional magnetic resonance imaging (fMRI).

Since the first studies, many others have expanded our knowledge of the mirror neuron system. Mirror neurons are found in many parts of the brain that overlap with the social cognition network outlined above, especially the motor-related areas. Iacoboni et al. (1999) used fMRI to image the brains of students as they made finger movements and watched the experimenters make finger movements. Iacoboni et al. found activity in some of the same areas of the frontal cortex and the parietal lobule in both situations.

Action, understanding, empathy and imitation

Mirror neurons appear to play a role in several areas of social cognition, including action, understanding, empathy, and imitation. When we see someone carry out an action (such as picking up an apple) our mirror neurons are activated as if we had personally picked up the apple. This neural 'mirroring' action could enable the observer to identify the goal or intention they would have if personally carrying out the behaviour, and then mentally attribute this to the person they are observing ('If I picked up an apple I would be hungry, therefore X is hungry'.).

Scanning studies have also shown that observing someone in pain activates the same brain systems that are activated when you feel pain yourself (Rizzolatti et al., 2006). So we directly experience the same sensations as the other person, which is the foundation of empathy. The mirror neuron system in humans is less activated in people who score low on empathy scales (Gazzola, Aziz-Zadeh and Keysers, 2006) and in participants with autism (Oberman et al., 2005). Hadjikhani et al. (2006) studied participants with autism and found less cortical matter in areas associated with the mirror neuron system.

Mirror neurons also facilitate imitation. People with a normally functioning mirror neuron system can simply and automatically copy a movement that they have seen someone perform. Without a functioning mirror neuron system, we would need to consciously and painstakingly analyse a movement before attempting to copy it. Some studies have suggested that people with autism have difficulty imitating other people, especially when complex movements are involved. Iacoboni et al. argue that problems with imitation could lead to the mental retardation that co-occurs with autism 75 per cent of the time.

A defective mirror neuron system has been argued to be the basis of autistic problems with social communication and interaction. However, research has provided mixed support for the implication of mirror neuron deficits in autism. Some studies (such as Iacoboni, 2006) have provided support for the claim that people with autism have mirror neuron deficits. Others (such as Dinstein et al., 2010) have contradicted this. Dinstein et al. compared the fMRI scans of ten autistic adults with ten age-matched non-autistic controls who observed and then copied a series of hand gestures (thumbs up, high five). The researchers found no significant difference in the average mirror neuron response between the two samples.

Evaluation of the role of the mirror neuron system in social cognition

While the mirror neuron system is clearly important as a basis for social cognition, it is not enough in itself for complex social cognition. Monkeys have a mirror neuron system, but only limited social cognition in areas such as deception. The human brain mechanisms underlying social cognition have evolved far beyond the mirror system identified in monkeys.

Social cognition is a broad area and many of the concepts are poorly defined. It involves perception of social signals, socialization, theory of mind and mentalizing, and emotion. It will be very difficult to unravel the precise brain mechanisms underlying all of these different aspects and how they interact.

The explanation based on mirror neurons is reductionist, reducing a complex topic – social cognition – to a low-level explanation. It is important not to let a focus on the brain divert us from the study of the development of social cognition at behavioural, family and social levels.

KEY POINTS

- Selman used scenarios of social situations to explore the development of perspective-taking.
- He identified five stages as children move from egocentric reasoning to understanding multiple viewpoints.
- Theory of mind (ToM) is tested using false belief tasks such as the Maxi test and the Sally Anne test.
- Typically developing children show ToM between three and four years of age.
- One explanation for autism is the failure to develop mentalizing abilities such as ToM.
- Theory of mind deficits are not universal in people with autism.
- Mirror neurons fire when an animal acts or observes someone carrying out an action.
- Mirror neurons are implicated in action, understanding, empathy and imitation.
- Studies of mirror neurons in people with autism have yielded conflicting results.

You can investigate Piaget's stage of formal operations using the Tower of Hanoi puzzle. While Piaget believed that abstract thought (formal operations) developed around age 12, studies have suggested that it is by no means as universal as Piaget thought.

The Tower of Hanoi problem is a good way to examine abstract thought. The tower consists of three rods and three discs of different sizes. The discs are placed on the left-most rod and the task is to move them in as few moves as possible to the right-most rod.

Fig. 4.16 The Tower of Hanoi puzzle (three-disc version)

The rules are as follows:

- Each move consists of taking the uppermost disk from one of the stacks and placing it on top of another stack.
- A disk can only be moved if it is the uppermost disk on a stack and only one disk can be moved at a time.
- No disk may be placed on top of a smaller disk.

Test a sample of adults over the age of 16. Observe them as they are solving the problem and record how many moves they take (be prepared to demonstrate the correct solution yourself – you can find this on the Internet). After the activity is completed, ask your participants if they adopted a strategy and how they solved the problem.

You will need to think about which criteria you should use (number of moves, use of a strategy, or combination of these) in order to categorize people as having reached formal operations or not.

If you wish to make this a quasi-experimental study, compare a sample of science and non-science students and record the number of moves taken to solve the puzzle. You can use a statistical test to look for any differences between your conditions.

1   Which of the following is one of Piaget's stages of cognitive development? **(1 mark)**

   Conservation   Formal operations   Class inclusion
   Egocentricity

2   Explain what is meant by 'theory of mind'. **(3 marks)**

3   Read the item below and answer the questions:

   > A developmental psychologist carried out an experiment to test for theory of mind in children aged three and four using two dolls called Sally and Anne. The child was shown a scenario where Sally hid a marble in a basket and went out. Anne moved the marble to a box. The child was asked 'Where will Sally look for her marble when she comes back?'
   >
   > The psychologist obtained the following data:
   >
   > | Age of child | Three-year-old children | Four-year-old children |
   > |---|---|---|
   > | Sally will look in the basket | 5 | 18 |
   > | Sally will look in the box | 15 | 2 |
   >
   > The psychologist decided to carry out a statistical test to see if there was a difference between the scores of three- and four-year-old children.

   a)   Name an appropriate graph the psychologist could use to display the data in the table above. **(1 mark)**

   b)   Identify one statistical test the psychologist could use to analyse the data in the table above. **(1 mark)**

   c)   Justify your choice of test with reference to the research study described above. **(2 marks)**

4   Describe and evaluate Vygotsky's theory of cognitive development. **(16 marks)**

Exam focus

Read through the following example exam question, example student answer, and examiner comments. Then, have a go at answering the question yourself!

EXAMPLE EXAM QUESTION

Describe and evaluate Piaget's theory of cognitive development. (16 marks)

Jamie's answer

Piaget believed that children pass through four stages of cognitive development that are linked to age. In each stage, the child becomes able to deal with more complex mental tasks, and stages end when there is a shift in the child's way of thinking. The newborn baby possesses reflexes that develop into simple schemas (e.g. grasping) and applies these to new objects (assimilation). When a schema does not work, the child alters it (accommodation) to fit the new experience. Adult learning develops in the same way. Piaget thought that some of the key milestones were object permanence (around eight months of age), egocentricity, conservation (around age seven), and class-inclusion tasks.

> **Examiner comment:** Clear coverage of key concepts. The stages are not described in minute detail to save words; description is embedded into the next paragraph.

Piaget devised tasks to test children's thinking abilities such as the three mountains task. The child is asked to pick out a viewpoint of a 3D model from another perspective. Pre-operational children cannot do this and pick their own view. Piaget also devised conservation tasks where a substance is transformed, such as pouring juice from a short glass into a tall glass. Children under the age of seven are fooled and claim the tall glass has 'more'. After the age of seven, the child can reason that the juice could be poured back (reversibility) or that the height and width cancel each other out (compensation). The concrete-operational child can only reason with objects and doesn't develop abstract thought until around age 12, according to Piaget.

> **Examiner comment:** The description of methods does two things; it summarizes Piaget's findings about children's thinking (AO1) and it sets up the critical discussion about methods (AO3). Good use of specialist terminology here.

Piaget's work has been very influential but his methods have been criticized for lacking child sense. Many studies have shown that children can achieve things earlier if tasks are made easier. Hughes (1975) asked children to hide a boy doll from a policeman using a model and found that 3-4-year-olds could work out what other people can see. McGarrigle and Donaldson used a 'Naughty Teddy' to alter a row of counters and found that children can conserve before the age of 7. Some critics have said that these tasks are easier than Piaget's.

> **Examiner comment:** Good, succinct coverage of research findings here.

Piaget's theory has been widely accepted and most psychologists agree that children can reason using concrete objects before abstract thought. However, studies have shown that many people fail to reach the stage of formal operations (i.e. never develop the ability to do subjects that require abstract thinking, like chemistry).

Piaget saw young children as similar to scientists, trying things out and constructing knowledge actively. Vygotsky thought that children were more like apprentices, learning from others in a social environment. Piaget did not put much emphasis on other people and thought that stages couldn't be speeded up or slowed down. However, studies have shown that thinking can be developed through scaffolding (e.g. helping a child to do a jigsaw) and extending into their ZPD.

Examiner comment: Good use of Vygosky here, but focus on Piaget's theory is lost at the end of the paragraph.

Examiner comment: Knowledge of Piaget's theory is accurate and generally well detailed. Evaluation is thorough and effective. The answer is clear, coherent and focused. Specialist terminology is used effectively. Minor detail and/or expansion of argument sometimes lacking. Level four response – around 14 out of 16 marks.

COGNITION

Part 3: Issues and options in psychology

Chapter 5: Schizophrenia

Introduction

What kind of image does the word 'schizophrenia' conjure up in your mind? It may be that you have never really encountered the word, but if you have, it is quite possible that you relate this disorder with terms like 'split personality', 'dangerous', or even 'psychopath'. None of these are accurate. People with schizophrenia do not have a split personality (schizophrenia means 'split mind'), they are no more dangerous than non-sufferers, and schizophrenia is not untreatable, as we shall see. Indeed, it is quite possible that you have met a person with schizophrenia without even knowing it, as it is estimated there are approximately 640,000 sufferers in the UK alone. It is clear, then, that there are several myths about schizophrenia that you need to be careful to avoid. So what exactly is schizophrenia?

Schizophrenia is an example of a mental illness referred to as a psychosis (an abnormality of the mind). Like many mental illnesses, it is diagnosed as a consequence of a number of symptoms being present. While any of the symptoms might occur independently in a variety of people who are not schizophrenic, it is the *combination* of symptoms that mark a person as having schizophrenia.

In this chapter we will look at the characteristics that typify schizophrenia, showing how they can be split into those that are noticeable by their presence and those that are noticeable by their absence. We will explore how schizophrenia has been classified in the past, how it is classified today and the influences on its diagnosis. We then take a look at the biological basis of schizophrenia and evaluate the evidence that it can be explained from a genetic, neurotransmitter or neuroanatomical standpoint. Next we look at some of the psychological explanations that have been proposed, including the ideas that schizophrenia is a consequence of family upbringing, that it is the result of cognitive deficits or that it results from some form of social inadequacy.

Having explored the possible causes of schizophrenia, we will move on to possible treatments, considering biological ones such as drug therapy, and psychological ones such as family therapy and cognitive behaviour therapy. The chapter concludes by exploring some of the ways that researchers have tried to combine approaches in what are referred to as interactionist models.

What is covered in Schizophrenia?

SCHIZOPHRENIA

What is schizophrenia?

Symptoms of schizophrenia

Schizophrenia is characterized by a number of different symptoms (much in the same way as a person suffering from flu might have a runny nose, a sore throat, and so on). Schneider (1959) described what he thought were the most important symptoms that are nearly always present in a person with schizophrenia. These included auditory hallucinations and delusional thinking. Later, Mayer-Gross, Roth and Slater (1969) added a number of other symptoms, such as withdrawal and avolition, which they considered to be important in the diagnosis of schizophrenia. The symptoms displayed in schizophrenia are distinctive by virtue of the presence or absence of behaviours when compared to ordinary people. When a behaviour is present that is not normally present, it is referred to as a **positive symptom**. When a behaviour is missing that we would usually expect to be displayed, then we call this a **negative symptom**. A person with schizophrenia will display a number of specific positive and negative symptoms, and it is this combination of symptoms that leads to the diagnosis of schizophrenia.

Positive symptoms

There are three different kinds of positive symptom that are typically displayed by a schizophrenic: hallucinations, delusions, and disordered thinking. These are additional behaviours that the schizophrenic possesses that are not normally experienced by people.

Hallucinations

Patients often report auditory hallucinations. This is a phenomenon where they hear voices in their head that are not real. The voices will often comment on something personal, or will tell them what they should do or think. For example, a voice might tell the person that they are a bad person or that there is someone from an intelligence agency watching them. Some schizophrenics suffer visual or tactile (touch) hallucinations, during which they see or feel things that are not real, but auditory hallucinations are by far the most common.

Delusions

Delusions are beliefs that could not possibly be true even though they will seem very real to the patient. There are two forms of delusion:

- **Delusions of persecution**: when the belief creates fear and paranoia. A common persecutory delusion is that the person is being hunted by a government agency.

- **Delusions of grandeur**: when the person believes they are powerful and/or important. A common delusion of grandeur is the person believing that they are God or Napoleon (for some unknown reason, Napoleon is quite common).

Disordered thinking

Disordered thinking is when a person believes that their thoughts are being interfered with in some way. There are three forms of interference:

Fig. 5.1 Schizophrenia means 'split mind'. The term split mind captures the split between what is real and what is not. The patient has trouble knowing whether what they believe, think, or feel is real or imagined.

- **Insertions**: when the person believes that thoughts are being inserted into their mind.

- **Withdrawals**: when the person believes that thoughts are being removed from their mind.

- **Broadcasts**: when the person believes that their thoughts are being transmitted to others (perhaps via the radio or television).

Negative symptoms

Here, the characteristic is noticeable by its absence. In other words, the person fails to display behaviours we would normally expect to see. As with the positive symptoms, there are three different kinds of negative symptom: speech poverty, avolition, and flattening of affect.

Speech poverty

Poverty of speech is referred to as alogia. It is where the person tends to speak quite infrequently, and when they do speak the speech lacks fluency. The person might give a brief, empty reply to being asked a question, and they will rarely engage in spontaneous speech.

Avolition

Avolition is the inability to engage in goal-directed behaviours. A goal-directed behaviour is where a person makes a conscious effort to do something for a purpose (for example, going to school). A person with avolition may choose to sit in their house for hours every day and may come across as uninterested in the world around them.

Flattening of affect

Affect is the term used to refer to emotion (that is, when you are 'affected' by something). People with schizophrenia will tend not to provide the types of cues that we usually use to show our emotional involvement. They do not use facial gestures, body language or eye contact and their voice is often monotone.

ACTIVITY 5.1

Read the extract in which Molly Watson, a woman diagnosed with schizophrenia, describes her experiences. The piece is presented in her own words. Consider the following questions:

1. Can you identify the positive and negative symptoms she describes?
2. What does her story tell you about some of the myths surrounding schizophrenia?

A schizophrenic's experience

At the age of 37, I had a psychotic break, just 3 years short of a diagnosis of late-onset schizophrenia. Aside from situational depression a decade prior, this was my introduction to mental illness. I spent a year sleeping on my mother's sofa, fearfully locked in her apartment and wondering what became of me before diagnosis and treatment began. My doctor told me that my prognosis was good because of my age, even with the severity and speed of onset.

I now live with auditory hallucinations, formally classified as "outer space" hallucinations that I hear outside of myself and, for me, stem mostly from sounds in the environment. This is in contrast to "inner space" hallucinations that are perceived to be within the head itself. I am disturbed by sounds, especially by the hypnotic resonance of motors and fans, for they carry with them the most persistent voices. These voices refer to themselves as the Wherewho.

There's a droning noise in the background at work and I can't discern its source. Is it a fan or a motor above the ceiling tiles? Is it a server or other hardware in the cubicle next to mine? Am I hallucinating? I tense up over the low, continued hum. It remains in the back-ground, yet at the forefront of my attention, even as I turn on my MP3 player in the hope that music will drown it out. Instead, focusing on the static from my headphones only seems to increase the dull, monotonous sound. My head starts to throb as my anxiety increases. I've had enough for now, so I decide to step outside for a cigarette. Along the way, my attention is drawn to the elevator motor, the drinking fountain, and various other sources of sound. On the loading dock, one particularly large vent repeatedly utters, "I hate you," in continuation of the conversation I had with the fridge this morning:

…Two or 3 h later, I find myself wondering how so much time can pass without me noticing. The dishes in the sink collect and the laundry piles up because my free time is spent in internal conversation.

…Spaced out and terminally disconnected, I am not always able to focus even when trying my hardest. My new manager enjoys holding morning meetings with a group of us cramped into his small office as he attempts to fill my brain with information. My breathing is fast and shallow and my legs bob up and down as my uneasi-ness and anxiety increase. I know others notice and judge my ability. Not only am I uncomfortable in such a small space with others, penned in, I am also uncomfortable in my body. Weight gain from medications has added 45 pounds to me—my clothes constrain me as much as the pressure to perform.

[published in Schizophrenia Bulletin (vol. 41 no. 1 pp. 6-8, 2015)]

Classification of schizophrenia

The process of diagnosing a mental illness is not easy as most illnesses are made up of a number of different symptoms. In order to help with this, clinicians use a system of classification to help them decide which mental illness a patient is presenting with. The standard and most used classification system of all mental disorders is the *Diagnostic and Statistical Manual of Mental Disorders* (DSM). There is also another classificatory system, the International Statistical Classification of Diseases and Related Health Problems (ICD), but this is less well used for mental illnesses. The diagnosis of schizophrenia does not require that all of the possible symptoms are presented by the patient, but there are some symptoms that are considered better indications of schizophrenia than others. Up until the most recent version of the DSM, DSM-5 (version 5), which came out in 2013, a patient with schizophrenia would be diagnosed as having one of five separate sub-types of the disorder. These were paranoid schizophrenia, disorganized schizophrenia, catatonic schizophrenia, undifferentiated schizophrenia, and residual type schizophreniform disorder.

These labels were removed for DSM-5 as many clinicians found them not to be helpful when diagnosing patients. Instead, DSM-5 takes an approach that employs the symptoms together with the progression of schizophrenia over time. The main criteria are listed in Table 5.1. There must be at least one from of first three key criteria present and the symptoms must have been present for at least one month. The progression of the disorder over time is captured by specifiers.

Key criteria	Specifiers
1. Delusions.	1. First episode, currently in acute episode. This applies to the first manifestation of illness that meets all of the diagnostic criteria of schizophrenia. An acute episode is a time period in which characteristic symptoms (criterion A) are present.
2. Hallucinations.	2. First episode, currently in partial remission. Partial remission is a time period during which an improvement after a previous episode is maintained and in which the defining criteria of the disorder are only partially fulfilled.
3. Disorganized speech (e.g., frequent derailment or incoherence).	3. First episode, currently in full remission. Full remission is a period of time after a previous episode during which no disorder-specific symptoms are present.
4. Grossly disorganized or catatonic behaviour. *This is an abnormal condition characterized by stupor/inactivity, mania, and either rigidity or extreme flexibility of the limbs*	4. Multiple episodes, currently in acute episode. Multiple episodes may be determined after a minimum of two episodes, i.e., after a first episode, a remission and minimum one relapse. An acute episode is defined as above.
5. Negative symptoms (i.e., diminished emotional expression or avolition)	5. Multiple episodes, currently in partial remission. Multiple episodes may be determined after a minimum of two episodes, i.e., after a first episode, a remission and minimum one relapse. Partial remission is defined as above.
	6. Multiple episodes, currently in full remission. Multiple episodes may be determined after a minimum of two episodes, i.e., after a first episode, a remission and minimum one relapse. Complete remission is defined as above.
	7. Continuous. In order to categorize an individual as having a continuous course, symptoms fulfilling the diagnostic symptom criteria of the disorder must be present for the majority of the illness course with subthreshold symptom periods being brief relative to the overall course.
	8. Unspecified. Available information is inadequate to characterize course.

Table 5.1 The new criteria for schizophrenia under DSM-5.

ACTIVITY 5.2

Create a table listing each of the key characteristics of schizophrenia and briefly describe each one.

EXAMPLE EXAM QUESTION

Briefly outline the reliability of the classification of schizophrenia. (4 marks)

Exam hint

You will need to outline at least two separate issues concerning reliability. These might compare DSM and ICD classificatory systems. For example, you might point out that the current version of ICD has subtypes whilst the current version of DSM does not.

Reliability and validity in diagnosis

Reliability

As well as the DSM classification system, which is preferred here in the UK, there is another system of classification, the International Statistical Classification of Diseases and Related Health Problems (ICD). This system is produced by the World Health Organization. ICD-10 (the current version) lists seven subtypes of schizophrenia, while DSM-IV (current up until 2013) listed only five. As we have seen, DSM-5 has removed the classification subtypes and the new ICD-11 is due for publication in 2017. Despite a number of published studies showing differences among the ICD subtypes, the diagnosis of which subtype a patient is showing is not always clear and can change across time. Hence the diagnosis is generally unreliable. In terms of reliability of diagnosis at a single point in time, Rosenhan (1973) showed that it was possible for non-schizophrenic people to be diagnosed as having schizophrenia (see the *Key study* below). This study showed that it is easy to misdiagnose schizophrenia. However, more recent studies have shown inter-rater reliabilities as high as 98 per cent (Jakobsen et al., 2005). In terms of test–retest reliability, Read et al. (2004) showed a concordance rate of only 38 per cent. In other words, when a person is diagnosed with schizophrenia when a test is first administered, there is only a 38 per cent chance that they will be diagnosed again on a retest some time later. Overall, most people agree that the reliability of diagnosing schizophrenia has improved, but there is still a worrying level of misdiagnosis.

Research methods link

For more on reliability, see pages 41–42.

KEY STUDY: ROSENHAN (1973)

Rosenhan was interested in the reliability of diagnosis of abnormality. He devised a study to investigate whether healthy, sane people could be mistakenly diagnosed as having a mental illness. He asked eight people (three women and five men) to attend a hospital complaining that they were hearing a voice. The voice was reported by these pseudo-patients to simply repeat a single word ('empty', 'thud' or 'hollow'). They each tried to gain admission to a different hospital in the US. All were successful and seven of the eight people were diagnosed as having schizophrenia. Once in the hospital they all behaved quite normally and asked to be released. It took them between seven and 52 days to be released. What was remarkable was that, even though the medical staff never detected their lack of any mental illness, many of the other patients claimed the pseudo-patients were journalists or professors put there to check up on the hospital.

In a follow-up to the first study, staff at one hospital, who had been aware of the first study, were falsely told that during the following three months one or more pseudo-patients would try to enter the hospital. Even though there were no pseudo-patients, ten per cent of the admissions were judged by one psychiatrist and one other staff member to be fakes.

Together, Rosenhan's studies demonstrate that clinicians and other staff were unable to detect the presence or absence of a mental illness. As this was an observational field experiment, it has high ecological validity. However, we must remember that this study was carried out a long time ago under DSM-II and so the data may no longer be valid. Furthermore, it might be better that psychiatrists err on the side of caution when making a diagnosis. It might be preferable to diagnose a healthy person as ill than to diagnose an ill person as healthy.

Research methods link

For more on field experiments, see pages 9–10.

THINKING SCIENTIFICALLY: THE ETHICS OF USING DECEPTION

The British Psychological Society guidelines are very clear about when it is permissible to use deception. They state:

Avoid intentional deception of clients unless:

(a) deception is necessary in exceptional circumstances to preserve the integrity of research or the efficacy of professional services

At the time of the Rosenhan (1973) study there would have been no formal psychological guidelines available (the current American equivalent of the UK guidelines is very similar). The closest thing that he would have had to draw upon was the 'Principles of Medical Ethics'.

Nevertheless, it is clear that without deception we would not have learned about the dangers of misdiagnosing schizophrenia. Indeed, the study most likely contributed to the improvements seen in diagnosis between 1973 and the present day. However, the modern guidelines also state that the deception must not be allowed to continue longer than is absolutely necessary. We might question, therefore, whether it was ethical for Rosenhan to allow one person to remain in hospital for 52 days. After all, they would have had their liberty restricted and would have had to continually avoid taking any medication they were prescribed.

Validity of diagnosis

The research findings on whether the diagnosis of schizophrenia is valid are very mixed. Some researchers report that when you match patients diagnosed with schizophrenia to the DSM criteria there is a good correlation (Hollis, 2000), suggesting that diagnosis is valid. However, two diagnosed patients can differ greatly on the precise symptoms each displays (for example, one showing delusions and another not), suggesting that the idea of a single label of schizophrenia is not valid. Perhaps then it is more valid to use the presence or absence of positive and negative symptoms to distinguish different forms of schizophrenia, as DSM-5 does. However, there are other threats to validity such as co-morbidity, culture bias, gender bias, and symptom overlap.

Research methods link

For more on validity, see pages 42–44.

Exam hint

You will need to define what reliability means and then choose one aspect of reliability to concentrate on. Use a research example to illustrate how the diagnosis is unreliable. So, for example, having defined what reliability is, you might consider how reliably a diagnosis can be made and use the Rosenhan (1973) study to briefly illustrate the unreliable nature of diagnosis.

EXAMPLE EXAM QUESTION

Explain ONE reason suggesting that the diagnosis of schizophrenia is unreliable. (4 marks)

Co-morbidity

People with schizophrenia often have other substantial psychiatric problems as well, referred to as **co-morbidity**. These other psychiatric problems can sometimes make the diagnosis of schizophrenia difficult. For example, if a person is showing

SCHIZOPHRENIA

social withdrawal then it is hard to place whether this is part of schizophrenia, part of depression, or both. The most common problems to occur co-morbidly with schizophrenia are:

- depression
- anxiety
- substance abuse
- post-traumatic stress disorder
- obsessive–compulsive disorder.

Culture bias

One form of **culture bias** involves the way in which symptoms are viewed. Many of the symptoms of schizophrenia are not viewed in the same way throughout the world. In some parts of the upper Amazon, for example, people take hallucinogens in order to experience hallucinations that are seen as having spiritual significance. So, hallucinations can be seen as positive in one part of the world and negative in another. In Serbia, the belief that schizophrenics are harmful either to themselves or others still persisted until quite recently, and this represents a different way of interpreting the symptoms (see Fig. 5.2).

Another form of culture bias occurs in diagnosis. In the US and the UK it has been shown that a black person is more likely to be diagnosed with schizophrenia than a white person (Simon et al., 1973). This was even the case when there were no noticeable behavioural differences between the groups. Whaley (2004) has suggested that this might be due to differences in the way the two groups express their symptoms. This casts a shadow over the reliability and validity of the diagnosis of schizophrenia.

Gender bias

Schizophrenia appears to affect just as many men as women, but the usual age of onset is earlier for men (18–30) than it is for women (25–35). It is also commonly assumed that women with schizophrenia tend to have better functioning (including cognitive and social capabilities) prior to the development of their schizophrenia, a better course of illness, and different brain damage and cognitive deficits (Canuso and Pandina, 2007). In other words, females tend to show fewer signs of developing schizophrenia before their first psychotic episode and recover better once they have been diagnosed. However, these findings could be the result of a **gender bias** in sampling. Goldstein (1993) suggested that males are more likely to be involuntarily committed to psychiatric institutions (referred to as being hospitalized) when they show mild signs of schizophrenia, due to the risk of socially deviant behaviour. Females, on the other hand, are likely to be voluntary patients (even though they may too spend some time in hospital) because they are more likely to seek help. As a consequence of this, Nasser, Walders and Jenkins (2002) argue that much of the early work on gender differences in schizophrenia was carried out mostly on males as they

Fig. 5.2 Serbian psychiatric hospital. The photo was taken by George Georgiou, who worked in Kosovo and Serbia between 1999 and 2002. The person is in a straitjacket (tied up) so as not to do any harm to herself or others. She is also kept in isolation so that she does not frighten or incite any of the other patients.

would have been the higher population in hospitals. If this was the case then the research would have been highly gender biased.

Symptom overlap

None of the symptoms of schizophrenia are exclusive to this disorder and we have already seen that people often have other psychiatric problems. This makes the evaluation of schizophrenia research extremely difficult. Even something as specific as hearing voices is not exclusive to schizophrenia – it is estimated that 13 per cent of the non-clinical population hear voices (Beavan, Read and Cartwright, 2011), whereas only 1 per cent of the population have schizophrenia. Such data undermine the validity of diagnosing schizophrenia.

KEY POINTS

- Schizophrenia is characterized by a number of positive and negative symptoms.
- Positive symptoms include auditory hallucinations, delusions, and disordered thinking.
- Negative symptoms include avolition, poverty of speech, and flattening of affect.
- DSM-5 has radically charged the guidance for the diagnosis of schizophrenia.
- Rosenhan's 1973 study questions the reliability of diagnosis of schizophrenia.
- There are a number of threats to the validity of schizophrenia, including co-morbidity, culture bias, gender bias, and symptom overlap.

Biological explanations of schizophrenia

It is sometimes believed that the entire answer to the question 'what causes schizophrenia?' will be a detailed explanation of the biological and genetic correlates of the disorder. Within this topic we will examine the extent to which we can make that claim, both within the context of our current knowledge and by examining what it is we could or could not know from a biological viewpoint. First we will explore the idea that schizophrenia is genetically inherited and, moreover, why it persists in the gene pool if it is damaging to the species. We will then look at some of the brain areas that have been linked to schizophrenia and try to explain how malfunctions in these areas may give rise to some of the symptoms. Finally, we will look at the neurotransmitter substances that have been linked to schizophrenia and whether imbalances in these chemicals hold the key to an explanation of how and why schizophrenia exists. The main neurotransmitter we will examine is dopamine but we will also consider some others.

Before we look in detail at some of the theories and research that suggest a biological basis for schizophrenia, we must remember that schizophrenia is a collection of symptoms (see page 246–7). Consequently, we would expect to find a number of different biological markers, each having a different role to play in one or more of the symptoms. We are not likely, therefore, to be able to pinpoint a single gene, a single brain area or a single neurotransmitter substance as the root cause. As we will see, research has gradually been building up a more complete picture of the multiple deficits that occur.

Genetic causes

The genetic question explores the degree to which schizophrenia can be inherited. There are two clues that point most to the idea that schizophrenia has a genetic origin: the fact that it continues to be present in about 1 per cent of the population, and that there is a degree to which it runs in families. Schizophrenia has roughly the same **prevalence rate** of 1 per cent in all parts of the world. That is, at any one time about 1 per cent of the population has schizophrenia (not to be confused with the **incidence rate**, which is the percentage of new cases in a period of time). While 1 per cent of the world's population may not seem much, it amounts to around 51 million people, with approximately 600,000 people in the UK. It is when you start to think of it in these terms that the importance of understanding what causes schizophrenia becomes clear. So are there any genetic markers?

The possible genetic origin of schizophrenia has mainly been explored using three methodologies: twin studies, adoption studies and family studies. Twin studies look at the degree to which if one twin has schizophrenia, the other twin also has it. This is called the concordance rate. Adoption studies also look at twins but here the emphasis is on situations where one twin has been adopted into a different family. Finally, family studies are ones where the incidence rates of schizophrenia are compared among different family members.

Twin studies
Twin studies offer an opportunity to directly look at comparisons between siblings who were born at the same time and who have thus had early identical upbringings. They can be **monozygotic twins**

(MZ), meaning they share 100 per cent of their genes or **dizygotic twins** (DZ), meaning they share, on average, 50 per cent of their genes. One of the first main studies of twins was by Kallmann (1946). He found that the concordance rate was higher for MZ twins (86 per cent) than for DZ twins (15 per cent). Gottesman and Shields (1966) also investigated the concordance rates in twin pairs (see the *Key study* below) and similarly found that these were higher for MZ twins (92 per cent) than for DZ twins (22 per cent). More recently, MacDonald and Schultz (2009) have suggested that among MZ twins, schizophrenia in one twin makes it 99 times more likely that the other twin will also have schizophrenia. At first sight this might lead you to think that schizophrenia is genetic, as more pairs of twins had schizophrenia when they shared all of their genes. Even so, the concordance figure of 86 per cent is a little way short of 100 per cent and 15 per cent is quite a bit short of 50 per cent, so we might conclude that while genetics plays a role (possibly a major role) they are not the whole story.

KEY STUDY: GOTTESMAN AND SHIELDS (1966)

Gottesman and Shields (1966) used the twin study method to investigate the concordance rates of schizophrenia in MZ and DZ twins. They used patient records from a psychiatric hospital that spanned a period of 16 years from 1948 to 1964. They found 68 twin pairs with a diagnosis of schizophrenia, but due to various problems (such as one twin being overseas) they were only able to include 57 pairs in their final analysis. The participants were split roughly half and half between males and females and there were roughly 50 per cent more DZ twins than MZ twins.

	Female	Male	Total
Monozygotic	11	13	24
Dizygotic	16	17	33
Total	27	30	57

Table 5.1 The number of twin pairs as expressed by gender and twin type

Gottesman and Shields used a variety of sources of information, which included hospital notes, case histories, semi-structured interviews with the twins and their parents, audio-recorded samples of the interviews, and tests of disordered thinking and personality. From this information they were able to separate the twins into four distinct categories:

1. Both twins were diagnosed with schizophrenia and hospitalized.
2. Both had been hospitalized but only one twin had been diagnosed with schizophrenia (the other being diagnosed with a related disorder).
3. One twin had schizophrenia and the other had a very different psychiatric abnormality.
4. One twin had schizophrenia and the other twin was clinically normal.

SCHIZOPHRENIA

The results showed that if categories 1 and 2 were combined then the concordance rate was 54 per cent for MZ twins and 18 per cent for DZ twins. When category 3 was added in, the rates rose to 79 per cent and 45 per cent respectively. Gottesman and Shields also noted that concordance was higher among females (77 per cent) than among males (49 per cent).

These data clearly suggested a genetic link to schizophrenia but also showed that genetics could not explain the whole story (the MZ concordance rate was not 100 per cent – see *Thinking scientifically* below). Gottesman and Shields therefore concluded that genetics provide a propensity towards developing schizophrenia and that there must be one or more things in the environment that provide the trigger. The strengths of this study are that these findings have been replicated many times elsewhere (for example, Davis et al., 1995; Torrey, 1992) and that the methodology employed was rigorous regarding the diagnosis of schizophrenia and the methods used for data collection. However, they did not fully describe what they meant by a disorder related to schizophrenia (category 2) and they also did not explore what environmental life events might have contributed to whether or not there was concordance between the twins.

THINKING SCIENTIFICALLY: GENETIC PROBABILITIES

We have considered that MZ twins share 100 per cent of their genes, so it is reasonable to suppose that if schizophrenia were 100 per cent inherited then the concordance rate for these twins would be 100 per cent. We never see such concordance rates, so it is safe to assume that schizophrenia is not simply inherited in the same way as something like eye colour. The way genetics work is that there are two processes: one is the possession of a particular gene and the other is whether or not the gene is expressed. We can think of this in terms of whether or not the gene is switched on. In other words, it is one thing to possess a light switch it is another to decide whether the light is turned on or not. What is clear from research is that schizophrenia is a complex disorder made up of a number of different symptoms. Each of these symptoms might well have a genetic marker but it will be environmental triggers that determine which of these markers are expressed. So, even though identical twins will possess the same genetic characteristics and will therefore have the same propensity for developing schizophrenia, their individual environmental experiences will decide whether or not the problem genes are turned on or turned off.

Adoption studies

The advantage of **adoption studies** over twin studies is that we can look at twins where one lives with one family and the other lives with a different family. The important thing here is that we should be able to separate genetic factors from environmental factors – the twins will share their genetic inheritance but will not share their environment, so it should be possible to separate the two. One of the most important adoption studies was conducted by Kety, Rosenthal, Wender and Schulsinger (1968). They had access to the Copenhagen records of 5483 adopted children. Among them they found 33 with schizophrenia, so they set about interviewing the biological and adopted relatives of this group. They also studied matched controls (adopted children with no family history of schizophrenia) in a similar way. They found that the concordance rates were higher between the schizophrenics and their biological relatives than between the schizophrenics and their adopted relatives. Furthermore, if one of the adopted parents developed schizophrenia, this did not cause the adopted child to be more likely to become schizophrenic (compared to the matched controls).

Family studies

Family studies set out to establish whether or not schizophrenia runs in families. Here, it is not just twins who are of interest but the entire immediate family. Table 5.2 shows the percentage of **co-morbidity rates** found by Kallmann (1938). It is clear from these figures that the closer the genetic link, the higher the co-morbidity rate. However, Reed et al. (1973) showed that the relationship might not be that simple. Using parents with psychosis (rather than people with schizophrenia in particular), they found that if a mother had psychosis then the risk to her child was 20 per cent, whereas if the father had psychosis, the risk to his child was only 8 per cent.

Relationship type	Incidence of schizophrenia (%)
Monozygotic twins	85.8
Dizygotic twins	14.7
Full siblings	14.3
Parents	9.2
Half-siblings	7.0
Marriage partners	2.1
Step-children	1.8

Table 5.2 Co-morbidity between family members (figures extracted from Kallmann, 1938)

Evaluating the genetic cause

Having looked at the different ways that researchers have explored the degree to which schizophrenia is genetically inherited or

Key terms

Family study: a study that looks at the development of symptoms in the family of a person with a disorder. Usually this extends to the immediate family but it can look beyond this.

Co-morbidity rate: the rate at which two people show the same disorder. It is not to be confused with the version without the word 'rate' (co-morbid – also sometimes written as comorbid) that refers to two separate disorders in the same individual.

SCHIZOPHRENIA

environmentally influenced, it is clear that there is a strong argument for a genetic link. However, there is also compelling evidence to suggest that genetics do not tell the whole story about the development of schizophrenia. Gottesman and Shields (1976) produced a comprehensive review of all of the twin, adoption and family studies that had been carried out at that time. They concluded that 'both the genes and environment… are each necessary but not sufficient for developing schizophrenia'. As we learn more about genetics, it is becoming clear that the environment can have an influence on the way in which our genes are expressed (called epigenetics – see Silber, 2014 for more information) and so can influence whether or not a person with the potential to become schizophrenic will actually develop the symptoms of schizophrenia. A limitation of genetic studies is that we are dealing with correlations, so it is difficult to be sure that the links we see are causal. Furthermore, it is extremely difficult to separate out genetic influences from environmental ones, and studies that look at genes more directly are still a long way from finding clear genetic markers of schizophrenia.

EXAMPLE EXAM QUESTION

Briefly outline TWO different approaches to exploring genetic causes of schizophrenia. (4 marks)

Brain areas associated with schizophrenia

We have seen that there is a genetic component to schizophrenia, so it follows that we should ask how that genetic influence leads to the symptoms of schizophrenia that we encountered in the first part of this chapter. Two of the most likely biological ways that genetics get played out are in changes to the structure of the brain and in changes to the working of the brain. In this section we will examine changes to the structure of the brain that might be linked to the behavioural changes we see in schizophrenia.

Ventricular enlargement

Our brains are soft and squidgy, with the consistency of porridge, so the cerebral ventricles provide the supporting fluid of the brain and also keep everything in place by providing an internal pressure. If there is damage to the brain and parts of it die then the ventricles will enlarge to fill the space left, so **ventricular enlargement** is often a good indicator of brain damage. This ventricular enlargement was first seen in schizophrenia in the 1970s using CT scans (for example, Johnstone et al., 1976) and a good example is shown in Fig. 5.3. In this figure, the ventricular enlargement can clearly be seen on the right hand image of a monozygotic twin with schizophrenia. On the left is the normal brain of the other twin who did not develop schizophrenia.

Damage to the cerebral cortex

We saw earlier that the characteristic features of schizophrenia are a mixture of positive symptoms and negative symptoms. It seems obvious, therefore, to ask if the brain damage we see provides us with clues as to why these symptoms occur. Much of the available

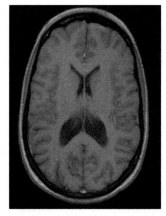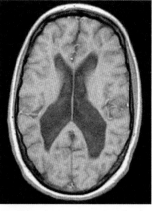

Fig. 5.3 An MRI scan of ventricular size in MZ twins. The healthy twin is seen on the left and the schizophrenic twin with enlarged ventricles is seen on the right.

data come from post-mortem examinations and from brain scans, particularly **MRI scans** (see *Thinking scientifically* on page 261).

One area of the brain that shows significant damage is one at the front called the dorsolateral prefrontal cortex. It resides in the frontal lobe (see Fig. 5.4). The damage appears to be to the supporting cells of the brain rather than to the neurons themselves (Gur et al., 2000) and the result is a reduction in the ability to solve problems and organise thoughts. Recent evidence by Ito et al. (2012) has suggested that this region of the brain might also be involved in deception and the perception of lies, things that a person with schizophrenia finds difficult to interpret.

Another cortical region that is damaged in schizophrenia is the primary visual area in the occipital lobe (see Fig. 5.4). Jibiki et al. (1991) showed that the activity in this part of the brain is disrupted, leading to the incorrect processing of visual stimuli. It is not difficult to see that visual misperceptions can result in the improper interpretation of such things as facial and emotional expressions and gestures, and these can result in deluded thinking.

The hallucinations suffered by a schizophrenic are almost always auditory, and we can trace these to brain damage too. Our brain auditory system allows for the interpretation of speech, and areas such as Wernicke's area (see Fig. 5.4) play an important role in speech comprehension. In addition, it seems we have two separate speech recognition systems. One is the 'what' system and determines the content of the speech. The other is the 'where' system and is involved in distinguishing internal speech from external speech. When you internally talk to yourself (for example, while thinking through a problem) you recognize this as being internal speech in your own voice. Plaze et al. (2011) have suggested that disruption to this 'where' system could lead to a person perceiving their own internal speech as coming from an outside person. This, then, would be an auditory hallucination. Of course, this alone does not explain why these hallucinations can be malicious, but if we add this to the disordered thinking and the possible lack of facial and emotional perception then a more complete picture might start to emerge.

Key terms

MRI scan: magnetic resonance imaging that provides a static image of the inside of the brain.

SCHIZOPHRENIA

BASAL GANGLIA

Involved in movement and emotions and in integrating sensory information. Abnormal functioning in schizophrenia is thought to contribute to paranoia and hallucinations. (Excessive blockade of dopamine receptors in the basal ganglia by traditional antipsychotic medicines leads to motor side effects.)

AUDITORY SYSTEM

Enables humans to hear and understand speech. In schizophrenia, overactivity of the speech area (called Wernicke's area) can create auditory hallucinations — the illusion that internally generated thoughts are real voices coming from the outside.

OCCIPITAL LOBE

Processes information about the visual world. People with schizophrenia rarely have full-blown visual hallucinations but disturbances in this area contribute to such difficulties as interpreting complex images, recognizing motion, and reading emotions on others' faces.

FRONTAL LOBE

Critical to problem solving, insight and other high-level reasoning. Perturbations in schizophrenia lead to difficulty in planning actions and organizing thoughts.

LIMBIC SYSTEM

Involved in emotion. Disturbances are thought to contribute to the agitation frequently seen in schizophrenia.

HIPPOCAMPUS

Mediates learning and memory formation, intertwined functions that are impaired in schizophrenia.

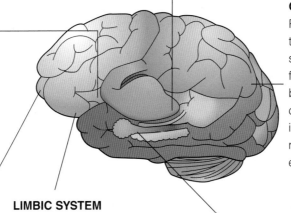

Fig. 5.4 Some of the areas of the brain affected by schizophrenia.

KEY STUDY: WHERE DO AUDITORY HALLUCINATIONS COME FROM?

In order to investigate the area of the brain that gives rise to auditory hallucinations, Plaze et al. (2011) used MRI brain imaging. They gathered MRI scans of 45 patients with schizophrenia and 20 control participants. The patients were split into two groups; those who heard hallucinations internally, as though coming from within their own heads, and those who heard hallucinations externally, as though the words were being spoken to them by someone else. They found differences in the MRI images in a region of the brain called the right temperoparietal junction. This region is known as the 'where' region of normal auditory processing. The images were then compared to those of the healthy controls. The researchers found a decrease in white matter (these are fibres that carry messages) for those who heard the hallucinations externally and an increase in white matter for those who heard them internally. It would thus appear that the way in which this region of the brain develops determines whether the hallucinations are perceived as originating from inside or outside the person's own body.

The use of imaging techniques has rapidly advanced our knowledge of how the brain works and why it sometimes does not. The MRI technique involves using radio waves and magnetic fields in order to construct a 3D image of the region being scanned (like the one seen earlier in Fig. 5.3). It is better than an X-ray because the quality of the image is so much better. For a complex disorder like schizophrenia it has an advantage over other methodologies in that a number of different brain regions can be examined at once. As it is a non-invasive technique, it has the added benefit of being able to be used with humans. Until imaging techniques were available we were left either to use animal models (not ideal for a disorder like schizophrenia) or to examine the brain post-mortem once it had been removed from the skull. However, schizophrenia has a young age of onset and is not a disorder that kills, so the time difference between developing the disorder and death renders a post-mortem examination of the brain almost useless, making the MRI scan much more useful. The more recent addition of fMRI (f standing for functional) allows us to see this clear 3D image change in real time rather than just being a snapshot of the brain at one moment.

Evaluating the evidence of the brain areas associated with schizophrenia

We should not be surprised that so many areas of the brain have been implicated in schizophrenia as we know that the condition is made up of multiple symptoms. We are starting to piece together the relationship between brain damage in one region and the behavioural deficits that may result from it. However, it is always difficult to decide whether brain damage causes or is the result of altered behaviour. It is possible that looking at brain areas is not refined enough to tell us what causes schizophrenia, so we will turn now to a look at the more intricate workings of the schizophrenic brain.

Neurotransmitter-related causes of schizophrenia

Our final look at biological explanations of schizophrenia takes us to the inner workings of the brain. The chemicals that are released when a neuron fires are called **neurotransmitter substances** and there are a number of different ones in the brain. Three key neurotransmitters have been implicated in schizophrenia and these are dopamine, glutamate and serotonin.

The dopamine hypothesis of schizophrenia

Dopamine is active in several areas in the brain and it is its over-activity in regions like the limbic system (see Fig. 5.4) that is linked to schizophrenia. There have been three versions of the dopamine hypothesis and it is worth looking at how each refinement emerged.

The first suggestion that dopamine was involved in schizophrenia came as a result of analysing how antipsychotic drugs worked. The drugs were first discovered in 1952, but it was not until ten years later that Carlsson and Lindqvist (1963) worked out that the drugs were reducing the effectiveness of dopamine in the brain. It was the addition of knowledge about how a recreational drug,

Key terms

Neurotransmitter substance: a chemical that is released from neurons when they fire. The neurotransmitter travels across a very small gap and attaches to a receptor on the next neuron to make a small effect on whether or not that next neuron fires.

Dopamine: a neurotransmitter substance thought to be overproduced in schizophrenia, and is believed to be one of the main reasons for the positive symptoms.

SCHIZOPHRENIA

amphetamine, works that pointed to dopamine being a candidate for schizophrenia. Amphetamines can produce psychotic symptoms similar to those seen in schizophrenia and a drug that reduced these symptoms, reserpine, was known to reduce the activity of dopamine. Putting all of this information together, researchers realized that if amphetamines induce psychosis by increasing dopamine activity and antipsychotic medicine reduces dopamine activity, then an increase in dopamine must be responsible for the psychotic symptoms in schizophrenia.

The second dopamine hypothesis was a refinement made in 1991. Like all neurotransmitters, dopamine is released from one neuron and then needs a specialised receptor on the receiving neuron for it to have its effect. There are several different receptors for dopamine and interest had focused on the one called the D_2 receptor. However, Davis et al. (1991) pointed out that in the prefrontal cortex (an area we looked at earlier – see Fig. 5.4) there are only D_1 receptors so it cannot be only D_2 receptors that are involved in schizophrenia. In addition, the activity of dopamine in this region seemed to be low rather than high. This gave Davis et al. the idea that reduced dopamine in frontal parts of the brain might be causing the negative symptoms, while increased dopamine in other regions was causing the positive symptoms. We are currently on the third version of the dopamine hypothesis, that has seen refinements that are beyond the scope of this text.

The glutamate hypothesis of schizophrenia

Glutamate is a major excitatory neurotransmitter in the brain, which means that it acts to encourage other neurons to fire. The receptor for glutamate (called the NMDA receptor) is present in regions of the brain that are linked to learning, attention and memory (all functions that are disrupted in schizophrenia). Since glutamate activity has been shown to be reduced in schizophrenics (Kim et al., 1980), this would fit with a reduced excitation in certain regions of the brain. The reduction seems to be linked to the NMDA receptors working less well than they should. Glutamate also acts to reduce dopamine activity in other areas of the brain. If glutamate activity is reduced then this paves the way for the increase in dopamine levels that we considered earlier.

The link between glutamate receptor malfunction and schizophrenia can also account for the timing of the onset of schizophrenia. The reduced NMDA functioning is present from birth but it becomes particularly problematic in puberty and adolescence, when there are major developmental changes that occur in the brain. It would appear, then, that the disruption to normal glutamate functioning leads to many of the deficits seen in schizophrenia.

ACTIVITY 5.4

List as many areas of the brain that you can that involve the activity of dopamine and glutamate. Which of these may play a role in schizophrenia?

The role of serotonin in schizophrenia

We have not yet considered one region of the brain identified in Fig. 5.4, namely the basal ganglia. In post-mortem analyses of schizophrenics, this region has been shown to have elevated levels of another neurotransmitter, serotonin. Serotonin plays a role in inhibiting the activity of dopamine in this part of the brain so an over-activity of serotonin here will depress the normal level of dopamine. Whereas elsewhere there is elevated dopamine functioning leading to positive symptoms, here the lower level of dopamine functioning can explain some of the negative symptoms.

The increase in serotonin in the basal ganglia also has its own effects. This region of the brain is involved in the integration of sensory information and is also involved in emotion processing. Disruptions to serotonin induced by drugs like lysergic acid diethylamide (LSD) have been shown to lead to hallucinations and paranoia, both symptoms of schizophrenia.

EXAMPLE EXAM QUESTION

Discuss biological explanations of schizophrenia. (16 marks)

Evaluating the neurotransmitter role in schizophrenia

It is fair to say that many of the positive symptoms seen in schizophrenia are the result of excessive dopamine activity – this supports the dopamine hypothesis of schizophrenia. However, it is also clear that this is not the whole story and that disruptions to other neurotransmitter substances, such as glutamate and serotonin, play an important role in both regulating the levels of dopamine and in producing some of the symptoms directly. In a very recent journal article (Pocklington et al., 2015), yet another major neurotransmitter called gamma aminobutyric acid (GABA) has also been implicated in schizophrenia, so the story is not yet complete. What is certain is that there are many systems of the brain that are affected in schizophrenia and they all contribute to the many and diverse symptoms that are displayed by the schizophrenic.

Exam hint

This question requires a discussion of at least two explanations. This means that you will need to keep your description of the explanations to a minimum (as this would be AO1) and move quickly into using the research evidence to either support or refute an explanation. Remember to evaluate the explanations by using research evidence to go beyond elaboration of the descriptions. You will need to do more than simply describe studies and should use evidence to give a critical evaluation of each explanation. Remember that critical is not the same as criticise – a critical analysis can be both positive as well as negative.

KEY POINTS

- Family, twin and adoption studies have all been used to explore the degree to which schizophrenia is genetically inherited.
- Genetic studies point to there being a genetic component to schizophrenia.
- Genetic inheritance is not the sole cause of schizophrenia.
- Damage to several regions of the brain has been correlated with schizophrenia, particularly the prefrontal cortex.
- Dopamine excess has been a frontrunner as a cause of the positive symptoms of schizophrenia.
- Glutamate and serotonin are also strongly implicated to have a role in schizophrenia.

Psychological explanations of schizophrenia

There are many areas of psychological explanation in relation to schizophrenia. Some try to explain the problems that a schizophrenic has in facing daily life and others try to explain how and why the symptoms developed. Some theories oppose the biological explanations and some work together with them. In this topic we will concentrate on two explanations: family and cognitive.

Family dysfunction explanations

Although Freud had little to say about any particular form of psychosis, many of the family-oriented theories of schizophrenia derive from his ideas about the id, ego and superego. Therefore, they are often more generally labelled as **psychodynamic** explanations. The ones we will consider here relate to family problems. We will look at the schizophrenogenic mother hypothesis, and some of the more general ideas about family dysfunction. Freud's own view of what we would now call schizophrenia was that it was caused by an imbalance of the id, ego and superego, but that such patients were not treatable through psychodynamic therapies. This is interesting in light of some of the psychodynamic treatments we will consider later in the chapter.

The schizophrenogenic mother hypothesis

This hypothesis was first introduced by Fromm-Reichmann in 1948 and put the blame for schizophrenia firmly on the mother's shoulders. Fromm-Reichmann argued that even though there had to be some genetic potential for a person to develop schizophrenia, the trigger was a domineering mother. Much of the supporting evidence was gained from studies that had looked at the families of schizophrenics and found the mother to be a domineering character within the family home (for example, Lidz and Lidz, 1949). For example, a mother might micromanage her child and refuse to acknowledge their independence. However, such studies can only establish correlations, so it is difficult to tell whether the mother simply became domineering as a response to the schizophrenic behaviour of the adolescent. Furthermore, we must appreciate that within family dynamics of the time (father at work and mother at home), the father would most likely have had much less interaction with the child.

By the 1970s, the focus was moving away from the mother and out towards the wider family. It was becoming evident that, from some of the studies looking at communication styles within families, the dominance in families with a schizophrenic child was coming from the father rather than the mother. However, results across studies were inconsistent, depending on which other factors were also being looked at in a study. So, for example, differences were found between families designated as low risk (less likely for the child to develop schizophrenia) and those designated as high risk, with mothers being dominant in high-risk families. What does start to become very clear is that there are many more family factors that are important in whether or not a child will develop schizophrenia and the notion of a schizophrenogenic mother being to blame for schizophrenia is, thankfully, no longer considered to be a viable explanation.

Family dysfunction

The two ideas we have considered so far are not the only ones that propose some kind of **family dysfunction** as the root of the expression of schizophrenic behaviours. A common theme that emerges is the difficulty in communication that is common to most schizophrenics. Wynne and Singer (1963) conducted a study involving 114 families, including ones where one sibling had schizophrenia. They used the **Rorschach inkblot** test (see Fig. 5.5) to examine how the family came to an agreement about what the figure represented. The dynamics of those families with a schizophrenic offspring were very different to the other families, in that the parents of the schizophrenic both showed high **communication deviance** scores. In other words, both parents were shown to use confusing and contradictory modes of communication. Furthermore, in families where only one parent showed communication deviance, the offspring was described as borderline schizophrenic. It also seemed to be the case that if the parents showed a communication deviance this was because they, too, had a predisposition to schizophrenia but one that was not expressed clinically (Subotnik et al., 2002). From a recent meta-analysis by de Sousa et al. (2013) it is clear that the link between communication deviance and schizophrenia has been confirmed across numerous studies. However, critics have said that without the use of properly conducted longitudinal studies, it would not be possible to confirm that communication deviance leads to schizophrenia.

Expressed emotion

One aspect of communication that has been extensively researched is that of **expressed emotion (EE)**. This refers to the hostile attitude that is often shown by relatives of a person with schizophrenia. A number of studies have indicated that EE is a major cause of relapse when patients return home after a period in hospital following a psychotic episode. For example, Brown et al. (1972) found that there were a number of families in which relatives showed EE towards the person with schizophrenia, even though there was no expressed emotion in the other direction.

EE has also been studied cross-culturally by Nomura et al. (2005). Their study not only compared the effect of EE in England and Japan, but is also interesting because they looked at the EE of the carers of schizophrenics rather than that of their relatives. The sample of carers investigated were 20 in each country. It was found that the frequency of critical comments was much higher among the English carers than among the Japanese carers. The authors argue that the very foundation of the two cultures is different and that this leads to differing perspectives on family relationships. They stated that, 'the Japanese family system, which is based on the collective group membership of a household and restricts each member's thought and behaviour, differs from English family system, which places

Fig. 5.5 An example of a Rorschach inkblot.

more emphasis on the relationships between individuals. Japanese people tend to be reserved in displaying their emotions in public and reluctant to overtly criticize their relatives, which probably affected a broad spectrum of EE responses in the Japanese samples.' This research clearly indicates that EE is less likely to play a role in schizophrenia within collectivist cultures.

KEY STUDY: SUBOTNIK ET AL. (2002)

Subotnik et al. were interested in examining the parents of patients who had been diagnosed with schizophrenia. There were three phases to the project and each phase examined around 100 biological parents of schizophrenic patients. The participants were interviewed to establish details about their family history, particularly whether or not there was a family history of schizophrenia. One of the tasks used to determine communication deviance was the Thematic Apperception Test (see Fig. 5.6). This test involves a person being given a card with a picture on it. The task is to make up a story saying what is occurring, what leads up to the scene depicted, how the characters are thinking and feeling and how the story might end. Scoring provides a measure of whether or not a communication deviance is being displayed.

The results showed that in families with a history of schizophrenia or related disorders, communication deviance was seen in mothers, but not in fathers. However, the personal history of the parent (whether or not they themselves had schizophrenia or a related disorder) had no bearing on the degree of communication deviance shown. The authors concluded that parents (especially mothers) can carry the gene or genes that predispose a person to developing schizophrenia without showing any obvious psychotic signs themselves. By looking at communication deviance scores in parents, we might be alerted to the potential development of schizophrenia in their offspring and could use this information to take preventative action (see the use of the drug olanzapine later in this chapter).

Fig. 5.6 The Thematic Apperception Test

The Subotnik et al. study used a combination of interviews and experimental tests to establish relationships between different sources of evidence. The tests gave the researchers information about whether or not a parent had a communication deviance. However, it was the information gained from the interviews about personal history that enabled the authors to explain why there were differences in communication deviance between parents. The approach of using both qualitative and quantitative approaches at the same time is called a **mixed methods approach**.

EXAMPLE EXAM QUESTION

Sarah is 19 and living at home. All through her teenage years she has had a difficult relationship with her immediate family and a year ago she suffered her first psychotic episode. While she has been out of hospital for several months, relationships within the family are tense and she often finds herself in arguments, especially with her mother. Most of these arguments are started by her misunderstanding something that has been said.

Briefly describe a psychological explanation that accounts for Sarah's situation. (2 marks)

Key term

Mixed methods approach: combines quantitative methods (e.g. experiments) with qualitative methods (e.g. interviews) within a single study.

Exam hint

The easiest explanation to use here is expressed emotion. As this is only a two-mark question you need to state that and then briefly explain what the term means.

Evaluating family explanations

There is some evidence to support the early family theories of schizophrenia, but much of the data are anecdotal and were not collected under proper scientific conditions. The theories have a certain degree of face validity. However, it is difficult to pinpoint whether these problems are causal or consequential. Either way, the family theories provide a more holistic approach to explaining schizophrenia than we saw with the biological explanations.

Research methods link

For more about face validity see page 43.

Link

For more information about holism, see page 106 of Chapter 1, *Issues and debates in psychology*.

ACTIVITY 5.5

Explore the characteristics of a dysfunctional family. Why might it be difficult to distinguish between a normal family with an unruly adolescent and a dysfunctional family with a schizophrenic?

Cognitive explanations of schizophrenia

It is suggested by the family explanations that schizophrenics might suffer from problems with their language processing. We can explore this a little further here and combine this with a look at other cognitive functions. In particular, it is useful to examine a schizophrenic's ability to process perceptual information (particularly face perception) together with their attention, memory and reasoning abilities. We will start with the schizophrenic's ability to comprehend the visual information coming in from the environment.

Perception deficits

The most interesting work that has been done in the field of perception has looked at face perception. To properly perceive a person's face we must process feature information (for example,

SCHIZOPHRENIA

Shin et al. set out to investigate whether or not schizophrenics have problems with configuration in facial recognition. They took 20 patients with a mean age of 26.8 and 20 age-matched healthy controls with a mean age of 25.6 and gave them a recognition memory test using the stimuli presented in Fig. 5.7.

- Set A: the configurational set – the faces differed by having the eyes of one face further apart or the distance between the nose and the mouth changed.
- Set B: the featural set – the faces differed by having one feature changed (for example, the eyes were from a different face).
- Set C: the control set – chairs were presented that might differ in features.

On each trial, two photos were presented for one second and the person was asked to say whether the two faces were the same or different. A total of 200 trials were presented. The results showed that even though the patients were poor at all tasks compared to the controls, they were particularly poor at recognizing configurational changes compared to featural changes. The authors claim that this deficit can explain the high levels of social dysfunction seen in patients with schizophrenia (see later in the chapter).

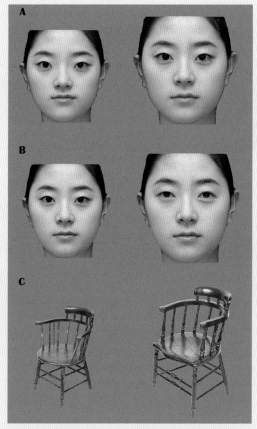

Fig. 5.7 Image sets used by Shin et al. (2008). Set A shows configurational differences, Set B featural differences, and Set C is a control set.

eyes, nose, mouth), specific features (whose eyes, nose, mouth) and configuration (for example, the distance between the eyes and the gap between the nose and the mouth). Shin et al. (2008) showed that schizophrenics were poor with configuration information. The importance of this is that it is the configuration information that tells us about the expression on a face. Not being able to properly interpret a person's facial expression can lead to a misperception of the person's intent and this seems to be precisely what happens in schizophrenia.

THINKING SCIENTIFICALLY: MATCHED CONTROL GROUPS

You will have read in many studies that control groups are used. These usually contain participants who are not exposed to the experimental variables and therefore can act as a comparison with the experimental group(s). In many areas of research it is important that the control group is matched to the experimental group on one or more factors. In studies of schizophrenia, it is important to use age-matched controls because we know that schizophrenia is sensitive to age, especially in the years surrounding the typical age of onset. In the Shin et al. study it was important that participant age did not interfere with the findings as a confounding variable. By making sure that the average age of the participants was within a small range, they ensured that any findings would be due to differences in recognition memory alone.

A number of studies have found that schizophrenics do poorly on tasks that require an appreciation of a facial emotional expression. When schizophrenics are asked to make judgements about the emotional expression of a face they often struggle to accurately describe the emotion being displayed (Ekman and Friesen, 1978). Similarly, they also struggle to state whether two faces presented side by side have the same or different emotional expressions. These results are probably due to the fact that schizophrenics tend to scan faces (using featural cues) rather than study them for the detail (using configurational cues) that would reveal an emotional expression.

Memory deficits

A well-evidenced finding of memory deficits in schizophrenics comes from **working memory**. Lee and Park (2005) have suggested that the poor perceptual processing could lead to poor encoding of material into working memory and, hence, a poor working memory. Furthermore, all parts of the working-memory system appear to be affected roughly equally, and evidence exists to show deficits in spatial working memory and the central executive. Most recently, the deficits in working memory have been linked to genetically inherited changes.

It is not just working memory that is affected in schizophrenia – the general memory of schizophrenics is also poor. They perform poorly on simple recall and recognition tasks and they underperform on a variety of long-term memory tasks. For example, in tests carried out by Leeson et al. (2010) they performed worse than controls on a task that required them to recall 15 nouns. Tests of memory were carried out immediately, after a distractor task, and then again after 25 minutes, and performances were poor on all three. Episodic and semantic memory are also both impaired and this collection of deficits has led some researchers to argue that the term schizophrenic amnesia should be used.

Research methods link

To review confounding variables, see page 12.

Key term

Working memory: used to hold information while it is being processed by other systems such as the language or reasoning systems.

Link

To review the working memory model, see pages 125–129 of Book 1.

SCHIZOPHRENIA

Reasoning deficits

As far as reasoning is concerned, the schizophrenic has two problems that give rise to **delusional thinking**. The first is having the deluded thoughts in the first place, but the second is a failure to reject such thoughts as beyond reality. In other words, it is one thing to have the thought that your best friend is trying to poison you, but it is quite another to then believe that the thought is true. Three different explanations for this latter component have been proposed. One is the 'jumping to conclusions' hypothesis, whereby a deluded person is more likely to make a more hasty decision about something than a non-deluded person. Garety et al. (2005) presented people with two jars of beads, both containing the same two colours of beads. The researchers said that in one jar two-thirds of the beads were colour A, and in the other jar two-thirds were colour B. On each trial they presented a bead from just one jar (the choice was not seen by the participant). Delusional patients were hastier in deciding that they knew which jar the beads were being drawn from. A second explanation for delusional thinking is an extreme attribution bias, in which the person is more likely to attribute a negative outcome to an external source and usually that source is a person. The final explanation is a lack of Theory of Mind. Theory of Mind (ToM) is the ability to recognize that other people may not hold the same thoughts, beliefs and feelings as you. Poor ToM is quite common in schizophrenics. In fact, there seems to be a relationship between the severity of the schizophrenia and the degree of deficit in ToM. This would seem to be a genetically inherited problem as there is a lower level of ToM in relatives of schizophrenics than in the rest of the population (Janssen et al., 2003). A lack of this ability might be the cause of believing delusional thoughts to be true.

Language deficits

The last of the cognitive explanations we will consider here is the idea that schizophrenics have poor language skills. According to some researchers (for example, Crow, 1997), it is the evolution of language that gave rise to the possibility of schizophrenia in the first place, referred to as the speciation hypothesis. Schizophrenics seem to have some parts of their language ability that are impaired while other aspects are perfectly normal. Many schizophrenics suffer from a language output impairment (as opposed to language comprehension) in terms of fluency, but the fluency problem seems only to be true of spoken language and not of written language. This might be because it is possible to write slowly (so the fluency deficit is not so easily detected), whereas speaking slowly will more obviously indicate a fluency deficiency. For many schizophrenics there is also a language comprehension deficit, especially in being able to relate the order of words in a sentence to the agents and recipients of actions. For example, you will understand the following sentence:

The team coach, whom the children liked a lot, was good at getting the best out of the players.

However, a person with schizophrenia may struggle to work out the middle part of the sentence (*whom the children liked a lot*). It is worth noting that the language deficits are easy to spot before the person has their first schizophrenic episode. While this alone would not indicate schizophrenia, it can be used alongside other markers to indicate those who may be at high risk of developing schizophrenia.

Evaluating cognitive explanations

It is clear that a lot of cognitive systems are impaired in schizophrenia. There is good evidence to support the dysfunction of nearly all areas of cognition. However, it is difficult to determine which of these is a cause of schizophrenia, and which is a consequence. Furthermore, the problems with cognition that have been identified are a partially reductionist explanation: on the one hand, a cognitive explanation reduces a complex disorder to a series of system impairments; on the other hand, it is itself merely the consequence of damage to the brain systems that serve these cognitive processes. Nevertheless, a coherent pattern of deficits is emerging and knowledge of these can form the basis of effective treatments. They can also explain other aspects of the characteristic behaviours of schizophrenia, such as the difficulties schizophrenics have managing social situations.

Link

For more information about reductionism see page 102 of Chapter 1, *Issues and debates in psychology*.

ACTIVITY 5.6

Consider how a combination of cognitive and family factors might lead to an explanation of the symptoms of schizophrenia. Which symptoms are easy to explain using these factors and which are hard to explain?

Evaluating psychological explanations

Psychological explanations of schizophrenia span a wide range of psychological perspectives. Some, like cognitive theories, are attempts to explain the consequences of underlying biological abnormalities. Others, like the family explanations, consider that there are non-biological causes of schizophrenia. There are also other explanations, such as social explanations, that take a different perspective and try to explain how schizophrenia affects the quality of life of the schizophrenic but also attempt to explain a role for the social environment in the development of symptoms. In many ways, these social theories point out some of the limitations of both family dysfunction and cognitive explanations of schizophrenia. For example, theories about faulty social perception show how schizophrenics can misinterpret the social world around them, and this provides an alternative view on how characteristics like a persecution delusion might emerge.

Taken together, the various theories of schizophrenia we have concentrated on here provide an incomplete picture – they are somewhat better at explaining the positive symptoms than the negative ones. Family dysfunction gives us some insight into how schizophrenia might emerge gradually from cognitive shortcomings that are evident from the schizophrenic's early years. These then come to a head with the first schizophrenic episode around the late teenage years or a little later.

Exam hint

You should briefly define what the term delusional thinking means and then you should provide a brief account of how one cognitive explanation would explain theory. An effective approach would be to use a specific delusion, e.g. paranoid, as an example.

EXAMPLE EXAM QUESTION

Briefly outline **one** cognitive explanation for the delusions seen in some people diagnosed with schizophrenia. (4 marks)

KEY POINTS

- There are many psychological explanations of schizophrenia, two of the main ones being family dysfunction and cognitive deficits.
- Family dysfunction has been derived from psychodynamic explanations that include notions like the schizophrenogenic mother and double bind.
- Family dysfunction argues that schizophrenia stems from communication deviance within the home .
- Cognitive deficits covering the whole range of cognitive processes have been suggested as causes of schizophrenia.
- These cognitive deficits include perception, attention, memory, reasoning and language.
- In evaluating psychological explanations of schizophrenia we must be mindful of other psychological arguments that come from areas like social psychology.

Drug therapy

Key term

Antipsychotics: drugs that are used to treat psychosis. These drugs usually target the positive symptoms of schizophrenia.

In this topic we will look at the drugs that have been developed to treat schizophrenia. While they are not the only form of biological treatment available, they are most definitely the first choice for psychiatrists. Whilst drug therapies are important, should be noted that around 30% of patients are resistant to drug therapy. The drugs are referred to as **antipsychotics**, as treating the psychosis of schizophrenia was originally the primary aim of them. The antipsychotics that have been developed have changed over time and they are now distinguishable into two separate types. The first are the older, original drugs and are referred to as the typical antipsychotics (also known as first-generation antipsychotics). The newer drugs are referred to as the atypical antipsychotics (also known as second-generation antipsychotics). Before discussing these, let us briefly consider how antipsychotics were first discovered.

The first antipsychotic drugs were discovered purely by a series of chance findings as a result of the development of a drug for a completely different purpose. This drug was chlorpromazine and in the early 1950s it was being developed as an antihistamine (the sort of drug you take in order to combat allergies like hay fever). One of the effects found from using the drug was that it lowered body temperature. The physician Henri Laborit thought this might be a useful effect during surgery so administered it alongside anaesthetic. Some of the effects seen in patients were calming, and in 1952 chlorpromazine was used on a manic patient, with the result that they were sent home from hospital after just three weeks. A clinical trial by Deniker and Delay later that year saw patients improve from their positive symptoms. By 1955, the drug was in full-scale production and was being favoured over the other biological treatments of the time, such as electroconvulsive therapy and brain surgery. Electroconvulsive therapy involved delivering large electrical shocks to the brain, which was found to have a pacifying effect on the patient. Brain surgery usually involved severing the connection between the frontal lobes and the rest of the brain. It, too, had a pacifying effect on the patient. However, neither was a solution that left the patient better able to function in the world.

Typical antipsychotics

The typical antipsychotics are so named because they were the first type of antipsychotic drug to be produced. As we shall see, they are effective in treating the positive symptoms of psychosis (delusions, disordered thinking and hallucinations) and some are effective in treating negative symptoms (blunted affect and withdrawal). However, they come at a price, which is that they all have severe side effects associated with them.

Chlorpromazine

When chlorpromazine (Fig. 5.8) was first discovered as an antipsychotic, nobody knew why it worked. They just knew that it was very effective in reducing the symptoms of psychosis, and it still remains an effective treatment today (Adams et al., 2005 – see the *Key study* below). We now know that the drug works by reducing the effect of dopamine at the dopamine receptors by physically blocking the receptors. However, it does so to almost all of the different types of dopamine receptor so it is not specific to those that are involved in schizophrenia. It also has an effect on a lot of other neurotransmitter systems. This leads to chlorpromazine having a number of side effects, as we shall see shortly.

Fig. 5.8 Chlorpromazine

As we saw in the section on biological explanations, a major hypothesis concerning the cause of schizophrenia is that it is the result of an excess of dopamine release. By blocking some of the dopamine receptors, chlorpromazine reduces the effect of this excessive dopamine release without actually reducing the amount of dopamine that is released. However, its effectiveness in doing this is fairly low, so we say that the drug has low **potency**. This means that a patient needs to take a high dose of the drug for it to work. If we now examine the side effects we can see why this is a problem.

Side effects of chlorpromazine

Chlorpromazine works on a number of other systems alongside the dopamine system. It blocks serotonin receptors and, while this leads to an anti-anxiety (anxiolytic) effect, it increases the chances of producing depression. The drug also works on acetylcholine receptors and noradrenaline receptors. The former leads to a dry mouth and the latter leads to lowered blood pressure (called hypotension). These side effects alone would be enough to cause concern, but chlorpromazine also comes with a massive risk to motor functions (the control of movement). Patients often report dystonia (a disorder that causes twisted and abnormal postures) that might be maintained for long periods of time. Another possible movement side effect is Parkinsonism. This is where a patient shows symptoms similar to those seen in Parkinson's disease (tremors [involuntary shaking], slow movement and stiff muscles). As we know these symptoms to be consequences of too little dopamine in certain parts of the brain, we can presume that they are the result of chlorpromazine reducing dopamine levels all over the brain.

KEY STUDY: ADAMS ET AL. (2005)

Adams et al. were interested in just how effective chlorpromazine is as an antipsychotic. It is the drug of choice all over the world, irrespective of the fact that there are a number of newer drugs and that chlorpromazine has some very severe side effects. It is a very cheap drug to produce, but that alone would not explain its widespread use in more affluent countries. Adams et al. carried out a systematic review of the published articles on chlorpromazine in order to establish if the drug should continue to be used as a treatment. While there are a number of qualitative articles about chlorpromazine, the authors only included studies in which there had been proper control procedures applied. Fifty articles were included in the review after several hundred had been rejected. The outcome of the review was that, even after 50 years, chlorpromazine comes out as an effective drug. It has a global positive effect on symptoms and, as a result, it is likely that schizophrenics will continue to take the drug. This is despite some very severe adverse side effects. The review concluded by recommending the continued use of chlorpromazine, especially in those countries that could not afford to use the more expensive new drugs on the market.

THINKING SCIENTIFICALLY: THE SYSTEMATIC REVIEW

The systematic review is a very powerful method of obtaining an overview of research in an area. Different studies might use slightly differing methods or techniques that make comparing one study with another difficult. This is especially the case when the participants are from a clinical population, as there are often too many variables to control for (for example, length of time showing symptoms, severity of symptoms, age, etc.). The systematic review analyses a large body of published research. It sets out certain criteria that must be met for a study to be included (for example, it must have a control group) and then uses only those pieces of research to gather an overall picture of findings. In this way, it is possible to draw conclusions based on very large sample sizes and across a period of time. In the field of mental illness, the systematic review is a very valuable tool for understanding a complex disorder like schizophrenia.

Haloperidol

Haloperidol (Fig. 5.9) is a very different kind of drug to chlorpromazine and is around 50 times more potent. Like chlorpromazine, it was originally developed for use with surgery. Again, as with chlorpromazine, the antipsychotic effects of haloperidol were quickly recognized. It is particularly effective in combating hallucinations and delusions. Given the high potency of haloperidol, the effective dose will be quite low. This is just as well, as the side effects with this drug are severe. Haloperidol is cheap to produce, which makes it attractive, but its side effects, can make alternatives look like a better choice.

Side effects of haloperidol

Haloperidol can produce some very severe side effects. According to a number of websites, there are more than 20 common or very common side effects, and even more less common or rare ones noted for haloperidol. In particular, the movement side effects are problematic with this drug, much more so than with chlorpromazine. Of the very common and common side effects, five relate to severe motor conditions. Some are also the opposite effects of each other. For example, some patients report difficulty sleeping while others report sleepiness. The severity of the side effects often leads to the patient not taking their medication at all.

> **EXAMPLE EXAM QUESTION**
>
> Briefly describe the side effects of ONE typical antipsychotic. (2 marks)

Evaluating the typical antipsychotics

The typical antipsychotic are effective in treating the positive symptoms of schizophrenia but are much less effective at treating the negative symptoms. The main issue with them is the severity of the side effects, which can decrease **drug adherence**. This is especially a problem if the patient has delusions of persecution as they are likely to believe that the drugs are being prescribed to harm them, and the severity of the side effects will simply serve to enhance that belief. The likely outcome in this circumstance is that the patient will cease to continue to take the drug.

Atypical antipsychotics

We have come a long way since the 1950s in our knowledge of the biological underpinnings of schizophrenia. This has helped pharmacologists to develop more tailored drugs that attempt to maintain the potency of the antipsychotic effect while reducing the side effects. The atypical antipsychotics first came into use in the 1970s. Their main benefit was the reduction of side effects but they also had other advantages. In particular, they seemed to produce a faster positive outcome for those patients having their first psychotic episode. We will examine three of these newer drugs as they provide different kinds of effectiveness for different kinds of patients.

Clozapine

Clozapine (Fig. 5.10) is a very effective antipsychotic drug and was introduced in the 1970s. It has proved to be very useful in reducing positive symptoms with most patients, but some are resistant to treatment with this drug. While clozapine does not have any motor side effects there is one side effect that has made some psychiatrists reluctant to prescribe it. The side effect is called agranulocytosis and it causes a decrease in white blood cells. In some patients this decrease can be large enough to result in death. Therefore, any psychiatrist prescribing clozapine will insist that the patient has regular blood tests to catch any decrease in their white blood cell count before it

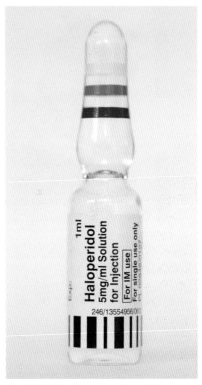

Fig. 5.9 While chlorpromazine is delivered as a pill, haloperidol can be usefully used as an injection in people who cannot reliably take the oral form.

Key term

Drug adherence: the degree to which a patient will continue to take a drug. Adherence is a particular problem for schizophrenics, who suffer delusions of persecution.

SCHIZOPHRENIA

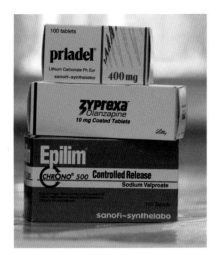

Fig. 5.10 Clozapine

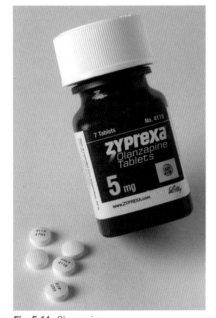

Fig. 5.11 Olanzapine

Key term

Placebo: a simulated treatment that is not a real treatment. For example, if the treatment is in pill form then the placebo might be a sugar pill that is made to look like the real pill.

gets to dangerous levels. Its continued use is because of its greater effectiveness than other drugs (Essali et al., 2009).

Olanzapine

Olanzapine (Fig. 5.11) is a drug that is only prescribed very early in a patient's experience of schizophrenia. It is extremely effective on both positive and negative symptoms but is never used long term. This is because the drug causes obesity and/or diabetes in many patients if used for any extended period. However, the drug has also been found to be useful in prodromal schizophrenia. A prodromal schizophrenic is a person who is at high risk of developing schizophrenia but who has not yet displayed any symptoms. One of these risk factors might be communication deviance in a parent where there is a family history of schizophrenia (see page 256). McGlashan et al. (2006) showed that those prodromal individuals who were given olanzapine had a lower incidence of developing schizophrenia than those who had not been given the drug.

KEY STUDY: MCGLASHAN ET AL. (2006)

While many drugs are available for treating psychosis when it occurs, some drugs have been looked at as potential drugs to prevent psychosis from developing. One such drug is olanzapine, and McGlashan et al. (2006) carried out a study to test this. The researchers carried out a study over six years that involved four separate American clinics. The study occurred in stages. The first stage was a screening stage to establish which people were at risk of developing a psychosis (prodromal patients). There then followed a year of treatment with olanzapine or a **placebo** in a double blind (see *Thinking scientifically* below) trial. This was followed by a year of no treatment. Of the 60 people originally recruited for the study, 27 dropped out during the treatment or placebo phase, leaving 19 people on the placebo and 14 on olanzapine. The number of people who became psychotic was measured and there were fewer in the olanzapine group (five people) than in the placebo group (11 people), although this was not a significant difference. However, the five in the olanzapine group developed their psychosis within the first four weeks of the treatment year, whereas the placebo group developed psychosis throughout the year. The researchers suggested that the five patients were already on the cusp of psychosis and so not really prodromal patients after all. The small sample size left at the end of the study makes it difficult to draw any firm conclusions about this. However, these results demonstrated that olanzapine is potentially effective in reducing the chances that a psychosis will develop. It would seem that for every five 'at risk' individuals that are treated, one would be prevented from developing psychosis. While that may not seem a lot, it is a start and is certainly of benefit to those individuals.

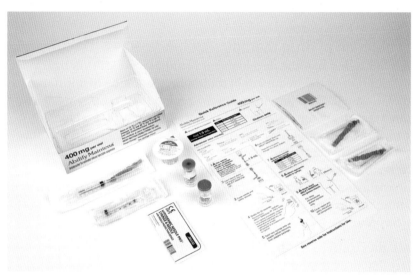

Fig. 5.12 Aripiprazole

Aripiprazole

Aripiprazole (Fig. 5.12) is a unique drug among the antipsychotics. Rather than blocking dopamine receptors, aripiprazole is what is called a partial agonist – it sits at receptor sites and promotes a partial response that is weaker than the effect of real dopamine. Hence, where dopamine activity is too high, it lessens the overall effect. In addition, aripiprazole has other benefits. Where there is too little dopamine in the brain, there will be receptor sites that have not been filled with a dopamine molecule. When aripiprazole attaches to these receptors it boosts the dopamine response. So it can help with overproduction of dopamine where that is occurring and underproduction where that is occurring. It might be for this reason that, unlike most of the other atypical antipsychotics, aripiprazole does not lead to obesity and has only rarely been associated with diabetes. That is not to say it does not have any side effects: patients do sometimes complain of nausea and insomnia.

Evaluating the atypical antipsychotics

The atypical antipsychotics are better than the typical antipsychotics, but this is mostly because of the reduction in side effects, especially the unwanted movement problems. However, they are not free from side effects, and obesity and diabetes are very real threats with long-term use. Having said that, these drugs are particularly useful for cases of first-episode schizophrenia and for pretreatment of those at risk of developing schizophrenia. The reduction of side effects helps here, as first-episode patients are often cautious of taking medication for fear that they might be being given with the intention of doing them some harm. So drug adherence is better than is seen with the typical antipsychotics. Another advantage of the typical antipsychotics is that they are more effective at treating the negative symptoms of schizophrenia.

> **ACTIVITY 5.7**
>
> If the atypical antipsychotics are so much better than the first-generation ones, discuss why we need different atypical antipsychotics.

Evaluation of drug therapy

It is fair to say that the development of antipsychotic drugs has revolutionized the treatment of schizophrenia. In the first instance, they elevated schizophrenia from the notion that it was a 'madness' that was largely untreatable without drastic measures and for which the only option was incarceration, to a treatable disorder that gave many patients an opportunity to lead a relatively normal life. Nevertheless, drug therapies assume that schizophrenia is biological in origin and so these treatments ignore any other causes. In this sense, they represent a reductionist perspective on the treatment of schizophrenia.

Another concern for the drug treatment of schizophrenia is the fact that drug treatments are mostly aimed at solving the problem of dopamine excess. However, we saw earlier in the chapter that dopamine is not the only neurotransmitter substance implicated in the symptoms of schizophrenia. In particular, none of the current drug treatments that work on the glutamate neurotransmitter system are being used to treat schizophrenia, though Javitt (2012) has suggested that those drugs that alter glutamate activity could be very effective against both positive and negative symptoms.

For both types of drug treatment we have seen that adherence is a problem. While this is more of a problem for typical antipsychotics, if one cannot get a schizophrenic to take their medication on a regular basis then it does not much matter which drug has been prescribed. It is here that we might see the most advantage to an interactionist approach and we will consider this at the end of the chapter, once we have looked at some of the psychological treatments that are available.

> **Exam hint**
>
> For each feature you choose you should explain why it is a strength/limitation and provide an example. The example could be in the form of a piece of evidence or it might be a contrast to alternative therapies.

> **EXAMPLE EXAM QUESTION**
>
> Briefly describe ONE strength and ONE limitation of drug therapy. (4 marks)

KEY POINTS

- Drugs used to treat schizophrenia are referred to as antipsychotics.
- Antipsychotics were accidentally discovered when looking for treatments for allergies.

- Chlorpromazine was the first antipsychotic to be used.

- Similar drugs soon followed and these are all called typical antipsychotics.

- The typical antipsychotics have very severe side effects, particularly motor effects.

- Newer drugs are referred to as atypical antipsychotics.

- These have fewer side effects and the side effects are less severe.

- Most antipsychotics are aimed at solving the dopamine problem so they only have limited efficacy.

Psychological therapies

The treatment and management of schizophrenia has drawn on a wide range of psychological approaches (see Silber, 2014 for a comprehensive overview). From the psychodynamic and social perspectives have emerged a selection of interventions that come under the general term of family therapy. From the cognitive and behavioural perspectives we have seen the emergence of cognitive behaviour therapy. Another behavioural approach that has been used to manage schizophrenia is token economy. Each of them represents an approach to treatment that derives from a particular set of beliefs about the causes of schizophrenia.

Family therapy

Some of the early approaches to treating schizophrenia considered treating the patient in isolation. **Family therapy** emerged once it was realised that the best way to help the schizophrenic was to involve at least the immediate family (parents and siblings) in the therapy process (See Figure 5.13). Family therapy proceeds as a number of distinctive stages. The first step in family therapy is a process called **psychoeducation** (this is also a therapy in its own right). Most of the family of a schizophrenic initially know little about the symptoms that their relative will be displaying and why they are behaving the way that they are. Knowing about what schizophrenia involves can help the family to understand what the person is going through and can lessen feelings of anger, shame and guilt that are often associated with discovering that a close relative has a mental illness. Once some of this knowledge has been established, the therapist will start to tackle the family stress levels and put the family in touch with sources of social support. Controlling stress levels is important to create a more tolerant environment for the schizophrenic. This is not an easy task as the family may be quite used to reacting angrily or aggressively to the schizophrenic's behaviours. The social support may emerge from within the family but can be facilitated by using the social support networks that exist. The purpose is to enable calm but frank discussion of the problems so that workable resolutions can be found. It is worth pointing out that this is of enormous value to the patient. With a better supported family environment, the schizophrenic is much more likely to engage in any personal therapy and to stick to the drug regimen that has been prescribed.

> **Key terms**
>
> **Family therapy:** includes all of the family or close relatives as part of the treatment.
>
> **Psychoeducation:** informing relatives about the nature of schizophrenia.

Fig. 5.13 Family therapy

Key terms

Behavioural family therapy: therapy that concentrates on problem-solving and communication skills and which involves the entire family.

Relatives group: therapy that only involves key members of the schizophrenic's family and may not include the patient themselves.

Exam hint

As this is only worth two marks, it is best to give a brief definition followed by just one example of an aspect of family therapy.

The last stage of family therapy involves trying to raise problem-solving skills and communication skills. This therapy can either be delivered to the whole family or to selected family members across a number of families. Some forms, for example, **behavioural family therapy (BFT)**, involve the family and include the patient. Others, such as **relatives group (RG)** therapy, just involve one or two key family members from a number of different families. Neither appears to be any more effective than the other (Montero et al., 2001) in terms of preventing relapse but there are some small differences between the two in favour of BFT (see the *Key study* below).

EXAMPLE EXAM QUESTION

Briefly describe what is meant by family therapy. (2 marks)

KEY STUDY: MONTERO ET AL. (2001)

There has been a lot of research undertaken on the value of various forms of family intervention but little has looked at these therapies from a cultural perspective. Different cultures have different approaches to how schizophrenia is perceived and treated (see *Thinking scientifically* below). Montero et al. decided to investigate whether BFT and RG therapy achieved the same or different outcomes in a group of patients from Valencia in Spain. One type of outcome measure is the relapse and readmission rate, and Montero et al. hypothesized that there would be no differences here. However, they also hypothesized that there would be differences on other outcome measures, such as social functioning, delusions and thought disorders.

There were 41 participants in the RG group and 46 participants in the BFT group. All patients were encouraged to continue with the medication they had been prescribed. Treatment consisted of two psychoeducation sessions followed by 12 months of either RG therapy or BFT. In both cases, relatives were seen weekly for the first six months, every two weeks for the next three months and monthly for the last three months. BFT was carried out in the patient's home with the whole family and concentrated on education about schizophrenia, training in communication skills and teaching problem-solving techniques. RG therapy included the patient in the initial psychoeducation sessions but after that, the patients were not present. Training took place at a health centre and consisted of teaching problem-solving techniques, training to reduce criticism, over-involvement and the amount of social contact between the patient and the relatives, and training to lower the expectations of the relatives.

The results showed that while there were no differences between the groups in terms of relapse and readmission rates, the BFT gave significantly better outcomes concerning social functioning and the delusions and disordered thinking. Montero et al. suggested that the inclusion of the patient was the reason for the improvements. Also, by involving the whole family, BFT reduces the stress in the environment as a whole rather than just that between the patient and the relatives who undergo RG (usually only consistently the mother).

As an evaluation of the study, the dropout rate for the study was quite high. Of the participants, 26 per cent did not attend any therapeutic sessions after the initial psychoeducation and only 60 per cent (52 families) completed the whole course of treatment. This is a small sample so the findings need to be treated with caution. Nevertheless, the study does show that within the context of Spanish family life, BFT provides significant additional advantages to RG as a treatment that sits alongside medication.

THINKING SCIENTIFICALLY: CULTURAL CONSIDERATIONS

When considering treatment of schizophrenia with antipsychotic drugs, it is easy to ignore cultural differences as being irrelevant to the effectiveness of the treatment. This is clearly not the case when we consider psychological treatments like family therapy. The way in which family therapy is delivered will be determined by the concept of the family within the local cultural setting and how this relates to the local concept of a mental illness. In the UK and the US, families will vary between those that have members living in close proximity to one another and those that are fragmented, with relatives living in different places. In other parts of the world there may be a more traditional family unit and closer ties between family members. This will affect the feasibility of BFT rather than RG therapy and will also play a role in the degree to which the family members want to be involved in helping. In addition, the westernized countries tend to view schizophrenia as a stigmatized mental illness, but in other parts of the world (for example, Africa and South America) it is treated with more compassion. According to Lefley (1990), patients in developing countries may function better simply because of the greater kinship that provides a greater tolerance to aberrant behaviours.

SCHIZOPHRENIA

Cognitive behaviour therapy

Fig. 5.14 The focus of CBT. As the diagram illustrates, CBT concentrates on finding ways to reshape a person's thoughts, feelings and emotions.

Cognitive behaviour therapy (CBT) is a widely used talking therapy that aims to help a person manage their thoughts, feelings and physical sensations (see Fig. 5.14). It aims to break a problem like negative thinking down into smaller component parts so that each can be tackled separately and more manageably. Hence, unlike other therapies, it concentrates on trying to resolve problems in the here and now. While it is usually used for problems like anxiety and depression, it can be modified for use with schizophrenia. However, CBT is not offered widely as a treatment for schizophrenia, despite there being a growing body of evidence concerning its value.

CBT can be used effectively to help overcome delusional thinking. The stages involve first identifying the delusory belief. For example, the patient may have noticed a trade van that parks outside their block of flats at 12.15 every day. The van waits there for about half an hour and then drives off. The patient concludes that the van is a disguised MI5 van that is checking in each day to report on whether the patient is at home. The next stage is to challenge those beliefs by looking at the evidence that the patient is using to support them. In our example, the patient might be asked to consider how many flats there are in the building and the likelihood that the van is there because of them. They might be asked to consider that perhaps the van parks there each day so that the driver can eat his lunch. Such alternative explanations are presented so that the patient can try to examine their own delusory thoughts in terms of alternative explanations.

As a consequence of the delusional thinking that is outlined above, many patients do not take the medication that they have been prescribed. In addition, even the newer drugs have side effects, such as obesity and diabetes, which dissuade patients from taking their medication. Morrison et al. (2014) have used cognitive therapy (a particular form of CBT) with such patients and this has proved to be very effective (see the *Key study* below). They discovered that cognitive therapy can reduce the symptoms of schizophrenia and this confirms the idea that CBT-based therapies can reduce the incidence of delusional thinking.

KEY STUDY: MORRISON ET AL. (2014)

Morrison et al. carried out a single blind, randomized control trial on 74 patients who were not taking any medication. Of them, 37 were provided with the 'treatment as usual' offered to those not on medication and 37 were given cognitive therapy alongside the treatment as usual. The study included patients from a number of different health trusts so it was not possible to describe in detail what 'treatment as usual' consisted of. To prevent this from being a confounding variable, the same number of patients from each trust were assigned to both conditions (cognitive therapy and no cognitive therapy).

The cognitive therapy was delivered as 26 therapy sessions for a maximum of nine months. The treatment for every patient was individual to that patient, but all treatments aimed to help them to consider the faulty judgements that they made, test these out using behavioural experiments and then to modify their cognitions to remove unhelpful cognitive and behavioural responses to situations.

The results were very positive. At nine months, positive clinical outcomes were achieved in more than twice as many patients who received the cognitive therapy as those who didn't. Furthermore, these figures were maintained after an 18-month follow-up. As well as the clinical outcomes, cognitive therapy had improved the patients' personal and social functioning, so it seems that CBT-based therapies can also fulfil some of the roles of family therapy. The researchers concluded that, 'cognitive therapy significantly reduced psychiatric symptoms and seems to be a safe and acceptable alternative for people with schizophrenia spectrum disorders who have chosen not to take antipsychotic drugs.' However, we must be a little cautious, as this study used a small sample and the researchers themselves conceded that a larger trial would be needed to confirm the results.

Research methods link

For more on confounding variables, see page 12.

THINKING SCIENTIFICALLY: DIFFICULTIES IN COLLECTING CLINICAL DATA

We saw in the Morrison et al. (2014) study that in order to gain enough participants, the researchers had to use patients from a number of different health care trusts. In the UK, each trust has some autonomy to make decisions about how treatments are organized. For those patients who take their medication the treatment is relatively simple, but for those who choose not to, the alternative treatments offered can vary. This was a potential problem for the researchers as they needed to be sure that any differences they measured were due to the addition of cognitive therapy and not due to other outside influences. To do this, they used what is called stratified sampling. This involves ensuring that the numbers of participants are balanced within each grouping that they have identified. In the Morrison et al. study, the groupings (or strata) were the different trusts. Hence, instead of just saying they wanted 37 in one group and 37 in the other group, the researchers made sure that if they had five cognitive therapy patients from one trust they also had five non-therapy patients from the same trust. Stratified sampling can be a really useful technique whenever participants are being recruited from different populations that might not have identical characteristics.

Other research has involved using CBT with adolescents who were at risk of developing schizophrenia. While the CBT did not reduce the number of people who developed a first psychotic episode, it significantly reduced the severity of that episode (Morrison et al., 2012). During the first episode of psychosis, the patient will be confused about what is happening to them and may also suffer depression as a result of the traumatic events they are suffering. The suggestion is that the CBT helps to reduce this depression and anxiety and thereby reduces the impact of the first psychotic episode.

Research methods link

For more on stratified sampling, see page 32.

SCHIZOPHRENIA

David is a 17-year-old who has recently been diagnosed with schizophrenia. He is showing the classic signs of paranoid delusions and he hears voices telling him that his family and the doctors are trying to harm him. While he has been prescribed an antipsychotic drug, his willingness to take it is erratic. His immediate family argue a lot, not just with him but among themselves. Since the diagnosis, David's relationship with his parents has deteriorated as they blame his behaviour for the disharmony among the family members.

Consider how psychological therapies might help David's situation.

Exam hint

You should start by describing what CBT is and then briefly explain how it is used with schizophrenics. To illustrate one strength you could refer to a piece of research support or you could show how it is effective for certain kinds of problem faced by the schizophrenic.

Key term

Token economy: a behaviour management technique where tokens are given out for good behaviour. The tokens can later be exchanged for things the person wants (e.g. treats).

EXAMPLE EXAM QUESTION

Briefly outline how CBT is used to treat schizophrenia and explain ONE strength of its use. (4 marks)

Token economy

A **token economy** is a behaviour modification technique that uses the principles of operant conditioning. The rationale behind it is that good behaviours are rewarded with the presentation of a token that can be used later to obtain something that the person wants. For example, imagine that a parent decides to reward their daughter with a star every time she tidies her bedroom and that they record her progress on a visible chart (see Fig. 5.15). The parent might have said to her that once she has obtained ten stars she can have a trip to the cinema. This is a token economy system. The reward is a star that, in itself, has no value. The value comes from what the stars can be traded in for later; in this case, a trip to the cinema.

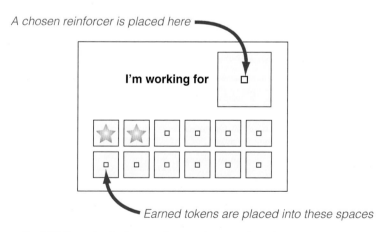

A chosen reinforcer is placed here

I'm working for

Earned tokens are placed into these spaces

Fig. 5.15 Example of a chart used to record progress in a token economy system

The use of token economies with schizophrenics was very popular in the 1960s and 1970s and were commonly used in hospitals and residential treatment centres. The method was aimed at improving the negative symptoms, such as social withdrawal and poor motivation. Ayllon and Azrin (1968) used a token economy system with 45 schizophrenic women in a psychiatric hospital. Before the token economy was introduced, the patients exhibited a variety of undesirable behaviours, such as screaming, being mute, and not using cutlery while eating. Tokens were rewarded for positive behaviours and these could be exchanged for benefits like listening to music. The researchers reported that within 20 days, patients were showing an average of 40 improved behaviours.

While much of the use of token economies has been superseded by social skills training, it is still used in some circumstances. Indeed, a major review of treatment recommendations (Lehman et al., 2004) advocated the token economy system as an effective method for promoting changes in behaviour. However, they reported that there was little evidence to suggest that this method was useful outside of this rather narrow context of a hospital or residential setting. Social Skills Therapy has now replaced token economies and has gained a lot of support as this is one area where the schizophrenic performs particularly poorly. Liberman et al. (2002) claim that this form of therapy is extremely successful and can allow the patient to feel comfortable in engaging in social contact.

Evaluating the psychological therapies

Family therapy fares well against the other kinds of psychodynamic and social therapy, but only if the treatment is extended over a period of more than three months. This makes this kind of therapy expensive, especially when compared to drug therapy. Furthermore, it relies on there being at least one family member who can provide the support. This is not always the case and many schizophrenics live alone without any contact with their family (often because of stigma). CBT can be an effective therapy but it seems to work best with the delusional thinking. It is especially effective when the delusional thoughts are preventing the person from taking their medication. Token economies have only a limited use and social skills training is effective only for those specific behaviours that are worked on in the sessions. All in all, the effectiveness of psychological treatments is variable and it is safe to say that these treatments are best used as accompaniments to drug therapy.

ACTIVITY 5.9

Henry is an 18-year-old newly diagnosed schizophrenic. He has a tendency to perceive even calm refusals by people as a deliberate act of sabotage and reacts in an aggressive manner (usually verbally rather than physically). For example, if his mother says that there is no cheese in the house so he cannot have a cheese sandwich, he considers the lack of cheese to be deliberate and proceeds to aggressively swear at her.

Compare how you might tackle this behaviour using a token economy or social skills training.

Interactionist approaches to schizophrenia

To conclude this chapter we need to consider how well all of the different elements we have discussed fit together. How well do biological explanations and psychological explanations complement each other? How much more effective are biological treatments if they are combined with psychological treatments? Finally, how well do theories about the causes of schizophrenia inform us about effective treatments? In order to consider these issues, we need to consider the development of the **interactionist approach** and the importance of the diathesis–stress model in understanding schizophrenia.

The diathesis–stress model

Throughout this chapter we have considered each element as a separate entity. We have looked at biological explanations, biological treatments, psychological explanations and psychological treatments. Our look at each of these has been in relative isolation. However, we all know that a complete understanding of schizophrenia could never be that simple. The most likely scenario is that the explanation comes from a mixture of biological and psychological factors and the best treatment combines drugs and other kinds of therapies. The **diathesis–stress model** acknowledges the complexity of most psychologically interesting disorders and describes the need to consider the interplay between biology and psychology. It recognizes that this interplay must be between the genetic inheritance of the individual and the life stresses that have arisen from their own unique environmental circumstance. Put more formally, we might define diathesis–stress as:

The combination of a genetic vulnerability to an illness and the stress needed for it to become a reality.

Key term

Interactionist approach: this approach suggests that the best explanations combine biological and psychological elements and the best therapeutic outcomes are obtained by using a combination of drug therapies and psychological therapies.

Key term

Diathesis–stress model: the most well-known kind of interactionist model, where a disorder (schizophrenia, in this case) is seen as the result of a combination of biological and psychological factors.

The diathesis–stress model and schizophrenia

You will have realized by now that schizophrenia is a collection of symptoms and that if a patient has enough of those symptoms then they will be diagnosed with schizophrenia. Within these parameters it makes perfect sense to talk of the diathesis–stress model. We have seen earlier in the chapter that there is very good evidence for a genetic basis for schizophrenia – this represents the diathesis side of the equation. Diathesis simply means 'a tendency to suffer from a particular medical condition'. If we construct a list of points in favour of the role of genetics, it might look like the following:

- Concordance rates are higher for MZ twins than for DZ twins, but the fact that the rate for MZ twins is not 100 per cent shows that genetics do not tell the whole story.
- Each of the symptoms can be traced to altered functioning of either a brain area or of a neurotransmitter system.
- We can assume that these changes are genetically inherited since there is nothing systematic about the early environment of patients that would point to the cause of these changes.
- It is possible to detect signs of symptoms prior to a patient having their first schizophrenic episode.
- Not everyone with schizophrenia has all of the symptoms associated with its diagnosis (those listed in DSM-5).
- Not everyone who displays a significant number of signs early in life goes on to develop full-blown schizophrenia.

These points indicate that the genetic changes that ultimately lead to brain changes represent a vulnerability for developing schizophrenia, rather than a certainty that it will develop.

When we looked at the psychological explanations for schizophrenia we examined many of the environmental stresses that a person with these genetic markers might face. We looked at the social and cognitive problems that usually arise from having the collection of brain and neurotransmitter problems that are typical in a schizophrenic brain. We also considered in detail the various ideas around the family environment and how it might magnify the problems that reduced social and cognitive functioning bring. The stress that might arise would be the stress part (or triggering mechanism) of the diathesis–stress model.

We can illustrate two different ways in which these factors might come together. In both examples we will assume the same biological changes have taken place and that both people are socially awkward in that they often misattribute the reasons behind a person's intentions from what they have said or done. They also think that they hear voices, but as they have never come across this they find it difficult to describe what they hear. Finally, they have a tendency to jump to conclusions (often the wrong ones) when faced with a problem-solving task. Before reading past the end of case 2, make a decision about what you think the outcome is for both cases. You can choose that the person develops schizophrenia or that they will only ever show signs of schizophrenia-like behaviour without ever having a schizophrenic episode.

Case 1

Person 1 comes from a loving, supportive family and is one of three siblings, having one older brother and one younger sister. At the age of five, the person showed signs that they did not always understand what was going on in the world around them. They would get frustrated at not being very good at schoolwork and they found making friends difficult. The family accepted that the person was 'a bit dim' and often made light-hearted remarks about the 'dim sheep of the family'. At the age of 15, the person started to hear voices. Their mother put this down to a lack of social contact with people of their own age and thought that they were just creating friends in their own head. The family were puzzled by the fact that the imaginary friend was making nasty suggestions, but simply put it down to a 'phase they are going through'. Although the person's behaviour was getting more erratic, the family wanted to support the child through this and it never occurred to them that there might be something seriously wrong. There was a noticeable change in the atmosphere in the house but the whole family tried to accommodate the strange behaviours as best they could, and this often meant avoiding contact altogether. This was especially true for the siblings, who now spent as much time as possible avoiding the inevitable confrontations.

Case 2

Person 2 comes from a family where the mother and father both have full-time jobs and the total family income makes them reasonably well off. The person is an only child and their early life was mostly spent with a mixture of child minders or at the home of grandparents. They would often spend the night at a grandparent's house because their parents would be getting back from work too late to put them to bed. There were seldom family meals as both parents tended to eat whenever they could find time in their busy schedules. With an unstable home base, the person found it difficult to make friends at school, as they couldn't easily engage in common social activities like a visit to the park or a sleepover. At the age of 12, the person complained that they were struggling to concentrate at school and often perceived that the teacher was picking on them for no reason. This was mostly met with the suggestion to 'pull your socks up' or with a story of how things for children are so much better now than they used to be. When the person started to hear voices they kept it a secret, believing that no one would be interested.

Case 1 or case 2?

Having read both cases, you might be thinking that it is difficult to decide which one developed schizophrenia and which one didn't. You would be right to find it difficult. It is quite possible that both of them developed schizophrenia and had a psychotic episode. In both cases the stress component could have been sufficient to act as the trigger for the underlying genetic propensity. What is noticeable about both cases is that they demonstrate social isolation and an inability for the family to deal with the signs of the person hearing voices and their delusional thinking. In the first example, the response was 'there, there', and in the second the family were unaware of many of the signs. The point about these cases is that they demonstrate that there is not one identifiable set of triggers. In families that are not aware of schizophrenia, there is no reason to see the behaviours that are displayed as anything other than a bit odd or as part of the natural variation in children growing up quite normally.

How does stress trigger schizophrenia?

In order to consider how stress triggers schizophrenia, we need to consider what we mean by stress. Stress as a trigger has often been associated with the presence of major life events (Day et al., 1987). Hultman et al. (1997) have suggested that these events usually occur no more than three weeks before a patient has a relapse. However, it might be that not all forms of stress act as a trigger. The distinction has been made between uncontrollable and controllable stress – it is the former that seems to act as a trigger. Uncontrollable stress occurs when a person believes that the source of the stress is external to them and so cannot be controlled by them. Frenkel et al. (1995) have suggested that this is a likely trigger in adolescents.

There have been a number of different theories about what stress does to the body to trigger a schizophrenic episode. As far back as the 1980s, there was a suggestion that stress could lead to an increase in the production of dopamine (Braden, 1984). This would certainly lead to an expression of the positive symptoms of schizophrenia even if it did not trigger a full-blown psychotic episode. However, Braden was using animal models to show the increase in dopamine, and there was no certainty that these changes would also occur in humans, as they would process a stressful situation very differently.

More recently, attention has turned to the effects of stress on cortisol levels. Cortisol is a hormone that is released in times of stress and serves to increase the availability of glucose (a source of energy). Naturally, stress occurs in a fight or flight situation in which the person needs to stand and fight or run away (for example, when confronted by a bear). In situations where there is long-term stress (as in the family situations described above), the prolonged release of cortisol is not good for one's health and that includes one's mental health. It might be that when a person with a propensity towards schizophrenia encounters situations of uncontrollable stress, the prolonged activation of cortisol generates the trigger for either a first psychotic episode or for a relapse (Jones and Fernyhough, 2007).

- It is becoming increasingly clear that no single explanation of schizophrenia is good enough.

- Interactionist models provide a way of combining alternative explanations to give a more complete picture of schizophrenia.

- Interactionist models also help to explore combinations of treatments that might be more effective than individual treatments.

- The diathesis–stress model is the most useful way to understand the interactionist approach.

- The diathesis–stress model proposes that psychological stresses act as a trigger for the expression of underlying biological vulnerabilities.

ACTIVITY 5.10

Using the two case profiles described in the text, consider how you might examine the degree to which the diathesis–stress model would explain the onset of schizophrenia.

Exam hint

This question carries a lot of marks so you need to be thorough in your answer and provide more than a superficial outline of the interactionist approach. One way to do this would be to provide a biological and a psychological explanation separately and then show how combining these explanations provides a more satisfactory explanation. Alternatively, you might explain the diathesis–stress model and provide examples of how that model explains the causes of schizophrenia.

EXAMPLE EXAM QUESTION

Discuss the advantages of an interactionist approach to explaining schizophrenia. (16 marks)

At the very beginning of this chapter we briefly explored how schizophrenia is portrayed by the public, and the collection of symptoms that characterize schizophrenia. This practical activity requires you to create a questionnaire to explore the general public's knowledge and perception of people with schizophrenia. The questionnaire should allow you to understand general knowledge about the disorder as well as attitudes towards schizophrenics.

As a methodology, you might want to use a combination of multiple-choice questions to explore people's knowledge together with Likert scale statements that allow you to understand attitudes towards people with schizophrenia.

Use the themes within the chapter to construct your questions and statements. These might include:

Knowledge

- What kinds of hallucinations do people with schizophrenia have?
- What is delusional thinking?
- How many schizophrenics are there in the UK?
- What type of drug is given to a person with schizophrenia? (Choice from antipsychotic, antidepressant, etc.)

Attitude

- All schizophrenics are dangerous.
- It is important to integrate people with schizophrenia into the community.
- People with schizophrenia should not be allowed to have children.
- A person with schizophrenia could never be a leader.
- There is no point giving drug treatments to a schizophrenic as they will not take them.

Think about how you would need to analyse the different elements of the questionnaire and what hypotheses you would be testing.

1. Read the text below and then answer the questions that follow.

    > Jordan was diagnosed with schizophrenia three years ago when he was
    > 19 years old. His grandmother on his father's side was autistic and his father
    > shows some cognitive deficits but has not been diagnosed with schizophrenia.

    a) Using the text above and your knowledge of schizophrenia, briefly discuss whether schizophrenia can be genetically inherited. **(6 marks)**

    b) Briefly outline dysfunctional thought processes that are typically seen in schizophrenia. **(6 marks)**

    c) Discuss the use of drug therapy and cognitive behaviour therapy in the treatment of schizophrenia. **(16 marks)**

2. Discuss biological explanations of schizophrenia. **(16 marks)**

3. a) Outline and evaluate the role of family dysfunction in schizophrenia. **(12 marks)**

    b) Outline and evaluate the use of CBT to treat schizophrenia. **(12 marks)**

Exam focus

Read through the following example exam question, example student answer, and examiner comments. Then, have a go at answering the question yourself!

EXAMPLE EXAM QUESTION

Jack is a 24-year-old who suffers from auditory hallucinations and delusions of persecution. He has only recently been diagnosed with schizophrenia so his family are uncertain how this has come about.

Use **one** biological and **one** psychological theory to explain to Jack's family why he is suffering from these symptoms. (16 marks)

Deepak's answer

One biological explanation of why Jack is suffering from schizophrenia suggests that it has been genetically inherited. This means that it has been passed down from his parents. Studies to support this idea are twin studies. Several twin studies have shown that monozygotic twins have a higher chance that both twins suffer from schizophrenia than dizygotic twins. This fits with the fact that monozygotic twins inherit the same DNA whereas dizygotic twins inherit different DNA. The DNA that Jack has inherited has therefore caused him to suffer from schizophrenia. However, we must be careful to interpret twin study data as we cannot be sure that the results are not due to the effect of the environment.

> **Examiner comment:** Needs a little elaboration. Use of MZ and DZ twins in these studies is meant to control for environmental effects.

A psychological explanation of Jack's symptoms is that he is suffering from cognitive deficits. His auditory hallucinations might be the result of him not being able to process language information properly and so not being able to recognize that the voices are being generated by himself and not by another person. The delusional thoughts might arise because of a deficit in cognitive reasoning. Garety et al. (2005) has shown that schizophrenics have a tendency to jump to conclusions and so misinterpret the things that happen around them. This can lead them to perceive the world to be against them when it isn't. However, while this might explain some persecution delusions (like being spied on), it cannot explain more extreme delusions (for example, that the city's water supply has been poisoned).

> **Examiner comment:** Good use of research evidence, a key source of elevation and explanations.

To evaluate these explanations, the genetic explanation has a lot of supporting evidence, and as the studies are carried out in the real world they have ecological validity. There are also studies that have been carried out in a number of different cultures. However, it is difficult to separate out genetic from environmental influences. For the cognitive explanations, these come from laboratory studies and so they lack ecological validity, though they have good control over the variables. The cognitive explanation is reductionist and most of the studies have taken place in westernized countries.

> **Examiner comment:** Could refer to family and adoption studies as well as twin studies. Could also refer to concordance between MZ twins never being 100%, so genetics are not the only cause.

> **Examiner comment:** Knowledge of genetic and, especially, cognitive deficits/dysfunctional thought processes is accurate and generally well detailed. Evaluation includes some effective reference to research evidence, but some points are too brief to be fully effective. Answers need to demonstrate understanding of e.g. reductionism and cultural relativity. Overall, a reasonable answer, good use of specialist terminology. Level 3, 10 marks out of 16.

SCHIZOPHRENIA

Part 3: Issues and options in psychology

Chapter 6: Eating behaviour

Introduction

For much of evolutionary history, our human ancestors experienced a constant struggle to find sufficient, safe food to survive – a struggle that continues today in many parts of the world where famine is rife. This provides a stark contrast with the position many of us take for granted today in affluent parts of the world, where food is in surplus and we can afford to buy and eat many different kinds of cuisines. This chapter begins by examining how our evolutionary history has influenced the food preferences shown today, before examining the influence of learning and of culture on eating behaviours.

Eating behaviour is of particular interest to psychologists as it involves many different levels of explanation. We cannot understand eating behaviour without considering the underlying biological systems. The basis of eating behaviour is our need to take adequate nutrition in order for our body's physiological systems to work effectively. The chapter examines the biological systems that underpin eating behaviour, including brain structures such as the hypothalamus, and hormones such as ghrelin and leptin, which send signals of satiety (fullness) to the brain. We examine how these biological factors may play a role in eating disorders such as anorexia nervosa. However, eating is not a purely biological activity. We also eat when we are not hungry because we can override our biological systems by continuing to eat long after we have taken sufficient food, if pleasing foods are available.

We then move on to examine some of the more common problems with eating that are seen in the westernized countries. Obesity is arguably the most important health issue facing the western world today, with levels at an all-time high and continuing to increase. Some estimates suggest that children born today will have shorter lives than their parents because of poor diet. What can psychology tell us about modern eating behaviours?

What is covered in Eating behaviour?

Explanations for food preferences

Evolutionary factors in food preferences

Link

You can remind yourself about natural and sexual selection by looking back at page 235 of Book 1.

Evolutionary psychologists are interested in how the characteristics shown by modern humans – in this case eating behaviours – may have their roots in the past. According to evolutionary theory, behaviours and characteristics that produce an advantage in terms of survival or reproduction are passed on to offspring, who inherit the characteristic. Over time, most members of the species come to possess the behaviour or characteristic.

We can distinguish between two kinds of psychological explanation. **Proximate explanations** are used in most fields of psychology and focus on the immediate causes of a behaviour. For example, the question 'Why is my child reluctant to try unfamiliar foods' could be answered by focusing on the influence of the child's best friend who refuses to eat certain foods. **Ultimate explanations** used by evolutionary psychologists, focus on how a particular behaviour may have evolved and the possible advantage it brought. An ultimate explanation for a reluctance to try new foods would focus on the advantages to our foraging ancestors of eating familiar foods and avoiding unfamiliar foods that might be poisonous.

Evolutionary psychologists are interested in how modern eating behaviours have been influenced by the history of our species. Some eating behaviours that are considered maladaptive today, such as bingeing, would have been extremely advantageous in a world where food was scarce and our ancestors did not know where or when the next meal would be found.

It is, of course, impossible to go back in the past and to see how our ancestors lived, what and how they ate. For this reason, evolutionary psychologists draw on a range of sources of evidence, including:

- Archaeological/fossil evidence: the shape and size of teeth can tell us about the diet of our ancestors, for instance whether they ate meat or not. Stone tools can tell us about the type of animals that were hunted for food.

- Comparisons with modern hunter-gatherer societies: there are still a few societies, such as the !Kung San of the Kalahari Desert, who follow a hunter-gatherer lifestyle, foraging for plants and berries, hunting animals and fishing. An examination of their eating patterns can tell us about the likely diet eaten by our ancestors.

- There are comparisons that can be made between the diets of humans and other apes. Between five and seven million years ago, we shared a common ancestor with the 'great apes' (chimpanzees and gorillas) and with monkeys. The diets of chimpanzees can tell us what our early ancestors were likely to have eaten, and comparison of ape and human digestive systems can tell us roughly when the human diet changed to include meat.

Fig. 6.1 The !Kung San people of the Kalahari Desert

Evolution of the human diet

For most of our existence, humans have lived as hunter-gatherers, eating a wide variety of foodstuffs, including grains, fruits, berries and grubs. These were in short supply and there was a constant struggle to find food. The pursuit of food was a high-energy, time-consuming business for our ancestors, with most of the day devoted to finding enough to stay alive. Which factors would have been important in ensuring survival and reproductive success for early humans? They would need to distinguish between edible foods and those that were poisonous or contaminated by bacteria. Acute senses of taste and smell would enable early humans to spot crucial differences between good and poor food sources. Modern human taste receptors reflect our evolutionary history as they are specialized to identify the following tastes:

• Sweet receptors: a sweet taste identifies that a food source is rich in carbohydrates and will provide important calories, replacing those burned up via energy expenditure.

• Salt receptors: salt is critical to the normal functioning of cells in the body and is lost during strenuous physical activity. It is important to be able to identify salty foods to replace this important nutrient.

• Umami: this has been discovered relatively recently and represents a meaty or savoury quality. This would indicate a good source of protein.

Early humans would also have developed taste receptors to help them detect and avoid dangerous foodstuffs. These included taste receptors for bitter and sour tastes: bitter-tasting foods indicate the presence of poisonous plant chemicals and a sour taste is associated with food that has gone off (such as milk or meat) and that may contain harmful bacteria.

Fig. 6.2 Facial expression when tasting a lemon

So our ancestors developed taste receptors that enabled them to identify foods rich in salt, sugar and fat, which were crucial to survival, and to identify and avoid poisonous or contaminated foods. These preferences are reflected in newborn babies (neonates). Studies of the facial expressions of neonates exposed to different tastes suggest innate preferences for sweet and salty flavours and a dislike of bitter and sour tastes (Steiner 1979, Rosenstein and Oster, 1988). As we will see, an innate preference for high-energy foodstuffs causes problems for modern humans, who generally lead less physically active lives and require fewer calories and less salt replacement.

Why did early humans become meat eaters?

Modern apes and monkeys live largely on fruit, nuts and plants. Chimpanzees may occasionally eat meat in the form of grubs, insects and smaller monkeys if they get the chance. However, the amount of meat eaten by chimpanzees is very small and estimated at a maximum of 4 per cent of their diet (Buss, 2008). While chimpanzees, gorillas and monkeys have a relatively long large intestine, specialized for the digestion of plant materials, humans are specialized to eat meat – we have a relatively long duodenum and small intestine for the digestion and absorption of protein. The human evolutionary line split from the great apes about six million years ago, and it is likely that early humans became full omnivores – animals that regularly eat meat as well as fruit, nuts and plants – at around that time.

Why did early humans become meat eaters? Meat is a rich source of protein and it is far more efficient to obtain protein from hunting than by foraging for plants and leaves. It is likely that meat eaters were more successful at surviving and reproducing; the behaviour rapidly spread through the species. However, there are also disadvantages to meat eating: meat is a major source of food poisoning, even today. During human development various methods evolved to make meat safer to eat, including cooking and spicing.

- Cooking, introduced at least half a million years ago (Wrangham et al., 1999) reduced the presence of harmful bacteria and made food easier to chew. Fossil remains show that our chewing teeth, the molars, have decreased in size during evolution (Lucas et al., 2006).

- Spices such as onion and garlic are extremely effective at killing bacteria. More spices are used in hot countries where food goes off more quickly, and in meat, which is far more dangerous if spoiled (Sherman and Hash, 2001). The use of spices is likely to have been spread by cultural transmission rather than by natural selection.

It is likely that the advantages of eating meat outweighed the disadvantages so the behaviour spread through the human population. Large occasional kills meant that early humans spent less time feeding themselves than when they foraged. Hunting led to the development of specialized skills, including making and using tools and weapons. The shift to hunting also led to a division of labour between the sexes: the physical demands of hunting were more suited to males, while females, who were occupied with child care, would forage, gathering berries, leaves, and fruits closer to the camp. Hunting required skills of navigation and social cooperation. Social cooperation itself puts pressure on the evolution of language and other high-level social skills (for example, deception, altruism). These skills would provide the selection pressure for a larger brain – individuals with brains capable of these complex actions would have been more likely to survive and breed.

In modern hunter-gatherer societies, meat still makes up a large proportion of the diet, between 20 and 90 per cent depending upon the season. Successful hunters share their kill with other members of the group outside their own families, and in some modern tribes women can divorce husbands who are not successful at providing food (Buss, 2008). Skilled hunters acquire prestige and power within the group and the ability to bargain for sexual favours. Kaplan and Hill (1985) studied the Ache tribe of Paraguay and found that good hunters reaped a range of benefits for their skills: they were more likely to be chosen as lovers by the women of the tribe and fathered more illegitimate children. Their offspring received preferential treatment in the social group. The ability to bargain for sexual favours is sometimes referred to as the 'sex for meat' hypothesis!

Food neophobia

Neophobia is another evolutionary aspect of food preferences. 'Neophobia' means 'fear of the new'. Applied to food it means that animals have a powerful tendency to avoid foods they have not come across before. Although this can lead to a dull diet, it ensures that foods are safe and new foods that may be harmful are avoided.

A longitudinal study of children's diet and food preferences is ongoing in Australia (Perry et al., 2015). In one element of the study, 330 parents were asked to keep a 48-hour food diary for their two-year-old children. They were also contacted by a researcher out of the blue and asked what foods their child had eaten in the previous 24 hours. The researchers found a relationship between food neophobia and lower consumption of fruit and vegetables in two-year-olds.

Food neophobia peaks between two and six years of age, then decreases naturally. However, it can be overcome by repeated exposure (trying the child with a food until it becomes familiar) and by modelling – showing an older child eating it. We tend to show greater liking for foods as they become more familiar (Frost, 2006).

Taste aversions

If we eat something that is poisonous or contaminated, it would be an evolutionary advantage to avoid that food in future – assuming we survive. This is referred to as a **taste aversion**. Babies and young children show an extensive range of taste aversions. Some of these

Key terms
Neophobia: a tendency to avoid unfamiliar foods.
Taste aversion: avoiding foods that produce an unfavourable response.

dislikes are understandable: some vegetables, such as broccoli and Brussels sprouts, contain chemicals that can be toxic to the very young (Nesse and Williams, 1994). Taste aversion was dramatically demonstrated in a study carried out using non-human animals by Garcia et al. (1977).

KEY STUDY: GARCIA ET AL. (1977)

Garcia et al. (1977) studied a group of wild wolves and coyotes. They wrapped mutton (sheep meat) in raw sheepskins and laced it with lithium chloride, a mild poison. The wolves and coyotes ate the mutton and were unsurprisingly and rapidly extremely sick. The researchers then observed what happened when live sheep were placed in the same field where the wolves could approach them. The wolves approached the live sheep, sniffed them and then turned away, retching as if they were going to be sick. The wolves had rapidly learned to associate the smell of the foodstuff with a bad response.

Fig. 6.3 The wild wolves and coyotes in Garcia's study learned a taste aversion to sheep

The study shows how taste aversion learning is highly specific and extremely intense. Just one experience will affect the animal's behaviour for months. From the evolutionary standpoint, a response of this nature would have been highly advantageous, contributing to keeping animals alive.

THINKING SCIENTIFICALLY: CLASSICAL CONDITIONING

Garcia et al.'s study demonstrates a form of learning called **classical conditioning**. Classical conditioning generally takes several trials, as in the famous examples of Pavlov's dogs (Pavlov, 1927) and Little Albert (Watson, 1920). The Garcia study shows that classical conditioning can happen extremely quickly through a single experience. This is referred to as 'one-trial learning'. It is likely that we have evolved a predisposition for this kind of rapid learning given the advantages in evolutionary terms. While the Garcia study used animals, most people can recall their own examples of taste aversions from a bad experience of food poisoning, Psychologists sometimes refer to a food aversion as a 'Garcia effect'.

Taste aversions during pregnancy

Many women demonstrate taste aversions in the early stages of pregnancy. Morning sickness is found in at least 75 per cent of women and has a convincing evolutionary explanation – the embryo protection hypothesis (Profet, 1992). Surveys show consistently that the foods most avoided by pregnant women are coffee, tea, meat, alcohol, eggs and vegetables (Buss, 2008). Alcohol, along with coffee and tea (which contain caffeine), can damage the baby's major organs. Meat and eggs are common sources of toxins such as bacteria, while some vegetables contain toxic chemicals harmful to the developing foetus. The sickness reaction therefore helps the mother to avoid foods that may be harmful, while vomiting prevents any toxins entering the mother's bloodstream and affecting her baby. Morning sickness is most severe in the early weeks of pregnancy, when the baby's major body organs are developing and the baby is most vulnerable. It generally eases off and disappears as the baby becomes fully formed and can no longer be affected by potential toxins. Of course, standards of hygiene are now fairly rigorous and morning sickness is therefore something of an evolutionary hangover. It is an impressive example of how evolution selected changes in feeding preferences that would help survival of the species.

Key term

Classical conditioning: learning by association.

Link

To review Pavlov and Watson's experiments, see pages 221–223 of Book 1.

ACTIVITY 6.1

Design a questionnaire to assess food preferences. Your questionnaire should be suitable to use with sixth-form students and should include a mixture of open and closed questions. You should devise questions to measure how often foods such as meat, fruit and vegetables are consumed. You may also want to include questions on taste aversions and favourite foods. You will need to think carefully about which type of question (open or closed) will yield the most useful data.

EXAMPLE EXAM QUESTION

Sarah has a two-year-old son, Aaron. She wants Aaron to have a varied diet and encourages him to try the food she and her partner are eating, such as spaghetti bolognaise. Aaron is very reluctant to try new foods and on some days he refuses to eat anything but yoghurt.

Using your knowledge of the evolution of food preferences, explain why Aaron is reluctant to try different foods. (4 marks)

Exam hint

This is an application question. Look carefully for the 'hooks' in the scenario. You could develop your answer by referring to relevant research but remember that you must apply these to the scenario.

Evaluation of evolutionary explanations of food preferences

The evolutionary approach can explain how many features of our digestive system, such as our range of taste receptors, are highly specialized to respond to sweet and salty tastes and to avoid sour or bitter tastes. The evolutionary approach can also explain some unusual aspects of food preferences and taste aversions, such as those shown in pregnancy.

Fossil evidence of changes to our digestive system (for example, our teeth, the structure of the digestive system, etc.) support hypotheses on the evolution of meat eating and the shift to a hunter-gatherer society. However, there is a limited amount of fossil evidence, and evolutionary explanations are often speculative. The shift to meat eating helps to explain the selective pressure on brain evolution in order to cope with new technical and social skills.

However, as noted at the start of this topic, much evolutionary psychology is based upon educated guesswork about how things must have been. As part of the biological approach, evolutionary explanations are reductionist. They do not take into account cultural transmission of behaviours related to food and feeding, and they do not place enough emphasis on social and cultural changes in, for example, the widespread availability of food. In western societies we no longer behave as hunter-gatherers, and the evolutionary approach is therefore limited.

The role of learning in food preferences

As we have seen, evolution has equipped us to prefer certain kinds of foods, notably those with high energy that contain sugar, fats and salts. These preferences were highly adaptive in the past when food was in short supply and our ancestors expended large amounts of energy hunting and gathering. Given this predisposition, what role does learning play in the development of eating patterns?

Learning explanations focus on learning through association (classical conditioning) through rewards and reinforcement (operant conditioning) and through social learning (observation and modelling). We have already seen how taste aversions can be formed rapidly through association of sickness with a particular food – the Garcia effect. We will now examine how operant conditioning and social learning are also influential in the development of children's eating habits.

Parental attitudes and food preferences

It seems rather obvious that parents' attitudes to food will influence eating habits. Parents, often mothers, make decisions about which foods will be bought and served in the household. If parents are concerned over health aspects of food they will work hard to make sure that their children have a balanced diet with unhealthy foods being restricted. If parents are less aware or less concerned over health issues such as obesity, they may take less care over their child's diet. As expected, there is a significant correlation between the diets of mothers and children (Ogden, 2007).

Parents often make systematic efforts to shape their children's eating habits through rewards, encouraging children to eat particular foods (often vegetables) and reward them for doing so. Rewards can include praise or treats such as sweets or ice cream, which are given after a healthy food has been eaten. However, research has shown that this approach is counterproductive: the more children are rewarded for eating certain things, the less they like them!

KEY STUDY: BIRCH ET AL. (1984)

Does the use of rewards shape what children eat?

Birch et al. studied a sample of 45 preschool children, 20 boys and 25 girls aged between three and five years old, to assess the effects of rewards on food preferences. They designed seven different flavoured milk drinks (including strawberry, chocolate and prune) and asked the children to say whether they liked or disliked each drink or whether the drink was 'OK'. The OK drinks were selected for the experiment as liking for the drinks could potentially increase or decrease.

The children were divided into an experimental condition (N=31) and a control condition (N=14). The experiment took place during 'snack' time at the preschool, over a period of four weeks. Each child was provided with the same drink twice a week, making a total of eight tastings. In the experimental condition, the children were given various rewards for finishing the drink. For some this was verbal praise ('Well done, you drank that all up') and for others, a physical reward was promised for drinking up ('If you drink it all up you can go and see a film'). Children in the control condition were exposed to identical procedures but were not rewarded for drinking the drink. Control children also received a promise to see the film but it was not linked to consumption of the drink.

At the end of the four weeks, the children were asked again to rate the drink, which they had originally thought was OK. Children who had been given a reward – regardless of the nature of the reward – liked the drink *significantly less* than they had at the start. Liking for the drink increased in the control condition where children had not been rewarded for consuming the drink, but the increase was not significant. Birch et al. concluded that providing rewards for eating a food is counterproductive and leads to the child liking the food less.

THINKING SCIENTIFICALLY: ANALYSIS OF BIRCH ET AL. (1984)

One advantage of the experimental method over methods of research is the ability to control all the variables that may affect the DV, with the exception of the IV. The researchers had designed special drinks for the purpose of the experiment to ensure that the children had not tasted them before. If they had used existing drinks, the children could already have had preferences for them or been influenced by advertising. The use of a wide range of flavours is also commendable as children with different kinds of food preferences could take part in the study on an equal basis.

Exam hint

It is a good idea to choose two ethical issues that are clearly separate in questions of this nature, rather than issues that are two sides of the same coin, such as consent and deception.

Research methods link

You can remind yourself about ethical issues by looking at pages 35–38.

EXAMPLE EXAM QUESTION

1. Explain ONE way in which Birch et al. could have allocated children to the experimental and control groups in this study. (2 marks)
2. Identify TWO ethical issues that the researcher would need to consider in this study and explain how they could have dealt with these issues. (6 marks)

Role models also play an important role in the development of children's eating patterns. In one intervention study, Lowe et al. (1998) used videos of 'food dudes', older children who modelled the consumption of refused food such as vegetables. Lowe et al. found that children exposed to the food dudes increased their consumption of the foods they had previously refused. Jansen and Tenney (2001) carried out an experiment on the impact of adult models on the consumption of unfamiliar yoghurt drinks. They found that children developed the greatest liking when they consumed a novel drink alongside an adult model who showed that they liked the drink.

Parents also affect the emotional context in which food is consumed. Observational studies have shown that negative parental comments about a child's eating habits ('S/he is so fussy') are associated with lower consumption of food whereas positive comments ('S/he is such a good eater') are associated with greater food consumption (Koivisto et al., 1994).

ACTIVITY 6.2

Based on the research you have read about in the above section, write a set of guidelines for parents of children aged between two and five. The guidelines should include dos and don'ts to encourage toddlers to eat a healthy diet.

Cultural influences on food preferences

Culture also has a range of effects on eating behaviour. In some parts of the world, food is scarce and there are high levels of malnutrition and starvation. Also, the availability of different types of food varies across regions of the world. Eskimos, for example, live largely on seal meat because that is what is available. Culinary practices, such as the use of spices in cooking, are more prevalent in hot countries as a method of increasing the safety of meat.

Many religions prohibit certain foods or require foods to be prepared in particular ways. For instance, Judaism divides foods into kosher (allowed) and trefa (forbidden) and Islam makes a similar distinction between halal (allowed) and haram (forbidden). Both Judaism and Islam promote periods of fasting, during Yom Kippur and Ramadan respectively. Religions including Buddhism and Rastafarianism consider living things to be sacred, and promote vegetarian or vegan diets. Leshem (2009) compared the diets of religious communities living close to each other in Israel with equal access to shops and food. In the Muslim community, intake of carbohydrates was twice that of the Christian group, and they also took in higher levels of protein, fats and salt. Though there were such differences, the mean body mass index was almost the same for both groups.

Another study carried out by Leshem, along with colleagues Saadi, Alem and Hendi (2009), demonstrates how cultural differences in diet have been shaped by evolutionary pressures.

KEY STUDY: LESHEM ET AL. (2009)

Leshem et al. examined the diets of the Negev Bedouin Arab women. The Negev Bedouin traditionally lived in the desert where summers are very hot, water is scarce and there is little shade. Today, some Negev Bedouin have migrated to live in cities close by.

Leshem et al. compared the diets, with a particular interest in salt intake, of two groups of women: 31 who were desert dwellers and 15 who had migrated to live in an urban area in the same climate zone. The researchers compared their diets with a group of 15 Jewish women living in

Fig. 6.4 Negev Bedouin women

the same city. They found that the two groups of Bedouin women had virtually identical diets, which were very high in salt. Salt intake was around 25 per cent higher than the sample of Jewish urban women. The overall calorie intake and fluid intake were both substantially higher in the Bedouin sample.

High salt intake is likely to have evolved in relation to the high fluid and salt loss associated with living in the desert. This adaptation had continued in the city dwellers, despite the move to an urban community with easy access to a range of foods. Leshem et al.'s study shows how urban Bedouins have retained cultural practices despite the move to a very different environment.

THINKING SCIENTIFICALLY: QUASI-EXPERIMENTS

Leshem's study is an example of a quasi-experiment. In a quasi-experiment, participants cannot be randomly allocated to conditions, as these are pre-existing. In quasi-experimental studies, it is important to match participants as carefully as possible to ensure that other variables such as age, or educational background do not affect the dependent variable (in this instance, diet).

Evaluation of the effects of culture on food preferences

Leshem et al.'s findings show that cultural influences on diet are profound and persist even where there is equal access to the same foods. These differences may originate in adaptations to previous environments, as with salt intake in the Bedouin people. In some groups there are strict religious guidelines on what may or may not be eaten, and these will survive whatever the surrounding environment.

Research methods link

You can remind yourself about quasi-experiments by looking at page 9.

However, cultural differences are being reduced with the spread of highly processed fast foods with high saturated fat content. Exposure of ethnic groups to new diets can have dramatic effects. Studies on the Pica Indians of New Mexico show that those who stay in their communities have low levels of obesity but that those who move to areas heavily influenced by American culture and diet develop high levels of obesity (Ravussin et al., 1994).

Benton (2004) conceptualizes the development of eating behaviour as a three-stage process in which nature (biology) and nurture (learning and experience) both play an important role:

- We are born with biological tendencies to like pleasant tasting, high-energy foods and to avoid unfamiliar foods.

- From infancy, we learn to associate different food tastes with both physiological and psychological consequences (for example, feeling full, rewards, treats, etc.).

- These experiences lead to the development of attitudes and beliefs about food that drive adult eating habits.

KEY POINTS

- Modern humans are omnivores and we use a wide range of foods to supply the nutrients that we need. Our digestive system, in particular our sense of taste, has evolved to identify safe foods and avoid harmful foods.

- The introduction of meat as an important part of the human diet led to the evolution of the hunter-gatherer society. This, in turn, gave a selective advantage to the evolution of skills such as weapon-making and tool use, and social cooperation.

- Our food preferences are affected by food neophobia, the inherited avoidance of unfamiliar foods.

- Taste aversion learning is a powerful form of learning based on a single bad experience with food. It helps animals to avoid foods that are dangerous.

- Morning sickness involves avoidance of certain types of food in the early stages of pregnancy. The embryo protection hypothesis states that the sickness probably evolved to protect the developing baby from foods that might harm it.

- Feeding preferences in babies and young children reflect a balance between neophobia and learning through familiarity. Repeated exposure increases food preference.

- Parents, especially the mother, influence food preferences in children by providing the child's diet and acting as role models. The mother's attitudes towards food are crucial. Later, peers become an important model in the social learning of food preferences.

- The parents' awareness of health risks associated with diet can influence the child's attitude to food.

- Culture can have significant effects on diet as a result of the availability of food, specific environments and religious beliefs.

Biological control of eating

From a biological point of view, eating is a bit of a guessing game. While there are many cues telling us that we are hungry, the decision to stop eating has to be based on a prediction about our future energy needs. Since we cannot know for sure when we will obtain our next meal, our body has to provide us with an educated guess. The mechanisms involved in **hunger** and **satiation** must be complicated, otherwise we would simply always eat until we were bursting and eat again and again every time the opportunity arose, just in case. The regulation of our food intake is necessary for **homeostasis**, as the nutrition gained from eating provides the energy needed for homeostatic mechanisms such as temperature regulation, breathing rate and many others. The regulation of our eating behaviour is also important in our ability to maintain an ideal body weight, hence the processes that initiate eating and stop us eating must use signals from which we are able to direct our behaviour. We can split the biological mechanisms that control eating behaviour into two broad areas. The first are hormonal mechanisms and the second are neural mechanisms.

Hormonal mechanisms of eating behaviour

There are a number of different hormones that are involved in controlling when we eat and how much we eat. The first ones we shall consider are insulin and glucagon. These regulate the amount of glucose in the blood and hence the amount of available energy our cells have to draw on. The others we will consider here are leptin and ghrelin. These hormones are partly responsible for making us want to start or stop eating.

Insulin and glucagon

Glucose is the main source of energy within our body and the amount of it in our bloodstream has to be maintained at the correct level for our current needs. When we are resting, our bodies need less available energy that when we are running or fighting. In order to have more energy available to us when we need it, we must store energy when we have more than we currently need, and have a mechanism for quickly releasing that energy when necessary. Glucose energy is stored in our body as **glycogen**. The hormone **insulin** is released from the **pancreas** (where it is made) and converts the glucose into glycogen that is then stored in our liver. Insulin also has two other important functions: it helps glucose to enter our cells, where it can be used to help power whatever that cell is designed to do; it also helps our body to store fat. When we eat fat it gets absorbed from our digestive tract into our bloodstream. The insulin takes it from our blood and lays it down as fatty deposits in **adipose cells**. These adipose cells are the body's fat stores and the changing quantity of them is largely responsible for alterations in our body weight.

Key terms

Hunger: a drive that causes an animal to change its behaviour towards one of obtaining food.

Satiation: the removal of the drive for hunger.

Homeostasis: the maintenance of a constant internal environment.

Glucose: a sugar that is the main source of easily useable energy. It travels in the blood where it can be transported to every one of the body's cells.

Glycogen: excess glucose stored by the body.

Insulin: the hormone made by the pancreas that converts blood glucose into glycogen for storage. It also helps fat to be stored in adipose cells.

Pancreas: the endocrine gland that makes insulin and glucagon. It is situated near the liver.

Adipose cells: the fat storage cells of the body.

Glucagon: This is a hormone that helps facilitate the release of glucose from the liver where it has been stored as glycogen.

Diabetes: a disease caused by low blood levels of insulin. Without enough insulin any excess of blood glucose cannot be stored as glycogen.

Leptin: the hormone that is released from adipose cells and travels to the hypothalamus where it acts as a satiety signal.

Satiety: the state in which the body believes it has eaten enough food to sustain itself for a period of time.

In order to get the stored glycogen and fat into a useable form of energy again we need another hormone called **glucagon**. Glucagon is also released from the pancreas and its job is to make the liver cells convert the stored glycogen back into glucose and then release that glucose into the bloodstream. Glucagon can also cause the release of fats from adipose tissue and these fats can then be converted into useable glucose or other forms of energy. However, the main hormone responsible for the breakdown of fats into useable energy is adrenaline and this is massively released during a fight or flight scenario.

The importance of insulin is demonstrated by the condition called **diabetes**. When a person has diabetes their insulin levels are low because of a failure of production by the pancreas and so they do not store the excess glucose in the blood. This causes a number of problems, including confusion that can lead to delirium and loss of consciousness. A lack of insulin can also result in a heart attack or blindness, and so those with severe diabetes have to inject themselves with insulin daily. Failure of the pancreas to produce insulin can happen because of damage to the cells early in life (type 1 diabetes) or can be due to a gradual decline of function later in life (type 2 diabetes). Type 2 diabetes is far more common and is linked to obesity, which we discuss later in this chapter.

Leptin

As already mentioned, when there is excess fat in the blood, it gets stored in adipose tissue. There is a hormone in fat cells that gets released as the fat gets stored called **leptin**. As more fat gets stored, so more leptin is released and this acts as a trigger for the person to stop eating (a **satiety** signal). The discovery of this hormone arose from the study of a genetically obese strain of mice referred to as 'ob' mice. The reason that these mice are obese is because they lack the gene that leads to the production of leptin. It seems that without leptin, the animal fails to become satiated (the feeling of having had enough to eat) and so keeps on eating. Further evidence to support this view is the fact that injections of leptin into 'ob' mice stops them eating as much.

ACTIVITY 6.3

Using the diagram, copy out the list of labels below and match them to the correct number in the cycle.

- the pancreas releases insulin into the bloodstream
- blood glucose levels drop to normal
- blood glucose levels rise to normal
- the liver begins storing glucose as glycogen
- the liver begins converting stored glycogen into glucose
- the pancreas secretes glucagon into the bloodstream

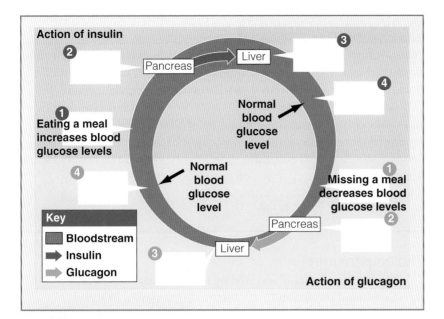

EXAMPLE EXAM QUESTION

Briefly outline the role of leptin in the control of eating behaviour. (2 marks)

Exam hint

As this question is worth two marks you should aim to say two things about the role of leptin.

Ghrelin

Ghrelin is a hormone that works in the opposite direction to leptin. When the stomach is empty, it releases **ghrelin** as a signal to the animal to start foraging for food. The amount of ghrelin that is released is proportional to the emptiness of the stomach. Although much of the research in this area was originally done on animals, the effect was also shown by Cummings et al. (2004) using human participants. When food is eaten it stretches the stomach wall and this stretching reduces the amount of ghrelin that is released. Ghrelin is known to act on a number of brain sites (e.g. the hypothalus) that are involved in the control of eating behaviour.

Key term

Ghrelin: the hormone that is released from the emptying stomach to signal to the hypothalamus that more food is required.

KEY STUDY: CUMMINGS ET AL. (2004)

Cummings et al. were interested in the relationship between the level of ghrelin release and the emptiness of the stomach. They asked six participants to agree to have blood samples at five-minute intervals taken from a catheter inserted into a vein, from when they ate a meal at lunchtime until they said they would like their evening meal. The blood samples allowed the researchers to monitor their levels of ghrelin. In addition, participants were asked every 30 minutes to report on their level of hunger.

The level of ghrelin was found to fall immediately after eating lunch and the drop lasted for around 70 minutes. After this, the level of blood ghrelin rose gradually until the participant reported wanting a meal and the experiment was stopped. Moreover, the level of blood ghrelin correlated extremely well with the level of reported hunger in five of the six participants. The authors concluded that the level of ghrelin was directly related to the emptiness of the stomach and that it also contributed to the level of hunger a person felt.

Research methods link

For more on sample sizes, see pages 31–33.

Much of Cummings et al.'s study points to the employment of very rigorous methodology. For example, the participants were isolated from any time cues so that there could be no influence from anticipating the approach of mealtime. The researchers also provided fully informed consent, and approval from the Ethics Committee had been obtained. There was also a full debriefing given after the study. The main problem with the study is that the sample size was very small and all of the six participants were male. We can ask the question as to whether the results can be generalized to the rest of the population and, in particular, to females. While it is hard to imagine why there might be gender differences in such a mechanism, we cannot be sure without further investigation. In addition, the data collected only provided correlations and not causes, so some caution would be needed in interpreting the results.

Key term

Cholecystokinin: the hormone released from the duodenum that signals to the hypothalamus that food is being digested and that eating may not need to continue.

Cholecystokinin

This is a hormone that is secreted by the first part of the small intestine called the duodenum. The food that passes from the stomach to the duodenum stimulates the release of **cholecystokinin (CCK)** from its walls. Its function seems to be as a satiety signal and it acts to oppose the effects of ghrelin. It also causes a slowing down of the movement of food through the digestive tract and thereby allows for greater absorption of nutrients into the blood. Injecting CCK can reduce the meal size that an animal or a human will eat (Gibbs et al., 1973), though it does also cause nausea, which makes its use as an appetite suppressant limited.

Neuronal control of eating

The main pathway of the food that we eat is through our digestive tract. This starts at the mouth, where we put food in, and ends at the anus, where we excrete waste products that we have no need for. Some key things happen along the way and the first of those occurs as soon as we put food in our mouths. Even before food enters your mouth, you begin to salivate and the saliva contains enzymes that start to break down the food. Our interest here, though, is in how signals from the digestive tract let the brain know how much food has been consumed.

The role of the stomach

One of the earliest studies to investigate the stomach was one by Cannon and Washburn (1912). Washburn, Cannon's student, was persuaded to swallow a balloon that could be inflated, and his stomach contractions were measured alongside his reports about his level of hunger. Whenever a stomach contraction occurred, Washburn reported having a hunger pang. This suggested that the contractions of the stomach were sending a message to the brain to indicate the degree of hunger being experienced. The finding was reinforced when a man who had swallowed acid, leading to the need to feed him directly into his stomach, also reported hunger in tandem with stomach contractions. However, it became obvious that the stomach was only one of many signalling systems when it was discovered that people who need to have their stomach surgically removed are still able to feel hunger.

The role of the hypothalamus

The discovery of the brain area most involved in hunger and satiety did not come until 30 years after Cannon and Washburn's discovery. By carrying out lesion studies on rats, Hetherington and Ranson (1942) discovered an area of the **hypothalamus** that seemed to be involved in stopping an animal from eating. This area is known as the **ventromedial nucleus** (VMH – indicating the ventromedial hypothalamus) and its removal causes an animal to overeat to the point of becoming morbidly obese. In fact, it will eat until it is about twice its normal weight (see Fig. 6.5).

Fig. 6.5 A rat that has had its ventromedial hypothalamus removed. It is typically known as a VMH rat.

The lesion seemed to be affecting the animal's **satiety centre** and so it did not register that it was full. Signals that indicate there is sufficient food in the body (for example, a lack of stomach contractions, a decreased release of ghrelin, a rise in blood glucose and an increased release of leptin) all travel to the VMH and switch off the animal's desire to go foraging for food.

A short time after this discovery, Anand and Brobeck (1951) discovered that lesions to another part of the hypothalamus would stop an animal from eating (a condition known as **aphagia**). This region is the **lateral hypothalamus** (LH) and it rapidly became referred to as the **feeding centre**. Activation of this region of

Key terms

Hypothalamus: the structure in the brain that controls a number of different regulatory functions of the body, including eating and the cessation of eating.

Ventromedial nucleus: part of the hypothalamus and is said to be the seat of the brain's satiety centre.

Satiety centre: the region of the brain that when activated causes an organism to stop eating.

Aphagia: a failure to eat when hungry.

Lateral hypothalamus: the part of the hypothalamus said to be the seat of the brain's feeding centre.

Feeding centre: the region of the brain that causes an organism to start eating.

the brain come from the signals indicating a decline in the level of nutrients. These signals include decreased blood glucose levels, stomach contractions and an increase in the release of ghrelin.

KEY STUDY: ANAND AND BROBECK (1951)

During the 1940s, a number of studies had discovered that damage to the ventromedial nucleus of the hypothalamus had led to overeating. There had also been suggestions of aphagia from researchers that had been investigating the role of the hypothalamus in temperature regulation. They decided, therefore, to systematically investigate the hypothalamus for regions that might control eating in the same way that the ventromedial hypothalamus controls satiety.

Anand and Brobeck used 94 rats to investigate areas of the hypothalamus near to the ventromedial nucleus. Some rats received large lesions (a method of destroying brain tissue) until candidate areas for aphagia had been located. They then gave other rats smaller lesions in that area so as to pinpoint exactly where in the hypothalamus the control of eating occurred. They discovered that there was a feeding centre within the hypothalamus and that it lay in the LH. They were even able to locate the precise centre to the most lateral part of the LH.

THINKING SCIENTIFICALLY: EXTRAPOLATING FROM ANIMALS TO HUMANS

It is always difficult to decide whether things we discover using animals may or may not apply to humans. In terms of findings from brain research, we must decide on the answer to two main questions. Firstly, is the animal that was used close enough (in evolutionary terms) to humans to reasonably assume that the areas of its brain are equivalent to the areas of a human brain? Secondly, is the function under investigation basic enough to be likely to be carried out the same way by this animal and by humans?

In the case of the Anand and Brobeck study, the animal was a rat and, since it is also a mammal, we can make the case that it is evolutionarily close enough to have a brain similar to that of a human. It is also the case here that the function under investigation was eating, so it is reasonable to assume that a rat's basic drives for eating and satiety are similar to a human's drives. However, we must also be mindful of the fact that humans are likely to be more sophisticated in their decision-making as to whether to continue eating or to stop eating, and so biological hunger will only be one of the factors guiding behaviour.

Confirmation of these findings came from studies using electrical stimulation rather than lesions. It was found that stimulating the LH would cause an animal to start foraging for food (or eating if food was present) and stimulating the VMH would cause an animal to stop eating. The whole process of hunger and satiety can therefore be seen as a cycle that is controlled by the hypothalamus (see Fig. 6.6)

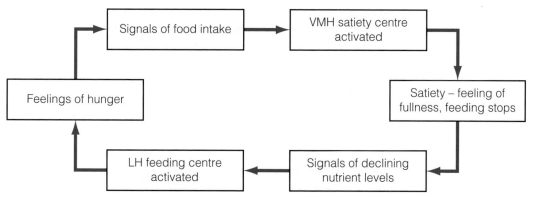

Fig. 6.6 Feeding, hunger and satiety centres – the dual centre model of feeding

Serotonin and eating

There has been research spanning the last 40 years that has suggested that serotonin (also known as 5-hydroxytryptamine or 5-HT) is involved in feeding behaviour; specifically, that increased levels of serotonin reduced food intake, whereas reduced availability of the neurotransmitter or blocking the receptors for it could induce feeding. Serotonin is one of the active neurotransmitter substances in the hypothalamus and is found in regions of the LH which, as we have seen, is considered to be a feeding centre. It is no surprise then that serotonin is believed to be involved in the regulation of feeding.

ACTIVITY 6.4

Discussion point: If the ventromedial hypothalamus controls satiety and the lateral hypothalamus controls feeding, what would you expect to be the effect if an animal had both areas of the hypothalamus removed?

The dual hypothalamic theory of the regulation of eating

As mentioned before, it is easy for the body to detect that it needs more food as this can be signalled by energy levels falling below a certain point. However, it is more difficult to make the judgement as to when to stop eating, as the food will not yet have been digested and the energy value of the food assessed. The ultimate goal is for the body to maintain a certain level of body fat. This is referred to as the set point and is monitored by the hypothalamic centres responsible for hunger and satiety. There have been two main theories as to how the set point is maintained: the glucostatic theory and the lipostatic theory.

The glucostatic theory

The **glucostatic theory** maintains that it is the blood glucose levels that are monitored by the hypothalamus to determine when it is time to eat and when it is time to stop eating. Blood glucose levels

> **Key term**
>
> **Glucostatic theory:** the theory that glucose levels in the blood are the main signal to the hypothalamus as to whether to start or stop eating and that they control the short-term regulation of food intake.

rise quite rapidly after food intake so this was a prime candidate. However, it was found by Alfenas and Mattes (2005) that blood glucose levels do not fluctuate enough between hunger states and satiated states to act as a trigger. Furthermore, the blood glucose levels of diabetics is often generally high and yet they do not have significantly smaller appetites than non-diabetics. Indeed, both type 1 and type 2 diabetics are more likely to be overeaters. A more recent version of the theory suggests that it might be glucose utilization rather than blood glucose levels that acts as the trigger. Since the lack of insulin in diabetics would reduce glucose utilization, this could account for some cases of diabetic overeating and obesity.

Exam hint

You will need to briefly state what the theory is. You might then evaluate it by referring to how well (or not) it explains a disorder like diabetes.

Key term

Lipostatic theory: the theory that fat levels in the blood are an important signal to the hypothalamus as to whether to start or stop eating and that they control the long-term regulation of food intake.

EXAMPLE EXAM QUESTION

Briefly evaluate the glucostatic theory of the control of eating behaviour. [4 marks]

The lipostatic theory

The **lipostatic theory** maintains that there is a set point for body fat. Here, then, the level of body fat is monitored and eating is regulated to keep the level of fat to a set point. Clearly, fat levels are going to change less rapidly than glucose levels, so the lipostatic theory has been suggested as an explanation of a long-term regulatory system, with the glucostatic theory explaining short-term regulation. The lipostatic theory would explain why short-term diets tend not to work – once the diet is over, the body will be driven to eat to return the level of body fat to 'normal'.

A modern approach

The two theories referred to above do not account for the roles of leptin and ghrelin, nor the roles of the other hormones we have looked at, such as cholecystokinin. It is clear that the regulation of food intake is a complex process and our knowledge of its complexity helps us to understand the biological influences on both anorexia and obesity that we shall look at later in this chapter.

KEY POINTS

- Hunger and satiation are two of the body's homeostatic mechanisms that help to maintain a stable internal environment.
- A number of hormones act as markers for how much nutrition is available to the organism at any given time.
- How much to eat is, to a degree, educated guesswork as the organism cannot know when it will next be able to feed.
- Insulin and glucagon help to maintain the level of available glucose in the blood.
- Leptin is a satiety signal based on the level of stored fat.
- Ghrelin is released as the stomach gets empty to signal the need to eat.
- There are a number of neural mechanisms that control feeding and satiation.

- The most important brain structure in the control of eating is the hypothalamus.

- The ventromedial hypothalamus is the satiety centre and the lateral hypothalamus is the feeding centre.

- The glucostatic and lipostatic theories both try to explain how either glucose or fat are monitored to maintain the organism's body weight.

Biological explanations of anorexia nervosa

Diagnosis of anorexia nervosa

When they are ill, people with anorexia nervosa don't seek or respond to the kinds of comforts and pleasures most of us enjoy, including food. They also resist and ignore feedback that signifies their precarious state of health. They don't see an emaciated figure in the mirror, they ignore the most obvious warning signs and dismiss comments from loved ones that suggest they are seriously and medically ill. People with anorexia nervosa have extreme self-denial, not only of food, but often of many comforts and pleasures in life. (Dr Walter Kaye, professor of psychiatry at the University of Pittsburgh School of Medicine)

The diagnostic criteria for **anorexia nervosa** (AN) includes:

- Restricting energy intake: eating less than is needed to maintain a body weight, leading to significantly low weight for age, sex and physical health.

- Either an intense fear of gaining weight or of becoming fat, or behaviour that interferes with weight gain (even though person is already a significantly low weight).

- Problems with body image: denying how serious their current low body weight is, or having a distorted image of their own shape/ weight, or allowing their shape/weight to unduly influence their self-worth.

In addition, there are two subtypes of AN. The **restricting type** involves a refusal to eat, whereas the **binge-eating/purging type** involves episodes of binge-eating followed by purging (removing weight from the body through vomiting or laxatives). Both of these subtypes of AN are associated with significant weight loss.

Anorexia nervosa is relatively rare, affecting around 0.3 per cent of males and 0.9 per cent of females. It affects young women far more than any other group (around 90 per cent of cases are female) and is extremely resistant to treatment. Some 30–40 per cent will show no improvement after five years. Anorexia nervosa is associated with a mortality rate of about 8 per cent, often through suicide (Polivy and Herman, 2002).

> **Key term**
>
> **Anorexia nervosa:** an eating disorder characterized by restriction of energy intake and an extreme fear of gaining weight. Subtypes include restricting and binge eating/purging.

Biological mechanisms associated with anorexia nervosa

Having looked at the biological mechanisms of normal eating, we are now in a position to examine what might go wrong in eating disorders. In this section we will examine the biological mechanisms associated with anorexia nervosa.

To explore the possible biological explanations of AN, we will first look to see if there is a genetic link by examining twin and family studies and the possible involvement of particular genes. We then look at the role of the neurotransmitters serotonin and dopamine and ask whether changes in these cause AN or if these changes are the effect of having AN. Finally, we will look at the possibility that AN results from neurodevelopmental events such as birth complications.

Genetic links to anorexia nervosa

It is difficult to understand why a person would simply choose to stop eating to the point where they endanger their own life. In looking for an explanation, we must examine whether or not this behaviour is inherited through DNA. One way of doing this is to carry out a **twin study**, in which we examine the likelihood of one twin having anorexia if the other twin has it. Of course, we must take into account whether the twins are identical or non-identical. Identical twins share 100 per cent of their DNA as they form from a single zygote (created from one egg and one sperm), hence they are called **monozygotic (MZ) twins**. Non-identical twins share, on average, 50 per cent of their DNA as they grow from two separate zygotes that develop together in the womb, hence they are referred to as **dizygotic (DZ) twins**. In fact, DZ twins share the same amount of DNA as any siblings do. The advantage of using twins is that, being born at the same time, they will have had virtually identical environments as they grew up. Furthermore, since MZ twins have twice the shared DNA as DZ twins, we should find twice the genetic influence. This can be measured through the **concordance rate**, which for this topic is the percentage of twin pairs who both show anorexia.

Holland et al. (1984) carried out a twin study and found that there was good evidence for arguing that AN is partly inherited. They found that the concordance rate for MZ twins (56 per cent) was significantly higher than for DZ twins (7 per cent). In a further study (Holland et al., 1988), they used a larger sample and found similar results. This time they had more twin pairs (45 compared with 34 in the earlier study) and they also collected family data. Concordance rates were found to be similar to the previous study (56 per cent and 5 per cent respectively). However, the addition of family data meant that they could calculate **heritability** scores in addition to looking at concordance rates. This showed even more clearly that there is a very strong genetic influence on the development of AN.

Fig. 6.7 The Olsen twins. When Mary-Kate (left or right?) was admitted to hospital suffering from AN her sister, Ashley (left or right?), was not suffering from AN at the time.

KEY STUDY: HOLLAND ET AL. (1984)

Holland et al. (1984) were interested in finding out the degree to which AN was genetically inherited. They hypothesized that if AN is inherited then if one MZ twin develops AN the other twin should also develop it. Furthermore, if one DZ twin develops AN then the other twin should have a 50 per cent chance of developing it. They studied 34 twin pairs to establish these concordance rates. The twin pairs were made up of 30 female pairs and 4 male, where one twin had already been diagnosed with AN. Whether or not the twins were MZ or DZ was established using a physical resemblance questionnaire. A blood test was only used if the questionnaire result was deemed to be inconclusive. Standard clinical tests were used to establish whether or not a twin had developed AN.

On examining the female twin pairs, Holland et al. found that the concordance rate for MZ twins was much higher than that for DZ twins. Concordance of AN was found in 9 of the 16 MZ twin pairs (56 per cent) and only one of the 14 DZ pairs (7 per cent). This would seem to provide a strong argument for saying that AN partly is caused by genetic inheritance. However, there are two problems with this study. The first is that the sample was very small and was also very gender-biased. The second is the assumption that the environment of twin pairs is identical. While similar, the environmental similarity might be stronger for MZ twins than for DZ twins.

THINKING SCIENTIFICALLY: EVALUATING TWIN STUDIES

The assumption that is made with twin studies is that twins are brought up in the same environment and so any concordance rates are a pure indicator of genetic inheritance. The argument is that they will be treated identically by their parents, they will play together and they will grow up in the same environment. On this basis, then, we would expect that if AN is purely down to genetic inheritance, MZ twins should show 100 per cent concordance and DZ twins should show 50 per cent concordance, on average. However, there is good reason to believe that MZ twins are treated more similarly than DZ twins and so part of the difference in concordance rates between MZ and DZ twins could reflect environmental effects. So if we examine the results of Holland et al.'s 1984 study we can see that there is evidence for a genetic component to AN but that we must also look to other, environmental explanations.

Alongside twin studies, researchers have tried to assess the genetic influence on AN by carrying out family studies. These investigate the family history of AN to try to establish whether or not there are inheritance factors in its development. One such study was carried out by Strober et al. (1985). They looked at the families of 60 anorexic patients and 95 non-anorexic patients who had a different psychiatric illness. They interviewed all of the first-degree relatives (immediate family) and as many second-degree relatives (aunts and uncles) as they could. They found 35 cases of eating disorders among the relatives and 27 of those (77 per cent) were relatives of patients with AN. This finding supports the view that there is a significant genetic component of AN.

It is fair to say that the studies referred to above are quite old and that interest in the genetics of AN has moved on and has now swung to finding the precise genes that are responsible for the variety of factors that give rise to AN. As we will see through the rest of this topic, the biological factors involved in AN go beyond those of the feeding and satiety centres and involve perceptual systems, anxiety and impulse control and the interpretation of harm and pleasure.

ACTIVITY 6.5

While the concordance rates for MZ twins are not 100 per cent, they are always larger than those for DZ twins. Discuss what this means in terms of the genetic influence on the development of anorexia nervosa.

Serotonin

Serotonin (also known as 5-hydroxytryptamine or 5-HT) is a brain neurotransmitter that is involved in a number of different functions. These include mood and impulse control and so dysfunction of this system has been shown to be involved in depression and obsessive–compulsive disorder. Serotonin also plays a role in feeding, as we saw earlier in the chapter. In order to make serotonin, the body needs **tryptophan**, an amino acid that we obtain directly from our food. How, then, might all of this come together to explain AN?

One of the clues to the role of serotonin in AN was the finding that sufferers of AN have reduced levels of **5-hydroxyindoleacetic acid (5-HIAA)** in their urine. This is a **metabolite** of serotonin. In other words, it is what is left when serotonin gets used up and this compound then gets excreted. If there is less 5-HIAA in the urine then there must be less serotonin being used. However, the reduced 5-HIAA is found in those who already have AN, so it could be that having AN leads to a reduction of serotonin metabolism and not the other way around. Kaye et al. (2005) examined the density of receptors for serotonin. There are two different serotonin receptors, 5-HT_{1A} and 5-HT_{2A}. It is the number of 5-HT_{2A} receptors that seem to be reduced in AN, leading to the lowered levels of serotonin use. What Kaye et al. suggested is that a person with AN starts out as someone with high levels of anxiety because of high levels of serotonin. High levels of serotonin also leads to the suppression of appetite. The person quickly learns that by eating less they can reduce their anxiety (the reduced intake of tryptophan reduces the amount of serotonin produced). The brain's reaction to the reduced serotonin levels is a reduction in the receptors for it and this occurs in an area

Key terms

Serotonin: a major brain neurotransmitter substance that is involved in various brain functions.

Tryptophan: an amino acid that is obtained from our diet and is used in the making of serotonin.

5-hydroxyindoleacetic acid (5-HIAA): when serotonin is used by the brain it gets broken down into 5-HIAA. The presence of 5-HIAA in a person's urine is an indicator that serotonin has been active.

Metabolite: any breakdown product that is the result of a chemical being used in the body.

of the brain that is responsible for impulse control. So, all in all, reducing food intake leads to reduced anxiety, but also to a reduced impulse control, so the impulse to eat due to the lowered serotonin is not acted on and the person continues to be driven by the satisfaction of the reduction in anxiety.

One of the limitations of this explanation of AN is the response of patients to the prescription of serotonin-specific reuptake inhibitors (SSRIs). These are drugs that lead to an elevation in the levels of serotonin. If the AN is caused simply by reduced levels of serotonin then taking SSRIs should alleviate the symptoms. However, it has been found that these drugs are only effective once a person's body weight has returned to normal. They do not help the person who is already chronically underweight. Another limitation of most of the AN research is that it is carried out almost exclusively on women. In general, 25 per cent of all eating disorders occur in men and AN itself is not exclusively a female problem.

Dopamine

As well as serotonin, another neurotransmitter substance, **dopamine**, has been linked to AN. Frank et al. (2005) reported on the dopamine activity of those recovering from AN compared to healthy controls. They used **positron emission tomography (PET)** scans to measure the levels of dopamine activity in a part of the brain known as the basal ganglia. Neurons in the basal ganglia are known to be involved in the interpretation of harm and pleasure. The researchers found that those recovering from AN had increased dopamine receptor activity, particularly at a particular kind of receptor called the D2 receptor type. This is associated with hyperactivity and an inability to comprehend the importance of stimuli. As a result, they do not obtain the usual pleasure from eating food. It is thought, therefore, that the overactivity of dopamine in the basal ganglia allows the AN patient to lose weight, resist eating and over-exercise.

Another study that supports the suggestion that dopamine levels are elevated in AN is the finding by Castro-Fornieles et al. (2006) that adolescent girls with AN have a higher level of **homovanillic acid** in their urine. Since this is a waste product of the metabolism of dopamine, we can conclude that dopamine activity must have been increased. While the above results are impressive, there is no consistency in the findings of studies linking dopamine to AN. Across a number of studies there are those that find an increase, decrease or normal levels of dopamine activity in AN patients when compared to healthy controls. We must remember also that the Frank et al. (2005) study used women who had recovered from AN rather than those currently suffering from it. We must be careful, therefore, not to ascribe cause to the increased dopamine activity found.

Key terms

Dopamine: a major brain neurotransmitter substance that is involved in various brain functions.

Positron emission tomography (PET): a type of imaging technique. A person first ingests a mildly radioactive form of glucose. When a part of the brain increases its activity it requires more glucose and some of this will be the ingested radioactive glucose. The imaging scanner detects this radioactivity and so we can see, in real time, which parts of the brain are active.

Homovanillic acid: the substance into which dopamine used by the brain gets broken down. The presence of homovanillic acid in a person's urine is an indicator that dopamine has been active.

Exam hint

A good way to approach this question is to use research evidence to illustrate the role of dopamine. The use of PET scans can be used to illustrate the link between an excess of dopamine activity and anorexia nervosa.

EXAMPLE EXAM QUESTION

Outline the role of dopamine in anorexia nervosa. (4 marks)

Key terms

Obstetric complications: medical problems that occur either during pregnancy or in the process of giving birth.

Attachment style: the kind of bond that develops early on between the primary caregiver (usually the mother) and the baby.

Neurodevelopmental explanations

Neurodevelopment refers to changes that occur while the foetus is developing in the womb or during the early part of an infant's development. There are three main neurodevelopmental aspects that have been suggested as a cause for AN. These are obstetric complications, maternal nutrition and season of birth.

Obstetric complications

Obstetric complications involve difficulties concerning the birth itself and one such difficulty is premature birth. Cnattingius et al. (1999) showed that among parents whose children go on to develop AN, 25 per cent of the mothers may have experienced severe obstetric complications, compared with only 7.5 per cent of those not experiencing such complications. In addition, Ward et al. (2000) have suggested that premature birth can increase the chances of the child developing AN by two to three times. Lindberg and Hjem (2003) later confirmed the relationship between premature birth and the development of AN. The likely reason for the link is that birth complications can lead to hypoxia, a lack of oxygen. If there is a lack of oxygen to the brain during birth then this can lead to brain damage.

Another possible mechanism for the development of AN could be the effect of birth complications on the way a mother relates to her child. During the early part of infancy, the baby creates important bonds with the primary caregiver (usually the mother). Mothers who have gone through obstetric trauma often have heightened anxiety and this can lead to the development of a dismissive **attachment style** (Ward et al., 2001). This can lead to reduced emotional expression of the mother which, in turn, might impair the development of the child's emotional regulation and its capacity to resolve trauma and loss later on. This attachment style can have very real effects on how the infant brain develops, particularly a region called the hypothalamic-pituitary-adrenal axis (HPA). The HPA system is very important to an organism's ability to respond to stress, and a lack of its proper development could lead to deficits in emotional recognition that often accompany AN.

Maternal nutrition

Alongside these possible causes, there is a potential problem with maternal nutrition. If the mother is suffering from AN during pregnancy, then the foetus will not be receiving enough nutrition. This is likely to lead to a lack of proper development of the foetus and can also cause birth complications. This also represents a double disadvantage, as the child will suffer from a genetic propensity to AN plus the effects of damage caused by a lack of nutrition.

EXAMPLE EXAM QUESTION

Outline what is meant by the term neural explanations in the context of anorexia nervosa. [4 marks]

Exam hint

As this question is for four marks there is scope to first define the word neural and then use two or three areas of development to illustrate how they can explain AN. For each area you will need to briefly say what it is and give an example of a research finding.

Season of birth

The idea that the time of year in which you are born can affect your mental health outcome is not a new one. This relationship has been suggested for a wide range of disorders and AN is no exception. Eagles et al. (2001) have suggested that those born in spring and summer are more susceptible to AN. Indeed, a recent meta-analysis of the effect of birth season was conducted in the UK by Disanto et al. (2011). They surveyed the month of birth data from 1293 anorexic cases in the UK (from a pool of nearly 22 million recorded anorexic cases between 1950 and 1980). They found that there was a significant excess of births from March to June and a significant lack of births from September to October. It is likely that these differences are due to environmental effects that have an impact on development around a critical time, such as early gestation or the early postnatal period. The authors suggested that candidate environmental events include seasonal changes in temperature, sunlight exposure and vitamin D levels, maternal nutrition and exposure to infections.

ACTIVITY 6.6

Within this section we have seen arguments that AN is partly genetically inherited and arguments that it is the result of neurodevelopmental problems. Discuss the relative merits of these two very different types of explanation for AN.

KEY STUDY: EAGLES ET AL. (2001)

The purpose of this study was to investigate whether the chances of becoming anorexic are related to the season in which a person is born. Eagles et al. analysed the birth dates from 446 female AN patients born in the northeast of Scotland between 1965 and 1997. They discovered that there was a significant increase in AN among females born in the first six months of the year, with the greatest rise being among those born between March and June.

Eagles et al. noted that these months were also associated with increases in other disorders, such as schizophrenia. They concluded that the most likely explanation was an intrauterine effect of diseases that were picked up by the mother during the winter months.

The Eagles et al. (2001) study provides us with some interesting significant results but the difficulty lies in interpreting what they mean. Firstly, such data only shows correlations and cannot tell us much about causes. While we can speculate about the features of the winter months that might contribute to AN, they must remain speculation. Furthermore, we cannot be sure that the clinical diagnosis of AN remained constant over the 30-year-period or that those making clinical diagnoses were doing so under common criteria. However, the study's analysis included a large sample size (albeit only a female one) so we can have some confidence that there is an association that needs further investigation.

KEY POINTS

- Twin studies suggest there is a genetic link to AN but that this does not tell the whole story of how AN develops.
- Family studies that look at first-degree relatives to see if there is a pattern within families have shown further support for the heritability of AN.
- A number of neurotransmitter systems have been linked to AN.
- Serotonin has been linked to AN, with high levels leading to appetite suppression and lowered anxiety but also a lowered impulse to eat.
- Dopamine has also been linked with AN, in the form of elevated levels that lead to people with AN getting less of a reward from the pleasure of eating.
- There are a number of potential neurodevelopmental causes of AN, including obstetric complications, lowered maternal nutrition and even the season in which a person is born.

Psychological explanations of eating disorders

We have seen that anorexia runs in families. However the lack of 100 per cent correlation between identical twins indicates that AN is not wholly explained by biological factors. A range of psychological factors play a part in the development of anorexia, including a cultural emphasis on thinness, family relationships and beliefs and attitudes about body size and shape. Here we examine the explanations put forward by social learning theory, the psychodynamic approach and the cognitive approach.

As you read this topic, try to avoid seeing these explanations as 'either/or'. It is helpful to think of AN as a jigsaw, with each explanation filling in a different element of the puzzle. It is rare that complicated human experiences have a single cause.

Social learning theory: modelling, reinforcement and media images

As you read in Book 1, social learning theory (SLT) focuses on the importance of learning from other people through observation

Link

You can remind yourself about SLT by looking back at pages 227–228 of Book 1.

and imitation of their behaviour. This is referred to as **modelling**. Behaviours or qualities that are seen to bring rewards to role models are most likely to be copied. This is **vicarious reinforcement**.

How might social learning influence the development of AN? Children are exposed to a range of role models including parents, siblings and peers. They are also exposed to images through television, the Internet and magazines, which provide messages about desirable body shape and size. Over the last 50 years, the desirable shape for women has gradually got thinner – pictures of actress Marilyn Monroe, the most famous beauty of the 1950s and 1960s, show how much ideals about women's bodies have changed. In contrast, the desirable body for boys and young men now emphasizes a muscular, toned physique rather than slenderness, encouraging young men to work out and bulk up. Exposure to a particular kind of ideal body shape can have a dramatic impact on how people think and feel about the adequacy of their own bodies.

Fig. 6.8 Marilyn Monroe had the desirable body shape of the 1950s and 1960s

Fig. 6.9 Model Rosie Nelson petitioned the government in 2015 to introduce legislation to stop the use of dangerously thin models. Nelson was already slim when she was told by an agency to slim 'down to the bone'.

Cross-cultural studies examining the incidence of AN provide an important source of evidence about exposure to thin models. Becker et al. (2002) investigated the incidence of eating disorders in Fiji before and after the introduction of television. While there was an absence of eating disorders before exposure to western television, five years after the introduction of television there were significant numbers of women with anorexia nervosa and bulimia nervosa. In support, Hoek et al. (1998) found lower rates of AN in the black inhabitants of the Caribbean island of Curaçao compared to the white population. They concluded that this was because the white population aspired more to western lifestyles, especially in relation to idealized images of women, while the black population still valued larger female bodies.

Reinforcement is another element of learning theory. Positive reinforcement includes compliments for weight loss and negative comments/teasing about bodies. Hill and Franklin (1998) found that the mothers of girls with eating problems were more critical of their daughter's appearance than the mothers of healthy girls.

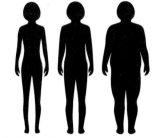

Fig. 6.10 The girls were shown three outline figures

Recent evidence suggests that girls start to internalize the idea that success equals thinness at a very young age indeed. Harriger (2014) studied a sample of 102 American girls between three and five years of age. The girls were shown three silhouettes (see Fig. 6.10) and then asked 'point to the girl who you think would be smart/mean/nice etc.'). Girls as young as three years of age allocated positive qualities to the thin image and negative qualities to the normal-sized and larger images.

One explanation of media effects is objectification theory (Fredrickson and Roberts, 1997). According to this approach, girls are aware that they are looked at and judged for their bodies and they rapidly learn to look at their body from an observer's perspective. This is **self-objectification**, literally seeing oneself as an object. Self-objectification occurs more in girls for two reasons:

- Girls are exposed to more critical comments about their bodies than boys.

- The media is saturated with images of female bodies, which are commented on and constantly evaluated.

In such a climate, 'girls are socialized into treating themselves as objects to be evaluated' (Mahendran, 2015). Stevens Aubrey (2006) asked a sample of American students, both male and female, to record their consumption of media images from television and magazines over a period of one year. She then measured their self-esteem and tendency to self-objectify. Those who consumed more media had higher levels of self-objectification: this was true of both women and men.

Fig. 6.11 Selfie or self-objectification?

Evidence and evaluation

As we have seen, there is a wealth of evidence for the importance of social learning in the development of AN. This approach can explain why AN is much more common in girls than boys, through the emphasis on slenderness as the ideal body shape rather than muscularity. It can also explain the increase in the incidence of AN between the 1970s and the 1990s (Keel and Klump, 2003) as the female ideal body became smaller. The approach is supported by considerable evidence from cross-cultural research, which indicates that greater exposure to western media is associated with increases in disordered eating.

Where SLT is less successful is in explaining who develops eating disorders. In our western culture, people are exposed all the time to images of ideal bodies – but only a small number go on to develop the clinical criteria for AN. This points to the conclusion that some people may be more vulnerable to this influence than others. In many families, one child develops AN but the others do not, pointing to the importance of some form of biological or psychological vulnerability. Anorexia is common in high-achieving girls from middle-class academic families where there is pressure to succeed. It is also more common in people with perfectionist tendencies. One area that has been looked at is the psychological characteristics of people with eating disorders and their families.

Psychodynamic explanations of anorexia

The psychodynamic approach emphasizes the importance of unconscious processes in behaviour. According to this approach, difficult or uncomfortable experiences, often from childhood, are locked away in the unconscious mind (or repressed) where they continue to affect adult behaviour. Freud believed that sexual development was particularly important and disruptions to development in the psychosexual stages could have lasting effects.

Link

You can recap the psychodynamic approach by looking at pages 216–220 of Book 1.

Anorexia typically starts during late childhood or early adolescence. Puberty marks the start of menstruation along with bodily changes – girls develop breasts and their hips broaden. The self-starvation integral to AN reverses or prevents these changes. Menstruation ceases, allowing the girl to put off decisions about sexuality and intimacy and the body resembles that of a pre-pubescent child. A simple explanation put forward by Crisp (1980) proposed that AN was an attempt to remain in a pre-pubertal state and postpone the onset of adulthood.

Anorexia as a struggle for autonomy

Hilde Bruch, a German doctor and therapist, carried out case studies examining the family backgrounds of people she was treating for anorexia. She identified a number of common characteristics, including the observation that two-thirds of her clients had sisters but no brothers. Bruch found that the mothers of AN people used food as a reward/comforter and anticipated their daughter's feeding needs. Bruch argued this could lead girls to feel confused about whether they were hungry or not and to feeling controlled. She referred to the family of the anorexic as 'a golden cage' (Bruch, 1978), protective and constraining, with few opportunities for self-determination. In this environment, Bruch believed that children struggle for autonomy – to feel independent from their parents. Bruch characterized AN as an attempt to exert control.

Bruch believed that AN served a number of functions, giving the sufferer a sense of control and self-esteem – self-starvation is, after all, difficult to achieve. Anorexia allowed the individual to withdraw from relationships and put off issues about adulthood and sexuality. Eating was one area that the sufferer could control (increase their self-efficacy) and feel autonomous. Within this context, the psychodynamic approach makes sense of AN as a 'desperate way of coping with problems involved in becoming an autonomous person' (Edwards, 1994).

Family systems theory and enmeshment

Key term

Enmeshment: a lack of boundaries and privacy within a family. Autonomy refers to the ability to make and implement decisions without being influenced or pressured by others.

Minuchin (1978) carried out a statistical study examining the families of adolescent anorexics and identified four common factors. These were **enmeshment**, over-involvement, rigidity and avoidance of conflict. The most important of these was enmeshment, which Minuchin characterized as lack of privacy and lack of boundaries within the family, that there are no closed doors. Over-involvement referred to parents taking part in all elements of the child's life, and rigidity to an unwillingness to change. Families also avoided overt conflict (arguments).

Minuchin, Rosman and Baker (1978) developed a family systems approach to AN. They suggested that the child develops AN as a means of diverting attention away from other family problems. For example, if parental relationships are breaking down, anorexia can function as a (misguided) attempt to keep the family together.

Evidence and evaluation

There is no doubt that most cases of eating disorders involve complex interactions between children and parents. However, it can be difficult to identify family problems that come before the eating disorder and those that are caused by the eating disorder. It is unsurprising that parents would be extremely protective of their offspring when they refuse to eat. While there is evidence for some of these ideas, most of the work in the area is based on case studies of families. These have issues of reliability, as they cannot be replicated. Although psychodynamic interpretations seem to fit descriptions of some cases, they are difficult to test using rigorous scientific methods.

The psychodynamic approach underpins much of the therapy offered to sufferers of AN. Kog et al. (1985) called Minuchin's model 'one of the best-known and influential' in family therapy but also noted that some of the concepts such as enmeshment were rather loosely defined. Various forms of psychotherapy and family therapy have been used in the treatment of eating disorders and they can be effective (Wilson, Grilo and Vitousek, 2007).

Cognitive theory: distortions and irrational beliefs

The cognitive explanation of anorexia focuses on thoughts and beliefs. The clinical characteristics of AN include distortions in experience of the body and in beliefs about size and shape. Fairburn (1997) viewed cognitive distortions as the 'core psychopathology' shown in anorexia. Two particular cognitive distortions have received a great deal of interest:

- Body image distortions – do anorexics overestimate their size in a way that is different to non-anorexics?

- Irrational beliefs – do anorexics possess irrational beliefs about body size/shape and the importance of thinness?

Fig. 6.12 'Nothing tastes as good as skinny feels' – Kate Moss. This controversial quote gathered many complaints from body image campaigners, who said it encouraged eating disorders.

Distortions and irrational beliefs

The question of body image distortion has generated a considerable amount of research. Many studies (for example, Garner and Garfinkel, 1976) comparing anorexics and controls have shown that anorexics are significantly more likely to overestimate how big they are. However, just as many studies have found no difference between anorexics and controls (for example, Steger et al., 1989), suggesting this kind of overestimation of size takes place in women of all shapes and sizes. A range of research (for example, Cooper et al., 1997, 2007) has shown cognitive distortions in people with anorexia, such as 'I am special because I am thin' and 'If I put on weight, it means I am out of control'. One of these studies is described in depth below.

KEY STUDY: COOPER ET AL. (2007)

Cooper et al. used semi-structured interviews to explore the beliefs and feelings about body size/shape in three groups of women:

- 16 women who had been diagnosed with AN
- 15 women who were currently dieting but had not been diagnosed with AN
- 17 control women (no eating disorder, not dieting).

The interview format contained a mixture of open questions about experiences and feelings along with some closed questions measured with a Likert scale.

Cooper et al. found that feeling fat was common in all three groups of women, indicating that this experience is normative and not characteristic of an eating disorder. However, those in the AN group reported feeling fatter and were more distressed by feeling fat. They experienced more negative cognitions such as 'I am useless' and 'I am feeble for wasting money on food'. They were also more sensitive to auditory references to fat, for instance in television cooking programmes, and to visual images related to size and shape.

THINKING SCIENTIFICALLY: EXPLORATORY STUDY

This is a small-scale, detailed study that Cooper et al. referred to as an 'exploratory study'. The use of interviews provides the opportunity for rich and detailed data to be gathered. The mixture of open and closed questions allows both qualitative and quantitative data to be collected, which is another strength of the interview method. The all-female sample means that findings cannot be generalized to male sufferers of AN. There are few studies of male anorexics, despite the recent increase in cases of AN in boys and men.

Evaluation of cognitive theory

Cooper et al.'s (2007) findings indicate that feeling fat is common to women regardless of whether they have an eating disorder, are dieting or neither of these. The difference between dieting and developing AN may that be AN requires beliefs about weight and shape *and* negative beliefs about the self to develop. In contrast, dieting is based solely on beliefs about size and shape.

This view is echoed in other research. Jones et al. (2007) suggested that people with AN do not just possess irrational beliefs about shape and size but a range of other cognitive distortions. Beck (1967) referred to the idea of core beliefs about the self, the world and the future, which affect how people with depression view the world: Jones et al. argued that these core beliefs may be key to explaining why some people go on to develop AN. The focus of cognitive research into AN is now on examining the importance of negative 'core' beliefs about the self as well as beliefs about shape and size.

One problem with research into cognitions and eating disorders is that beliefs are only examined after people have been diagnosed (that is, studies are retrospective rather than prospective) and this makes it difficult to see if the negative beliefs preceded AN or developed after it. Nonetheless, therapies involving some cognitive behavioural element can make an important contribution to helping people with anorexia.

Link

You can remind yourself about Beck's work by looking back at page 204 of Book 1.

EXAMPLE EXAM QUESTION

Which of the following concepts are NOT part of the psychodynamic explanation of eating disorders? (2 marks)

- Modelling
- Enmeshment
- Struggle for autonomy
- Reinforcement
- Irrational beliefs
- Distortions

Exam hint

You can use a process of elimination on multiple-choice questions by identifying and ruling out the behavioural and cognitive concepts in the list of terms.

Psychological explanations: putting it all together

Anorexia involves a complex range of behaviours, feelings and experiences, making a simple explanation unlikely. It may be that there are different 'routes' to anorexia and that the same kinds of experiences can produce different outcomes for different people – triggering anorexia in one person but depression for another.

It is likely that all of these explanations play some part. Girls internalize culturally defined standards of female beauty, including slimness (in western cultures), and in some girls this creates a tension between the real self and the ideal self. This leads to dissatisfaction with their own body weight and shape, which in turn leads to dieting and an obsession with food. In vulnerable girls who hold negative beliefs about the self, dieting can lead to a fully-fledged eating disorder. The process may be advanced by imitation of role models (social learning) and direct reinforcement by praise from family and friends for losing weight (operant conditioning).

- Anorexia nervosa is a rare psychological problem that involves restricting food intake and an intense fear of gaining weight
- Social learning theory emphasizes the importance of role models and reinforcement in the development of AN. Exposure to western media has been shown to increase rates of AN in cross-cultural studies.
- Social learning theory struggles to explain why only a small number of people develop AN when most are exposed to images of ideal body shapes.
- The psychodynamic explanation focuses on the unconscious, childhood and sexuality.
- Bruch characterized AN as a struggle for autonomy.
- Minuchin believed that AN was more common in enmeshed and over-protective families.
- The psychodynamic approach is difficult to test but family therapy is one of the more effective treatments for AN.
- The cognitive explanation focuses on irrational beliefs and distorted body image.
- Research shows that many women, not just anorexics, feel fat and overestimate their size.
- Some research suggests that those with AN possess other negative core beliefs about themselves, in line with Beck's work.
- AN is complex and it is likely that many factors play a role in its development.

Biological explanations of obesity

What is obesity?

Obesity was included in early versions of the DSM as an eating disorder but it was removed in the 1980s. The DSM-5 manual states:

Obesity is not included in DSM-5 as a mental disorder. Obesity (excess body fat) results from the long-term excess of energy intake relative to energy expenditure. A range of genetic, physiological, behavioral, and environmental factors that vary across individuals contributes to the development of obesity; thus, obesity is not considered a mental disorder.

How is obesity defined?

The most widely used method of defining obesity makes use of the **body mass index (BMI)**. BMI is calculated by dividing weight in kilograms by the square of height in metres. A BMI of 19–24.9 is considered normal.

- 25–29.9 = overweight
- 30–39.9 = obese
- 40+ = severely obese

Key term

Body mass index (BMI): the most common method used to define obesity, calculated by dividing weight in kilograms by the square of height in metres.

However, a BMI reading of 30+ can be attained by heavily muscled individuals who are physically fit (for example, rugby players). An alternative measurement based on excess body fat around the waist can be used. The following waist measurements are associated with increased risk of health problems:

- for men, a waist circumference of 94 cm

- for women, a waist circumference of 80 cm.

ACTIVITY 6.7

The rapid increase in cases of obesity over the last 20 years means that it is now the largest category of problems associated with eating behaviour. Here are some statistics from NHS England regarding the growth in obesity:
- In 1993, 13 per cent of men and 16 per cent of women were obese – by 2011 this had risen to 24 per cent for men and 26 per cent for women.
- The proportion of adults with a normal BMI between 1993 and 2013 decreased from 41.0 per cent to 31.2 per cent among men and from 49.5 per cent to 40.8 per cent among women.

Display the data above using an appropriate graph(s).

Why has obesity increased?

Weight gain occurs when calorific intake exceeds energy expenditure (we consume more than we use). Over the last 20 years, a number of social changes have fuelled the increase in weight gain:

- A decrease in physical activity: children play outside less, and children and adults walk and cycle less and travel more by car. The increase in television-watching and playing computer games matches the increase in childhood obesity over the last 20 years. Early research suggested that each extra hour's viewing per day increases levels of obesity by 2 per cent (Dietz and Gortmaker, 1985).

- An increase in the availability and consumption of fast food and soft drinks over the last 20 years: fast food generally has higher energy content (calories), often in the form of fat rather than carbohydrates, and lower nutritional content, while soft drinks also have a high energy content in the form of sugar. Portions have also increased in size (Anderson and Butcher, 2006). The increase in the number of working parents means that there is less time for meal preparation and more reliance on fast food.

- The food industry invests substantial sums of money into researching aspects of food that make it more attractive, such as taste and colour: it has been very effective in using research into feeding behaviour to persuade us to eat foods that have high energy content and little nutritional value.

Biological influences associated with obesity

In this section, we will examine what biological influences are associated with a person becoming obese and consider whether the biological correlates we see are causes or consequences of obesity. As we go through the ideas to explain obesity, you might like to reflect on whether or not they are just the reverse of the ideas we explored for anorexia. As with AN, we will first explore the genetic factors that might contribute to obesity and then we will look at the neural explanations.

Genetic explanations of obesity

We are often being told by the media that, as a nation, we are becoming more obese and that it is our poor diet that is to blame. We are particularly warned that childhood obesity is on the rise. They are quick to capitalize on the problem (see Fig. 6.13) and are ready to blame parents, fast-food outlets, schools and government as the cause. In this section we examine whether or not there might be a case for arguing that some obesity, at least, is the result of genetics rather than poor eating habits.

ACTIVITY 6.8

Using the information presented on the heritability of obesity, look at Fig. 6.13 and discuss whether or not the regional figures support a genetic explanation.

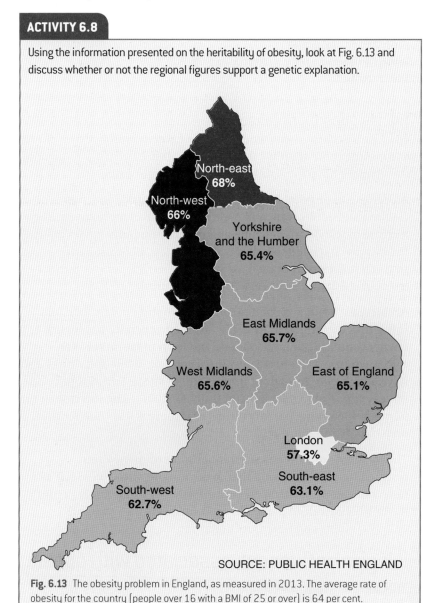

SOURCE: PUBLIC HEALTH ENGLAND

Fig. 6.13 The obesity problem in England, as measured in 2013. The average rate of obesity for the country (people over 16 with a BMI of 25 or over) is 64 per cent.

Family studies

There is a strong public belief that obesity runs in families. **Family studies** are the best way to test whether these family traits are real or are simply stereotypes. Garn et al. (1981) carried out a longitudinal study in the US in which they tracked 564 girls and 553 boys for a period of 18 years between 1960 and 1978 and measured the thickness of the folds of skin below the shoulder blade (subscapular) and on the upper arm (triceps). They compared these **skinfold changes** by grouping the children into low-income families and high-income families. They found that while the low-income children were initially leaner at the start of the study, they had gained more fat than the high-income children during adolescence and beyond. This finding suggests that it is the eating habits of low-income children rather than their genetic inheritance that determines the fat gain. However, we must be cautious here because even though the sample was large, it was all taken from one US city. Furthermore, we can question whether skinfold measurements are an accurate way to examine obesity.

A more recent longitudinal family study by Chaput et al. (2014) examined the heritability rates of a number of factors (Table 6.1). The study initially looked at 1650 people from 375 families in Quebec in 1979 and the study ran until 2002. At each measurement point some families had dropped out and new families were recruited to keep the sample size high. Some of the markers came out to show very high heritability scores. Of particular interest are BMI, abdominal and visceral fat, metabolic rates and physical activity level, as these are known to have DNA markers associated with them (meaning they can be related to genetic causes).

Key terms

Family studies: studies that try to establish whether or not a feature tends to run in particular families and so has a genetic component.

Skinfold changes: a measure of obesity that is obtained by measuring the thickness of a fold of skin. This is usually done on the shoulder blade or the upper arm. Changes in this thickness over time can indicate markers for the development of obesity.

Body fat and fat distribution	Body mass index	40%
	Per cent body fat	55%
	Waist circumference (WC)	57%
	WC adjusted for BMI	51%
	Total abdominal fat	52%
	Subcutaneous abdominal fat	42%
	Visceral abdominal fat	56%
Energy intake and eating behaviours	Energy intake/kg	30%
	Carbohydrate (%)	36%
	Lipid (%)	39%
	Protein (%)	44%
	Cognitive dietary restraint	6%
	Susceptibility to hunger	28%
Energy expenditure and physical activity (PA) level	PA level	27%
	Exercise participation	12%
	Inactivity	25%
	Moderate to strenuous PA	16%
	Total daily activity	19%
	Leisure time PA (h/week)	17%
	Resting metabolic rate	47%

Table 6.1 Heritability percentages (adapted from Chaput et al., 2014)

A final thing to note about family studies is that they seem to find the same result regardless of where in the world the study is carried out. Maes et al. (1997) reviewed a number of studies that had been done. The analysis showed that results from the UK, US, Brazil, Italy, Canada, Israel and a number of other countries all found similar levels of heritability.

Twin studies

The findings for twin studies show little difference from those of family studies. Twin studies concentrate on the direct genetic line by comparing MZ and DZ twins. According to Maes et al. (1997), heritabilities across a number of studies range from 0.50 to 0.90. Studies have indicated a relationship between twins for BMI in adolescence and adulthood and for skinfolds. Stunkard et al. (1990) studied 93 sets of twins and found that 66–70 per cent of the twin pairs shared similar weights. However, it was more likely that they shared similar weights if they were thin than if they were obese, so this does raise the question of to what degree obesity can be shown to be genetically inherited. In a more recent study, Silventoinen et al. (2009) found that genetic factors were very influential on BMI and this was the case for different ages of twin pairs.

The FTO gene

Having established that there is a genetic component to obesity, the search has been on to try to identify the gene (or genes) that are responsible for the overeating behaviour. One candidate is the **fat mass and obesity-associated (FTO) gene**. The discovery of the possible link between this gene and obesity came while investigating type 2 diabetes. As we saw earlier in the chapter, type 2 diabetes is often associated with obesity. Frayling et al. (2007) have shown that this gene is linked to an effect on BMI that leads to obesity and has been shown to be effective at all ages, including in children. They examined the BMI data from 38,759 individuals and showed that possession of the correct variant of the gene increases BMI. The **recessive alleles** of the gene seem to be the critical component. Possession of one recessive allele leads to an average weight increase of 1.2 kg and possession of both recessive alleles (about 16 per cent of those sampled) showed an average of a 3 kg increase in body weight. That represents a 1.67-fold increase in the chances of becoming obese.

Basal metabolic rate theory

One of the ways in which a genetic predisposition towards obesity can show itself is through changes to our **basal metabolic rate (BMR)**. Metabolic rate is a measure of the current level of activity needed to keep all of our bodily functions going along at the required pace. The rate can change depending on what you are doing. So if a person is exercising, the rate might temporarily increase. The BMR, then, is the rate when they are at rest. The basal metabolic rate theory suggests that we inherit our rate through our genes (Bouchard et al., 1990). If you have a low BMR then you will not use up calories very quickly when at rest and so you are more likely to put on weight. If BMR is inherited then we can see that some people will be more naturally prone to obesity. Of course, obesity will only occur if the calorie intake exceeds the calorie usage, so a person with a low BMR can choose to reduce their food intake or exercise more regularly to offset the low BMR.

Not everyone agrees with the theory surrounding BMR. O'Rahilly and Farooqi (2006) have suggested that the inherited factors are more likely to be changes in hunger, satiety and food intake rather than BMR. They therefore argue that the genetic link to obesity is more likely to be neurobehavioural than metabolic. Furthermore, Tarantino et al. (2008) have suggested that while low BMR might initially be a cause of obesity, once obese a person is more likely to have a high BMR. Furthermore, this high BMR found in obesity when combined with diabetes has been linked to metabolic syndrome, which can lead to heart disease or stroke.

Another explanation for the association between BMR and obesity comes from research on a protein called the **kinase suppressor of Ras 2 (KSR2)**. According to Pearce et al. (2013), variations in KSR2 can lead to abnormal cell fat and glucose metabolism. The consequence of this can be hyperphagia (excessive eating) in childhood, low heart rate, reduced basal metabolic rate and severe insulin resistance.

Appetite control

We saw earlier the role of leptin in hunger control. According to Montague et al. (1997), leptin production is controlled by the **OB gene**. The ob mouse has two recessive alleles of this gene (ob/ob) and is unable to synthesize leptin. The lack of leptin means that the mouse does not possess the signal to stop eating and so becomes obese (see Fig. 6.14). Interestingly, injections of leptin into these mice allowed them to stop eating and led to gradual weight loss (Campfield et al., 1995).

Montague et al. (1997) reported that they had examined the DNA of two severely obese children and had found that the gene that codes for leptin, which is found on chromosome 7, showed an abnormality.

Key terms

Kinase suppressor of Ras 2 (KSR2): a protein that is involved in the metabolism of glucose and fat. Abnormal function of this protein might lead to obesity.

OB gene: the gene that codes for the production of leptin. The capital O and B indicate the dominant alleles. The use of capital letters here refers to the more usual dominant allele form of the gene. The use of lower case letters would indicate possession of the recessive alleles (as in ob mice).

Fig. 6.14 An ordinary mouse and an ob mouse. The ob mouse is unable to synthesize leptin.

When Montague et al. undertook their study there was increasing evidence that a lack of leptin was responsible for the obesity found in ob mice. Administration of leptin reversed their obesity and giving leptin to normal mice caused them to lose body fat. However, by 1997 date no similar gene abnormalities had been found in humans. In this study, the researchers carried out a thorough DNA analysis of two children who had extreme obesity. Both children were of Pakistani origin and, even though they had been normal weights at birth, both had become obese at an early age. Neither had any clinical features for which obesity was a known consequence and neither had any brain abnormalities. Each child had two siblings of normal weight and none of the parents were obese.

When the DNA of both children was examined, it was found that part of the coding sequence on the leptin gene was found to be missing a piece. This led to a lack of production of leptin, which, in turn, led to an absence of the signal to the hypothalamus that halts the activity of the hunger centre. Examination of the DNA of the parents showed that both parents were heterozygous (they both had Ob/ob genes – so one dominant and one recessive allele). In both cases, their offspring had inherited the ob part of the gene (the recessive allele) to make them ob/ob. Possessing the recessive gene was what caused the coding to go wrong and resulted in the lack of leptin production.

This finding allows us to understand the genetic circumstances under which a person might have a genetic disposition towards obesity. The research also sparked the idea that leptin supplements could be used with humans to reverse obesity caused by this genetic inheritance.

THINKING SCIENTIFICALLY: AVOIDING CONFOUNDING VARIABLES

In the Montague et al. (1997) study, the two children that were observed were both of Pakistani origin. There was a varied set of control participants also used, those being the family members of the children and a number of unrelated individuals. The unrelated individuals consisted of both adults and children so that controls could be compared to the children who were central to the study and the family members, who were mostly adults. At first sight this seems like a very thorough set of controls to ensure that the data obtained from the children were not due to other factors. However, all of the unrelated control participants (adults and children) were white Caucasians, whereas the children and their family members were all Pakistani. This presents a confounding variable of cultural origin. We are, therefore, left uncertain about whether data we might collect from unrelated Pakistani individuals would confirm or refute the conclusion that the children's obesity was caused by mutations in the leptin gene.

Set-point theory

Set-point theory proposes that our body regulates its food intake in order to maintain a particular level of fat stores (and hence a particular weight). This 'ideal' level of fat storage is referred to as the set-point. Obese people are believed to have a high set-point, either as a consequence of genetics or as a result of a disease like diabetes or thyroid disease, and hence they eat to maintain this high level of fat storage. Some of the evidence for this idea comes from the difficulty that obese people have in losing weight. Research has suggested that when an obese person loses weight their metabolic rate lowers. This lowering of metabolic rate is an attempt to conserve energy in what the body thinks is a time of famine. Decreased BMR leads to a decrease in energy output and so the calories ingested will contribute to fat storage and weight gain. However, this theory is not universally accepted and some researchers do not agree that weight regain in obese people who have lost weight is due to the influence of a set-point.

> **Key term**
>
> **Set-point:** the level of fat in the body. It is suggested that the food regulatory system tries to maintain this fat level.

EXAMPLE EXAM QUESTION

Outline any TWO theories that relate obesity to genetic causes. (4 marks)

> **Exam hint**
>
> Your answer should be able to correctly name and briefly describe two theories. It would help if you could give an example from each of the theories you outline.

Evolution and obesity

Humans have a higher proportion of fat in their bodies than other animals. While most animals are 4–8 per cent fat, most average men have 13 per cent fat and most average women have 25 per cent fat (Wells, 2006). Given this, it is relevant to ask whether or not this excess of fat has somehow conferred an evolutionary advantage on humans over other animals. A number of theories suggest this might be the case, and the thrifty gene hypothesis is a good example of this. An alternative explanation comes from the drifty gene hypothesis, where the suggestion is that the continued prevalence of obesity is a chance evolutionary occurrence.

The 'thrifty gene' hypothesis

The **thrifty gene hypothesis** was first proposed by Neel (1962). The term thrifty refers to careful management of something (usually money in a modern context). Neel was interested to know why diabetes remained in the population when it was linked to a reproductive disadvantage; surely if it was maladaptive it should have died out. He hypothesized that diabetes, with its associated obesity, would have been useful in Palaeolithic times as it would allow individuals to fatten up when food was plentiful in order to survive any lean times ahead. Hence the gene that coded for diabetes was a thrifty gene. There is little modern support for this idea as the gene that Neel was suggesting has never been located and we now believe that obesity is unlikely to be a single-gene effect.

> **Key term**
>
> **Thrifty gene hypothesis:** the evolutionary theory that offers an explanation for why obesity persists in the population even though it is maladaptive.

The drifty gene hypothesis

This hypothesis, first proposed by Speakman in 2007, suggests that some genes predispose us to obesity, but are neutral and have been drifting over evolutionary time. Speakman (2013) explains that some genetic components are neither advantageous nor disadvantageous. If they crop up in an individual that has other advantages then they will be transferred to offspring. So, even though they do not have any positive effect, they continue to crop up in the population. Equally, other individuals who do not possess these obesity-conferring genes also have offspring. This leaves us with a situation in which some individuals are obesity-prone and others obesity-resistant.

The polygenic approach

If we review what we have discovered so far about obesity, it is becoming clear that there is a significant genetic influence on whether a person is or is not prone to obesity. However, it is also fair to say that it is difficult to isolate a single genetic element that could account for the multitude of reasons why a person might become obese. The **polygenic** approach recognizes this and proposes that there are a number of different genes that are responsible for controlling food intake, and that a person's tendency towards obesity is most likely to be the result of a combination of factors rather than due to a single gene defect (though the latter is possible in some cases).

Neural explanations of obesity

To finish our analysis of biological explanations of obesity we must turn to neural mechanisms and try to explain how the genetic propensities play out in terms of real physiological effects. We will examine just two ideas here, one being the dual hypothalamic theory that we saw earlier and the other being the role of the orbitofrontal cortex.

The dual hypothalamic theory

If you recall, earlier in the chapter we established that the hypothalamus has both a feeding centre and a satiety centre. The latter is located in the ventromedial hypothalamus (VMH). It stands to reason, therefore, that if the VMH is damaged, the organism will not be able to respond to satiety signals such as leptin, and will therefore continue to eat. Over time, this will lead to obesity. Evidence to support this comes from Shimizu et al. (1997), who showed that male rats will overeat to obesity after bilateral lesions to the VMH.

The orbitofrontal cortex

Alongside the VMH, there is another part of the brain that has been linked to obesity. The **orbitofrontal cortex (OFC)** has been linked to the brain's reward system and, in particular, to dopamine function. Volkow et al. (2008) have shown that there is a reduction in D2 dopamine receptors in morbidly obese people. It seems that this reduction in D2 receptors occurs in a region of the brain called the orbitofrontal cortex (see Fig. 6.15).

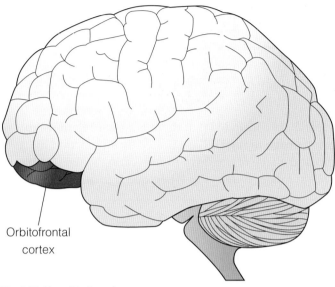

Orbitofrontal cortex

Fig. 6.15 The orbitofrontal cortex

The OFC has been implicated in the motivation to feed (Rolls, 2004). Therefore, abnormalities in the OFC could enhance food-oriented behaviour and encourage a person to become obese. Maayan et al. (2011) (see the *Key study* below) have shown that the volume of the OFC is reduced in obese patients, so there are good grounds for suggesting that this region plays a role in the reduced regulation of feeding.

EXAMPLE EXAM QUESTION

Outline ONE neural explanation of obesity. (2 marks)

Exam hint

This question is only worth two marks so you should name the explanation and then explain how the relevant part of the brain is involved in producing obesity. You might want to very briefly refer to a piece of research to underline your understanding.

KEY STUDY: MAAYAN ET AL. (2011)

Maayan et al. were interested in the disinhibited eating behaviour seen in obese people. They wanted to see if this excessive eating was associated with the level of activity in the orbitofrontal cortex. They studied 91 adolescents, of whom 37 were lean and 54 were obese according to their BMI scores. They gave each person a neuropsychological assessment followed by the Three-Factor Eating Questionnaire (TFEQ). This questionnaire has three scales: one that assesses a person's cognitive control over eating, one that assesses the person's susceptibility to eating in response to emotional factors and one that assesses the person's susceptibility to eating in response to feelings of hunger. They also used MRI imaging to measure the volumes of frontal brain regions, including the OFC.

The researchers found that the obese participants had higher levels of disinhibition than lean participants on all three factors measured by the TFEQ. There were also significant associations between the TFEQ scores and both BMI (positive association) and the volume of the OFC (negative association). However, the OFC association was for the lean participants rather than the obese ones. It would seem, then, that for lean people, disinhibition of eating is associated with a decrease of OFC volume. We can assume that for obese people the OFC is already reduced in volume and so we do not see any changes with the level of obesity.

The researchers concluded that there is a clear relationship between damage to the OFC (indicated by a reduction in its volume) and a lack of the drive to stop eating when one has had enough (no longer hungry) or when one is in an emotional state.

THINKING SCIENTIFICALLY: CROSS-SECTIONAL RESEARCH

The Maayan et al. (2011) study was a piece of cross-sectional research. This is where the researchers take a snapshot of the situation at a given point in time. This has both advantages and disadvantages. The advantage of cross-sectional studies like this one is that it captures the state of the brain at that moment in time and this can be related to the current state of cognitive appraisal. However, without longitudinal data it is impossible to assess the time course of the development of obesity. This means that we cannot be sure that the brain changes observed are causally related to the obesity. Furthermore, we cannot know if the brain changes caused obesity or vice versa.

ACTIVITY 6.9

You have now covered the brain correlates of normal eating, anorexia nervosa and obesity. Copy the unlabelled brains provided and label them with the parts of the brain involved in eating behaviour. For each part identified, state whether it has a role in normal eating, and/or anorexia nervosa, and/or obesity.

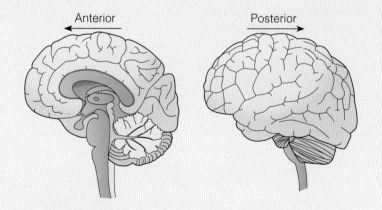

Anterior   Posterior

- Most, but not all, family studies point to a degree of heritability of obesity.

- Twin studies provide similar results to those of family studies.

- The FTO gene has been suggested as being partly responsible for obesity.

- One theory suggests that we inherit our basal metabolic rate and that this determines our weight, but not all researchers agree with this theory.

- The OB gene has also been implicated in controlling our appetite.

- Set-point theory suggests that our body regulates its food intake to maintain a level of fat stores.

- Several evolutionary theories (e.g. the thrifty gene hypothesis) suggest that obesity has a survival value.

- Dysfunction of the hypothalamus and the orbitofrontal cortex have both been linked to obesity.

Psychological explanations of obesity

Obesity appears on the surface to be easy to explain and treat – people should do more and eat less – so what role does psychology have in offering explanations? Psychological research studies comparing dieters (usually referred to as 'restrained eaters') with non-dieters ('unrestrained eaters') show that attempts to restrict intake by dieting often leads people to eat more rather than less. We will examine one of these studies carried out by Herman and Mack (1975) below then move to examine a number of explanations including restraint theory and the boundary model.

KEY STUDY: HERMAN AND MACK (1975)

Herman and Mack (1975) carried out one of the earliest studies using the 'preload/test method'. In this approach, eaters are given some sort of food (a preload) then exposed to other foods to see how much they eat.

Herman and Mack selected a sample of 45 female students. The participants were told that the experiment was a study of taste experiences. Fifteen participants were randomly allocated to three conditions:

- Group 1 received no preload.
- Group 2 were given one milkshake as a preload.
- Group 3 were given two milkshakes as a preload.

Groups 2 and 3 were asked to rate the taste qualities of the milkshakes. All 45 participants were then given three tubs of ice cream of different flavours and given ten minutes to rate their taste qualities. They were told they could eat as much of the ice cream as they wanted.

Finally all the participants were given a questionnaire to assess their degree of dietary restraint (dieting). Herman and Mack divided the participants into restrained eaters (those dieting) and unrestrained eaters and compared the amount of ice cream eaten by them.

- Herman and Mack found that low-restraint participants ate less of the ice cream in the third condition (two milkshakes) than in the first or second conditions. This is what common sense would predict: they would be 'fuller' after two milkshakes compared to one or zero preloads and would eat less ice cream.
- However, high-restraint (dieters) ate significantly more ice cream in the second and third conditions (preloads) than in the first condition (no preload). While they should have been less hungry, it appeared that the preload had the opposite effect, leading them to eat more.

Herman and Mack also calculated the relationship between the score on the eating restraint questionnaire and the amount of ice cream eaten. They found a significant positive correlation: the more the participants were attempting to diet, the more they ate!

THINKING SCIENTIFICALLY: METHODOLOGICAL ISSUES

The restraint questionnaire was given after the feeding tests, so the division of each group into high- and low-restraint participants was what we call post hoc – that is, after the study had been designed and carried out. Ideally this should be done before the study, but Herman and Mack felt that giving the questionnaire before the feeding tests would have alerted the participants to the general purpose of the experiment. This might have biased the results.

This meant that the distribution of high- and low-restrained participants differed across the groups. For example, there were nine high-restraint and only six low-restraint participants in the second group. This uneven pattern reduces the reliability of the findings. Group sizes were also small (especially after the division into high- and low-restraint participants).

Exam hint

The key element here is comparison between dieters and non-dieters, hence your graph should show this clearly. Remember to include a title and appropriate labels.

EXAMPLE EXAM QUESTION

Here is a sample of data from Herman and Mack's experiment. The table shows the mean amount of ice cream in grams consumed in the first and third conditions.

Mean amount of ice cream eaten in grams	No preload	High preload
Non-dieters	220	130
Dieters	100	175

Draw an appropriate graph to display the data. (4 marks)

Restraint theory

Herman and Mack explained their findings with **restraint** theory. They argued that restrained eaters aim to eat less and sometimes achieve this. However, they also show periods of overeating often triggered by anxiety or other moods. Once a dieter has started to eat, their inhibitions about eating are reduced and they continue. This is sometimes referred to as the 'what the hell effect'. **Disinhibition** can arise from a preload, from emotional distress (mood eating) or from intoxication (the munchies). In the long term, dieting leads to increased food intake.

Restraint theory offered a new approach to understanding eating behaviour and was supported by a range of evidence showing that dieters often paradoxically eat once more once their diet is broken (Ogden, 2007). However, it said little about the physiological mechanisms involved in eating and was replaced by the boundary model in 1984, which attempted to integrate the findings about restraint with biological mechanisms.

The boundary model

Herman and Polivy (1984) argued that food intake in a normal eater is controlled by physiological mechanisms. These mechanisms tell us when we are hungry and stop us eating when we are satiated. The eater listens to their body's signals and eats in response to these.

In contrast, the restrained eater, or dieter, sets an additional 'cognitive' boundary in between hunger and fullness, which is lower than the physiological boundary. This is what they *think* they should eat (number of calories, specific foods) set by the demands of the diet. The dieter replaces the physiological control with a cognitive control. If a low-calorie preload (for example, a tub of cottage cheese) is consumed that is within the cognitive boundary, the diet will continue. If the preload exceeds the cognitive boundary (for example, a large bag of crisps), the dieter will eat in an uncontrolled manner until they reach satiety.

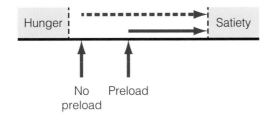

Fig. 6.16 Food intake boundaries in unrestrained eaters and restrained eaters

Key terms

Restraint: controlling food intake through dieting.

Disinhibition: eating more once restraints have been loosened.

Evaluation of the boundary model

Herman and Mack's 1975 experiment provides clear support for the boundary model. The model is commendable as it combines physiological and psychological factors to explain feeding behaviour. Restrained eaters have a 'cognitive' dieting boundary for food intake and once this is overcome (by the milkshake preloads in Herman and Mack's experiment) the 'what the hell' effect takes over and eating is disinhibited. So they eat *more* in the preload condition than in the zero preload condition – the opposite pattern to low-restraint participants.

However, much of the experimental work was carried out under controlled conditions in the laboratory. This gives it high levels of reliability but low levels of ecological validity. Dieting in the real world may involve more complicated issues than are studied in the laboratory.

The boundary model does not specify precisely the cognitive and emotional (affective) processes that lead to the 'what the hell' effect. Other characteristics of restrained eaters have been identified that contribute to their problems maintaining a diet. Restrained eaters (in common with people diagnosed with anorexia or bulimia nervosa) tend to become preoccupied with food and thoughts of food. They may then try to deny that food is important and suppress their thoughts about it. However, studies have shown that when instructed not to think about something, we actually think about it more (Ogden, 2007). Restrained eaters may therefore overeat as a rebound effect from trying not to think about food.

Explanations for the success and failure of dieting

A small number of people lose weight through dieting and maintain that weight loss, but most people do not (Mann et al., 2007) – counterintuitively, they often end up eating more, as shown in Hermann and Mack's 1975 comparison of restrained and unrestrained eaters.

Estimates suggest that around 80 per cent of women aged 40–60 are trying to lose weight but have difficulty losing it or maintaining the weight loss. A multimillion-pound dieting industry has grown up over the last 20 years, advertising various diets and strategies guaranteed to lead to weight loss. This industry is aimed at girls and women. Many women diet when only mildly overweight if at all because their actual body size and shape does not match their ideal size and shape. Lohman et al. (2002) carried out a prospective study examining who is most successful at dieting.

KEY STUDY: LOHMAN ET AL. (2002)

Lohman et al. followed a group of dieters through the first four months of a two-year weight-loss programme. Their aim was to identify the factors associated with successful and unsuccessful diet attempts.

The programme was advertised on US television and an initial sample of 446 women enquired about taking part. Of these 142 met the criteria, which were:

- aged between 40 and 55 years
- BMI between 25 and 38 (just overweight to obese)
- non-smokers.

This group further decreased to 112 women as 30 failed to comply or dropped out before the study started.

Each of the participants was given a battery of psychological tests before the intervention began. The intervention consisted of a weekly meeting lasting two and a half hours, following a Weight Watchers format: weekly weigh in, diet advice, group discussion and a one-to-one chat with an adviser. The group met for 16 weeks in total. Eighty-nine of the 122 starters completed the programme, showing a dropout rate of 21 per cent.

The researchers divided the completers into three groups: successful dieters who lost 6.4 kg or more, moderately successful dieters who lost 2–6.3 kg, and unsuccessful dieters who lost less than 1.9 kg or gained weight. They then scanned the data collected at the start to identify any differences between the groups and found the following to be significant:

- The unsuccessful dieters had made a higher number of previous attempts at dieting, had greater expectations about weight loss, higher body dissatisfaction and lower self-esteem.
- In comparison, the successful dieters had more reasonable expectations about how much they wanted to lose and had fewer previous diet attempts.

THINKING SCIENTIFICALLY: PROSPECTIVE AND LONGITUDINAL

Lohman et al.'s study is commendable as it is prospective and longitudinal – the research team followed a group from the start of the weight-loss programme. There is also a very detailed range of measurements providing clear information about the differences between successful and unsuccessful dieters. The sample here is rather homogenous – women of a narrow age range who are non-smokers – making it difficult to apply these findings outside the research setting.

Explanations for the failure of dieting

There are both biological and psychological reasons why diets often do not work. In biological terms, dieting to reduce weight below the body weight set-point is difficult because the body will try to restore the set-point in any way it can. Besides increased feelings of hunger, the body will reduce its basal metabolic rate (BMR) as weight is lost. A lower BMR *reduces* energy expenditure, making weight loss difficult even on a diet. Effectively the body treats a diet as a period of famine and puts measures in place to survive.

This effect is most notable with 'crash' diets, where calories are severely restricted with the aim of rapid weight loss. Slow weight loss of one to two pounds a week is more sustainable – but slow weight loss often reduces the motivation to stick to the diet. An alternative approach involves diets such as the 5:2 system, where calories are restricted to 600 calories on two days of the week. Evidence is still being gathered on the effects of this, but some studies suggest that it may be as effective as calorie-counting and may reduce the risks of breast cancer and type 2 diabetes (Harvie and Howell, 2010/2012).

Reviews of controlled studies of dieting in the real world similarly conclude that reducing calorie input through dieting is not an effective method of losing weight (Mann et al., 2007). Dieters alternate between periods of restriction and periods of overeating. In the long term, between one- and two-thirds of dieters end up actually regaining more weight than they lost on the diet. Restriction of food can lead to an increased preoccupation with food and increased eating (Warren and Cooper, 1988). Repeated attempts at dieting (called 'yo-yo' dieting) can in the long term increase the chances of heart disease.

Successful dieting

Research suggests that successful weight loss is possible when combined with lifestyle changes (Powell, Calvin and Calvin, 2007). These involve low-calorie (especially low-fat) diets with lifestyle changes such as physical exercise, group and individual support. An increase in physical exercise prevents the body reducing the BMR and can even increase it. Self-monitoring is also useful: the person is encouraged to keep a diary and records to monitor their progress. This encourages their sense of being in control.

It is also important to set realistic goals. Although on average weight loss was only seven pounds on the programmes reviewed by Powell et al., it was sustained over at least two years, and this level of weight loss has significant health benefits for the overweight.

ACTIVITY 6.10

Design a presentation to provide information about how psychological research can help to maximize weight loss. You should base your presentation on what you have read in this chapter about the biology of eating behaviour and obesity. The audience is a Weight Watchers-type group. You should include a list of dos and don'ts in your presentation.

KEY POINTS

- Obesity is the most common problem associated with eating today.

- Obesity results when calorific intake exceeds energy expenditure over a long period of time.

- Restrained eaters (dieters) often eat more after a preload than non-dieters.

- The boundary model suggests that dieters impose a cognitive boundary between hunger and fullness. When this boundary is passed, the 'what the hell' effect takes place (disinhibition).

- The boundary model combines psychological and physiological factors and is supported by research. However much of this is lab-based.

- Dieting often fails and there are both biological and psychological reasons for this.

- Dieting often leads people to eat more.

- Successful dieting involves slow and consistent weight loss accompanied by lifestyle changes such as increased activity/exercise and permanent changes to eating habits.

The topic of eating behaviour is sensitive and this is particularly so for disordered eating. For this reason, both of these activities ask you to collect data using yourself as a participant.

The first activity focuses on link between mood and eating. Keep a food diary for a period of at least two days in which you record everything you eat (including snacks!). Record your mood at the same times each day (for instance, at 8 AM, 12 PM, 4 PM and 8 PM) while you are keeping the food diary. Use a scale of 1–5 where 1 represents a low or bad mood and 5 represents a very good mood. When you have completed your diary and your mood log, look to see if you can identify any patterns. Do you tend to eat more when in a low mood and do the types of foods you choose appear to lead to improved or further lowered mood? Based on your findings, identify one or more hypothesis that you would like to test about the possible relationship between eating behaviour and mood.

The second practical activity focuses on the claims made by some of the more popular diets today. One example of these is the Paleolithic diet, which argues that we should base our eating habits as closely as possible on those which our hunter-gatherer ancestors would have followed. A range of claims is made for the benefits of the Paleolithic diet, including prevention of heart disease, cancer, arthritis, etc.

Start by finding out about the Paleolithic diet using Internet sources. Identify the foods that are recommended and those that are prohibited. Then find one or two studies that have suggested benefits and scrutinize these using your knowledge of research methods. You might like to consider sample size, how allocation to conditions was achieved, the existence or otherwise of a control group and the possibility of demand characteristics. Based on the evidence you have identified, what scientific conclusions (if any) can be drawn about the effects of the Paleolithic diet on health and well-being?

Example exam questions

1. Briefly outline the biological explanation for anorexia nervosa. **(2 marks)**

2. Explain TWO limitations of the biological explanation for anorexia nervosa. **(6 marks)**

3. Read the item below and answer the question that follows.

> Sandra has recently joined a Weight Watchers group and is discussing her experiences of dieting with other members of the group. Sandra says that every time she goes on a diet, she becomes obsessed with food and ends up putting on even more weight. Simon says that once he breaks the diet he eats until he feels uncomfortably full.

Discuss explanations for the success and failure of dieting. Refer to the material above in your answer. **(16 marks)**

Exam focus

Read through the following example exam question, example student answer, and examiner comments. Then, have a go at answering the question yourself!

EXAMPLE EXAM QUESTION

Discuss evolutionary explanations of food preferences. [16 marks]

Annie's answer

Evolutionary psychologists are interested in how modern eating behaviours have been influenced by evolutionary factors. For thousands of years, our ancestors lived as hunter-gatherers. Food was scarce and there was a constant struggle to find enough to eat. Modern eating problems such as obesity probably relate to our evolutionary past.

Examiner comment: A claim is made but no explanation or evidence.

Early humans evolved acute senses of taste and smell to help them identify edible and poisonous foodstuffs when foraging. This is reflected in the taste receptors shown by modern humans, who are adept at recognizing foods that are sweet and rich in calories. We also have salt receptors that would have helped with salty foods, which was valuable in the past when our ancestors led physically active lives hunting.

Examiner comment: Well-written second paragraph, clearly focused on food preferences.

Studies have shown that preferences for sweet and fatty foods are shown by newborn babies (neonates), supporting the claim that we have innate preferences for sweet and salty flavours (Steiner). However, these innate preferences cause problems for modern humans and are leading to obesity now we are less active.

Examiner comment: Succinct use of research evidence to provide support.

An important development in our evolution was the shift to meat eating. Early humans probably became meat eaters because meat is a rich source of protein and it was more efficient to obtain protein from hunting than by foraging for plants and berries. Studies comparing chimpanzees and humans show that chimpanzees have a long large intestine that is specialized for digesting plants, whereas humans have a long duodenum and small intestine specialized for eating protein (meat). This supports the claim that early humans became meat eaters just after the evolutionary split from chimps. However, today many people are vegetarian, which shows that meat eating isn't universal and it might be more down to upbringing and cultural evolution.

Examiner comment: Good use of comparative evidence here.

Examiner comment: Rather a weak critical comment.

Other evolutionary factors include food neophobia and taste aversions. Neophobia is the avoidance of new or unfamiliar foods, which is shown in many children. While this is irritating for parents, food neophobia probably evolved because it was safer for our foraging ancestors to stick with eating familiar foods that they knew were safe rather than trying new foods, which might be poisonous. Taste aversions were demonstrated by Garcia, who showed how wolves could learn to avoid mutton after the meat was laced with poison. The taste aversion happened in just one trial – contradicting the behaviourist idea that learning takes several trials.

> **Examiner comment:** This material needs linking back to show how evolution has played a role.

Evolutionary explanations of food preferences are based on fossil evidence, which support hypotheses on the evolution of meat eating. However, there is limited fossil evidence, and evolutionary explanations are often speculative. It is said that evolutionary psychology is just guesswork about how our ancestors must have lived – it is clear that lots of other factors also affect food preferences including learning and culture (e.g. the use of spices to make meat safe was probably passed on through cultural evolution). In western societies we no longer behave as hunter-gatherers, and the evolutionary approach is therefore limited.

> **Examiner comment:** Knowledge of evolutionary explanation of food preferences is accurate and generally well detailed. The essay is well focused with good use of research evidence. There are one or two places where critical comments could be further elaborated. Terminology is used reasonably effectively but reference to natural selection at the start would have been useful. Level four response around 13/16 marks.

Chapter 7: Stress

Introduction

'Stress' is part of modern life. The term is used to describe situations we have to cope with (for example, an interview or driving test are 'stressful') and is also used to explain illness ('he's been under lots of stress lately') or even death ('the heart attack was brought on by stress at work').

The work of Hans Selye from the 1930s onwards was instrumental in the development of stress research in psychology. Key elements of his work are explored later in this chapter, but in brief Selye identified a link between physical stress and illness in rats. He also identified the major pathways underlying the physiological responses to stress. By the 1970s, it was widely accepted that stress could be a major factor in illness, especially heart disease.

The study of stress poses a range of challenges for the psychologist. Scientific research relies on variables that are clearly defined and quantifiable, so the first step in doing research into stress is to have an agreed definition. Unfortunately, as we have seen above, the term stress is used in different ways. Psychologists have developed various ways of defining and measuring the various sources of stress, often through the use of questionnaires. Physiological measures have also been developed to examine the relationships between stress and illness.

Despite the common view that stress leads to illness, it is quite clear there are substantial individual differences in responses to stress. Most of us know people who appear to be under extreme stress but sail through with no ill effects whilst others succumb easily to infections at the slightest hint of stress in their lives.

Stress-related illness is recognised as a major political and economic factor, responsible for increased absenteeism and low productivity at work. 'Stress management' has become a major industry, both at the level of organisations and for individuals. The final section of the chapter examines the methods used by organisations and by individuals to reduce and manage stress.

What is covered in Stress?

STRESS

What is stress?

Before considering the physiological aspects of stress we need to have a definition of what we mean by stress. We would all agree that bereavement and redundancy, for instance, are stressful. But we also know that their effects on people would vary from person to person. The key to this is how we *perceive* the stressful situation and how we *perceive* our ability to cope with it (i.e. we assess our internal resources and whether they are sufficient to cope with the stressful situation). This leads to the widely accepted *transactional* definition of stress (the term 'transaction' refers to the interaction between the individual and his/her environment), developed by Lazarus (Lazarus & Folkman, 1984):

> '**Stress** exists when a person appraises the demands of a situation as exceeding their perceived coping resources'.

The consequence of this is that the person feels that their well-being is threatened.

The importance placed on appraisal, the *perception and assessment* of the situation and of coping resources is critical. People will vary in their appraisals, and this can account for individual differences in responses to stress, and also informs psychological methods of coping with stress. Students who appraise examinations as highly demanding and their coping resources as inadequate will be highly stressed; students who appraise examinations as less demanding and their coping resources (knowledge, revision, practice, etc.) as substantial will be less stressed. This may have no bearing on performance, as appraisals can be wrong, but simply on the *experience* of taking the examination.

Remember this definition as you read through the chapter, while we refer to it directly when looking at individual differences in stress and coping with stress.

The physiology of stress
Sympathomedullary pathway (SAM)

The **sympathetic nervous system (SNS)** is part of the autonomic nervous system that controls our internal organs, such as various glands, the heart and the circulatory system, and the digestive system. Nerve pathways of the SNS originate in the brainstem (part of the brain just above the spinal cord) and travel via the spinal cord and spinal nerves to the various body organs. One of these pathways runs to the adrenal medulla, which along with the adrenal cortex makes up the adrenal gland.

The SNS functions to control our internal organs automatically, without our conscious control, and plays a vital role in stress responses. When appraisal processes in higher brain centres detect a stressful situation, the hypothalamus activates the SNS centres in the brainstem and the pathways running to the adrenal medulla (SAM pathway). When activated, the SNS stimulates the adrenal medulla to release the hormones **adrenaline** and **noradrenaline** into the bloodstream. You covered the role of adrenaline in the fight and flight response last year.

The SNS itself has direct connections to the heart and activation speeds up heart rate and raises blood pressure. These effects are increased and sustained by the release of adrenaline and noradrenaline from the adrenal medulla via the SAM pathway; these act on heart muscle to increase heart rate, and also on blood vessels to constrict them and so raise blood pressure. The end result is that oxygen is rapidly pumped to the muscles of the skeleton allowing for increased physical activity.

Link

You can look back at this material on pages 258–265 of Book 1.

Key terms

Adrenaline: a hormone which acts on heart and the circulatory system to increase heart rate and blood pressure.

Noradrenaline: a hormone, which mobilizes the body for action, by increasing arousal and alertness.

STRESS

ACTIVITY 7.1

Your pulse rate is an easy indicator of how your body is responding to daily stressful situations. Take your pulse three or four times at an un-stressful (and convenient) time of day and calculate the average of the measurements to establish a 'resting' baseline rate. Now take your pulse in a range of different and mildly stress situations (e.g. waiting for a late bus/train, working on a piece of demanding homework, after an argument) to see how it varies. If you want to do this activity in a more systematic (and fun) way you could buy a set of commercial bio dots, which measure your stress levels and change colour to indicate these.

Hypothalamic–pituitary–adrenal system (HPA)

Key term

Hypothalamic–pituitary–adrenal system: a stress response system which operates via the release of the hormones and which results in the release of corticosteroids from the adrenal cortex.

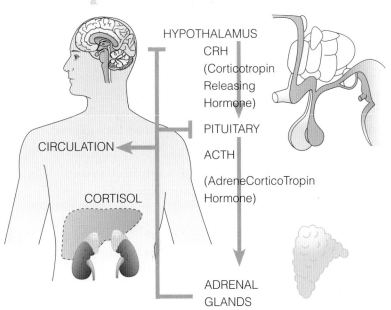

HYPOTHALAMUS

CRH (Corticotropin Releasing Hormone)

PITUITARY

ACTH (AdreneCorticoTropin Hormone)

CIRCULATION

CORTISOL

ADRENAL GLANDS

Fig. 7.1 Hypothalamic–pituitary–adrenal system

Pituitary gland: the 'master gland' of the body, which instructs other glands to release hormones.

Cortisol: a steroid hormone which instructs the release of stored sugars into the bloodstream for energy.

The second stress response system is the HPA. The **pituitary gland** sits just beneath the brain, connected to the hypothalamus by a short stalk (the infundibulum). The pituitary is the master gland of the body, releasing a number of hormones into the bloodstream. A major function of these hormones is to control other glands spread around the body involved in vital functions such as reproduction and growth. Although released from the pituitary gland, ultimate control of these hormones is located in the hypothalamus, and their release depends upon hypothalamic activity.

The key pituitary stress hormone is adrenocorticotrophic hormone (ACTH). The hypothalamus stimulates the release of ACTH from the pituitary into the bloodstream. The hormone travels to the adrenal cortex, part of the adrenal gland; we have two adrenal glands, located close to the kidney on each side of the body. When ACTH reaches the adrenal cortex it stimulates the release of corticosteroids such as **cortisol** into the bloodstream. Cortisol has major effects on the body as we will examine.

The role of cortisol

Cortisol is one of the main corticosteroid hormones released from the adrenal cortex when the HPA is activated. In fact cortisol is being released all the time and this release usually follows a circadian biological rhythm. Levels are lowest at night, then surge in the morning, then gradually decline during the day. Stress increases cortisol levels over and above the normal level for the particular time of day. After activation of the HPA in response to a stressor, levels of cortisol peak at about 20–30 minutes.

Link

For more on circadian biological rhythms, see page 289 in Book 1

Energy is taken in in the form of fats, sugars and carbohydrates in our diet. After digestion sugars and carbohydrates are converted to **glycogen** and stored in muscles and, especially, the liver. Fats are stored in the body's fatty tissue. The major role of cortisol is to reverse this process by releasing glycogen stored in the muscles and liver and promoting its conversion back to sugars in the bloodstream. These sugars can then be used as an energy source by the brain and by skeletal muscle, and burnt up in vigorous activity. Under conditions of excessive stress, cortisol can also promote the liberation of fats from our fat stores. These enter the bloodstream as free fatty acids and can be another important source of energy for muscles and brain.

Key terms

Glycogen: the key source of fuel for the body which is made by and stored in the liver.

The immune system: a complex set of inter-related systems which provide the body's defence again infections.

Raised levels of corticosteroids, if sustained over a long period, also have the effect of suppressing the body's **immune system**. This system is the body's defence against infection, and consists of a variety of complex subsystems vital in keeping the person healthy.

A lining to the brain's blood vessels, the blood-brain barrier, protects the brain from many chemicals and hormones circulating in the bloodstream but some, such as cortisol, can penetrate this barrier and freely enter the brain. The brain has receptors for cortisol and so can detect levels of this hormone in the bloodstream. As levels rise, the hypothalamus inhibits release of ACTH (see earlier) and so reduces release of cortisol from the adrenal cortex. This is a neat negative feedback system, restoring baseline levels of cortisol after a rise in release. However this negative feedback system can be overridden if stress continues, and levels of cortisol will remain high for as long as the stressor lasts. A negative feature of cortisol's ability to enter the brain is that it can reduce activity of the neurotransmitter serotonin. Low levels of serotonin are associated with depression (some antidepressant drugs work by increasing activity of serotonin), and so a side effect of prolonged stress can be low levels of brain serotonin and consequent depression.

EXAMPLE EXAM QUESTION

Figure 7.2 shows the major hormones released through the HPA and SAM pathways. Write the following labels into the correct places on the diagram: adrenal medulla; pituitary gland; ACTH; adrenal cortex. (4 marks)

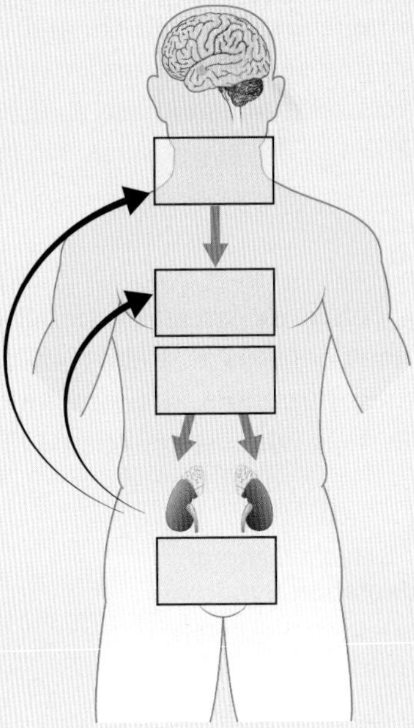

Fig. 7.2 Major hormones released through the HPA and SAM pathways

Exam hint

It is probably easiest to work backwards with this kind of question. Begin with the stress responses (corticosteroids/adrenaline) then trace your way back through the respective pathways, identifying the stages and applying the labels for each stage.

The stress response systems are extremely old in evolutionary terms, and as you can see their main effects are to allow for physical energy expenditure (e.g. fight or flight) in times of stress-related emergencies. This makes sense when stressors, such as predators, required a physical response and a zebra needed to run fast to escape the lion. However the life of modern humans is very different, as fast running isn't usually an effective coping response for the stress of exams or difficult relationships. In these cases it is thought that the body's response to stress can become pathological (i.e. may lead to illness). One of the earliest and most influential models of the body's response to stressors was introduced by Selye, and this remains a useful way of picturing the process.

General adaptation syndrome (GAS)

One of the first influential models of the effects of stress on the body was put forward by Selye in the 1930s. Selye noticed that rats given repeated daily injections developed similar stress-related symptoms,

Key term

General adaptation syndrome: a three stage model of the body's general response to stress.

such as gastric (stomach) ulcers. On the basis of many studies he developed a three-stage model of how the body responds to stressors, and called this the general adaptation syndrome (GAS) as he thought it described how the body responds to any stressor:

Stage 1: Alarm

A stressor is perceived by higher brain centres and signals are sent to the hypothalamus. The HPA axis and the SAM pathway are activated. Levels of stress-related hormones surge, heart rate and blood pressure increase, and energy reserves are mobilised.

Stage 2: Resistance

If the stressor persists the body's response systems, HPA and SAM maintain their activation, with levels of stress-related hormones and bodily arousal remaining above normal. The individual appears to be coping but the response systems are under strain. The individual becomes vulnerable to stress-related illness as the immune system, after the initial activation of the alarm stage, becomes suppressed by long-term stress.

Stage 3: Exhaustion

Long periods of stress ('**chronic**' stress) eventually exhaust the body's defence systems and energy reserves, and its ability to maintain high levels of circulating stress hormones. Immune function remains suppressed. This is the stage when stress-related illnesses may develop.

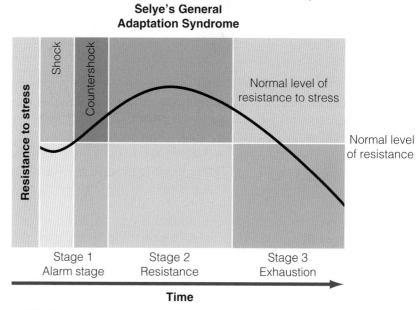

Fig. 7.3 Selye's general adaptation syndrome

Evaluation of Selye's work

Selye's work has been extremely influential in developing the whole area of research into stress. He identified the central roles of the HPA system and the SAM pathway, which we will explore in detail next. He also emphasised the links between chronic stress and illness.

Selye emphasized that the GAS was a common response to all stressors. He ignored individual differences and the cognitive elements of perception and appraisal, which are vital to the way we perceive and appraise situations as being stressful or not. Remember that much of Selye's early work was based on rats and a narrow range of physical stressors, so it is perhaps unsurprising that he downplayed individual differences and the role of cognitive processes.

Additionally, it is now thought that stress-related illnesses are not caused by exhaustion of the body's physiological stress responses. Rather, it is the effect of chronic long-lasting raised levels of stress hormones such as cortisol that eventually can lead to illness.

EXAMPLE EXAM QUESTION

Mike is newly qualified teacher, who has just finished his first term working in a school. Mike has found the work stressful. He has spent most evenings preparing lessons or marking children's homework. He is looking forward to his Christmas holiday but he becomes ill the weekend after finishing school with a cold which is followed by a stomach bug. Mike has just about recovered when it is time to go back to school.

Use your knowledge of the General Adaptation Syndrome to explain Mike's experiences. (4 marks)

Exam hint

In order to answer this question, you will need to map Mike's experiences onto the stages of the GAS. Avoid giving too much descriptive detail about the stages as marks are awarded for application.

KEY POINTS

- Stress occurs when the perceived demands of a situation exceed the perceived ability to cope.
- Two key pathways play a role in the body's response to stress - the hypothalamic–pituitary–adrenal axis (HPA) and the sympathetic–adrenomedullary pathway (SAM).
- Activation of the HPA results in the release of ACTH from the pituitary gland. This hormone stimulates the release of corticosteroids including cortisol from the adrenal cortex.
- Cortisol increases the mobilization of stored energy reserves so that levels of glucose and fatty acids rise in the bloodstream. Cortisol also supresses the immune system, leaving the body vulnerable to illness and infections.
- Selye put forward a three-stage model of the body's generalized response to stress known as the General Adaptation Syndrome.
- Activation of the SAM results in the secretion of adrenaline and noradrenaline from the adrenal medulla.
- Adrenaline acts directly on the heart and circulation system to speed up the heart rate and raise blood pressure.

The role of stress in illness

As we have seen, the body's response to stress involves a cascade of hormonal and chemical changes along with increases in heart rate and blood pressure. It is a feature of the action of corticosteroids such as cortisol that they can also suppress the activity of our immune system, potentially leaving us vulnerable to illness and infection. Increases in heart rate and blood pressure put severe mechanical strain on our heart and circulatory system, increasing the possibility of cardiovascular disorders such as strokes and heart attacks.

It is commonly believed that stress leads to illness. Conditions such as eczema, gastric (stomach) ulcers, hypertension (long-term raised blood pressure), irritable bowel syndrome, some cancers and most cardiovascular disorders have all been linked to stress. Stress is also – unsurprisingly – linked to increased levels of depression and anxiety and related symptoms such as sleeplessness and poor performance at work and at college. Before accepting these beliefs about the effects of stress, it is important for psychologists to assess the evidence.

Stress and **immunosuppression**

The immune system is an immensely complex set of interacting processes that provides the body's defences against infection and illness. It is made up of various cells and circulating proteins and is designed to cope with a variety of hostile viruses, bacteria and infectious processes. We have two basic systems:

- **Natural immunity** – this is a primitive system made up of white blood cells (leucocytes) in the bloodstream. These attack and ingest (absorb) invading pathogens such as viruses and bacteria; a major subdivision of this natural immunity system is made up of natural killer cells (NK cells), and these have been used as a popular index of immune function in studies on stress. Natural immunity is non-specific, attacking any invading pathogens it comes across.
- **Specific immunity** – Specific immunity is a more sophisticated system. Cells of the specific system (made up of various types of lymphocyte, produced in the lymph glands of the body) can learn to recognise invading pathogens and then to produce specific antibodies to destroy them. This is the basis of immunization; a small dose of a pathogen is given to stimulate the production of antibodies, so that in future that person is protected against the pathogen.

The natural immune system reacts rapidly to invasion by bacteria and viruses, but in a non-specific fashion. Specific immunity takes days to develop as it involves 'learning' about the invader so that specific antibodies can be produced. Together the two systems provide a defence against infection that is usually effective. The question is whether stress can suppress the immune system so that illness and infections are more likely to occur.

This has been a fertile area for research and many different studies have been carried out using different stressors and different measures of immune function. Two examples will illustrate this range.

ACTIVITY 7.2

As you read the two key studies below, identify the similarities and differences between them in relation to research method used, measure of immune functioning, sample, outcome and ethical issues. Which do you think provides the best measurement of the effects of stress on the immune system and why?

KEY STUDY: COHEN ET AL (1993)

These researchers investigated the role of general life stress on vulnerability to the common cold virus. Three hundred and ninety four participants completed questionnaires on the number of stressful life events they had experienced in the previous year. They also self-rated their degree of stress and their level of negative emotions such as depression. The three scores were combined into what the researchers called a 'stress index'.

The participants were then exposed to the common cold virus, leading to 82 per cent of them becoming infected with the virus. After seven days the number whose infection had developed into a clinical cold was recorded. The findings were that the chance of developing a cold (i.e. failing to fight off the viral infection), was significantly positively correlated with scores on the stress index.

Cohen et al concluded that life stress and negative emotions reduce the effectiveness of our immune system, leaving participants less able to resist viral infections.

Research methods link

You can refresh your memory for correlational research, and cause and effect explanations by looking at pages 22–25.

THINKING SCIENTIFICALLY: METHODOLOGICAL ISSUES

Cohen's study measured actual illness outcomes (i.e. whether participants developed a cold or not) rather than measuring immune functioning. Activity of the immune system was inferred from the presence or absence of a clinical cold. Other studies have supported the claim that the probability of developing a cold is correlated with high levels of negative events in the preceding days (Evans & Edgington, 1991).

Cohen used a correlational study, so cause and effect between the stress index and illness cannot be confirmed. In addition, the measurement of stress (the stress index) was made up of life events, self-rated level of stress, and levels of negative emotions. The study does not tell us which of these is more or less important in relation to stress-related illness.

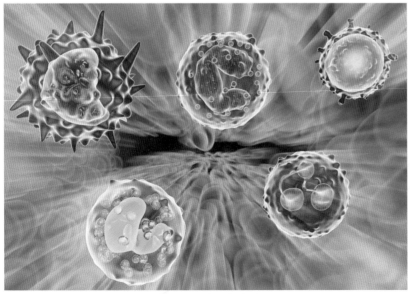

Fig. 7.4 Different types of white blood cells. Top left: basophil, top middle: monocyte, top right: lymphocyte. Bottom left: neutrophil, bottom right: eosinophil.

KEY STUDY: KIECOLT-GLASER ET AL., 1984

In an influential study Kiecolt-Glaser and her research group looked at naturalistic life stressors and their impact on measures of immune function. They used 75 medical students preparing for their final examinations. As a measure of immune function they used natural killer (NK) cell activity, part of our natural immunity system.

Measures of NK cell activity were recorded from blood samples taken one month before exams (low stress) and during the exam period (high stress). Participants also completed questionnaires on stressful life events and levels of social isolation. Findings were that NK cell activity was significantly reduced in the high-stress samples, compared to the low-stress samples. In addition, the greatest reductions were in students reporting the highest levels of social isolation.

Kiecolt-Glaser et al concluded that a relatively brief natural stressor such as an examination can significantly reduce immune function, potentially making people more vulnerable to illness and infections. The effects are more noticeable in students experiencing high levels of social isolation.

Link

You can read more about physiological measurements of stress in the section of the chapter on page 369.

THINKING SCIENTIFICALLY: METHODOLOGICAL ISSUES

There was no direct measure of illness outcomes, unlike Cohen's study; it may be that the significant reductions in immune function were still too small to increase the chances of stress-related illness. In her research Kiecolt-Glaser does not manipulate an independent variable (e.g. examination stress) but takes advantage of natural stressors. A cause and effect relationship cannot be confirmed, but a range of findings from a number of different studies consistently point to a relationship between life stress and reduced immune function.

This experiment used a sample of medical students and it could be argued that findings cannot confidently be generalized to other populations. However, in further research, Kiecolt-Glaser's research group (1987, 1991) have shown reductions in immune function in a variety of highly stressed groups, including dementia carers and women going through stressful divorces, implying that these findings can be representative of different populations.

Research methods link

This is an example of a natural experiment, in which the independent variable occurs without manipulation by the researcher. You can remind yourself of the by advantages and disadvantages of natural experiments looking at pages 9–10 of the Research Methods chapter.

Follow-up studies by Kiecolt-Glaser and her group have shown that small wounds (inflicted under controlled conditions and with ethical approval) take longer to heal in highly stressed groups such as carers for dementia patients, who also show significant reductions in immune function (Kiecolt-Glaser et al., 1991; 1995). Kiecolt-Glaser's research group have also shown that short-term marital conflict can also produce reductions in immune function and prolong the healing of small wounds (Malarkey et al., 1994; Kiecolt-Glaser et al., 2005). She has therefore demonstrated a link between life stress, reductions in immune function, and some health outcomes.

Commentary

Different researchers use different stressors and different measures of immune function. To bring some sense to the field it is necessary to combine the findings of many studies and to look for consistencies in the data. This method is known as **meta-analysis** and it provides a much more reliable picture of relationships between variables.

Segerstrom and Miller (2004) performed such a meta-analysis on studies of stress and the immune system. They combined the findings of 293 studies and came up with a number of conclusions. The most important ones were:

- Short-term stressors produced an increase or upregulation of natural immunity, as measured for instance by an increase in the number of natural killer cells in the bloodstream. This makes sense as natural immunity is a fast response system that would be activated by the immediate onset of a stressor.
- Chronic or long lasting stressors were found to consistently downregulate or suppress all measures of immune function, both natural and specific. These suppressive effects of chronic stress were also consistent across gender and age groups.

- A further analysis by Segerstrom and Miller used those studies that involved life event questionnaires such as the Social Readjustment Ratings Scale (see p. 367) as well as measures of immune function. Overall they found no relationship between life events and immune function. However, in the subgroup of participants aged over 55 the meta-analysis found that life events did correlate with a reduction in immune function.

(see p. 367)

Key term

Meta-analysis: a statistical analysis of the findings of separate studies which have used the same method, to test the data for statistical significance and resolve discrepancies.

Fig. 7.5 Final exams, an acute stressor

STRESS

ACTIVITY 7.3

You have now read about two ways of studying the immune system – measuring natural killer cells (Kiecolt-Glaser) and measuring illness outcomes (Cohen). Devise a questionnaire to measure illness over a specified period, such as the last four weeks. Your questionnaire should be suitable to use with fellow students and adults and is likely to cover areas such as days off work/school number of coughs/colds, number of 'over the counter' remedies such as paracetamol consumed. You should use closed questions and devise a scoring system for your questions. You can use your questionnaire in the practical activity at the end of this chapter.

Research methods link

For more on closed questions, see page 19.

For more on closed questions, see page 19.

EXAMPLE EXAM QUESTION

Discuss research into stress and immunosuppression. (16 marks)

Exam hint

Start your answer with a short definition of the term 'immunosuppression' and identify the different methods which have been used to examine the effects of stress on the immune system. Comparison of the strengths and weaknesses of correlation and natural experiments is a good source of AO3 marks.

Stress and cardiovascular disorders

The ultimate purpose of the alarm stage of the stress response is to provide the energy required for rapid responses – fight or flight. Activation of the HPA system leads to increased blood levels of sugars and fatty acids to provide fuel for muscular activity. Activation of the SAM pathway leads to increases in heart rate and blood pressure to speed oxygen to the muscles so that they can work most effectively.

However, long-term increases in blood pressure can physically damage the linings of blood vessels, eroding the lining and so providing sites at which circulating fatty acids (or 'plaques') can accumulate. Plaques

A **heart attack** occurs when the blood supply to the heart is cut off, leading to a death of heart muscle.

A **stroke** occurs when the blood supply to part of the brain is cut off, leading to death of brain tissue.

cause narrowing of the blood vessel and may eventually lead to a **heart attack** or, if it occurs in the brain's circulatory system, a **stroke**.

In our evolutionary past, the stress response was highly adaptive, providing the energy to escape from predators. The sugars and fats were burned up in the physical activity of fight or flight. The HPA and SAM worked together to allow enable the adaptive response to occur. As human culture evolved we moved away from these basic survival stressors. They still existed but we began to worry in addition about more complex stressors such as relationships, money and job security. These modern stressors are just as effective at activating the stress pathways as being confronted by an angry rhino. However the response to our contemporary stressors no longer involves intense muscular activity, so we do not burn up the high levels of sugars and fatty acids; they remain in the bloodstream, contributing to the furring up of our arteries.

There is even more research on the link between stress and cardiovascular disorders than on immune suppression. Studies have examined the impact of acute stressors such as earthquakes or the lesser stress of public speaking, and chronic stressors such as the on-going stress involved in daily life, work and family relationships.

One study examined the immediate impact of the 1999 Taiwan earthquake on heart rate. Twelve patients were undergoing monitoring before the earthquake struck and the monitoring caught the immediate impact on their bodies of the sudden natural disaster. The earthquake led to a dramatic increase in heart rate (Huang, Chiou, Ting, Chen and Chen, 2001). Another study found an increase in pulmonary embolism (blockages in the artery which carries blood from the heart to the lungs) after the 2004 earthquake in Nigeria (Watanabe et al., 2008).

Public speaking is a source of short-term, acute stress for many people. Dimsdale and Moss (1980) measured the levels of adrenaline in a sample of junior doctors who were giving presentations at a conference. On average, the levels of adrenaline increased threefold during the presentation.

KEY STUDY: THE INTERHEART STUDY (ROSENGREN ET AL., 2004)

The INTERHEART study has examined the effects of psychosocial stress on heart attacks in a substantial sample of people drawn from 52 countries of the world across all continents. Around 11,000 people who had experienced a heart attack were matched for age and sex with controls who had not had a heart attack. All the participants were asked to report on the stress levels in their lives, with questions relating to four stress arenas – work, home, financial stress and life events.

The researchers found that the sample that had experienced heart attacks reported significantly higher levels of stress than the matched controls. Those who reported suffering from permanent stress had more than 2.1 times the risk of a heart attack than the control group. The differences were significant across all ethnic groups regions and genders.

THINKING SCIENTIFICALLY: GENERALIZATION

This is a substantial, international study with an extremely large sample size, making generalization possible. The measurement of stress was self-reporting and therefore subjective in nature. However, as we have already discussed, stress is a subjective experience, arising when the perceived demands of a situation exceed the individual's perceived ability to cope. Person A's stress nightmare may not even be registered as a stressful event by Person B.

Rosengren et al note that one problem lies with the retrospective nature of the INTERHEART study. Patients who have experienced a heart attack may be more likely to remember the past as stressful, or to try and recall stressful events, which have taken place, than the control group. This 'distortion of history' may introduce bias to the results.

Commentary

All of these stress-related conditions can be caused by factors other than stress, such as genes, or lifestyle factors such as diet, environmental toxins and pollutants. One of the key problems with investigating the link between stress and heart disease is that people experiencing high levels of stress may engage in less healthy behaviours. For example, they may be more likely to smoke, drink larger amounts of alcohol and less likely to spend time on exercise, especially if they are time pressured. These factors may act as confounding variables in relationships between stress and cardiovascular disorders. There are substantial individual differences in vulnerability and resilience to stress – as we will explore in the next section.

Link
You can read more about the link between stress and heart disease in the section on Type A behaviour on p. 376.

EXAMPLE EXAM QUESTION

Describe findings of research into stress and cardiovascular disorders. (4 marks)

Exam hint
Avoid including methodological detail in your answer as this will not be awarded credit. Aim to summarize the findings of at least two research studies.

KEY POINTS

- The immune system provides the body's defences against infection.

- Cohen found that participants with higher scores on a stress index were more likely to develop a clinical cold when exposed to the cold virus.

- Kiecolt-Glaser found a reduction in natural killer cells in medical students undergoing exams.

- Meta-analyses show that short-term stressors lead to an upregulation of natural immunity (increase in natural killer cells) but chronic, on-going stressors lead to downregulation of immune functioning.

- The SAM and HPA stress responses act on the cardiovascular system, releasing stored sugars for energy and increasing blood pressure.

- Cardiovascular disorders include heart attacks and strokes.

- Studies show that natural disasters such as earthquakes produce immediate and dramatic increases in heart rate and increases in cases of pulmonary embolism shortly afterwards.

- The INTERHEART study has found that heart-attack victims report significantly higher stress levels than matched controls.

- It is difficult to establish direct cause and effect relationships between stress and illness as illnesses are effected by genetics and lifestyle factors such as smoking.

Measuring stress

Research methods link

You can remind yourself about self-report techniques by looking at pages 20–22.

There are a variety of different ways of measuring the degree of stress in someone's life. Some of the more common methods include **self-report scales**, semi-structured interviews in which participants talk through their life stressors with a trained interviewer and **physiological measures**. Specific tools have been developed for different sources of stress such as **life events**, **daily hassles** and stress at work. This section examines some of the more commonly used measures, before going on to explore what these have told us about the different sources of stress in people's lives.

Self-report scales

Self-report scales are questionnaires in which respondents are asked about the incidence/frequency of stressful events in their lives. Some self-report scales are pen and paper whereas others are completed online. Two influential self-report scales are the Social Readjustment Rating Scale (SRRS) devised by Holmes and Rahe in 1967 and the Hassles and Uplifts Scale (Kanner 1981). Self-report measures can be quickly administered to large numbers of participants and they can provide honest data when they are completed privately and anonymously. However, response rates can be varied and there is no guarantee that those who do send them back are representative of the overall population.

The Social Readjustment Rating Scale

Thomas Holmes and Richard Rahe were doctors. Whilst working in hospitals they noticed that many patients, in particular those with heart disease, reported that they had experienced events such as getting married, losing a job, or moving house in the preceding year. Holmes and Rahe introduced the concept of a **life event** as a change in life circumstances requiring a degree of adjustment on the part of the individual. Holmes and Rahe examined the medical records of over 5000 patients and made a list of 43 life events which preceded their hospital admissions.

Holmes and Rahe then asked 394 people to rate the impact of the 43 life events. In order to do this they were asked to compare each event with marriage in terms of the degree of adjustment necessary. Marriage was given an arbitrary value of 500 and the participants were asked to award a score to the other events relative to this baseline: if an event was perceived as more stressful as getting married, the score would be higher than 500. In order to create the finalized scale, the average score for each event was divided by 5 and referred to as a **Life Change Unit (LCU)**. The complete scale (see Table 7.1) was referred to as the Social Readjustment Rating Scale (SRRS).

Death of a spouse (life partner) was rated as the event requiring the most adjustment, and therefore the most stressful, with divorce and marital separation following, but a long way behind. At the bottom were events such as minor law breaking, Christmas and holidays. In the next section we will examine what research using the SRRS has shown about the impact of life events.

Evaluation of the SRRS

The SRRS is easy to use, as you simply add up the LCUs for life events occurring during the preceding year to produce an overall score. However, the original scale took no account of the *nature* of the event (i.e. was the impact positive or negative?). Some events, such as marriage, are chosen and although these events still involve some stress, the changes are generally positive. Holmes and Rahe assumed all events, regardless of their nature, involved readjustment and were therefore stressful.

The Social Readjustment Rating Scale (SRRS)
Example items
Rank life event (LCU)
1 Death of a spouse (100)
2 Divorce (73)
4 Jail term (63)
6 Personal injury or illness (53)
7 Marriage (50)
8 Fired at work (47)
10 Retirement (45)
12 Pregnancy (40)
17 Death of a close friend (37)
22 Change in responsibilities at work (29)
23 Son or daughter leaving home (29)
25 Outstanding personal achievement (28)
27 Begin or end school (26)
28 Change living conditions (25)
30 Trouble with boss (23)
33 Change in schools (20)
36 Change in social activities (18)
41 Holiday (13)
42 Christmas (12)
43 Minor violations of the law (11)

Table 7.1 Holmes and Rahe Social Readjustment Rating Scale (SRRS)

The scale provides a single generalized score for each event, which takes no account of individual circumstances. A divorce, for example, may be perceived very differently by each of the partners; the partner who seeks the divorce may feel lower levels of stress than the partner who is being divorced. This relates to the *cognitive appraisal of stressful situations*, which in fact determines whether we find them highly stressful or relatively harmless.

Other life-event scales have been developed that try to avoid some of the problems above. The Life Events Scale (LES; Sarason et al. 1978) allows people to rate 57 life events in terms of severity of impact and whether the impact is positive or negative. This allows for individual differences. In addition, specialized sections can be added for particular groups, such as students. The LES produces three scores – negative change, positive change, and total change (similar to the SRRS). In general, negative life-change scores correlate more highly with illness outcomes.

The Hassles and Uplifts Scale

Major life events, by their nature, are relatively rare. The regular sources of stress in people's lives tend to arise from the on-going problems of day-to-day living, such as travel problems, relationships, keeping up with college work. etc. Lazarus, one of the key stress researchers of the last 30 years, felt that hassles were more significant for health than major life events. His research group (Kanner et al., 1981) devised the Hassles Scale specifically to assess these sources of stress.

Kanner's original Hassles Scale had 117 items covering all aspects of daily life. Lazarus felt that life also contained positive events, known as **uplifts** that could counteract the negative effects of daily hassles. An Uplifts Scale was created with 135 positive items, such as getting good grades or getting on well with friends.

Ten Most Frequent Hassles and Uplifts ($N = 100$)[a]	
Item	% of times checked
Hassles	
1. Concerns about weight	52.4
2. Health of a family member	48.1
3. Rising prices of common goods	43.7
4. Home maintenance	4.28
5. Too many things to do	38.6
6. Misplacing or losing things	38.1
7. Yard work or outside home maintenance	38.1
8. Property, investment, or taxes	37.6
9. Crime	37.1
10. Physical appearance	35.9
Uplifts	
1. Relating well with your spouse or lover	76.3
2. Relating well with friends	74.4
3. Completing a task	73.3
4. Feeling healthy	72.7
5. Getting enough sleep	69.7
6. Eating out	68.4
7. Meeting your responsibilities	68.1
8. Visiting, phoning, or writing someone	67.7
9. Spending time with family	66.7
10. Home (inside) pleasing to you	65.5

[a] Items are those most frequency checked over a period of nine months. The "% of times checked" figures represent the mean percentage of people checking the item each month averaged over the nine monthly administrations.

Table 7.2 Ten most frequent hassles and uplifts

ACTIVITY 7.4

Locate online copies of the SRRS and the Hassles and Uplifts Scale and complete these to establish your own score. Based on your scores, have major life events or hassles caused you most stress in the last year? Now, take one of the two scales and consider how well the items reflect the hassles *or* life events of students around your age today. Identify any items which you think are outdated and see if you can decide on what sort of items might replace these. (If you do not have access to computers in the classroom, why not try this as a homework activity?)

Evaluation of the Hassles and Uplifts Scale

Kanner's Hassles and Uplifts Scale has proved a useful way of measuring the degree of stress from minor everyday niggles. The scale has been modified for specific groups such as students, where items such as study problems and unfriendly tutors are particularly relevant. Studies using the Hassles Scale have indicated that hassles may be closely linked to psychological well-being.

The original Hassles Scale contains 117 items, making completion a time-consuming exercise. However, the original scale has been modified by Lazarus and Folkman into a shorter version, the HSUP scale, which measures daily hassles, daily uplifts and a combined score.

Physiological measures, including skin conductance response

As the body's stress response involves a number of physiological processes it seems obvious that a more objective method of measuring stress would be to use these physiological processes. We have already seen examples of this approach in the section on stress and the immune system; blood levels of natural killer cells could be seen as a physiological measure of stress – low levels may indicate high levels of stress.

However, measuring immune function is not straightforward and other physiological measures have traditionally been far more popular. These involve direct recording of SAM activity for example:

- Heart rate – this increases with activation of the SAM pathway in stressful situations. It tends to return to baseline (normal levels) fairly quickly, but can provide an index of immediate reactions to a stressor.
- Blood pressure – this is increased by SAM pathway activation in response to short-term stressors, but can also show persistent increases in situations of chronic stress. In fact raised blood pressure ('hypertension') over a long period is seen as a key indicator of chronic stress.
- **Skin conductance response** – SAM activation, besides its effects on the circulatory system, increases the activity of sweat glands in the skin. It is a common experience that in stressful situations or in situations involving anxiety or fear our hands can feel damp and clammy – this is caused by increased sweat-gland activity secreting more sweat on to the skin surface. This increased sweat secretion changes the electrical characteristics of the skin, and this change

Key term

Skin conductance response: a measurement of sweat secretions using electrodes to assess the electrical activity of the skin.

can be detected by recording electrodes placed on the hand. It is known as the skin conductance response. The older term for this measure is 'galvanic skin response', or GSR.

Evaluation of the SCR

The SCR is highly sensitive, and in fact is the basis of the lie detector – lying is usually stressful, so when someone lies it can activate the stress pathways; this changes sweat-gland activity and is detected as an SCR. In theory therefore, the SCR could be used to assess an individual's stress reactions to a particular situation.

Heart rate, blood pressure and the SCR can all be measured using recording electrodes on the surface of the body. The electrodes are connected to a machine called a polygraph, and this is routinely used to record all three measures simultaneously. In this way we can generate a picture of the arousal state of the body, reflecting activation of the SAM pathway.

Exam hint

This question requires succinct coverage of the methods you choose. It is a good idea to select one self-report measure and one physiological measurement to avoid repetition in your answer.

EXAMPLE EXAM QUESTION

Outline two methods of measuring stress. (6 marks)

KEY POINTS

- Stress can be measured using self-report scales and physiological measurements.
- Self-report scales include the SRRS to measure life events and Hassles and Uplifts Scales.
- The SRRS has 43 items each with a score. The most stressful item is death of partner.
- The Hassles and Uplifts Scales have been adapted to use with different groups.
- Self-report measures are good ways of getting large amounts of data relatively easily. However, there is no guarantee that those who return them will form a representative sample.
- Physiological measurements of stress focus on the bodily response and include heart rate and blood pressure.
- Skin conductance response is a measurement of the electrical activity of the skin. It forms the basis of lie-detector tests.

Sources of stress
Life changes and daily hassles

As we have seen, the work of Holmes and Rahe (1967) on life changes has been central to the development of life event scales. Holmes and Rahe defined a score of over 150 LCUs as a *life crisis* and a score over 300 LCU's as a *major crisis*.

Subsequent research carried out by Holmes and Rahe (Holmes & Masuda, 1974; Rahe & Lind, 1971) using the SRRS found a significant relationship between LCU scores and stress-related disease. A score of over 150 LCUs increased the chances of a stress-related illness by 30 per cent and a score over 300 LCUs increased the illness risk by 50 per cent. However, these studies were **retrospective**. This means that people already undergoing treatment for heart disease and other stress-related

Key term

Retrospective: studies which require participants to recall events which happened in the past.

illnesses were asked to recall life events from the previous year. As we discussed in relation to stress and cardiovascular disorders, memories for life events may be distorted. This can be a particular problem when people are already ill, as they may be looking for explanations for their illness and therefore exaggerate the number of life events.

KEY STUDY: RAHE ET AL (1970)

Rahe et al. (1970) investigated the stress–illness link in a sample of healthy participants. Over 2000 US Navy personnel filled in the SRRS for the previous six months. They were then followed up over the following seven-month tour of duty, and all stress-related illnesses recorded and rated for number and severity, producing an overall illness score.

The findings were that there was a positive correlation of 0.118 between levels of stress in terms of LCU scores, and illness scores. Although this is a relatively low correlation (remember that correlation coefficients can vary from +1.0 through 0 to −1.0) it was statistically significant due to the very large sample involved in the research. Rahe et al. concluded that there is a relationship between life events and the development of stress-related illness.

Research methods link

You can remind yourself about the strength of correlation coefficients by looking at Figure 9 on page 24 of the Research Methods chapter.

Key term

Prospective studies involve following participants over a period of time from the start of the study. An example would be studies of life stress and health.

THINKING SCIENTIFICALLY: PROSPECTIVE STUDIES

This is a **prospective** study which has advantages over retrospective research. Prospective studies involve an assessment of participant's LCU units before they have become ill. Participants are then followed up to see if illness develops. This avoids some of the problems associated with retrospective studies which were discussed earlier.

Rahe's study uses a correlational method. As you know, correlations do not imply causality. Divorce may be a factor correlated with

depression, but perhaps the depression of one partner led to the marriage break up rather than the other way round.

Although this study was carried out on American sailors and you might argue that the results are difficult to generalize, others studies have produced very similar findings regarding the correlation between life events and illness. However some studies find no significant relationship, while even when significant the correlation coefficients are usually low.

Although the work of Holmes and Rahe was extremely valuable in its attempt to measure or quantify the levels of stress in people's lives and show some associations with health, it did not address other sources of life stress. Subsequent research using the Hassles and Uplifts Scale has suggested that for most people, more stress occurs from small daily stressors than from life events.

KEY STUDY: KANNER, COYNE, SCHAEFER AND LAZARUS (1981)

Kanner et al. carried out a longitudinal study comparing the impact of life events and hassles on psychological wellbeing. A sample of 100 middle-aged adults drawn from a local community were asked to compete the Hassles and Uplifts Scale each month for a duration of ten months. They were also asked to complete the SRRS to establish a LCU score. Finally, the participants completed a measure of psychological well-being including feelings and anxiety and depression.

Kanner et al. found that the hassles score was more closely related to psychological wellbeing than the SRRS score, implying a stronger relationship between well-being and minor daily stressors. Interestingly, uplift scores were related to better psychological well-being for women but not for men.

THINKING SCIENTIFICALLY: LONGITUDINAL STUDIES

This study is commendable as it is longitudinal in nature, following a group of participants over a sustained period of time. This provides a more detailed measurement of the relationship between the variables than a snapshot single measurement. As with Rahe's study, the method is correlational, making it difficult to establish cause and effect. The length of the Hassles Scale (117 items) and the Uplifts Scale (135 items) in this study may have been tedious for completion for the participants.

Other studies have supported Kanner et al's claim that scores on the Hassles Scale correlate with stress-related problems, in particular depression and anxiety. De Longis et al. (1982) did a study comparing scores on both the Hassles Scale and a Life Event Scale and found that correlations with health outcomes were greater for the hassles scores. Uplifts were unrelated to health outcomes. Similarly, Jandorf et al. (1986), using a different measure of daily events (the Assessment of Daily Experience scale, ADE: Stone & Neale, 1984), found higher positive correlations between daily events and health outcomes than between major life events and health.

Workplace stress, workload, and control

Over recent years one source of stress has attracted a huge amount of interest from public and psychologists alike. Workplace stress is now considered one of the major sources of stress for many people; every week there are reports of the increasing levels of stress attached to a variety of jobs, such as nursing, police work, and teaching. This type of stress is considered even more important because it not only distresses the individual but can lead to poor performance at work, increased absenteeism, and stress-related illness. It is therefore important for organizations to identify and minimize sources of stress in the work environment, and to help employees cope with them.

Every workplace is different. However some areas of stress apply to most organisations including:

- *Environment* – heating, lighting and the physical arrangement of the workplace are all potential sources of stress. Many studies have shown that intense noise and increases in temperature can lead to frustration, stress and in some cases aggression. The physical layout of the workplace can affect the psychological wellbeing of the employee in terms of 'personal space' and privacy. It is unsurprising that call centres are rated by many as stressful working environments!

- *Organizational factors* – these are elements such as opportunities for promotion, involvement in decision-making, relationships with other workers.
- *Home–work interface* – with many people having to balancing the competing demands of home and work, in particular parents with small children, this potentially very stressful area has become the subject of much debate. The concept of **'work–life' balance** refers to the ideal situation where an individual has time for both work and home responsibilities, leading to less stress and better psychological adjustment.

Workload and control

Workload is one of the most obvious factors in workplace stress. Workload refers to the amount of work to be done: interestingly research shows that it is not just work overload that can be stressful (Dewe, 1992), but that having too little to do can have similar effects.

Control has been a central focus of research into workplace stress. The degree of control a person has over their workload (sometimes referred to as 'decision latitude') has been shown to directly affect the level of stress experienced. High levels of control lead to lower levels of stress, while low levels of control, typically experienced by workers lower down the organization hierarchy, can increase stress levels.

Karasek's 1979 model (see Fig. 7.6) has been a popular way of picturing the relationship between job demand (workload) and levels of control. He suggests that the most stressful jobs involve high

Key terms

Work–life balance refers to ideal situations where workers have sufficient time for work and family responsibilities.

Workload refers to the amount of work to be completed within a particular time period.

Control refers to the amount of power an individual has to make decisions about their work.

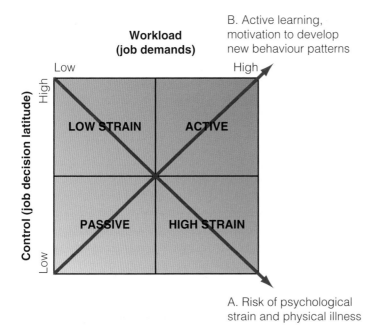

Fig. 7.6 Karasek's workload/control model

demand and low control, and the least stressful involve low demand and high control. Research supports the idea that a combination of high demand and low control is the most stressful combination, but also shows that these relationships can be modified by other factors, such as social support.

KEY STUDY: MARMOT ET AL. 1997

Since the 1960s a long-term study has been running on the relationships between workplace stress, health, and various individual and social risk factors such as smoking, blood pressure and cholesterol levels, obesity and socio-economic status. Participants are taken from London-based government civil servants, and the studies are therefore referred to as the Whitehall studies. In the first, Whitehall I, a clear gradient in heart problems and mortality rates was established, with workers in lower grades having twice the rate of workers in the highest grade. Differences in risk factors (e.g. workers in lower grades tend to smoke more and have higher levels of blood pressure) accounted for about a quarter of this difference.

Marmot et al. (1997) analysed data from over 7000 participants in the Whitehall II study, which began in 1985. Participants were followed up over five years. All were free of heart problems when the study began. The data showed a similar gradient in heart disease to Whitehall I, with the rate in the lowest grades being 1.5 times the rate in the highest grades. When the researchers analysed the data in detail they found that risk factors such as smoking, obesity, and hypertension could account for some of the increase in lower grades, but the most significant factor was the degree of 'decision latitude' or control that participants felt they had.

- Lack of control had a significant effect independent of socio-economic and other risk factors
- Note that in relation to Karasek's model, workload was less important than control (decision latitude)

THINKING SCIENTIFICALLY: BIASED SAMPLES

The study was largely based on self-report questionnaires, which raises issues of biased responding by participants, for instance underestimating risk factors such as smoking. Some factors that were not measured may have contributed to the results, for example workers in lower grades may have in common some characteristic that makes them vulnerable to heart disease but that was not measured in the study. The sample was of government civil servants. Although males and females were represented, this is otherwise a biased sample and it would be difficult to automatically generalize the results to other groups of workers. However the findings are supported by many other studies that have demonstrated a clear relationship between stress at work and lack of control.

In a very different workplace, Johannson et al (1978) found higher levels of stress hormones and stress-related illness in a group of highly-skilled sawmill employees whose work was machine-paced (i.e. giving them little or no control over their workrate). In general, research supports a key role for level of control in workplace stress, with actual workload being of less importance (Jones and Bright, 2001).

Measuring and dealing with workplace stress

In addition to the sources of stress mentioned above there are several others, such as role ambiguity (being unsure of your responsibilities), relationships with other employees and career progression. There are a variety of questionnaire packages available to assess workplace stress and employee characteristics. The Occupational Stress Indicator (Cooper et al., 1988), for instance, uses self-report questionnaires to measure the sources of stress as perceived by the employee. In addition it measures characteristics such as social support, Type A behaviour, and coping strategies. The eventual outcome is a profile of the individual and the organization in terms of sources and degree of stress in its workforce.

These findings are then used to devise strategies to reduce the negative effects of stress on the individual (health problems) and on the organization (absenteeism, lowered productivity). These can include individually-tailored stress management programmes for employees, and changes to the way the organization is structured and managed.

Research methods link

For more on content analysis and thematic analysis, see pages 26–28.

ACTIVITY 7.5

A psychologist asked a group of students to write about stress in their part-time jobs. Read the two extracts below and think about how these relate to the research you have read about on workplace stress. You can also consider how you might analyze this type of qualitative data. Two possible methods are content analysis and thematic analysis.

'The worst thing about my job is the hours: I have to work a very long Saturday, as the shop stays open until 8pm. I am tired when I get there from school, but much more tired when I finish. The other staff are friendly enough but because I am a casual worker, I am sure I get more than my fair share of the most boring jobs. The customers are generally OK but often they bring things back when they have worn them, which is cheeky. Most customers expect that you will change items if they make enough of a fuss.'

'I work in a fast-food restaurant. Most of the other staff are students and we have a good laugh. The most stressful thing is the customers; they often complain (in the hope of getting a free meal!) i and the noise when the restaurant is busy. The kitchen is incredibly hot and the chefs also get stressed about the pressure of work when it is busy and take it out on the waitresses.'

EXAMPLE EXAM QUESTION

A group of researchers carried out a study to assess the relationship between workplace stress and illnesses. A sample of 100 workers at a large company were asked to complete a self-report measure of workplace stress once a month for six months. The researchers also recorded the number of days' absence they had taken due to illness over the same period.

(a) Explain what is meant by a self-report measure of stress. (2 marks)
(b) Identify one graph which the researchers could use to display the relationship between workplace stress and absence. (1 mark)
(c) Identify one statistical test, which the researchers could have used to assess the relationship between workplace stress and absence. Justify your choice of statistical test with reference to the research study. (3 marks)

KEY POINTS

- Research has shown a positive correlation between life changes and illness in a variety of populations, however, correlations are relatively small.
- Daily hassles may be more strongly related to psychological wellbeing than life events.
- The workplace is a major source of stress for many people.
- Karasek's model argues that the most stressful jobs are those with high demand and low control. Least stressful jobs involve low demand and high control.
- Marmot's 'Whitehall' studies suggest that lack of control is more stressful than high demand.

Individual differences in stress

So far we have reviewed various sources of stress in people's lives, from major life events through daily hassles to stressors specific to the workplace. One thing that stands out across all these areas is the role of individual differences. People vary in their vulnerability to stress-related problems. This may be because they **react** to stressors differently, or perhaps they have different methods of **coping** with stress. In the next sections we review both of these possibilities.

Personality types

Type A

The study of human personality is extremely complicated, with a variety of different approaches leading to a variety of different models. Potentially there are literally hundreds of characteristics that could be studied in relation to stress, but unfortunately only a few of these have generated significant amounts of research.

Type A behaviour (TAB)

Type A behaviour refers to a pattern of behaviours and attitudes that has been long linked to a vulnerability to stress-related illness. The pattern is shown in Table 7.2.

Key term

Type A behaviour: a behaviour pattern characterized by hostility, competitiveness and time pressure which is linked to stress-related illness.

Characteristics	
Time pressured	• Always working to deadlines • Unhappy doing nothing • Multi-tasking; doing several jobs at the same time
Competitive	• Always oriented towards achievement • Plays to win, whether at work or on the sports field
Hostility	• Becomes easily irritated and impatient with co-workers • Easily angered • Anger can be directed inwards

Table 7.3 Type A Behaviour

The Type A concept evolved from the work of Friedman and Rosenman in the 1950s and 1960s. They studied the characteristics of patients with coronary heart disease (CHD) and identified a particular pattern of behaviour that seemed to be associated with a vulnerability to heart disease. The characteristics are listed in Table 7.2. They also defined a **Type B** pattern that was essentially the opposite of Type A, i.e. relaxed, not competitive, and not hostile.

Early studies by their research group suggested that a Type A person was around twice as likely to develop CHD as a Type B. One of these pieces of research is described below.

Key term

Type B behaviour: a relaxed and non-competitive style of behaviour.

KEY STUDY: ROSENMAN ET AL 1976

Rosenman et al. (1976) studied 3454 middle-aged men on the West coast of the US. They were categorized as either Type A or Type B by structured interview. This is an interview where the questions are pre-planned. As the participant answers the questions the trained interviewer also notes behavioural signs of the Type A pattern. For instance, time pressure can be seen by the rate of speech and by interruptions to speed up the interviewer. Other behavioural signs of Type A behaviour include tapping fingers on the table, fidgeting and restlessness. Answers to the questions and the general behaviour are put together to provide an overall assessment of TAB.

The participants were followed up for 8.5 years. During that time there were 257 heart attacks, 69 per cent of which were in the Type A group. This was a significant effect even when lifestyle risk factors such as obesity and smoking were controlled for. Rosenman et al. concluded that the high TAB individual was vulnerable to heart disease.

Research methods link

You can remind yourself about structured interviews by looking at pages 21–22.

THINKING SCIENTIFICALLY: GENERALIZATION

This sample is extremely specific in terms of gender, age and cultural background of the participants, making the ability to generalize very limited indeed. The assessment of TABP focuses on both what is said and observation of non-verbal behaviours, making this a sensitive measure. There are many individual and lifestyle variables that can affect vulnerability to heart disease. Although some of these were controlled for, it is possible that some important variable was missed. The study has high ecological validity, but such real-life studies do not have perfect control over all variables

Evaluation of Rosenman et al 1976

Results like this seem to make intuitive sense, in that the competitive and pressured life makes the Type A person appear highly stressed. However, it soon became apparent that the link between TAB and heart disease was not reliable. Shekelle et al (1985) studied over 12,000 male participants, with TAB assessed by a self-report questionnaire and structured interview. They found over seven years that there was no difference in the incidents of heart disease between the Type A and the Type B groups. A number of general reviews (e.g., Matthews and Haines, 1986) suggest that only about half of the studies on TAB and CHD find a significant link. The general picture that emerged was that TAB was not a strong predictor of heart disease.

TAB is a complex combination of characteristics and one interesting question is whether particular characteristics are more important than others. Booth-Kewley and Friedman (1987) reviewed a number of studies in this area and concluded that the component of **hostility** and other negative emotions was a key element in linking TAB and CHD. In fact, Dembroski et al. (1989) found that hostility was more strongly linked to CHD than the overall TAB score. This was supported in a meta-review by Miller et al. (1996) who identified hostility as a risk factor in its own right.

> **Key term**
>
> **Hostility:** an unfriendly, antagonistic or aggressive response to people and events.

ACTIVITY 7.6

Devise an observational checklist (see pages 16–17) to measure Type A behaviour pattern. Your checklist should consist of behavioural categories to measure the components of Type A behaviour (time pressure, competitiveness and hostility). These must all be characteristics that can be observed (i.e. finger tapping, number of interruptions) and counted rather than concepts such as impatience. Carry out a short observation either in real life or using a YouTube clip ('The Apprentice' is ideal) to test your checklist. You should use event sampling (see page 17). Now reflect on your checklist. How easy it is to observe and record Type A behaviour?

Fig. 7.7 Observing behaviour patterns in a meeting

> **Key term**
>
> **Type C behaviour:** a behaviour pattern characterised by patient, co-operative behaviour, with little expression of negative emotions such as anger.

Type C behaviour

Since Friedman and Rosenman's work, interest has turned to other personality types associated with stress. Unsurprisingly these have been named Type C and D! Type C behaviour was identified by Temoshok (1979) whilst working in a melanoma (skin cancer) clinic. Temoshok interviewed 150 patients who were being treated for melanoma and found a very similar pattern of behaviour in over 3/4 of them, which she referred to as **Type C behaviour**. In simple terms, Type C's were 'pleasers': they were patient and co-operative and often seemed more concerned about the impact of their illness on family or friends than themselves. They were self-sacrificing and unassertive. They did not express emotions such as anger, fear or sadness but preferred to 'bottle these up'.

In a subsequent study (Temoshok et al., 1985) Temoshok and colleagues studied the relationship between Type C behaviour and size of tumours in a sample of patients aged between 18 and 72. They found a strong association between tumour size and Type C personalities in cancer sufferers under the age of 55.

What can we conclude from research into Types A, B and C behaviour? Friedman and Rosenman's introduction of the Type A behaviour stimulated an enormous amount of interest and research. It focused interest onto personality factors and health, and demonstrated that there could be links between personality and heart disease. Subsequent research has identified Type C behaviour, which appears to be linked to a higher risk of cancer.

As early findings failed to be replicated, the TAB concept was analyzed in more detail, and this led to the identification of the hostility dimension as an important risk factor for heart disease. The fact that some Type A individuals seem to cope well with stress suggests that some of their characteristics may protect them against the negative effects of stress. This brings us to a consideration of stress hardiness.

EXAMPLE EXAM QUESTION

Describe what is meant by Type A behaviour and explain how you might establish if someone shows this behaviour pattern. (6 marks)

Exam hint

This question asks you to summarize the characteristics of Type A behaviour and explain how it might be measured. You could summarize the structured interview method used by Rosenman, or alternatively refer to the use of an observational checklist.

Hardiness

The concept of the **hardiness** was introduced by Kobasa (1979) who was interested in factors that might protect or buffer people against the effects of stress. In an influential study, Kobasa examined the effects of personality type on a group of male business executives.

Key term

Hardiness: a personality type which shows strong resilience in the face of stress, characterized by control, commitment and challenge.

KEY STUDY: KOBASA (1979)

Kobasa studied male executives working for a large public company, with demanding and responsible jobs. The original sample consisted of over 800 workers. Each worker was asked to complete a measurement of stress (Holmes and Rahe's SRRS) and a measurement of stress-related illness.

Kobasa used the results of the two questionnaires to select a smaller sample of participants who showed similarly high levels of stress on the Holmes and Rahe's scale: However, one group (86 executives) did not show signs of stress-related illnesses despite the high stress score whereas a second group of 75 executives had developed various stress-related illnesses. These two groups constituted the two conditions of the independent variable.

Kobasa then administered a range of measures to assess personality differences between the two groups, including a locus of control scale, and a commitment scale. She found significant differences between the two groups, which were referred to under the umbrella term of 'hardiness'.

The group who did not suffer stress-related illnesses scored significantly higher on three dimensions. They showed higher levels of commitment to their jobs, had a strong internal locus of control and in Kobasa's words showed 'an attitude of vigorousness towards the environment' seeing stressful events as challenges to be overcome. These three components – control, commitment and challenge – made up the hardy personality.

Kobasa's work is an example of a natural experiment. The independent variable occurs without manipulation from the researcher. Natural experiments can show high levels of ecological validity but it is more difficult to establish causes and effect relationships as there may be other differences between the two groups which have affected the stress-related illness, acting as confounding variables.

This study of hardiness used mainly male, white-collar workers and you could argue that it lacked generalizability. However, the findings have been supported by later studies (Kobasa et al. 1982) and in particular by Beasley et al. (2003) who investigated the effects of life stress in university students. Students who scored more highly on hardiness showed reduced levels of psychological distress.

Research by Klag and Bradley (2004) suggests that the protective effects of hardiness may differ between males and females. Klag and Bradley compared a sample of 50 male and 80 female university staff and found in agreement with Kobasa, that hardiness acted as a buffer between stress and illness in males but not in females.

Evaluation

The area of research into personality and stress has a number of controversies and disagreements. However, there are some obvious connections between the work on TAB and Kobasa's concept of hardiness. According to Kobasa, high levels of control, commitment, and challenge protect against the harmful effects of stress. If you look back at the characteristics of people who score highly on TAB you will see that they have high levels of competitiveness and are very achievement oriented. You could argue that people with these characteristics are showing commitment and also see life as a series of challenges to be overcome. Commitment and challenge are key components of hardiness, so an overall conclusion might be that the Type A behaviour pattern also contains aspects of hardiness. Some characteristics of TAB such as time pressure and hostility may increase vulnerability to stress. Other characteristics such as commitment and challenge may increase resistance to stress. This mixed pattern might explain why the results of studies trying to link Type A behaviour and heart disease are inconsistent. In addition, personality is one of several variables which can influence stress – others include coping style and gender which we will explore in the next section of the chapter.

Fig. 7.8 Hardy individuals often set themselves challenges!

EXAMPLE EXAM QUESTION

Discuss research into individual differences in response to stress. (12 marks)

KEY POINTS

- Type A behaviour was associated with stress-related illness by Rosenman (1976). Type A individuals were more likely to develop heart disease than Type Bs.

- Subsequent research has indicated that hostility is the most significant component of Type A behaviour in relation to heart disease.

- Research by Temoshok suggests that Type C behaviour is associated with a higher risk of some cancers.

- Some individuals appear to be resistant to stress and show hardiness (Kobasa). Hardy people feel in control of their lives, have high levels of commitment and see stressful events as challenges.

- Some evidence suggests that that hardiness may buffer the effects of stress on illness more strongly in men than women.

Exam hint

This is a fairly open question, which allows you to choose which personality types you want to talk about. If you choose Type A behaviour (which has been studied most extensively) you can use the material on hardiness to evaluate this.

Managing and coping with stress

Drug therapy

Stressful situations are usually associated with feelings of anxiety. Drugs used in the treatment of anxiety are therefore prescribed for people complaining of 'feeling stress'. Up to the 1960s, anxiety was treated with drugs from the barbiturate family. Although these could be effective, barbiturates are lethal in overdose and also produce high levels of dependency. In the 1960s a class of drugs called the **benzodiazepines (BZ)** was introduced, and these rapidly took over from the barbiturates in the treatment of anxiety.

BZs act in the brain. They increase the action of the **neurotransmitter** GABA; **GABA** is an inhibitory neurotransmitter meaning that its role is to dampen down the activity of other neurotransmitter pathways throughout the brain. By increasing this inhibitory action of GABA, BZs therefore produce heightened inhibition of neurotransmitter activity in the brain, and there is some evidence that the inhibition of noradrenaline and serotonin are particularly important for the anti-anxiety effect of BZs.

Librium and Valium are successful anti-anxiety drugs and are often prescribed for the stress and anxiety associated with life events such as bereavement. However, as with all drug treatments for psychological conditions there are weaknesses as well as strengths associated with the use of BZs.

BZs reduce feelings of fear and anxiety associated with stressful situations. Compared with the barbiturates they are relatively safe in overdose. They may help people recover from specific life events such as marriage break-up or bereavement, but even then a psychological grieving or mourning process has to be gone through.

Link

For more on neurotransmitters, see page 251 of Book 1.

Key terms

Benzodiazepines (BZ): anti-anxiety drugs which increase the availability of GABA in the brain. BZs The best-known examples of these drugs are Librium, Valium and Mogadon.

Neurotransmitters: chemicals which enable nerve impulses to pass across the synapse.

GABA: an inhibitory neurotransmitter, which suppresses the activity of other neurotransmitters in the brain.

Link

For more on psychological conditions, see Chapter 4 of Book 1.

Physical dependence: The physical need to engage in a behaviour. Failure to engage results in physical (i.e. bodily) effects.

Withdrawal: Symptoms that occur when someone stops taking a drug to which they have become physically dependent.

Link

You can remind yourself about the distinction between excitation and inhibition by looking at page 253 of Book 1.

Key term

Beta-blockers: drugs which reduce activity in the sympathetic branch of the autonomic nervous system.

Link

For more on the automatic nervous system see page 258 of Book 1.

The major problem with BZs is that they can lead to a state of **physical dependence**. This means that if the drug is stopped the person goes into a **withdrawal syndrome**. The symptoms of withdrawal include sleeping problems, sweating, tremors, and raised heart rate. Although not as severe as barbiturate dependency, the dependency problems with BZs have led to them being prescribed only for short periods. BZs have a range of side effects. They can produce feelings of tiredness and sedation, and impaired motor co-ordination. There is also evidence for memory impairment, especially during long-term treatment with BZs. Because they can lead to dependence and may also have a range of distressing side effects, fully informed consent should be obtained before they are prescribed. It is possible that some people with severe stress-related anxiety would not be fully competent to give informed consent.

BZs do not target the sources of stress or help the individual develop more effective coping strategies. Effective stress management should specifically target sources of stress in one's life and/or ones available coping resources. This reduces the gap between perceived demands and perceived resources. The use of BZs is most effective if combined with psychological methods that address the causes of stress.

Beta-blockers

This group includes drugs such as Propranolol and Alprenolol. These drugs act directly on the heart and circulatory system of the body. They reduce activation of the cardiovascular system by sympathetic fibres of the autonomic nervous system. In this way they directly reduce increases in heart rate and blood pressure associated with stressful situations, and are also used in the management of chronic hypertension (raised blood pressure). Beta-blockers are sometimes prescribed for musicians and snooker players whose smooth motor-control can be upset by high levels of arousal.

Beta-blockers target the physiological stress response, acting directly to reduce heart rate and blood pressure in stressed individuals. They act rapidly and have a life-saving function in people with life-threatening high blood pressure (hypertension.) Although they can interact with other drugs, especially those taken for asthma, beta-blockers do not have severe side effects, mainly because their main action is in the body and they do not penetrate the brain easily.

However, beta-blockers do not target the sources of stress but only the physical symptoms, therefore they are inappropriate for the long-term management of stress-related arousal. For maximum efficiency, beta-blockers should be combined with psychological methods of stress management in the hope of providing a long-term non-drug solution.

Psychological approaches: Stress Inoculation Training

As we discussed at the start of this chapter, stress occurs when the perceived demands of a situation exceed the perceived coping abilities. Stress therefore involves two appraisal processes: appraisals of the demands being made and appraisals of coping resources. High levels of stress may be experienced when individuals make faulty appraisals; for instance, overestimating the demands of a situation, such as the difficulty of an examination or underestimating their ability to cope – for example, their level of preparation.

These broad characteristics of stress provide ways of tackling harmful levels of stress by identifying and possibly changing cognitions. If stress is caused by faulty appraisal and evaluation, one approach to stress management might be to target those faulty cognitions. Approaches that target people's perception and evaluation of stressful situations come from a category of therapies known as Cognitive Behavioural Therapy (CBT). We covered CBT in detail in Chapter 4 of Book 1 in relation to explanations of psychological disorders. However, it is a general approach to understanding and changing behaviour that can be applied in many different areas, including stress management. One approach to stress management is Meichenbaum's **Stress Inoculation Training** (SIT). This consists of three stages:

> **Key term**
>
> **Stress Inoculation Training**: a cognitive approach which tackles stress through conceptualization skills training and application to the real world.

1. Conceptualization

In this stage the client works with the therapist to identify the sources of stress in their lives. This may involve thinking back to stressful encounters and trying to identify the key features. In addition, they would be encouraged to keep a diary to record stressful experiences during the day. The therapist may also challenge some of the client's appraisals of stressful situations if they seem exaggerated.

At the end of this stage the client and therapist should have a clear understanding of the major sources of stress. They can then move on to the second stage.

2. Skills Training and Rehearsal

It is possible to acquire specific skills to address some of the common stressors in people's lives. A common source of stress is social anxiety, that is, interacting with other people either at work or socially. People with social anxiety often have poor non-verbal communication, for example not making eye contact or appearing unapproachable. They can be shown to improve their social communication through skills training and practice.

Another source of stress is sitting examinations. The stress of examinations is often related to their perceived difficulty and/or importance. This leads to high levels of arousal and a failure to perform well. In this case, a client can be helped towards a realistic appraisal of the examination and also trained in revision techniques. Coping self-statements can also be used ('I have revised thoroughly – if I forget names and dates, it won't be a disaster')

A background issue in most stressful situations is physiological arousal. Regardless of the particular source of stress, training in relaxation is always useful. So whether it is entering a room full of people, or the examination hall, the individual will have a relaxation technique they can use to keep their bodily arousal under control.

3. Application in the Real World

After practising specific skills and relaxation techniques in the therapeutic setting the client is then encouraged to apply them in the real world. That is not the end of the story as the client and the therapist continue monitoring the success or failure of the therapy. A key to the approach is that the client should learn from experience, by reflecting on the success or failure of their new skills. If necessary, there would be opportunities for further training and rehearsal.

KEY STUDY: JAY AND ELLIOTT (1990)

Jay and Elliot assessed the effectiveness of Stress Inoculation Training using parents of children who were ill with leukemia. The children were required to undergo surgical procedures as part of their treatment and the researchers assessed how well SIT reduced the understandably high levels of anxiety felt by the parents before and during the surgery.

One hour before their child was due to go to the operating theatre, parents were shown a short 'SIT' film of a parent who demonstrated the use of coping self-statements, relaxation and coping imagery. The parents were encouraged to practice the skills they had seen and were compared with a second group of parents who received the usual support but did not view the SIT film.

After the procedure, both groups of parents were asked about their anxiety levels during and after the procedure. The parents who had received SIT showed significantly less anxiety and better coping skills.

THINKING SCIENTIFICALLY: EFFECTIVENESS OF SIT

Jay and Elliot's field experiment demonstrates the effectiveness of SIT in a real situation, where the stressful event (child undergoing surgery) is acute and time limited. Videotaped SIT modeling films have been shown to be effective in a variety of clinical settings. This kind of real world research has serious ethical considerations. The parents who took part are in an extremely stressful situation-hence obtaining fully informed consent would be very important. It is also imperative that the researchers emphasize the right to withdraw at any time-along with the right to refuse to take part in studies of this nature.

Evaluation of Stress-Inoculation Therapy

SIT is a cognitive-behavioural approach that focuses on the different elements involved in stress. The first stage in managing stress involves identifying the sources of stress in your life and assessing how well you have dealt with them in the past. SIT starts with this important step. Stress exists where there is a gap between perceived demands and the resources you have to cope with them. The cognitive element of SIT is aimed at producing a realistic appraisal of demands, while the training in relevant skills is aimed at increasing resources to cope with those demands. Training in specific relaxation techniques gives clients some control over any stressful situation. However, SIT, like most forms of cognitive behavioural therapy, takes time, commitment and money. It is not, therefore, suitable or available to everyone.

EXAMPLE EXAM QUESTION

Jamie is a young football player who is preparing for a trial for his city team. Jamie is worried about stress affecting his game during the trial. In the last few training sessions, Jamie has becomes extremely anxious and he is convinced that his shots at goal will go wide. His anxiety is so crippling that he has started to 'freeze' on the pitch. His promising career is under threat because of his nerves.

Explain how Stress Inoculation Training could be used to help Jamie manage his stress. (6 marks)

Exam hint

This is an application question so look very carefully for the cues in the scenario. Use these to structure your coverage of the three stages of SIT in your answer.

STRESS

Biofeedback

Biofeedback is a stress management technique that combines physiological and psychological methods. The individual is wired up to machines that provide feedback on physiological processes related to stress such as heart rate. This information is displayed on a monitor and a buzzer sounds if the heart rate goes above a specific level. The individual is then taught psychological techniques to reduce physiological arousal, such as breathing techniques, visualisation of calm scenes (a cognitive technique) and meditation. The buzzer/visual display indicates when the techniques are successful and the heart rate has lowered. In this way, the person is helped to develop their own psychological techniques to lower their own heart rate and blood pressure, using the biofeedback as a guide as to when they are successful.

Key term

Biofeedback: a technique that involves providing feedback about the bodily stress response and teaching techniques to reduce these responses.

After training the individual is then encouraged to apply the techniques in real life, and be confident that even without immediate biofeedback they are reducing their physiological arousal.

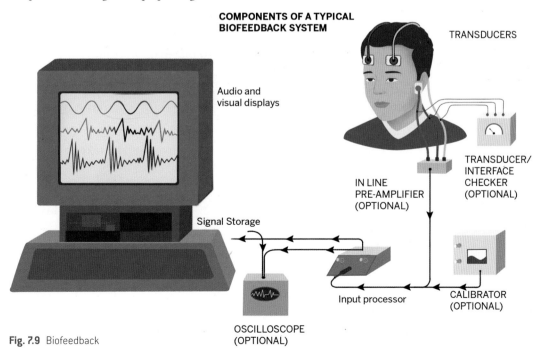

COMPONENTS OF A TYPICAL BIOFEEDBACK SYSTEM

TRANSDUCERS

Audio and visual displays

TRANSDUCER/ INTERFACE CHECKER (OPTIONAL)

IN LINE PRE-AMPLIFIER (OPTIONAL)

Signal Storage

Input processor

CALIBRATOR (OPTIONAL)

OSCILLOSCOPE (OPTIONAL)

Fig. 7.9 Biofeedback

KEY STUDY: NESTORIUC ET AL., 2008

In this study the researchers performed a **meta-analysis** on 53 studies of biofeedback for the treatment of tension headaches. Most studies used feedback from the frontalis muscle that covers the forehead ('electromyographic feedback'). Electrodes attached to the skin record the state of tension in this muscle, and the participant is encouraged to reduce this level of muscle tension. In some, but not all studies, biofeedback was combined with systematic relaxation training.

The results of the meta-analysis showed that biofeedback was highly effective at reducing the frequency and intensity of tension headaches in children, adolescents and adults. In addition, biofeedback was significantly more effective than relaxation alone. The most effective combination was biofeedback *combined* with relaxation.

THINKING SCIENTIFICALLY: STATISTICAL POWER

The large number of participants from combined studies provides statistical power - the ability to detect patterns, which may not be found with smaller samples. There has been a long debate about whether relaxation is as effective as biofeedback plus relaxation. Nestorius's meta-analyses suggest strongly that biofeedback is significantly more effective than relaxation alone in particular areas such as managing tension headaches.

Evaluation of biofeedback

The above meta- analysis provides clear evidence that biofeedback is effective for controlling heart rate and in the treatment of headaches caused by muscle tension. Attanaso et al. (1985) showed that biofeedback for tension headaches was especially effective in children, probably because of the exciting machinery involved. Biofeedback has clearly been shown to be effective in coping with stress, leading to long-term reductions in heart rate, blood pressure, and muscle tension. The process has no side effects but it does require motivation and commitment for the training programme, which will consist of several sessions, to be successful.

Biofeedback training involves recording apparatus and takes place in a laboratory or other quiet place. It is not easily accessible to most people. It also requires several sessions, so involving financial and time commitments. This again restricts the range of people who can use it. In particular they must be highly motivated. As the training takes place in a laboratory there may be issue over generalising to the real world. The person must be disciplined and able to apply the cognitive/relaxation techniques when faced with real life stressors.

Social support and coping with stress

On a common sense level, **social support** refers to the network of family, friends, and co-workers that you rely on in times of stress. Social support is difficult to define precisely as it is extremely varied. Support could be provided by your five a side football team or by a close relationship with a partner. One approach is to focus on the different types and functions of social support provided by social networks:

Types of social support

1. Instrumental support – involves support in the form of practical help, for instance the friend who lends you money or mends your car is providing instrumental support.
2. Emotional support – involves listening, expressing concern and providing reassurance. Emotional support can occur face-to-face or online.
3. Esteem support – the presence of people who care about you helps to boost self-esteem, raising morale and helping people feel they can cope with life's stressors.
4. Informational support – includes providing information about a particular stressor (e.g. a health problem) along with advice about how to deal with it.

Note: informational support is not named on the A level specification so you cannot be asked questions directly on it.

Research into the effects of social support

Many, many studies over the last 40 years have shown that social support is a critical factor in reactions to a range of stressful situations, ranging from physiological responses to immediate stressors, to coping with life threatening illnesses such as cancer and heart disease. We have space to refer to just a few of these to provide a flavour of this rich research area.

One effect of social support is reducing physiological responses to stressful situations. In a laboratory experiment, heart rate and blood pressure during a difficult and stressful arithmetic task were lower in women with a companion than those who did the task alone (Kamarck et al., 1998). Allen et al. (2002) found that the presence of a pet lowered heart rates during the performance of stressful tests. Social support is not just provided by people!

Social support also reduces vulnerability to stress related illnesses. Death from heart disease is lower in those with higher levels of social support, as measured by size of social network (Vogt et. al., 1992). Cohen et al. (1997) found that vulnerability to the common cold was greatest in participants with the smallest social networks.

Uchino, Cacioppro and Kiecolt-Glaser (1996) carried out a meta-analysis of studies of social support in the context of coping with stress.

STRESS

They concluded that the amount of social support showed a consistent relationship with reduced blood pressure (an index of reduced stress) in 28 different studies. There was a significant association between level of social support and immune functioning in 19 studies. For instance, carers for dementia patients showed reduced immune function, and this was particularly marked in those reporting the lowest levels of social support.

How does social support reduce stress?

(Jones and Bright, 2001) identify two approaches to explaining the effects of social support:

1. The buffering hypothesis suggests that social support has specific effects only in stressful situations. It 'buffers' or protects the individual against the negative effects of stress, by either reducing the demands or by increasing coping resources.
2. The direct effects hypothesis suggests that social support has positive effects on health in general which are independent of stress.

Urchino's study showed that social support is consistently effective in reducing blood pressure and heart rate, effects that would be beneficial to health in general. These effects would be even more striking under conditions of high stress suggesting that the answer is probably a combination of these two effects. Overall there is more support for the direct effects hypothesis than for the buffering hypothesis, as it seems unlikely that social support would only influence health in stressful situations.

Evaluation of research into social support

As we saw at the start of this section, there are a number of different types of social support and this leads to methodological problems for researchers. They have to decide what type they are looking at, and how to operationalise (measure) it. Different studies look at different types and measure them in different ways. This makes it difficult to compare findings from different studies. We can draw general conclusions about social support, but there is relatively little consistent research on the different *types* of social support.

Another challenge for researchers in this area is the issue of individual differences. particularly those related to gender and personality. There is some evidence (Jones and Bright, 2001; Halamandaris and Power, 1999) that women rely on and use social support more effectively than men, while people scoring high on neuroticism tend to report lower levels of social support. The final section of this chapter examines the issue of gender, coping and stress.

ACTIVITY 7.7

Design a laboratory experiment to assess the effects of a pet on heart rate during a stressful situation. You should use a repeated measures design. Identify the stressful task you would use and explain how you would control order effects. Your experiment should comply with ethical principles for conducting research.

Callum has lost his job and wants to take his employer to court for unfair dismissal. His friend Vic was in a similar position last year so Callum meets him for a chat. Vic tells Callum about the steps he took to prepare for the court appearance and also encourages Callum to talk about his worries.

Name one type of social support that Vic is providing to Callum. (2 marks)

Discuss research into the effects of social support on the reduction of stress. (10 marks)

Exam hint

There are ten marks available for the second part of this question hence you have little space to include detail. Summarise the findings of two or three studies then discuss some of the difficulties in studying the effects of social support.

Gender differences in coping with stress

As we have seen, everyday life involves a variety of stressors from hassles and major life events to stress at work. **Coping** refers to the range of strategies which people use to reduce the demands of stress outside of formal stress management. Folkman and Lazarus (1980) divided coping strategies into two basic types:

Key term

Problem focused coping involves tackling the stressor.

1. Problem focused coping – this approach involves tackling the stress with the aim of reducing or removing it entirely. For example, a problem with a difficult boss at work could be tackled by approaching them and asking them to alter their behaviour-or by changing jobs!
2. Emotion focused coping – this approach involves attempting to regulate our emotional response to the stressor, for example, keeping calm when the boss is difficult and meeting friends after work to 'offload'.

Emotion focused coping involves regulating the emotional response to the stressor

Research has implied that there may be gender differences in use of these coping strategies (Miller and Kirsch 1987) with men tending to prefer problem focused coping methods and women opting for emotion focused coping. However, findings are mixed. Tamres et al (2002) carried out a meta review of studies on gender and coping and found that women tended to use a greater variety of different strategies to cope with stress than men who by and large, used ventilation (off-loading) and avoidance. The use of coping strategies was investigated in a large-scale study carried out by Matud (2004).

KEY STUDY: MATUD (2004)

Matud examined the amount of stress experienced by a sample of 1566 women and 1250 men living in the Canary Islands, along with their preferred coping strategies for dealing with stress in their lives. Each participant completed a number of self-report questionnaires measuring life events, hassles and chronic on-going stressors. Matud found that women reported higher levels of chronic, on-going stressors and daily hassles than men although life event scores were similar.

Coping style was measured using Roger, Jarvis, and Najarian's Coping Style Questionnaire CSQ (1993) The CSQ asks respondents to report how frequently (always, often, rarely or never) they have used four coping strategies over a recent period :

- Rational coping (analysing the problem)
- Detached coping (shutting off)
- Avoidance coping (trying not to think about the problem)
- Emotional coping (becoming angry or tearful)

Men were significantly more likely to use rational and detached coping styles than women who reported the use of avoidance and emotional coping. However, whilst differences were significant, they were relatively small.

THINKING SCIENTIFICALLY: QUESTIONNAIRES

The data on stress and coping was collected using self report methods (questionnaires) It is possible that men and women might differ in their willingness to report stress in their lives and to report the coping methods they used. In addition, collection of data was retrospective (participants were asked to think back over the previous months and recall how they coped with stress).

Link
Link you can read more about self report questionnaires on page 366.

Where do gender differences originate?

Two explanations for gender differences in coping are socialisation and role constraint.

1. The traditional female role emphasised dependence and emotional expression (showing feelings) whereas the traditional male role emphasised action and assertion. Carver (1989) argues that men and women who were socialised to behave in strongly masculine or feminine ways would be more likely to adopt the respective ways of coping with stress- tackling it head on (men) versus showing feelings (women).
2. A second explanation relates to role constraints, suggesting that man have traditionally had greater power and resources (i.e. financial wealth) to tackle stress whereas women have had less access to these resources.

Matud's findings are more consistent with the first of these explanations. However, Matud also notes that the different methods of coping are amenable to different to different types of stressful situations. In the past men were more likely to experience work place stress and to deal with family finances-both of which are best tackled by problem solving approaches. In contrast, women operating tin the domestic arena would experiences tresses relating to family relationships, and caring responsibly, which may account for the choice of emotion focused strategies. Felston (1998) notes that gender differences in coping are decreasing and more recent studies using samples of university students suggest that gender differences in coping are no longer visible.

KEY POINTS

- Benzodiazepines and beta-blockers are two types of drugs used to manage the effects of stress.

- BZs increase the action of the neurotransmitter GABA.

- Beta-blockers reduce activity in the sympathetic nervous system.

- Drugs can be useful for short periods of stress but for maximum efficiency they should be combined with psychological methods.

- Stress Inoculation Training is a form of CBT, which involves analysing the source of stress, developing coping skills and applying these to the real world.

- SIT is effective for a range of different stressful situations.

- Biofeedback combines biological measurement of stress responses with psychological techniques to reduce arousal. It is particularly effective for tension headaches.

- Social support is difficult to define and measure. It can involve practical help (instrumental support), emotional support and boosts self esteem.

- SS reduces arousal in stressful situations and reduces vulnerability to a range of stress related illnesses.

- Gender differences in coping have been found in some research with men preferring problem-focused coping and women choosing emotion-focused coping. These differences appear to be reducing as gender socialisation moves toward greater equality.

Chapter 7: Stress   391

PRACTICAL ACTIVITY

In section four of this chapter, *Measuring stress,* you constructed a self-report questionnaire to measure health (see page 366). This practical activity requires you to collect data using your health questionnaire, to measure stress from life events, and to assess the relationship (if any) that exists between the life events and illness. You will find a shortened copy of Holmes and Rahe's SSRS on page 367 and you can locate full versions of the SRSS online if you would prefer. We suggest you work in a group of two or three students and each collect data from three or four people making between ten and twelve people in total. You can pool your data for analysis.

The first stage in the activity is to produce sufficient copies of your health questionnaire and SRRS. You will then need to identify a sample of fellow students (preferably non-psychologists!) who are willing to act as participants. You will need to draft a consent form providing information about the study to your potential participants so they can decide whether or not to take part.

You will also need to decide which order to administer the two questionnaires: life events before health or health before life events (there are pros and cons to both of these). When the questionnaires have been completed you should debrief your participants answering any questions they have. Calculate two scores for each participates – a life event score (SRRS) and a health score. You can plot these on a graph (scattergram), which will provide a visual display of any relationship between the co-variables. Finally, you can calculate the correlation between the two variables using an appropriate test of correlation.

Example exam questions

1. Briefly outline the general adaptation syndrome. **(2 marks)**

2. Evaluate self-report methods of measuring stress. **(6 marks)**

> Jamie has just started work as a junior chef in a busy restaurant. His job is to prepare vegetables and ingredients for the key dishes. Different chefs are in charge of the starters, main courses and puddings and all three make demands on Jamie at the same time to complete work for them. Jamie is finding the job extremely stressful.

a) Use your knowledge of workplace stress to explain why Jamie is finding his new job stressful. Refer to relevant research in your answer. **(4 marks)**

b) Discuss the effectiveness of SIT and biofeedback in the management of stress. **(12 marks)**

Exam focus

Read through the following example exam question, example student answer, and examiner comments. Then, have a go at answering the question yourself!

> **EXAMPLE EXAM QUESTION**
>
> Discuss research into stress and immunosuppression. (16 marks)

Maryam's answer

Examiner comment: A good start here with clear definitions of the key terms in the title!

The immune system is the body's method of protecting itself from incoming danger in the form of bacteria and viruses. The immune system is made up of natural immunity and specific immunity. Immunosuppression refers to a reduction in the efficiency of the immune system. Many studies have investigated the relationship between stress and reduced immunity.

Examiner comment: Clear identification of research method setting up the later evaluation.

Examiner comment: This isn't quite accurate: a correlational study has co-variables rather than IV and DV. The point is also not fully developed.

One method to assesses stress and immune suppression involves correlation. This basically involves measuring how much stress people are under, and how ill they become. Cohen investigated this relationship by measuring the amount of stress in a large group of participants then exposing them to the cold virus. Cohen found that people who scored higher on the stress index were more likely to develop a cold. Cohen's research used illness outcomes as the dependent variable: this measurement does not involve direct measurement of the immune system but infers that it has been suppressed. In addition, this is correlational research so we cannot conclude that stress caused the ill health–it may be that stressed pps in Cohen's study drank or smoked more to deal with the stress and this led to the development of a cold. This is known as the 'third variable problem'.

Examiner comment: Essay is losing focus on immunosuppression here.

Because of the ethical issues involved most experiments in this area make use of naturally occurring stressors such as exams or caring of an elderly relative. Kiecolt-Glaser studied a group of medical students measuring their natural killer cells in blood samples before and during exams. She found that NK cells reduced significantly during the exam period and immunosuppression was most noticeable in students who were lonely. This relates to social support–as more social support is associated with lower levels of stress related illnesses. Social support also reduces heart rate during stressful tasks A second study by Kiecolt-Glaser found reductions in immune functioning in women caring for relatives. This is a long term chronic stressor whereas exams are a short term acute stressor.

Kiecolt-Glaser used a direct measurement of immune functioning in comparison to Cohen. However, as this is a natural experiment (for ethical reasons as stated earlier) there is a lack of control over the variables. Once again students are likely to sleep less and perhaps drink more coffee during revision and these could also affect the immune system.

A meta analysis is a good way of bringing together many different research studies. One meta-analysis found that short-term stress increased the efficiency of the immune system (i.e. boosted it) but long-term chronic stress led to immune suppression. As with cardio vascular disorders, it would appear that our bodies have evolved to cope with some stressors better than others!

Examiner comment: A well written and well informed essay. Research examples are well selected and the comparison of different methods is a good source of A03 marks.
Top band - one or two minor inaccuracies and a slight loss of focus make this around 13/16 marks.

Chapter 8: Aggression

Introduction

Aggression is a very complex behaviour, and psychologists commonly divide it into two basic subtypes. *Hostile aggression* stems from a feeling of anger, done with the intention to cause pain or injury. *Instrumental aggression* is an intention to harm but done as a means to attain a particular goal. The study of aggression is a good example of how psychologists and others are trying to understand and find solutions to social problems, and aggression is at the heart of one of the most pressing problems facing humanity. It is estimated that well in excess of 250 million people died as a result of war and conflict in the twentieth century alone. The global population is currently estimated at over 7 billion, with it set to hit 11 billion by 2050. With growing density, coupled with increasing inequalities and dwindling natural resources, there is every possibility of a continued trend to further destruction as individuals and nations aggress.

The study of aggression is a good example of how human behaviour can be explained in more than one way. Some researchers take a social psychological approach, and consider aggression to be the result of various situational and dispositional influences. Others prefer a more biological approach, looking for the origins of aggressive behaviour in brain structures and chemicals, or clues in the behaviour of our animal cousins and distant ancestors. In this chapter we will consider some of the main social psychological and biological explanations for aggression. We will also look at aggressive behaviour in an institutional context, namely prisons. Aggression in prisons is a major problem: figures released by the UK government in 2014 showed a 30 per cent increase in grievous assaults and 69 per cent increase in suicides within British prisons, with record prison populations. We will also look at an issue that has drawn heated debate for many years – the influence of media on aggressive behaviour.

What is covered in Aggression?

Neural and hormonal mechanisms in aggression

There is no doubt that neural and hormonal mechanisms are important in human aggression. What is less clear is the role played by the various biological mechanisms implicated in aggressive behaviour. What is certain, however, is that the relationship between biology and behaviour is an extremely complex one, and like other behaviours human aggression is the outcome of a variety of causes.

The limbic system

Key term

Limbic system: the name given to a number of connected brain areas located deep inside the brain.

The **limbic system** (Fig. 8.1) is made up of a number of connected components, situated deep inside the brain. These include the amygdala, cingulate gyrus, diencephalon (the thalamus and hypothalamus), and hippocampus. The limbic system connects the brain stem (responsible for basic vital life functions, like heartbeat, breathing, blood pressure and reflexes) to the cortex (associated with higher brain functions such as thought and deliberate action). In addition to controlling essential behaviours like eating and drinking, the limbic system plays an important role in controlling a range of emotional behaviours, such as fear and mood.

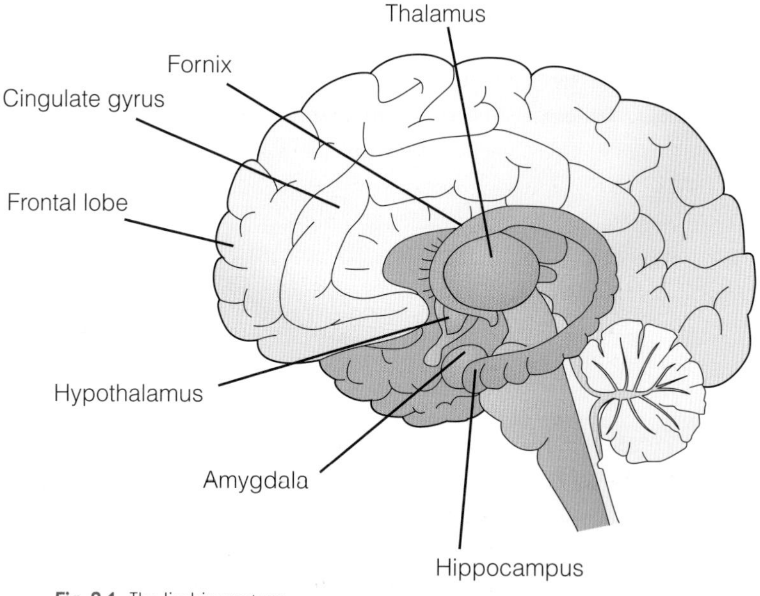

Fig. 8.1 The limbic system

The limbic system has long been associated with aggressive behaviour. For instance, it appears that the hypothalamus serves a regulatory role in aggression. In 1937, Bard and Mountcastle separated the cortex (the outer layer of the brain, which controls higher-level functions) from the limbic system in cats and found that, after further destruction of the hypothalamus, the cats were predisposed to ferocious behaviour. It has also been found that destruction of a particular part of the hypothalamus (called the ventromedial nuclei) causes cats, within a couple of weeks of surgery, to develop permanent 'savage behaviours'.

The amygdala appears to be important for the perception of emotions and the control of aggressive responses through modulating (altering the activity of) other brain areas, such as the hypothalamus. Stimulation of the amygdala can cause an animal to respond to things in the environment in fearful and aggressive ways. Egger and Flynn (1963) found that stimulation of the amygdala can increase or decrease aggression, depending on which region of it was stimulated. Destruction of the amygdala results in tameness in animals and calmness in humans (characterized by a reduction in emotional responsiveness). For example, an amygdalectomy (surgical removal of the amygdala) reduces violent behaviour. Further evidence comes from instances of temporal lobe epilepsy where the seizures originate in the amygdala. Seizure characteristics in these individuals typically involve aggressive behaviour.

Serotonin

Neurotransmitters influence all behaviours, including aggression. Serotonin in particular has been consistently implicated in aggressive behaviour. Serotonin has an inhibitory effect so that in normal quantities it has a calming effect and maintains a stable mood. It is thought that it achieves this effect by working in the frontal cortex to inhibit activity in the amygdala (a brain area important in the control of aggressive behaviour). Unsurprisingly perhaps, reductions in serotonin can result in more impulsive and possibly aggressive behaviour. Lindberg et al. (1985) compared the serotonin levels of 16 males convicted for violent crimes (specifically, murder), 22 males who had attempted suicide, and 39 healthy males. They measured concentrations of 5-HIAA (a substance produced by the breakdown of serotonin in the brain) in their cerebrospinal fluid (CSF). Low levels of 5-HIAA would indicate low levels of serotonin. They found the lowest levels in those who had killed a partner or who had attempted suicide. According to Davison et al. (2000), individuals prone to violence and aggression have serotonergic projections (neural pathways that use serotonin) into the prefrontal cortex that are faulty. This prevents them regulating their emotions, resulting in negative emotions and impulsive behaviour.

> **Key term**
>
> **Neurotransmitter:** a brain chemical (such as serotonin) that communicates information between neurons (cells in the brain).

AGGRESSION

KEY STUDY: PASSAMONTI ET AL. (2012)

Passamonti et al. (2012) altered the serotonin levels in healthy participants by manipulating their diet to contain, on consecutive days, either no or normal levels of tryptophan. This substance is essential for manufacturing serotonin, so with no tryptophan in the diet serotonin levels would be low. The participants were also given a questionnaire to assess their tendencies towards behaving aggressively. The researchers used fMRI scans to measure how brain regions reacted when participants were shown pictures of faces with angry, sad, and neutral expressions.

The researchers found that on low serotonin (no tryptophan) days communication between the prefrontal cortex and the limbic system was weaker compared to normal serotonin days. This communication appeared particularly weak in those assessed by the questionnaire to have an existing tendency to behave aggressively.

This research suggests that when serotonin levels are low, it is more difficult for the prefrontal cortex to control emotions generated by limbic structures. Individuals predisposed to aggression are particularly sensitive to reductions in serotonin, and are therefore more susceptible to allowing aggressive impulses to become aggressive behaviours.

THINKING SCIENTIFICALLY: A RANDOMIZED DOUBLE-BLIND PLACEBO CONTROLLED EXPERIMENT

This study is an example of a randomized double-blind placebo controlled experiment. This means that participants were randomly assigned to either the experimental or placebo condition. Because it was double-blind, neither participants nor researchers knew which participants were actually taking the drink that depleted tryptophan and which were taking the inactive (placebo) drink. Such procedures significantly reduce the influence of demand characteristics and experimenter effects. Because of this, scientists consider well-designed and conducted randomized double-blind placebo studies the 'gold standard' in experimental research.

The role of serotonin in aggressive behaviour is far from clear, however. While research has consistently linked low levels of serotonin with aggression, high levels of serotonin have also been associated with aggression (see discussion of the MAOA gene later in this topic). It is highly unlikely that any behaviour is the result of a single neurotransmitter. It appears that the influence of serotonin is through complex interactions with other neurotransmitters, hormones and neural circuits, with particular interactions giving rise to different types of aggressive behaviour in differing circumstances. In this way, both low and high levels of serotonin might give rise to aggressive behaviour, but do so through different routes.

Exam hint

Take care to select neural mechanisms here – the specification identifies these as the limbic system and serotonin (testosterone is a hormonal, *not* neural, mechanism). Keep the answer straightforward – describe each mechanism and some research into it.

Key term

Testosterone: the most important male hormone, produced mostly by the testes (with a small amount produced by the adrenal glands). Females also have testosterone, but normally at a much lower level in the body than males.

EXAMPLE EXAM QUESTION

Outline and evaluate neural mechanisms in aggression. (12 marks)

Testosterone

Testosterone is an androgen (a male sex hormone), secreted by the testes in males and, to a lesser degree, the ovaries in females (males have about eight times more testosterone than females). It is essential for physical health and well-being, and is necessary for reproductive growth and the development of male secondary sex characteristics, such as beard growth and a deepening voice.

Experiments with animals have consistently demonstrated a link between testosterone and aggression. For example, Wagner et al. (1979) observed reduced levels of aggression in male mice following castration. Furthermore, they were able to return aggression to pre-castration levels with injections of testosterone.

The relationship between testosterone and aggression in humans is much less clear, however. Kouri et al. (1995) investigated the possibility that testosterone causes aggression. They gave participants increasing doses of testosterone over a three-week period. Before and after the testosterone injections participants were given a press-button task by which they could either accumulate points exchangeable for money or subtract points from what they thought was an opponent (this was a ruse – there was no opponent). Another group of participants had exactly the same experience except that their injections were placebos (unknown to participants, the injections contained a harmless, inert substance). Aggression was measured by how participants responded to having points deducted by the fictitious opponent. It was found that the testosterone-receiving participants were much more likely to respond themselves by deducting points, which Kouri et al. interpreted as an act of aggression.

Some researchers have argued that increased levels of testosterone associated with aggression are in fact the *result* of the aggressive behaviour, rather than the cause of it. Support for this idea comes from Klinesmith et al. (2006). They took saliva samples from participants to test testosterone levels before and after completing a task. Participants were either given a gun to interact with or a child's toy to assemble. Following this, they were asked to add as much hot pepper sauce as they wished to a cup of water they believed another participant would have to drink – this was the measure of aggression. Those participants who had interacted with a gun not only added more pepper sauce, but they were also found to have increased levels of testosterone following the task.

The research into the relationship between testosterone and aggression gives inconsistent results. While some studies have found a correlation between levels of testosterone and aggression, other studies have failed to find this. Harrison et al. (2000), for example, found a consistent relationship between testosterone and aggression. Only some of their participants given testosterone showed an increase in aggressive tendencies in response to a frustrating computer game. Some research has even found increased testosterone levels associated with *less* aggression. Some of this inconsistency is possibly due to differences in how aggression has been operationalized. There are different types and degrees of aggression and testosterone levels, and it is possible that testosterone levels are related to only some of them. It has also been suggested that the relationship between testosterone and aggression is an indirect one, mediated by complex interactions between neurotransmitters, neural circuitry, and social contexts.

Exam hint

You are only being asked to evaluate here, so you do not need to explain what testosterone is or what it does in the body. The most straightforward way to answer this is to present the findings of two or three research studies. Remember, only six marks here, so do not go over the top – the number of findings you use will depend on the amount of detail you are able to provide for each.

EXAMPLE EXAM QUESTION

Evaluate the role of testosterone in aggression. (6 marks)

Genetic factors in aggression

A role for genetics in animal aggression has been conclusively demonstrated by the effects of selective breeding. This is the process of choosing animals with the desired characteristics – in this case, aggression – and allowing them to breed only with each other. The offspring showing the strongest sign of the desired characteristic are again the ones selected to breed with others showing these same characteristics. This process is repeated over generations to produce an animal with the desired dominant characteristic – aggression.

The effects of selective breeding for aggression can be seen in the altered physical structure and behaviours of animals bred over generations for this purpose, such as fighting cocks, pitbull dogs and Spanish fighting bulls. It has also been demonstrated experimentally. For example, Hood and Cairns (1989) were able to breed mice with significantly higher levels of aggression in just four generations. They also demonstrated how the environment can alter the expression of aggressive genes. For instance, while consistently more aggressive than other mice, highly aggressive mice tended to show reduced aggression when reared with siblings than when reared in isolation. Clearly, while genes appear to increase the propensity for aggression in animals, aggression itself is mediated by environmental factors. Although selective breeding studies have revealed some of the mechanisms of inherited aggression, the extent to which we can generalize the findings to humans is debatable.

Twin studies

Ethics and practicalities obviously prohibit selective breeding studies using humans, so researchers have had to approach the investigation of genes and human behaviour in other ways. Studies of aggressive behaviour in twins is a potentially rich source of information. Identical or monozygotic (MZ) twins share 100 per cent of their genes. If aggression has a significant genetic component, then aggression in one twin should be positively correlated with aggression in the other. Non-identical or dizygotic (DZ) twins, however, share only 50 per cent of their genes so, if aggression is genetic, it is far less likely that aggression in one twin is positively correlated with aggression in the other. Researchers assume that the upbringing of MZ and DZ twin pairs are very similar, so the influence of potential environmental influences are naturally controlled. Coccaro et al. (1997) used a questionnaire designed to measure hostility in order to assess aggressive tendencies in 182 MZ and 118 DZ twin pairs. Their analysis suggested a genetic contribution to specific types of aggression: 47 per cent contribution to direct assault, 40 per cent to indirect assault, 37 per cent to irritability, and 28 per cent to verbal assault. As the genetic contribution was never 100 per cent, environmental influence clearly accounted for much of the twin aggressive tendencies.

Fig. 8.2 Selectively bred chicken, made to be a fighting cock

However, twin studies are not without their shortcomings. For example, many psychologists disagree with the assumption of shared environments in such research, and point out that because MZ twins nearly always have a much closer relationship than DZ twins, they are more likely to influence each other's behaviour. Therefore, separating out the relative contributions of genes and environment is extremely problematic. Technological advancements and increasing understanding of genes have meant that some researchers have turned to a search for specific genes associated with aggression.

ACTIVITY 8.1

Research by McGuffin and Gottesman (1985) indicated that if one MZ twin is aggressive then there is an 87 per cent likelihood of the other twin also being aggressive, compared to 72 per cent in DZ twins.

What does this difference between MZ and DZ twins tell us about the contributions of genetic and environmental factors in aggressive behaviour?

What problems do researchers face when investigating genetic contributions to aggressive behaviour?

The MAOA gene

The individual differences seen in levels of aggression are the result of complex interactions between genes and environment. Research has identified a number of genes possibly associated with aggressive behaviour, and the monoamine oxidase A (MAOA) gene has attracted the most attention. This gene controls levels of an enzyme (also called monoamine oxidase A). This enzyme breaks down the neurotransmitters serotonin, dopamine and noradrenaline after they have been used for communication across a synapse. The MAOA gene was first suggested as a candidate following research by Brunner et al. (1993). They investigated the case of a Dutch family whose male members had been particularly aggressive over many generations. Subsequent research found that males in the family had a faulty MAOA gene, resulting in higher than normal levels of serotonin.

A role for MAOA in aggression was finally established through studies with mice. Cases et al. (1995) found that they could create highly aggressive mice by disabling the MAOA gene in the X chromosome. Only male mice were affected by this procedure however; female mice have two X chromosomes so could compensate for the lack of an MAOA gene in one with the MAOA gene in the other. This explains why only males in the Brunner et al.'s study had a history of violence. Cases et al. were able to return male mice to a normal state of behaviour by restoring the function of the MAOA gene in their X chromosome.

And yet, the role of the MAOA gene in aggression remains vague. It is highly unlikely that a complex behaviour like aggression is the result of a single gene. It is more likely that an MAOA defect has an influence on aggressive behaviour in some individuals in specific circumstances. Individuals with defective MAOA genes do not all behave aggressively, or respond in the same way to factors that might

AGGRESSION

be triggers for aggressive behaviour. Research seems to suggest that a combination of a faulty MAOA gene *plus* significant environmental stress brings about increased aggression, not a faulty MAOA gene alone (Caspi et al., 2002).

KEY POINTS

- A range of neural and hormonal mechanisms have been found to be important in human aggression.
- The limbic system controls emotional behaviours such as fear and mood, and parts of this system seem to control aggressive responses.
- Low levels of serotonin have been related to aggressive behaviour, but the exact role of this neurotransmitter remains unclear.
- Testosterone is associated with increased levels of aggression in animals, though the evidence for its role in human aggression is far less clear.
- Selective breeding in animals has shown conclusively that genes are important in aggression, but the exact role of genes in aggressive behaviour remains to be discovered.
- One candidate gene is MAOA, which regulates monoamine oxidase A. Defective MAOA genes results in excess serotonin and other neurotransmitters and appears to be associated with aggressive behaviour.

The ethological explanation of aggression

Key term

Ethology: the study of animals in their natural environment within the context of evolution theory.

Ethology is the study of animals in their natural environment within the context of evolutionary theory. Ethologists argue that only by studying animals as they naturally behave can natural behaviour be observed. There is no distinction between humans and animals, except to acknowledge that humans are complex animals. One consequence of this is the ethological assumption that humans and animals share many similar drives, so that what is found to be the case for animals could also the case for humans.

Innate releasing mechanisms and fixed action patterns

According to leading ethologist Konrad Lorenz, aggression is an instinct that has evolved to serve a number of important functions (Lorenz, 1966). For example, it ensures that only the strongest and fittest males pass on their genes to the next generation. Aggression also serves the useful purpose of more widely distributing a species. This ensures that territorial resources are exhausted less quickly and that disease has less impact. Finally, aggression also helps to maintain important hierarchies in socially organized animals.

Lorenz noted that social animals (i.e. those who live in groups) tend to inflict relatively little harm on members of their own species. This is because they show *ritualized aggression*, where aggression is used to assert power and maintain status. It is a series of escalating threat displays that may or may not end in physical contact (from which injuries are rare). The escalation ceases when one of the aggressing animals displays an appeasement gesture – a behaviour that signals defeat and submission, thus stopping the aggression of the other animals (Fig. 8.3).

Fig. 8.3 Dogs use appeasement as a tactic to suppress the aggressive behaviour of other dogs

For Lorenz, aggression only happens when there are cues in the environment to trigger it. Energy for an instinctive act (called action-specific energy) builds up within an animal. The greater the build-up of this energy, the greater the pressure to release it as a behaviour, and the lower the stimulation from something in the environment needed to trigger it. When apparent random aggression occurs it is because the build-up of energy is so great that it has to be released – very little is needed to trigger the aggressive behaviour thus it can sometimes appear unprovoked. The action-specific energy is prevented from being released by an *innate releasing mechanism* (IRM). The IRM is hard-wired, an inherited neural network that is part of an animal's biology. In response to an environmental stimulus (called the 'releaser' if it is another animal, or a 'sign stimulus' if it is some other sensory stimulus), the IRM allows the release of the action-specific energy as a *fixed action pattern* (FAP). This is an instinctive behavioural sequence that always runs to completion – that is, once begun it will not stop until finished.

ACTIVITY 8.2

During breeding season the bill of adult herring gulls turn a bright yellow with a red spot at the tip. When a herring gull chick sees this colourful bill it pecks at it. In response to the pecking the adult regurgitates food for the chick.
What is the sign stimulus and what is the fixed action pattern in this gull behaviour?
Can you think of a human behaviour that is a fixed action pattern? What does your conclusion mean for how these ethological ideas can be applied to human behaviour?

Later ethologists disagreed with Lorenz. For example, it has been pointed out that FAPs are most common in animals with relatively simple cognitive abilities and that are high in instinctive behaviour. Human adults are devoid of such stereotypical behaviours, which in humans can only be seen as vestigial instincts in infants. For example, the grasping reflex, where the hand grips in response to touch, is said to have evolved in our ancestors to enable infants to hold on to mother as it is carried around. It is also clear that human aggression does not appear to be ritualistic. Indeed, Niko Tinbergen, another eminent ethologist, suggested that humans are the only species *without* ritualized aggression. While animal aggression towards a conspecific (a member of their own species) rarely results in harm, in humans the goal of aggression appears to be a deep-rooted desire to harm another.

Just because behaviours look similar does not mean that underlying functions and motivations are also similar, and so most psychologists reject the notion that rules of behaviour that apply to animals unequivocally also apply to humans. That is not to say that evolutionary influences are absent from human behaviour – humans and animals experience similar evolutionary pressures, but have responded to these in different ways. Humans are unique in the complexity of their emotions, intelligence and social relationships, and so human evolution has uniquely shaped the way that aggression is displayed.

Exam hint

Sometimes, the difficulty of a question comes from the demand to be selective and concise. Here is a good example – this question could be asked for more marks but the task here is to select the core ideas that briefly summarize the ethological explanation.

EXAMPLE EXAM QUESTION

Briefly outline the ethological explanation of aggression. (4 marks)

Evolutionary explanations of human aggression

Evolutionary psychologists argue that aggression has its origins in our evolutionary past, having once served useful survival advantages. Kenrick et al. (1996) proposed that male aggressive behaviour evolved because it once led to greater reproductive success. It derived from male competition for access to females, with dominant males, able to employ aggressive tactics to maintain their dominance, more able to pass on their genes to the next generation. Aggressive tendencies would also have been useful when competing for limited resources, and also in aiding hunting activities.

Females would also have been choosy when selecting a mate. They invest much more in their offspring than do males, such as months of pregnancy, health risks of childbirth, and years of subsequent childcare. It would have been advantageous therefore for females to select males who appeared most able to provide for them and their offspring, i.e. males who were more dominant and aggressive. This selection process resulted in these males having more opportunities and passing on the characteristics that made them successful (for example, dominance and aggression) to the next generation.

One source of aggression with roots in our evolutionary past is male sexual jealousy. This is where the exclusive access of a male to a sexual partner is threatened, either in an imaginary or real sense. For males, infidelity has to be prevented at all costs. While females can always be 100 per cent certain that a child they are carrying is theirs, a male can never be so sure. Thus, they risk investing effort and resource into raising offspring that do not carry their genes. Jealousy involves a number of mate-retention strategies aimed at holding onto a mate once found and avoiding cuckoldry (a cuckold is a male with an unfaithful partner). These include vigilance, where females are closely watched by their male partners, and guarding, where males restrict the access of other males to claimed females.

This is supported by Buss and Shackelford (1997). They investigated mate retention strategies in 19 married couples. Matching the predictions of evolutionary psychology, they found that men were more likely than women to use resource display (for example, status) as a tactic, while women were more likely than men to use appearance enhancement (for example, youth and perceived physical attractiveness). In terms of aggression, the use of physical threat was much more likely to be used by men than women.

ACTIVITY 8.3

For some psychologists, male violence against females has its roots in our evolutionary past.

How might this view of human aggression be useful in preventing male violence against women?

How might other approaches in psychology explain male violence against women?

EXAMPLE EXAM QUESTION

Statistics from the United States indicate that nearly two-thirds of murders involve a male offender and male victim, less than a quarter involve a male offender and female victim, and less than a tenth involve a female offender and female victim. Use your knowledge of evolutionary explanations of aggression to explain these statistics. [4 marks]

Exam hint

There are a number of ways of answering this question, so make a choice; do not try to do everything for only four marks. For example, you could focus on why males kill males (such as sexual rivalry and guarding), why males kill females (such as sexual jealousy), or even why females are much less likely to murder than males.

Daly and Wilson (1988) point out that while acts of aggression by men against their spouses varies considerably across cultures, there is much less variation in the motives for such violence. They analysed crime data of murder and assaults to see if there was a pattern to the violence of men against women. They found that:

- rates of wife murder were much higher in estranged couples than cohabiting couples

- murder and assault by husbands was greatest on the youngest wives and decreased with age

- murder and assault by husbands was much higher in non-marital than marital relationships

- the highest rate of violence was when a woman was cohabiting but had a child by another man.

Daly and Wilson argued that these findings reflect attempts at coercive control by males, and differed in degree according to male perceptions of cues that indicate a wife's likelihood of infidelity.

Evolutionary explanations of human aggression have been criticized for being impossible to test empirically, and therefore being unscientific. Explanations are based on understanding behaviour that came from many thousands of years ago, an understanding that is ultimately based on conjecture rather than sound evidence. Furthermore, aggression is a complex behaviour. It has many forms and triggers, and individuals vary considerably not only in their levels of aggression but also how they respond to it – some may respond to aggression with aggression, while others may be passive or attempt to avoid confrontation. Evolutionary explanations appear far too simplistic for such complex behaviour.

KEY POINTS

- The ethological explanation argues that aggression is an instinctive behaviour, and that it occurs in humans for much the same reason that it occurs in other animals.

- Innate releasing mechanisms release action-specific energy, which results in the fixed action pattern.

- The fixed action pattern can be an aggressive behaviour. However, such stereotyped patterns of behaviour are not seen in humans.

- Evolutionary explanations of human aggression claim that we see aggressive behaviour now because it was a useful behaviour for our evolutionary ancestors.

- Aggression would have been useful for gaining resources and access to females, and may have been selected by females as a desirable characteristic in a potential mate.

- The vestiges of this evolved behaviour can be seen in mate-retention tactics and responses to acts of sexual jealousy.

Social psychological explanations of human aggression

Aggression is essentially a form of social behaviour, and has therefore drawn the interest of social psychologists. Social psychological explanations of aggression focus on how aggressive behaviour results from our interactions with the social world. A range of theoretical perspectives and social determinants have been suggested to explain aggression.

Social learning theory

According to social learning theory, aggression is learned through the observation and imitation of aggressive behaviour. Bandura (1963) called this process modelling. This is not a case of blindly copying behaviour seen in a model, however. A behaviour is more likely to be copied if the observer considers the model similar to them (for example, in age, sex or attitude), or if the model is in a position of power (for example, an admired celebrity or authority figure). The extent to which the observer feels able to imitate the modelled behaviour (called self efficacy) is also important. This may be a matter of confidence or capability. Learning can also take place through observing the consequences of a model's behaviour: imitation is more likely if a model is rewarded (reinforced) for their behaviour than if it is punished. This is called vicarious reinforcement. While this modelling can be seen in humans of any age, children are particularly vulnerable to the influence of a potential role model.

Bandura also described a number of processes that were essential if imitation of an observed behaviour was to occur (Fig. 8.4).

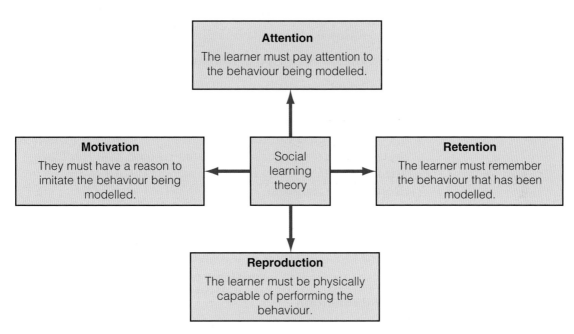

Fig. 8.4 Social learning theory

Early support for social learning theory came from a series of experiments conducted between 1961 and 1963 by Bandura and colleagues that became known as the bobo doll studies. They were able to demonstrate the effects of observing a violent role model on the behaviour of children (see *Key study*).

KEY STUDY: BANDURA, ROSS AND ROSS (1963)

Bandura, Ross and Ross studied a sample of 96 children (48 boys and 48 girls) aged between 35 and 59 months old. They were place in one of four conditions. There were three experimental groups and one control group, with 24 participants in each. The experimental groups were further divided into two conditions, so that half were exposed to same-sex models and half to models of the opposite sex.

Experimental condition 1: Real-life aggression

Each child was brought into a room by the female experimenter to play, and an adult model (either male or female) who was waiting nearby was also invited to take part. While the child played at a table with crayons and paper, the model went to another part of the room where there was a bobo doll and proceeded to kick and punch it, adding verbally aggressive comments. The attack lasted around ten minutes.

Following this, the child was taken to another room containing very attractive toys to play with. Once they had started to play they were frustrated: they were stopped from playing and told that the toys were for other children and were shown to another room containing rather dull toys and a bobo doll. The children were observed for 20 minutes through a one-way mirror in this room, and assessed for imitative aggression.

Experimental condition 2: Human-film aggression

The procedure was similar to condition 1 but this time, instead of a real-life model joining them, the children were told that as they played a movie would be shown on a screen. The colour film was of the same male or female adult from the real-life condition engaged in the same behaviour towards the bobo doll. This film lasted ten minutes, and at the conclusion the children were escorted to the test room, as in condition 1.

Experimental condition 3: Cartoon-film aggression

This was similar to condition 2 but this time the procedure involved playing a film of a cartoon character, 'Herman the Cat', behaving in a similarly aggressive way towards the bobo doll.

Control condition

Everything was exactly the same except that the children were not exposed to an aggressive model.

Bandura, Ross and Ross found that all the children in experimental conditions 1, 2 and 3 showed higher levels of aggression towards the bobo doll in the test room than children in the control condition. Boys showed more aggression than girls in all experimental conditions.

Research methods link

For more on face validity, see page 43.

Social learning theory has face validity (that is, it looks as though it is right). It is widely observed that young children readily imitate what they see in others and the media – most people can easily recall examples from their own or others' childhoods where the behaviour of television characters and pop stars were imitated. There is some debate, however, about how influential observed behaviour really is in the long term, as experimental studies only show the short-term effects of observing aggressive models.

Support for social learning theory also comes from observations of cultures that apparently have little or no aggression. The !Kung San people of the Kalahari Desert, for instance, raise their children in ways that discourage overt aggressive behaviour, for example by avoiding physical punishment and dissipating tensions between children. The society disapproves of aggression between its members and so adults do not provide aggressive models for the children.

There is a convincing body of evidence to show that factors unrelated to social learning are important in aggressive behaviour. Research has identified a number of candidate genes for aggression that appear to contribute to increased aggression seen in some individuals. Hormones such as testosterone also appear to influence aggressive behaviour. Aggression is a complex behaviour with many possible causes, which can therefore be understood from a variety of perspectives.

Deindividuation

Aggressive behaviour is almost universally socially unacceptable. In western cultures, legal sanctions are in place as a deterrent, and a negative social stigma comes with such behaviour. In some circumstances, however, changes to accepted norms of behaviour can occur. One example of this is behaviour when part of a larger group. It was first noted by Le Bon (1895) that a 'collective mind' emerges in a crowd. This is primitive in nature, and causes uninhibited behaviour in individuals, including antisocial acts like aggression. This loss of individual identity while in a crowd was later referred to as **deindividuation** (Festinger et al., 1952). For Festinger et al., the more extreme actions of individuals while in a large group are caused by a sense of anonymity and a feeling of a lack of personal responsibility. Individuals in a group no longer see themselves as individuals so do not feel that they are being singled out as such by others. This loosens restraints against behaviours that would otherwise be inhibited.

Diener (1980) argues that this lack of self-awareness caused by group membership is key to understanding deindividuation effects. We are normally self-aware and we use this self-awareness to regulate our own behaviour. In a crowd, however, the group becomes the focus of attention, through such behaviours as chanting and clapping, and the subsequent decrease in self-awareness leads to deindividuation.

More recently, Reicher (1987) proposed the social identity model of deindividuation effects (SIDE), which broadens the context of deindividuation effects to include settings such as the Internet, where people frequently identify themselves with avatars and pseudonyms. This theory sees self-identity not as a single entity but something more complex, shaped by aspects of personal identity (personal attributes that uniquely identify a person) and social identity (knowledge and understanding of a particular group and emotional significance associated with membership). When a person becomes part of a group, sense of self is not lost, as Diener suggests, but is shifted from personal to social identity. Thus, behaviour is now guided (as opposed to dictated – not all control of behaviour is lost) by what

> **Key term**
>
> **Deindividuation**: the loss of individual identity when in a group so that individuals fail to see the consequences of their actions.

AGGRESSION

membership of that group entails. The more a person is immersed in a group, the greater the shift to social identity. In these circumstances, the effects of anonymity, for example reduced feelings of individual difference, serve to increase the prominence of social identity still further. Deindividuation then is the result of a combination of group immersion and a reduced personal identity (thus reduced self-awareness and regulation). It is the shift to a social identity that produces a deindividuated state.

Exam hint

Sometimes the most obvious answer is the best one – anonymity is at the core of deindividuation, so use this as the basis for a brief rationale for the behaviour of painted warriors.

EXAMPLE EXAM QUESTION

Research has shown that, during conflict, warriors who wear face and body paint are more aggressive than those who do not.

Use your knowledge of deindividuation theory to explain this. (4 marks)

There is some evidence to support the role of reduced personal identity and situational cues in deindividuation. The Stanford Prison experiment (Zimbardo et al., 1971) showed that deindividuation effects are particularly marked in environments where self-identity is reduced. In a mock prison study, some participants were dressed for the role of guards and some dressed as prisoners. Despite it being a simulation, the behaviour of both guards and prisoners soon became extreme. Participants had become anonymous members of their groups, their individuality had become lost to the powerful roles they found themselves in, and thus they became deindividuated.

There is considerable disagreement among psychologists about what the key contributor to deindividuation is. Zimbardo (1970) argued that it is *anonymity*. He demonstrated this in a Milgram-like study that required female participants to deliver electric shocks to another participant. Some participants wore lab coats and hoods, were not referred to by name and were kept apart from other participants during the study, so that they were anonymous. Other participants wore normal clothes, a name tag, were referred to by name and were able to see each other during the study. Even though all the participants could see the victim receive their electric shocks, those participants who were made to feel anonymous delivered shocks for twice as long as participants without anonymity. Some studies outside of the laboratory have supported the role of anonymity in aggressive behaviour. Silke (2003) analysed 500 violent attacks occurring in Northern Ireland between 1994 and 1996. He found that 206 attacks were carried out by people who wore disguises, thus hiding their identities.

However, Diener (1977) points out that anonymity does not always lead to a deindividuated state. Indeed, his review of research into the causes of deindividuation suggests that this state does not inevitably follow from being part of a group, and even when deindividuation does occur antisocial behaviour is not necessarily the outcome. For example, prosocial behaviour is typically the result of large crowds gathering at music festivals.

ACTIVITY 8.4

Ask as many participants as possible to answer the following question on a piece of paper. It is important to *guarantee* participants complete anonymity otherwise this will not work, so be careful how you do this.

'If you could be totally invisible for 24 hours and were completely assured that you could not be detected or held responsible for your actions what would you do?'

1 How many of the responses contain behaviours that could be classified as prosocial?
2 How many of the responses contain behaviours that could be classified as anti-social?
3 How do your findings support deindividuation theory of aggression?
4 Is this a valid way of testing deindividuation?

Exam hint

This 16-mark question requires an accurate and detailed knowledge of deindividuation theory to get your answer into the top band of marks. Learn the theory in detail, and use the findings of two or three studies to effectively evaluate the study.

The frustration–aggression hypothesis

The **frustration–aggression hypothesis** was proposed by Dollard et al. (1939). According to their original theory, aggression is caused by frustration, and the greater the frustration, the greater the aggressive response. They defined aggression as any behaviour intended to injure the person to whom it is directed. Frustration occurs when a goal-directed behaviour is blocked, that is, we are prevented from doing something we really want or need to do.

Key term

Frustration–aggression hypothesis: the theory that aggression stems from some sort of frustration.

Miller (1941) modified the frustration–aggression hypothesis to acknowledge that aggression was only one of a number of possible responses to frustration. Miller pointed out that individuals often successfully manage frustrating situations without resorting to aggression. Aggression becomes the dominant response to frustration when such behaviour has been rewarded in the past.

Many studies have successfully demonstrated the link between frustration and aggression. For example, in the bobo doll study of Bandura, Ross and Ross (1963), aggression was instigated by frustrating the participants – the children were stopped from playing with the good toys, leading them to imitate the adult or film depictions of aggression by enacting their frustration as aggression against the bobo doll.

However, the frustration–aggression hypothesis is over-simplistic. Burstein and Worchel (1962) point out that frustration does not always lead to aggression, and is most likely a response only when the frustration is perceived to be unjustified. Even then, aggression is not inevitable. When frustration arises from an understandable cause – it might feel unjustified but the 'victim' understands why it occurred – aggression becomes only one of a number of possible behavioural responses. Instead of aggression, the impulse could be to engage in an alternative response to the one that produced frustration, or even to simply give up.

- According to social learning theory, aggression is learned through the observation and imitation of aggressive behaviour.

- According to deindividuation theory, aggression is due to the loss of individual identity when in a group. Perceived anonymity might then lower a sense of personal responsibility towards behaving aggressively.

- According to the frustration–aggression hypothesis, aggression is the result of frustration created by a blocked goal.

Institutional aggression

It is rare that a behaviour occurs in the absence of environmental influence, and some environments have been observed to exert a particularly strong influence on behaviour. One such is an institution. Institutions are social structures or organizations with clearly prescribed sets of rules, roles and expectations meant to govern the behaviour of individuals within them. The police, the military and hospitals are good examples of this, as are schools and churches. Some behaviours are more prevalent in some institutions than in others. Aggression, for example, is particularly associated with the institution of prison. Prisons are a unique and extreme form of institution because of the explicit and social-sanctioned way that they guide and control behaviour. Quite why prisons in particular are associated with aggression and other forms of misconduct has attracted considerable debate, but explanations basically fall into two types: situational and dispositional.

Aggressive behaviour in prisons: situational explanations

Some of the most famous and dramatic studies in psychology have been those that demonstrate the influence of the situation in which a person finds themselves on their behaviour. The Stanford Prison experiment illustrated a number of situational factors that help to explain the influence of institutions. The aim of the experiment was to see if the widespread brutality seen in American prisons at the time was the result of characteristics of the people in prison, or to do with the situation that prisoners find themselves in. Zimbardo et al. (1971) set up a mock prison in a basement of a university. Within a day, the students selected to participate had radically changed their behaviour. Those selected to take part as guards became more punitive and aggressive in their treatment of those selected as prisoners. In response, the prisoners began to rebel, with a number becoming passive and apparently depressed. Although intended to run for two weeks, the experiment was halted after just six days. While the study has been widely criticized for the ethical issues it raises, most researchers agree that it vividly demonstrated the influence of roles and how identities and moral values can quickly become lost in situations involving imbalances in power and status. The powerful social roles of both prisoner and guard appeared to create conditions ripe for conflict and aggression. Furthermore, a deindividuated state may have been created by the wearing of uniforms (which for guards also involved reflective sunglasses) and the lack of use of personal names. This further increased the likelihood of aggressive behaviour.

The Stanford Prison experiment appears to support the idea that the situation a person finds themselves in, such as prison, has a significant effect on their aggressive behaviour. This idea is sometimes referred to as the deprivation model – aggression being the consequence of the prison experience. Prison confinement comes with many deprivations, such as the imposition of harsh rules, loss of power and autonomy, loss of personal freedoms, restricted access to family and friends, and reduced privacy. Sykes (1958) referred to these multiple deprivations as the 'pains of imprisonment'. Inmates adjust to these 'pains' in different ways and to varying degrees. For Mackenzie and Goodstein (1985), a key deprivation affecting adjustment to prison and subsequent prisoner misconduct is loss of personal control. Very control-limited environments like prisons are very stressful, and it is the effect of this stress that lies at the root of much aggression seen in prisons. This is supported by studies that have attempted to address the psychological problems associated with imprisonment. Samuelson et al. (2007), for example, assessed the outcomes of mindfulness-based stress reduction (MBSR) in six correctional institutes, involving 1350 inmates. They found post-course improvements in a range of measures, including hostile and aggressive attitudes, low self esteem and mood disturbance.

ACTIVITY 8.5

It has been said that, 'If you put good apples into a bad situation, you'll get bad apples.'
What do you think he meant by this? Which explanation of institutional aggression does this support?

Aggressive behaviour in prisons: dispositional explanations

While situational explanations focus on factors in the prison environment that might bring about aggressive behaviour, dispositional explanations focus on aspects of the individual as a cause of aggression – what the prisoner brings with them to prison. In the context of institutional aggression, this is sometimes referred to as the importation model.

A number of studies have linked dysfunctional behaviour in inmates to levels of testosterone. Dabbs et al. (1995) measured testosterone levels in the saliva of 692 adult male prisoners. Using data from prison records, they found that those committed for violent crimes had higher testosterone levels and were more aggressive in prison than those committed for non-violent crimes (such as theft and drug crimes). However, research into the effects of testosterone and behaviour do not support a direct involvement in aggressive and violent behaviour. According to Mazur and Booth (1997), the two appear linked because of the role aggression serves in asserting and maintaining social dominance in prisons. The suggestion then is that both situational and dispositional factors need to be considered when understanding institutional aggression.

Irwin and Cressey (1962) pointed out that inmate behaviour is a reflection of their pre-prison characteristics and behaviour. In order to fully understand aggression in a prison context it is important to recognize the personal and social histories that individuals bring with them to prison. DeLisi et al. (2011) analysed the family background and offender records of 2520 male prison inmates. Their findings suggest that life events in childhood 'cascade' to predict both antisocial behaviour during adolescence and misconduct, including aggressive behaviour, during periods of imprisonment. Consistent with the importation model, substance abuse problems, gang involvement and previous crime history were important factors predicting behaviour while in custody. However, they argued that prison misconduct is more complex than a straightforward importation of subcultural attitudes and beliefs. Personal experiences including poverty, family criminality, and abuse directly contributed to periods of juvenile detention. Such confinements greatly restricted opportunities for prosocial development, a conclusion they supported with the finding that age of first confinement was a consistent predictor of later prison misconduct.

Exam hint

Take care – the question uses the plural *explanations*, so you have to use the two explanations for institutional aggression, situational and dispositional. Outline both explanations and use research evidence effectively, for instance be clear how it supports (or otherwise) the explanation.

EXAMPLE EXAM QUESTION

Discuss explanations for institutional aggression in the context of prisons. (16 marks)

KEY POINTS

- Institutional aggression is aggression that occurs in environments with clearly prescribed sets of rules, roles and expectations that are meant to govern the behaviour of individuals within it.

- Situational factors have been identified, such as powerful social roles, deindividuation, and stress from multiple deprivations.

- Dispositional factors include aspects of ones biology (e.g. testosterone) and aspects of the personal and social histories that individuals bring to institutions.

Media influences on aggression

There has been a heated debate amongst psychologists for some years now concerning whether or not exposure to violence in media (notably television, films and computer games) produces negative psychological effects, and if so, how these can be explained. While this is ongoing in psychology, every so often this debate enters the public domain and itself becomes a media issue. This is prone to occur after high-profile cases where individuals have committed acts of violence attributed to the consequences of watching violent media. However, the effects of watching violence are much more subtle and complex than news media and popular commentators make out. Indeed, there is considerable disagreement among psychologists about the influence of media on social behaviour.

Fig. 8.5 Some researchers argue that early exposure to violence predicts aggressive behaviour in adulthood.

One influential longitudinal study was carried out by Huesmann et al. (2003). Children were first studied in 1977 when they were aged between five and eight years, and again in 1991 when they were in their twenties. Huesmann et al. found that the viewing of violent television shows when the children were between six and nine years of age correlated significantly with measures of adult aggression in both men and women in the sample. This correlation was significant for physical aggression in both men and women and for 'indirect' aggression in women only. The more a child had identified with same-sex violent television role models, the more likely they were to be aggressive in later life. Those men classed as high-violence viewers in boyhood had three times the crime conviction rate of low-violence viewers.

Huesmann et al.'s study indicated that children copy aggressive and violent behaviour and that this continues into ongoing aggressive behaviour patterns in adulthood, even linking to involvement in crime. Other studies have supported this general finding. Anderson and Bushman (2002) conducted a large-scale meta-analysis of studies using a variety of methods to investigate media influences on aggression, accumulating over 48,000 participants in total. They found that watching violence had a significant effect on later aggressive behaviour. The effect was strongest in laboratory experiments, but there was still a substantial effect in field and longitudinal studies.

Anderson and Bushman (2002) argued that the link between watching violence and acting aggressively can be understood by using the analogy of smoking and lung cancer:

- Some smokers get lung cancer, but some do not. Some watchers end up acting violently, but others do not.

Research methods link

For more on meta-analysis, see page 50.

- People differ in how susceptible they are to smoking-induced cancer. People differ in how susceptible they are to film and television violence.

- Researchers knew that smoking caused cancer long before they understood the precise mechanisms involved. Researchers know that watching violence 'causes' violence, although they have not entirely teased out the mechanisms.

It is important to note, however, that not all studies support a causal link between media violence and aggressive behaviour. Charlton et al. (2002) conducted a natural experiment into the impact of the introduction of television to the geographically remote community of St Helena, a British colony in the southern Atlantic Ocean with a population of 6000. In 1993, two years before the introduction of television, Charlton et al. studied the children to provide a baseline measure of aggressive behaviour. They returned in 1998, three years after the introduction of television.

They found no overall increase in aggressive behaviour post-television. Children with higher antisocial behaviour scores before television was introduced, however, were most likely to watch a large number of cartoons, implying that children with an interest in violence may select programmes with that sort of content.

Comstock and Paik (1991) argued that although there is a link between watching aggressive media and acting aggressively, the two factors correlate rather than one (watching violence) causing the other (acting aggressively). They noted that a fairly large number of characteristics relating to family background and personality also correlate with watching violence and acting aggressively. So, for example, children from lower socio-economic classes tend to watch more television, as do children with lower levels of measured intelligence. This may be due to a number of different reasons, such as the dislike of alternative, more cognitively demanding activities, or the cost of alternative forms of entertainment. According to this approach, the 'link' that can be seen between watching violence and acting aggressively can be understood by considering the underlying variables that 'cause' greater exposure to violent media and apparent imitations of media aggression.

ACTIVITY 8.6

Conduct an experiment into the influence of music on behaviour. First of all, read about laboratory experiments to remind yourself of important considerations when designing an experiment (for example, ethics, control). Find two songs of approximately the same length – one with an aggressive tone and lyrics and one with a non-aggressive tone and lyrics. You will also need to create a stimulus to measure the effects of listening to the music. Create a list (about six items) of gapped words that could be completed to reflect aggression or non-aggression. For example, H*T could be HIT or HAT. Once you have selected participants, give those in the control the list to complete immediately after listening to the non-aggressive song. Do the same with the participants in the experimental condition after they have listened to the aggressive song.

Do your findings support your hypothesis? What do your findings suggest about the influence of aggressive media?

Research methods link

For more on experiment design, see pages 10–13.

The effects of computer games

The attention of researchers has increasingly turned to the influence of computer games on aggressive behaviour. The gaming sector is the fastest-growing entertainment industry – worldwide, the computer gaming market is estimated to have exceeded £60 billion in 2015. Technological advances in computer graphics and game delivery (for example, virtual gaming) have meant that the depictions of violence have become more immersive and realistic. Some of the most popular games are, according to their ratings, intended for adults. Haninger and Thompson (2004) examined 80 computer games aimed at teenagers and found that 94 per cent contained some form of aggression. It was only in 2012 in the UK that games began to be rated in line with European standards by the Video Standards Council (VSC), forcing retailers to comply with laws on age-appropriate sales. This does not however apply to games bought online as downloads.

There appear to be a range of effects of playing computer games that may be linked to antisocial and aggressive behaviour. Sheese and Graziano (2005) suggested that playing violent games may serve to undermine cooperative and prosocial behaviours. Their participants played either a violent or a non-violent version of the video game *Doom* in pairs. They were then separated and given individual tasks that allowed them to either cooperate with their partner for mutual gain, exploit their partner for their own benefit, or withdraw from the task. Sheese and Graziano found that those who had played the violent version of *Doom* were more likely to choose to exploit than cooperate or withdraw.

Möller and Krahé (2009) conducted a longitudinal study into the relationship between exposure to violent computer games and aggressive thoughts and behaviours. A group of German secondary school pupils aged between 13 and 16 were assessed by questionnaires for violent video game usage and for various aggressive tendencies. This happened at the start of the study and again after 30 months. The researchers found increases in aggressive beliefs, attitudes and behaviours were associated with exposure to violent video games. Möller and Krahé pointed out that the findings were particularly worrying given the short time in which the effects were seen to emerge in a sample whose exposure to violent games was low (rated 2 on a scale of 0 to 20). They suggested that effects could be expected to be much greater in those with higher exposure to aggressive computer games over a longer period of time. Also, as measures of aggressive tendencies did not predict violent video game use, Möller and Krahé argued that the changes must be due to exposure over time to violent media.

Not all researchers support the view that there is a link between playing violent computer games and aggressive behaviour, however. Van Schie and Wiegman (1997) surveyed 346 children and found no relationship between time spent playing computer games and levels of aggression, although a reduction in prosocial behaviour was noted. In another study, Unsworth et al. (2007) measured players for aggressive feelings before, during, and after playing *Quake II* and found that only those that were already aggressive before the game were more angry after playing it. This suggests that individual differences need to be taken into consideration when predicting the outcomes of playing violent computer games. This is supported by Guimetti and Markey (2007). They assessed their participants for personality traits associated with anger and then assigned them to play either a violent game or non-violent action game. After playing the game they were asked to complete a series of stories, which were assessed for aggressive content. They found that only those assessed at the start as 'angry' became more aggressive after playing the violent game, supporting the idea that personality traits such as an aggressive disposition are important in mediating people's responses to playing computer games.

While some research has found a link between violent video game usage and aggression, it is also important to understand possible underlying mechanisms. A number of possibilities have been put forward to explain why exposure to aggressive media might influence behaviour, including desensitization, disinhibition and priming.

The role of desensitization

Key term

Desensitization: regular exposure to aggressive media means that normal physiological arousal tends to reduce maybe even disappear, making people less sensitive and responsive to aggression.

Watchers of films containing horror, violence and action will remember the experience of a stress response at particularly scary, unpleasant or exciting moments – a sense of shock, increased heartbeat, a change in breathing. Such individuals will also recall how, on second and subsequent viewings of the same scenes, this arousal is much reduced or even absent. The feeling of a need for films of ever-increasing excitement or violence in order to get the same initial reaction might also be familiar. This is an example of **desensitization**. With regular watching, arousal tends to reduce and may even disappear altogether, so that each time aggressive media is watched the person's physical and emotional reaction reduces.

Comparing the brain responses of habitual gamers with those who do not play violent games, Bartholow (2007) found reduced brain response in the gamers, which he interpreted as evidence of desensitization. Carnagey et al. (2007) examined the effect of playing violent computer games on later responses to real-life violence. A sample was questioned about their playing habits and were then randomly allocated to either play a violent or a non-violent game for 20 minutes. Following this, all participants watched a film that depicted real-life violence while wired to measure their physiological responses (heart rate and galvanic skin response, the latter being a change in the electrical conductivity of the skin caused by emotional change). Those who had played the violent game had lower measures of both, suggesting that gaming leads to desensitization to real-life violence.

'Today's sophisticated computer games require players to pay constant attention, and violent acts are continually repeated throughout the game. They engage on a deeper level – physically and emotionally – than people do when watching a movie or TV.'

Outline the role of desensitization in explaining the possible effects of exposure to violent computer games. (4 marks)

Exam hint

The quote here is used to guide your thinking. It does not provide you with the answer exactly, but gives you a hint as to why desensitization might be a useful explanation for some responses to playing violent computer games. Always read quotes carefully – they are there to help, not hinder, and can sometimes 'tune you in' to the right things to say in an answer.

The role of disinhibition

According to Berkowitz (1962), people are naturally aggressive. Impulses to behave aggressively, however, are mostly held in check, and thus aggressive behaviour is usually *inhibited*. Exposure to media aggression, however, leads viewers to feel that aggression is an acceptable behaviour. One consequence of this is that inhibitions to behave aggressively are weakened, increasing the likelihood of the viewer behaving in similarly aggressive ways. In other words, exposure to media aggression results in a *disinhibition* to behave aggressively. According to Berkowitz, disinhibition effects are most likely when the perpetrator of aggression is seen to be rewarded, when opportunities to behave aggressively closely resemble those witnessed in the aggressive media, and when there is a target for aggression that is seen as legitimate (for example, when someone feels provoked).

The role of cognitive priming

Cognitive priming theory refers to the idea that exposure to aggression in media such as films, television and computer games leads to the storage of memories associated with aggression in the observer. Huesmann et al. (2003) refers to these as 'scripts'. Scripts are memories for the sequence of basic actions needed to complete a more complex behaviour. Once created, these scripts are available for retrieval. When an individual is subsequently exposed to a situation that is in some way linked to aggression (for example, a real-life situation similar to one where an aggressive response was observed in the media), these scripts are triggered, making aggressive behaviours available to the observer as a possible response. An observer of media aggression is thus 'primed' to react in similar ways to a provocation.

Recently, advances in brain scanning have supported the idea that scripts are stored in long-term memory. Murray et al. (2006) used functional magnetic resonance imaging (fMRI) to compare the brain areas that were active when a sample of eight children watched both violent and non-violent television programmes. In both conditions, the regions that process visual motion were active, as would be expected. However, when the children watched the violent film, a network of right-hemisphere regions was activated associated with emotional regulation, arousal and attention. As well as this, the areas of the brain responsible for storing episodic memories were active, implying that the acts seen may have been stored as aggressive scripts for later use.

Key term

Cognitive priming: exposure to aggressive media leads people to store memories of aggression that are then available to be retrieved or activated later, increasing the likelihood of individuals behaving in similar ways.

AGGRESSION

Exam hint

There are only six marks available so you can see that the issue here is not the number of words you use but your ability to carefully select and then use knowledge effectively in the context of the scenario.

EXAMPLE EXAM QUESTION

Recent research has found that two-thirds of all television programming contains violence, and that programmes designed for children contain more violence than those designed for adults. By age 18, the average American child will have seen 200,000 violent acts and 16,000 murders on TV.

Explain the possible influence on aggressive behaviour of exposure to such media. Refer to psychological theory and/or research in your answer. (6 marks)

KEY POINTS

- Media influence has been explained by social learning theory, using concepts of observation and modelling as a result of a deindividuated state and as a consequence of frustration.
- There has been considerable debate about the effects of watching violence on later aggressive behaviour.
- Some studies show that watching violence during childhood has an effect on aggressive behaviour in adulthood. However, some researchers argue that there are no direct effects of exposure to media violence.
- Computer games are different to other media in that they ask the player to take an active role.
- Computer games have been shown to increase arousal, decrease helping behaviour and lead to desensitization to game and real-life violence. But some researchers argue that there is a lack of convincing evidence.
- Cognitive priming suggests that watching violent media can lead to aggressive scripts that may be recalled in real-life situations.
- Watching violence leads to initial arousal followed by desensitization.
- Watching media violence might lead to the weakening of inhibitions against acting similarly.

PRACTICAL ACTIVITY

Conduct a content analysis of British television to investigate the frequency and/or representation of aggression on television (first, remind yourself about content analysis by reading the relevant section in the Research Methods chapter).

1. State the aim and hypothesis for this investigation.
2. Decide on a sample – that is, set limits on what is going to be analysed. For instance, three different TV channels between 8pm and 9pm Monday to Friday, or you might restrict yourselves to popular soaps.
3. Develop a coding system. For instance, you will need criteria for deciding whether an observed event constitutes aggression or not, and you might want to record other variables, like the sex of perpetrator and victim, and type of aggression, etc. Your coding system should produce quantitative data, for example the number of times the event occurs.
4. Represent your findings in simple bar charts.
5. Interpret your findings in terms of the hypothesis.
6. Reflect: What problems did you encounter doing the content analysis? How did you overcome them? What does this exercise tell you (a) about the amount of aggression on British television, and (b) the strengths and limitations of content analysis?

Example exam questions

1. Discuss the role of **either** genetic **or** neural factors in aggression. **(16 marks)**

2. Briefly outline and evaluate the findings of ONE research study into the role of testosterone in aggression. **(4 marks)**

3. Discuss evolutionary explanations of human aggression. **(16 marks)**

4. Outline and evaluate one social psychological explanation of human aggression. **(12 marks)**

5. Outline the dispositional explanation of institutional aggression. **(4 marks)**

6. Briefly outline one limitation of the dispositional explanation of institutional aggression. **(2 marks)**

7. Tom spends many hours playing games on his computer. He used to enjoy games in which he controlled characters as they jumped between platforms and overcame obstacles. He no longer finds such games exciting and is now playing ever more action-packed and violent shooter games.

   Use your knowledge of psychology to explain the change in Tom's behaviour. **(4 marks)**

Exam focus

Read through the following example exam question, example student answer, and examiner comments. Then, have a go at answering the question yourself!

EXAMPLE EXAM QUESTION

Describe and evaluate deindividuation theory of aggression. (16 marks)

Dev's answer

Deindividuation is a social psychological theory of aggression. It states that anonymity leads to increased aggression because when a person is anonymous they cannot be identified. Deindividuation is most likely to occur when in a group, for example a crowd, but it can occur when a person is alone, such as on the Internet.

> **Examiner comment:** A core principle of deindividuation is here (anonymity) but the description lacks detail. Missing, for example, are reduced sense of personal responsibility, lack of self-awareness, a shift in social identity.

The theory is supported by Zimbardo's Stanford Prison experiment. Students were selected to participate in a mock prison experiment (the prison was really the basement of the university set up to look like a prison with cells, etc.). Some participants were guards, and given uniforms and dark glasses to wear. The prisoners wore simple overalls and were given numbers to identify them rather than names. They were all observed and filmed during the study. It was found that even though it was supposed to last two weeks, the study was stopped after six days. This is because the guards became more and more aggressive towards the prisoners, who became distressed and depressed. There are ethical problems with this study however, as there was clear distress caused to participants, maybe even psychological harm. Also, they weren't given the right to withdraw.

> **Examiner comment:** A common problem – getting caught up in the procedure of a study and not getting to the point, which here is the implication of the finding for deindividuation, for example, *how* does it support the theory?

> **Examiner comment:** This is irrelevant – the ethics of the study have no bearing on what it means to deindividuation theory.

Another study supporting deindividuation is one involving female participants giving electric shocks to female participants. Zimbardo found that participants who could not be identified (because they were wearing cloaks) gave higher shocks than those who wore their own clothes and used their own names. This is because they felt anonymous and so were deindividuated. However, this was a lab experiment and the findings cannot be generalized to real, everyday life, so it lacks ecological validity.

> **Examiner comment:** Even though it lacks clarity, this is better use of a study. The findings are clearly related to deindividuation.

> **Examiner comment:** Again, this criticism of the study is serving no real purpose and so is irrelevant.

Deindividuation also occurs in real-life situations. It has been found that during the conflict in Northern Ireland many of the violent attacks were carried out by people who hid their identities with masks. This also supports deindividuation theory.

> **Examiner comment:** Potentially good, but not used effectively here – how exactly does this support deindividuation theory?

> **Examiner comment:** There is some understanding of deindividuation theory in the answer. Knowledge however lacks detail and understanding. There is evaluation of the theory but this is only partly effective, e.g. it is not always clear what the implications of the studies for deindividuation are. A general lack of clarity means that this answer falls into Band 2. The ideas here however are sound and with more detail and effective use of knowledge it could get into the top band.

Part 3:
Issues and options in psychology

Chapter 9: Forensic psychology

Introduction

Within the broad field of psychology, forensic psychology is a specialism concerned with the application of psychology to the legal process. It developed out of a need for psychological evidence to be used as part of the law and legal process. In its broadest sense, incorporating investigative and criminological psychology, it can be applied to the criminal investigation, psychological explanation of crime and the treatment of criminals. The first recorded use of expert psychological testimony in court was in 1896, when in a murder case Albert von Schrenck-Notzing argued that due to the huge pre-trial publicity the witnesses would not be able to distinguish between what they had actually seen and what they had read in newspapers. James McKeen Cattell conducted the first studies of legal testimony in 1895 and Hugo Munsterberg published the first papers on forensic psychology in 1908. From these early beginnings forensic psychology has developed into an important applied area of professional psychological practice. Forensic psychologists work in many areas, some of which will be touched on in this chapter. To become a forensic psychologist, one has to have a degree in psychology and undertake a specialized postgraduate course. Forensic psychologists are employed mainly by the prison service, but also work in secure psychiatric hospitals, police and probation service, government departments, private practice and in universities.

The subject areas of forensic psychology not only involve a range of knowledge from different areas of psychology but touch on areas of sociology, moral philosophy and law too. It requires a special ability in terms of being able to think about and consider broader issues in relation to crime as well as being able to focus on the individual involved. In this chapter we will be looking specifically at some examples of areas that concern forensic psychology. This will include the problems in identifying and measuring crime and how to deal with it. These involve issues of great importance and debate in today's society. We will also examine possible explanations as to why people engage in crime and the techniques of profiling used by the police and forensic psychologists to help bring criminals to justice. Throughout this chapter the terms criminal and offending behaviour will be used fairly interchangeably as they are in most contexts.

What is covered in Forensic psychology?

FORENSIC PSYCHOLOGY

Problems in defining crime
What is a crime?

We probably all have an idea as to what is meant by the word 'crime'. For most, it would be seen as 'breaking the law', for which if caught we would expect to be punished. From an early age most of us are set 'rules' of behaviour by our carers as part of normal socialization. These will vary from family to family but overarching these are societal 'rules' that we are all expected to comply with, and some of these are backed up by legal statute. For example, I will not be prosecuted for jumping a queue, or not saying please and thank you or excuse me when I sneeze, although they might be breaking societal norms (or social rules). However, if I buy drinks while underage, exceed the speed limit while driving or racially abuse someone in the street, I am clearly committing a crime. This highlights two types of crime:

- acts that break the law – legal definition of crime

- acts that cause offence to moral norms or values held by society like religious belief – normative definition of crime.

Key term

Crime: an act the breaks the law (legal definition) or an act that causes offence to societal norms and values (normative definition).

Sometimes these two definitions can be used to describe the same crime and sometimes the two types seem at odds. For example, if I find a £5 note in a busy street and choose to keep it, along the lines of 'finders keepers' as my grannie used to say, am I not committing a legal **crime**? How many people would report this sort of find to the police in our society? The point being that a legally defined crime may not match up to the norms of socially accepted behaviour. The way we view crime is a social construction that depends on how we see it from both legal and a normative stance.

Exam hint

As there are only two marks for each problem you should state and briefly describe each one, illustrating with an example if appropriate. Sample problems are cultural variations, legal vs normative issues, impact of the crime.

EXAMPLE EXAM QUESTION

Briefly explain TWO problems in defining crime. (4 marks)

Crimes clearly vary across cultures (for example, topless sunbathing is a crime in some places) as indeed, as we shall see later, does our response to it.

Ways of measuring crime

Every year the Home Office publishes the latest crime statistics and trends for England and Wales. These sorts of statistics are compiled by most developed nations of the world, but in different ways. In England and Wales these are based on two main sources of data: the British Crime Survey/Crime Survey for England and Wales (BCS/CSEW) and official statistics recorded by the police and the Home Office.

Official statistics

Official statistics can take many forms, some examples of which are explored here.

Police statistics on reported/recorded crimes

Due to the need for detailed police reporting procedures, police statistics provide a rich and up-to-date record of crime. However, they are affected by reporting biases, as some victims regularly report to police and others choose not to for various reasons, such as considering it a waste of time or too much hassle. There are also no guarantees the police record events as crimes in a consistent way across authorities or time. Crimes recorded by the police themselves are not the same as crimes reported to the police. Every year the recording procedures are reviewed and they are determined by the HOCR (Home Office Counting Rules). For example, in the year ending December 2014, there were over one million convictions for non-notifiable offences (up 3 per cent from the year ending December 2013) that are not covered in police-recorded crime or the CSEW looked at later in this chapter (for example, being drunk and disorderly or committing a speeding offence).

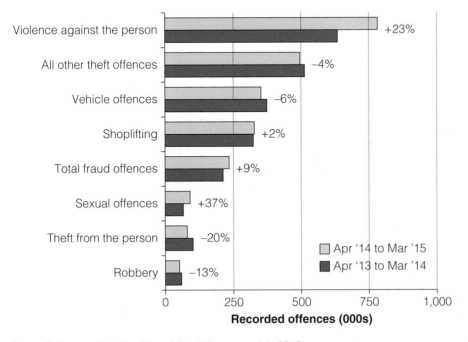

Source: *Police-recorded crime, Home Office © Crown copyright 2015*

Fig. 9.1 Selected victim-based police recorded crime offences in England and Wales: volumes and percentage change between year ending March 2014 and year ending March 2015

The most dramatic increase in this recent example recording period is for sexual offences recorded by the police, which increased by 37 per cent compared with the previous year, to a total of 88,219 across England and Wales in the year ending March 2015. Within this, the number of offences of rape increased by 41 per cent and the number of other sexual offences increased by 36 per cent. These increases are likely to be due to an improvement in crime recording by the police and an increase in the willingness of victims to come forward and report these crimes, due in part to the societal concerns of not reporting in the past and increased assurances regarding confidentiality. The statistics are also compounded in very recent years by the reporting of historic offences following Operation Yewtree. This is the ongoing police investigation into sexual abuse allegations, predominantly the abuse of children, against the British media personality Jimmy Savile and others. The investigation, led by the Metropolitan Police Service, started in October 2012.

Court statistics

These give an indication of the numbers and types of crimes being processed by the courts and also the sentencing patterns. The obvious potential bias here is the factors that were considered in prosecuting (as opposed to not charging), which can and do vary across areas and time.

Prison statistics

This data provides information on the numbers in prison, offence categories and sentence duration. There is no shortage of data here, as the Ministry of Justice publishes weekly update figures of the prison population, which can be accessed online. They also publish projections, and from a 2015 figure of around 86,000 prison inmates it is estimated that this may rise to 90,000 by 2020. The vast majority of prisoners are male, at around 95 per cent. The main bias here is that sentencing policies can vary over time and place, especially if there is a cultural focus on specific crimes (for example, racist attacks, child pornography).

Victim surveys

The annual British Crime Survey (BCS), started in 1982, asks a random sample of households about a range of crime-related matters, including their fear and experience of crime over the preceding year. The sample size currently comprises over 35,000 adults, and since 2009 includes 3000 children between the ages of 10 and 15 in England and Wales. Since the late 1980s it has been misleadingly titled, as Scotland (which has its own distinct legal system) was excluded, so in 2012 this was eventually rectified and the BCS is now called the Crime Survey for England and Wales (CSEW). Scotland and Northern Ireland carry out their own crime surveys. All of them can be accessed online. The main objective of the survey is to provide information about the levels and nature of crime, and public attitudes to crime and punishment, to help inform Home Office policy. It is hoped that this survey will produce a true reflection of the extent of crime. Despite reported levels of most crime falling, public perception still appears to be that it is high nationally. There are subgroup differences in perception, with women more worried than men about burglary and violent crime, and people with poor health the most worried about crime and twice as likely to be worried about burglary.

The CSEW consistently reveals a far higher number of crimes than that reported by the official Home Office statistics (see Fig. 9.2). This is because fewer than half of the crimes reported in the CSEW have been brought to the attention of the police, and of them about half are not recorded as crimes by the police as they do fit their defined categories for recording crime.

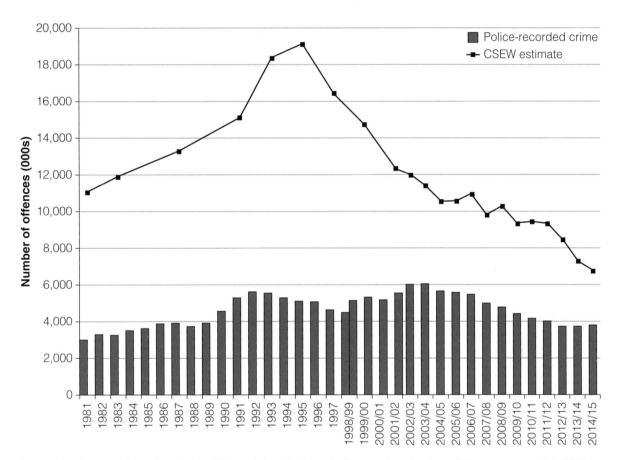

Source: Crime Survey for England and Wales, Office for National Statistics / Police recorded crime, Home Office © Crown copyright 2015

Fig. 9.2 Graph showing police-recorded crime and BCS/CSEW estimates

Fig. 9.3 from the 2015 CSEW shows how crimes involving violence have been generally falling since the peak in the mid-1990s. However, this conflicts with the 23 per cent increase in the police statistics shown earlier (see Fig. 9.1). Like sexual offences this anomaly may be due to increased confidence in reporting these offences to the police. This does illustrate how researchers have to be very cautious when using and interpreting statistics of all kinds.

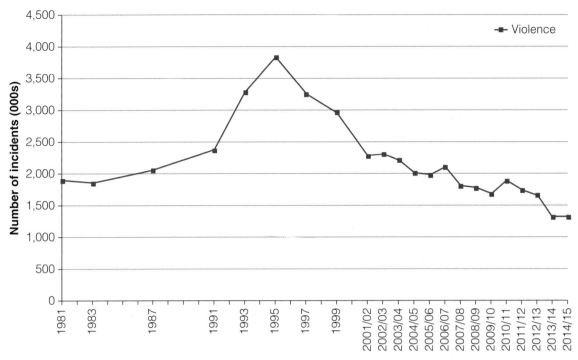

Source: Crime Survey of England and Wales: Office of Public Statistics © Crown copyright 2015

Fig. 9.3 Trends in Crime Survey for England and Wales involving violence, year ending December 1981 to year ending March 2015

ACTIVITY 9.2

Crimes of various sorts are reported in newspapers. Either on your own or in a group, gather some recent papers and make a list of the types of crime reported and the words used to describe the offences. When you have completed this review, look at what sorts of crimes the media tends to focus on and the kind of language used to describe them. Think about whether this gives a fair reflection of the nature of UK crime.

Research methods link

For more about the nature and problems of surveys, see page 18.

One of the big issues with surveys such as the CSEW and its forerunner the British Crime survey (BCS) is that they are questionnaire-based and because of that there may be methodological pitfalls. Respondents may exaggerate and 'over-report' or be embarrassed/anxious and 'under-report'. The questionnaires are completed unsupervised in the home environment, but they do secure a good response rate of about 75 per cent. The most significant issue is that as society changes, its attitudes to certain crimes do, and this may be reflected in CSEW responses. For example, crimes such as fraud and cybercrime are currently excluded, but this is under review. As we have already noted, people are more likely to report domestic violence and sexual offence crimes now than they used to be. A broader issue is that occasionally 'moral panics' lead to certain crimes being more heavily featured such as muggings, animal cruelty, or stalking. Recently, there has been an upsurge of media coverage relating to child sexual abuse, in some cases featuring media celebrities, and this will impact on the public's attitudes and perceptions.

The term 'moral panic' was first introduced by Cohen in 1972 following his study of the phenomenon of youth crime in Britain in the 1960s.

At the time two opposing teen factions, Mods (motor scooters) and Rockers (motor bikes), came to the attention of the media and therefore the public. Clashes between the two groups, usually at weekends or holidays and in seaside towns, were reported way out of proportion with the actual scale of the phenomenon. This fuelled an exaggerated public response to this threat of youth violence being out of control, which became a form of moral panic.

Fig. 9.4 Mods versus Rockers

EXAMPLE EXAM QUESTION

Describe a victim survey. (4 marks)

Exam hint

Note that the question is worth four marks and asks for description only. You will need to say what a victim survey is, probably using the CSEW as an example. You can mention the method and sample and its range of question areas. You could also mention that it gives a more realistic view of the 'hidden' nature of crime not picked up by official crime statistics.

Offender surveys

An alternative way to gather information about the extent and nature of crime is to focus on the perpetrators rather than the victims. Surveys in this area can be of known offenders or more general population surveys where offenders can identify themselves while remaining anonymous. Such surveys can help gauge not only the incidence of crime (number of offences) but also the prevalence of criminal activity (number of people committing crime). These sorts of surveys can possibly throw more light on the true nature of crime and the fact that much is neither reported nor detected. A survey conducted by Belson (1975) is a classic example, as in his random sample of 1445 London boys aged 13–16, 70 per cent said they had stolen from a shop and 17 per cent from private property. Since these are prosecutable offences it would seem to be indicative of a high figure for unreported crime.

Evaluation of ways of measuring crime

As can be seen, there is a wide variety of data sources available on crime, its nature and its victims, however reconciling all these different types of sources is not easy. The official statistics only give us part of the picture, the tip of the iceberg in a way, as they are simply based on records of recorded crime, convictions and sentencing. Sometimes it is difficult to know if there are instances of multiple or double counting of the same criminal, who may have repeated offences or committed multiple ones. Across police authorities and even courts there may be slight local variance in recording practices. Victim and offender surveys involve self-report methodology, which may have issues with:

- Reliability: the respondents may exaggerate and over-report or be anxious and under-report.

- Biased sample: those with literacy issues may be excluded, as may be the most dangerous criminals, or the rich and powerful who may have been involved in certain corporate crimes.

- Biased selection of crime: the focus tends to be on 'traditional' crimes and new trends like cybercrime are not picked up.

KEY POINTS

- There are two definitions of crime: the legal one and the normative one.

- Crime is measured in official statistics recorded by the police, courts and prisons.

- Surveys relating to crime are carried out with victims and offenders.

- It is very difficult to get a true picture of crime levels due to issues relating to how crime is defined and the types of data available.

Offender profiling

The term **offender profiling** is also known as criminal profiling, psychological profiling, behavioural profiling, offender analysis or simply 'profiling'. Whatever it is called, its primary aim is to assist investigative practice and provide advice to police to help solve crime and identify offenders. Historically it is most commonly associated with the crimes of serial killers, but the field is now extending to other criminal areas such as burglary and even white-collar crime. The field has attracted considerable media attention due to certain high-profile cases and popular television programmes such as *Cracker*, *Silent Witness*, *Waking the Dead* and the various *CSI* series. The popular fictional detective character Sherlock Holmes was able to narrow his suspects down based on his analysis of the crime scene and behavioural analysis.

ACTIVITY 9.3

As you read through this chapter you will read names of a number of infamous case studies. These are narrative accounts of notorious criminals. Many of them you may not have heard of, and although some make gruesome reading, you might like to research a sample of them through online searches to help appreciate the background to psychology work in this area. Read them in the role of a forensic psychologist looking for evidence and insights into behaviour and patterns.

In reality, offender profiling is much less glamorized and much more painstaking than the media portrayal. Ebiske (2008) suggests that profiling involves using an understanding of human behaviour, motivation, and pathology so that a picture of the psychological characteristics of a perpetrator can be built. Contemporary profiling has a long history of case study examples where suggestions were made regarding the type of person or future behaviour likely to

Research methods link

For more information on reliability and bias, see pages 41–42.

Key term

Offender profiling: the collection of empirical data in order to build up a picture of the characteristics of those involved in a certain type of crime.

Fig. 9.5 Sherlock Holmes

happen. The first of these involved the police pathologist Thomas Bond, who profiled the infamous Jack the Ripper, the terror of the streets of Whitechapel in London in the late 1880s. He inferred that the offender might be suffering from satyriasis (excessive and uncontrollable sexual desire in males), which was very different to the popular belief at the time that he was a butcher or surgeon with specialized anatomical knowledge. In 1929, another pathologist, Karl Berg, dealt with a similar case, known as the Dusseldorf Vampire. Berg speculated that the offender was a narcissistic psychopath due to the degrading treatment of his victims. In 1943, American psychiatrist Walter Langer was asked by the US Strategic Services to provide a specific psychological profile – this profile described an individual who was a neurotic psychopath and who would commit suicide in the face of failure. The focus of the profile was Adolf Hitler, who did indeed die that way in a Berlin bunker two years later.

According to Petherick and Turvey (2008) two underlying logical processes emerge for criminal investigation and the data, and these tend to inform the different approaches taken in this field. The first is individual case study, leading to in-depth knowledge about the characteristics of a particular individual. This was the way Sherlock Holmes operated. In contrast, a more statistically based process is one that uses the 'average' – it is more like generating a theory rather than specifically relating to a single case. In the following sections it can be seen how these approaches have impacted on the field of offender profiling in what are sometimes called the top-down or bottom-up approaches to profiling. It is important to consider as you read whether profiling is just 'common sense' or if it does indeed have some basis in scientific method. This will be taken up later in the evaluation of offending profiling.

Top-down approach (FBI)

In 1972, the FBI set up the Behavioural Science Unit (BSU) with the remit to develop methods for identifying unknown offenders in unsolved major cases. The unit was highly influenced by the early pioneering work of James Brussel, who drew up profiles for the New York Bomber in 1956 and the Boston Strangler in 1968. The BSU developed a technique known as Criminal Investigative Analysis (CIA), commonly called crime-scene analysis or the **top-down approach**. It tries to develop an evidence base on offenders. Initially researchers at the unit undertook a series of systematic studies especially in relation to serial murders. One particular study focused on 36 imprisoned sexual killers, many of whom were interviewed to produce what eventually became systematic descriptions of this type of offender and their behaviour patterns.

Crime-scene profiling has four key stages: data assimilation, crime classification, crime reconstruction and profile generation.

Key term

Top-down approach: sometimes referred to as crime-scene analysis. Evidence from the crime scene is compared to patterns from previous crimes in order to make predictions about more crimes and the likelihood of when and where they will occur. The approach starts with the big picture and then fills in the details.

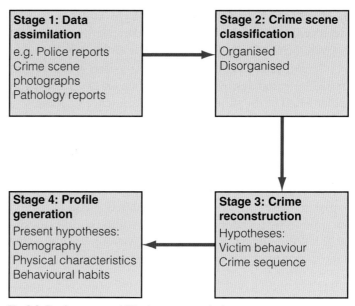

Fig. 9.6 The four stages of FBI crime scene analysis

Organized and disorganized offender types

A key component of stage 2 is using the data gathered from the crime scene and reports to establish whether the offences have been committed by 'organized' or 'disorganized' offenders. The crime scene for an **organized offender** would typically show signs of careful planning and control, and the victim would be a 'targeted' individual. For a **disorganized offender** there will be little evidence of planning in terms of state and choice of site, weapon or nature of attack, and the victim would appear to be random. Based on background research underpinning this classification approach, certain key attributes are usually associated with these two offending types in relation to murder/assault crimes.

- **Organized offender**: leads an ordered life and kills after some critical life event. Their actions are premeditated and planned. They will bring weapons and restraints to the murder site and carefully remove them afterwards. They are likely to be very intelligent and employed.

- **Disorganized offender**: more likely to have committed the crime on impulse when emotionally aroused. There will be no evidence of premeditation and evidence is likely to be left behind such as weapon, personal items, blood, semen, etc. This offender type is likely to be less socially competent and more likely to be unemployed.

Building on these basic dimensions, researchers have developed typologies in other areas. This includes crimes such as stalking, arson and burglary. For an example see Fox and Farrington's burglar typology in Table 9.1. Fox and Farrington have additional types for this crime, labelled 'opportunistic' and 'interpersonal', and their data is based on a database of the Statistical Patterns of Offending Typology (SPOT).

Key terms

Organized offender: often said to be psychopathic, highly organized in most facets of life, cleans up crime scene and removes or covers up evidence.

Disorganized offender: often said to be psychotic, with a disorganized and chaotic lifestyle, makes little or no attempt to tidy up crime scene.

Offence style	Offense description	Offender description	
Opportunistic	Unlawful entry – entry left open No preparation or tools Unoccupied residence Low-value items stolen Little evidence left behind	Young offenders Adolescent onset Short criminal career Low offending frequency Do not know victim	Mostly male, but some female offenders Versatility, prior petty theft/shoplifting arrests Do not have a car
Organized	Clean but forced entry Tools brought to scene No evidence left behind High-value items stolen that often require fence/network	Older offenders Adolescent onset High offending frequency Limited versatility – prior arrests for theft/burglary	Often have a car Cohabiting or have partner May have met victim
Disorganized	Forced entry Scene left in disarray Tools and/or evidence left Low-value or no items stolen	Young offenders Early onset Long criminal career High offending frequency	Versatility – past arrests for drug offences Do not know victim
Interpersonal	Occupied residence Target is victim, not objects Attempted, threatened, or committed violence at scene Personal items stolen	Adult-aged Late criminal onset Solo offender Have a car Single/not cohabiting	No record, but if arrested, usually for violence Select female victims Know of victim

Table 9.1 SPOT burglary styles

ACTIVITY 9.4

Over Easter weekend in 2015 there was an audacious robbery of security boxes in a highly protected vault in Hatton Garden, London.

HATTON GARDEN VAULT HEIST

1 The raiders abseil down a lift shaft to the basement where the vault is located

2 They break through a wall and disabled the alarms

3 They cut through the 18inch thick vault door

4 Once inside the vault they break into at least 60 security boxes filled with gold, jewellery and loose diamonds

Graphic: Nick Coles

Fig. 9.7 Hatton Garden robbery

- How would you go about doing a CIA style investigation of this crime?
- What evidence would you use?
- What sort of profile do you think would emerge – organized or disorganized?

Exam hint

You will need introduce the background to this term, and define and illustrate it with some example characteristics relating to specific crimes. It is only four marks, so you will need to be brief, but ensure you go beyond just listing characteristics. You could use a burglary example from Fox and Farrington's SPOT styles.

Key term

Bottom-up approach: an approach developed in the UK that uses statistical databases to look for consistencies in an offender's pattern of behaviour when committing a crime.

Key term

Investigative psychology: statistically based attempts to identify patterns in different crime characteristics and the consideration of geographical factors in undertaking crime.

EXAMPLE EXAM QUESTION

Outline what is meant by an 'organized' offender. [4 marks]

Bottom-up approach

The **bottom-up approach** most associated with offender profiling in the UK looks for consistencies in an offender's behaviour during the crime. No initial assumptions are made about the offender and the approach relies heavily on statistical databases. It tries to predict how an offender will behave in future crimes and in other aspects of their life. A bottom-up approach starts with the details and creates the bigger picture.

Investigative psychology

This approach to offender profiling is most associated with the work of Professor David Canter and has been labelled investigative psychology. Canter's pioneering work and reputation was built on his success in helping to create a psychological profile that led to the capture of the 'Railway Rapist' and serial killer John Duffy in 1986.

The main focus of **investigative psychology** is assessment of the crime scene to analyse behaviour and social interactions between offender and victim. For example, Canter and Larkin (1993) identified two types of offending, the 'marauder' and the 'commuter'. The marauder does not stray far from their home base, whereas the commuter will move well away from it to commit their crimes. This links in to geographical profiling (covered later in this topic). There is strong support for most crime being committed by the marauding type, as illustrated by 87 per cent of sexual assaulters in Canter's 1993 study.

Canter's profile of the Railway Rapist

Between 1975 and 1986, 23 women aged 15 to 32 were raped at or near railway stations in and around London. Based on his behavioural profiling, Canter drew up some key profile criteria that helped narrow down the 2000 suspects the police had already linked by blood group. Duffy, who was imprisoned for other serious offences, was eventually identified (along with an accomplice David Mulcahy). Compare the accuracy and any differences in the Canter profile presented below.

Canter's profile of the rapist	John Duffy
Male	Male
Mid to late 20s	Matched age at time
Right-handed	Right-handed
Lives in area of offences	Lived in Kilburn
Probably has girlfriend/wife	Had ex-wife and a girlfriend
Possibly no children	No children
Fairly solitary	Only one or two close friends
Semi-skilled, including weekend work	Railways carpenter
Knowledge of railway system	
Previous experience with police	Interviewed after 'domestic' incident with ex-wife

Table 9.2

Key psychological principles

Canter (1994) suggested certain key psychological principles inform and assist the profiling process. These are:

- **Interpersonal coherence**: the actions of the offender will be the norm to them. For example, the type of victim may reflect the subgroup the offender belongs to/has a grudge against.

- **Time and place significance**: the offender needs to be in control so they will choose a specific place. For example, marauders vs commuters.

- **Criminal characteristics**: analysis of crimes/offenders assists classifying and identifying behaviour patterns.

- **Criminal career**: number of times crime repeated, and with growing confidence may increase.

- **Forensic awareness**: previous contact with police may assist criminal in covering their tracks.

Fig. 9.8 John Duffy

Two features that emerge from these principles that help identify if crimes are committed by the same offender. The first is whether the offender has behaved in the same way each time they commit a crime – this is known as the 'offender consistency hypothesis' (Canter, 1995). The second is that, besides offenders being relatively consistent in their crime behaviour, the investigators will also look for evidence of 'behavioural distinctiveness', sometimes known as the criminals 'signature' (Woodhams et al., 2007; Canter, 2000).

Canter's belief was that by adopting this approach the principles were far more scientific than the FBI Crime Scene Analysis and were based on statistical modelling. Despite these assertions, there has been much criticism of their use and success has been mixed. For example, Copson (1995) did a survey of detectives working in offender profiling and found that the profile only succeeded in catching the offender in 3 per cent of cases. However, one must be aware of the flaws of survey research and potential 'demand characteristics', as this was very soon after the ideas were introduced and there was widespread scepticism among those used to more 'traditional' detective work.

Research methods link

For more about demand characteristics, see pages 34–35.

KEY STUDY: CANTER AND HERITAGE (1990)

Canter and Heritage were interested in whether there were particular patterns of behaviour occurring across similar crimes. They undertook a detailed qualitative content analysis on 66 sexual offences committed by 27 offenders. The reports came from a range of police forces in the UK, and were therefore less likely to be ethnocentrically biased due to variations in policing practice. Canter used a computer program he had developed called smallest-space analysis to support their research methodology. The findings indicated that there were five key variables relevant to all 66 cases. These were:

- no reactions to victim
- impersonal language

- surprise attack
- vaginal intercourse
- victims clothing disturbed.

The general underlying pattern of behaviour suggested the attacks were impersonal and sudden and the victim's response irrelevant to the offender. These five factors became to be known as the 'five-factor theory' in relation to sexual offences, as they have been shown to contribute to all such offences. Individual offenders will create their own patterns around these key factors and careful analysis of such patterns allows the police to decide if an offence has been committed by the same individual.

THINKING SCIENTIFICALLY: **LARGE SAMPLE SIZE**

This study had the strength of bringing together information from a large sample of offences. This should have increased the representativeness of the sample and the generalizability of the findings, which became widely known as the five-factor theory. The researchers used a qualitative method of analysis called content analysis. Although such methods can have subjectivity if they are done systematically, they produce a 'rich' set of data for addressing research questions: in this case, what are the common factors that occur in sexual attacks?

Geographical profiling

Research methods link

For more on content analysis, see pages 26–27.

Key term

Geographical profiling: the examination of spatial features of crime to help establish patterns relating to specific crimes and offenders, and to assist detection and prevention.

First touched on by Canter's early work **geographical profiling** (geoprofiling) is now one of the fastest-growing fields of investigative psychology (Canter, 2007). Its pioneer, Kim Rossmo (1995), focused on one key question: What does the location of the crime say about the where the offender might live? Essentially, this type of profiling makes use of the non-random nature of criminal behaviour, especially in relation to their movements (consistency hypothesis again). Wilson (2003), (cited in Turvey, 2012) wrote, 'Crimes are not just random – there's a pattern. It has been said criminals are not so different from shoppers or even lions hunting prey. When an offender has committed a number of crimes, they leave behind a fingerprint of their mental map, and you can decode things from that.'

The geoprofiling approach consists of three key areas:

- studies of criminal spatial activity

- development of decision-support tools based on research findings

- exploring the effectiveness of these support tools in helping police investigations.

The focus of this method is to try to establish how the location of a crime scene can provide vital clues about the offender. It tries to assess and predict key profile information, such as the most likely area the offender would live, work, socialize and travel in. Information about any of these would help the police narrow down the field of suspects and centre of inquiry.

To develop a geographical profile a number of procedures are carried out:

- examination of the case file including witness statements, psychological and autopsy reports

- analysis of crime scene

- discussions with crime-investigating team

- analysis of demographic data and local crime-scene statistics

- study of local transport, neighbourhood and street maps

There are some theoretical underpinnings that contributed to the development of geographic profiling and these will be briefly introduced.

The least-effort principle

This is something, criminal or not, that we can all identify with because at its most fundamental level it suggests that given two alternatives for any course of action people will choose the one requiring least effort. That will account for you looking at things on your phone rather than tidying your bedroom! Translated to the offending world, the principle suggests that crimes will be committed where it involves least effort to get to commit them (for example, own neighbourhood, on easily accessible travel routes, etc.).

Distance decay

Distance decay refers to the idea that crimes will decrease in frequency the farther away an offender travels from their home. Distance decay is the geographical expression of the least-effort principle and results in offenders preferring closer crime sites. Most criminals will apply some common sense here and realize they are more likely to be recognized in their immediate neighbourhood, so Rossmo (2000) quite rightly suggests there is a 'buffer zone' directly around the offender's own home.

The circle hypothesis

There seems to be a fascination amongst geographical profilers for determining geometric circular shapes to define the criminal's operational 'field', but the 'circle hypothesis' has evidence backing it up, including studies on a sample of arsonists (Kocsis and Irwin, 1998) and on sexual assaulters (Canter, 1993).

One can see all these aspects being supported in a retrospective analysis of the infamous 'Yorkshire Ripper', Peter Sutcliffe, who was a serial killer of 13 women (and seven attempted murders) over an extended period throughout the 1970s. He committed his crimes in an area easily accessible from his home (but outside a buffer zone), with more attacks taking place closer to home than further away, and all could be encircled in a pattern (see Fig. 9.10). In essence, he largely fitted the 'marauding' type, although there was the odd 'commuter' attack. He worked as a local lorry driver at the time of the attacks.

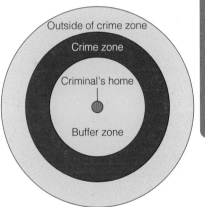

Fig. 9.9 Crime activity and the most likely area

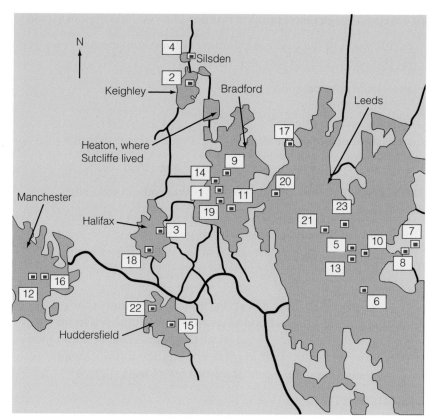

Fig. 9.10 Map of murders/attacks believed to have been committed by Peter Sutcliffe

At the time of the 'Yorkshire Ripper' investigation there were none of the sophisticated profile computing systems that are now widely used to account for these human behavioural patterns. There are many examples in use, but one uses a computer database called Criminal Geographic Targeting (CGT). Spatial data relating to the distance, movement and time to and from a crime scene are analysed to produce a three-dimensional model known as a 'jeopardy surface'. The jeopardy surface can be superimposed on a map of the crime-scene area and provides the investigating team with a computer-derived indication of where the offender may live and work. This software provides a very useful tool, not only in investigating specific crimes but in additional broader research into spatial behaviour patterns of offending populations and trends. Such is the interest in these techniques, their use has now extended well beyond crime investigations. For example, Rossmo has been involved with other research teams mapping the hunting patterns of white sharks in South Africa and the foraging patterns of pipistrelle bats in Scotland using CGT-style techniques. (Le Comber et al., 2006; Martin et al., 2009).

Exam hint

Only an outline is required but you need to say what it is and mention the three underlying concepts of least effort, distance decay and circle hypothesis.

EXAMPLE EXAM QUESTION

Outline the nature of geographical profiling. (4 marks)

Does offender profiling work?

Having presented the main areas and types of profiling it has to be said that, with the exception of topics like unidentified flying objects (UFOs) and other paranormal activities, few things have received as much attention and credibility with so little scientific evaluation conducted on it as offender profiling has. Although in the absence of such evidence belief in UFOs is limited to restricted groups, offender profiling has been widely embraced and used by a substantial number of law enforcement agencies across the globe. What evidence is there that supports this widespread interest and adoption of its techniques?

Attempts to evaluate have tended fall into two areas: customer satisfaction surveys and comparative profiler ability studies.

Customer satisfaction surveys

Like any evaluations of an instrument or service, the most direct way to evaluate is to ask the users how satisfied they are with it. In trying to evaluate the success of offender profiling methods, the police have been asked to express their satisfaction with it. This is based on the obvious premise that valid and useful profiles would lead to greater police levels of satisfaction, and ineffective results would lead to police dissatisfaction and the police no longer wanting to use profiles as part of their investigative work.

There have been many surveys of this kind conducted over the years (for example, Pinizzotto, 1984; Copson, 1995; Snook, Taylor and Bennell, 2007) and they have all indicated that the police generally believe profiles benefit their investigations in some way, though the exact nature and extent of the benefit still remains a little unclear.

The early US-based survey by Pinizzotto (1984) reported that 77 per cent of police departments reported that the FBI profiles significantly helped their investigations and 17 per cent stated that the profiles lead directly to the suspect being identified. That said, less than half the cases involving profiling were solved, and 17 per cent felt the profiles 'were not useful at all'. Another, more recent US study in 2001 by Trager and Brewster seems to be in line with this and found 63 per cent of surveyed officers said the profiles were useful and 38 per cent indicated that they directly assisted in identifying the suspect. This has to be balanced against the 25 per cent who said the profiles actually 'hindered' their investigation in some way.

With a different approach to profiling, a United Kingdom study by Copson (1995) interestingly produced similar figures to the US studies, with 83 per cent of police finding profiles useful. They aided understanding of the case (61 per cent), opened new lines of inquiry (16 per cent) and actually directly helped solve the case (14 per cent).

One of the most recent survey studies was done in Canada (Snook, Gendreau, et al., 2008) and found even higher satisfaction figures, with 94 per cent of officers feeling that profiles helped solve cases. This study also supported an important perceived benefit of profiling – that of opening new leads in a case. 52 per cent of officers felt it did this and 74 per cent felt that the profile was accurate in predicting the characteristics of the offender found guilty.

Despite this seemingly very positive customer survey evidence, there are methodological flaws with it. There have been suggestions that police satisfaction with profiles does not necessarily provide proof of true accuracy of the offender profile. Further research evidence also indicates that individuals' beliefs about the professional standing of the profiler, and more importantly, their own beliefs in profiling, are likely to lead to positive attitudes on such surveys. This is an example of the 'Barnum effect', named after the showman P.T. Barnum's circus trick where intentionally ambiguous details are so ambiguous they fit almost every possible case. This is something we might experience when reading horoscopes for example, even though they are not for our star sign. In simple terms, we believe what we want to believe.

Comparative profiler ability studies

The findings and concerns of the consumer surveys have led some researchers to explore a different approach to evaluating criminal profiling. In essence, how can we compare the actual accuracy of a profiler with a non-profiler? This could be seen as comparative studies of the 'expert' versus the 'novice'.

The first study of this kind compared the predictions of psychologists, detectives, college students and FBI profilers in terms of matching the offender characteristics in rape and murder cases with the actual offender from a multi-choice 'line-up' of varied trait descriptions. The FBI profilers were by far the most accurate, although the detectives did better in the combined rape and murder cases (Pinizzotto and Finkel, 1990).

Following this pioneering study, Kocsis et al. did a series of studies (2000 et seq.) to further evaluate the accuracy of profilers compared to other groups that have potential profiling aptitudes, such as the police (field experience), psychologists (human behaviour knowledge), science undergraduates (logical reasoning aptitude) and psychics (pure intuition). Results of these studies found that the profilers surpassed all the other groups in terms of relative accuracy in predicting offenders from crime scene information. However, the absolute differences were not as great as one would imagine. For example, in the 2000 study the profilers had 46 per cent accuracy compared with 40 per cent for students and 38 percent for psychics. Subsequent reviews of this work suggest that comparative accuracy has still not been fully determined (Snook, Eastwood et al., 2007).

What this overview of evaluations indicates is that there are still clear gaps in a scientific assessment of how profiling impacts on the 'real world' outcomes and performance in actual police investigations. In a research article trying to look behind the 'smoke and mirrors' of profiling, Snook, Cullen et al. (2008) made a plea for more evaluative studies in this area. Although Snook was advocating for more scientific evidence on the effectiveness of offender profiling, it has to be acknowledged that the lack of it is due to it being such a challenging research area. One very recent study conducted by Fox and Farrington (2015) claims to be the first of its kind in the profiling literature, and may trigger more much-needed research to move the field from largely conjecture to proof that it works.

Fox and Farrington set out to conduct the experimental evaluation on the effect of offender profiles when applied in active ongoing police investigations. Specifically, what they set out to do was to compare police agencies using profiling with ones that used 'traditional' police methods, to measure the impact profiling had on burglary arrest rates over a one-year period.

The study was based in Florida in the United States, and the researchers' first task was to find four police departments that were well matched before the experimental intervention. They took into account jurisdiction size, location and number of serving officers. Most crucially, they undertook careful analysis of the burglary statistics and data for four years prior to the study and tried to match as near as possible on this. This baseline data would form the foundation for the comparison with the same data for the year after the experimental intervention in the participant groups. The experimental intervention consisted of using the SPOT burglary profiles (see Table 9.1) in a three-week training period involving class-based and field activities with the chosen police department at all levels. After the three weeks of training the burglary arrest rates and data was collected for just under a year (see Fig. 9.11). The other three police departments received no training and were unaware the study was taking place.

The statistical analysis was complex but a comparison was made with the four-year baseline data and the 'experimental' year.

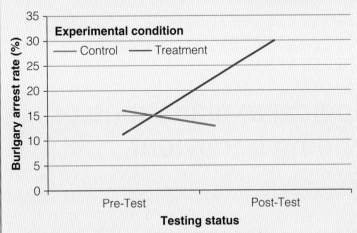

Fig. 9.11 Burglary arrest rate in the Fox and Farrington study

The statistical conclusions indicated that the arrest rates were three times higher for burglary in the experimental department compared with the control ones. This appeared to demonstrate that the offender profiling intervention had had a positive effect in this first controlled experimental study in the field.

Groundbreaking though the Fox and Farrington study is, what criticisms might be levelled at it? The independent variable in this study was the training, and the main dependent variable burglary arrest rates. The writers themselves acknowledge some shortcomings, such as the experimental group not being randomly chosen (it was convenience-sampled, being the closest to the researchers' workplace), police officers' prior attitudes to profiling were not monitored or controlled, and since the police officers would in a sense be the 'profilers', there was no discussion or exclusion of cases already underway. This latter point could have led to a portion of the arrest rate increase being due to the extra attention officers gave to burglary cases after receiving the profiling training. This is an example of the 'Hawthorne effect' and not necessarily due to the use of the burglary profile. This effect is so-called after it was noticed that there were improvements in workforce productivity in a series of 1930s studies at the Hawthorne works of the General Electric Company in the US, purely due to the interest shown in the workers by the researchers rather than any changes imposed. Most research on the Hawthorne effect suggests if it does occur, the spike in improved results typically declines within eight weeks. The researchers maintain therefore that the extended one-year data collection period would not be overly affected. This illustrates some of the difficulties in conducting research of this sort in such an applied setting.

Exam hint

This question is potentially broad so you need watch your timing and make every word count. You will need to define what criminal profiling is then describe the two main approaches to profiling. This would be the US FBI top-down and investigative (UK) bottom-up approaches. This should include mention of organized/disorganized types for the former and geoprofiling for the latter. As it is a discuss question, you will need to present some evaluation points in relation to the approaches, citing studies and issues/debates. The latter could include reference to how scientific or not the process is.

Link

For more about nature–nurture, see pages 94 of Chapter 1, *Issues and debates in psychology*.

EXAMPLE EXAM QUESTION

Discuss approaches to criminal profiling. (16 marks)

KEY POINTS

- The top-down approach to profiling is associated with crime-scene analysis and the FBI. One aspect of this is identifying organized or disorganized offenders.

- The bottom-up approach is most associated with David Canter and what is known as investigative psychology, which has a statistical basis.

- Geographical profiling examines the spatial features of a crime to help narrow down the profile using models based on the least-effort principle, distance decay and the circle hypothesis.

Biological explanations of offending behaviour

Underlying all the theoretical approaches to offending is the role of the nature–nurture debate. The fundamental question is are criminals born or are they made? Consider some of the most serious serial murderers over the last century such as Peter Sutcliffe (discussed in the profiling section in the previous topic – victims were women), Ian Brady and Myra Hindley (the 'Moors murderers' – victims were children), and Dr Harold Shipman (victims were patients). What was it in their psychological and/or biological make up that drove them to such depravities? We can also think of child murderers, such as the ten-year-olds Jon Venables and Robert Thomson, who kidnapped and murdered Jamie Bolger in 1993. Over the years various theories have emerged to try and explain why people offend and they can be divided into those on the nature side (biological) and the nurture side (psychological). They are both of such importance that they will be treated as separate themes and reviewed at the end.

The theories taking the biological approach study either the physiological form of the offender (historical approach) or the underlying biological factors such as genetics and neural causation.

Physiological explanations
Lombroso's atavistic form theory
It was the Italian criminologist Cesare Lombroso in the 1870s who introduced the concept of the **atavistic form**. He claimed that criminals were at a more primitive stage of evolutionary development and had different physical features, which he labelled atavistic. These features included a narrowing sloping brow, prominent jaw, high cheekbones, large ears and possibly extra nipples, fingers or toes. He went a little bit further and suggested different subtypes of criminal could be identified by their physical features. For example, he claimed murderers had bloodshot eyes, curly hair and a prominent jaw.

> **Key term**
>
> **Atavistic form:** the specific physical features that are associated with criminal subtypes.

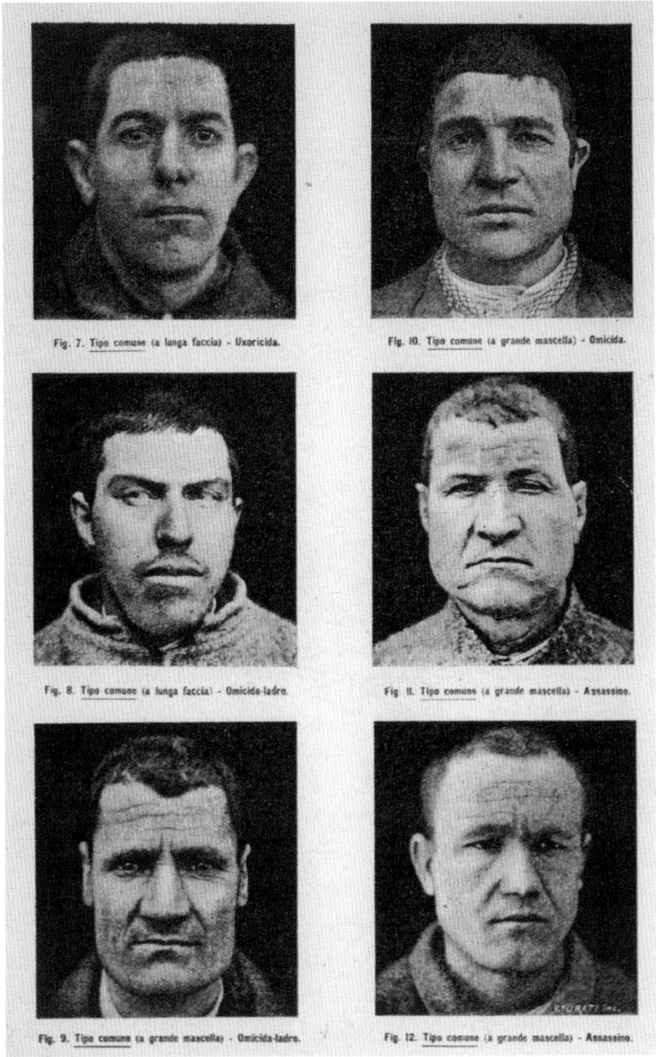

Fig. 9.12 A plate of photographs of murderers from Lombroso's study

FORENSIC PSYCHOLOGY

Chapter 9: Forensic psychology   447

Clearly these features are heritable, so in his early writings Lombroso was clearly on the side of the 'nature' argument. In his later writings he modified his views and claimed that only a third of criminals directly inherited their criminal behaviour and the rest it was due environmental factors (Lombroso, 1911).

In evaluating Lombroso's work a number of points can be made, mainly to do with methodology. One of the most critical is that his sample only consisted of criminals – he had no comparison group of non-criminals. No doubt some of the physical features he identified can be possessed by non-criminals too. His sample also consisted of many individuals who had other psychological disorders, so maybe there was some confusion between criminality and psychopathology. There was debate at the time with other researchers about his definition of criminality. And later, Goring et al. (1972) compared the physical features of 3000 English criminals and non-criminals and found no significant difference in the physical features. That sounds quite convincing and certainly less dubious than Lombroso's conclusion, but there were criticisms of Goring's methodology too. To his credit, Lombroso's lasting contribution was to move explanation away from a general 'wickedness' view to trying to study the area more scientifically, and many regard him as the father of modern criminology.

Exam hint

This is only worth two marks, so you will need to briefly describe only the key details. No evaluation is required, so restrict your response to Lombroso's basic premise that refers to earlier stages of evolution and the presence of specific physical features (perhaps with an example).

EXAMPLE EXAM QUESTION

What is meant by 'atavistic form' in relation to offending? (2 marks)

Sheldon's body-type theory

An alternative theory of criminal and aggressive behaviour based on physical appearance was proposed by Sheldon (1949) in his theories on constitutional psychiatry. His theory proposed three body types, also known as somatotypes:

- Endomorph: fat and soft physique. A relaxed, sociable, loving nature.

- Ectomorph: thin and fragile physique. Solitary, introverted, self-conscious nature.

- Mesomorph: muscular and hard physique. Aggressive, callous, unfeeling – more likely to be criminally minded.

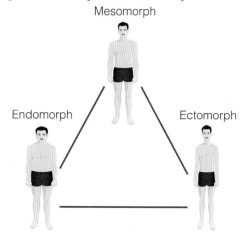

Fig. 9.13 Sheldon's three body types

Sheldon stated that it was rare for someone to be a pure somatotype – that individuals would display a combination of each personality type based on their own individual somatotype. Initially Sheldon's theory was seen as more scientific as he supported it with a key study.

KEY STUDY: SHELDON (1949)

Method: Full-length photographs of 200 male delinquents were compared to those of 200 male college students and rated on a 7-point scale according to the three body types.

Findings:

Body build	Students	Criminal delinquents
Endomorph	3.2	3.4
Ectomorph	3.4	1.8
Mesomorph	3.8	5.4

Table 9.3 Body types and ratings

This table suggests that students had similar body types on average, whereas the male criminal delinquents were significantly more mesomorphic, thus supporting Sheldon's theory that those with a more muscular and hard physique were more prone to criminality.

THINKING SCIENTIFICALLY: CRITICISMS OF THE SHELDON STUDY

In spite of the findings, this study has been subject to much criticism. Two issues were that the legal definition of 'delinquency' was not used in identifying his sample group, and that the ratings may have been unreliable, as although there is some research to show a link between mesomorphy and offending behaviour, other psycho-social factors need to be taken into account. For example, a child/young adult with a muscular body type may find early success in getting what they want if they act in an aggressive and dominant way, so it becomes a learned response behaviour. A muscular body type is attractive to gang cultures so those with that body type may be encouraged to join and get involved in offending type behaviour.

In overall terms, the evidence for physical appearance and links to offending behaviour are interesting but lacking in empirical depth.

ACTIVITY 9.5

In Sheldon's study photographs were rated on a 7-point scale according to the three body types. How would you rate yourself and four others from your family or friends? If you wish you could ask a friend to do the ratings on the same people independently. Having done this consider how accurate the process is and what the limitations are.

Genetic explanations of offending behaviour

Moving away from the simple physical-based theories of Lombroso and Sheldon, interest has focused on possible genetic contributions to criminal behaviour. Twin studies have been used in this area, as the use of monozygotic (MZ) twins who have identical genes can be compared to dizygotic (DZ) twins who have different genes and

Link

For more on the nature–nurture debate and role of twin studies see pages 94 of Chapter 1, *Issues and debates in psychology*.

are no more alike than siblings. The research assumes each twin has similar life experiences, so evidence from this area should be able to support a 'nature' argument over a 'nurture' one.

Cloninger et al. (1978) found there was a 0.7 correlation between MZ twins and 0.4 for DZ twins in terms of their criminality versus their non-criminality. This would suggest a genetic connection; however, critics of this research cite the fact that MZ twins are much more likely to be treated and brought up in the same way than DZ twins (Guthrie, 1998). The fact that they are brought up so similarly might also contribute their shared likelihood of entering into offending behaviour.

In this area there is also interest in what are called 'adoption studies', where the child's relationship to both the adoptive parents and their natural biological parents can be compared. A very large study by Mednick, Gabrielli, and Hutchings (1984) sampling over 14,000 adopted individuals found a correlation between criminal convictions of the adoptee and their natural parent, but no relationship with their adoptive parents. The correlation was only true of certain types of crime like theft, but not true for violent crime. Critics would point out that often children are adopted into family situations similar to those of their biological parents, thus making it difficult to differentiate nature–nurture influences.

For a number of years there has also been the XYY chromosome hypothesis. In genetics our sex is basically determined by chromosomes, with women having two X chromosomes and men an X and a Y chromosome. Occasionally some men are born with two Y chromosomes – that is, XYY rather than XY – which is known as Klinefelter's syndrome. As it is the Y chromosome that makes males male rather than female, those with the extra Y might be considered as extra-masculine. This in turn may lead to them being more aggressive due to their hyper-masculinity. Based on this it was conjectured that there may be a larger proportion of XYY men in prison or psychiatric populations. Indeed, research seemed to back this up, as although they are rare in the general population they are more common in men involved in crime (Epps, 1995). However, it has to be noted that many of these criminals were not involved in violent crime, which might have been expected from the XYY chromosome hypothesis. An infamous serial killer of at least 13 women in the US called Arthur Shawcross had this chromosomal pattern, but it has not been found in other such cases so it is discredited as the causal link. Due to the lack of any substantive evidence, XYY theory is now largely defunct in the forensic psychology field.

Neural explanations of offending behaviour

Neural mechanisms, especially the limbic system, influence many of our social behaviours, particularly those associated with emotions and motivation. There is a considerable body of research in this area, and perhaps not unsurprisingly, some work has been done trying to establish possible links with offending patterns of behaviour. Some studies look at 'structural' evidence and others look at 'functional' evidence. In simple terms, they ask if there are links with actual physiological structures or if it is in some way more associated with what individuals do and how they work.

Structural evidence

Raine et al. (2000) studied 21 individuals with antisocial personality disorder (ASPD) and compared them to matched groups of substance users and a non-offending control group. They found an 11 per cent reduction in the size of the orbital prefrontal cortex in the ASPD group. This area of the brain is considered to be critical in managing the neural networks associated with emotions and behaviour. Other researchers such as Laakso et al. (2002) found that ASPD groups had smaller temporal lobes compared to normal control groups. Sterzer et al. (2005) found reduced grey-matter volumes in adolescent samples who had been diagnosed with 'conduct disorder'. Schiffer et al. (2007) found paedophile men had less grey-matter volume than comparison groups of heterosexual and homosexual men. Another area of research provides some evidence to suggest that brain damage can result in more offending types of behaviour. This can be due to problems at birth (perinatal damage) or due to subsequent accidents and injuries.

Functional evidence

Neural circuitry

Blair (2003) and others have argued psychopathic characteristics reflect abnormal functioning in the neural circuitry involving the amygdala and prefrontal cortex. Birbaumer et al. (2005) supported this with a study involving conditioning tasks with a sample of psychopaths. The lack of amygdala neural activity indicated little fear or emotional response, and would suggest it is easier to offend as such individuals are not capable of recognizing or understanding the mental state of their victims. This reduced emotional response has been found in a number of other well-controlled studies with adolescents with conduct disorder backgrounds (Kiehl et al., 2004; Sterzer et al., 2005).

Executive functioning

Executive functioning is another functional area of interest in this area. This refers to the higher-order cognitive control processes that include decision-making and inhibition. Extensive neuro-imaging research has established that the lateral prefrontal cortex plays an important role in executive functioning.

Morgan and Lilienfeld (2000) did a meta-analysis of 39 studies examining the relationship between executive dysfunction and antisocial behaviour. They found a significant effect in juvenile delinquency and conduct disorder. This has been supported in studies of both adolescent and adult psychopaths. In summary, these studies seem to suggest that the lack of executive functioning means these individuals lack the ability to plan, act rationally or control their impulses.

EEG activity

Slower and abnormal EEG activity in children and adolescents has been found to be associated with later criminal behaviour. In one of Raine's studies (1990) it was demonstrated that 15-year-old boys with lower EEG arousal levels were more likely to become criminals by age 24 than those with higher levels. It is felt that EEG abnormalities are in some way linked to cortical immaturity, which reduces reasoning and emotional regulation.

Exam hint

This is an outline and you are only required to present one explanation. As it is an outline you only need to present a description with a study or two as supporting evidence. You could focus on the structural explanation put forward by Raine (2000) or one of the functional explanations based on the amygdala, executive functioning or EEG abnormalities.

EXAMPLE EXAM QUESTION

Outline ONE neural explanation of offending behaviour. (4 marks)

ACTIVITY 9.6

Imagine you have been asked to offer an explanation for someone's offending behaviour. Based on the material provided in this topic, make a list of all the possible explanations in a table. For each explanation try to decide whether it would support the nature or nurture side of the debate and rate its 'scientific' base from 1 (not scientific) to 5 (very scientific). Try and think of at least one criticism of each explanation.

Evaluation of neural explanations

The neural evidence has been based on very scientific methodology and measuring techniques and many studies have been replicated. However, there are issues relating to the samples used, as many of the offending research participants come from poor backgrounds and it is difficult to establish whether the neural effects are related to that (for example, poor diet, substance-abusing parents) or innate physiological factors. Often the comparison groups cannot be well matched – it is very difficult as they come from different backgrounds. Brain damage studies can be flawed because it is not always possible to establish when and how the damage occurred.

KEY POINTS

- The historical atavistic form theory of Lombroso suggested criminals had distinctive physical features and Sheldon later proposed those of a particular body type (mesomorphs) were more likely to be criminals.

- Twin and adoption studies provide evidence for a possible genetic link to criminal behaviour, but like the XYY chromosome hypothesis, this is contentious.

- There is both structural and functional evidence that neural factors are associated with potential criminal and antisocial behaviour.

Psychological explanations of offending behaviour

As an alternative to the more biologically based approaches to trying to explain offending behaviour, a range of other approaches are presented here. They tend to favour the 'nurture' side of the argument, but not exclusively. Some of these approaches are personality-based and others are more influenced by our cognitive development and later behaviours.

Psychodynamic approach

In psychodynamic theory, the likelihood of developing or exhibiting offending behaviour is very much determined by the level of conflict between the id and the superego – the id being governed by the 'pleasure principle' and the superego by the 'morality principle'. As children we have no concept of morality until the superego is fully formed.

According to psychodynamic theorists, having a harsh or weak superego leads to an imbalance between the three components of personality (id, ego and superego). A harsh superego can result in huge feelings of guilt and obsession when the id attempts to get satisfaction. People with strong superegos tend to be law abiding, although it is argued that on occasions forces from the their id become so overwhelming that they feel guilty and commit antisocial or deviant behaviours so as to be punished. Much more common, and to be expected based on this theory, is offending behaviour arising from a weak or undeveloped superego. Here the individual is led by the demands of the id with little or no experience of conscience about their behaviours. According to psychodynamic theory, underdeveloped superegos (or egos) can lead to psychosis and the inability to feel sympathy for the victims of crime (DiNapoli, 2002). Since it is felt that our parents play a key role in the development of a fully functioning superego, having unloving or absent parents can be very damaging. This formed the basis of Bowlby's maternal deprivation hypothesis. His 1944 study of teenage thieves established that delinquency in that group was strongly related to maternal deprivation in childhood. This ties in well with the work of Aichorn, a psychoanalyst who felt that stress only produced crime in those who had a particular mental state known as latent delinquency. Latent delinquency, according to Aichorn, results from inadequate childhood socialization and manifests itself in the need for immediate gratification (impulsivity), a lack of empathy for others, and the inability to feel guilt (Aichorn, 1935).

The psychoanalytic perspective is criticized because it lacks empirical support, and much information has been derived from therapists' subjective interpretations of interviews with a very small number of patients (Englander, 2007). However, it is important to note that psychodynamic principles have had a major impact on the subsequent development of criminological thought. For example, many other theories of violent crime have come to stress the importance of the family and early childhood experiences.

> ### EXAMPLE EXAM QUESTION
>
> Briefly describe the psychodynamic explanation for offending behaviour. (4 marks)

> **Exam hint**
>
> The context here is offending behaviour and the injunction word is describe. However, it is for four marks only and needs to be brief and focused. Long descriptions of Freudian psychodynamic theory are not required and neither is evaluation. You should focus on the role of the superego and the role parents have in developing it.

Eysenck's theory of the criminal personality

Eysenck, a well-known type-trait personality theorist, believed that crime arises from certain personality traits that are biological in origin. Originally Eysenck (1969) stated that an individual's personality traits could be reduced to two key dimensions: neuroticism (N) and extroversion (E). An individual high on the neuroticism dimension is prone to anxiety, variable moods and depression, whereas someone low on neuroticism is emotionally stable. The extroversion dimension refers to the amount of external stimulation an individual craves, with those seeking large amounts being labelled extrovert and those who require low amounts being labelled introvert. A typical characteristic of many extroverts is impulsiveness, which is relevant in relation to much of offending behaviour. The Eysenck Personality Inventory (EPI) was developed as a psychometric measure of these key traits, and in the majority of the population the types are normally distributed.

Eysenck's personality theory posits that the extroversion and neuroticism personality traits are related to the central nervous system. Extroversion is associated with autonomic arousal and the lower this is, the more stimulation a person seeks from their environment. According to the theory, neuroticism is linked to the stability of the central nervous system. A high neuroticism score shows that the individual has high anxiety levels and their nervous system reacts strongly to aversive stimuli. Eysenck believed that these individuals find it difficult to learn socially appropriate behaviours, for example not behaving aggressively to others.

Eysenck theorized that criminal behaviour is associated with individuals who score high on both extroversion and neuroticism dimensions (see Fig. 9.14). This combination means that such individuals can be impulsive and constantly seek stimulation (due to being high on extroversion) but do not learn from their punishments (due to being high on neuroticism). In a later development of his theory, Eysenck added a third personality dimension: psychoticism (P). Individuals high in psychoticism are uncaring, aggressive and solitary and could also be more likely to be involved in criminal activity.

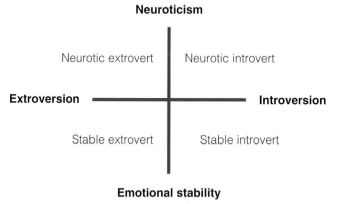

Fig. 9.14 Eysenck's typology. He found that criminals were more likely to be in the neurotic extrovert category.

In evaluation, Eysenck and Eysenck (1971) offered their own supporting evidence based on sampling members of the prison population and compared them to a normal population. The evidence confirmed that there were proportionally more prisoners in the neurotic extrovert typology. Farrington et al. (1982) did a review of several studies of official and self-reporting offenders. They concluded that high N (but not E) was related to official offending, and high E (but not N) was related to self-reporting offenders. Interestingly, high

P (psychoticism) was high on both, although the questions on that scale do tend to be connected with antisocial behaviour, so that may be the explanation. Other research has found inconsistencies with the theory, with some supporting the high extroversion case but others not, and it continues to be an area of debate. One of the problems with any prison-based research is that samples are rarely controlled for the nature of the crimes or duration of sentence. Research has also found a higher percentage of the prison population having lower intelligence scores, which could be a confounding variable when faced with psychometric questionnaires.

Learning theory approach

The learning theory explanation of crime relates to the principles of both classical and operant conditioning. Essentially, offending is learned in the same way as we learn other behaviours. For example, a child may learn to associate stealing sweets from a shop with a feeling of excitement, and stealing behaviour becomes a classically conditioned response. Operant conditioning focuses on the consequences of the child's actions, so if a child is punished for stealing sweets the behaviour would decline. However, if the child receives positive reinforcement, possibly in the form of praise from peers, the offending behaviour is more likely to be repeated. Social learning theory based on the work of Bandura et al. (1973) would suggest the importance of role models and vicarious reinforcement in offending behaviour. If we see role models rewarded or punished it would increase or decrease the likelihood of us behaving in the same way. Studies have also found that people who live in violent communities learn to model the aggressive behaviour of their neighbours (Bartol, 2002).

In terms of aggressive offending, behavioural theorists have argued that the following four factors help produce violence:

1. a stressful event or stimulus, such as a threat, challenge or assault, which heightens arousal

2. aggressive skills or techniques learned through observing others

3. a belief that aggression or violence will be socially rewarded (by, for example, reducing frustration, enhancing self-esteem, providing material goods or earning the praise of other people)

4. a value system that condones violent acts within certain social contexts.

Early empirical tests of these four principles have been promising in terms of providing supporting evidence. (Bartol, 2002).

An issue for learning theory as an explanation of offending is that it is rather deterministic. It states that an individual's offending behaviour is as a result of their learning experiences and observations of role models that surround their environment. The theory fails to acknowledge the importance of free will.

Link

For more on free will see pages 84 of Chapter 1, *Issues and debates in psychology*.

Differential association theory

A specific learning theory is the **differential association theory**, first proposed by Sutherland in 1939. This socio-psychological theory is based on the idea that criminal offending behaviour is learned through exposure to criminal norms. Social learning studies like Bandura's have demonstrated the way in which children learn by simple imitation and this is more likely to occur if rewarded. If children or young adults are exposed to crime and criminal activities they are more likely to copy such activities, and because of the environment they are in, this will be likely to be reinforced as it will be part of their normality. In essence, we will take on the values and attitudes of those key people who surround us (usually parents and peers). It was Burgess and Akers (1966) who added in the element of differential reinforcement of deviant behaviours to Sutherland's original notion of simple association – that the rewards come, for example, in the form of not being caught, the thrill and the possession of items not usually attainable and social encouragement from a similarly minded peer group. Interestingly, the theory claims to apply at different strata in society. The process of learning offending behaviour in more middle-class settings may encourage more perceived middle-class crimes such as tax evasion, fraud, etc. This pattern of behaviour can then become internalized (Siegel et al., 2006). There is empirical research to support this idea, as demonstrated by Rebellon (2006), who used the notion of vicarious reinforcement to show that if delinquent behaviour was rewarded (by attention or other gratification), others will also raise their own delinquent behaviour levels. This view of differential association theory can help explain why gang culture might also develop where young people are subjected to peer pressure and social labelling.

ACTIVITY 9.7

Gangs or close social groupings are common in adolescence and you may well belong to one yourself or know friends who are.

How could you use differential association theory to explain how this happens?

Do you think some individuals are more likely to seek out groups than others? Why?

In evaluation, the theory could be perceived as a little vague and untestable. How can we measure unfavourable attitudes and at what point does it become truly 'offending' behaviour? The main problem is, that in trying to make a causal link between the environmental experience and later offending attitudes and behaviour, it does not account for the fact that some children, despite the most violent and poor backgrounds, do not go on to become criminals or engage in such activities. It needs a more individual perspective. This alternative view is offered by **rational choice theory** (Cornish and Clarke, 1998). A rational choice is one where a decision is made to commit offending behaviour based on weighing up the consequences, especially in terms of rewards. This is done at an individual, not group, level. Guerrette et al. (2005) suggested that rational choice theory means that the choice to commit a crime will vary with the type of crime and its specific purpose for the potential offender. Individuals will apply a cost–benefit decision-making analysis in choosing whether to commit a crime or not. This will be heavily influenced by each person's self-concept and moral code. What the theory does not explain is exactly how these internal decisions are made.

Cognitive approach

The basis of the cognitive approach to explaining offending behaviour is to focus on the cognitive processes we engage in when dealing with moral issues and some of the distortions we may have in our thinking in this area.

Level of moral reasoning

Moral reasoning refers to how individuals reason about and justify their behaviour in relation to moral issues. The most well-known psychological approach to moral reasoning is the cognitive developmental theory, initially proposed by Piaget (1932) and subsequently developed by Kohlberg (1969, 1984). Kohlberg's theory is based on six developmental stages of moral reasoning, which one progresses through with reasoning becoming more complex and abstract. This theory has more recently been revised by Gibbs (2010), giving more emphasis to the roles of social perspective-taking and empathy.

Immature moral reasoning		Mature moral reasoning	
Stage 1 Unilateral and physicalistic	Stage 2 Exchanging and instrumental	Stage 3 Mutual and prosocial	Stage 4 Systemic and standard
Reasoning refers to powerful authority figures (e.g. parents, teachers) and the physical consequences of behaviour. Individuals show little or no perspective-taking.	Reasoning incorporates a basic understanding of social interaction. This typically is seen in terms of cost–benefit deals, with the benefits to the individual being of most importance.	Reasoning reflects an understanding of interpersonal relationships' norms and expectations. Empathy and social perspective-taking are apparent, along with appeals to one's own conscience.	Reasoning reflects an understanding of complex social systems, with appeals to societal requirements, basic rights and values, and character/integrity.

Table 9.4 The four stages of Gibbs' theory

Gibbs' theory focuses only on the first four stages of Kohlberg's theory (see Table 9.4). Moral reasoning becomes more mature as one goes up the stages, and at stage 3 shows an understanding of interpersonal relationships and other people's needs and at stage 4, societal needs. Social perspective-taking reasoning skills are crucial at these stages to allow for emotions such as empathy to play a part in motivating decisions about reasoning and behaviour (Hoffman,

2000). Looking at Kohlberg's/Gibbs' theories a justification can be made for offending behaviour at each of the stages:

- Stage 1 – offending can be morally justified if punishment avoided

- Stage 2 – offending can be morally justified if the individual receives benefits that outweigh the costs

- Stage 3 – offending can be morally justified if it maintains personal relationships

- Stage 4 – offending can be morally justified if it maintains society or is sanctioned by a social institution.

Although offending can be justified at each stage, in practice research has established that the circumstances in which it usually occurs reflect moral reasoning at the less mature stages (Palmer, 2003; Stams et al., 2006). This moral immaturity in young offenders has been found to extend across a range of values and not just those relating to offending (Palmer and Hollin, 1998).

Cognitive distortions

Beck (1972) first introduced the idea of **cognitive distortions** in his early developments of cognitive behavioural therapy with depressives, and his student Burns (1989) popularized them with his publications on self-help. For some time these distortions have been considered important in increasing the likelihood of engaging in criminal activity. Gibbs (2003, 2010) has investigated the role cognitive distortions play in the relationship between moral reasoning and offending behaviour. Cognitive distortions occur when an individual forms distorted attitudes and thoughts that legitimize the offending behaviour.

Gibbs believes the main distortion used to support offending is egocentric bias. This is characteristic of both immature moral reasoning and the thinking style of offenders (Antonowicz and Ross, 2005). An egocentric bias is a type of cognitive bias in which someone thinks about things solely from their own point of view, which leads to a skewed pattern of thinking. This type of bias makes the individual think that their influence and importance are greater than they actually are. An everyday example would be that people working in a group setting with egocentric bias often believe they contributed more to the group project than they actually did. A particular focus for cognitive distortion has been on sex offenders. Lindsay et al. (2007) developed and used the Questionnaire on Attitudes Consistent with Sexual Offending (QACSO). This has a series of scales that evaluate attitudes to rape, voyeurism, exhibitionism, dating abuse, homosexual assault, child sexual abuse and stalking. The research established that six of the seven scales were valid and reliable indicators of cognitive distortions held by sex offenders (the exception being homosexual assault). Examples of cognitive distortions in this area are related to the perceived sexual nature of children, the distorted view of helping them learn, and how their behaviour signals sexual interest and so forth. When confronted with their criminal activities a key distortion will be denial, a mental process by which offenders reject the consequences of their actions

Key term

Cognitive distortion: an exaggerated or irrational thought process that means that the way a person is thinking about something does not necessarily match up with the reality of what is going on.

and/or blame someone else. According to Salter (1988), denial can take many forms in sex offenders:

- denying that the abuse actually took place

- denying the seriousness (fondled but no sexual contact)

- denying that there is anything wrong with them (for example, they have found God and don't need therapy or help)

- denying responsibility (for example, saying that the child seduced them).

All but the first denial are ways of trying to 'play down' the significance of their criminal activity, which is known as **minimization**. In a sample of paedophiles and rapists, Barbaree (1998) found that a substantial number denied their involvement and approximately 40 per cent went on to minimize the seriousness of the offence or the extent of their culpability. Minimization and denial are almost used interchangeably, and they are commonly used as examples of criminals' cognitive distortions across a spectrum of crimes, not just sex-related ones.

Another cognitive distortion is **hostile attribution bias**. This is where ambiguous events/social interactions are interpreted as hostile. At its basic level, it is a bias the individual uses that infers aggressive intent. This is along the lines of 'he was looking at me in an odd way', interpreting that as hostile and inappropriately reacting aggressively to them and their presence. There is convincing evidence for hostile attribution bias as a cognitive processing distortion. Orobio de Castro et al., (2002) did a meta-analysis of 41 attribution studies, concluding that the bias had a very strong relationship with aggressive behaviour among children and adolescents. More recently, Bailey and Ostrov (2008) demonstrated this relationship held into adulthood.

ACTIVITY 9.8

Although we have been trying to relate cognitive distortions to offending, they often feature in our own life or daily experience. Take some time to reflect on at least one example for each of where you have personally experienced egocentric bias, minimization, and hostile attribution bias.

EXAMPLE EXAM QUESTION

Outline ONE cognitive distortion that could be involved in criminal thinking. (2 marks)

KEY POINTS

- Personality-based explanations based on Freud and Eysenck suggest certain personality types are more likely to be involved with crime.

- Learning and differential association theory provide evidence that criminal behaviour is a learned behaviour as a result of reinforcement and modelling.

- Cognitive explanations focus on moral development and cognitive distortions playing a key role in the likelihood of being involved in criminal activity.

Dealing with offending behaviour

Dealing with offenders has been an issue for society throughout history. In times past, public hangings for major offences or even minor ones by contemporary standards (like animal theft) regularly took place at towns throughout the United Kingdom. Public punishment could also be meted out to local miscreants by having them put in the stocks to be publically humiliated by taunting and throwing rubbish at them.

Fig. 9.15 Stocks

In the Victorian era there were particular concerns about crime as crime levels rose sharply. Offences went up from about 5000 per year in 1800 to about 20,000 per year in 1840. This was linked to the Industrial Revolution – although it created wealth for owners of factories and mines, it brought workers into dense urban environments to live in relative poverty, which led to more crime. One attempt to stop the growth of crime had been through making punishments severe. During the eighteenth century there were about 200 crimes punishable by hanging, with murder and treason at the serious end but right down to pick-pocketing or stealing food at the lower end of the scale. This had started to cause public concern, and by the time Queen Victoria came to the throne in 1837, fewer crimes carried a compulsory death sentence and punishments for minor offences were less severe.

The Victorian era saw new ideas being tried out. They included the building of new jails (prisons) and looking at how these could be used to stop criminals from reoffending. Prison buildings and daily life within them changed dramatically to reflect the beliefs of the time. Prison regimes came to be based on the concepts of separation, silence, hard labour and moral guidance.

During the eighteenth century, the practice of transportation was used as an alternative punishment to hanging. Convicted criminals were transported to the colonies to serve their prison sentences. Most never returned. It had the advantages of removing the criminal from society and being cheaper than keeping them in custody.

The Victorian era played a significant role in encouraging society to review strategies for dealing with crime. Previously, criminals were seen as the lowest form of life in society and had to be severely punished. Towards the end of the era there was some acknowledgement that mental illness and parental upbringing may play a part in many criminals' life choices, and that rehabilitation and punishment need to be more balanced. More contemporary approaches to crime and punishment consider various options, most of which are based on psychological and moral principles.

Aims of custodial sentencing and punishment

Traditional views of punishment could relate it to the way B.F. Skinner introduced it with his learning theory approach. The concept of reinforcement and punishment belongs to the area of learning theory known as operant conditioning. In operant conditioning theory, punishment is the reduction of a behaviour due to the application of an adverse stimulus (*positive* punishment) or removal of a pleasant stimulus (*negative* punishment). Extra chores, or in the bad old days, a 'clip round the ear', are examples of positive punishment, while making a naughty child lose relaxation or play privileges are examples of negative punishment. Removal of all electronic devices (for example, phones/tablets/computers or gaming technology) seems to be the most powerful form of negative punishment available to most parents in today's society, in contrast to being sent to your bedroom where many of these items are often located, which would certainly not be effective!

Fig. 9.16 Negative punishment: removal of all electronic devices

Think what your first instincts would be if you were assaulted in your street or you arrived home to find you had been burgled. You would probably like to do various things to the offenders that are best not repeated here. If we were to take the law into our own hands it would be a recipe for disorder and social breakdown. This is why the criminal justice system exists. In our developed society it is acknowledged that crimes against us as individuals are in fact also against the laws and norms of our society, therefore responsibility for dealing with offenders lies with the state.

At the present time there are four main aims for punishment and custodial sentencing that can be considered: retribution, deterrence, rehabilitation and incapacitation.

Retribution

Link

For more on free will, see pages 84 in Chapter 1, *Issues and debates in psychology*.

The essence of retribution as a theory of punishment is the idea of 'just desserts', in which punishment is inflicted on the offender because it is 'deserved' by the crime which he or she has committed. The offender 'pays for' his or her crime by means of a punishment that should fit the crime. The offender, in suffering the punishment inflicted by the state, makes reparation to society. A secondary aspect of retribution is that by inflicting the punishment, society is demonstrating its disapproval of, or censure, of the crime. In the retributive approach punishment is therefore entirely concerned with the past behaviour of the offender – with the crime that he or she has committed. It acknowledges that the offender has committed the offence of their own free will and therefore had the choice not to.

In modern societies retributive punishment usually takes the form of loss of liberty or resources through imprisonment or fines. The determination of the length of an imprisonment sentence or level of fine for various types of offences is known as the 'tariff'.

There are many problems such an approach faces. For example:

- There is inequality in society, therefore fines have different impacts depending on offenders' socio-economic circumstances.

- Would a particular tariff have the same effect on offenders at different stages of their life cycle?

- How do we decide the seriousness of all types of crime in terms of 'just desserts'?

- Cultural differences in retribution (for example, a first-time car vandalism offence in the UK results in a fine, in Singapore it results in four months in prison and maybe caning and a fine too).

The conclusion is that for retribution to work as a form of punishment it depends on moral arguments about 'just desserts' (does the punishment fit the crime?) and some level of societal agreement about the nature of harm, crime causation, and how it should be dealt with. This is a contentious area, which is why the media have stories that reflect conflict among members of the judicial service, media and the public concerning the appropriate 'just desserts'.

Deterrence

Instead of retribution, which focuses on the crime committed and paying the price, deterrence theory is oriented on the nature of the offender, their future behaviour and what punishment will stop them offending again. This is called individual deterrence.

If the problems facing retribution are considered more related to moral and philosophical issues, then those facing deterrence theory tend to be psychological and sociological. The idea that a particular sentence will deter someone from committing the same crime again may make assumptions about their personality and background. Deterrence theory assumes people are rational and that they calculate that if the gain from the crime is less than the pain of the punishment then they will not repeat the criminal behaviour. However, that assumption about rationality means the theory has some problems:

- Offenders may focus on the chance of getting caught more than the severity of the sentence.

- Crime could be seen as an exciting and challenging activity and that the risk of being caught is the reason for doing it.

- In a subculture like that of professional criminals, actually having a prison sentence is status-enhancing rather than a deterrent.

It could be argued that deterrence works best on the offender who is not associated with a criminal subculture. For example, a middle-class motorist who would fear the implications of a drink-driving ban for their lifestyle, as opposed to the poorest offenders in society who have little to lose from punishment and therefore are least likely to be deterred by a prison sentence or other punishment.

Deterrence can also be aimed at the future behaviour of the rest of the population. This is called 'general deterrence'. This is where

FORENSIC PSYCHOLOGY

judges might hand out sentences that seem disproportionate as an 'exemplary sentence', with the aim being to discourage others. This flies in the face of retribution theory as it seems to inappropriately punish one person unjustly as an example to others.

The problem here is that the justification for general deterrence, like individual deterrence, relies on there actually being consequences in terms of reducing offending. For example, in 1973 a mugger in Birmingham was given a sentence of 20 years. At the time there had been a 'moral panic' about a UK-wide spate of muggings, and the judge decided to 'send a message' to anyone else thinking of engaging in this form of antisocial activity. However, there was no noticeable change in the crime rate following the sentence and researchers concluded that the young people most likely to engage in street theft were also least likely to know about the sentence that had been handed down.

Rehabilitation (or reform)

With increasing societal concerns the objective of punishment has been seen as not simply deterring the offender but attempting to reform the offender's outlook on life to a more positive one so that they will be less likely to offend again.

In some cases this can be done by psychological or psychiatric intervention to address the offender's personality, attitudes and behaviours. In other cases, what is seen as important is education and skills training in order to try to equip the offender with some minimal life skills so that, on coming out of prison, they will not immediately regress to old ways and start offending again.

A problem that arises with rehabilitation strategies is the extent to which they can integrate with retribution and deterrence sentencing. There can be a conflict between what may be seen as 'just desserts' as a deterrence and the requirements for effective rehabilitation and re-education. When prisoners can only be released upon successful completion of the rehabilitation programme there is a danger of indeterminate sentences occurring, especially if there are resource and provision issues. (Examples of rehabilitation programmes [such as anger management] are covered in more detail later in this topic).

Incapacitation (protection of society)

Incapacitation is concerned with the fact that some offenders are dangerous and need to be removed from society to protect the public. In 2009, those serving life sentences, as a proportion of all prisoners, was 9.5 per cent in the US and 19.3 per cent in England and Wales (Griffin and O'Donnell, 2012). This represents a large number of criminals effectively removed from society and incapacitated, because protection of the public has become of increasing concern.

There are problems with incapacitation. Like rehabilitation there can be issues of indeterminate sentences. Does a life sentence mean exactly that? If incapacitation is to work as a strategy it must be based on evidence that the risks of reoffending are very high indeed, and that no amount of rehabilitation will make such individuals no longer dangerous to society and worthy of rejoining it.

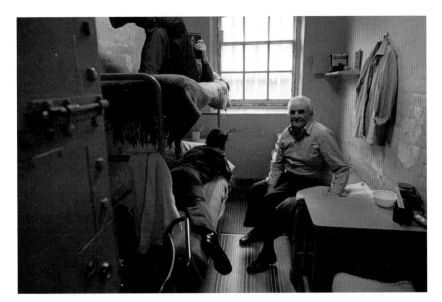

Fig. 9.17 The harsh realities of imprisonment

Psychological effects of custodial sentencing

Once a person enters prison, whether for a short or long sentence, they are essentially being removed from normal society and immersed into a new institutional culture with its own rules and social norms. These can vary from institution to institution but there are some common factors and experiences. Research is rather limited in this area but what is apparent is that the experience of a first-time prisoner is different to a 'repeater'. Liebling and Maruna (2005) report that restlessness, anxiety and sleeplessness tend to occur at the start of an imprisonment term when adjustments have to be made. Common initial reactions to imprisonment are feelings of depression, guilt and anxiety. It has long been established that suicide rates are higher in prison than in normal society, and in the US it has been noted that about half of suicide attempts occur on the first day of confinement.

Studies of long-term prisoners tend to concentrate on prisonization theory (Thomas and Petersen, 1977), which has as its focus the negative effects of socialization in prison, including the process of acceptance and role adaptation. Early studies in this area tended to neglect psychological effects, but in the 1990s there was some interest in longitudinal-designed studies covering behaviour and the cognitive and emotional experience associated with long-term confinement. Zamble (1992), in his seven-year longitudinal study of long-term inmates, found that emotional deprivations were experienced more than physical, except for missing sex. Emotional aspects of support, safety, freedom, and privacy were most missed. Although the number of friends an inmate had did not change, there was a decrease in time spent socializing, mainly as a way of avoiding conflict, and as a result prisoners felt like they lost emotional connection.

A large number of the longitudinal studies found high and increasing levels of mental illness among the prison population. There is also evidence to suggest that middle-class and white-collar criminals are more adversely affected by imprisonment than working-class inmates. Dudeck et al. (2011) reported that 14 per cent of European inmates exhibited high levels of post-traumatic stress disorder symptoms following imprisonment. As many as 50 per cent of their sample were in need of psychological treatment as a result of their imprisonment and a third had contemplated or attempted suicide. One of the problems with any research done in this area is that it is virtually impossible to say whether imprisonment caused this increase in risk or if medical and psychological problems are simply compounded conditions that already existed.

One psychological effect of the 'institutionalization' of prison life is that there is evidence to suggest incidents of aggression can increase. This is believed to be linked to the importation model (Irwin and Cressey, 1964) or deprivation model (Sykes, 1958), both cited in Thomas and Foster's evaluative study (1973). There was evidence of this institutionalization in the infamous prison study conducted by Haney, Banks and Zimbardo (1973), which was called off after six days as there were serious concerns about how the student wardens and prisoners were behaving.

Link

For more on the importation and deprivation models, see pages 414–416 of Chapter 8, *Aggression*. To read about the Zimbardo study, see pages 81–83 of Book 1.

All convicted criminals have to live with the fact they will become victims of 'labelling theory' (Becker, 1974). When they are released they will have to adjust to society treating them as 'ex-cons'. Many crimes will carry potentially very stigmatizing labels that will impact on both the offender and social interactions with them (for example, rape or child abuse). This is illustrated by Sheffield United and Wales footballer Ched Evans (see Fig. 9.18), who was released in 2014 after being sentenced to five years imprisonment for rape. His release raised all sorts of moral debates as to whether he should be allowed to return to his career as a professional footballer – despite having served his punishment, the label 'rapist' endured.

Fig. 9.18 Ched Evans

Effects on families of offenders

One possibly neglected area is not so much the psychological impact on the prisoner but the impact on their families. Travis and Waul (2003) wrote extensively about the effects of incarceration and re-entry on children and family, acknowledging that the vast majority of prisoners have families in the wider community. These effects will in turn impact on prisoners' perceptions of hopelessness, isolation and anxiety.

KEY STUDY: MURRAY AND FARRINGTON (2005)

Impact of parental imprisonment on sons

Background: Prisoners' children appear to suffer profound psychosocial difficulties during their parent's imprisonment. However, no previous study had examined later-life outcomes for prisoners' children compared to children separated from parents for other reasons. This study aimed to examine the hypothesis that parental imprisonment predicts boys' antisocial and delinquent behaviour.

Method: The study used longitudinal data from the Cambridge Study in Delinquent Development (CSDD). The CSDD includes data on 411 inner-London males and their parents. This study compared boys separated by parental imprisonment during the first ten years of their lives with four control groups: boys who did not experience separation, boys separated by hospital or death, boys separated for other reasons (usually disharmony), and boys whose parents were only imprisoned before their birth. Individual, parenting, and family risk factors for delinquency were measured when the boys were aged eight to eleven. Eleven antisocial and delinquent outcomes were assessed between ages 14 and 40.

Results: Separation because of parental imprisonment predicted all antisocial-delinquent outcomes compared to the four control conditions. Separation caused by parental imprisonment was also strongly associated with many other childhood risk factors for delinquency. After controlling for parental convictions and other childhood risk factors, separation caused by parental imprisonment still predicted several antisocial-delinquent outcomes, even up to age 32, compared with other types of separation.

Conclusions: Prisoners' children are a highly vulnerable group with multiple risk factors for adverse outcomes. Parental imprisonment appears to affect children over and above separation experiences and their associated risks. Further research on possible moderating and mediating factors, such as stigma, reduction in family income and reduced quality of care, is required to identify the mechanisms by which parental imprisonment affects children.

THINKING SCIENTIFICALLY: MURRAY AND FARRINGTON (2005)

This was a well-designed study in terms of studying children over an extended period. The control groups are a strength and the study used a range of established behavioural measures. Limitations were the lack of reported detail on finer points relating to family history (marriage, divorce, age/crime background of parents) and also ethnocentric factors. The sample was from inner London, an area of the UK that may have its own subcultural factors to take into account. The participants would also know they were being studied so demand characteristics could play a part: these could be from either the participants themselves or, even more likely, parental influences.

Recidivism

Given the role custodial sentencing plays in the criminal justice system, the most important psychological effect that should be investigated and evaluated is whether it helps to change and rehabilitate the offender's attitude and behaviour. An obvious measure of this would be the likelihood of reoffending after release, called **recidivism**.

The challenge faced by the government in tackling recidivism is continually being underlined by figures that reveal little change over the last ten years, other than a slight rise in the number of criminals returning to crime.

According to recent Ministry of Justice figures (2012), more than one in four criminals reoffend within a year of being released from jail, convicted or cautioned, committing nearly 500,000 offences between them. This equates to a reoffending rate of 26.8 per cent, up from 26.3 per cent in the previous annual set of figures. This of course is

> **Key term**
>
> **Recidivism:** the act of a person repeating an undesirable behaviour after he/she has either experienced negative consequences of that behaviour or been treated/ rehabilitated for it.

almost certainly an underestimate of the true level of recidivism as others will have reoffended and not been caught and recorded.

Interestingly, over 50 per cent of these repeat offences were committed by criminals with 11 or more previous offences, and 10 per cent of them were committed by nearly 11,000 criminals who had previously been jailed at least 11 times. There has been slight drop in first-time offenders reoffending.

There was also a notable rise in the proportion of criminals who reoffend being handed prison sentences of less than 12 months, which increased from 56.6 per cent to 57.8 per cent.

The main feature that comes out of the data is that a significant proportion of offenders are enmeshed in a 'circle of crime', and despite interventions, are reoffending soon after their release. The life cycle of offending behaviour has become a reinforced role that they continue to act out due to circumstance, peer patterns or the nature of their personality. The relationship to poverty is a recurring theme for many as well.

Family are an important part of the re-entry process for a released prisoner. Families provide an important link to life in the community while inmates are in prison, and offer a source of stability, support and encouragement during the challenging transition from prison to the home environment. Several studies have demonstrated that continued contact with families during and immediately after release reduces recidivism and fosters reintegration into the community (Naser and La Vigne, 2006). This is especially important during the critical period immediately following release in terms of offering emotional support and a place to stay.

Rehabilitation programmes

There are a vast variety of approaches to rehabilitation and in this section we will focus on the broad field of behavioural strategies, and more specifically on anger management and the more recent area of restorative justice.

Behaviour modification in custody

Behaviour modification (also known as behavioural therapy) has quite a long history in psychology, much of it developed in psychiatric institutions before the advent of more community care-related practices. The techniques are based on learning theory, especially the concepts relating to operant conditioning. Ayllon and Azrin (1968) worked extensively to develop programmes that would build up desirable behaviour – to increase the occurrence of desirable behaviours and decrease the occurrence of other less desired ones.

The idea is based on the notion that if criminal behaviour is learned in the same way as any other behaviour (through Skinner's principles of reinforcement and punishment), these inappropriate behaviours can be 'unlearned' in the same way.

Token economies are one such example that has been used historically both to manage and change behaviour in institutions. Essentially, if you behave well and produce the desired behaviours you will be reinforced by the use of some sort of 'token' (positive reinforcement) you can save up and exchange for certain privileges or primary reinforcements (for example, cigarettes or sweets). Within a prison context, desired behaviours might be, for example, rule compliance, completing chores and behaving in a socially acceptable way. This selective reinforcement encourages desirable behaviours to be learned and undesirable ones to be extinguished. Non-compliance can lead to privileges (such as exercise/social time) being removed in the form of negative reinforcement.

In terms of contemporary developments there are a large number of behaviour modification programmes now used to help offenders address aspects of their offending lifestyle. Treatments aimed at rehabilitating offenders are part of a rapidly developing and changing field, with a plethora of individual and group-based programmes available and being developed (see Table 9.5). As can be seen, they each have their own aims and potential client group. The aims can focus on specific behaviours (like drug abuse or violence), emotions (such as anger) or social skills (like relationships) and in some cases integrate all or a combination of these. Many of them are based on cognitive or learning theory approaches. They are designed to address the way issues are thought about and the way in which behaviour manifests itself.

Aggression Replacement Training (ART)	A group work programme for people convicted of violent offences or who have problems controlling their temper. It challenges offenders to accept responsibility for their behaviour.
Addressing Substance Related Offending (ASRO)	A drug and alcohol cognitive behavioural intervention designed to assist offenders in addressing drug- and alcohol-related offending and to reduce or stop substance misuse.
Building Skills for Recovery (BSR)	A psychosocial programme that is delivered in a group setting or on a one-to-one basis. It aims to reduce offending behaviour and problematic substance misuse, with an eventual goal of recovery.
Controlling Anger and Learning to Manage it (CALM)	An emotion-management programme designed for those whose offending behaviour is precipitated by intense emotions. The goals are to assist offenders in understanding the factors that trigger their anger and aggression and learn skills to manage their emotions.
Choices, Actions, Relationships and Emotions (CARE)	This is a course for female prisoners whose offending is related to difficulties with emotion control. The course aims to help participants identify and label emotions and develop skills for managing emotion.
Community Domestic Violence Programme (CDVP)	A domestic violence programme aimed at reducing the risk of violent crime and abusive behaviour towards women in relationships by helping male perpetrators change their attitudes and behaviour.
Drink-Impaired Drivers Programme (DID)	DID challenges attitudes and behaviour, aiming to reduce drink-driving.
Offender Substance Abuse Programme (OSAP)	This programme addresses drugs or alcohol misuse, using cognitive methods to change attitudes and behaviour to prevent relapse and reduce offending.
The Women's Programme	This is a cognitive and motivational programme specifically designed for women who have committed acquisitive offences (e.g. shoplifting) and are at risk of reconviction for non-violent crimes.
Thinking Skills Programme (TSP)	A cognitive skills programme that addresses the way offenders think and the behaviour associated with offending.

Table 9.5 Examples of offender behaviour programmes

The UK Prison Service has developed its own set of accredited programmes, which are a series of activities aimed at working with offenders to reduce reoffending. Accreditation shows these programmes are evidence-based and congruent with the 'What Works' literature (a 1990s government-supported initiative to improve and present consistent effective practice across the prison and rehabilitation sector). Programmes vary in length, complexity and mode of delivery, and are targeted according to risk and need.

In order to achieve accreditation, each programme will have demonstrated that it is based on sound evidence as to which techniques and interventions help offenders to change and which assessment tools are reliable in targeting the appropriate offenders for each intervention. For every intervention there is also a commitment to rigorous monitoring of the quality of programme delivery and an evaluation of the impact made by the programme on future reoffending.

These programmes are also subject to research scrutiny in terms of value and effectiveness. That said, the most evaluative work that appears to have been done to date has been on sex offender programmes, some of which have a long history and are high profile. However, there are increasing numbers of other evaluation studies and research papers being published. Blud et al. (2003) did a large-scale evaluation of the impact of two programmes on over 4000 UK prisoners and found significant positive short-term effects.

There is growing international evidence that the type of cognitive behavioural techniques that these accredited programmes apply are the most effective in reducing offending behaviour. However, in evaluation it has to be noted that it is rare and difficult to undertake long-term studies into their effectiveness.

Exam hint

This is worth four marks, so you need to briefly describe what behaviour modification is with the key details only. You then need briefly to name and describe one behaviour modification application, such as token economy or any listed in Table 9.5.

EXAMPLE EXAM QUESTION

Describe what is meant by behaviour modification and give ONE example of an intervention that uses it with offending behaviour. (4 marks)

Anger management

A specific area that raises many challenges in the offender population is the strong emotion of anger. For some this can be the cause or a contributing factor in their offending behaviour (for example, domestic assaults, violence, rioting) and for others it becomes an issue that arises during imprisonment. Among the many programmes aimed at prisoners are some focusing on the nature of anger and how to manage this (for example, CALM in Table 9.5).

These approaches usually involve some adaptation of cognitive behavioural intervention, usually based on Albert Ellis's (1991) ABCD model, as in Fig 9.19. Ellis developed RET (rationale emotive therapy), which is widely used in various clinical and therapeutic contexts. The basis of the model is that a stimulus event (A) creates beliefs (B) that have

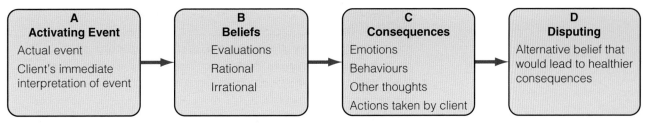

Fig. 9.19 The ABCD model of anger

consequences (C). To deal with them effectively we need to 'dispute' (D) with our beliefs and come up with alternative healthier (non-aggressive/offending) responses. There is a 'worked' example in Fig. 9.20.

A
Activating event

I am waiting at a very busy bus stop on a Friday evening on the way home from work, tired after another busy week. As the bus approaches, several people push in front of me and start to board. In this situation, I will almost certainly get frustrated and start to feel angry. According to Ellis, I will engage in 'self-talk', which could be along the lines of 'How dare they?', 'Bunch of inconsiderate jerks', 'Should I swear and shout at them?'

⬇

B
Beliefs

The basis of Ellis's model is that under these circumstances many of my beliefs will appear in irrational self-talk saying things like, 'They obviously don't care about anyone but themselves – they must be so selfish', ' They should queue like everyone else', 'People should be more considerate of my feelings', ' They are probably not British'. Essentially, I expect everyone to behave like me and comply with my social expectations of the situation.

⬇

C
Consequences

As I am now angry, I will have all the internal physiological reactions associated with that (increased heart rate, etc.) and will be agitated. I will most likely internalize this unhealthy anger or I will act out and say something. Under these circumstances I am personally extremely unlikely to try to throw several people off a bus or start a fight, but others might! For those with anger management issues, this is the 'explosive' stage and what follows are the negative consequences of the post-explosion phase.

⬇

D
Disputes

It is often better to change your outlook by disputing your beliefs and creating an internal self-talk that is more rational and adaptive. Ellis' approach consists of identifying irrational beliefs and disputing them with more rational or realistic views. I have clearly got angry, and may think that I was not treated fairly and that it is not right, as I expect to be treated fairly. Rather than continue with these beliefs, I must try to dispute them. From an anger management perspective, it is better in this example to accept the unfairness and lack of interpersonal norms that are a feature of living in a busy urban society. Thus, to dispute this belief, it is helpful to tell myself, 'I can't be expected to be treated fairly by everyone.'

I could also say to myself, 'I have no power over things I cannot control', or 'I have to accept what I cannot change'. These are examples of ways to dispute beliefs, which are used in other cognitive behavioural programmes, such as Alcoholics Anonymous. By trying to reframe our beliefs we change our perceptions and response to the event. In simple terms we are putting it into a more realistic perspective.

Fig. 9.20 An example of ABCD model in practice

ACTIVITY 9.9

Try to recall the last time you felt angry, then use the ABCD model to analyse your response. What caused it? What did you think? How did you react and feel afterwards? Then use the 'dispute' strategy to think how you could have engaged in more neutral/positive self-talk.

Then try to put it into practice next time you get angry. This can even work when you get cross in an exam when the paper doesn't quite have what you were expecting. If you get angry and blame the exam setter, you will probably underperform. Difficult as it is, try to reframe and think about what you can do, not what you can't!

Restorative justice programmes

Key term

Restorative justice: an approach to justice that focuses on the needs of the victims and the offenders, as well as the involved community, instead of satisfying abstract legal principles or punishing the offender. Victims take an active role in the process, while offenders are encouraged to take responsibility for their actions.

With the increasing costs and concerns about the effectiveness of custodial sentencing and other related strategies there has been a countermovement over recent years towards redefining punishment away from hurting the offender (perpetuating the 'cycle of harm') to redressing the offence by compensating the victim. Programmes taking this stance are called **restorative justice programmes**. De Haan and Loader (2002) discuss this in terms of redistributive justice and a means of reconnecting offenders and their victims in a way that actively seeks to redress the balance of harm. In part it reflects more recognition of the neglected rights and needs of the victim too. Look how often in the news and on television we hear of or see victims' families attending the public galleries in court cases as their only way of trying to grasp an understanding of why and how the crime happened. This is also perhaps their only opportunity to have some sort of face-to-face contact with the offender and it may be an important part in their own victim rehabilitation.

In its most direct form restorative justice involves the offender and victim meeting in the presence of other professionals and attempting a reconciliation, with the offender making reparations to the victim by trying to explain themselves. The explanation may be enough in itself, or depending on the crime, offenders can pay the victim back directly or in some other way, such as through work or agreed community tasks. In these negotiations the offender is made aware of the impact their offending had on the victim and quite likely their family too. A study by Sherman et al. (2005) evaluated four such restorative justice face-to-face programmes for a range of crimes in both Australia and the UK and found that they were successful in victims feeling less angry/revengeful, less self-blaming and more forgiving. These programmes therefore appear to work as a policy for reducing harm to victims, and although it is believed that they might help reduce recidivism, this has still to be determined by substantive research rather than individual samples.

There were a number of changes introduced in the Criminal Justice Act 2003 to improve the community sentencing regime and produce a more responsive and flexible approach to sentencing. Community punishment orders focus on offenders having to undertake unpaid work for the community, usually in areas where they have offended, and the orders may contain special provisions for drug and alcohol treatment, anger management classes, curfews and exclusions. They are usually all under the supervision of probation or criminal justice social workers. The idea is that the offenders are redressing their crimes by giving something back to the community as well as redefining life skills for themselves.

EXAMPLE EXAM QUESTION

Discuss two ways of dealing with offending behaviour. (16 marks)

KEY POINTS

- The aims of custodial sentencing are varied and can cover retribution, deterrence, rehabilitation and incapacitation.
- The psychological effects of custodial sentencing impact on emotions, behaviour, identity and family.
- Recidivism rates are high and raise concerns regarding current sentencing practice.
- Developments in treatment programmes based on behavioural modification, anger management and restorative justice can be effective in the rehabilitation process.

ACTIVITY 9.10

Now that we have covered all these areas of forensic psychology, it would be worthwhile reflecting on your own position regarding some key contentious questions in this area. You can use material from the chapter to support your argument or you may like to engage in additional reading for your own interest. The area of crime and police work is a feature in our daily newspapers and other forms of media, so keeping up to date with current affairs will also help inform your own views on such issues.
Some key questions to explore:
- Is profiling really scientific and does it work?
- Are criminals born or made?
- What purpose does punishment really fulfil for the criminal and for society?
- Is inequality the motivation for most crime?
Can you think of any other key questions?

Exam hint

The first point to note is only two are required, so you have to make your choices from custodial sentencing, behaviour modification, anger management or restorative justice. The second aspect is that it is a discussion question, so although some description is needed, evaluative and comparison points will be important for higher band marks. This should help to influence your choice. Remember to set your two ways of dealing with offending behaviour in the context of the aims of punishment and sentencing (retribution, deterrence, rehabilitation, incapacitation).

PRACTICAL ACTIVITY

This practical involves the construction and analysis of a survey questionnaire. Your study can explore social attitudes to aspects of crime and punishment. You could use Likert scales to collect quantitative data and/or open questions to collect qualitative data to explore areas of your choice such as:

- What is a crime?
- Which crimes are most serious?
- What is the level of fear of crime?
- What views do people have about the causes of crime?
- What views do people have about justice and punishment?

In addition, you might want to collect some relevant demographic data (such as gender, age, crime victim).

You will need to carefully consider the sampling method and sample size you are going to use and ensure ethical procedures are followed. This means your brief should cover informed consent, anonymity, and the right to withdraw at any time. You will also need a debriefing. You must ensure that you keep data secure and destroy questionnaires once the data have been analysed. Before starting your survey, you should ensure that your questionnaire and accompanying briefings have 'ethical approval' from your teacher.

To analyse the data you could look at answers to specific questions or look at the overall data. For quantitative questions, overall scores could be derived, and by making use of the demographic data simple analyses could be done for two different 'groups'. Qualitative data could be reviewed using content analysis for any recurring themes.

Finally, after you have completed your research you should consider the strengths and limitations of your study and how it could be improved. Did it stimulate other ideas for more research and link with material in this chapter?

1. Briefly outline what is meant by an offender survey. **(2 marks)**

2. Describe differential association theory as a psychological explanation of offending behaviour. **(4 marks)**

3. Read the item below and answer the question that follows.

> The vast majority of cases that come to court involve repeat offenders who are a major cost to our society.

   Referring to the above outline, what is meant by recidivism. **(2 marks)**

4. Describe biological explanations of offending behaviour. **(16 marks)**

Exam focus

Read through the following example exam question, example student answers, and examiner comments. Then, have a go at answering the question yourself!

EXAMPLE EXAM QUESTION

Discuss TWO psychological explanations of offending behaviour.
(16 marks)

Maddie's answer

Examiner comment: Maddie has made a decision to go for a broad interpretation of psychological explanation, which is acceptable as long as it is clear at the outset that this approach is being taken.

Psychologists for many years have been expected to help explain why some people offend and others do not. There are various psychological explanations of offending behaviour and in this essay the focus will be on discussing broad-based personality and learning theory explanations.

Examiner comment: There's always a danger with such a big theory to go into long descriptive detail about features that are not really relevant to offending. This response has not done that and has provided at least one supporting study.

The two main theories that have offered a personality-based explanation are those offered by Freud and Eysenck. In Freud's theory, the most relevant aspect is how the id, ego and superego work together. The id is the unconscious component, driven by the 'pleasure principle', the sole goal of which is to gain pleasure and satisfaction regardless of real-world demands (ego). The superego is the conscience and plays a key role in keeping our behaviour at a socially acceptable level. Our superego is developed as result of our upbringing, and parents and school play a significant part. A weak superego will result in a greater likelihood of offending. The Bowlby 1949 study of teenage thieves demonstrated that maternal deprivation was a significant feature in their lives. This therefore could be used to support the idea that in the absence of a key parent conscience development is harmed and the id has free rein.

Examiner comment: This is rather brief but the focus is fine. It would have been good to have had another study cited, and mention of psychoticism.

Eysenck felt that there were two key dimensions to personality, these being neuroticism (N) and extroversion (E). Eysenck's own research based on comparing prisoners and a general population sample found that there were more neurotic extrovert types in prison compared to other types.

Examiner comment: Again, it would be easy to describe all the theory. This response has focused on the basics that are relevant.

Learning theory explanations are based on classical and operant conditioning, and claims that offending behaviour is a learned behaviour just like any other. Sutherland's differential association theory suggests that if we are exposed to criminal behaviour we will model the behaviours and values of those around us by simple association. Burgess and Akers (1966) added the idea of differential reinforcement, where deviant behaviours are rewarded and thus are more likely to be repeated.

The problem with these two types of explanation is that although they explain why some people enter crime, there are always exceptions. The theories tend to offer a group perspective and alternative views might focus more on the individual. The rational choice and cognitive theories do this, and there is considerable evidence that biological factors may play an important role in explaining criminal activity too.

Examiner comment: This flags that evaluation is being introduced, and although the paragraph offers alternative approaches, it could be clearer and better developed.

Examiner comment: This response just about makes the bottom of level 3, getting around 9 out of 16 marks. Knowledge of two broad types is sound. It is an ambitious effort trying to have more breadth rather than depth. The response is mainly descriptive and it is only at the end some general evaluation is included. There could have been more points made in relation to the explanations offered, hence it only just scrapes into this band. The answer is mostly clear and organized. Specialist terminology is mostly used effectively. An alternative approach would have been to have focused on two specific explanations (e.g. Freud and Eysenck) and covered them in more detail and depth.

Chapter 10: Addiction

Introduction

Having an addiction can be a burden on the entirety of a person's life. Not only can it threaten the person's own health (physical or psychological), but it can also impact on the people around the addict. In this chapter we explore how addiction is defined, explained and treated, and we consider two addictions in some detail. The chapter starts with an attempt to define addiction but, as we will see, it is not an easy task. Where, for example, is the boundary between a habit and an addiction? We then look at the risks in becoming an addict and consider both biological (genetic) risks and psychological risks such as peers, personality and the media. The two main addictions that the chapter explores in some detail are nicotine addiction and gambling addiction. In each case we explore explanations for the initiation, maintenance and relapse of these addictions and we do this from biological, learning theory and cognitive perspectives. The penultimate topic looks at some of the forms of treatment that are available to the addict, from drug therapies to behavioural therapies to CBT. Finally, we look at some of the models that have been created to explain behaviour, such as the theory of planned behaviour, and the Stages of Change model.

What is covered in Addiction?

ADDICTION

Descriptions of addiction

You might be surprised to know that the earliest identified alcoholic drink dates from around 7000 BCE. While we cannot be sure, it is probable that this period in history also saw the first alcoholic. Yet alcoholism was not officially declared a disease until 1956. Similarly, the use of the opium poppy and of cannabis can both be traced back to 4000 BCE. It would seem, therefore, that the concept of **addiction** is nothing new, and you might think that we would have a good definition of what it is by now. You would be wrong. Addiction might loosely be defined as the compulsion to indulge in a behaviour. Many common definitions include concepts like needs and urges and very often refer to a lack of control. Definitions by experts, however, tend to emphasize the compulsive aspect along with the idea of a physical dependence. They too, though, also highlight the lack of control aspect of addiction (Walters and Gilbert, 2000). If we look at official definitions we discover that the World Health Organization does not even use the term addiction. Instead it refers only to **dependence**. Also, the DSM classification (the main clinical diagnostic manual) has only recently been expanded, in DSM-5 (2013), to include addictions other than those involving substance misuse. Given this lack of agreement on a definition, perhaps a good place to start is by defining some of the key concepts used in addiction research.

Dependence

According to the online Oxford Dictionary, dependence is defined as:

the state of relying on or being controlled by someone or something else

This definition clearly identifies control as a key element. The source of that control comes in the form of a need rather than merely a desire (such as a need for another cigarette, another drink or another flutter on the horses). It is when we consider what we mean by need that the concept of dependence becomes interesting. Suppose you are sitting watching television and you decide that you need a cup of tea. Suppose, also, that you find the kettle to be broken so you cannot have that cup of tea. You are likely to become a little frustrated by this situation. Do you imagine that your frustration would be a physical one (because you physically need a cup of tea rather than any other kind of drink) or a psychological one (because you want tea and do not want any other kind of drink)? In other words, is it your body that is craving tea or is it your mind? If we now switch from tea to nicotine, the question becomes a little trickier to answer. If you are a smoker and are denied a cigarette, is your craving a physical one or a psychological one? It is likely that the answer is a mixture of both. If this is the case, then we might want to know how much of the need is due to **physical dependence** and how much is due to **psychological dependence**. In order to be able to do this, we can try to characterize the separate signs that would indicate a difference between the two forms of dependence.

Physical dependence

As the name suggests, physical dependence is about the bodily need for addictive activity. Hence, we might expect to see some signs of physical distress if the person is denied the ability to indulge in the activity. These signs might take the form of changes in heart rate and blood pressure, sweating, or even the emergence of tremors. For example, in the case of nicotine dependence, the physical signs that might occur if the person stops smoking might be nausea, decreased heart rate and an increased appetite. A similar set of physical signs are seen with withdrawal from all types of addictive behaviour, even those that do not involve taking a physical substance.

Psychological dependence

If you are a smoker and you are unable to smoke (perhaps you are on a long-haul flight of nine hours' duration) then it is likely that as time goes on you think more and more about wanting a cigarette. In addition to the physical symptoms described above, it is likely that you will start to feel anxious, become irritable and feel sad or depressed. These are the signs of psychological dependence and they go beyond the physical need for nicotine. As with physical dependence, these symptoms also occur with addictive behaviours that do not involve a physical substance.

Tolerance

Whenever we engage in an activity that we find enjoyable, we have a natural desire to carry out that activity again. However, we may find that when we do so for a second time, the experience is not quite as good as it was the first time. We are then faced with a choice: do we not bother engaging with this activity again (it was good to do it just the once) or do we seek ways to make the experience as good as it was? If we choose the latter, we may find that we need to engage in the activity more intensely in order to repeat the original experience. This need to do more in order to get the same effect is called **tolerance**.

While tolerance does not apply to every activity, there are a surprisingly large number of things for which it is true. Many of the examples often used to explain tolerance are taken from interactions with drugs. We can usefully ask whether tolerance occurs to other kinds of behaviours. Can tolerance develop, for example, to gambling behaviour? The answer would appear to be yes, as many gamblers report that not only does their frequency of betting increase over time but that the amount of money they bet with also increases, sometimes to the point at which they accrue massive debts. However, not all addictive behaviours will display tolerance. For example, smokers may increase the number of cigarettes they smoke in the early days (perhaps before they actually become addicted), but once they have reached a satisfying level (for example, 20 cigarettes per day) they will plateau in their behaviour. So here tolerance does not seem to play a part. It seems, therefore, that tolerance might well be a key feature of addiction, although it is not a defining one.

> **Key term**
>
> **Tolerance**: the decrease in effect that occurs over time for same input (e.g. a single cigarette). Where it occurs, it means that the addict must increase their dose for the same level of satisfaction.

ADDICTION

Tolerance versus obsession

It is easy to confuse tolerance with habit and obsession as they both lead to an increase in a particular activity. In addition, these words, along with the term addiction, are used differently in everyday language to the way in which we might use them academically. Being obsessed by something (in an academic/clinical sense) requires that there is a physical reaction if the person is prevented from engaging in that activity. Having an obsession, therefore, compels the person to engage in an activity again and again. How might this be different to having an addiction? Perhaps one of the defining features of an addiction is tolerance. Tolerance dictates not only that the frequency of the activity will be high, but that the level of engagement will increase over time. For example, a person could be obsessed about checking that they have turned the gas off when leaving the house (clinically, this might prevent them leaving the house) but they cannot gain tolerance to this as they cannot check that they have turned the gas off any more rigorously than they did before. Compare that with, say, taking cocaine. Here, the experience with repeated use can only be matched by taking more cocaine than before.

EXAMPLE EXAM QUESTION

Define what is meant by the term tolerance. (4 marks)

Withdrawal

You have probably heard smokers declare that they could give up if they wanted to. The reality, though, is that it is not that simple. Trying to give up something you are addicted to invariably produces unpleasant feelings and these are what we refer to as **withdrawal symptoms**. The most usual form of withdrawal experienced is physical withdrawal from a behaviour and it is usually associated with substance addiction. For example, there are physical effects of stopping smoking, such as increased threat-induced anxiety (Hogle et al., 2010 – see the *Key study*) at the behavioural level and an effect on acetylcholine neurotransmitter receptors (called nicotinic receptors) that had themselves been altered by the process of smoking (Antolin-Fontes et al., 2015) at the physiological level.

KEY STUDY: HOGLE ET AL. (2010)

Previous research had indicated that drug addiction leads to changes in the way that the brain responds to stress. However, all of this research had been conducted on animals, so Hogle et al. investigated whether or not the effect is also seen in humans. Instead of measuring activity in the brain directly, they measured the startle response when a small shock was applied.

There were 117 participants who took part and half of them (58) were asked to refrain from smoking for 24 hours (their compliance was checked by measuring the carbon monoxide in their exhaled air). Experiment 1 involved unpredictable shock, whereby participants viewed successive trials of a square being shown that was one of two different colours. During these presentations 12 shocks were delivered randomly. Experiment 2 involved predictable shock, and consisted of the same set-up but the shocks only occurred when one colour was presented and the participants knew which colour this was. In order to measure the effect that the shocks were having, the **startle response** was elicited during the shock session by presenting white noise (like the static on a radio) trials. Each white noise burst acted as a surprise event and caused the person to blink as a natural response. The response that was measured (the DV) was this eye-blink movement using equipment similar to that shown in Fig. 10.1. For control participants only the white noise trials were presented and they received no shocks. The size of the eye blink was used to indicate the level of the startle response.

The results showed that nicotine withdrawal increased the startle response for unpredictable shock (compared to the no-shock controls) but showed no difference for predictable shock. The researchers concluded that when a smoker refrains from nicotine they are more likely to interpret unpredictable scenarios as stressful and that this will increase the chances of a relapse (if quitting) or the development of an addiction (if relatively new to smoking).

Fig. 10.1 The apparatus required to measure the startle response (here, the electrodes are being used to measuring facial muscles but in stress research they are placed close to the eye).

THINKING SCIENTIFICALLY: USING MODELS TO INFER MECHANISMS

The Hogle et al. (2010) research refers to the fact that animals, rather than humans, are typically used in sensitive areas of research. After all, it would be unethical to ask non-smokers to start smoking so that you could obtain a truly random sample. As a consequence, animals are often used to model the behaviour. Apart from the ethics of animal research, discussed elsewhere in the book, we cannot be sure that humans would behave in the same way.

Another problem is that Hogle et al. were interested in changes in the brain. Again, modelling proved to be useful. They were able to use the startle response as an indicator of changes that would be taking place in the brain without having to implant electrodes or use intrusive techniques such as imaging.

Addiction

Link

For more on the ethics of animal research, see Chapter 1, *Issues and debates in psychology*, page 122.

Key term

Salience: the importance of something to that particular person. What is salient to one person is not necessarily salient to another person.

Now that we have considered the main concepts used in describing addiction, are we better able to provide a definition of the term? Unfortunately, the answer is no. We can point to some characteristic features that typify an addict but nothing that specifically defines one. An addict is likely to have a biological dependence on the focus of the addiction, will suffer withdrawal symptoms if the activity is withheld and may have built up a tolerance that gradually requires more of the behaviour to reach a level of satisfaction (referred to as satiation). One thing, though, that we have not yet discussed is the way in which the addictive behaviour interferes with everyday life. Perhaps the key quality of an addiction is that the addictive behaviour takes a higher level of importance than anything else in the person's life. In other words, addictive behaviours have **salience**. This salience can lead to the addict performing the behaviour even though they know it is harmful to themselves and/or those around them. The addicted gambler cannot stop, even though the rising debt will mean their family will go without certain things. Initially this might be luxuries, but addictive gambling can lead to there not being enough money to buy food and, ultimately, to a breakdown of the family. For the alcoholic, neither the thought of the physical harm to their body or the changes that can occur in the social environment (losing a job, losing a family, becoming aggressive, etc.) are enough to allow the person to quit.

Some researchers have tried to define the most important aspects of addiction. Griffiths (1996) characterizes an addictive behaviour as having six elements (see Table 10.1). Walters (1999) has suggested the four Ps:

- progression – to a higher tolerance and a greater risk of withdrawal
- preoccupation – cannot stop thinking about the behaviour
- perceived – a loss of control over the behaviour
- persistence – continuing to indulge in the behaviour despite the negative consequences.

Feature	Explanation
Salience	The behaviour is the most important thing in your life
Mood modification	The activity provides an excitement (often referred to as a 'buzz')
Tolerance	The need to increase the amount of the behaviour to get the same size of effect
Withdrawal symptoms	The negative feelings that arise when the person is prevented from undertaking the behaviour
Conflict	When problems arise between you and those around you as a direct result of your engagement in the behaviour
Relapse	The return to the behaviour when you have attempted to give it up

Table 10.1 Characteristics of addictive behaviour as characterized by Griffiths (1996)

Any useful definition of addiction is going to have to go beyond drug addiction and will also have to embrace new forms of addiction such as online gambling, online gaming and online sex addictions. Furthermore, as with modern issues of drug addiction, these new addictions are more easily accessible to children and adolescents than was the case in the 1950s when many of the theories around addiction were beginning to emerge. Kuss and Griffiths (2011) have recently reviewed the literature on online gaming addiction as this poses a particular addiction threat to the well-being of children and young adolescents. Having reviewed the 30 empirical research papers published since 2000, they concluded that online gaming addiction can be classified as a true behavioural addiction that has many similarities with online gambling.

KEY STUDY: KUSS AND GRIFFITHS (2011)

The researchers investigated online gaming addiction in children and adolescents. They were interested in this because it represented a test of some of the beliefs about addiction. One was that addictions often start around this time of a person's life and another was that behavioural addictions are true addictions rather than disorders of impulse control. They decided to review the literature published between 2000 and 2011, and found 30 articles that met all of their criteria, including participants aged between 8 and 18 and some assessment of online gaming addiction.

Kuss and Griffiths discovered that there were some differences in the way the gaming addiction was being measured (some based on gambling addiction criteria and some on substance abuse criteria). They also found that online gaming showed tolerance and other characteristics that make it appear more like substance abuse than like a gambling addiction.

The researchers concluded that online gaming addiction is becoming more prevalent due to the increased accessibility of online gaming platforms and the success of complex online games, such as *World of Warcraft*.

THINKING SCIENTIFICALLY: THE VALUE OF A LITERATURE REVIEW

It can sometimes be hard to gain an overview of a field of research from reading just one or two pieces of research. This might be because there are different ways in which studies have been conducted (for example, different methodologies used or different measures taken), or because the research spans a long period of time in which different ideas have been popular, or even because there are too many variations within a single field (for instance, the number of different kinds of memory). For the area of online gaming being explored by Kuss and Griffiths, a number of these were the case. There was no agreed-upon definition of how online gaming addiction might be measured, so studies had adopted different scales. While addiction research has a long history, online gaming is a new phenomenon so in the beginning nobody really knew how to approach it, leading to lots of different opinions. Finally, the area of interest for these authors was the effect of online gaming on children and young adolescents, so not all of the addiction research ideas would be relevant.

The literature review was able to concentrate on a few key questions, such as how online gaming was defined, whether addictive online gaming more closely resembled pathological gambling or pathological substance misuse, and the value of parental reports. They were able to conclude that the criteria for pathological gambling fitted quite well with online gaming addiction but that refinements to the criteria were needed.

Our inability to properly define addiction is not going to deter us from looking at the risks to becoming an addict, to explore two addictions in detail (nicotine and gambling) or to look at ways in which addiction might be reduced. Let us start by looking at who is the most likely to be vulnerable to developing an addictive behaviour.

ACTIVITY 10.1

Compare the suggestions by Griffiths (1996) and Walters (1999) in terms of how well they characterize the main features of addiction. Are there any addictions you can think of that do not fit with these accounts?

Exam hint

This question requires that you understand which things are the essential components of an addiction. One way to answer it would be to refer to the DSM-5 criteria. However, you could simply refer to three or four of the main ones. In either case, the terms dependence, tolerance and withdrawal should be considered in your answer.

EXAMPLE EXAM QUESTION

Describe the key features of addiction. (6 marks)

KEY POINTS

- It is difficult to define exactly what is meant by addiction.
- Addiction is a clinical condition referred to in DSM-5, though the WHO refers to it as dependence.
- There are two types of dependence (physiological and psychological) that act independently of each other.
- Tolerance is the gradual need to increase the amount of the addictive behaviour for the same size of effect.
- When a person tries to quit their addiction they will suffer withdrawal symptoms.
- There have been attempts to define addiction by the use of key characteristics.

Risk factors in addiction

From our description of addiction above it is clear that having an addiction is generally a bad thing. However, millions of people smoke cigarettes and/or gamble in some way (for example, do the lottery on a regular basis), so we might expect to find that the risk of becoming an addict was more a consequence of social and environmental factors than biological ones. Could it really be that the entire human race is genetically programmed to be at risk of becoming an addict? Or are the chances of becoming an addict tied in to the pressures of life such as peers, stress or the way in which our personality develops? To discover whether there is a case for saying that humans become addicts because they are humans, we will first examine if there are **genetic risk factors** associated with addiction, with specific reference to nicotine and gambling addictions.

ACTIVITY 10.2

Before reading any further, list as many things as you can think of that might put a person at risk from engaging in an addictive behaviour. When reading through this topic, tick off those you identified and consider whether those on your list that are not included here are factors that should be included or might not really be risk factors at all.

Genetic markers for addiction

Clearly a key question regarding genetic vulnerability is, can you inherit an addiction from your parents? There is a lot of evidence to suggest that addictive qualities can be inherited but, as we shall see, there is no single addiction gene.

A number of family, adoption and twin studies have been carried out on a variety of forms of addiction and they all seem to conclude that there is a strong case for a genetic component to addictive behaviours. **Family studies** point to the fact that first-degree relatives of addicts are at greater risk of addiction (Merikangas et al., 1998). Similarly, **adoption studies** have found greater links among biologically related individuals (Uhl et al., 1995) and **twin studies** have found greater concordance rates among monozygotic (MZ) twins than among dizygotic (DZ) twins for a number of different forms of addiction (Kendler et al., 2006). Agrawal and Lynskey (2008) compared MZ and DZ twins and concluded that there was a moderate to high concordance rate (0.3 to 0.7) for addiction to a variety of drugs. This implies that there is a strong nature component to addiction.

More recent interest has been focused on the genetic mechanisms that are involved in this inheritance and on whether the inheritance is of a general vulnerability to addiction or different vulnerabilities to different forms of addiction.

Much of the research on the details of the genetics underlying addiction has been carried out on mice, and there is only a small amount of research on human genetic effects. Through these studies a number of specific examples have been discovered that might link genetic effects to addiction vulnerability. In humans, non-smokers appear to carry an inactive form of the gene CYP2A6 (Tyndale and Sellers, 2002), and a dopamine receptor gene called the DRD2 gene has been found to have a variation that is more common in people addicted to nicotine (Comings et al., 1996), alcohol (Dick and Foroud, 2003) or cocaine (Noble et al., 1993) than in other non-addicted people.

We can see, therefore, that there are clear indicators that genetic inheritance can lead to a vulnerability towards addiction.

Key terms

Genetic risk factor: within the context of this topic, it is any genetic mechanism that causes the likelihood of a person becoming an addict to increase.

Family studies: studies that look at whether a particular genetic trait runs in families.

Adoption studies: studies that look at whether a person (usually a twin) develops more in line with the traits of their adopted family or with the traits of their biological family. Often the behaviour of the adopted twin is compared with that of a non-adopted twin.

Twin studies: studies that look at the relative traits of two twins who are brought up in the same environment. The twins can be identical (monozygotic) or non-identical (dizygotic).

ADDICTION

Furthermore, some genes tend to make it more likely that you will acquire a specific addiction, whereas others seem to give a more general vulnerability.

The influence of peers

We have seen that some people have a propensity towards becoming addicted because of their genetic constitution, but genetics is not the whole story. Throughout our lives, **peers** provide an enormous pressure for us to conform and fit in. If the group we are associating with engage in addictive behaviours, such as smoking, we are likely to feel obliged to take part as well. This behaviour has been characterized through the social identity theory developed by Tajfel and Turner (1979). According to this behaviourist theory, the reward for engaging in the behaviour is acceptance and popularity within the group. There is a lot of evidence that peers do influence the actions of others. For example, Sussman and Ames (2001) found that peer use of drugs was one of the best predictors of future drug use by others. Similarly, new members to a group of smokers are encouraged to smoke. Indeed, Eiser et al. (1989) showed that smokers provide others in the group with positive rewards like popularity and social status if they too take up smoking. Interestingly, where smoking is not a common feature of a group then peer pressure can equally persuade a new member who smokes to give up (or at least not to smoke in the group's presence). However, peer pressure is unlikely to be present for all addictions, especially those that the person is trying to hide (for example, sex addiction), though a combination is also possible (for example, where a person is encouraged to gamble when at the bookmakers but hides their behaviour from their family).

Personality factors

Another feature of becoming an addict is whether or not there exists a set of personality characteristics that make you more likely to become an addict. Eysenck produced a personality theory that had three dimensions: introversion–extroversion, neuroticism and psychoticism. An extrovert is someone who is outgoing. Someone who is neurotic tends to be moody and anxious, and someone who is psychotic tends to be cold, impulsive and aggressive. According to Francis (1996), people who are dependent on drugs like alcohol, heroin and nicotine have higher than normal scores on the neuroticism and psychoticism scales. Terracciano and Costa (2004) showed that smokers scored higher on neuroticism than those who had never smoked, with former smokers scoring between the two other groups. This suggests that there may be personality characteristics typical of those addicted to nicotine. However, we must remember that these data are only correlational and so it is unclear whether any causal relationships exist (and, indeed, which might cause which).

While these general measures of personality are useful to a degree, they are rather crude measures of a fairly specific set of behaviours. More recently, Anderson et al. (2011) have suggested that there might be certain personality characteristics (for example, a love of excitement, an impulsive nature and an inability to quit) that are typical of someone who is vulnerable to becoming an addict. These characteristics are collectively referred to as an **addiction-prone personality** (APP) and the researchers have developed a scale designed to measure this. Originally, the scale was focused on alcohol abuse, as its questions were based on a Canadian drinking survey. The scale was quickly found to be applicable to general drug use and could discriminate drug addicts from non-addicts and also predict the severity of addiction and the likelihood of recovery (Barnes et al., 2000). The APP scale has been used successfully by Franco Cea and Barnes (2015) in a study that looked at APP traits in biological and adoptive families. They wanted to see whether or not genetics or the environment better explained the development of an APP. Their results pointed to a greater role for the environment than for genetic inheritance.

KEY STUDY: FRANCO CEA AND BARNES (2015)

Franco Cea and Barnes were interested in whether or not an addictive personality can be inherited and/or passed on to children through social mechanisms. To do this, they looked at how well an adult's score on an APP measure predicts the scores for their offspring or their adopted children.

The authors measured the APP scores from 328 members of biological families and 77 members of adoptive families. Each family member completed the APP, and then seven years later 405 offspring completed the same measure. Their results showed no differences between biological and adoptive influences, but the APP scores of the adults were good predictors of the APP of the children. This indicates that there is a significant influence of parental socialization on the development of addiction and there is not such a strong genetic influence, at least in terms of personality.

THINKING SCIENTIFICALLY: DEVELOPING A PERSONALITY MEASURE

Franco Cea and Barnes used a personality measure to assess how prone a person was to becoming addicted. This test was devised by Barnes et al. (2006) becuase the only tests of addiction around at the time were those for people who were already addicted. The development of personality measures is a complex process. Most measures use a Likert scale in which statements are presented and the person must decide whether or not they agree with the statement. Usually this is on a 5-point scale from strongly agree to strongly disagree.

Each test item must be statistically checked for its relevance to the measure so that there are no statements that have no value. Getting the statements right can be a long process, especially if the test is to span extremes of the measure and have a portion of the scale that indicates a clinical level of performance. The scale must then be tested on thousands of individuals so that the validity and reliability of the measure can be thoroughly tested. Only then can the authors be sure that the test is a valuable measure of the personality trait.

EXAMPLE EXAM QUESTION

Describe and briefly evaluate the role of personality as a risk factor for addiction. (6 marks)

Stress

We have all heard people making excuses that they smoke/drink/ use drugs for a reason related to stress. Driessen et al. (2008) showed that people suffering from post-traumatic stress disorder (PTSD) were more likely to turn to drugs or alcohol for comfort. Ogden and Fox (1994) found that some teenage girls were using smoking to control their weight, as the thought of putting on weight was causing them to feel stressed. The relationship between stress and addiction is a complicated one. On the one hand, people report that they use addictive behaviours to reduce their stress levels but, on the other hand, many addictions are known to increase stress. For example, smoking has been found to actually increase stress levels, so we have to question why there is a perceived opposite relationship between stress and this particular addictive behaviour.

There is a lot of research that links stress to addiction vulnerability. Some research has looked at the relationship between negative life events and the use of drugs. This link would appear to be especially strong if the negative life event occurs in childhood or adolescence. The negative life events that have been linked to stress include loss of a parent, parental divorce and conflict, emotional or physical abuse and low parental support, to name just a few. For example, Wills et al. (1992) conducted a study looking at how life events and family support affected substance use in 11–13-year-olds. They found that negative life events (measured using a life-events scale) were associated with high levels of substance use (cigarettes, alcohol and marijuana were looked at in this study), but that parental support and/or academic competence seemed to be protective against developing such substance use.

Stress can also have a cumulative effect on a person that leads to a vulnerability to addiction. A series of studies have shown that the likelihood of drug or alcohol dependence is correlated with the number of stressful life events you have suffered (Lloyd and Turner, 2008). The timing of the events seems not to be important, so the cumulative effect can happen over many years. Researchers have also found that these effects are not gender-specific, though there was some ethnic variation among the sample of American participants used in the studies.

The mechanisms by which stressful events lead to vulnerability to addiction are starting to be mapped out biologically. They involve the reward systems of the brain that are mediated by the neurotransmitter dopamine and also the frontal brain systems that allow us to exert control, particularly self-control. The effects of stress include a release of a hormone called **cortisol** and this is known to increase dopamine

Cortisol: a hormone that is released when the body requires more energy. Most often this is when there is a stressful situation. Another of cortisol's actions is to increase the activity of dopamine, which stimulates the reward system.

function in some parts of the brain. The way in which these factors combine to increase the vulnerability to addiction have been modelled in a schematic by Sinha (2008) and this is presented in Fig. 10.2.

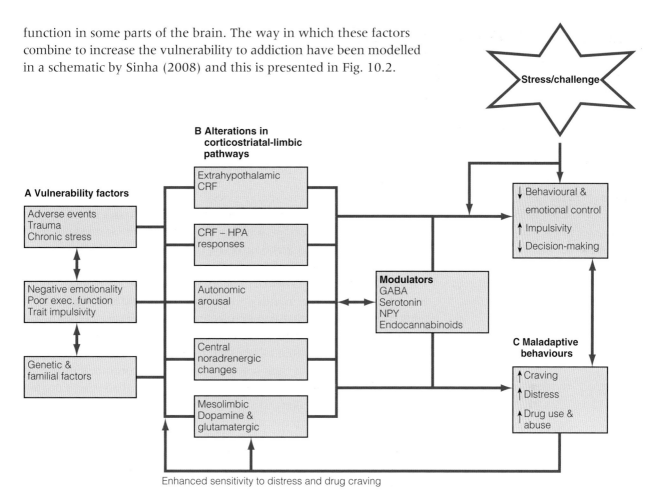

Fig. 10.2 A schematic model of stress effects on addiction, representing the cross-sensitization (becoming sensitized to one thing as a result of having been sensitized to another thing) of stress and drugs on behavioural and neurochemical responses that are mediated by the stress and reward pathways. (CRF refers to corticotrophin-releasing factor, which promotes the release of cortisol, and HPA refers to the hypothalamic-pituitary-adrenal axis, a stress response pathway that leads to an increase in adrenaline).

A further consideration is the effect that stress in childhood, or even prenatally, can have on later addictive behaviour. Stress early in childhood can cause alterations to the structure of the brain and this can affect how information is processed. This can particularly lead to changes in salience, and this will affect the way in which a stressful scenario is perceived. It can also serve to enhance the perceived reward associated with drug misuse. As the brain undergoes significant changes during late childhood and early adolescence, this is a potentially critical time for the effects of vulnerability. There has most recently been a suggestion that even prenatal stress in the mother can lead to increased vulnerability in the unborn offspring by altering the way in which the brain develops. Said et al. (2015) has shown that prenatal stress can affect dopamine receptor development and make the offspring vulnerable to nicotine addiction. However, we must be cautious, as almost all of the work on prenatal stress has been carried out on rats, and it is therefore difficult to relate these findings to humans. Furthermore, we must also remember that stress is a personal phenomenon and is defined as the response to a perceived threat to the individual's well-being.

Age

We have already seen that adolescents seem to be at the most risk of becoming addicted. For example, Shram (2008 – unpublished PhD thesis) explored the different responses to self-administered nicotine in adolescent and adult rats using various **reinforcement schedules**. She has shown that adolescents are more susceptible to the drivers for the acquisition of nicotine use (reinforcement and reward), whereas adults are more susceptible to the drivers that maintain nicotine use (resistance to extinction).

> **Key term**
>
> **Reinforcement schedule**: a pattern of rewards that can be given after a response. Reinforcements can be given after a fixed period of time (fixed interval) or number of responses (fixed ratio). Alternatively, the time or number of responses required before a reinforcement is given can be variable from trial to trial (variable interval and variable ratio, respectively).

The effect of peer pressure also seems to be related to age. During early adolescence, peers are highly influential, and if your friends are engaging in smoking and drug use then there is an enormous pressure on you to do likewise (Rozi et al., 2015). As you move into late adolescence the influence of peers is reduced and is replaced by the influences of close friends and romantic partners. However, the addictive behaviours that you indulge in early in life can stay with you into adulthood. In a British longitudinal study by Fidler et al. (2006), 5863 11-year-old children were asked to fill out a questionnaire once a year that asked about their smoking habits. This continued until the children were 16 years old. Those 11-year-olds who had tried smoking just once were more likely to take up smoking later on (before the age of 16), even if they had not smoked for three years after their initial trial. We must be mindful, though, that the data were self-report data and those claiming to have only tried smoking once may, in fact, have smoked more often. Also, while the yearly response rate was high (74–85 per cent), the total students who took part every single year was only 35 per cent of the original sample.

Addiction risk is not just a young person's problem. A report by the Institute of Alcohol Studies in 2013 showed that while people of 65 and over do not consume more alcohol than those at younger ages, more of them drink on at least five days of the week, and this is true of both men and women. It seems that those over 65 drink little and often and this can have serious consequences for their health. It could be that the drinking is often a way to reduce stress, as those in this age bracket are likely to suffer an increase in negative life events (stopping working, loss of loved ones and social isolation).

Media as a risk factor

The media can have both a positive and negative effect on addictive behaviours. Smoking advertising is now banned from television in the UK and there are public information films about the dangers of smoking and drug use. However, this is contrasted with the multitude of advertisements encouraging gambling behaviour, from the lottery on mainstream television to sports betting on the sports channels. Advertising for alcohol is still permitted, and in a German study, Sargent and Hanewinkel (2009) showed that adolescents who have a television in their bedroom are more likely to try alcohol.

Another issue concerning the media is that television focuses on young people, even though we have seen that there are alcohol risks for the over 65s and it is estimated that a third of all alcoholics develop their addiction during retirement. Within the written press there are countless stories about how bad drug users are, but there is little focus on other kinds of addiction – in modern times it would be relatively unusual to find a newspaper article about smoking.

Alongside media influences from television and the written press we see addictive behaviours portrayed in film. Sulkunen (2007) examined 140 scenes from 47 films and found that many films promoted risky activities such as smoking, drinking and drug taking. Whether or not these images have an effect on behaviour is a contentious issue. Dalton et al. (2003) showed a correlation between adolescent exposure to smoking in films and the likelihood of starting to smoke, and a similar result was found by Sargent and Hanewinkel (2009). However, Boyd (2008) has noted that there are equally many films that portray the negative consequences of drinking and drug taking. It is, therefore, just as likely that adolescents will be put off these activities as encouraged to engage in them.

KEY STUDY: SARGENT AND HANEWINKEL (2009)

Sargent and Hanewinkel (2009) were interested in the relative influence of smoking in films and tobacco advertising on children's likelihood of smoking. Their study was conducted in Germany, where the advertising of tobacco products had not yet been banned. 5626 adolescents between the ages of 10 and 15 were asked to complete a survey in 2005 and then a follow-up survey in 2006. Within the survey there were questions that asked them to describe (if they could) their favourite television tobacco advertisement and to tick a list of 50 films for whether or not they had seen them. All of the films contained people smoking. Each participant was also asked to estimate how many cigarettes they had smoked in their life up to that point and how often they smoked at the time of the survey.

The results showed that smoking in films has a stronger effect on a person starting to smoke, whereas tobacco advertising has a stronger effect on persuading a youth to experiment with tobacco after they have already tried it once. They also found age and gender differences, with older adolescents more likely to progress from onset to experimentation, and more girls progressing to higher levels of smoking than boys.

THINKING SCIENTIFICALLY: CULTURAL VARIATION

The Sargent and Hanewinkel (2009) study was conducted in Germany, whereas most of the previous research had been based in the US. However, the findings here were similar to those studies in the US, so from that point of view the findings could be said to be externally valid. However, both of these countries have westernized societies and both have slowly been moving from a culture where tobacco smoking was acceptable and promoted to one where smoking tobacco products is seen as antisocial. Furthermore, all of the samples only used white participants, so we must question whether these results would be replicated among other cultures.

Evaluating risk studies

Many of the studies in this field are conducted in real-life settings, so they have good external validity but are low on internal validity. Many of the studies are correlational, so it is not possible to argue cause and effect. However, there are a very large number of studies that nearly all point in the same direction so we can have a high degree of satisfaction that the evidence presented is likely to be accurate. Some studies have looked across gender differences, but few have looked at cultural differences, so the evidence is very much drawn from western populations (predominantly the US and Europe). Finally, there are a number of animal studies in this field and we must be cautious in our interpretation of such data.

ACTIVITY 10.3

Find five people who smoke and five people who have never smoked. If possible, vary the ages of your participants. Conduct a short interview (no more than five minutes each) that asks about how they first got into smoking or why it is they have never smoked. See if you can pick out any common themes across the two groups. Do those themes fit the headings in this topic or are there other things that researchers need to consider? Remember that you need to conduct the mini study ethically with a consent form, debrief, etc.

Exam hint

As there are only two marks for each factor you should name and describe each factor and provide an example to illustrate your understanding.

EXAMPLE EXAM QUESTION

Outline TWO risk factors for addiction. (4 marks)

Link

For more on the nature–nurture debate, look back at Chapter 1, *Issues and debates in psychology*, pages 22–28.

In terms of the nature–nurture debate it is clear that there are some well-defined genetic vulnerabilities that might make an individual at greater risk of developing an addiction. However, the environment plays a critical part, and without the means and mechanisms available it is unlikely that a person with an addictive genetic make-up will fall into an addiction. Against that, though, there are numerous social opportunities to engage in addictive behaviours and with the online environment these are becoming more easily accessible. Furthermore, we have seen that there are vulnerable periods in a person's life (particularly adolescence) when the risk of addiction is greater. We are now well placed to take a look at two forms of addiction in some depth.

KEY POINTS

- There are multiple biological and psychological risk factors associated with addiction.
- Whether or not addiction can be inherited has been explored using family studies, twin studies and adoption studies.
- Peers can have a major role to play in whether an addictive behaviour is continued once it has been tried.

- There have been attempts to define personality characteristics that make a person vulnerable to addiction and these characteristics make up what is referred to as an addiction-prone personality.

- Stress has been strongly linked as a risk factor for addictive behaviours, as these behaviours are often seen as ways to relieve stress though, in fact, they often do the opposite.

- The media has also had a big part to play in promoting or warning against addictive behaviours.

Nicotine addiction

Cigarette smoking is a leading cause of preventable disease and premature death, so it is almost unthinkable that people would engage in such an activity. However, this serves only to underline just how addictive tobacco smoking must be. Addiction to nicotine is recognized as combining a number of different factors, from the physical dependence caused by nicotine itself to the behavioural and cognitive drivers that make people continue smoking, even in the face of strong incentives to quit. Despite its commonality within society, there are no agreed-upon criteria for nicotine addiction. The US Surgeon General has presented the following list of criteria in an effort to try to define nicotine addiction:

- drug use that is highly controlled or compulsive with psychoactive effects
- stereotypical patterns of use
- continued use despite harmful effects
- relapse following abstinence accompanied by recurrent cravings.

In the UK there are around 10 million smokers (as of 2013), with 22 per cent of men and 17 per cent of women smoking on a regular basis. Despite strong advertising campaigns and easy access to good information, the 20–24-year-old age group have the highest percentage of smokers (30 per cent), which means that the problem is not slowly going away as one might expect. So what drives someone to start smoking, to keep smoking and to have difficulty in giving up smoking? We will look at each of these three problems within different domains of investigation. We will start with the biological explanations and then look at learning theory (behavioural) and cognitive explanations. Some potential problems with the research into nicotine addiction will be explored briefly at the end of this topic.

Biological reasons to be a smoker

You might think that the idea that there could be a biological reason for being a smoker suggests that it is not the person's own responsibility. However, we shall see that the explanation provided by biology only permits an understanding of vulnerability and not certainty. Furthermore, we need to recognize that much of the data is correlational and so we cannot imply causation.

Research methods link

For more on correlations, see pages 22–25.

Initiation of smoking

In the last topic we explored some of the genetic risks associated with addiction in general. Reference was made to the work of Comings et al. (1996) that showed a genetic link between the A1 **allele** (a variation of the DRD2 gene) and the likelihood of a person becoming a smoker. This gene variant is known to reduce the number of dopamine receptors and dopamine is known to be a neurotransmitter involved in the brain reward (mesolimbic) system (see Fig. 10.3). It is likely, therefore, that this gene variant will lower a person's natural reward levels, and since nicotine raises the level of brain dopamine it will be favoured in providing brain reward. Kendler et al. (1999) has estimated the heritability of nicotine dependence to be as high as 70 per cent.

Key terms

Allele: one of two or more versions of a gene on a chromosome. An individual inherits two alleles for each gene, one from each parent.

Enkephalins and endorphins: two kinds of naturally occurring neurotransmitter substances (referred to as opioids because opiates like heroin have the same effect) that have the effect of reducing pain and providing pleasure.

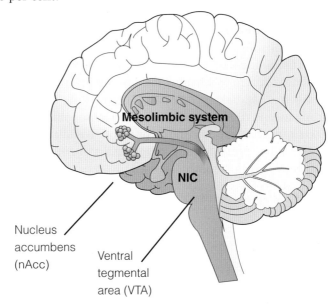

Fig. 10.3 Mechanism of action of nicotine in the central nervous system. Nicotine predominantly binds to the nicotinic acetylcholine receptors located in the mesolimbic-dopamine system of the brain. Nicotine specifically activates nicotinic receptors in the tegmental area, causing an immediate dopamine release.

Nicotine also stimulates the brain's internal opioid system by activating **enkephalins** and **endorphins**. These are the brain's natural neurotransmitters that are released when we experience pleasure. Hence, nicotine use will be perceived as pleasurable by the smoker. In fact, both the dopamine and opiate reward pathways are stimulated with every puff on the cigarette (around 20 per cigarette) and the nicotine only takes about 15 seconds to reach the brain. This speed of response is powerfully reinforcing and so encourages repeat behaviour.

As well as genetic determinants, there may be other biological determinants of smoking initiation. Silverstein et al. (1982) found that by changing the biological conditions under which college students with little smoking experience smoked a cigarette they could manipulate the positive or negative experiences associated with smoking. This can be linked to whether or not a person will take up smoking. Interestingly, they only found the effect in women, not in men.

Research methods link

For more on ethical issues, see pages 35–38.

Silverstein et al. were interested in the factors that lead to someone becoming an addicted smoker. When they conducted their study it was already known that many people feel sick when they smoke their first cigarette. However, previous studies had suggested that only 20 per cent of those who went on to smoke felt sick, whereas 80 per cent of those who didn't go on to be smokers felt sick. Furthermore, women are more likely to feel sick on first smoking than men. It was also suggested that the acidity or alkalinity of a person's urine could be linked to whether or not a person took up smoking. Silverstein et al. wanted to investigate these things simultaneously.

They took 34 college students (18 men and 16 women) with very little smoking experience and split them into two groups. One group had their urine made acidic by drinking cranberry juice and eating some glutamic acid hydrochloride tablets. The other half drank grapefruit juice and ate some sodium bicarbonate tablets, thereby making their urine alkaline. Males and females were divided equally across the conditions. One hour later, the urine was measured and the students were asked to take eight two-second puffs of a cigarette. Twenty-five minutes later they were asked if they would be willing to volunteer for a second experiment that involved smoking a number of cigarettes over a week. This was never actually run, but the researchers recorded whether a person was willing or not to take part (the dependent variable).

The results showed that 75 per cent of the acidic urine women volunteered but only 13 per cent of the alkaline urine women volunteered. For the men this was 56 per cent and 44 per cent, respectively. Hence, it seems that the acidity or alkalinity of urine affects whether women are likely to become smokers after their first cigarette but seems not to affect whether or not men will. This research pointed to a number of factors that could lead to acid urine, such as nutrition, stress, drug use, and so on. These would all need to be accounted for in the quest for reasons why some people become addicted to nicotine.

In the Silverstein et al. (1982) study we have some interesting ethical debating points. Firstly, was it ethical to give cigarettes to people who did not smoke? Secondly, was it ethical to randomly assign volunteers to conditions that could make them more likely to become addicted to nicotine (the acidity condition in this case)? Thirdly, was it right to deceive them into thinking there was a real follow-up study? The first issue might be debated against the fact that the participants were volunteers and we have to assume that they were giving their informed consent. For the second issue, the researchers did not know which condition, if any, would have an effect, and the amount of smoking required was very low. As for the deception, this was at a very low level as there was no further study and the question only asked about their willingness to take part.

All in all, we might consider that the research was conducted in as ethical a way as possible given the questions the researchers were trying to answer. You might think differently. However, this does show that there are no clear-cut answers regarding ethics and that is why all modern research is submitted to an ethics panel before it can be allowed to go ahead.

Maintenance of smoking

With nicotine affecting the brain's reward centre, the behaviour of smoking is maintained by wanting to re-experience the pleasurable sensation. However, the overstimulation of the reward centres with dopamine causes them to become desensitized. This means that they work less well in response to the same amount of dopamine (referred to as downregulation). In order to get the same pleasurable feeling as before, the person has to smoke more – this is what we call tolerance. Not only does tolerance develop, but the downregulation leads to withdrawal symptoms if the level of nicotine is not maintained. Khaled et al. (2012) discovered that depression levels were higher among smokers than those who had never smoked because of this need to maintain the nicotine level. Schachter et al. (1977) proposed what they called a nicotine-titration model to explain how smokers continue to smoke just to keep a certain level of nicotine in their body. To test this model, they gave smokers cigarettes with different levels of nicotine, and found that those on low-nicotine cigarettes smoked 25 per cent more. This shows that it is the nicotine content and not the act of smoking that is important in maintaining the behaviour.

Smoking relapse

As has already been stated, nicotine has a high tolerance level and stopping the nicotine intake leads to withdrawal symptoms that include irritability, weight gain and an increased blood flow in brain areas associated with memory, attention and reward. This serves to remind the smoker of the past enjoyment and so to avoid these symptoms the smoker relapses and begins smoking again. Even if a person stops smoking they may still be susceptible to a small intake of nicotine. After stopping for just a short while the nicotine from just a single cigarette will produce an even bigger hit than when they first started smoking and this will drive them to want to start smoking again.

ACTIVITY 10.4

Construct your own family tree as best you can going back to at least your grandparents. For each person on the tree write down what you know about their smoking activity as follows:

*   Did they smoke?
*   Are they still alive?
*   Do they have any smoking-related problems (breathing difficulties, lack of taste or smell, etc.)?
*   Have they tried to give up?

From your family tree, decide whether or not you think smoking (or not smoking) is genetically linked. Compare your family tree with those of others in your group.

EXAMPLE EXAM QUESTION

Briefly describe dopamine's involvement in nicotine addiction. (4 marks)

Exam hint

This question requires you to refer to the dopamine reward system. You should try to describe very briefly its role in addiction. One or two research examples would enhance your description.

Learning theory explanations of smoking

If the biological theories are referring to the reward centres of the brain, it makes sense to ask whether learning theory perspectives on reinforcement and reward might have something to offer in explaining the addiction to nicotine.

Initiation

Learning theory suggests that we will continue to do things that we find rewarding. Social learning theory (SLT) adds that the rewards do not have to happen directly to us but can be vicarious by observing the positive effects of actions for others. SLT could therefore explain why smoking is seen as an acceptable behaviour by many. When a child observes adult role models (such as parents and celebrities) smoking, they are more likely to also associate those role models with positive effects like popularity, rather than negative effects like disease. This will then encourage that person to try smoking when they are older as they will want to obtain those same rewards. The media might also have had a role to play in encouraging smoking in the past. Brynner (1969) showed that the media often portrayed smokers as being attractive and tough, and adolescents would see this as a desirable behaviour. We might question whether this is still the case today.

Another reason why people may start to smoke is provided by operant conditioning. The initiation of smoking might be encouraged by peers and the person will smoke in order to gain the reward of popularity. Indeed, Mayeux et al. (2008) found a positive correlation between boys who started smoking at the age of 16 and their popularity when they had reached the age of 18. This correlation was not, however, seen for girls. It would also appear to be the case that the correlation for boys only works where a boy is not already popular. Boys who are already popular at age 16 are less likely to start smoking and are more likely to engage in other risky behaviours.

Classical conditioning can also provide an explanation of why smoking behaviour might be initiated. The association made is between smoking and increased mood. Partly this will be the direct effects of nicotine on our brain reward system, but it might also include the mood enhancement derived from engaging in smoking while enjoying yourself with friends.

Maintenance

The most influential learning theory argument for the maintenance of smoking behaviour comes from operant conditioning. Just as the rewarding elements of smoking were responsible for its initiation, so

ADDICTION

these same rewards are responsible for maintaining the behaviour. In addition, the negative effects of withdrawal provide a potent source of negative reinforcement, and so the smoking behaviour is used to prevent these negative effects.

An additional element that comes into play regarding maintenance is **cue reactivity** (also sometimes called cue exposure). Once a smoker has become established, they engage in very ritualized behaviours around smoking. For example, you might see a smoker tap the end of the cigarette on a flat surface before lighting it. In addition, the smoker develops cues that trigger the desire for a cigarette (a trip to the pub or the end of a meal). The sight of one of these cues is sufficient to make the individual crave a cigarette. These cues are so strong that Carter and Tiffany (1999) discovered that the addict reacts to the cues alone in the same way that they react to smoking. However, there can be problems with this kind of laboratory-based research – cues to smoking are not the same as cravings produced by the passage of time since the last cigarette. Sayette and Tiffany (2013) have suggested that if a participant enters the laboratory in a partially craving state and the lab is full of smoking cues, then baseline questioning about their urge to smoke might be partially due to craving and not wholly due to the cues.

Another driver for the continuation of smoking is **self-efficacy**. This refers to the confidence a person has in being able to exert control over the things they want to do. It has been found that adolescents often believe they have self-efficacy, and so they see smoking as something they could easily give up if they wanted to. By contrast, adults who smoke a lot have little self-efficacy and believe that it would be impossible for them to give up. In both cases, self-efficacy leads to the person maintaining their smoking addiction.

A final behavioural explanation comes from tension reduction theory (Conger, 1956). This theory suggests that behaviours like smoking are particularly maintained in situations that provoke fear or anxiety (the idea that smoking calms your nerves). Smoking does have the effect of reducing inhibitions by creating a pleasurable mood (via the release of dopamine), and so if a person has survived an anxiety-provoking scenario once with a prior smoke, the individual is encouraged to smoke each time an anxiety-provoking scenario arises.

Relapse

There is little to say about the reasons for relapse that have not already been said about maintenance. Cue reactivity and operant conditioning processes concerning the effect of withdrawal symptoms account for almost all of the learning theory explanation of smoking relapses. The possible addition to make is that there may be a classical conditioning component. If we assume that there develops a strong association between the cues to smoking and the pleasure of smoking, then the pleasure experienced with the cue alone will eventually fade away due to extinction. To rekindle the pleasant feeling, the urge to smoke once more is likely to surface.

Cognitive explanations of smoking

Cognitive explanations of smoking behaviour emphasize the way in which events are perceived and interpreted. We will see that sets of faulty cognitions are responsible for the initiation and maintenance of smoking. Shadel and Mermelstein (1993) described the cognition surrounding smoking in terms of a vicious cycle in which people engage in smoking as a way of coping with stresses in their lives. This leads to financial, social and medical problems that create a low mood. Smoking is then, again, used to try to cope with the low mood. As we will see, other models involve expectancy (the expectation about the outcome of engaging in the behaviour) and the self-efficacy that we saw with learning theory accounts.

Initiation

Smith (1980) provided an expectancy account of how smoking behaviour starts with his perceived effects theory. This argues that we have expectations about the effects of smoking that include being able to engage in social interactions and a reduction in stress levels. Some even believe that smoking will provide a performance enhancement and this encourages them to start. A further aspect of this is that veteran smokers tend to provide positive expectations to novices, and so instead of being put off by the idea, they are encouraged (Eiser et al., 1987).

Another theory about the cognitive influence on initiation is the self-medication model. This suggests that the initial decision to start smoking is conscious and deliberate and is an attempt to relieve stress or some other negative psychological symptom. This theory is similar to the rational choice theory, which suggests that people make a conscious decision that the short-term satisfaction and benefits outweigh the possible future costs such as ill-health and financial hardship.

Maintenance

As with learning theory explanations, many of the cognitive theories that explain initiation also explain maintenance. In terms of expectancy theory, there are still the expectations that smoking will lead to positive effect. However, it is possible that the expectations change from being controlled at a conscious level to being unconscious expectations about outcome. This fits with the idea that once smoking behaviour has become established it becomes part of a person's automatic processing. This is underlined by the experienced smoker's frequent lack of knowledge about when they had their last smoke and how much they have smoked that day. The process of lighting up can become automatic and have little to do with conscious control.

The self-medication model continues to explain maintenance even though it involves some faulty thinking. The reason why self-medication initiated smoking was to relieve stress. Continued smoking, in reality, leads to higher than average stress levels.

However, the smoker continues to believe that the act of smoking is reducing their stress, and the real increased stress just encourages the person to smoke more.

When a person starts to smoke the idea of any ill-health outcomes is a long way in the future, and we have seen that rational choice theory can explain the decision to go for immediate satisfaction. As smoking becomes addictive, the threat of ill health becomes ever more real, especially if the person starts to notice a lack of stamina or a decreased sense of taste and/or smell. Nevertheless, **cognitive myopia** takes over and the person creates an active preference for the immediate satisfaction over the long-term benefits of not smoking.

Relapse

The cognitive theories around relapse centre on the person's ability to exert control over their actions. From a **locus of control** perspective, those with an internal locus of control are likely to have more success with giving up. Those that have an external locus of control are more inclined to believe that their actions are determined by outside forces and they, therefore, find it easier to place any blame for failure on someone or something else. This puts less pressure on them to succeed with their quest to give up.

Self-efficacy will also come into play with regard to quitting and relapse. Those with low self-efficacy may feel incapable of being able to change their behaviour and their defeatist attitude is likely to lead them to give in to the craving quite soon after trying to stop. Condiotte and Lichtenstein (1981) studied self-efficacy in cigarette smokers who were on cessation programmes and found that a period in which the person had a low degree of self-efficacy was associated with a likelihood that they would relapse.

KEY STUDY: CONDIOTTE AND LICHTENSTEIN (1981)

Condiotte and Lichtenstein were interested in whether the level of self-efficacy a person has can predict the chances that a person would relapse after they had tried to quit smoking. At the time, success rates for stopping smoking were only 20 per cent, and so the authors wanted to discover if there was any simple reason for this common success rate. Bandura (1977) had already suggested that self-efficacy theory can explain psychological and behavioural changes that arise from a number of different clinical treatments, and the authors wished to explore if this could account for the success or failure of stopping smoking. The authors hypothesized that if a programme increased self-efficacy then it ought to reduce relapse rates.

They took 78 smokers who were trying to quit using one of two programmes. These were the Oregon Smoking Control Programme, which was US-government funded (n = 35), and the Five Day Plan, which was a national US program run by the Seventh Day Adventist Church (n = 43). The group of 78 smokers was comprised of 38 males and 43 females, and their age ranged from 16 to 70.

A number of baseline measures were taken prior to commencing the treatment, such as a report on the number of cigarettes they smoked each day and the name of an informant whom the researchers could contact to see how well the person was coping with quitting. Pre-treatment and post-treatment confidence measures were used to assess efficacy. Success or failure of the treatment was monitored for three months after the treatment had ended.

The results showed that the greater the self-efficacy, the greater the success of the treatment (the correlation coefficient was 0.62). This suggests that self-efficacy is a good predictor of relapse rates. However, we must exercise caution. We do not know the social circumstances of these smokers in terms of the support for quitting they may have received, how many other smokers there might have been in the house, and so on. Also, the sample size was quite small. Nevertheless, the data are quite impressive in terms of the size of the correlation.

THINKING SCIENTIFICALLY: HOW BIG SHOULD A SAMPLE BE?

It is difficult to know what the right size should be for your sample to ensure that your findings are generalizable. Partly, the decision will depend on the size of the population – if you want to investigate something just within your own school/college, then the sample size need only be fairly small (which will depend on the size of the school/college). However, Condiotte and Lichtenstein's study looked at smokers and used just 78, so you might question how representative of the general population they were. Furthermore, the age range was very large and so there may have only been one or two people in a given age group. There are statistics that you can use to calculate the minimum sample size, but that is beyond the scope of this book.

In terms of expectancy, Tate et al. (1994) told some smokers that they would suffer no negative experiences during a period in which they stopped smoking and told other smokers that they would suffer negative experiences. A third group were not told anything and this acted as a control condition. Those that were given the positive message reported fewer physical and psychological effects compared to the controls. This shows that a person's expectations can dramatically affect their ability to control their own behaviour.

One final model to consider here is the theory of planned behaviour. We will deal with this model in greater detail later in the chapter. For now, we can consider briefly what the model predicts about smoking relapse. The model attempts to reconcile how behavioural intentions, behavioural attitudes, perceived control and social norms combine to produce a behavioural outcome. According to this model, even

Research methods link

For more on sampling, see pages 31–33.

ADDICTION

though a person may have an intention to stop smoking they will fail to do so if they have a positive attitude towards smoking, believe that smoking is important within their social context and do not feel that they can exert the appropriate control necessary to stop this behaviour.

ACTIVITY 10.5

Sarah is an executive in an advertising company that advertises a range of products that includes tobacco products and cosmetics. She has been in advertising for 25 years and has seen some dramatic changes during that time. She first started smoking around the time when there was a lot of pressure on cosmetics companies to stop testing their products on animals. Some of the cosmetics Sarah was involved in advertising did still use animal testing and this caused Sarah a great deal of stress. She started smoking as she believed this would make her less stressed. Even though she knows that smoking is bad for her health, she feels that if she gives up she will not be able to cope with the pressures on her at work.

Explore how each of the perspectives covered would explain Sarah's initiation into smoking and why she continues to smoke.

Exam hint

This question requires a brief description of both explanations followed by at least two similarities and at least two differences. Remember to evaluate these either with research examples or by referring to methodological issues.

EXAMPLE EXAM QUESTION

Compare and contrast behavioural and cognitive explanations of nicotine addiction. (12 marks)

Evaluating nicotine addiction research

As mentioned earlier, much of the research that has been carried out has been, necessarily, correlational (ethically, researchers cannot force people to smoke). The biological research only provides an idea of the propensity to smoke and many people who carry the appropriate genetic make-up never actually start smoking. No single explanation provides a complete picture of why people smoke and so a diathesis–stress explanation is probably the most likely to provide a more complete picture (see the last part of this chapter).

Learning theory models of smoking behaviour are often simplistic in that they do not consider that humans are able to impose cognitions on top of their more basic behaviours. However, in denying a role for conscious decision-making, this explanation might partially account for why it is so difficult to stop smoking. The very idea that the motivating forces to smoke are not under conscious control might explain why having a desire to stop is in conflict with the ability to do so.

KEY POINTS

- Smoking has been biologically linked to the DRD2 gene that controls the number of dopamine receptors.
- Smoking increases the activity of the brain's natural reward and pleasure system.

- Nicotine has a high tolerance level, which makes stopping difficult and increases the chances of relapse.
- Learning theory explanations of smoking involve classical conditioning, operant conditioning and social learning.
- Part of the mechanism for maintenance and relapse involves cue reactivity.
- Cognitive explanations suggest that smokers wrongly perceive smoking to relieve stress (self-medication).
- Another cognitive factor in smoking behaviour is locus of control.

Gambling addiction

Having a gambling addiction is a recognised clinical disorder under DSM-5. A person is described as having a gambling disorder if the following is true.

A Persistent and recurrent problematic gambling behaviour leading to clinically significant impairment or distress, as indicated by the individual exhibiting four (or more) of the following in a 12-month period:

1. Needs to gamble with increasing amounts of money in order to achieve the desired excitement.
2. Is restless or irritable when attempting to cut down or stop gambling.
3. Has made repeated unsuccessful efforts to control, cut back, or stop gambling.
4. Is often preoccupied with gambling (for example, having persistent thoughts of reliving past gambling experiences, handicapping or planning the next venture, thinking of ways to get money with which to gamble).
5. Often gambles when feeling distressed (for example, helpless, guilty, anxious, depressed).
6. After losing money gambling, often returns another day to get even ('chasing' one's losses).
7. Lies to conceal the extent of involvement with gambling.
8. Has jeopardized or lost a significant relationship, job, or educational or career opportunity because of gambling.
9. Relies on others to provide money to relieve desperate financial situations caused by gambling.

B The gambling behaviour is not better explained by a manic episode.

Specify if: **Episodic:** Meeting diagnostic criteria at more than one time point, with symptoms subsiding between periods of gambling disorder for at least several months. **Persistent:** Experiencing continuous symptoms, to meet diagnostic criteria for multiple years.

Specify if: **In early remission:** After full criteria for gambling disorder were previously met, none of the criteria for gambling disorder have been met for at least 3 months but for less than 12 months. In sustained remission: After full criteria for gambling disorder were previously met, none of the criteria for gambling disorder have been met during a period of 12 months or longer.

Specify current severity: **Mild:** 4–5 criteria met. **Moderate:** 6–7 criteria met. **Severe:** 8–9 criteria met.

Recent estimates put the prevalence rates for pathological gambling between 0.5 per cent and 2.5 per cent (compare this with 1 per cent for schizophrenia). Estimates for gambling rates that are at a problematic but sub-clinical level are as high as 15 per cent (Shaffer and Hall, 2001). In 2007, a survey in Britain showed that 68 per cent of the population had engaged in some form of gambling behaviour, even if that was only playing the lottery. In this topic we will look at the possible reasons why people develop an addiction to gambling. There are many areas that researchers have used to explain pathological gambling. The three we will consider here are biological, learning theory, and cognition. For each type of explanation we will consider the initiation of gambling, its maintenance and then the risks of relapse when attempting to quit.

Biological explanations of gambling

Unlike the case for nicotine addiction, it is difficult to pinpoint biological explanations of gambling as it is a complex behaviour. However, it is possible to look at inheritance rates as an indicator of a genetic component and we can also examine the brain and neurotransmitter functions to look for changes that would indicate the types of behaviour typical of someone who gambles (such as changes in the reward system).

Initiation

If we ask why people are drawn to gambling in the first place, we are bound to run into the question of how much is nature and how much is nurture. To examine the nature side, we can look to studies of genetic inheritance and studies of brain abnormalities that might be linked to the behaviours associated with gambling.

Genetics explanations

As you might expect, genetic studies have involved family studies, twin studies and direct investigations of the biology of genes. Black et al. (2006) studied 31 pathological gambling (PG) **probands** and 193 of their first-degree relatives (along with similar numbers of controls) to establish whether or not there were family links to gambling. They found that gambling activity was significantly more prevalent in the relatives of the PG probands than of the controls. These relatives were also more likely to have engaged in other addictive behaviours (such as substance abuse or alcoholism). In a twin study, Eisen et al. (1998) carried out a telephone interview study with 6718 male/male twins (a mixture of over 3000 **monozygotic twin** pairs and **dizygotic twin** pairs) who served in the US military during the Vietnam War era (1955–75). They found that inherited factors explained 62 per cent of the diagnosis of pathological gambling (which was then DSM-III – Revised). However, the fact that only military males were used decreases the external validity of the study.

In terms of more direct genetics research, Comings et al. (2001) carried out a genetic analysis on 139 pathological gamblers and found that seven genes that code for the regulation of dopamine, serotonin and noradrenaline neurotransmitters were all implicated in the risk of developing pathological gambling. As the study also used 139 age-, race- and sex-matched controls we can be reasonably sure that the results relate to activities that are associated with gambling. This fits with lots of previous research that has shown increased levels of dopamine and noradrenaline activity in problem gamblers. Even drugs that increase dopamine as a treatment of Parkinson's disease have been known to cause gambling problems in a small number of recipients (Grosset et al., 2009), underlining the importance of dopamine activity in gambling addiction.

Many of these previous studies have been carried out exclusively on men. However, Slutske et al. (2010) carried out a telephone survey of 2889 Australian twin pairs, of whom 57 per cent were women. They found that genetic factors accounted for 49.2 per cent of the liability for disordered gambling (DSM-IV) and that there were no differences between men and women. This means that the genetic markers for gambling behaviour are likely to be the same for both sexes.

Other biological correlates

Alongside the research that points to a genetic component of pathological gambling, other research has shown abnormalities in the way that the brains of gamblers function. These include changes to neurotransmitter function, especially in areas of the brain that use dopamine, serotonin and noradrenaline. In addition, **electroencephalographic (EEG)** research has shown that pathological gamblers (PG) have abnormalities in their EEG pattern. Regard et al. (2003) showed that 65 per cent of their sample of pathological gamblers had abnormal EEG patterns, whereas only 26 per cent of the healthy controls had abnormal EEG. In addition, 81 per cent of the PG group had a medical history of neuropsychological problems. These kinds of findings are also seen in individuals with other sorts of addictions.

> **Key term**
>
> **Electroencephalograph (EEG):** a way of looking at brain activity (Fig. 10.4). From electrodes placed on the scalp, it allows us to examine which parts of the brain are more active at any given time (say, when reading, as you are doing now) without having to plant electrodes inside the brain.

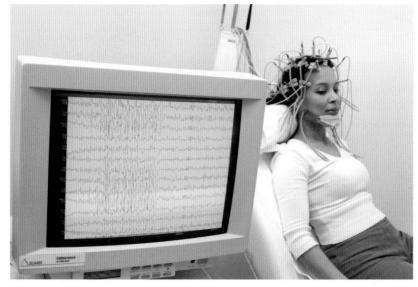

Fig. 10.4 Example of an EEG trace

Maintenance

The biological maintenance of gambling behaviour is most likely to be a combination of factors. Increases in dopamine within the reward centres of the brain will maintain the pleasant feelings associated with gambling. In addition, increases in heart rate and cortisol levels have been found when pathological gamblers engage in gambling activities, but not when non-gamblers play the same games without any monetary gain (Meyer et al., 2004). These changes are part of the stress response and add weight to the idea that gambling behaviour is being maintained by activating mechanisms associated with fear and excitement, both of which are a part of the thrill of gambling. However, a recent study by Geisel et al. (2015) did not find any elevation in cortisol levels when comparing pathological gamblers and matched healthy controls.

Relapse

When gamblers attempt to quit they are faced with a number of physical withdrawal symptoms. These include insomnia and loss of appetite. The symptoms are remarkably similar to those seen when drug addicts try to stop using. Rosenthal and Lesieur (1992) found that 65 per cent of pathological gamblers reported at least one physical side-effect, such as insomnia, headaches and loss of appetite. In addition, 91 per cent of them felt cravings to return to gambling, so the chances of relapse are very high. While there were no gender differences reported, the strength of the symptoms did correlate with the number of hours spent gambling and the severity of the gambling addiction (as evidenced through DSM-IV).

ACTIVITY 10.6

Adrian is a monozygotic twin aged 15. His mother does the lottery every week and his father used to gamble quite heavily but gave up when he was 35 years old. His paternal grandfather is an addictive gambler betting every day on horse racing and this led to his wife divorcing him before the twins were born. His grandmothers both go to bingo once a week and one of them buys a scratch card two or three times a week. Adrian has not yet gambled in any way but his twin quite regularly plays the slot machines at the local arcade. None of Adrian's friends are into any form of gambling.

From a genetics perspective, how likely do you think it is that Adrian will become a gambler? What other factors might influence whether or not Adrian takes up gambling later in life?

Learning theory explanations of gambling

Learning theory explanations argue that gambling is a learned response that is under the control of reinforcement and reward. These explanations also include the idea of social learning through imitation or observation. We have already seen that the brain reward systems have been implicated in gambling behaviour so it makes sense that these theories could have some value in explaining pathological gambling.

Initiation

Many forms of gambling are perfect examples of operant conditioning, where the driver for the behaviour comes in the form of **partial reinforcement**. This is where a reward is provided on some occasions when a behaviour is displayed, but not all occasions. For instance, slot machines work on the principle of **variable ratio reinforcement schedules**, whereby a reward is obtained after a variable number of responses. It is the fact that the next attempt might lead to a jackpot win that keeps you putting in your money. Occasional smaller winnings are reinforcements that maintain your willingness to keep playing. By the same token, if you won on every spin then you would either quickly get bored or fail to continue the first time the machine failed to pay out. The power of the variable ratio reinforcement schedule was demonstrated by Skinner in the 1950s. However, this alone would not explain why some people go on to develop pathological gambling habits while others remain only occasional gamblers. Furthermore, it would not explain gender differences in gambling behaviour.

Attempts to understand the nature of the reinforcement have provided a number of different ideas concerning what might constitute a reward. Moran (1970) suggested that the all-important reward was the size of the winnings, whereas Brown (1986) suggested it was the level of excitement. Negative reinforcement has also been suggested as the source of reward with gambling serving as an escape from life problems, thereby reducing stress (Blaszczynski and McConaghy, 1989). A study by Diskin and Hodgins (1999) showed that this negative reinforcement might be achieved by the gambler narrowing their attention during the activity.

Key terms

Partial reinforcement: where a reward (reinforcement) is not provided after every correct behavioural response but is given only after some responses.

Variable ratio reinforcement schedule: an operant conditioning schedule in which a reinforcement (which, in the case of gambling, would be a pay-out) is provided after a variable number of attempts. In the slot machine scenario, a pay-out might occur somewhere between one and 50 tries, with the additional factor that the amount of the pay-out would be weighted towards the small amounts (e.g. pays out 100 of the lowest amounts for every large pay-out). Together these mean that there is just enough hope of a jackpot win while ensuring that most people lose money over a session.

KEY STUDY: DISKIN AND HODGINS (1999)

Diskin and Hodgins' research was an extension of previous studies that had suggested that types of gambling like video lottery gambling are favoured by individuals who are seeking distractions from life problems. While playing, the gambler is able to block out all of the sights and sounds around them and often lose track of time in the process. However, these previous studies had all used self-report measures and so Diskin and Hodgins wanted to test the theory using a more empirical approach.

Two groups of participants were used. In one group there were 12 pathological gamblers (six men and six women) and in the other group 11 occasional gamblers (four men and seven women). A video lottery terminal (see Fig. 10.5) was used, but was rigged with four LED lights located around the video terminal. While playing the game, the LED lights would randomly come on (one at a time) and the player had to press the response bar as soon as they noticed the light on. Their reaction time was recorded.

Diskin and Hodgins found that pathological gamblers were slower to respond, suggesting that they focused more intensely on the game. This was further supported by the fact that seven pathological gamblers missed a total of 29 trials altogether, whereas only three

ADDICTION

of the occasional gamblers missed a total of four trials. Due to the small numbers, gender differences were not examined. So, it seems that pathological gamblers pay less attention to their surroundings than other people. Again, this focus on the game to the exclusion of everything else suggests that negative reinforcement is acting here as an escape from the external world and its problems.

Fig. 10.5 A video lottery terminal

THINKING SCIENTIFICALLY: SAMPLE SIZES IN CLINICAL AREAS

The Diskin and Hodgins study only used 23 people in total. Only 12 of these were pathological gamblers. At first, we might want to criticize the researchers for using too few participants to be able to generalize their findings to the rest of the population. However, we must be careful not to condemn them too quickly. The use of pathological gamblers is going to require recruitment from a relatively small population of people, so it becomes noticeable that studies involving rarer clinical problems often have small sample sizes. While in the case of gambling there may be many pathological gamblers around, those that have been diagnosed as such are a much smaller number.

Could the researchers at least have used a larger number of occasional gamblers? While they could have, this would have caused other problems, as unequal sample sizes can pose problems when it comes to the statistical analysis.

Another part of the learning theory argument for the initiation of gambling comes from social learning. Having an early experience of someone else's winning success through gambling can reinforce the idea of gambling through vicarious reinforcement. This is what Skinner referred to as a person's reinforcement history (Skinner, 1953). He argued that if the behaviour of gambling was reinforced early in a person's life, then later on in life the frequency of winning did not have to be high to maintain the gambling behaviour. Similarly, Custer and Milt (1985) have suggested that a big win early in an adult gambling career can trigger a move towards pathological gambling.

Classical conditioning has also been used to explain the initial phases of gambling. The unconditioned stimulus would be sitting with a group of friends (or at least like-minded people) and the unconditioned response would be a pleasant feeling, such as feeling relaxed or excited. If this unconditioned stimulus is then paired with the conditioned stimulus of gambling, then this too will come to elicit the conditioned response of feeling relaxed or excited. Drummond and Glautier (1994) showed that alcohol-related stimuli (such as sitting in a pub) result in the same physiological responses as alcohol itself, so it would seem reasonable to make the same argument for gambling-related activities.

Maintenance

Why does a person continue to gamble even though the majority of the time is spent nursing the wounds of their losses? The operant learning theory explanation for this is the power of variable ratio schedules in resisting **extinction**. Extinction is the term used to describe the reduction of a behavioural response as a result of the removal of a reward. If you get rewarded each time you perform a task and then you suddenly cease to be rewarded, you will quickly stop doing the task. The fact that gamblers *only* win occasionally and that they never know if the next attempt will be that one big victory keeps them playing and playing. The fact that they do win occasionally keeps them wanting to play for that really big win. If they get that big win on say, a slot machine, then classical conditioning might explain the desire to seek out bigger and better environments for gambling (such as progressing to casinos).

> **Key term**
>
> **Extinction:** the gradual reduction of a conditioned behavioural response because of the removal of the reward that had become associated with that response.

Another maintenance explanation is cue reactivity. This is when an external cue triggers the behaviour. In the case of the gambler, watching a football match on television might trigger the desire to place a bet on the game.

Relapse

Cue reactivity can also be used to explain relapse back into addiction. For the person who is trying to stop gambling, it is virtually impossible for them to steer clear of reminders. Watching television provides cues in the form of sports, advertisements and so on. Walking along a high street brings with it the likelihood of walking past a betting shop. Even in the supermarket the National Lottery is all too obvious.

Another reason for relapse is negative reinforcement. The withdrawal symptoms from gambling were mentioned earlier – a return to gambling provides the negative reinforcement of those withdrawal symptoms. Rosenthal and Lesieur (1992) found a positive correlation between the number of hours a person spent gambling and the extent of their withdrawal symptoms.

EXAMPLE EXAM QUESTION

Outline the learning explanation of gambling addiction. (4 marks)

Cognitive explanations of gambling

The cognitive theories of gambling centre on a person's beliefs about what is happening in the gambling scenario. Hence, many of the theories try to explain the sources of faulty thinking that the gambler has, especially about the control they think they have over the immediate environment. It might also be the case that some of the cognitive reasons why gambling appeals to the pathological gambler are a consequence of the attitudes of parents and others towards gambling during childhood.

Initiation

The most influential cognitive process that initiates problem gambling is a person's own beliefs about the gambling environment. Some involve misperceptions about probability and are commonplace. For example, if you are tossing a coin, you tend not to believe that a long run of heads will occur (even though it is possible simply by chance), but a short run is acceptable and the more heads you toss, the more certain you become that the next toss will be a tails. By this logic, to the gambler, a run of bad luck must be followed by good luck, a belief known as the gambler's fallacy. Another fallacy often applied by gamblers is the sunk cost fallacy. This is where prior expenditure makes people reluctant to abandon their projects and may encourage them to throw bad money after good. For the gambler this represents an attempt to win back the money they have already lost.

The more control the person believes they have over the gambling environment, the more likely that they will become addicted. When a game is perceived to have a level of skill, such as playing a card game like poker, then the budding gambler is led into a false sense of having control over the outcome (Langer, 1975). This then leads the gambler to overestimate their chances of winning and encourages them to continue playing for that one big win.

Maintenance

One of the most useful cognitive explanations of maintenance is referred to as **cognitive bias**. This leads a person to continue to gamble despite suffering frequent, and sometimes heavy, losses. Unfortunately though, this can be a wrong decision that is influenced by things like motivations, emotions and social pressures. Gamblers tend to hold two kinds of bias: belief that they can influence the outcome (directly or indirectly), and belief that they can correctly predict the outcome. These are exacerbated if the activity gives them a degree of choice (for example, choosing your own ticket) and/or is familiar to them (a roulette wheel they have played before) and/or involves them in some way (they personally throw the dice). These biases lead the gambler to believe they have some degree of control

Cognitive bias: a sort of thinking short-cut in that there are rules of thumb that allow people to make quick decisions. These decisions are based on expectations that are drawn from past experiences. Mostly they are helpful and accurate but they can sometimes be erroneous and lead to false beliefs.

over the outcome. Another source of bias stems from a belief that the outcome involves some sort of skill. So in gambling on horse racing the gambler will overestimate the chances of winning (Reid, 1986), whereas in a bet on the lottery the belief the gambler has in winning is reduced. Furthermore, Reid pointed out that instead of seeing a near miss as a loss the gambler sees it as a near win and so is encouraged to gamble again. Kassinove and Schare (2001) have looked in detail at the effects of a near miss on slot machine gambling and have found that gambling only persists when the frequency of near misses is within an acceptable range.

KEY STUDY: KASSINOVE AND SCHARE (2001)

There has been a lot of interest in the conditions under which a person wants to continue gambling. Kassinove and Schare (2001) wanted to examine the relative effects of big wins and near misses. Based on previous research, the researchers predicted that a big win or a moderate number of near misses would keep a person gambling. The big win would tempt the gambler to play again if there was believed to be skill involved in the game and the near misses provide a sense of being close to being lucky.

The study involved 180 undergraduate students who played on a four-wheel slot machine. A near miss was defined as having the first three numbers the same and the last number different (for instance, 2, 2, 2, 5). Participants receiving near misses were in three groups, with the near-miss rate set at 15 per cent, 30 per cent or 45 per cent of trials. For the big-win condition, on trial 8 the person won $10 (each spin cost a notional $0.25 – they did not spend their own money – and a normal win paid out $2.25). In all conditions there were 50 near-miss trials. At the end of this period, participants could continue to play but there were no more near misses, big wins or ordinary pay-outs, so these trials were extinction trials. The dependent variable was how many extinction trials the person engaged in before they decided to quit. To make that decision a real one, participants were paid any money they had won before leaving the experiment.

The results showed that the 30 per cent near misses yielded the least extinction (that is, the participants played for longer after the first 50 spins) and there was no difference between 15 per cent and 45 per cent. This gave an inverted U-shaped distribution. Whether or not players had received the big win seemed to make no difference to the outcome. The researchers concluded that the near misses seem to suggest to the gambler that, for games involving pure chance, a big win is just around the corner. However, this does not explain why the 30 per cent near-miss condition was the most effective in keeping the gamblers playing. It might be that 15 per cent is too little to maintain interest and 45 per cent is too much, given that the pay-outs did not follow frequently enough. So it might be the relationship between near misses and pay-outs that maintains the gambler's desire to continue playing.

The Kassinove and Scharle study provides a good example of the problems with conducting laboratory studies. On the surface, the study might look like a good test of the circumstances under which gamblers will continue to play slot machines. However, it would be unethical to ask players to risk losing their own money, so each spin only cost a notional 25 cents. We can ask whether or not players would have made different decisions had they been using their own money. We are left, therefore, with a trade-off situation in which the researcher must decide whether to use real-life self-reports of gambling behaviour (with the possibility that participants might lie) or to use laboratory situations (where a participant is not playing for real).

According to Sharpe and Tarrier (1993) gambling may be initially maintained by operant conditioning but that this is soon superseded by cognitive processes. Their argument centres on faulty coping skills. Instead of being able to challenge false cognitions and apply appropriate problem-solving skills, the gambler's continued losses usually cause them to have low self-esteem, financial difficulties and to be under stress so that their normal coping strategies do not get applied appropriately.

Exam hint

This answer requires you to accurately outline two explanations. However, to ensure maximum marks you should provide either an example or a research study to expand your description.

EXAMPLE EXAM QUESTION

Outline ONE learning theory explanation and ONE cognitive explanation for addictive gambling. (4 marks)

Relapse

The cognitions that prevent a gambler recovering from their addiction involve mood and the sense of a vicious cycle. Gambling can help a person to cope with negative mood states that can result from boredom and can also lead to positive mood states created by the excitement of gambling. These can be strong incentives to take gambling up again, even after a decision has been made to stop. The vicious cycle explanation complements this by suggesting that the gambler believes that the low mood that is created from having financial difficulties can be offset by a return to gambling and the chance to win enough to pay off the debts.

ACTIVITY 10.7

Find someone you know who gambles (excluding the lottery or scratch cards) on a fairly regular basis (at least once every week) and someone who rarely or never gambles (again, excluding the lottery or scratch cards). Ask them about the things that drive them either to gamble or that prevent them from gambling. Include questions about their family, their attitude towards gambling and any gambling experiences they might have had (of others gambling for the non-gamblers).

See how well the information you have gathered fits with the theories you have covered. Which theory seems to fit best with the behaviours that have been described?

Evaluating explanations of gambling

We have seen that none of the theories on offer provide a complete explanation of pathological gambling. While some theories have a lot of supporting research evidence, this evidence is often obtained from small sample sizes or is gender biased in that a lot of the research focuses on males.

The learning theory explanations can be said to be deterministic. This is because many of the ideas behind these theories have been derived from research using animals and so they fail to take into account the higher-order thinking that humans are capable of. However, the fact that these theories deny a role for conscious awareness on the part of the gambler could explain why people have difficulty in resolving the conflict between the desire to cease gambling and the forces that compel them to continue.

For all of the types of theory, data are often obtained from survey research so it is difficult to establish cause and effect. They generally present simplistic solutions and the complexities behind gambling addiction are often ignored. In particular, each type of theory tends not to consider those ideas offered by the other theories and none of them explain very well the reasons why some people are able to gamble occasionally whereas others are drawn into an addictive and pathological pattern of gambling activity.

KEY POINTS

- Twin studies suggest that gambling behaviour may be genetically inherited but, to date, no genes have been identified.
- Pathological gamblers have abnormalities in their EEG pattern.
- Many forms of gambling situations involve, and can be explained by, operant schedules of reinforcement.
- Variable ratio schedules are important for initiation and maintenance, and provide a resistance to extinction.
- Cognitive theories about gambling suggest that the gambler often wrongly believes that they can control their environment.
- Cognitive explanations of gambling maintenance suggest the involvement of cognitive bias.
- The increase in online gambling opportunities is worrying.

Methods for reducing addiction

Now that we have looked at some of the risks and causes of addiction, we can explore whether any of the theories we have considered help us to reduce or remove addictive behaviours. Most of the treatments have come from three areas. The first is biological treatments that treat addiction as a chemical disorder – by targeting the brain systems that are behaving abnormally, the hope is that the person will cease to indulge in their addiction. The second basis for treatment supposes that the addictive behaviour has been learned and so it is possible for it to be unlearned. By creating new learning concerning the triggers for the addictive behaviour, the attempt is to break the links and to reduce the appeal of the addiction. The final version of treatment is based on the belief that addiction is the result of faulty thinking. Hence, if the addict can be taught to think about the stimuli that give rise to the behaviour in a more positive way, they will better cope with the temptations and resist acting out their addiction.

Drug therapy

From a biological perspective, an addiction can be thought of as a disease (although the term biological abnormality might be more accurate). As such, the solution ought to come in the form of a drug that can be administered to correct whatever biological system is malfunctioning. The more we discover about the biological basis of addictions, the better we are at being able to provide addicts with drugs to replace their addiction. Most **drug therapy** works by attempting to replace the addiction with a drug that has similar physical effects. You might think that this would be likely to simply replace one addiction (such as smoking) with a different addiction (for example, to nicotine gum) and you would, in part, be correct as this is a very real risk. However, the principle behind drug therapy is that the drug can take care of the physical dependence while the person does other things to reduce or remove the psychological dependence. Once this has happened, the idea is that the physical reliance on the drug can then be slowly reduced until it is not needed at all.

With this in mind, we can look at some examples of the way in which drugs have been used with nicotine and gambling addictions.

Smoking

Different drug therapy approaches have been taken to help people stop smoking. The most well-known one is called nicotine replacement therapy (NRT) and it is relatively effective (Watts et al., 2002). The various types of this therapy include the readily available nicotine patches, gum, tabs (placed under the tongue), nasal spray, etc. that people can use to try to stop smoking. With gum, tabs and nasal spray there is a fixed and immediate shot of nicotine, and this is believed to not only reduce the craving but also provides positive reinforcement because the nicotine is stress relieving too. Patches deliver a steady stream of nicotine, so they reduce the physiological craving but do not provide the positive reinforcement. However, NRT does not provide any help to the psychological components of the addiction and only treats the physical addiction. It does, though, help prevent relapse as NRT causes a gradual desensitization of the nicotine receptors. After a time, this makes the smoking of a real cigarette quite unpleasant, as the effect of its nicotine dose will be too strong.

Key term

Drug therapy: a treatment that involves giving a person a drug to mimic or replace the drug they are receiving through their addictive behaviour.

Other forms of drug therapy used with smokers are an antidepressant called bupropion and a nicotine agonist (activates the same receptors as the natural neurotransmitter) called varenicline. Both of these increase dopamine activity and reduce the number of nicotine receptors. Since the drug increases dopamine, if the person then smokes the effect of the cigarettes will be less pleasurable. Varenicline has been shown to be marginally more effective than bupropion. Tonstad et al. (2006) used varenicline in their study and found that smokers who managed to stop smoking for at least seven days by the end of 12 weeks of varenicline treatment showed significantly greater continuous abstinence in weeks 13 to 24 compared with those given a placebo. This advantage was also maintained at follow-up to week 52.

KEY STUDY: WATTS ET AL. (2002)

Watts et al. carried out a review of the various drug therapies available to help people stop smoking. They compared literature published between January 1999 and January 2001 and looked at research involving treatment with nicotine patches (27 studies), nicotine gum (13 studies), nicotine inhaler (four studies), nicotine nasal spray (three studies), bupropion (two studies) and combination therapy (usually bupropion combined with one of the other methods – three studies). They looked at three aspects for each type of treatment: safety and tolerability, efficacy, and price. Most of the studies they found compared a treatment method against a placebo.

The results showed that there was not much to choose between the treatment methods and that all of them were effective in increasing abstinence rates over trying to quit without the use of a treatment. The cheapest treatments were found to be bupropion and the nicotine patches, but as the study was conducted in the US, prices elsewhere could differ. One word of caution was mentioned by the researchers and that was that the treatments will only work alone if the person is motivated to quit. If this is not the case, then they advised that the treatment be used in conjunction with a counselling intervention designed to increase person's motivation.

THINKING SCIENTIFICALLY: MAKING COMPARISONS ACROSS STUDIES

Review articles are good at determining whether or not there is a general case to be made for something. In the Watts et al. study there was clear evidence that all of the nicotine replacement therapy methods were effective. However, it can often be difficult to make comparisons across studies if the methodologies used are different, the ages, genders, etc. are different or if the outcome measures are different. This is often the case in clinical research. The studies used by Watts et al. all compared treatment with a placebo, but not all clinical studies might do this and so the review sample might be reduced as a consequence. Watts et al.'s review was not able to monitor differences in the extent of smoking of the participants (frequency of smoking, cigarettes versus pipe or cigars, etc.) and was also unable to take into account the length of time that participants had been smoking.

We must therefore treat reviews with some caution, even though they often provide the only way to see the extent to which a finding can be replicated.

Gambling

Gambling represents a non-substance addiction and this has also been shown to be treatable with a variety of drugs. Grant and Kim (2006) reviewed the effectiveness of some of these drugs when compared with a placebo and found many of them to be effective (see Table 10.2). However, they point out that there has been little research in this area, given that prevalence rates of pathological gambling arc on a par with, for example, schizophrenia.

Medication	Subjects	Mean daily dose	Outcome
Fluvoxamine (Luvox)	15 enrolled 10 completed	195 mg	Fluvoxamine superior to placebo
Naltrexone (ReVia)	89 enrolled 45 completed	188 mg	Naltrexone group significantly improved compared with placebo
Fluvoxamine (Luvox)	32 enrolled 13 completed	200 mg	Fluvoxamine not statistically significant from placebo
Paroxetine (Paxil)	53 enrolled 41 completed	51.7 mg	Paroxetine group significantly improved compared to placebo
Paroxetine (Paxil)	76 enrolled 45 completed	50 mg	Paroxetine and placebo groups with comparable improvement
Lithium carbonate SR (Lithobid SR)	40 bipolar-spectrum subjects enrolled 29 completed	1170 mg	Lithium group significantly improved compared with placebo
Sertraline (Zoloft)	60 enrolled 44 completed	95 mg	Similar improvement in both groups
Nalmefene	207 enrolled 73 completed	25 mg, 50 mg or 100 mg	Nalmefene group significantly improved compared to placebo

Table 10.2 Table from Grant and Kim (2006) showing the use of drugs with pathological gambling. It is worth noting the number of completions as well as whether or not the drug use was successful.

ACTIVITY 10.8

Imagine that you are an addict and you are offered a drug that will help you to quit your addiction. You know you ought to quit your addiction but you are not fully committed to stopping. What might be the barriers to you engaging with the drug therapy?

EXAMPLE EXAM QUESTION

Briefly evaluate the effectiveness of drug therapy for smoking addiction. (6 marks)

Exam hint

Although the question only asks for an evaluation, you will have to very briefly describe the drug you have chosen and which addiction it is used for. Having done this, the best way to approach this question is to use research evidence to assess the efficacy of the drug. As an evaluation, you could compare it with another drug or you might want to evaluate the quality of the studies themselves.

Behavioural interventions

Behavioural interventions work on the principle that an addiction is maintained by the principles of conditioning. These can be classical conditioning, operant conditioning or influences such as social learning. We will consider here only two of the methods, one that is derived from classical and operant conditioning and one that is derived solely from operant conditioning, namely **aversion therapy** and **covert sensitization**, respectively. Aversion therapy tries to make a person feel unwell if they engage in the behaviour. Covert sensitization tries to do the same as aversion therapy but without physically engaging in any behaviour.

Aversion therapy

Here we will focus on the behavioural component of aversion treatment and the involvement of conditioning techniques. More accurately, the process is to provide extinction training (that is, the aim is to extinguish the unwanted behaviour). The principle behind this therapy is to change the pairing of feelings associated with the addictive behaviour from pleasant ones to unpleasant ones (hence classical conditioning initially but then becoming operantly controlled) in the hope that the new pairing will undo the old one. Aversion therapy has been used with a large number of addictions, including smoking, alcoholism and gambling. In each case the behaviour is paired with something unpleasant – for example, the drug disulfiram is used with alcoholism and is an emetic. However, other techniques have also been used, such as giving a mild electric shock paired with smoking or drinking alcohol. There used to be lots of support for aversion therapy solutions and there were many different forms that had claims of success. For example, Danaher (1977) showed that a technique called rapid smoking had good therapeutic value. However, not all treatments using aversion therapy claimed to be successful, and Miller et al. (1973) found no differences between using high or low levels of shock treatment and the effectiveness of group therapy. This technique is now mostly only used with alcohol abuse as far as addiction is concerned, though it is still used to reduce other kinds of behaviours.

Covert sensitization

Covert sensitization is aversion therapy of a very different sort. It was first described by Cautela (1967) and involves a person imagining carrying out their addictive behaviour rather than actually doing it. For example, the nicotine addict might be asked to imagine smoking a cigarette in their living room but to also imagine that the cigarette is making them feel nauseated. Indeed, the person is asked to imagine feeling so nauseated that they are vomiting uncontrollably over their

Key terms

Aversion therapy: therapy designed to extinguish the addictive behaviour by pairing it with something unpleasant.

Covert sensitization: therapy that tries to pair the addictive behaviour with an unpleasant feeling but does so by using the person's imagination rather than live stimuli.

ADDICTION

living room furniture. In later sessions the person is asked to imagine being offered a cigarette in their living room but refusing to accept it. The hope is that in refusing the cigarette they are spared the feeling of nausea and that this removes the desire to have a cigarette. Kraft and Kraft (2005) detailed six case studies in which this technique had been used successfully. The six cases involved alcoholism, cigarette smoking, cannabis smoking, nail tearing, overeating and chocolate addiction, so the technique has offered success across a range of addictions. However, this technique will not work with everyone and is likely to require a high degree of motivation for it to be successful. As the technique does not address the motivational aspects of the addictive behaviour, the person remains susceptible to relapse.

Cognitive behaviour therapy

The principle behind **cognitive behaviour therapy (CBT)** is that behaviours are determined by thoughts and so bad behaviours must be determined by bad thoughts. If a person can change the way they think about something then their behaviour should change as a consequence. So the reason that a person gambles, smokes or drinks alcohol addictively is because they hold unhealthy thoughts about their activity. CBT is becoming a method of choice for use with many forms of addiction. While there are many forms of this (for example, rational emotive behaviour therapy and dialectic behaviour therapy), the main components of them all are the same, so let us look at how CBT is used and what successes have been reported.

Firstly, the patient and the therapist work together to establish the circumstances under which the addictive behaviour occurs. They consider together the motivations to act and the feelings that are experienced when carrying out the behaviour for all time periods surrounding the action (those feelings and motivations before, during and after the addictive behaviour has been performed). The next step is to apply some skills training. This is where the therapist teaches the patient a number of effective ways to cope with the desire to behave. These coping strategies will help the patient to unlearn their old habits and to take on new ones that do not involve carrying out the addictive behaviour. All the time the patient is encouraged to apply positive thinking and this helps them to embed the belief that they can beat the addiction. In addition, patients with addictions often suffer from feelings of low self-worth, so the process is designed to improve the patient's self-esteem. The patient also has to learn to say no to offers to engage in the behaviour. This is often achieved by having the patient practise saying no in a non-threatening environment so that they are then later able to do the same in real life.

A big advantage of CBT over other kinds of therapy is that it is very cost-effective. It can be completed over a relatively short space of time (about 10–15 sessions) and there is no need for any residential component, as is the case with some of the other methodologies. This significantly keeps the cost of treatment to its lowest possible level.

There are numerous examples in the literature of the success of CBT in treating a wide range of addictions. Ladouceur et al. (2001) have shown that CBT is more effective than no treatment for those with pathological gambling. The data are impressive, because 86 per cent of the 33 gamblers given CBT went from being pathological gamblers to not being pathological according to DSM-IV (the relevant version at the time). That this method has widespread use was demonstrated by King et al. (2012), who showed that cognitive behaviour techniques could be successful with Internet addiction in children. This was a case study using a single 16-year old male with pathological Internet addiction, so we would need to be cautious about the general validity of this finding. However, the positive finding regarding CBT and Internet use has been reported several times (for example, Young, 2007; Cao et al., 2007; Li and Dai, 2009).

KEY STUDY: YOUNG (2007)

Internet addiction is a relatively new clinical disorder and so there is not much of an understanding of how to treat it. While it seems obvious to try the methods that work for similar kinds of addiction, the evidence for the effectiveness of each treatment type must be collected. Young (2007) conducted a study to look at the efficacy of CBT in treating Internet addiction. Internet addiction is defined as the inability to control Internet use in such a way as to cause relational, social and occupational problems.

Young used a survey methodology with 114 participants (42 per cent female) who were confirmed as online addicts using the Internet Addiction Test (IAT). Participants were given 12 online CBT sessions that provided strategies for avoiding particularly problematic applications and managing any behavioural issues they may have had. A questionnaire was administered after the third, eighth and twelfth sessions, and then again at a six-month follow-up. The questions included ability to control online abuse, motivation to quit and improvements in relationships.

The results showed that the most frequently reported problem by the participants at the start of the treatment was one of time management followed by problems with their relationships. Improvements were shown in their motivation, their control over computer use and their relationships, and these improvements were maintained up to the six-month follow-up. In this way, Young showed that CBT is an effective treatment for Internet addiction. However, this study did not separate out various forms of Internet abuse (online gaming, online shopping, etc.) and so there may be some types of online addiction for which CBT works better, or worse, than for other types.

It is always difficult to know how long a follow-up period should be before you can say that a treatment has long-term effectiveness. With any treatment that involves a human intervention there is always the danger that a treatment is effective because of the attention being paid to the participant during treatment. It is therefore essential to be able to state that the treatment works beyond the period of contact with the therapist. What is not clear is how long this should be after treatment has ceased. In Young's (2007) study, the follow-up was conducted after six months. It is therefore impossible to say whether the improvements seen would still be in place a year or more after treatment. However, we do know that the longer abstinence occurs, the more likely it is to have a lasting effect.

It is hard to find studies that have shown CBT not to work at all, but there are a few that suggest it is only as good as other treatments. For example, Morgenstern et al. (2001) found CBT to be no better than another method in treating alcoholics. However, that is not a statement that CBT failed to work, only that it does not always outperform other methods. We can conclude, therefore, that when CBT is compared to no treatment it is clearly better, but when it is compared to other treatments, the data are not as conclusive.

ACTIVITY 10.9

Almost all of the methods discussed in this topic suggest that being motivated will increase your chances of the treatment being successful. Which, if any, of the treatments do you think would have the best success with someone who doesn't really want to quit? What are your reasons for thinking this?

Exam hint

One way to tackle this question is to choose one biological and one psychological method, as this will give you more to talk about in the evaluation. However, to do this effectively you would need to have good and accurate knowledge of the different drugs and their uses in the different kinds of addiction. An alternative approach would be to choose behavioural and cognitive behaviour methods and use their different psychological principles (that is, no reference to mental phenomena versus reference to thinking, respectively) as a way of evaluating each.

EXAMPLE EXAM QUESTION

Describe and evaluate TWO methods of reducing addiction. (16 marks)

KEY POINTS

- Drug therapy is a common means for treating some kinds of addiction.
- The use of drug therapy is very successful but often needs to be combined with some form of support mechanism.
- Behavioural interventions often involve aversion therapy or covert sensitization.
- Behavioural therapies either try to make a person feel sick at the thought of carrying out the addictive behaviour or make them feel relaxed so they do not need the behaviour.
- Cognitive behaviour therapy is the main cognitive intervention used to treat addicts.
- Most studies involving CBT have shown a successful treatment outcome compared to no treatment.

Applying behaviour change models to addictive behaviour

In this final topic of the chapter we look at two models of behaviour change and how well they can be applied to addictive behaviours. The first is the **theory of planned behaviour** (TPB), initially devised by Ajzen (1985) from an earlier idea called the theory of reasoned action (Fishbein and Ajzen, 1975). It has been periodically refined to its current version (Ajzen and Fishbein, 2005). It suggests that a behaviour results from a combination of attitude, social pressure and behavioural control. The other model we will consider is **Prochaska's stage model of behaviour change** (also known as the transtheoretical model or TTM). The original model (Prochaska and DiClemente, 1983) had only five stages, but a later version by Prochaska and Velicer (1997) included a sixth step.

The theory of planned behaviour

The theory of planned behaviour (TPB) is a theoretical model that attempts to describe the components involved in making a behavioural decision. While the model does not explicitly state how to change a behaviour, many researchers and therapists have used the model to devise treatment schemes designed to address each component of the model.

The TPB model

The purpose behind the TPB is to allow a prediction of what a person's intention to act is. The first thing to note is that the model is not about whether an action definitely will or will not occur, only about whether the intention is there and the fact that this makes the behaviour likely. According to the model, there are three kinds of belief controlling the intention: behavioural beliefs, normative beliefs and control beliefs (see Fig. 10.6).

ADDICTION

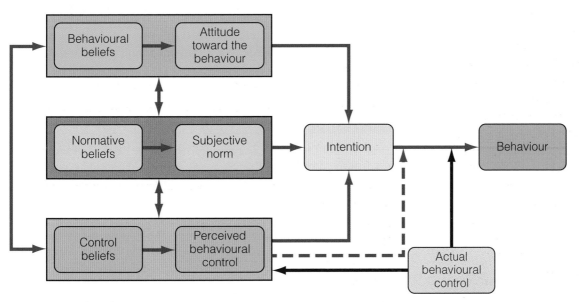

Fig. 10.6 Azjen's (2006) version of the theory of planned behaviour showing the three belief systems involved in creating an intention to act

Behavioural beliefs

A behavioural belief is a belief about the consequences of a behaviour. An example of a behavioural belief might be that if I stop smoking I will decrease the chances that I will develop lung cancer. However, the way in which a behavioural belief works is not quite that simple because aligned to that belief is a behavioural attitude. The attitude towards a behaviour is the overall evaluation of that behaviour as positive or negative. On the positive side, decreasing my health risks is good, but on the negative side I might have to stop going to smoky environments (such as a good friend's house) to avoid the temptation of smoking. The balance of perceived positive and negative outcomes gives rise to my overall attitude to the behaviour.

Normative beliefs

A person's normative beliefs involve a consideration of normative beliefs and the effect of subjective norms on these normative beliefs. A normative belief is a person's perception of the pressures to perform, or not perform, a particular behaviour. In Britain, the social norm concerning smoking has changed from one of it being a good thing to smoke to one of it being an unacceptable behaviour (for the most part). A subjective norm is the influence friends and family (and other significant people) have on your own perception about a behaviour. For example, some might frown upon smoking marijuana, which might encourage you to quit, but others might think it is a cool thing to do, which would encourage you not to quit. The combination of these will influence your belief about the pressure to behave one way or the other.

Control beliefs

Control beliefs concern your own perceived behavioural control. This is the degree of control you believe you have over the behaviour. For example, you might honestly believe that you are capable of giving up smoking. The perception is based upon the degree to which you think there are factors that might impede your ability to carry out the behaviour. For example, if your partner smokes and is not willing to quit at the same time that you do, you might feel that you will have no control over whether there are cigarettes present in the house. This will influence the degree to which you believe you are capable of giving up within these circumstances.

ACTIVITY 10.10

Jeremy has been a smoker for 15 years and is desperate to give up, as he wakes up every morning with a severe chesty cough. While the first cigarette of the day tends to make his cough go away, he knows that this is not a good situation for him to be in and his long-term health prospects are being damaged by his smoking. Jeremy's best friend is also a smoker, and when Jeremy has previously mentioned the possibility of quitting his friend has made it very clear that he will not be joining in. In fact, his friend has commented that if Jeremy does try to quit he should not expect the friend to not smoke in his presence. Jeremy is reasonably determined to quit and so he believes that he can control his addiction but he might have to avoid going to his friend's house for a time.

Using the theory of planned behaviour, decide whether Jeremy has a strong intention to stop smoking.

EXAMPLE EXAM QUESTION

Briefly describe the theory of planned behaviour. (4 marks)

Exam hint

You will need to describe the three components of the model and refer to the fact that together they lead to an intention that is then more likely to lead to a behaviour.

Applying the TPB model to addiction

The TPB has been applied to a wide range of addictive behaviours, from smoking cessation (Bledsoe, 2006) to sorority (a social group of undergraduate women) alcohol consumption (Huchting et al., 2008). The model has been quite successful in helping clinicians to devise programmes to help people change their behaviour (usually to remove unwanted behaviours). For example, Slater et al. (2011) used TPB to inform their campaign to reduce marijuana use in adolescents. They focused on attitudes towards behavioural control and called one of the campaigns 'Be under your own influence'. Indeed, many campaigns that attempt to stop a negative behaviour focus on the element of control in the form of willpower.

The TPB is not just useful in understanding addictions that use psychoactive substances. Kuss and Griffiths (2011) reviewed the literature on addiction to social networking and found that the TPB has been used in this area. Pelling and White (2009) found that social networking activity is influenced by attitudinal and normative elements predicted by the TPB, but that this is not the whole story, as an additional component that they measured, self-identity, also contributed to predicting intentions and behavioural outcome.

KEY STUDY: **PELLING AND WHITE (2009)**

Models like the TPB are useful if they can lead to good predictions about who is and who is not vulnerable to an addiction. The model has been shown to be effective in predicting many kinds of addictive behaviour, and Pelling and White set out to explore its value in predicting people's use of social networking websites (SNWs), such as Facebook or Bebo. As some previous researchers had claimed that TPB alone does not capture all of the potential predictors of addiction, the researchers decided to include some extra measures: self-identity (the importance of the activity to the person's feelings of self-worth) and belongingness (the need to be involved with, accepted by and valued by others). Addictive tendencies (the six criteria defined by Griffiths [1966], referred to at the beginning of the chapter) were also measured.

The study involved 233 undergraduate students (149 female and 84 male) aged 17–24. They were asked to complete two questionnaires, one week apart. The first questionnaire asked some standard TPB questions together with specific questions to explore self-identity, belongingness, addictive tendencies and various demographic details. The follow-up questionnaire simply asked participants the number of days on which they had made four or more separate visits to a SNW.

The results showed that attitude and subjective norm were good predictors of future SNW behaviour but perceived behavioural control was not (see Fig. 10.6 for a reminder of the three components of the TPB). The additional measure of self-identity was also a good predictor of SNW behaviour, but belongingness was not. Both, though, were good predictors of addictive tendency. Overall, then, there was some support for the use of the TPB in predicting whether or not a young person is likely to engage in high-frequency use of SNWs.

Evaluating the TPB model

On the plus side, the TPB has an advantage over previous theories as it is able to take into account unconscious behaviours. Furthermore, the inclusion of the control beliefs recognized that the relationship between intention and action has to include a person's belief about their own capabilities. Another positive component of the TPB is that it is relatively easy to devise questionnaires that tap into each of the belief components.

Armitage and Conner (2001) carried out a meta-analysis of 185 studies using the TPB that had been published by the end of 1997. Their conclusion was that TPB is a good predictor of intentions and behaviour. They did, though, point out that prediction is superior for self-reported rather than observed behaviour. However, Manstead and Parker (1995) have argued that, despite its huge success, TPB has a number of methodological and theoretical issues.

The TPB is a purely cognitive model and is, therefore, somewhat reductionist. As a consequence of this, one of the theoretical limitations of the TPB is that it does not take into account emotional factors that might influence behaviour. However, we must remember that the model only aims to assess the intention to act and was not really meant to assess whether or not the behaviour will occur. One final problem for the model is that much of the research data are correlational and collected in the field so, while high in external validity, the model suffers from a lack of internal validity.

Research methods link

For more on validity, see pages 42–44.

Prochaska's stage model of behaviour change

This model of behaviour change differs from planned behaviour because it tries to define the stages that a person must go through in order to change their behaviour. It uses some core constructs about change to elicit processes of change that are explicit instructions about how to act. The model behind these processes describes six stages that a person must pass through in order to change. The complete model is called the transtheoretical model (TTM) and the stages of change are a component of that model.

The TTM model

The TTM model is a model of intentional behaviour change. That is, it describes the processes involved when someone deliberately tries to change their behaviour. As such, it has become one of the major models that inform health interventions. It was first conceived by Prochaska and DiClemente in 1977 but the model did not really take shape until it was published a few years later (Prochaska and DiClemente, 1983). The model consists of a number of different components and these are four constructs, ten processes, six stages, decision balance and self-efficacy. The main focus here will be on the six stages.

Stages of change

The six stages are described in Fig. 10.7 and are often represented in a form that indicates an ascending spiral (see Fig. 10.8) to underline the fact that it is possible to slip back some stages as well as progress through them.

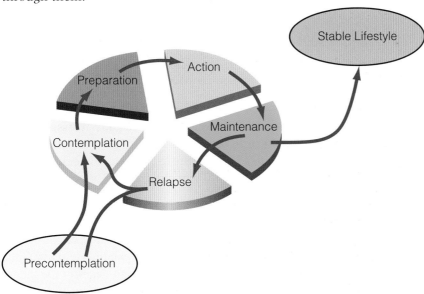

Fig. 10.7 Prochaska and DiClemente's stages of change

The stages in the model span a time period from before you even start to think about changing your behaviour to a period in the future where you barely remember the time when you needed to change. The possibility of relapse is also indicated in many diagrammatic versions of the model. Of course, making these changes is not that easy, so the stages capture landmark turning points.

Pre-contemplation

At this stage, the individual is not even thinking about changing their behaviour. Indeed, they may not even see the behaviour as a problem (for example, I don't drink all that much) and so the thought that they should change it has not even crossed their mind. Of course, they may well have encountered the problem in various ways before (for instance, someone points it out to them) but at this stage their response is dismissal. Therefore, the person in the pre-contemplation stage is not considering the need to change their behaviour.

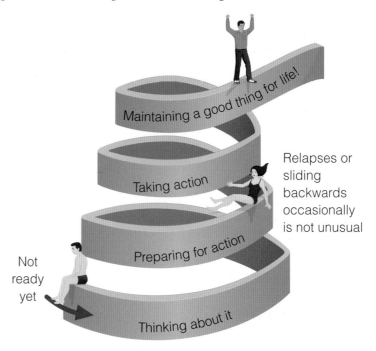

Fig. 10.8 The stages of Prochaska's model represented as a spiral to indicate that moving through the stages often involves steps forwards and lapses backwards

Contemplation

The person has now reached the stage where they are willing to consider that they might need to change a behaviour (for example, I suppose I did drink quite a bit over the last couple of weeks) and are willing to explore ways that they might do this. However, they have not yet made any commitment to change, they are merely considering it as a possibility.

Preparation

This is the stage in which the person starts to make plans for changing the behaviour. They have now made a determined decision to change (for example, it is about time I took control of my life and stopped drinking so much) and is exploring the various ways by which they might achieve that change. At this stage, their plan is likely to include a consideration of the possible problems they will encounter and they will have thought about how they will overcome these obstacles.

Action

The person is now putting their plan into action. Often this stage involves a public disclosure of their intentions (for example, hey everyone, I have decided to stop drinking) and this is often so that they can receive support and so that they can, as far as possible, avoid situations in which they might be tempted to abandon their plan (for example, someone saying to them, are you sure you wouldn't like just a half?). This action stage usually lasts a few months and it is only then that the person can move on to the next stage.

Maintenance

At this stage, the change in behaviour has become reasonably well established (for example, I do not drink alcohol anymore). The temptation to revert back to the old behaviour lessens. The person may have established personal landmarks (for example, three months without a drink) and has now achieved a few of those landmarks. They are not completely free of the behaviour but are getting there and feeling more confident about their ability to make this a permanent change.

Termination

This is the ultimate goal. The person has reached this stage when there are no remaining temptations that would send the person back to their previous behaviour. They are also no longer tempted at all by others' engagement in the behaviour (for example, saying it does not bother me if you are having a drink). The fear of a relapse has now passed and the person can relax in the knowledge that their behaviour change has been a success.

Other elements of the model

You will see from Fig. 10.7 that one of the segments is labelled 'relapse'. This is the possible alternative stage that can come into play from any of the other stages apart from termination. Relapse implies that the person has reverted back to their old behaviour. At this point they will need to make a decision whether or not to try again.

Applying the stages of change to addiction

The stages of change model has been applied to a number of clinical settings in which a behaviour change is desired, and this includes cases of addiction. In fact, it is widely accepted as a good model with which to understand the barriers to changing an addictive behaviour and as a good starting point for the treatment of addiction. It has been widely applied, especially in the treatment of substance abuse. One of the first examples of its use was by the original researchers to explain smoking behaviour.

KEY STUDY: PROCHASKA AND DICLEMENTE (1983)

Prochaska and DiClemente (1983) were interested in the stages and processes that people go through when they decide to quit on their own. Almost all of the previous research had looked at people who were trying to quit via a formal cessation programme, even though less than 30 per cent of those Americans who quit at the time used such programmes. Prochaska and DiClemente aimed to examine the processes of change that accompanied each of the stages of change.

There were 872 participants from two US states (Rhode Island and Texas) and each was assigned to a group depending on their quitting status. These were long-term quitters (247), recent quitters (134), contemplators (187), immotives (pre-contemplators) (108) and relapsers (196). They used a process of change test to measure the ten processes of change. The test consisted of a 40-item questionnaire with four items for each process. The researchers also took saliva samples to validate the participants' self-reported smoking status. The participants filled in the questionnaires and were given a short interview every six months for a period of two years.

Table 10.3 shows the results in a simplified form. The highest (H) and lowest (L) scores for each process are shown for each stage. The top five processes are experiential (thinking) and the bottom five are behavioural. It is not surprising that contemplators and relapsers show mostly experiential processes and recent quitters show mostly behavioural processes. The authors concluded by suggesting that this model and the data presented could be used to improve treatment programmes and make them more appealing and also to improve self-help manuals for those who want to quit on their own.

	Immotives	Contemplators	Recent quitters	Long-term quitters	Relapsers
Consciousness-raising	L	H			
Self-liberation	L		H		
Social liberation		H	L		
Self-re-evaluation	L				H
Environmental re-evaluation	L			H	H
Counterconditioning	L		H		
Stimulus control	L		H		
Reinforcement management	L		H		
Dramatic relief	L	H			
Helping relationship	L		H		

Table 10.3 Simplified results from Prochaska and DiClemente (1983). It is clear that pre-contemplators (immotives) are low in all processes and that different stages are associated with different processes of change.

Earlier in the chapter we saw the problem of having small sample sizes when the addiction being investigated does not have large numbers of people who are clinically diagnosed. In the case of smoking it is easy to find participants, so the test of the stages of change model could be done with a large number of participants. In Prochaska and DiClemente's particular study it was also necessary to have a large initial sample as it could not have been known how many participants might drop out between the initial questionnaire and the final one two years later. This highlights the need to plan carefully when conducting a study.

The use of stages of change has had claims of a reasonable degree of success in treating a wide range of addictions. However, despite there being a huge literature on the stage of change model, most of the addiction studies have concentrated on only smoking cessation. A review of the effectiveness of stage-based interventions to promote smoking cessation (Riemsma et al., 2003) showed that it generally had little effect. Only one of 11 studies where stage-based interventions were directly compared with other interventions showed a significant advantage of the stage-based interventions. In any case, evaluating the degree of success is not very easy. If termination is the ultimate goal then how long must one wait before assessing that termination has occurred? It is not unreasonable for a clinician to expect that treatment will take up to five years.

Describe some possible behaviours associated with the preparation and action stages of the stages of change model for a smoker and a gambler. In both cases, what might constitute having reached termination?

Evaluating the stages of change model

Despite the positives surrounding the stages of change model, there are some limitations to it. One issue is that it does not account for all possible behavioural outcomes. For example, I may have gone through the stages up to action and my action decision may be not to change my behaviour. In other words, I am making an active decision, but not one that leads to a cessation of my addictive behaviour. This might be because I fear that changing my behaviour will change other aspects of my life that I quite like (for example, the friends I have because of my use of cannabis).

Another problem with the model is that it implies that the steps to change are fixed. In other words, the expectation is that one moves from contemplation to planning before moving to action. This might not always be the case. For example, some people give up smoking without really planning anything about how it will happen. They move directly from contemplating giving up to acting, without planning a ceremonial throwing away of cigarettes, planning to drink at a different pub, and so on.

ADDICTION

EXAMPLE EXAM QUESTION

Discuss the theory of planned behaviour and the stages of change model. (8 marks)

Despite these shortcomings, it must be remembered that this model was devised when we had little idea about the processes and stages that explain behaviour change. Prochaska's original idea provided an excellent starting point from which to try to develop a holistic model of behaviour change. Since these beginnings other refinements have emerged and taken into account more elements of the process.

KEY POINTS

- There are two key behaviour change models that have been used to explain addictive behaviour.
- The theory of planned behaviour (TPB) model suggests that behaviours arise from the intention to behave.
- The TPB tries to explain the sources of an intention to behave and therefore the likelihood that a behaviour will occur.
- The TPB has three components that drive intention: behavioural beliefs, normative beliefs and control beliefs.
- The stages of change model tries to explain the different stages a person goes through when trying to quit an addictive behaviour.
- The full stages of change model includes the possibility of no longer being addicted as well as the possibility of relapse.
- The stages of change are: pre-contemplation, contemplation, preparation, action, maintenance and relapse.

This practical involves the construction and analysis of a questionnaire. Choose a either nicotine addiction or gambling addiction as the focus of the survey. Use about ten statements and a Likert scale to explore each of the following four areas with respect to your chosen addiction.

- How is the addiction defined?
- What are the risks of becoming addicted?
- What drove initiation and maintenance of the addiction?
- What treatments has the person tried and were there any relapses?

In addition, you might want to collect some demographic data, such as gender and age.

A reminder about the ethics procedure

Ensure that you have also created a briefing sheet and consent form, along with a debriefing and making sure that the questionnaires are completed anonymously. Also ensure that you are able to keep the data secured and that it is destroyed after completion of the study (once the data have been analysed). Finally, you must have your questionnaire approved as ethical by your teacher before you can collect any data.

To analyse the results you could look at the answers to individual questions and see how they relate to the research you have read about. You could also score the themes and carry out some simple analyses by using the demographic data to produce separate groups.

Example exam questions

1. Briefly outline Prochaska and DiClemente's stage model of behaviour change. You may outline either the five-stage or the six-stage version of the model. **(6 marks)**

2. Explain ONE strength of this model. **(2 marks)**

3. Outline and evaluate explanations of gambling addiction. **(16 marks)**

Exam focus

Read through the following example exam question, example student answer, and examiner comments. Then, have a go at answering the question yourself!

EXAMPLE EXAM QUESTION

Outline TWO explanations for nicotine addiction. (4 marks)

Emily's answer

One explanation for nicotine addiction is that it is genetically inherited. A genetic link has been made to the DRD2 gene and this changes the number of dopamine receptors in the mesolimbic system. This system is associated with reward and so a person gets a reward when they have a cigarette because the nicotine activates the reward centres of the brain.

A second explanation for nicotine addiction is cue reactivity. This is when a person has learned to associate certain cues with smoking. For example, if you are used to smoking while at a friend's house and you are trying to give up, just being at the house will make you want a cigarette more as the environment acts as a cue for smoking. This is a learning theory explanation for why it is so difficult to give up an addiction like smoking.

Examiner comment: This is a good paragraph as it shows an appreciation of the genetic explanation for smoking. There is a reference to a relevant gene and to a neurotransmitter system and so even though there is not a lot of detail, there is enough coverage for two marks.

Examiner comment: Again this is a very good answer for two marks. It names the explanation and gives an example that makes it clear to the examiner that the candidate understands the term. The explanation is also noted as being one that comes from learning theory. Again, therefore, the candidate has done enough for two marks and the answer as a whole receives full marks.

Ben's answer

One explanation comes from learning theory and involves faulty cognitions. People believe that smoking relieves stress even though research has shown that it actually increases stress. Smoking becomes a form of self-medication so this acts as a positive reinforcement.

A second explanation is a biological one. This suggests that smoking is genetically inherited and the evidence for this comes from twin studies using monozygotic (MZ) and dizygotic (DZ) twins. MZ twins show higher rates of smoking than DZ twins and they share 100 per cent of their genes so this shows that smoking is an inherited trait.

Examiner comment: There is confusion between learning theory and cognitive explanations. However, outside of that, the answer has a relevant point about the belief of stress relief. There is enough for one mark but there is not enough detail to overlook the initial confusion.

Examiner comment: This answer is very vague and does not relate specifically to smoking behaviour. While the essence of the argument might be correct, this set of statements could equally be made about gambling or a host of other disorders. Hence, there is nothing that relates to the question well enough for any marks to be awarded.

Examination skills

Introduction

As we reminded you in the Year 1 book, it can be helpful to think of A Level exams in the same way as your driving test. You prepare for your driving test by familiarizing yourself with exactly what is required and then regularly practising the different components and manoeuvres to become skilled at them. This is a very good approach to apply to A Level assessments. In this section we take a close look at the examinations you will be undertaking and illustrating the skills you will need to develop for success in the second year of your A Level study. You may have already completed Papers 1 and 2 as an AS qualification at the end of your first year – this will have provided a flavour of the type of questions you will meet at the end of Year 2.

A reminder about assessment

A good place to start is to remind you of what will be required in your exams. The Psychology examinations assess three main skills, or 'Assessment Objectives':

1. AO1: You should be able to **demonstrate knowledge and understanding** of psychological ideas, processes, techniques and procedures.
2. AO2: You should be able to **apply your knowledge** and understanding of psychological ideas, processes, techniques and procedures in different contexts and when handling data.
3. AO3: You should be able to **analyse, interpret and evaluate** psychological information and evidence, to make judgements and reach conclusions and to develop and refine designs and procedures when carrying out or planning research.

So, you can expect the exam papers to contain questions that require you to use the different kinds of cognitive skills you have developed over the course: to demonstrate knowledge of theories, research studies and methods; to apply your knowledge to novel situations; and to analyse and evaluate theories, research studies and methods. Some exam questions combine these objectives – for example, asking you to show knowledge of a topic and then apply your knowledge to a novel situation, or demonstrate knowledge of a theory and then analyse/evaluate the theory. Your understanding of research methods will form an important element of assessment of your second year of study.

By way of reminder:

- Paper 1 contains more A01 (knowledge) marks
- Paper 2 contains more A02 (application) marks
- Papers 1 and 3 contain more A03 (analysis and evaluation) marks than Paper 2.

Throughout the book you will find examples of the different types of question that will be used in your exam papers, along with some helpful hints about how to tackle these, and some things to avoid! We strongly advise you to write answers to these questions as part of your exam preparation: this will help you to hone your writing skills for the different kinds of question.

General guidance for A Level Psychology exams

There are three assessments for A Level Psychology: Papers 1, 2 and 3. These are equally weighted, so each provides 33 per cent of your final mark for A Level. All three question papers will include a mixture of multiple-choice questions, short questions and extended writing (essay-style) questions.

Time management

You have two hours to complete each exam paper and each paper is worth 96 marks. As you will need reading time, this makes a rough rule of just over one minute for each mark. The number of marks provides a guide for how much to write, and you should look carefully at how marks are allocated in each section of the examination when planning your answers. It does not make sense to write for ten minutes on a question that is worth four marks then try to tackle a ten-mark question in five minutes. You should plan to spend around **ten minutes on an eight-mark question** and around **20 minutes on 16-mark question**. It is a good idea to practise writing against the clock when preparing for your exams. It can also be a good idea to put your watch on the desk in the examination and keep a close eye on how time is going – it is very easy to overrun!

Decoding questions

Many students are concerned that, under the pressure of the exam, they may misread or misinterpret a question. Years of marking student responses have shown us just how common this can be. Often, students who know a great deal of information and have clearly revised thoroughly write a good answer to a different question to the one that has been set – albeit in the same area – and sadly, gain few marks. Other students include material that cannot be awarded marks – for instance, including evaluation when the question has asked only for description of a topic area.

Each question will be comprised of one or more injunction words (instructions) and content words. Common injunction words include *outline*, *describe* and *summarize*, which relate to the assessment objective A01; *apply*, which relates to A02; and *evaluate* and *discuss*, which relate to A03. Each of these has different meanings and you should make sure you are familiar with these common terms and the differences between them. For instance, an outline is a sketch of the main features with little detail, whereas a description provides more detail about the main features of a theory, study or explanation.

It can help to underline the injunction and content words on the question. Let's have a look at an example:

Sam is a police officer. She has just started working the night shift and after a week, she finds that she has difficulty sleeping during the day and is becoming tense and irritable. Sam is also worried that she is less alert during the night shift itself.

Using your knowledge of endogenous pacemakers and exogenous zeitgebers, explain Sam's experiences. (4 marks)

The injunction word in this question is 'explain' and you are asked to use your knowledge of zeitgebers and endogenous pacemakers in your explanation. Hence, this question requires you to explain why Sam has the experiences described in the scenario and your explanation should draw on your knowledge of endogenous pacemakers and zeitgebers.

ACTIVITY 1: DECODING QUESTIONS

Read the following questions and identify the injunction words and content words. Roughly rephrase/rewrite each question in your own words.

1. Discuss psychological research into self-disclosure. (16 marks)
2. Explain what is meant by 'androgyny' and outline one method of measuring androgyny. (5 marks)
3. Discuss explanations for the success and failure of dieting. (16 marks)
4. Briefly outline TWO positive symptoms of schizophrenia. (4 marks)
5. Describe and briefly evaluate the role of personality as a risk factor for addiction. (6 marks)
6. Compare and contrast behavioural and cognitive explanations for nicotine addiction. (12 marks)

How will my answers be marked?

Your paper will be scanned and then marked online – which makes it very important to write clearly! The examiners who mark your paper will use a '**Level of response**' mark scheme. This mark scheme identifies the key characteristics of a good, reasonable, or basic answer for each question.

- Short questions (i.e. 4 marks) generally have two levels of response.
- Moderate length answers (i.e. 6 or 8 marks) have three levels of response.
- Extended writing questions (i.e. 12 or 16 marks) have four levels of response.

The descriptor for the level shows the average performance for the level. The examiner will read your response carefully and check if it fits the criteria in the lowest level before moving up the levels to see where your response fits. They will consider the overall quality of your answer to do this, rather than 'picking holes' in small and specific parts of the answer and looking for areas where you have not been as clear as you might. It is worth noting that the top level does not require a perfect answer.

Here is an example of a Paper 2 question and the relevant mark scheme:

> Dominic is unhappy and lacks confidence. He also thinks he is not very good-looking and not very clever. He goes to a counselling therapist for help. The therapist suggests that Dominic lacks congruence.
>
> Outline what is meant by 'congruence'. Explain ONE way in which Dominic might achieve 'congruence'. (4 marks)
>
> *(AQA Specimen Material)*

This question has two injunctions (instructions): 'outline' and 'explain'.

Level	Marks	Description
2	3–4	Outline of congruence is clear and coherent with appropriate use of terminology. Application to Dominic is appropriate with description of need to reduce the gap and how to achieve this.
1	1–2	Outline is limited, i.e. shows some knowledge that congruence involves different aspects of the self. Application is vague. The answer as a whole is not very clearly expressed.
	0	No relevant content.

(AQA Specimen Material)

ACTIVITY 2

The mark scheme identifies two levels of response. What should your answer include in order to be awarded a mark in Level 2?

So, this mark scheme provides you with goalposts, identifying exactly what you should aim for in your answers to score well.

What about maths?

The standard of maths in the Psychology assessment is at least the standard of higher-tier GCSE mathematics, and at least **10 per cent of the marks** at A Level will require you to use your mathematical skills. Questions could require you to:

- calculate descriptive statistics (e.g. mean scores or ranges from a set of data)
- comment on which descriptive statistics to use in a particular data set (mean, median or mode)
- display data in an appropriate graph
- explain the difference between probability levels $p \leq 0.05$ and $p \leq 0.01$
- use critical value tables (i.e. statistical tables) to decide whether to reject or retain the null hypothesis.

Paper 2, Psychology in context

Paper 2, Psychology in context, assesses your knowledge of three **compulsory** topic areas. There are no options on this paper and you will be required to answer all the questions. The paper is worth 96 marks and **half** of these marks are awarded for your understanding of research methods. The sections are as follows:

- Approaches in psychology (24 marks)
- Biological psychology (24 marks)
- Research methods (48 marks)

As with Paper 1, questions will be mixture of multiple-choice, short answer and extended writing. Marks for these questions are likely to vary and you should look carefully at the number of marks available as a guide for how much to write. You should aim to spend about 30 minutes on Section A and 30 minutes on Section B. This will allow around an hour for Section C, Research methods.

Many of the questions on this paper will expect you to **apply your knowledge** (A02) so let's have a look at gaining good marks on application questions.

Advice for tackling Paper 2

How to gain good A02 marks on application questions

The assessment objective A02 requires you to apply your knowledge in different contexts. Hence, the key to good A02 marks is thorough application to the scenario. How do you go about applying knowledge? Each scenario on the examination will have been carefully constructed to provide a series of clues, or 'hooks'. You should start by reading the scenario very carefully to identify the key hooks – it can help to underline these on the exam paper.

The question is about the effects of working night shifts

Sam has worked nights for one week

Sam has problems with sleeping during the day

feeling irritability, lack of sleep?

loss of alertness at night

> Sam is a police officer. She has just started working the night shift and after a week, she finds that she has difficulty sleeping during the day and is becoming tense and irritable. Sam is also worried that she is less alert during the night shift itself.
>
> Using your knowledge of endogenous pacemakers and exogenous zeitgebers, explain Sam's experiences. (4 marks)

So the scenario refers to several effects of working nights, including difficulty sleeping during the day, irritability and lack of alertness while working at night. These effects arise when there is conflict between the external cues or zeitgebers (such as daylight and darkness), which conflict with messages from the internal endogenous clock.

Once you have identified the key 'hooks', construct your answer to the scenario by referring to each hook carefully, preferably in the order they occur in the stem. You should not waste your time describing other research into bodily rhythms as no marks are available for description: remember that marks are awarded for showing your understanding through *application* to the example.

Tackling the research methods component of Paper 2

Your understanding of research methods is tested on Paper 2, Psychology in context, and accounts for half of the marks on this paper (48 out of 96). This section of the paper will present you with a description of one or more (fictional) research studies – such as an experiment, correlation or observation – and you will be asked a series of questions about this piece of research. Some common questions are:

- Identify the IV and DV and operationalize these.
- Write a hypothesis for the study.
- Identify and comment critically on the experimental design that has been used.
- Identify controlled variables and potential confounding variables.
- Identify the type of sample used and comment on the implications of this, for example in terms of generalizability.
- Identify the ethical issues inherent in the research study and comment how they have (or have not) been handled.

You should tackle the research methods questions by reading the whole scenario through at least once, and preferably twice. It can also help to annotate the exam paper, jotting down the IV, DV, etc. while you are reading. Resist the temptation to start answering the questions without reading to the end, as you will probably miss important information. One of the most common errors students make is failing to apply knowledge sufficiently and precisely to the scenario – for instance, identifying a confounding variable, which could not occur in the experiment described.

A very good way to prepare for this type of question is to focus on some of the 'key studies' you have met and work through the bulleted list above, identifying answers.

Design a study to …

Another potential component of the research methods element of Paper 2 is for you to design a piece of research, often building on one you have already answered questions about. You will probably have carried out several pieces of practical work in your psychology lessons and it is a good idea to look back over these in preparation for the exam. Once again, you should read these questions very carefully, and it may help to underline on the paper what you are required to include in your answers. It is very easy to go off target!

ACTIVITY 5

Design an observation study to investigate possible differences in mobile phone use between male and female students in a college cafeteria. (12 marks)

In your answer you should provide details of:

- the behavioural categories to be used and how the data will be recorded
- how reliability of the data collection might be established
- ethical issues to be considered.

Paper 3: Issues and options in psychology

Paper 3, Issue and options in psychology, covers **one compulsory topic** area, Issues and debates, and **three options**. Each of the four sections is worth 24 marks and the paper is two hours long, which allows for about 30 minutes per section.

The sections are as follows:

- Issues and debates: compulsory: 24 marks
- Relationships OR Gender OR Cognition and development: 24 marks
- Schizophrenia OR Eating behaviour OR Stress: 24 marks
- Aggression OR Forensic psychology OR Addiction: 24 marks

Advice for tackling Paper 3

How to gain good A01 marks

The assessment objective A01 requires you to demonstrate knowledge and understanding of theories, methods or research studies. Typical A01 terms include 'outline' and 'describe'. An outline is a sketch of the main features without much detail. A question which asks for an outline is likely to have fewer marks awarded for A01. If you are asked to describe, more detail is required and there are likely to be more marks available. For an outline you will need to select the most important information to include. For example, if you were asked to outline the filter theory of attraction, you would identify the three filters and the time periods at which they operate. If you were asked to describe filter theory, you could also include Kerckhoff and Davis' longitudinal study (see page 142) to illustrate the different filters in action.

1. Here is an answer to the question 'Describe Prochaska's six-stage model of behaviour change [6 marks]'. Read the answer and then convert this into a three-mark *outline* of the model. Aim to make your summary less than 100 words in length.

Prochaska's model identifies six stages that people go through when attempting to change a behaviour, such as giving up smoking or increasing exercise. The stage of pre-contemplation occurs before the individual has identified the need to change. Contemplation follows and this involves thinking about giving up smoking or starting an exercise programme. The next stage is preparation: the decision for change has been made and the person starts to plan how they will reach their goal, for instance telling family colleagues they intend to stop smoking, and getting rid of ashtrays in the house. The stage of action occurs when the plans are put into effect – at this stage there is danger of slipping back into the old ways. The stage of termination occurs when the danger is past and the person now sees himself or herself as a non-smoker who is no longer tempted to relapse.

Compare your answer with the example given at the end of this chapter.

2. Now have a go at constructing answers to the two following questions:
   a) Briefly outline TWO positive symptoms of schizophrenia. [4 marks]
   b) Describe TWO positive symptoms of schizophrenia. [6 marks]

Your outline should name the two symptoms and briefly explain the nature of both, and your description should provide more detail, showing the different characteristics of the symptoms. You might find it easier to write the six-mark description first, then edit it down to a four-mark outline.

How to gain good AO3 marks

The assessment objective AO3 requires you to analyse and evaluate theories, research studies, and methods. What do we mean by analysis and evaluation? These are critical skills that indicate that you can go further than simply describing theories and studies, and you can engage in discussion about how useful or important they are. Evaluation is literally putting a value on something – telling us how much it is worth or how useful it is.

A good start to evaluation is to identify strengths and weaknesses of a theory or a study. Many students assume that critical analysis consists only of negative points, but it is fine to be positive: all the research you have read about in this book has made a valuable contribution to psychological knowledge at some point, even though some insights may have been superseded by more recent (and possibly scientific) understanding of a topic.

In the exam guidance for Book 1 we explored the differences between evaluating research studies (e.g. Bandura's bobo doll study) and evaluating explanations. We also considered the importance of elaboration – developing your critical points. These skills still apply here, but a further skill to develop in Year 2 is the establishment of *a line of argument*. This is most important on Paper 3 where there are likely to be more essay-style, 16-mark questions.

Establishing a line of argument

What is a line of argument? In simple terms, a line of argument refers to an essay that moves clearly and logically towards a conclusion via a series of steps along the way.

Let us examine an example. Read the following answer to a 16-mark essay on aggression and jot down your responses to the questions below:

- Is the answer well informed and accurate?
- Does it include relevant evidence?
- Is the argument clear throughout the essay?
- What do you think the question was?

Aggression occurs in all societies and is socially unacceptable in most of them. In western cultures, legal sanctions are in place as a deterrent, and a negative social stigma comes with such behaviour. Aggression has been shown to increase when people are anonymous and cannot be identified. Zimbardo (1970) demonstrated this in a Milgram-like study that required female participants to deliver electric shocks to another participant. Some participants wore lab coats and hoods, were not referred to by name and were kept apart from other participants during the study, i.e. they were anonymous. Other participants wore normal clothes, a nametag, were referred to by name and were able to see each other during the study. Even though all the participants could see the victim receive their electric shocks, those participants who were made to feel anonymous delivered shocks for twice as long as participants without anonymity. Other studies outside of the laboratory have supported the role of anonymity in real-life aggressive behaviour. Silke (2003) analysed 500 violent attacks occurring in Northern Ireland between 1994 and 1996. He found that people who wore disguises, thus hiding their identities, carried out 206 attacks.

Aggression often occurs in a crowd. An explanation was developed from the ideas of Le Bon (1895) who noticed that in crowds, a 'collective mind' emerges, leading to uninhibited behaviour and antisocial acts such as aggression. Festinger et al. referred to this loss of individual identity while in a crowd as deindividuation. Festinger argued that anonymity and a reduced personal responsibility lead people in a group to cease to see themselves as individuals or to be deindividuated.

Diener (1980) argues that we are normally self-aware and use this to regulate our own behaviour. In a crowd, the group becomes the focus of attention through such behaviours as chanting and clapping, and the subsequent decrease in self-awareness leads to deindividuation. There is disagreement therefore about which elements of being in a crowd are most important.

Social learning theory emphasizes learning from role models and the frustration–aggression approach sees aggression as a drive, which comes from being prevented from achieving a goal.

Reicher (1987) argues that when a person becomes part of a group, for example of football supporters, there is a shift of identity rather than a loss of identity. The shift is from personal identity (for example, being Jack Smith) to a social identity or sense of oneself as a group member (for example, being an Everton supporter). Deindividuation, according to Reicher, occurs when we are a member of a group which emphasizes social rather than personal identity. Deindividuation is not the only social psychological explanation of aggression. Finally, in some crowds, deindividuation can produce peaceful rather than aggressive behaviours (for example, at a music festival).

You probably wrote that the answer is accurate and contains a range of research. However, you may have found it difficult to establish a line of argument or to identify the title of the essay, which was:

Discuss one social psychological explanation of human aggression. (16 marks)

There are two reasons why this answer is difficult to follow:

1. It is disorganized, lacking a clear structure
2. There is no 'line of argument'.

A simple way to structure material for an answer of this nature in an exam could be:

- Stage 1: An outline of the explanation you have chosen
- Stage 2: An examination of the evidence *for* the explanation
- Stage 3: An examination of evidence *against* the explanation or critique of the explanation
- Stage 4: Drawing together the argument to reach a reasoned conclusion.

ACTIVITY 7: ESTABLISHING A LINE OF ARGUMENT

Using the above steps, construct an answer using only the material in the essay above. You can move material around and group it into sensible sections. You can compare your answer with an example at the end of the section.

Your essay now should be clearly and logically ordered. In order to make the line of argument clear, you should signpost throughout your essay. Signposting refers to using the first (and sometimes last) line of each paragraph to explain what will be covered in each section. Here are some useful signposts for you to insert into your essay:

- A range of evidence shows that aggression is more likely when people are anonymous, supporting deindividuation theory.
- However, Diener (1980) argues that it is not anonymity but reduced self-awareness, caused by being in a crowd, which leads to deindividuation.
- One social psychological explanation of aggression is deindividuation.
- Another criticism of deindividuation has been put forward by Reicher (1987).
- These are arguably better explanations of why individuals are aggressive (for instance, picking a fight) when they are not anonymous or in a crowd.

Activity answers

Activity 1 Decoding questions

Qu	Injunction words	Content words	So the question is asking you to...
1	Discuss	Research into self-disclosure	Summarize and talk critically about psychological theories and/or studies into self-disclosure
2	Explain and outline	Androgyny and measuring androgyny	Explain what androgyny is and briefly summarize one method that can be used to measure androgyny
3	Discuss	Explanations for success and failure of diets	Summarize explanations of why diets succeed and fail. Talk critically about the explanations you have covered
4	Briefly outline	Two positive symptoms of schizophrenia	Provide a brief sketch of the characteristics of two positive symptoms
5	Describe and briefly evaluate	The role of personality as a risk factor for addiction	Describe how personality influences addiction and talk critically about the importance of personality in addictions
6	Compare and contrast	Behavioural and cognitive explanations of nicotine addiction	Summarize the behavioural and cognitive explanations of nicotine addiction, then identify similarities and differences between them

Activity 2: Mark schemes

A Level 2 (top band) response requires:

- Outline of congruence is clear and coherent with appropriate use of terminology. Application to Dominic is appropriate with description of need to reduce the gap and how to achieve this.
- An outline that is clear and coherent with appropriate use of terminology.
- Appropriate application to the scenario including description of how to reduce the gap.

Activity 3: Application

Sam has just started working night shifts and this is disrupting her sleep–wake cycle, which is a circadian rhythm. As Sam now works shifts, she needs to be awake when it is dark and asleep when it is daylight. The darkness will lead to the production of melatonin (the sleep hormone) and this what makes Sam feel less alert and sleepy during the night shift. When Sam goes home from work and tries to go to sleep, zeitgebers, such as light and noise like the birds singing, are cues to be awake, making it difficult for Sam to sleep during the day. This disruption of her rhythms is what makes Sam tense and irritable – she may also be suffering from sleep deprivation, which is common in night-shift workers.

Activity 6: Outline versus describe

1) Prochaska's model identifies six stages of behaviour change. The model begins with pre-contemplation before the individual has identified the need for change. This is followed by contemplation, which involves thinking about changing the behaviour. Once the decision has been made, the next stages are preparation (making plans for change) and action (putting the plans into effect). Termination is the last stage, occurring when the new behaviour is firmly established.

2a) Two positive symptoms of schizophrenia include auditory hallucinations and delusions. Auditory hallucinations are often referred to as 'hearing voices' that are not real. The voices often provide a running commentary on the person's behaviour that can be negative or derogatory (e.g., telling the schizophrenic that they are a bad person). Some schizophrenics also suffer visual or tactile hallucinations such as spiders crawling on the body, but auditory hallucinations are most common.

A second positive symptom is delusions, Delusions are beliefs that could not possibly be real (for example, I am Adolf Hitler), though they seem very real to the patient. Common delusions include persecution (thinking MI5 are after you) and delusions of grandeur (for example, I am David Beckham). Delusional beliefs cannot be argued with and however much counterevidence is presented the person continues to believe their delusions.

2b) Two positive symptoms of schizophrenia include auditory hallucinations and delusions. Auditory hallucinations are experienced as 'hearing voices', which provide a running commentary on the person's behaviour. Delusions are beliefs that could not possibly be real (for example, I am Adolf Hitler), though they seem very real to the patient. Common delusions include persecution and delusions of grandeur. Delusional beliefs are extremely resistant to change and are held onto despite evidence against them.

Activity 7: Establishing a line of argument

One social psychological explanation of aggression is deindividuation. This explanation developed from the ideas of Le Bon (1895), who noticed that in crowds a 'collective mind' emerges, leading to uninhibited behaviour and antisocial acts such as aggression. Festinger et al. referred to this loss of individual identity while in a crowd as deindividuation. Festinger argued that anonymity and a reduced personal responsibility lead people in a group to be deindividuated.

> **Examiner comment:** Theory clearly named at the start of the essay.

A range of evidence, which shows that aggression is more likely when people are anonymous, has supported the deindividuation theory. Zimbardo (1970) demonstrated this in a Milgram-like study that required female participants to deliver electric shocks to another participant. Some participants wore lab coats and hoods, were not referred to by name and were kept apart from other participants during the study, i.e. they were anonymous. Other participants wore normal clothes, a nametag, were referred to by name and were able to see each other during the study. Even though all the participants could see the victim receive their electric shocks, those participants who were made to feel anonymous delivered shocks for twice as long as participants without anonymity. Other studies outside of the lab have supported the role of anonymity in real-life aggressive behaviour. Silke (2003) analysed 500 violent attacks occurring in Northern Ireland between 1994 and 1996. He found that people who wore disguises, hiding their identities, carried out 206 attacks. These examples support the claim that anonymity leads to increased aggression.

> **Examiner comment:** Clear signpost explains what the paragraph will cover.

However, Diener (1980) argues that it is not anonymity but reduced self-awareness caused by being in a crowd that leads to deindividuation. We are normally self-aware and use this to regulate our own behaviour. In a crowd, however, the group becomes the focus of attention, through such behaviours as chanting and clapping, and the subsequent decrease in self-awareness leads to deindividuation. There is disagreement about which elements of being in a crowd are most important.

> **Examiner comment:** Next stage of argument clearly indicated at the start of the section.

Another criticism of deindividuation has been put forward by Reicher (1987). Reicher argues that when a person becomes part of a group, for example of football supporters, there is a shift of identity rather than a loss of identity. The shift is from personal identity (e.g., being Jack Smith) to a social identity or sense of oneself as a group member (e.g., being an Everton supporter). Deindividuation, according to Reicher, occurs when we are a member of a group, which emphasizes social rather than personal identity. Deindividuation is not the only social psychological explanation of aggression. Social learning theory emphasizes learning from role models and the frustration–aggression approach sees aggression as a drive that comes from being prevented from achieving a goal. These are arguably better explanations of why individuals are aggressive (for instance, picking a fight) when they are not anonymous or in a crowd. Finally, in some crowds, deindividuation can produce peaceful rather than aggressive behaviours (for example, at a music festival).

Revising and preparing for exams

When you come to start revising, it is important to ask yourself the following questions: Do you actually know how to revise? And do you know how you best learn? In order to find this out, you should see if you are primarily a visual, auditory or kinaesthetic learner. This will help you to use revision strategies that play to your strengths.

Visual learning strategies: seeing is believing

If you are a visual learner, your revision strategy needs to reflect this. Activities you could use to revise include the creation of illustrations, for example tables, graphs, diagrams, pictures, or video. There are online applications that can be used to produce visually rich material too, such as mind-maps. It is commonly reported that visual learners revise most effectively in a quiet environment.

Auditory learning strategies: learning by listening

Auditory learners need to hear the content they are learning. If this is you, try recording your notes with a sound recorder and playing them back. Test yourself on small sections that you've just heard. You could also try to repeat facts out loud from your notes with your eyes closed. Word association works well when trying to remember key facts or notes. You could also arrange a revision forum with friends. Hearing ideas and discussing them strengthens your knowledge.

Kinaesthetic learning strategies: activated by action

The kinaesthetic learner likes a 'hands on' approach, and if this is you, then you should consider this when planning your revision. It is of utmost importance that your revision activities get you involved in the work, perhaps by working through a student workbook or a 'companion guide' that encourages you to read and then interact with the material. Why not create little tasks, such as a mix and match activity where the details for a topic have to be matched with its broader explanatory details? Since you learn best from participating in the learning, why not revise by carrying out studies that might have been done to support the points you are trying to learn? Kinaesthetic learners need variety, so don't just make use of one technique, but do different activities during each revision session.

Exam calendar

'Spec check': Organizing your knowledge

The checklist for Part 1: Introductory topics in psychology and Part 2: Psychology in context (Approaches in psychology, Biopsychology, and Research methods) are in your A Level Year 1 and AS book.

Part 3: Issues and options in psychology Compulsory content		Have I got notes?	Revised?
3.1 Issues and debates in psychology	• Gender and culture in psychology – universality and bias. Gender bias including androcentrism and alpha and beta bias; cultural bias, including ethnocentrism and cultural relativism.		
	• Free will and determinism: hard determinism and soft determinism; biological, environmental and psychic determinism. The scientific emphasis on causal explanations.		
	• The nature–nurture debate: the relative importance of heredity and environment in determining behaviour; the interactionist approach.		
	• Holism and reductionism: levels of explanation in psychology. Biological reductionism and environmental (stimulus–response) reductionism.		
	• Idiographic and nomothetic approaches to psychological investigation.		
	• Ethical implications of research studies and theory, including reference to social sensitivity.		
Optional			
Option 1			
3.2 Relationships	• The evolutionary explanations for partner preferences, including the relationship between sexual selection and human reproductive behaviour.		
	• Factors affecting attraction in romantic relationships: self-disclosure; physical attractiveness, including the matching hypothesis; filter theory, including social demography, similarity in attitudes and complementarity.		
	• Theories of romantic relationships: social exchange theory, equity theory and Rusbult's investment model of commitment, satisfaction, comparison with alternatives and investment. Duck's phase model of relationship breakdown: intra-psychic, dyadic, social and grave dressing phases.		
	• Virtual relationships in social media: self-disclosure in virtual relationships; effects of absence of gating on the nature of virtual relationships.		
	• Parasocial relationships: levels of parasocial relationships, the absorption–addiction model and the attachment theory explanation.		
3.3 Gender	• Sex and gender. Sex-role stereotypes. Androgyny and measuring androgyny including the Bem Sex Role Inventory.		
	• The role of chromosomes and hormones (testosterone, oestrogen and oxytocin) in sex and gender.		
	• Atypical sex chromosome patterns: Klinefelter's syndrome and Turner's syndrome.		
	• Cognitive explanations of gender development, Kohlberg's theory, gender identity, gender stability and gender constancy; gender schema theory.		
	• Psychodynamic explanation of gender development, Freud's psychoanalytic theory, Oedipus complex; Electra complex; identification and internalization.		
	• Social learning theory as applied to gender development. The influence of culture and media on gender roles.		
	• Atypical gender development: gender identity disorder; biological and social explanations for gender identity disorder.		

Part 3: Issues and options in psychology Compulsory content		Have I got notes?	Revised?
3.4 Cognition and development	• Piaget's theory of cognitive development: schemas, assimilation, accommodation, equilibration, stages of intellectual development. Characteristics of these stages, including object permanence, conservation, egocentrism and class inclusion.		
	• Vygotsky's theory of cognitive development, including the zone of proximal development and scaffolding.		
	• Baillargeon's explanation of early infant abilities, including knowledge of the physical world; violation of expectation research.		
	• The development of social cognition: Selman's levels of perspective-taking; theory of mind, including theory of mind as an explanation for autism; the Sally Anne study. The role of the mirror neuron system in social cognition.		
Option 2			
3.5 Schizophrenia	• Classification of schizophrenia. Positive symptoms of schizophrenia, including hallucinations and delusions. Negative symptoms of schizophrenia, including speech poverty and avolition. Reliability and validity in diagnosis and classification of schizophrenia, including reference to co-morbidity, culture and gender bias and symptom overlap.		
	• Biological explanations for schizophrenia: genetics, the dopamine hypothesis and neural correlates.		
	• Psychological explanations for schizophrenia: family dysfunction and cognitive explanations, including dysfunctional thought processing.		
	• Drug therapy: typical and atypical antipsychotics.		
	• Cognitive behaviour therapy and family therapy as used in the treatment of schizophrenia. Token economies as used in the management of schizophrenia.		
	• The importance of an interactionist approach in explaining and treating schizophrenia; the diathesis–stress model.		
3.6 Eating behaviour	• Explanations for food preferences: the evolutionary explanation, including reference to neophobia and taste aversion; the role of learning in food preference, including social and cultural influences.		
	• Neural and hormonal mechanisms involved in the control of eating behaviour, including the role of the hypothalamus, ghrelin and leptin.		
	• Biological explanations for anorexia nervosa, including genetic and neural explanations.		
	• Psychological explanations for anorexia nervosa: family systems theory, including enmeshment, autonomy and control; social learning theory, including modelling, reinforcement and media; cognitive theory, including distortions and irrational beliefs.		
	• Biological explanations for obesity, including genetic and neural explanations.		
	• Psychological explanations for obesity, including restraint theory, disinhibition and the boundary model. Explanations for the success and failure of dieting.		
3.7 Stress	• The physiology of stress, including general adaptation syndrome, the hypothalamic pituitary–adrenal system, the sympathomedullary pathway and the role of cortisol.		
	• The role of stress in illness, including reference to immunosuppression and cardiovascular disorders.		
	• Sources of stress: life changes and daily hassles. Workplace stress, including the effects of workload and control.		
	• Measuring stress: self-report scales (social readjustment ratings scale and hassles and uplifts scale) and physiological measures, including skin conductance response.		
	• Individual differences in stress: personality types A, B and C and associated behaviours; hardiness, including commitment, challenge and control.		
	• Managing and coping with stress: drug therapy (benzodiazepines, beta blockers), stress inoculation therapy and biofeedback. Gender differences in coping with stress. The role of social support in coping with stress; types of social support, including instrumental, emotional and esteem support.		

Part 3: Issues and options in psychology Compulsory content		Have I got notes?	Revised?
Option 3			
3.8 Aggression	• Neural and hormonal mechanisms in aggression, including the roles of the limbic system, serotonin and testosterone. Genetic factors in aggression, including the MAOA gene.		
	• The ethological explanation of aggression, including reference to innate releasing mechanisms and fixed action patterns. Evolutionary explanations of human aggression.		
	• Social psychological explanations of human aggression, including the frustration–aggression hypothesis, social learning theory as applied to human aggression, and deindividuation.		
	• Institutional aggression in the context of prisons: dispositional and situational explanations.		
	• Media influences on aggression, including the effects of computer games. The role of desensitization, disinhibition and cognitive priming.		
3.9 Forensic psychology	• Problems in defining crime. Ways of measuring crime, including official statistics, victim surveys and offender surveys.		
	• Offender profiling: the top-down approach, including organized and disorganized types of offender; the bottom-up approach, including investigative psychology; geographical profiling.		
	• Biological explanations of offending behaviour: an historical approach (atavistic form); genetics and neural explanations.		
	• Psychological explanations of offending behaviour: Eysenck's theory of the criminal personality; cognitive explanations; level of moral reasoning and cognitive distortions, including hostile attribution bias and minimalization; differential association theory; psychodynamic explanations.		
	• Dealing with offending behaviour: the aims of custodial sentencing and the psychological effects of custodial sentencing. Recidivism. Behaviour modification in custody. Anger management and restorative justice programmes.		
3.10 Addiction	• Describing addiction: physical and psychological dependence, tolerance and withdrawal syndrome.		
	• Risk factors in the development of addiction, including genetic vulnerability, stress, personality, family influences and peers.		
	• Explanations for nicotine addiction: brain neurochemistry, including the role of dopamine, and learning theory as applied to smoking behaviour, including reference to cue reactivity.		
	• Explanations for gambling addiction: learning theory as applied to gambling, including reference to partial and variable reinforcement; cognitive theory as applied to gambling, including reference to cognitive bias.		
	• Reducing addiction: drug therapy; behavioural interventions, including aversion therapy and covert sensitization; cognitive behaviour therapy.		
	• The application of the following theories of behaviour change to addictive behaviour; the theory of planned behaviour and Prochaska's six-stage model of behaviour change.		

Your calendar of action for effective exam preparation and completion

One month (plus) before the exam	• Success is built upon preparation. So ensure that you have all your notes. • Make use of the 'spec check' earlier to ensure your notes cover the whole specification. If not, speak to your teacher about getting additional notes for it. • Identify your preferred learning style (visual, auditory, kinaesthetic), and develop activities that complement this. • Bearing in mind your preferred method of learning, plan out times for revision that allow for the specification to be covered, and more than just superficially. • Develop a set of goals that are achievable as you go through your revision. Maybe reward yourself with certain numbers of rest periods that can be used how you like, e.g. time with friends.
Two weeks before	• Revision is well under way. Make sure that you complement your learning of the theory with good practice of the examination questions. • Theory is not everything – being aware of the question type, style and layout is just as important. • Make use of the exam questions and guidance throughout this book to get you started. Why not also try to use your own imagination – you can use the specification check and some of the specimen questions to create your own questions. • Remember, practice makes perfect. • Ask your teacher to look at your attempts. Note down any issues that seem to recur and ask for help in rectifying these. • Now is the time for refining your skills, and clearing up last-minute anomalies in understanding.
One week before	• In this week, focus on the issues that you might find most difficult. There is still time, but be more efficient with it! • Your mind will rest easier if you know the material well. So in a self-rewarding way, tick off on the spec check the areas that you have covered and know well. Identify the areas that need to be revisited in order to clarify understanding. • The use of highlighters is a good idea, colour coding the areas of the specification that might be well learned (green); in need of a little more (orange); really don't understand (red).
The night before	• Should you cram until the last minute, or rest? Most teachers would say that what you don't know by the night before, you will never know. • As a general guide, however, ensure that you have plenty of rest the evening before. Go to sleep early – next morning you will need all the extra energy your body can generate. Remember, your body requires sleep, and a late night of revising may reduce your effectiveness.
The day of the exam	• If it is a morning examination, make sure you have a good breakfast. The examination will require a lot of mental energy, so slow release energy foods are often the best – for example, porridge, or bananas. • If your exam is in the afternoon, you have some more time to fine-tune your revision. Don't do this excessively. • Get to your examination location with plenty of time to spare. Try to reduce all avoidable sources of stress. • Once in the exam location, make sure you complete the necessary administration. • Start the exam – remember to enjoy it – you have worked hard and prepared for it well, now simply show the examiner what you can do. • After the exam – avoid too much unnecessary dissection of what you have done. This will worry you, and may affect future exam performance.

References

Agrawal, A., and Lynskey, M.T. (2008). Are there genetic influences on addiction: evidence from family, adoption and twin studies. *Addiction*, 103(7), pp.1069–1081.

Aichorn, A. (1935). *Wayward Youth*. New York: Viking Press.

Ajzen, I. (1985). From intentions to actions: A theory of planned behavior. In J. Kuhl and J. Beckmann (eds), *Action Control*. Berlin, Heidelberg: Springer Berlin Heidelberg.

Ajzen, I. and Fishbein, M. (2005). The influence of attitudes on behavior. In D. Albarracín, B.T. Johnson, and M.P. Zanna (eds), *The Handbook of Attitudes*. Mahwah, NJ: Erlbaum.

Allen, K., Blasovich, J., and Mendes, W.B. (2002). Cardiovascular reactivity and the presence of pets, friends, and spouses: the truth about cats and dogs. *Psychosomatic Medicine*, 64, pp.727–739.

Anderson, C.A. and Bushman, B.J. (2002). Human aggression. *Annual Review of Psychology*, 53, pp.27–51.

Anderson, R.E., Barnes, G.E., and Murray, R.P. (2011). Psychometric properties and long-term predictive validity of the Addiction-Prone Personality (APP) scale. *Personality and Individual Differences*, 50(5), pp.651–656.

Antolin-Fontes, B., Ables, J.L., Görlich, A., and Ibañez-Tallon, I. (2014). The habenulo-interpeduncular pathway in nicotine aversion and withdrawal. *Neuropharmacology*, 96, pp.213–222.

Anton, R.F., Drobes, D.J., Voronin, K., Durazo-Avizu, R., and Moak, D. (2004). Naltrexone effects on alcohol consumption in a clinical laboratory paradigm: temporal effects of drinking. *Psychopharmacology*, 173(1–2), pp.32–40.

Antonowicz, D.H. and Ross, R.R. (2005). Social problem solving deficits in offenders. In M. McMurran and J. McGuire (eds), *Social Problem-solving and Offending; Evidence, Evaluation and Evolution*. Chichester: John Wiley and Sons, Inc.

Archer, J. and Lloyd, B. (1982). Sex and gender. In W. Stainton Rogers and R. Stainton Rogers (2001) *The Psychology of Sex and Gender*. Maidenhead: Open University Press.

Argyle, M., Henderson, M., Bond, M., Iizuka, Y., and Contarello, A. (1986). Cross-cultural variations in relationship rules. *International Journal of Psychology*, 21(1–4), pp.287–315.

Armitage, C.J., and Conner, M. (2001). Efficacy of the theory of planned behaviour: A meta-analytic review. *British Journal of Social Psychology*, 40(4), pp.471–499.

Asch, S.E. (1951). Effects of group pressure upon the modification and distortion of judgment. In Guetzkow, H. (ed.), *Groups, Leadership and Men*. Pittsburgh, PA: Carnegie Press.

Atkinson, R.C., and Shiffrin, R.M. (1968). Memory: A proposed system and its control processes. *The Psychology of Learning and Motivation*, 2, pp.89–195.

Ayllon, T. and Azrin, N. (1968). *The Token Economy: A Motivational System for Therapy and Rehabilitation*. East Norwalk, CT: Appleton-Century-Crofts.

Azrin, N.H., Sisson, R.W., Meyers, R., and Godley, M. (1982). Alcoholism treatment by disulfiram and community reinforcement therapy. *Journal of Behavior Therapy and Experimental Psychiatry*, 13(2), pp.105–112.

Bailey, C.A. and Ostrov, J.M. (2008). Differentiating forms and functions of aggression in emerging adults: Associations with hostile attribution biases and normative beliefs. *Journal of Youth and Adolescence*, 37, pp.713–722.

Baillargeon, R., Spelke, E.S., and Wasserman, S. (1985). Object permanence in five-month-old infants. *Cognition*, 20, pp.191–208.

Bandura, A. (1973). *Aggression: A Social Learning Analysis*. Eaglewood Cliffs, NJ: Prentice Hall.

Bandura, A. (1977). Self-efficacy: Toward a unifying theory of behavioral change. *Psychological Review*, 84(2), pp.191–215.

Bandura, A. (1977). *Social Learning Theory*. Englewood Cliffs, NJ: Prentice Hall.

Bandura, A. (2002). Social cognitive theory of mass communication. In Bryant, J. and Zillmann, D. (eds), *Media Effects: Advances in Theory and Research*, 2nd ed., pp.121–154. Mahwah, NJ: Erlbaum.

Bandura, A. and Walters, R.H. (1963). *Social Learning and Personality Development*,. New York: Holt, Rinehart and Winston.

Bandura, A., Ross, D., and Ross, S.A. (1961). Transmission of aggression through limitation of aggressive models. *Journal of Abnormal and Social Psychology*, 63(3), pp.575–582.

Bandura, A., Ross, D., and Ross, S.A. (1963). Imitation of film-mediated aggressive models. *Journal of Abnormal and Social Psychology*, 66(1), pp.3–11.

Barbaree, H.E. (1998). Denial and minimisation among sex offenders: Assessment and treatment outcome. *Sex Offender Programming*, 3(4), pp.1–7.

Bard, P. and Mountcastle, V.B. (1948). Some forebrain mechanisms involved in expression of rage. *Research Publications – Association for Research in Nervous and Mental Disease*, 27, pp.362–404.

Barnes, G.E., Murray, R.P., Patton, D., Bentler, P.M., and Anderson, R. E. (2000). *The Addiction Prone Personality: Longitudinal Research in The Social Sciences*. New York: Plenum Publishers.

Baron-Cohen, S., Leslie, A. and Frith, U. (1985). Does the autistic child have a 'theory of mind'? *Cognition*, 21, pp.37–46.

Bartholow, B.D., Bushman, B.J., and Sestir, M.A. (2006) Chronic violent video game exposure and desensitization to violence: Behavioral and event-related brain potential data. *Journal of Experimental Social Psychology*, 42(4), pp.532–539.

Bartlett, F. (1932). *Remembering: An Experimental and Social Study*. Cambridge: Cambridge University Press.

Bartol, C. (2002). *Criminal Behavior: A Psychological Approach*. Upper Saddle River, NJ: Prentice Hall.

Beavan, V., Read, J., and Cartwright, C. (2011). The prevalence of voice-hearers in the general population: A literature review. *Journal of Mental Health*.

Beck, A.T. (1972). *Depression; Causes and Treatment*. Philadelphia, PA: University of Pennsylvania Press.

Becker, H.S. (1974). Labelling theory reconsidered. *Deviance and Social Control*, 3, p.41.

Beech, J.R. and Mackintosh, I.C. (2005). Do differences in sex hormones affect handwriting style ? Evidence from digit ratio and sex role identity as determinants of the sex of handwriting. *Personality and Individual Differences*, 39(2), pp.459–468.

Belson, W.A. (1975). *The Public and the Police*. London: Harper and Row.

Bem, S.L. (1974). The measurement of psychological androgyny. *Journal of Consulting and Clinical Psychology*, 42, pp.155–162.

Bem, S.L. (1981). Gender schema theory: A cognitive account of sex typing. *Psychological Review*, 88, 354–64.

Benton, D. (2004). Role of parents in the determination of the food preferences of children and the development of obesity. *International Journal of Obesity*, 28, pp.858–869.

Bergin, J. and Wade, T.D. (2014) Psychometric properties of the eating disorder belief questionnaire. *International Journal of Eating Disorders*, 47(6) pp.640–646.

Berkowitz, L. (1962). *Aggression: A Social Psychological Analysis*. New York: McGraw-Hill.

Berry, J.W. (1969). On cross-cultural comparability. *International Journal of Psychology*, 4(2), pp.119–128.

Best, D. and Williams, J. (1998). Masculinity and femininity in the self and ideal descriptions of university students in 14 countries. In G. Hofstede (ed.) *Masculinity and Femininity: The Taboo Dimension of National Cultures*. Thousand Oaks, CA: Sage Publications.

Billedo, C., Kerkhof, P. and Finkenauer, C. (2015). The use of social networking sites for relationship maintenance in long-distance and geographically close romantic relationships. *Cyberpsychology, Behavior, and Social Networking*, 18(3), March 2015, pp.152–157.

Birbaumer, N., Viet, R., Lotze, M., Erb, M., Hermann, C., and Grodd, W. (2005). Deficient fear conditioning in psychopathy: A functional magnetic resonance imaging study. *Archives of General Psychiatry*, 62, pp.799–805.

Birch, L.L., Marlin, D.W., and Rotter, J. (1984). Eating as the 'means' activity in a contingency: effects on children's food preferences, *Child Development*, 55(2), pp.431–439.

Black, D.W., Monahan, P.O., Temkit, M., and Shaw, M. (2006). A family study of pathological gambling. *Psychiatry Research*, 141(3), pp.295–303.

Blair, R. (2003). Neurobiological basis of psychopathy. *British Journal of Psychiatry*, 182, pp.5–7.

Blaszczynski, A. and McConaghy, N. (1989). Anxiety and/or depression in the pathogenesis of addictive gambling. *International Journal of the Addictions*, 24(4), pp.337–350.

Blaszczynski, A., McConaghy, N., and Frankova, A. (1990). Boredom proneness in pathological gambling. *Psychological Reports*, 67(1), pp.35–42.

Bledsoe, L.K. (2006). Smoking cessation: an application of theory of planned behavior to understanding progress through stages of change. *Addictive Behaviors*, 31(7), pp.1271–1276.

Blud, L., Travers, R., Nugent, F., and Thornton, D. (2003). Accreditation of offending behaviour programmes in HM Prison Service: 'What works' in practice. *Legal and Criminological Psychology*, 8(1), pp.69–81.

Bogartz, R.S., Cashon, C.H., Choen, L.B., Schilling, T.H., and Shinskey, J.L. (2000). Reply to Baillargeon, Aslin and Munakata. *Infancy*, 1, pp.403–446.

Bower, T.G.R. and Wishart, J.G. (1972). The effects of motor skill on object permanence. *Cognition*, 1, pp.165–72.

Bowlby, J. (1944). Forty-four juvenile thieves: Their characteristics and home-life. *International Journal of Psychoanalysis*, 25, pp.19–53.

Braden, W. (1984). Vulnerability and schizoaffective psychosis: A two-factor model. *Schizophrenia Bulletin*, 10(1), pp.71–86.

Brown, G.W., Birley, J.L.T., and Wing, J.K. (1972). Influence of family life on the course of schizophrenic disorders: A replication. *The British Journal of Psychiatry*, 121(3), pp.241–258.

Brown, R.I.F. (1986). Arousal and Sensation-Seeking Components in the General Explanation of Gambling and Gambling Addictions. *International Journal of the Addictions*, 21(9–10), pp.1001–1016.

Bruce, V. and Young, A. (1998). *In the Eye of the Beholder: The Science of Face Perception*. New York: Oxford University Press.

Bruch, H. (1978) *The Golden Cage: The Enigma of Anorexia Nervosa*. London: Open Books.

Brunner, H., Nelen, M., Breakefield, X., Ropers, H., and van Oost, B. (1993). Abnormal behavior associated with a point mutation in the structural gene for monoamine oxidase A. *Science*, 262(5133), pp.578–580.

Burgess, R.L. and Akers, R.L. (1966). A differential-reinforcement theory of criminal behaviour. *Social Problems*, 14(2), pp.128–147.

Burns, D. (1989). *The Feeling Good Handbook: Using the New Mood Therapy in Everyday Life*. New York: W. Morrow.

Burstein, E. and Worchel, P. (1962). Arbitrariness of frustration and its consequences for aggression in social situation. *Journal of Personality*, 30, pp.528–541.

Buss, D.M. (1989). Sex differences in human mate preferences: Evolutionary hypotheses tested in 37 cultures. *Behavioural and Brain Sciences*, 12, pp.1–49.

Buss, D.M. and Schmitt, D.P. (1993). Sexual strategies theory: An evolutionary perspective on human mating. *Psychological Review*, 100, pp.204–32.

Buss, D.M. and Shackelford, T.K. (1997). From vigilance to violence: Mate retention tactics in married couples. *Journal of Personality and Social Psychology*, 72, pp.346–361.

Cairns, R.B. and Scholz, S.D. (1973). Fighting in mice; Dyadic escalation and what is learned. *Journal of Comparative and Physiological Psychology*, 85, pp.540–550.

Cairns R.B., MacCombie, D.J., and Hood, K.E. (1983). A developmental genetic analysis of aggressive behavior in mice: I. Behavioral outcomes. *Journal of Comparative Psychology*, 97, pp.69–89.

Campbell, A., Shirley, L., and Candy, J. (2004). A longitudinal study of gender-related cognition and behaviour. *Developmental Science*, 7(1), pp.1–9.

Campbell, L.A., Smith, F.J., Guisez, Y., Devos, R., and Burn, P. (1995). Recombinant mouse OB protein: evidence for a peripheral signal linking adiposity and central neural networks. *Science*, 269(5223), pp.546–549.

Canter, D. (1994). *Criminal Shadows*. London: HarperCollins.

Canter, D. (1995). Psychology of offender profiling. In R. Bull and D. Carsons (eds) *Handbook of Psychology in Legal Contexts*. Chichester: John Wiley and Sons, Inc.

Canter, D. (2000). Offender profiling and criminal differentiation. *Legal and Criminological Psychology*, 5, pp.23–46.

Canter, D. (2007). *Mapping Murder: The Secrets of Geographical Profiling*. London: Virgin.

Canter, D. and Heritage, R. (1990). A multivariate model of sexual offences behaviour: Developments in offender profiling. *Journal of Forensic Psychiatry*, 1, pp.185–212.

Canter, D. and Larkin, P. (1993). The environmental range of serial rapists. *Journal of Environmental Psychology*, 13, pp.93–99.

Canuso, C.M. and Pandina, G. (2007). Gender and schizophrenia. *Psychopharmacology Bulletin*, 40(4), pp.178–190.

Cao, F., Su, L., Liu, T., and Gao, X. (2007). The relationship between impulsivity and Internet addiction in a sample of Chinese adolescents. *European Psychiatry: The Journal of the Association of European Psychiatrists*, 22(7), pp.466–71.

Carlsson, A. and Lindqvist, M. (1963). Effect of chlorpromazine or haloperidol on formation of 3methoxytyramine and normetanephrine in mouse brain. *Acta Pharmacologica et Toxicologica*, 20, pp.140–144.

Carnagey, N.J., Anderson, C.A., and Bushman, B.J. (2007). The effect of video game violence on physiological desensitization to real-life violence. *Journal of Experimental Social Psychology*, 43, pp.489–496.

Carroll, K.M., Rounsaville, B.J., Nich, C., Gordon, L.T., Wirtz, P.W., and Gawin, F.H. (1994). One year follow-up of psychotherapy and pharmacotherapy for cocaine dependence: delayed emergence of psychotherapy effects. *Archives of General Psychiatry*, 51, pp.989–997.

Carter, B.L. and Tiffany, S.T. (1999). Meta-analysis of cue-reactivity in addiction research. *Addiction*, 94(3), pp.327–340.

Cases, O., Seif, I., Grimsby, J., Gaspar, P., Chen, K., Pournin, S., Müller, U., Aguet, M., Babinet, C., and Shih, J.C. (1995). Aggressive behavior and altered amounts of brain serotonin and norepinephrine in mice lacking MAOA. *Science*, 268(5218), pp.1763–1766.

Caspi, A.J., McCray, J., Moffitt, T.E., Mill, J., Martin, J., Craig, I.W., Taylor, A., and Poulton, R. (2002). Role of genotype in the cycle of violence in maltreated children. *Science*, 297(5582), pp.851–854.

Cautela, J.R. (1967). Covert sensitization. *Psychological Reports*, 20(2), pp.459–468.

Charlton, T., Gunter, B., and Hannan, A. (2002). *Broadcast Television Effects in A Remote Community*. Mahwah, NJ: Lawrence Erlbaum Associates.

Chevallier, C. (2012). Theory of mind and autism: Revisiting Baron-Cohen's Sally Anne study. In A. Slater and P. Quinn (eds) *Developmental Psychology: Revisiting the Classic Studies*. London: Sage.

Choliz, M. (2015). Ethical gambling: Principles and proposals. *Journal Of Behavioral Addictions*, 4, p.9.

Chomsky, N. (1965). *Aspects of the Theory of Syntax*. Cambridge, MA: MIT Press.

Clark, R.D. and Hatfield, E. (1989). Gender differences in receptivity to sexual offers. *Journal of Psychology and Human Sexuality*, 2, pp.39–55.

Clegg, H. (2007). Evolutionary Psychology. In D. Miell, A. Phoenix, and K. Thomas *Mapping Psychology*, Milton Keynes, The Open University.

Cloninger, C.R., Christiansen, K.O., Reich, T., and Gottesman, I.I. (1978). Implications of sex differences in the prevalence of antisocial personality, alcoholism, and criminality for familial transmission. *Archives of General Psychiatry*, 35, pp.941–951.

Cnattingius, S., Hultman, C.M., Dahl, M., Sparén, P. (1999). Very preterm birth, birth trauma, and the risk of anorexia nervosa among girls. *Archives of General Psychiatry*, 56(7), pp.634–638.

Coccaro, E.F., Bergeman, C.S., Kavoussi, R.J., and Seroczynski, A.D. (1997). Heritability of aggression and irritability: A twin study of the Buss-Durkee aggression scales in adult male subjects. *Biological Psychiatry*, 41(3), pp.273–284.

Cohen, S. (1972). *Folk Devils and Moral Panics*. Oxford: Basil Blackwell.

Cohen, S., Doyle, W.J., Skoner, D.P., Rabin, B.S., and Gwaltney, J.M. (1997). Social ties and susceptibility to the common cold. *Journal of the American Medical Association*, 277(4), pp.1940–1944.

Cohen, S., Tyrrell, D.A.J., and Smith, A.P. (1993). Negative life events, perceived stress, negative affect and susceptibility to the common cold. *Journal of Personality and Social Psychology*, 64(1), pp.131–40.

Comings, D., Gade-Andavolu, R., Gonzalez, N., Wu, S., Muhleman, D., Chen, C., Koh, P., Farwell, K., Blake, H., Dietz, G., MacMurray, J.P., Lesieur, H.R., Rugle, L.J., and Rosenthal, R. (2001). The additive effect of neurotransmitter genes in pathological gambling. *Clinical Genetics*, 60(2), pp.107–116.

Comings, D., Muhleman, D., and Gysin, R. (1996). Dopamine D2 receptor (DRD2) gene and susceptibility to posttraumatic stress disorder: a study and replication. *Biological Psychiatry*, 40(5), pp.368–372.

Comstock, G.A. and Paik, H. (1991). *Television and the American Child*. San Diego, CA: Academic Press.

Condiotte, M.M., and Lichtenstein, E. (1981). Self-efficacy and relapse in smoking cessation programs. *Journal of Consulting and Clinical Psychology*, 49(5), pp.648–658.

Conger, J.J. (1956). Alcoholism: Theory problem and challenge. II. Reinforcement theory and the dynamics of alcoholism. *Quarterly Journal of Studies on Alcohol*, 17, pp.296–305.

Cooper, C.L., Sloan, S.J., and Williams, S. (1988). *The Occupational Stress Indicator*. Windsor: NFER-Nelson.

Cooper, P.J., Whelan, E., Woolgar, M., Morrell, J., and Murray, L. (2004). Association between childhood feeding problems and maternal eating disorder: Role of the family environment. *British Journal of Psychiatry*, 184(3), pp.210–215.

Copson, G. (1995). *Coals to Newscastle? Part 1: A study of Offender Profiling (Special Interests Series Paper 7)* . London: Home Office.

Cornish, D.B. and Clarke, R.V.(1998). Opportunities, precipitators and criminal decisions: A reply to Wortley's critique of situational crime prevention. *Crime Prevention Studies*, 16, pp.41–96

Costa, P.T. and McCrae, R.R. (1992). Four ways five factors are basic. *Personality and Individual Differences*, 13(6), pp.653–665.

Crow, T.J. (1997). Schizophrenia as failure of hemispheric dominance for language. *Trends in Neurosciences*, 20(8), pp.339–343.

Custer, R. and Milt, H. (1985). *When Luck Runs Out: Help For Compulsive Gamblers*. New York: Facts on File Publications.

Dabbs, J.M., Carr, T.S., Frady, R.L., and Riad, J.K. (1995). Testosterone, crime, and misbehaviour among 692 male prison inmates. *Personality and Individual Differences*, 18(5), pp.627–633.

Dalton, M.A., Sargent, J.D., Beach, M.L., Titus-Ernstoff, L., Gibson, J.J., Ahrens, M.B., Tickle, J.J., and Heatherton, T.F. (2003). Effect of viewing smoking in movies on adolescent smoking initiation: a cohort study. *Lancet*, 362(9380), pp.281–285.

Daly, M. and Wilson, M. (1988). *Homicide*. New York: Aldine de Gruyter.

Danaher, B.G. (1977). Research on rapid smoking: Interim summary and recommendations. *Addictive Behaviors*, 2(4), pp.151–166.

Davidson, R.J., Putnam, K.M., and Larson, C.L. (2000). Dysfunction in the neural circuitry of emotion regulation: A possible prelude to violence. *Science*, 289(5479), pp.591–594.

Davis, J.O., Phelps, J.A. and Bracha, H.S. (1995). Prenatal development of monozygotic twins and concordance for schizophrenia. *Schizophrenia Bulletin*, 21(3), pp.357–366.

Davis, K.L., Kahn, R.S., Ko, G., and Davidson, M. (1991). Dopamine in schizophrenia: A review and reconceptualization. *The American Journal of Psychiatry*, 148(11), pp.1474–1486.

Dawkins, R. (1976). *The Selfish Gene* (revised edition). Oxford: Oxford University Press.

Day, R., Nielsen, J.A., Korten, A., Ernberg, G., Dube, K.C., Gebhart, J., Jablensky, A., Leon, A., Marsella, A., Olatawura, M., Sartorius, N. Strömgren, E., Takahashi, R., Wig, N., and Wynne, L.C. (1987). Stressful life events preceding the acute onset of schizophrenia: A cross-national study from the World Health Organization. *Culture, Medicine and Psychiatry*, 11(2), pp.123–205.

De Dreu, C.K., Greer, L.L., Van Kleef, G.A., Shalvi, S., Handgraaf, M.J. (2011). Oxytocin promotes human ethnocentrism. *Proceedings of the National Academy of Sciences of the United States of America*, 108(4), pp.1262–1266.

De Haan, W. and Loader, I. (2002). On the emotions of crime, punishment and social control. *Theoretical Criminology*, 6(3), pp.243–253.

de Maris, A. (2007). The role of relationship inequity in marital disruption. *Journal of Social and Personal Relationships*, 24(2), pp.177–195. de Sousa, P., Varese, F., Sellwood, W., and Bentall, R.P. (2013). Parental communication and psychosis: A meta-analysis. *Schizophrenia Bulletin*, 40(4), pp.756–768.

de Vries, A., Noens, I., Cohen-Kettenis, P., van Berckelaer-Onnes, I., and Doreleijers, T. (2010). Autism spectrum disorders in gender dysphoric children and adolescents. *Journal of Autism and Developmental Disorders*, 40(8), pp.930–936.

DeLisi, M., Hochstetler, A., Johnson, G., Caudill, J.W., and Marquart, J.W. (2011). The road to murder: The enduring criminogenic effects of juvenile confinement among a sample of adult career criminals. *Youth Violence and Juvenile Justice*, 9, pp.207–221.

DeLongis, A., Coyne, J.C., Dakof, G., Folkman, S., and Lazarus, R.S. (1982). Relationships of daily hassles, uplifts, and major life events to health status. *Health Psychology*, 1(2), pp.119–136.

Deregowski, J.B. (1972). Pictorial perception and culture. *Scientific American*, 227(5), pp.82–88.

Dewe, P.J. (1992). Applying the concept of appraisal to work stressors: some exploratory analysis. *Human Relations*, 45(2), pp.143–164.

Di Napoli, P.P. (2002). Adolescent violent behaviour and ego development. *Journal of Adolescent Health*. 31(6), pp.446–448.

Di Pellegrino, G., Fadiga, L., Fogassi, L., Gallese, V., and Rizzolatti, G. (1992). Understanding motor events: a neurophysiological study. *Experimental Brain Research*, 91, pp.176–180.

Dick, D.M., and Foroud, T. (2003). Candidate genes for alcohol dependence: A review of genetic evidence from human studies. *Alcoholism: Clinical and Experimental Research*, 27(5), pp.868–879.

Diener, E. (1977). Deindividuation: causes and consequences. *Social Behaviour and Personality*, 5(1), pp.143–155.

Diener, E. (1980). Deindividuation: The absence of self-awareness and self-regulation in group members. In P.B. Paulus (ed.), *Psychology of Group Influence*. Hillsdale, NJ: Erlbaum.

Dimsdale J.E. and Moss J. (1980). Short-term catecholamine response to psychological stress. *Psychosomatic Medicine*, 42(5), pp.493–497.

Dindia, K. and Allen, M. (1992). Sex differences in self-disclosure: A meta-analysis. *Psychological Bulletin*, 112(1), pp.106–124.

Dinstein, I., Thomas, C., Humphreys, K., Minshew, N., Behrmann, M., and Heeger, D. (2010). Normal movement selectivity in autism. *Neuron*, 66(3), pp.461–469.

Diskin, K.M. and Hodgins, D.C. (1999). Narrowing of attention and dissociation in pathological video lottery gamblers. *Journal of Gambling Studies/Co-Sponsored by the National Council on Problem Gambling and Institute for the Study of Gambling and Commercial Gaming*, 15(1), pp.17–28.

Dollard, J., Doob, L., Miller, N., Mowrer, O., and Sears, R. (1939). *Frustration and Aggression*. New Haven, CT: Yale University Press.

Driessen, M., Schulte, S., Luedecke, C., Schaefer, I., Sutmann, F., Ohlmeier, M., Kemper, U., Koesters, G., Chodzinski, C., Schneider, U., Broese, T., Dette, C., and Havemann-Reinicke, U. (2008). Trauma and PTSD in patients with alcohol, drug, or dual dependence: a multi-center study. *Alcoholism, Clinical and Experimental Research*, 32(3), pp.481–488.

Drummond, D.C. and Glautier, S. (1994). A controlled trial of cue exposure treatment in alcohol dependence. *Journal of Consulting and Clinical Psychology*, 62(4), pp.809–817.

Drummond, K., Bradley, S., Paterson-Badali, M., and Zucker, K. (2008). A follow-up study of girls with Gender Identity Disorder. *Developmental Psychology*, 44(1), pp.34–45.

Duck, S. (1994). Meaningful relationships: Talking, sense and relating. In D. Miell and R. Dallos (1996) *Social Interaction and Personal Relationships*. Milton Keynes: Open University.

Duck, S. and Wood, J. (2006). What goes up must come down: Sex and gendered patterns in relational dissolution. In M. Fine and J. Harvey (eds), *Handbook of Divorce and Relationship Dissolution*. New York: Routledge.

Dunbar, R. and Waynforth, D. (1995). Lonely hearts analysis. Cited in R. Dunbar (1995) Are you lonesome tonight? *New Scientist*, 145(1964), pp.26–31.

Dunbar, R., Knight, C. and Power, C. (eds) (1999). *The Evolution of Culture*. Edinburgh: Edinburgh University Press.

Durkin, K. (1995). *Developmental Social Psychology*. Oxford: Blackwell.

Dwyer, D. (2000). *Interpersonal Relationships*. London: Routledge.

Ebiske, N. (2008). *Offender Profiling in the Courtroom: The Use and Abuse of Expert Witness*, Westport, CT: Greenwood.

Egger, D.M. and Flynn, J.P. (1963). Effects of electrical stimulation of the amygdala on hypothalamically elicited attack behavior in cats. *Journal of Neurophysiology*, 26(5), pp.705–720.

Eisen, S.A., Lin, N., Lyons, M.J., Scherrer, J.F., Griffith, K., True, W.R., Gldberg, J., and Tsuang, M.T. (1998). Familial influences on gambling behavior: an analysis of 3359 twin pairs. *Addiction*, 93(9), pp.1375–1384.

Eiser, J.R., Morgan, M., and Gammage, P. (1987). Beliefcorrelates ofperceived addiction in young smokers. *European Journal of Psychology of Education*, 2, pp.307–310.

Eiser, J.R., Morgan, M., Gammage, P., and Gray, E. (1989). Adolescent smoking: Attitudes, norms and parental influence. *British Journal of Social Psychology*, 28(3), pp.193–202.

Ekman, P. and Friesen, W.P. (1978). *The Facial Action Coding System*. Palo Alto, CA: Consulting Psychological Press.

Elliot, A., and Niesta, D. (2007). Romantic red: Red enhances men's attraction to women. *Journal of Personality and Social Psychology*, 95(5), pp.1150–1164.

Ellis, A. (1991). The revised ABC's of rational-emotive therapy (RET). *Journal of Rational-Emotive and Cognitive-Behaviour Therapy*. 9(3), pp.139–172.

Engel, G. (1977). The need for a new medical model: A challenge for biomedicine. *Science*, 196(4286), pp.129–136.

Englander, E. (2007). *Understanding Violence*, (3rd ed.). Mahwah, NJ: Lawrence Erlbaum Associates.

Epps, K.J. (1995). Sexually abusive behaviour in an adolescent boy with the 48, XXYY syndrome: A case study. In N.K. Clark and G.M. Stephenson (eds), *Investigative and Forensic Decision Making, Issues in Criminological and Legal Psychology No. 26*. Leicester: Division of Criminological and Legal Psychology, British Psychological Society.

Essali, A., Al-Haj Haasan, N., Li, C., and Rathbone, J. (2009). Clozapine versus typical neuroleptic medication for schizophrenia. *The Cochrane Database of Systematic Reviews*, (1), CD000059.

Evans, P.D. and Edgerton, N. (1991). Life-events and mood as predictors of the common cold. *British Journal of Medical Psychology*, 64(Pt 1), pp.35–44.

Eysenck, H.J. (1969). *The Biological Basis of Personality*. Revised 2006. New Brunswick, NJ: Transaction Publishers.

Eysenck, H.J. (1976). *The Measurement of Personality*. Baltimore, MD: University Park Press.

Eysenck, S.B.G and Eysenck H.J. (1971). A comparative study of criminals and matched controls on three dimensions of personality. *British Journal of Social and Clinical Psychology*, 10(4), pp.362–366.

Fagot, B.I., Leinbach, M.D. and O'Boyle, C. (1992). Gender labelling, gender stereotyping and parenting behaviours. *Developmental Psychology*, 28, pp.225–230.

Farrington, D.P., Biron, L., and Le Blanc, M. (1982). Personality and delinquency in London and Montreal. In J. Gunn and D.P. Farrington (eds) *Abnormal Offenders, Delinquency and the Criminal Justice System*. Chichester: John Wiley and Sons, Inc.

Felsten, G. (1998). Gender and coping: use of distinct strategies and associations with stress and depression. *Anxiety, Stress, and Coping*, 11(4), pp.289–309.

Festinger, L., Pepitone, A., and Newcomb, T. (1952). Some consequences of deindividuation in a group. *Journal of Abnormal and Social Psychology*, 47, pp.382–389.

Fidler, J.A., Wardle, J., Brodersen, N.H., Jarvis, M.J., and West, R. (2006). Vulnerability to smoking after trying a single cigarette can lie dormant for three years or more. *Tobacco Control*, 15(3), pp.205–209.

Fishbein, M. and Ajzen, I. (1975). *Belief, Attitude, Intention and Behavior: An Introduction to Theory and Research*. Reading, MA: Addison-Wesley Pub. Co.

Fitzgerald, D. and White, K. (2003). Linking children's social worlds: perspective taking in parent child and peer contexts. *Social Behavior and Personality*, 31(5), pp.509–522.

Folkman, S. and Lazarus, R.S. (1980). An analysis of coping in a middle-aged community sample. *Journal of Health and Social Behavior*, 21(3), pp.219–239.

Forest, A.L., and Wood, J.V. (2012). When social networking is not working: Individuals with low self-esteem recognize but do not reap the benefits of self-disclosure on Facebook. *Psychological Science*, 23(3), pp.295–302.

Fox, B.H. and Farrington, D.P. (2012). Creating burglary profiles using latent class analysis: A new approach to offender profiling. *Criminal Justice and Behaviour*, 39(12), pp.1582–1611.

Fox, B.H. and Farrington, D.P. (2015). An experimental evaluation on the utility of burglary profiles applied in active police investigations. *Criminal Justice and Behaviour*, 42(2), pp.156–175.

Francis, L.J. (1996). The relationship between Eysenck's personality factors and attitude towards substance use among 13–15-year-olds. *Personality and Individual Differences*, 21(5), pp.633–640.

Franco Cea, N. and Barnes, G.E. (2015). The development of addiction-prone personality traits in biological and adoptive families. *Personality and Individual Differences*, 82, pp.107–113.

Fredrickson, B.L. and Roberts, T.A. (1997). Objectification theory. *Psychology of Women Quarterly*, 21(2), pp.173–206.

Frenkel, E., Kugelmass, S., Nathan, M., and Ingraham, L.J. (1995). Locus of control and mental health in adolescence and adulthood. *Schizophrenia Bulletin*, 21(2), pp.219–226.

Fuller, R.K., Branchey, L., Brightwell, D.R., Derman, R.M., Emrick, C.D., Iber, F.L., James, K.E., Lacoursiere, R.B., Lee, K.K., Lowenstam, I., Manny, I., Neiderhiser, D., Nocks, J.J., and Shaw, S. (1986). Disulfiram treatment of alcoholism. *Journal of the American Medical Association*, 256(11), p.1449.

Gardner, R.A., and Gardner, B.T. (1969). Teaching sign language to a chimpanzee. *Science*, 165(894), pp.664–672.

Garety, P.A., Freeman, D., Jolley, S., Dunn, G., Bebbington, P.E., Fowler, D.G., Kuipers, E., and Dudley, R. (2005). Reasoning, emotions, and delusional conviction in psychosis. *Journal of Abnormal Psychology*, 114(3), pp.373–384.

Geary, D.C., Rumsey, M., Bow-Thomas, C.C., and Hoard, M.K. (1995). Sexual jealousy as a facultative trait: evidence for the pattern of sex differences in adults from China and the United States. *Ethology and Sociobiology*, 16, pp.355–383.

Gehring, D. and Knutson, G. (2005). Prevalence of childhood trauma in a clinical population of transsexual people. *International Journal of Transgenderism*, 8(1), pp.23–30. Geisel, O., Panneck, P., Hellweg, R., Wiedemann, K., and Müller, C.A. (2015). Hypothalamic-pituitary-adrenal axis activity in patients with pathological gambling and internet use disorder. *Psychiatry Research*, 226(1), pp.97–102.

Gibbs, J.C. (2003). *Moral Development and Reality: Beyond the Theories of Kohlberg and Hoffman*. Thousand Oaks, CA: Sage Publications.

Gibbs, J.C. (2010). *Moral Development and Reality: Beyond the Theories of Kohlberg and Hoffman*, 2nd ed.. Thousand Oaks, CA: Sage Publications.

Giumetti, G. and Markey, P. (2007). Violent video games and anger as predictors of aggression. *Journal of Research in Personality*, 41(6), pp.1234–1243.

Glaser, R. and Kiecolt-Glaser, J.K. (2005). Stress-induced immune dysfunction: Implications for health. *Nature Reviews Immunology*, 5(3), pp.243–251.

Goldin-Meadow, S., and Mylander, C. (1998). Spontaneous sign systems created by deaf children in two cultures. *Nature*, 391(6664), pp.279–281.

Goldstein, J.M. (1993). Sampling biases in studies of gender and schizophrenia: A reply. *Schizophrenia Bulletin*, 19(1), pp.9–14.

Goetz, S.M.M., Tang, L., Thomason, M.E., Diamond, M.P., Hariri, A.R., and Carré, J.M. (2014). Testosterone rapidly increases neural reactivity to threat in healthy men: A novel two-step pharmacological challenge paradigm. *Biological Psychiatry*, 76(4), pp.324–331.

Goring, C. (1972). *The English Convict: A Statistical Study Including the Schedule of Measurements and General Anthropometric Data*. Montclair, NJ: Patterson Smith.

Goswami, U. (1998). *Cognition in Children*. Hove: Psychology Press.

Gottesman, I. I. and Shields, J. (1966). Schizophrenia in twins: 16 years' consecutive admissions to a psychiatric clinic. *British Journal of Psychiatry*, 112(489), pp.809–818.

Gottesman, I. I. and Shields, J. (1976). A critical review of recent adoption, twin, and family studies of schizophrenia: Behavioral genetics perspectives. *Schizophrenia Bulletin*, 2(3), pp.360–401.

Grant, J.E. and Kim, S.W. (2006). Medication management of pathological gambling. *Minnesota Medicine*, 89(9), pp.44–48.

Greenberg, B.S. (1988). Some uncommon television images and the Drench hypothesis. In D. Giles (2003) *Media Psychology*. Lawrence Erlbaum: London.

Greenfield, P.M and Lave, J. (1982). Cognitive aspects of informal education. In K. Durkin (1995) *Developmental Social Psychology*. Oxford: Blackwell.

Green, R. (1997). Family co-occurence of 'gender dysphoria': Ten siblings or parent-child pairs. *Archives of Sexual Behaviour*, 29(5), pp.499–507.

Green, S., Lewis, R., and Willerton, J. (2015). *Oxford AQA Psychology: A Level: Year 1 and AS*. Oxford: Oxford University Press.

Greiling H., and Buss, D.M. (2000). Women's sexual strategies: The hidden dimensions of extra pair mating. *Personality and Individual Differences*, 28, pp.929–963.

Griffin, D. and O'Donnell, I. (2012). The life sentence and parole. *British Journal of Criminology*, 52(3), pp.611–629.

Griffiths, M. (1996). Behavioural addiction: An issue for everybody? *Employee Counselling Today*, 8(3), pp.19–25.

Grosset, D., Antonini, A., Canesi, M., Pezzoli, G., Lees, A., Shaw, K., Cubo, E., Martinez-Martin, P., Rascol, O., Negre-Pages, L., Senard, A., Schwarz, J., Strecker, K., Reichmann, H., Storch, A., Löhle, M., Stocchi, F., and Grosset, K. (2009). Adherence to antiparkinson medication in a multicenter European study. *Movement Disorders*, 24(6), pp.826–832.

Guerette, R.T., Stenius, V.M., and McGloin, J.M. (2005), Understanding offense specialization and versatility: A reapplication of the rational choice perspective. *Journal of Criminal Justice*, 33(1), pp.77–87.

Gur, R.E., Cowell, P.E., Latshaw, A., Turetsky, B.I., Grossman, R.I., Arnold, S.E., Bilker, W.B., and Gur, R.C. (2000). Reduced dorsal and orbital prefrontal gray matter volumes in schizophrenia. *Archives of General Psychiatry*, 57(8), pp.761–7688.

Guthrie, R.V. (1998). *Even the Rat Was White: A Historical View of Psychology*, 2nd edition. Boston, MA: Allyn and Bacon.

Haith, M.M. (1998). Who put the cog in infant cognition? Is rich interpretation too costly? *Infant Behaviour and Development*, 21, pp.167–179.

Halamandaris, K.F. and Power, K.G. (1999). Individual differences, social support and coping with the examination stress: A study of the psychosocial and academic adjustment of first year home students. *Personality and Individual Differences*, 26(4), pp.665–685.

Han, D.H. and Renshaw, P.F. (2012). Bupropion in the treatment of problematic online game play in patients with major depressive disorder. *Journal of Psychopharmacology*, 26(5), pp.689–96.

Hanewinkel, R. and Sargent, J.D. (2009). Longitudinal study of exposure to entertainment media and alcohol use among german adolescents. *Pediatrics*, 123(3), pp.989–995.

Haney, C., Banks, C., and Zimbardo, P.G. (1973). Interpersonal dynamics in a simulated prison. *International Journal of Criminology and Penology*, 1, pp.69–97.

Haninger, K. and Thompson, K.M. (2004). Content and ratings of teen-rated video games. *Journal of the American Medical Association*, 291(7), pp.856–865.

Hare-Mustin, R.T., and Marecek, J. (1990). *Making a Difference: Psychology and the Construction of Gender*. New Haven, CT: Yale University Press.

Harlow, H.F. (1958). The nature of love. *American Psychologist*, 13(12), pp.673–685.

Harriger, J. (2014). Age differences in body size stereotyping in a sample of preschool girls. *Eating Disorders*, 23(2), pp.177–190.

Harrison, L. and Gardiner, E. (1999). Do the rich really die young? Alcohol-related mortality and social class in Great Britain, 1988–94. *Addiction*, 94(12), pp.1871–1880.

Harrison, R.J., Connor, D.F., Nowak, C., Nash, K., and Melloni, R.H., Jr. (2000). Chronic anabolic-androgenic steroid treatment during adolescence increases anterior hypothalamic vasopressin and aggression in intact hamsters. *Psychoneuroendocrinology*, 25, pp.317–338.

Harvie, M. and Howell, A. (2012). Symposium 3: Obesity-related cancers. Energy restriction and the prevention of breast cancer. *Proceedings of the Nutrition Society*, 71(2), pp.263–275.

Harvie, M., Pegington, M., Mattson, M.P., Frystyk, J., Dillon, B., Evans, G., Cuzick, J., Jebb, S., Martin, B., Cutler, R., Son, T., Maudsley, S., Carlson, O., Egan, J., Flyybierg, A., and Howell, A. (2010). The effects of intermittent or continuous energy restriction on weight loss and metabolic disease risk markers: A randomised trial in young overweight women. *International Journal of Obesity*, 35(5), pp.714–727.

Held, R., and Hein, A. (1963). Movement-produced stimulation in the development of visually guided behavior. *Journal of Comparative and Physiological Psychology*, 56(5), pp.872–876.

Heylens, G., De Cuyper, G., Zucker, K., Schelfaut, C., Elaut, E., Vanden Bossche, H., De Baere, E., and T'Sjoen, G. (2012). Gender identity disorder in twins: A review of the case report literature. *Journal of Sexual Medicine*, 9, pp.751–757.

Hill, C.Y., Rubin, Z. and Peplau, A. (1976). Breakups before marriage: The end of 103 affairs. *Journal of Social Issues*, 32, pp.147–167.

Hines, M. and Kaufman, F.R. (1994). Androgen and the development of human sex-typical behaviour: Rough and tumble play and sex of preferred playmates in children with congenital adrenal hyperplasia. *Child Development*, 65(4), pp.1042–1053.

Hines, M., Brook, C., and Conway, G. (2004). Androgen and psychosexual development: Core gender identity, sexual orientation and recalled childhood gender role behavior in women and men with congenital adrenal hyperplasia (CAH). *Journal of Sex Research*, 41, pp.75–81.

Hoekzema, E., Schagen, S., Kreukels, B., Veltman, D., Cohen-Ketteris, P., and Delemarre-van-de Waal, H. (2015). Regional volumes and spatial volumetric distribution of gray matter in the gender dysphoric brain. *Psychoneuroendocrinology*, 55, pp.59–71.

Hoffman, M.L. (2000). *Empathy and Moral Development: Implications for Caring and Justice*. Cambridge: Cambridge University Press.

Hofstede, G. (1980). *Culture's Consequences: International Differences in Work-Related Values*. Beverley Hills, CA: Sage.

Hogle, J.M., Kaye, J.T., and Curtin, J.J. (2010). Nicotine withdrawal increases threat-induced anxiety but not fear: neuroadaptation in human addiction. *Biological Psychiatry*, 68(8), pp.719–725.

Hollenbaugh, E., and Everett, M. (2013). The effects of anonymity on self-disclosure in blogs: An application of the online disinhibition effect. *Journal of Computer-Mediated Communication*, 18, pp.283–302.

Hollis, C. (2000). Adolescent schizophrenia. *Advances in Psychiatric Treatment*, 6(2), pp.83–92.

Holmes, T.H. and Masuda, M. (1974). Life change and illness susceptibility in separation and depression: Clinical research aspects. In J.P. Scott and G. Sengy (eds), *Proceedings of the American Association for the Advancement of Science Symposium*, pp.161–186.

Holmes, T.H. and Rahe, R.H. (1967). The social readjustment rating scale. *Journal of Psychosomatic Research*, 11, pp.213–218.

Holt, C.L. and Ellis, J.B. (1998). Assessing the current validity of the Bem Sex-Role Inventory. *Sex Roles*, 39(11/12), pp.929–941.

Homans, G.C. (1961) Social Behaviour: Its elementary forms. In M.A. Hogg and G.M. Vaughan (2005) *Social Psychology*, 4th edition. Harlow: Pearson Education.

Hood, K.E. and Cairns, R.B. (1989). A developmental-genetic analysis of aggressive behaviour in mice: IV. Genotype-environment interaction. *Aggressive Behaviour*, 15, pp.361–380.

Horney, K. (1926). Flight from womanhood. *Feminine Psychology*. New York: Norton.

Huang, J., Chiou, C., Ting, C., Chen, Y., and Chen, S. (2001). Sudden changes in heart rate variability during the 1999 Taiwan earthquake. *American Journal of Cardiology*, 87(2), pp.245–248.

Huchting, K., Lac, A., and LaBrie, J.W. (2008). An application of the Theory of Planned Behavior to sorority alcohol consumption. *Addictive Behaviors*, 33(4), pp.538–551

Huesmann, R.L., Mois-Titus, J., Podolski, C., and Eron, L.D. (2003). Longitudinal relations between children's exposure to TV violence and their aggressive and violent behavior in young adulthood: 1977–1992. *Developmental Psychology*, 39(2), pp.201–221.

Hughes, M. (1975). Egocentricism in pre-school children. Edinburgh University, unpublished doctoral dissertation.

Hultman, C.M., Ohman, A., Cnattingius, S., Wiselgren, I.M., and Lindstrom, L.H. (1997). Prenatal and neonatal risk factors for schizophrenia. *British Journal of Psychiatry*, 170, pp.128–133.

Iacoboni, M., Woods, R.P., Brass, M., Bekkering, H., and Mazziotta, J.C. (1999). Cortical mechanisms of human imitation. *Science*, 286(5449), pp.2526–2528.

Irwin, J. and Cressey, R. (1962). Thieves, convicts, and the inmate culture. *Social Problems*, 10, pp.142–155.

Ito, A., Abe, N., Fujii, T., Hayashi, A., Ueno, A., Mugikura, S., Takahashi, S., and Mori, E. (2012). The contribution of the dorsolateral prefrontal cortex to the preparation for deception and truth-telling. *Brain Research*, 1464, pp.43–52.

Izzard, S. (2002). Deconstructing Oedipus. *European Journal of Psychotherapy, Counselling and Health*, 5(1), pp.1–12.

Jakobsen, K.D., Frederiksen, J.N., Hansen, T., Jansson, L.B., Parnas, J., and Werge, T. (2005). Reliability of clinical ICD-10 schizophrenia diagnoses. *Nordic Journal of Psychiatry*, 59(3), pp.209–212.

Jandorf, L., Deblinger, E., Neale, J.M., and Stone, A.A. (1986). Daily versus major life events as predictors of symptom frequency. *Journal of General Psychology*, 113(3), pp.205–218.

Javitt, D.C. (2012). Twenty-five years of glutamate in schizophrenia: Are we there yet? *Schizophrenia Bulletin*, 38(5), pp.911–913.

Jibiki, I., Takizawa, Y., and Yamaguchi, N. (1991). Visual dysfunction in treated schizophrenia suggested by visual evoked potentials from pattern-reversal stimulation. *European Archives of Psychiatry and Clinical Neuroscience*, 241, pp.61–64.

Johansson, G., Aronsson, G., and Linstrom, B.O. (1978). Social psychological and neuroendocrine stress reactions in highly mechanised work. *Ergonomics*, 21, pp.583–599.

Johnstone, E.C., Crow, T.J., Frith, C.D., and Husband, J. (1976). Cerebral ventricular size and cognitive impairment in chronic schizophrenia. *Lancet*, 30, pp.924–926.

Jones, F. and Bright, J. (2001). *Stress: Myth, Theory, and Research*. Harlow: Pearson.

Jones, S.R. and Fernyhough, C. (2007). A new look at the neural diathesis–stress model of schizophrenia: The primacy of social-evaluative and uncontrollable situations. *Schizophrenia Bulletin*, 33(5), pp.1171–1177.

Kallmann, F.J. (1938). *The Genetics of Schizophrenia*. Oxford: J.J. Augustin.

Kallmann, F.J. (1946). The genetic theory of schizophrenia. *American Journal of Psychiatry*, 103(3), pp.309–322.

Kamarck, T.W., Peterman, A.H., and Raynor, D.A. (1998). The effects of the social environment on stress-related cardiovascular activation: Current findings, prospects, and implications. *Annals of Behavioral Medicine*, 20, pp.242–56.

Kandel, D.B. (1978). Similarity in real-life adolescent friendship pairs. In M. Eysenck (2001) *Psychology for A2 Level*. Hove: Psychology Press.

Kanner, A.D., Coyne, J.C., Schaefer, C., and Lazarus, R.S. (1984). Comparison of two modes of stress measurement: Daily hassles and uplifts versus major life events. *Journal of Behavioural Medicine*, 1981, 4 (1), pp.1–39.

Kanner, L. (1943). Autistic disturbances of affective contact. *Nervous Child*, 2, pp.217–250.

Kaplan, H. and Hill, K. (1985). Hunting ability and foraging success among Ache foragers. *Current Anthropology*, 26, pp.131–133.

Karasek, R.A. (1979). Job demands, job decision latitude and mental strain: Implications for job design. *Administrative Science Quarterly*, 24, pp.285–308.

Kassinove, J.I. and Schare, M.L. (2001). Effects of the 'near miss' and the 'big win' on persistence at slot machine gambling. *Psychology of Addictive Behaviors*, 15(2), pp.155–158.

Keating, D.P. (1979). Adolescent thinking. In J.P. Adelson (ed.) (1980) *Handbook of Adolescence*. New York: Wiley.

Keinlen, K.K. (1998). Developmental and social antecedents of stalking. In L. McCutcheon, V. Scott, M. Aruguete and J. Parker (2006) Exploring the link between attachment and the inclination to obsess about or stalk celebrities. *North American Journal of Psychology*, 8(2), pp.289–300.

Kelly, E.L. (1955). Consistency of the adult personality. *American Psychologist*, 10(11), pp.659–681.

Kelly, T.H., Robbins, G., Martin, C.A., Fillmore, M.T., Lane, S.D., Harrington, N.G., and Rush, C.R. (2006). Individual differences in drug abuse vulnerability: d-amphetamine and sensation-seeking status. *Psychopharmacology*, 189(1), pp.17–25.

Kendler, K.S., Aggen, S.H., Tambs, K., and Reichborn-Kjennerud, T. (2006). Illicit psychoactive substance use, abuse and dependence in a population-based sample of Norwegian twins. *Psychological Medicine*, 36(7), pp.955–962.

Kendler, K.S., Neale, M.C., Sullivan, P., Corey, L.A., Gardiner, C.O., and Prescott, C.A. (1999). A population-based twin study in women of smoking initiation and nicotine dependence. *Psychological Medicine*, 29(2), pp.299–308.

Kenrick, D.T., Keefe, R.C., Gabrielidis, C., and Cornelius, J.S. (1996). Adolescents' age preferences for dating partners: Support for an evolutionary model of life-history strategies. *Child Development*, 67, pp.1499–1511.

Keppel, G., and Underwood, B.J. (1962). Proactive inhibition in short-term retention of single items. *Journal of Verbal Learning and Verbal Behavior*, 1(3), pp.153–161.

Kerchoff, A.C. and Davis, K.E. (1962). Value consensus and need complementarity in mate selection. *American Sociological Review*, 27, pp.295–303.

Kety, S.S., Rosenthal, D., Wender, P.H., and Schulsinger, F. (1968). The types and prevalance of mental illness in the biological and adoptive families of adopted schizophrenics. In D. Rosenthal and S.S. Kety, (eds), *The Transmission of Schizophrenia*. Oxford: Pergamon Press.

Khaled, S.M., Bulloch, A.G., Williams, J.V.A., Hill, J.C., Lavorato, D.H., and Patten, S.B. (2012). Persistent heavy smoking as risk factor for major depression (MD) incidence: Evidence from a longitudinal Canadian cohort of the National Population Health Survey. *Journal of Psychiatric Research*, 46(4), pp.436–443.

Kiecolt-Glaser, J.K., Dura, J.R., Speicher, C.E., Trask, O.J., and Glaser, R.S.O. (1991). Spousal caregivers of dementia victims: Longitudinal changes in immunity and health. *Psychosomatic Medicine*, 53, pp.345–362.

Kiecolt-Glaser, J.K., Garner, W., Speicher, G.M., Penn, G.M., Holliday, J., and Glaser, R. (1984). Psychological modifiers of immunocompetence in medical students. *Psychosomatic Medicine*, 46(1), pp.7–14.

Kiecolt-Glaser, J.K., Marucha, P.T., Malarkey, W.B., Mercado, A.M., and Glaser, R. (1995). Slowing of wound healing by psychological stress. *Lancet*, 346(8984), pp.1194–1196.

Kiecolt-Glaser, J.K., Ogrocki, P., Stout, J.C., Speicher, C.E., and Glaser, R. (1987). Marital quality, marital disruption and immune function. *Psychosomatic Medicine*, 49(1), pp.13–34.

Kiehl, K., Smith, A.M., Mendrek, A., Forster, B.B., Hare, R.D., and Liddle, P.F. (2004). Temporal lobe abnormalities in semantic processing by criminal psychopaths as revealed by functional magnetic resonance imaging. *Psychiatry Research Neuroimaging*, 130, pp.27–42.

Kim, J.S., Kornhuber, H.H., Schmid-Burgk, W., and Holzmüller, B. (1980). Low cerebrospinal fluid glutamate in schizophrenic patients and a new hypothesis on schizophrenia. *Neuroscience Letters*, 20(3), pp.379–382.

Kim, P., Evans, G.W., Angstadt, M., Ho, S.S., Sripada, C.S., Swain, J.E., Liberzon, I., Phan, K. L. (2013). Effects of childhood poverty and chronic stress on emotion regulatory brain function in adulthood. *Proceedings of the National Academy of Sciences of the United States of America*, 110(46), pp.18442–18447.

King, D.L., Delfabbro, P.H., Griffiths, M.D., and Gradisar, M. (2012). Cognitive-behavioral approaches to outpatient treatment of internet addiction in children and adolescents. *Journal of Clinical Psychology*, 68(11), pp.1185–1195.

Kistler, M. and Lee, M. (2010). Does exposure to sexual hip-hop music videos influence the sexual attitudes of college students? *Mass Communication and Society*, 13, pp.67–68.

Klinesmith, J., Kasser, T., and McAndrew, F. (2006). Guns, testosterone, and aggression: An experimental test of a mediational hypothesis. *Psychological Science*, 17(7), pp.568–571.

Kocsis, R.N., Irwin, H.J., and Hayes, A.F. (1998). Organised and disorganised criminal behaviour in arsonists: A validation study of a psychological profiling concept. *Psychiatry, Psychology and Law*, 5, pp.117–133.

Kocsis, R.N., Irwin, H.J., Hayes, A.F., and Nunn, R. (2000). Expertise in psychological profiling: A comparative assessment. *Journal of Interpersonal Violence*, 15(3), pp.311–331.

Kog, E., Vandereycken, W., and Vertommen, H. (1985). The psychosomatic family model. A critical analysis of family interaction concepts. *Journal of Family Therapy*, 7, pp.31–44.

Kohlberg, L. (1958). *The Development of Modes of Moral Thinking and Choice in the Years 10 to 16*. Chicago, IL: University of Chicago.

Kohlberg, L. (1966). A cognitive-developmental analysis of children's sex role concepts and attitudes. In K. Durkin (1995) *Developmental Social Psychology*. Oxford: Blackwell.

Kohlberg, L. (1969). *Stages in the Development of Moral Thought and Action*. New York: Holt, Rinehart and Winston.

Kohlberg, L. (1976). Moral stages and moralization: The cognitive-developmental approach. *Moral Development and Behavior: Theory, Research, and Social Issues*. New York: Holt, Rinehart and Winston.

Kohlberg, L. (1984). *The Psychology of Moral Development: Essays on Moral Development*, Vol. 2, New York: Harper and Row.

Koivisto, U-K., Fellenius, J., and Sjoden, P-O. (1994). Relations between parental mealtime practices and children's food intake. *Appetite*, 22, pp.245–258.

Kosfeld, M., Heinrichs, M., Zak, P.J., Fischbacher, U., and Fehr, E. (2005). Oxytocin increases trust in humans. *Nature*, 435(7042), pp.673–676.

Kouri, E.M., Lukas, S.E., Pope, H.E., Jr, and Oliva, P.S. (1995). Increased aggressive responding in male volunteers following the administration of gradually increasing doses of testosterone cypionate. *Drug and Alcohol Dependence*, 40, pp.73–79.

Kraft, T. and Kraft, D. (2005). Covert sensitization revisited: six case studies. *Contemporary Hypnosis*, 22(4), pp.202–209.

Kurdek, L.A. (1977) Structural components and intellectual correlates of cognitive perspective-taking in first through fourth grade children. *Child Development*, 48, pp.1503–1511.

Kuss, D.J. and Griffiths, M.D. (2011). Online social networking and addiction—a review of the psychological literature. *International Journal of Environmental Research and Public Health*, 8(9), pp.3528–3552.

Kusyszyn, I. and Rutter, R. (1985). Personality characteristics of male heavy gamblers, light gamblers, nongamblers, and lottery players. *Journal of Gambling Behavior*, 1(1), pp.59–63.

Kweitel, R. and Allen, F.C. (1998). Cognitive progress associated with gambling behaviour. *Psychological Reports*, 82(1), pp.147–153.

Ladouceur, R., Jacques, C., Ferland, F., and Giroux, I. (1999). Prevalence of problem gambling: a replication study 7 years later. *Canadian Journal of Psychiatry*, 44, pp.802–804.

Ladouceur, R., Sylvain, C., Boutin, C., Lachance, S., Doucet, C., Leblond, J., and Jacques, C. (2001). Cognitive Treatment of Pathological Gambling. *Journal of Nervous and Mental Diseases*, 189(11), pp.774–780.

Langer, E.J. (1975). The illusion of control. *Journal of Personality and Social Psychology*, 32(2), pp.311–328.

Langlois, J.H. and Downs, A.C. (1980). Mothers, fathers and peers as socialisation agents of sex-typed play behaviours in young children. In K. Durkin (1995) *Developmental Social Psychology*. Oxford: Blackwell.

Lawrence, M. (ed.) (1994). *Fed Up and Hungry: Women, Oppression and Food*, London: The Women's Press.

Lazarus, R.S. and Folkman, S. (1984). *Stress, Appraisal and Coping*. New York: Springer.

Le Comber, S.C., Nicholls, B., Rossmo, D.K., and Racey, P.A. (2006). Geographic profiling and animal foraging. *Journal of Theoretical Biology*, 240(2), pp.233–240.

Leaper, C., Anderson, K. J., and Sanders, P. (1998). Moderators of effects on parents' talk to their children: A meta-analysis. *Developmental Psychology*, 34, pp3–27.

Lee, J. and Park, S. (2005). Working memory impairments in schizophrenia: A meta-analysis. *Journal of Abnormal Psychology*, 114(4), pp.599–611.

Leeson, V.C., Barnes, T.R., Harrison, M., Matheson, E., Harrison, I., Mutsatsa, S., Ron, M.A., and Joyce, E. M. (2010). The relationship between IQ, memory, executive function, and processing speed in recent-onset psychosis: 1-year stability and clinical outcome. *Schizophrenia Bulletin*, 36(2), pp.400–409.

LeFebvre, L., Blackburn, K., and Brody N. (2012). Navigating romantic relationships on Facebook: Extending the relationship dissolution model to social networking environments. Talk presented at the International Association of Relationship Research Conference, Chicago, IL.

Lefley, H.P. (1990). Culture and chronic mental illness. *Psychiatric Services*, 41(3), pp.277–286.

Lehman, A.F., Kreyenbuhl, J., Buchanan, R.W., Dickerson, F.B., Dixon, L.B., Goldberg, R., Green-Paden, L.D., Tenhula, W.N., Boerescu, D, Tek, C., Sandson, N., and Steinwachs, D.M. (2004). The Schizophrenia Patient Outcomes Research Team (PORT): Updated treatment recommendations 2003. *Schizophrenia Bulletin*, 30(2), pp.193–217.

Leshem, M., Saadi, A., Alem, N., Hendi, K., (2008). Enhanced salt appetite, diet and drinking in traditional Bedouin women in the Negev. *Appetite*, 50, pp.71–82.

LeVay, S. (1991) A difference in hypothalamic structure between heterosexual and homosexual men. *Science*, 253, pp.1034–1037.

Levenson, H. (1981). Differentiating among internality, powerful others, and chance. *Research with the Locus of Control Construct*, 1, pp.15–63.

Lidz, R.W. and Lidz, T. (1949). The family environment of schizophrenic patients. *American Journal of Psychiatry*, 106, pp.332–345.

Li, G. and Dai, X. (2009). Control study of cognitive–behavior therapy in adolescents with internet addiction disorder. *Chinese Mental Health Journal*, 23, pp.457–470.

Liebling, A. and Maruna, S. (2005). *The Effects of Imprisonment*. Cullompton: Willan Publishing.

Light, P. and Oates, J. (1990). The development of children's understanding. In I. Roth *Introduction to Psychology*, Volume 1. Milton Keynes: Open University.

Lindberg, L., Tuck, J., Asberg, M., Scalia-Tomba, G., and Bertilsson, L. (1985). Homicide, suicide and CSF 5-HIAA. *Acta Psychiatrica Scandinavica*, 71, pp.230–236.

Lindsay, W.R., Whitefield, E., and Carson, D. (2007). An assessment for attitudes consistent with sexual offending for use with offenders with intellectual disabilities. *Legal and Criminological Psychology*, 12(1), pp.55–67.

Lloyd, D.A., and Turner, R.J. (2008). Cumulative lifetime adversities and alcohol dependence in adolescence and young adulthood. *Drug and Alcohol Dependence*, 93(3), pp.217–26.

Lombroso, C. (1911). *Crime, Its Causes and Remedies*. Boston, MA: Little, Brown.

Lorenz, K. (1966). *On Aggression*. London: Methuen.

Lutchmaya, S., Baron Cohen, S., and Raggatt, P. (2002). Foetal testosterone and eye contact in 12-month-old infants. *Infant behaviour and development*, 25, pp.327–335.

Lytton, H. and Romney, D.M. (1991). Parents' differential socialization of boys and girls: A meta-analysis. *Psychological Bulletin*, 109, pp.267–296.

McConaghy, N., Armstrong, M.S., Blaszczynski, A., and Allcock, C. (1983). Controlled comparison of aversive therapy and imaginal desensitization in compulsive gambling. *British Journal of Psychiatry*, 142(4), pp.366–372.

McConaghy, N., Blaszczynski, A., and Frankova, A. (1991). Comparison of imaginal desensitisation with other behavioural treatments of pathological gambling. A two- to nine-year follow-up. *British Journal of Psychiatry*, 159(3), pp.390–393.

McCutcheon, L., Scott, V., Aruguete, M., and Parker, J. (2006). Exploring the link between attachment and the inclination to obsess about or stalk celebrities. *North American Journal of Psychology*, 8(2), 289–300.

MacDonald, A.W. and Schulz, S.C. (2009). What we know: Findings that every theory of schizophrenia should explain. *Schizophrenia Bulletin*, 35(3), pp.493–508.

McGarrigle, J. and Donaldson, M. (1974). *Conservation accidents*, Cognition, 3, pp.341–350.

McGlashan, T.H., Zipursky, R.B., Perkins, D., Addington, J., Miller, T., Woods, S.W., Hawkins, K.A., Hoffman, R.E., Preda, A., Epstein, I., Addington, D., Lindborg, S., Trzaskoma, Q., Tohen, M., and Breier, A. (2006). Randomized, double-blind trial of olanzapine versus placebo in patients prodromally symptomatic for psychosis. *The American Journal of Psychiatry*, 163(5), pp.790–799.

McGuffin, P. and Gottesman, I.I. (1985). Genetic influences on normal and abnormal development. In M. Rutter and L. Hersov (eds), *Child and Adolescent Psychiatry: Modern Approaches*, Oxford: Blackwell Scientific.

McKenna, K., Green, A., and Gleason, M. (2002). Relationship formation on the internet: What's the big attraction? *Journal of Social Issues*, 58(1), pp.9–31.

MacKenzie, D.L. and Goldstein, L. (1985). Long-term incarceration impacts and characteristics of long-term offenders: An empirical analysis. *Criminal Justice and Behavior* 12(4), pp.395–414.

McKillip, J. and Riedel, S.L. (1983). External validity of matching on physical attractiveness for same and opposite sex couples. *Journal of Applied Social Psychology*, 13, pp.328–337.

Maguire, E.A., Gadian, D.G., Johnsrude, I.S., Good, C.D., Ashburner, J., Frackowiak, R.S., and Frith, C.D. (2000). Navigation-related structural change in the hippocampi of taxi drivers. *Proceedings of the National Academy of Sciences of the United States of America*, 97(8), pp.4398–4403.

Maguire, E., Woollett, K., and Spiers, H. (2006). London taxi drivers and bus drivers: a structural MRI and neuropsychological analysis. *Hippocampus*, 16, pp.1091–1101.

Maheswaran, D., and Shavitt, S. (2000). Issues and new directions in global consumer psychology. *Journal of Consumer Psychology*, 9(2), pp.59–66.

Malarkey, W.B., Kiecolt-Glaser, J.K., and Pearl, D. (1994). Hostile behaviour during marital conflict alters pituitary and adrenal hormones. *Psychosomatic Medicine*, 56(1), pp.41–51.

Maltby, J., Day, L., McCutcheon, L.E., Houran, J., and Ashe, D. (2006). Extreme celebrity worship, fantasy proneness and dissociation: Developing the measurement and understanding of celebrity worship within a clinical personality context. *Personality and Individual Differences*, 40, pp.273–283.

Manson, S., Shore, J., and Bloom, J. (1985). The depressive experience in American Indian communities: A challenge for psychiatric theory and diagnosis. In A. Kleinman (ed.), *Culture and Depression: Studies in the Anthropology and Cross-cultural Psychiatry of Affect and Disorder*. Berkeley, CA: University of California Press.

Manstead, A.S.R. and Parker, D. (1995). Evaluating and extending the theory of planned behaviour. *European Review of Social Psychology*, 6(1), pp.69–95.

Mareschal, D. and Kaufman, J. (2012). Object permanence in infancy: Revisiting Baillargeon's drawbridge study. In A. Slater and P. Quinn (eds) *Developmental Psychology: Revisiting the Classic Studies*, London: Sage.

Marmot, M., Bosma, H., Hemingway, H., Brunner, E., and Stasfield, S. (1997). Contribution of job control and other factors to social variation in heart disease incidence. *Lancet*, 350(9073), pp.235–239.

Martin, C.L. and Halverson, C.F. (1981). A schematic processing model of sex typing and stereotyping in children. *Child Development*, 52, pp.1119–1134.

Martin, R.A., Rossmo, D.K., and Hammerschlay, N. (2009). Hunting patterns and geographical profiling. *Journal of Zoology*, 279(2), pp.111–118.

Maslow, A.H. (1943). A theory of human motivation. *Psychological Review*, 50(4), pp.370–396.

Matud, M.P. (2004). Gender differences in stress and coping styles. *Personality and Individual Differences*, 37(7), pp.1401–1415.

Mayer-Gross, W., Roth, M., and Slater, E. (1969). *Clinical Psychiatry*, (3rd ed., by Slater, E. and Roth, M.). London: Baillière, Tindall and Cassell.

Mayeux, L., Sandstrom, M.J., and Cillessen, A.H.N. (2008). Is being popular a risky proposition? *Journal of Research on Adolescence*, 18(1), pp.49–74.

Mazur, A. and Booth, A. (1998). Testosterone and dominance in men. *Behavioural and Brain Sciences*, 21(3), pp.353–363.

Mednick, S.A. Gabrielli, W.F. and Hutchings, B. (1984). Genetic influences in criminal convictions. *Science*, 224, pp.841–894.

Merikangas, K.R., Mehta, R.L., Molnar, B.E., Walters, E.E., Swendsen, J.D., Aguilar-Gaziola, S., Bilj, R., Borges, G., Caraveo-Anduaga, J.J., DeWit, D.J., Kolody, B., Vega, W.A., Witchen, H.U., and Kessler, R.C. (1998). Comorbidity of substance use disorders with mood and anxiety disorders. *Addictive Behaviors*, 23(6), pp.893–907.

Meyer, G., Schwertfeger, J., Exton, M.S., Janssen, O.E., Knapp, W., Stadler, M.A., Schedlowski, M., and Krüger, T.H.C. (2004). Neuroendocrine response to casino gambling in problem gamblers. *Psychoneuroendocrinology*, 29(10), pp.1272–1280.

Miell, D. and Croghan, R. (1996). Examining the wider context of social relationships. In D. Miell and R. Dallos (1996) *Social Interaction and Personal Relationships*. Milton Keynes: Open University.

Migneault, J.P., Adams, T.B., and Read, J.P. (2009). Application of the Transtheoretical Model to substance abuse: historical development and future directions. *Drug and Alcohol Review*, 24(5), pp.437–448.

Milgram, S. (1963). Behavioral study of obedience. *Journal of Abnormal and Social Psychology*, 67(4), pp. 371–378.

Milgram, S. (1964). Issues in the study of obedience: A reply to Baumrind. *American Psychologist*, 19(11), pp.848–852.

Miller, N.E. (1941). The frustration-aggression hypothesis. *Psychological Review*, 48, pp.337–342.

Miller, P.M., Hersen, M., Eisler, R.M., and Hemphill, D.P. (1973). Electrical aversion therapy with alcoholics: An analogue study. *Behaviour Research and Therapy*, 11(4), pp.491–497.

Miller, S.M. and Kirsch, N. (1987). Sex differences in cognitive coping with stress. In R.C. Barnett, L. Biener, and G.K. Baruch (eds), *Gender and stress* New York: Free Press.

Minuchin, S. (1978). *Psychosomatic Families: Anorexia Nervosa in Context*. Cambridge, MA: Harvard University Press.

Moghaddam, F.M. (1998). *Social Psychology: Exploring Universals Across Cultures*. New York: W.H. Freeman and Company.

Möller, I. and Krahé, B. (2008). Exposure to violent video games and aggression in German adolescents: A longitudinal analysis. *Aggressive Behavior*, 34, pp.1–14.

Montero, I., Asencio, A., Hernández, I., Masanet, M.J., Lacruz, M., Bellver, F., Iborra, M., and Ruiz, I. (2001). Two strategies for family intervention in schizophrenia: A randomized trial in a Mediterranean environment. *Schizophrenia Bulletin*, 27(4), pp.661–670.

Moran, E. (1970). Varieties of Pathological Gambling. *British Journal of Psychiatry*, 116(535), pp.593–597.

Morgan, A.B. and Lilienfeld, S.O. (2000). A meta-analytic review of the relationship between antisocial behaviour and neuropsychological measures of executive function. *Clinical Psychology Review*, 20, pp.113–136.

Morgan, M. (1982). Television and adolescents' sex role stereotypes: A longitudinal study. *Journal of Personality and Social Psychology*, 43, pp.947–955.

Morgenstern, J., Morgan, T J., McCrady, B.S., Keller, D.S., and Carroll, K.M. (2001). Manual-guided cognitive-behavioral therapy training: A promising method for disseminating empirically supported substance abuse treatments to the practice community. *Psychology of Addictive Behaviors*, 15(2), pp.83–88.

Morrison, A.P., French, P., Stewart, S.L.K., Bentall, R.P., Birchwood, M., Byrne, R., Davies, L.M., Fowler, D., Gumley, A.I., Jones, P.B., Lewis, S.W., Murray, G.K., Patterson, P., and Dunn, G. (2012). Early detection and intervention evaluation for people at risk of psychosis: multisite randomised controlled trial. *BMJ* (Clinical Research Ed.), 344, e2233.

Morrison, A.P., Turkington, D., Pyle, M., Spencer, H., Brabban, A., Dunn, G., Christodoulides, T., Dudley, R., Chapman, N., Callcott, P., Grace, T., Lumley, V., Drage, L., Tully, S., Irving, K., Cummings, A., Byrne, R., Davies, L.M., and Hutton, P. (2014). Cognitive therapy for people with schizophrenia spectrum disorders not taking antipsychotic drugs: a single-blind randomised controlled trial. *Lancet*, 383(9926), pp.1395–1403.

Murray, J. and Farrington, D.P. (2005). Parental imprisonment: Effects on boys' antisocial behaviour and delinquency through the life course. *Journal of Psychology and Psychiatry)*, 46(12), pp.1269–1278.

Murray, J.P., Liotti, M., Ingmundson, P.T., Mayberg, H.S., Pu, Y., Zamarripa, F., Liu, Y., Waldorff, M.G., Gao, J-H., and Fox, P.T. (2006). Children's brain activations while viewing televised violence revealed by fMRI. *Media Psychology*, 8, pp.25–37.

Murstein, B.I. (1972) Physical attractiveness and marital choice. In R.D. Gross (1993) *Psychology: The Science of Mind and Behaviour*, 3rd edition. Bath: Hodder and Stoughton.

Naser, R.L. and La Vigne, N.G. (2006). Family support in prisoner re-entry process: Expectations and realities. *Journal of Offender Rehabilitation*, 43(1), pp.93–106.

Nasser, E.H., Walders, N., and Jenkins, J.H. (2002). The experience of schizophrenia: What's gender got to do with it? A critical review of the current status of research on schizophrenia. *Schizophrenia Bulletin*, 28(2), pp.351–362.

Neel, J.V. (1962). Diabetes mellitus: A 'thrifty' genotype rendered detrimental by 'progress'? *American Journal of Human Genetics*, 14(4), pp. 353–362.

Noble, E.P., Blum, K., Khalsa, M.E., Ritchie, T., Montgomery, A., Wood, R.C., Fitch, R.J., Ozkaragoz, T., Sheridan, P.J., and Anglin, M.D. (1993). Allelic association of the D2 dopamine receptor gene with cocaine dependence. *Drug and Alcohol Dependence*, 33(3), pp.271–285.

Nobles, W.W. (1976). Extended self: Rethinking the so-called Negro self-concept. *Journal of Black Psychology*, 2(2), pp.15–24.

Nomura, H., Inoue, S., Kamimura, N., Shimodera, S., Mino, Y., Gregg, L., and Tarrier, N. (2005). A cross-cultural study on expressed emotion in carers of people with dementia and schizophrenia: Japan and England. *Social Psychiatry and Psychiatric Epidemiology*, 40(7), pp.564–570.

Norman, P., Armitage, C.J., and Quigley, C. (2007). The theory of planned behavior and binge drinking: assessing the impact of binge drinker prototypes. *Addictive Behaviors*, 32(9), pp.1753–1768.

Nunes, T. (1992). Children doing mathematics. In D.J. Wood (1998) *How Children Think and Learn: The Social Contexts of Cognitive Development*. Oxford: Blackwell Publishing.

Oei, T.P.S. and Raylu, N. (2004). Familial influence on offspring gambling: a cognitive mechanism for transmission of gambling behavior in families. *Psychological Medicine*, 34(7), pp.1279–1288.

Ogden, J. and Fox, P. (1994). Examination of the use of smoking for weight control in restrained and unrestrained eaters. *International Journal of Eating Disorders*, 16(2), pp.177–185.

Orobio de Castro, B., Veerman, J.W., Koops, W., Bosch, J.D., and Monshouwer, H.J. (2002). Hostile attribution of intent and aggressive behaviour: A meta-analysis. *Child Development*, 73(3), pp.916–934.

Palmer, E.J. (2003). *Offending Behaviour: Moral Reasoning, Criminal Conduct and the Rehabilitation of Offenders*. Cullompton: Willan Publishing.

Palmer, E.J. and Hollin, C.R. (1998). A comparison of patterns of moral development in young offenders and non-offenders. *Legal and Criminological Psychology*, 3, pp.225–235.

Passamonti, L., Crockett, M.J., Apergis-Schoute, A.M., Clark, L., Roew, J.B., Calder, A.J., and Robbins, T.W. (2012). Effects of acute tryptophan depletion on prefrontal-amygdala connectivity while viewing facial signals of aggression. *Biological Psychiatry*, 71(1), pp36–43.

Pasterski, V., Brain, C., Geffner, M., Hines, M., Hindmarsh, P and Brook, C. (2005). Prenatal hormones and postnatal socialization by parents as determinants of male-typical toy play in girls with congenital adrenal hyperplasia. *Child Development*, 76(1), pp.264–278.

Pasterski, V., Hines, M., Neufeld, S., Spencer, D., Acerini, C., Hughes, I., Hindmarsh, P.C., and Zucker, K. (2014). Increased cross-gender identification independent of gender role behavior in girls with congenital adrenal hyperplasia: Results from a standardized assessment of 4- to 11-year-old children. *Archives of Sexual Behavior*, 44, pp.1363–1375.

Pawlowski, B. and Sorokowski, P. (2008). Adaptive preferences for leg length in a potential partner. *Evolution and Human Behavior*, 29(2), pp.86–91.

Pelling, E.L. and White, K.M. (2009). The theory of planned behavior applied to young people's use of social networking websites. *Cyberpsychology and Behavior: The Impact of the Internet, Multimedia and Virtual Reality on Behavior and Society*, 12(6), pp.755–759.

Penton-Voak, I.S. and Perrett, D.I. (2000). Female preference for male faces changes cyclically: Further evidence. *Evolution and Human Behaviour*, 21, pp.39–48.

Perner, J., Leekam, S.R., and Wimmer, H. (1987). Three-year-olds' difficulty with false belief: The case for a conceptual deficit. *British Journal of Developmental Psychology*, 5, pp.125–137.

Perrett, D.I., Lee, K., Penton-Voak, I., Burt, D.M., Rowland, D., Yoshikawa, S., Henzi, S.P., Castles, D., and Akamatsu, S. (1997–99). Sexual dimorphism and facial attractiveness. *Nature*, 394, pp.884–886.

Petherwick, W. and Turvey, B. (2008). Nomothetic methods of criminal profiling. In B.E. Turvey (ed. *Criminal Profiling: An Introduction to Behavioural Evidence Analysis*, (3rd edition). Burlington, MA: Elsevier Academic Press.

Phillips, D. (1974). The influence of suggestion on suicide: Substantive and theoretical implications of the Werther effect. *American Sociological Review*, 39, pp.340–354.

Piaget, J. (1932). *The Moral Judgement of the Child*. London: Kagan Paul.

Piaget, J. (1952). *The Origins of Intelligence in Children*. New York: International Universities Press.

Pike, J. and Jennings, N. (2005). The effects of commercials on children's perceptions of gender appropriate toy use. *Sex Roles*, 52(1–2), pp.83–91.

Pinizzotto, A.J. (1984). Forensic psychology: Criminal personality profiling. *Journal of Police Science and Administration*. 12, pp.32–40.

Pinizzotto, A.J. and Finkel, N.J. (1990). Criminal personality profiling: An outcome and process study. *Law and Human Behaviour*, 14, pp.215–233.

Plaze, M., Paillère-Martinot, M.-L., Penttilä, J., Januel, D., de Beaurepaire, R., Bellivier, F., Andoh, J., Galinowski, A., Gallarda, T., Artiges, E., Olié, J-.P., Mangin, J.-F., Martinot, J-.L., and Cachia, A. (2011). "Where do auditory hallucinations come from?" – A brain morphometry study of schizophrenia patients with inner or outer space hallucinations. *Schizophrenia Bulletin*, 37(1), pp.212–221.

Pocklington, A.J., Rees, E., Walters, J.T.R., Han, J., Kavanagh, D.H., Chambert, K.D., Holmans, P., Moran, J., McCarroll, S.A., Kirov, G., O'Donovan, M.C., and Owen, M J. (2015). Novel findings from CNVs implicate inhibitory and excitatory signaling complexes in schizophrenia. *Neuron*, 86(5), pp.1203–1214.

Poulin-Dubois, D., Serbin, L., Eichstedt, J., Sen, M., and Beissel, C. (2002). Men don't put on make-up: Toddlers' knowledge of the gender stereotyping of household activities. *Social Development*, 12(2), pp.166–181.

Pratt, M., Green, D., MacVicar, J. and Bountrogianni, M. (1992). The mathematical parent: Parental scaffolding, parent style and learning outcomes in long division mathematics homework. *Journal of Applied Developmental Psychology*, 13(1), pp.17–34.

Premack, D. and Woodruff, G. (1978). Does the chimpanzee have a theory of mind? *Behavioral and Brain Sciences*, 4, pp.515–526.

Prochaska, J.O. and DiClemente, C. (1983). Stages and processes of self-change of smoking: Toward an integrative model of change. *Journal of Consulting and Clinical Psychology*, 51, pp.390–395.

Prochaska, J.O. and Velicer, W.F. (1997). The transtheoretical model of health behavior change. *American Journal of Health Promotion*, 12(1), pp.38–48.

Puts, D.A. (2005). Mating context and menstrual phase affect women's preferences for male voice pitch *Evolution and Human Behaviour*, 26, pp.388–397.

Rahe, R.H. and Lind, E. (1971). Psychosocial factors and sudden cardiac death. *Journal of Psychosomatic Research*, 8, pp.487–491.

Rahe, R.H., Mahan, J., and Arthur, R. (1970). Prediction of near-future health-change from subjects' preceding life changes. *Journal of Psychosomatic Research*, 14, pp.401–406.

Raine A., Lencz, T., Bihrle, S., La Casse, L., and Colletti, P. (2000). Reduced prefrontal gray matter volume and reduced autonomic activity in antisocial personality disorder. *Archives of General Psychiatry*, 57, pp.119–127.

Rebellon, C. (2006). Do adolescents engage in delinquency to attract the social attention of peers? An extension and longitudinal test of the social reinforcement hypothesis. *Journal of Research in Crime and Delinquency*, 43(4), pp.387–411.

Reed, S.C., Hartley, C., Anderson, V.E., Phillips, V.P., and Johnson, N.A. (1973). *The Psychoses: Family Studies*. Philadelphia, PA: Saunders.

Regard, M., Knoch, D., Gütling, E., and Landis, T. (2003). Brain damage and addictive behavior: A neuropsychological and electroencephalogram investigation with pathologic gamblers. *Cognitive and Behavioral Neurology*, 16(1), pp.47–53.

Reicher, S. (1987). Crowd behaviour as social action. In J.C. Turner, M.A. Hogg, P.J. Oakes, S. Reicher and M.S. Wetherell (eds), *Rediscovering the social group: A self-categorization theory*. Oxford: Basil Blackwell.

Resner, G., and Hartog, J. (1970). Concepts and terminology of mental disorder among Malays. *Journal of Cross-Cultural Psychology*, 1(4), pp.369–382.

Rhatigan, D. and Axsom, D. (2006). Using the investment model to understand battered women's commitment to abusive relationships. *Journal of Family Violence*, 21(2), pp.153–162.

Ridley, M. (2004). *Nature Via Nurture*. London: HarperCollins.

Riemsma, R.P., Pattenden, J., Bridle, C., Sowden, A.J., Mather, L., Watt, I.S., and Walker, A. (2003). Systematic review of the effectiveness of stage based interventions to promote smoking cessation. *British Medical Journal* (Clinical Research Ed.), 326(7400), pp.1175–1177.

Rivera S.M., Wakeley, A., and Langer, J. (1999). The drawbridge phenomenon: Representational reasoning or perceptual preference? *Developmental Psychology*, 35, pp.427–435.

Rizzolatti, G., Fadiga, L., Gallese, V., and Fogassi, L. (1996). Premotor cortex and the recognition of motor actions. *Brain Research and Cognitive Brain Research*, 3, pp.131–41.

Rogers, C.R. (1951). *Client-centered therapy: Its current practice, implications and theory*. Boston, MA: Houghton Mifflin.

Roger, D., Jarvis, G., and Najarian, B. (1993). Detachment and coping: The construction and validation of a new scale for measuring coping strategies. *Personality and Individual Differences*, 15, pp.619–626.

Rosengren, A., Hawken, S., Ounpuu, S., Sliwa, K., Zubaid, M., Almahmeed, W.A., Blackett, K.N., Sitthi-amorn, C., Sato, H., Yusuf, S., and the INTERHEART investigators (2004). Association of psychosocial risk factors with risk of acute myocardial infarction in 11,119 cases and 13,646 controls from 52 countries (the INTERHEART study): case-control study. *Lancet*, 364(9438), pp.953–962.

Rosenhan, D.L. (1973). On being sane in insane places. *Science*, 179(4070), pp.250–258.

Rosenthal, R.J. and Lesieur, H.R. (1992). Self-reported withdrawal symptoms and pathological gambling. *American Journal on Addictions*, 1(2), pp.150–154.

Roskies, A. (2006). Neuroscientific challenges to free will and responsibility. *Trends in Cognitive Sciences*, 10(9), pp.419–423.

Rossmo, D.K. (1995). Place, space, and police investigations: hunting serial violent criminals. In J.E. Eck and D.L. Weisburd (eds) *Crime and Place: Crime Prevention Studies*, Vol. 4. Monsey, NY: Willow Tree Press.

Rossmo, D.K. (2000). *Geographic Profiling*. Boca Raton, FL: CRC Press.

Rozi, S., Mahmud, S., and Lancaster, G. (2015). Peer pressure and family smoking habits influence smoking uptake in school going male adolescents. *European Journal of Public Health*, 25(suppl. 3), pp.176–221.

Ruble, D.N, Balaban, T., and Cooper, J. (1981). Gender constancy and the effects of sex-typed television toy commercials. *Child Development*, 52, pp.667–673.

Said, N., Lakehayli, S., El Khachibi, M., El Ouahli, M., Nadifi, S., Hakkou, F., and Tazi, A. (2015). Prenatal stress induces vulnerability to nicotine addiction and alters D2 receptors' expression in the nucleus accumbens in adult rats. *Neuroscience*, 304, pp.279–285.

Salter, A.C. (1988). *Treating Child Sex Offenders and Victims: A Practical Guide*. Newbury Park, CA: Sage.

Samuelson, M., Carmody, J., Kabat-Zinn, J., and Bratt, M.A. (2007). Mindfulness-based stress reduction in Massachusetts correctional facilities. *The Prison Journal*, 87, p.254.

Sarason, I.G., Johnson, J.H., and Siegel, J.M. (1978). Assessing the impact of life changes: development of the life experiences survey. *Journal of Consulting and Clinical Psychology*, 46, pp.932–946.

Sargent, J.D. and Hanewinkel, R. (2009). Comparing the effects of entertainment media and tobacco marketing on youth smoking in Germany. *Addiction*, 104(5), pp.815–823.

Sayette, M.A. and Tiffany, S.T. (2013). Peak provoked craving: an alternative to smoking cue-reactivity. *Addiction*, 108(6), pp.1019–1025.

Schachter, S. (1977). Studies of the interaction of psychological and pharmacological determinants of smoking: I. Nicotine regulation in heavy and light smokers. *Journal of Experimental Psychology*, 106(1), pp.5–12.

Schachter, S., Silverstein, B., Kozlowski, L.T., Herman, C.P., and Liebling, B. (1977). Effects of stress on cigarette smoking and urinary pH. *Journal of Experimental Psychology, General*, 106, pp.24–30.

Schiffer, B., Peshel, T., Paul, T., Gizwski, E., Forsting, M., Leygraf, N., Schedlowski, M., and Kruege, H.C. (2007). Structural brain abnormalities in the frontostriatal system and cerebellum in pedophilia. *Journal of Psychiatric Research*, 41(9), pp.753–762.

Shimizu, N., Oomura, Y., Plata-Salamán, C. R., & Morimoto, M. (1987). Hyperphagia and obesity in rats with bilateral ibotenic acid-induced lesions of the ventromedial hypothalamic nucleus. *Brain Research*, 416(1), pp. 153–156.

Schneider, K. (1959). *Clinical Psychopathology*. New York: Grune and Stratton.

Segerstrom, S.C. and Miller, G.E. (2004). Psychological stress and the human immune system: a meta-analytic study of 30 years of inquiry. *Psychological Bulletin*, 130(4), pp.601–630.

Selman, R.L. (1976). Social-cognitive understanding: A guide to education and clinical practice. In Durkin, K. (1998) *Developmental Social Psychology*. Cambridge: Blackwell.

Selman, R. L. (1980). *The Growth of Interpersonal Understanding*. New York: Academic Press.

Selye, H.S. (1956). *The Stress of Life*. New York: McGraw-Hill.

Shadel, W.G. and Mermelstein, R.J. (1993). Cigarette smoking under stress: the role of coping expectancies among smokers in a clinic-based smoking cessation program. *Health Psychology*, 12, pp.443–450.

Sharpe, L. and Tarrier, N. (1993). Towards a cognitive-behavioural theory of problem gambling. *British Journal of Psychiatry*, 162(3), pp.407–412.

Sheese, B.E. and Graziano, W.G. (2005). Deciding to defect: The effects of video-game violence on cooperative behavior. *Psychological Science*, 16(5), pp.354–357.

Sheldon, W.H. (1949). *Varieties of Delinquent Youth: An Introduction to Constitutional Psychology*. New York: Harper.

Sherman, L.W., Strang, H., Angel, C., Woods, D., Barnes, G.C., Bennett, S., and Inkpen, N. (2005). Effects of face-to-face restorative justice on victims of crime in four randomised, controlled trials. *Journal of Experimental Criminology*, 1, pp.367–395.

Shinkareva, S.V, Malave, V.L., Mason, R.A., Mitchell, T.M., and Just, M.A. (2011). Commonality of neural representations of words and pictures. *NeuroImage*, 54(3), pp.2418–2425.

Shin, Y.-W., Na, M.H., Ha, T.H., Kang, D.-H., Yoo, S.-Y., and Kwon, J.S. (2008). Dysfunction in configural face processing in patients with schizophrenia. *Schizophrenia Bulletin*, 34(3), pp.538–543.

Shively, C.A., Mirkes, S.J., Lu, N.Z., Henderson, J.A., and Bethea, C.L. (2003). Soy and social stress affect serotonin neurotransmission in primates. *Pharmacogenomics Journal*, 3(2), pp.114–121.

Sieber, J.E., and Stanley, B. (1988). Ethical and professional dimensions of socially sensitive research. *American Psychologist*, 43(1), pp.49–55.

Siegal, M. (1987). Are sons and daughters treated more differently by fathers than by mothers? *Developmental Review*, 7(3), pp.183–209.

Siegel, L.J., Welsh, B.C., and Senna, J.J. (2006). *Juvenile Delinquency: Theory, Practice and Law*. Belmont, CA: Thomson Wadsworth.

Signorelli, N. and Morgan, M. (eds) (1990). *Cultivation Analysis: New Directions in Media Effects Research*. New York: Sage.

Silber, K. (2014). *Schizophrenia*. Basingstoke: Palgrave Macmillan.

Silke, A. (2003). Deindividuation, anonymity, and violence: Findings from Northern Ireland. *The Journal of Social Psychology*, 143(4), pp.493–499.

Silverman, I. (1971) Physical attractiveness and courtship. *Sexual Behaviour*, 4, pp.22–25.

Silverstein, B., Kelly, E., Swan, J., and Kozlowski, L.T. (1982). Physiological predisposition toward becoming a cigarette smoker: Experimental evidence for a sex difference. *Addictive Behaviors*, 7(1), pp.83–86.

Simon, R.J. (1973). Depression and schizophrenia in hospitalized black and white mental patients. *Archives of General Psychiatry*, 28(4), p.509.

Singh, D. (1993) Adaptive significance of female attractiveness: The role of waist to hip ratio. *Journal of Personality and Social Psychology*, 65, pp.293–307.

Skinner, B.F. (1938). *The Behaviour of Organisms: an Experimental Analysis*. Oxford: Appleton-Century.

Skinner, B.F. (1953). *Science And Human Behavior*. New York: Simon and Schuster.

Slaby, R.G. and Frey, K.S. (1975). Development of gender constancy and selective attention to same sex models. *Child Development*, 46, pp.849–856.

Slater, M.D., Kelly, K.J., Lawrence, F.R., Stanley, L.R., and Comello, M.L.G. (2011). Assessing media campaigns linking marijuana non-use with autonomy and aspirations: "Be Under Your Own Influence" and ONDCP's 'Above the Influence'. *Prevention Science: The Official Journal of the Society for Prevention Research*, 12(1), pp.12–22.

Slutske, W.S., Zhu, G., Meier, M.H., and Martin, N.G. (2010). Genetic and environmental influences on disordered gambling in men and women. *Archives of General Psychiatry*, 67(6), pp.624–630.

Smith, G.M. (1980). Perceived effects of substance use: a general theory. *NIDA Research Monograph*, 30, pp.50–58.

Snook, B., Cullen, R., Bennell., C., Taylor, P., and Gendreau, P. (2008).The criminal profiling illusion: what's behind the smoke and mirrors? *Criminal Justice and Behavior*, 35, pp.1257–1276.

Snook B, Eastwood, J., Gendreau, P., Goggin, C., and Cullen, R. (2007). Taking stock of criminal profiling: A narrative review and meta-analysis. *Criminal Justice and Behavior*, 34, pp.437–453.

Snook, B., Gendreau, P., Bennell, C., and Taylor, P. (2008). Criminal profiling: Granfalloons and Gobbledygook. *Skeptic*, 14(22), pp.36–41.

Soenens, B., Vansteenkiste, M., Vandereycken, W., Luyten, P., Sierens, E., and Goossens, L. (2008). Perceived parental psychological control and eating-disordered symptoms: Maladaptive perfectionism as a possible intervening variable. *Journal of Nervous and Mental Disease*, 196(2), pp.144–152.

Sprecher, S. (1998). Insiders' perspectives on reasons for attraction to a close other. In M.A. Hogg and G.M. Vaughan (2005) *Social Psychology*, 4th edition. Harlow: Pearson Education.

Stack, S. (2000). Media impacts on suicide: A quantitative review of 293 findings. *Social Science Quarterly*, 81, pp.957–971.

Stams, G.J., Brugman, D., Dekovi, M., van Rosmalen, L., van der Laam, P., and Gibbs, J.C. (2006). The moral judgement of juvenile delinquents: A meta-analysis. *Journal of Abnormal Child Psychology*, 34, pp.697–713.

Stein, A., Walters, E.A., and Fairburn, C.G. (1995). Eating habits and attitudes among mothers of children with feeding disorders. *British Medical Journal*, 310(6974), p.228.

Stein, A., Woolley, H., Cooper, S.D., and Fairburn, C.G. (1994). An observational study of mothers with eating disorders and their infants. *Journal of Child Psychology and Psychiatry*, 35(4), pp.733–748.

Stephenson, W. (1953). *The Study of Behavior; Q-technique and its Methodology*. Chicago, IL: University of Chicago Press.

Sterzer, P., Stadler, C., Krebs, A., Kleinschmidt, A., and Poustka, F. (2005). Abnormal responses to emotional visual stimuli in adolescents with conduct disorder. *Biological Psychiatry*, 57, pp.7–15.

Stevens Aubrey, J. and Frisby, C.M. (2011). Sexual objectification in music videos: a content analysis comparing gender and genre. *Mass Communication and Society*, 14, pp.475–501.

Stevens Aubrey, J. and Harrison, K. (2004). The gender role content of children's favorite TV programs and its links to their gender-related perceptions. *Media Psychology*, 6, pp.111–146.

Stever, G. (2010). Fan behavior and lifespan development theory: Explaining parasocial and social attachment to celebrities. *Journal of Adult Development*, 18, pp.1–7.

Stone, A.A. and Neale, J.M. (1984). New measure of daily coping: development and preliminary results. *Journal of Personality and Social Psychology*, 46, pp.892–906.

Subotnik, K.L., Goldstein, M.J., Nuechterlein, K.H., Woo, S.M., and Mintz, J. (2002). Are communication deviance and expressed emotion related to family history of psychiatric disorders in schizophrenia? *Schizophrenia Bulletin*, 28(4), pp.719–729.

Sulkunen, P. (2009). Images of addiction: Representations of addictions in films. *Addiction Research and Theory*, 15(6), pp.543–559.

Sussman, S.Y., and Ames, S.L. (2001). *The Social Psychology Of Drug Abuse*. Buckingham: Open University Press.

Sutherland, E.H. (1939). *Principles of Criminology*, 3rd ed. Chicago, IL: JP Lippincott Co.

Swaab, D.F. and Fliers, E. (1985). A sexually dimorphic nucleus in the human brain. *Science*, 228(4703), pp.1112–1115.

Sykes, D. (1958). *The Society of Captives: A Study of a Maximum Security Prison*. Princeton, NJ: Princeton University Press.

Tajfel, H. and Turner, J.C. (1979). An integrative theory of intergroup conflict. *The Social Psychology of Intergroup Relations*, 33(47), p.74.

Tamres, L.K., Janicki, D., and Helgeson, V.S. (2002). Sex differences in coping behavior: A meta-analytic review and an examination of relative coping. *Personality and Social Psychology Review*, 6, pp.2–30.

Tanaka-Matsumi, J., and Marsella, A.J. (1976). Cross-cultural variations in the phenomenological experience of depression: I. Word association studies. *Journal of Cross-Cultural Psychology*, 7(4), pp.379–396.

Tarbox, S.I., and Pogue-Geile, M.F. (2006). Spontaneous dyskinesia and familial liability to schizophrenia. *Schizophrenia Research*, 81(2–3), pp.125–137.

Tate, J.C., Stanton, A.L., Green, S.B., Schmitz, J.M., Le, T., and Marshall, B. (1994). Experimental analysis of the role of expectancy in nicotine withdrawal. *Psychology of Addictive Behaviors*, 8(3), pp.169–178.

Taylor, S.E., Klein, L.C., Lewis, B.P., Gruenewald, T.L., Gurung, R.A., and Updegraff, J.A. (2000). Bio-behavioral responses to stress in females: tend-and-befriend, not fight-or-flight. *Psychological Review*, 107(3), pp.411–429.

Tengco-Pacquing, C., Vega, B.C., Magpantay, J., Zapanta, J., Tolentino, R., and Varona, A. (2013). A brief report on celebrity attitude scale data collected in the Philippines. *North American Journal of Psychology*, 15(1), pp.213–214.

Terracciano, A. and Costa, P.T. (2004). Smoking and the Five-Factor Model of personality. *Addiction*, 99(4), pp.472–481.

Terrace, H., Petitto, L., Sanders, R., and Bever, T. (1979). Can an ape create a sentence? *Science*, 206(4421), pp.891–902.

Thibaut, J.W. and Kelley, H.H. (1959). The social psychology of groups. In M.A. Hogg and G.M. Vaughan (2005) *Social Psychology*, 4th edition. Harlow: Pearson Education.

Thomas, C.W. and Petersen, D.M. (1977). *Prison Organization and Inmate Subcultures*. Indianapolis, IN: Bobbs-Merrill.

Thorndike, E.L. (1898). Animal intelligence: An experimental study of the associative processes in animals. *The Psychological Review*, 2(4), pp.i–109.

Thornhill, R., Gangestad, S.W., and Comer, R. (1995). Human female orgasm and male fluctuating asymmetry. *Animal Behaviour*, 50, pp.1601–1615.

Tonstad, S., Tønnesen, P., Hajek, P., Williams, K.E., Billing, C.B., and Reeves, K.R. (2006). Effect of maintenance therapy with varenicline on smoking cessation: a randomized controlled trial. *Journal of the American Medical Association*, 296(1), pp.64–71.

Torrey, E.F. (1992). Are we overestimating the genetic contribution to schizophrenia? *Schizophrenia Bulletin*, 18(2), pp.159–170.

Travis, J. and Waul, M. (2003). *Prisoners Once Removed: The Impact of Incarceration and Re-Entry on Children, Families And Community*. New York: Universal Institute Press.

Triandis, H., Lambert, W., Berry, J., Lonner, W., Heron, A., Brislin, R., and Draguns, J. (eds) (1980). *Handbook of Cross-Cultural Psychology*. Boston, MA: Allyn and Bacon.

Tseng, W.-S., and Hsu, J. (1969). Chinese culture, personality formation and mental illness. *International Journal of Social Psychiatry*, 16(1), pp.5–14.

Turvey, B.E. (2012). *Criminal Profiling: An Introduction to Behavioural Evidence Analysis*, 4th ed. San Diego, CA: Elsevier.

Tyndale, R.F. and Sellers, E.M. (2002). Genetic Variation in CYP2A6-Mediated Nicotine Metabolism Alters Smoking Behavior. *Therapeutic Drug Monitoring*, 24(1), pp.163–171.

Uchino, B.N., Cacioppo, J.T., and Kiecolt-Glaser, J.K. (1996). The relationship between social support and physiological processes: A review with emphasis on underlying mechanisms and implications for health. *Psychological Bulletin*, 119, pp.488–531.

Uhl, G., Elmer, G., Labuda, M., and Pickens, R. (1995). Genetic influences on drug abuse. In F. Bloom and D. Kupfer (eds), *Psychopharmacology: The Fourth Generation Of Progress*. New York: Raven Press.

Utz, S. (2015). The function of self disclosure on social networking sites: Not only intimate but also positive and entertaining self-disclosures increase the feeling of connection. *Computers in Human Behavior*, 45, pp.1–10.

van de Vijver, Fons J. R. (2007). Cultural and gender differences in gender-role beliefs, sharing household task and child-care responsibilities, and well-being among immigrants and majority members in the Netherlands. *Sex Roles*, 57, pp.813–824.

Van Gool, E., Van Ouytsel, J., Ponnet, K., and Walrave, M. (2015). To share or not to share? Adolescents' self-disclosure about peer relationships on Facebook: An application of the Prototype Willingness Model. *Computers in Human Behavior*, 44, pp.230–239.

van Schie, E.G.M. and Wiegman, O. (1997). Children and videogames: Leisure activities, aggression, social integration, and school performance. *Journal of Applied Social Psychology*, 27(13) , pp.1175–1194.

Van Yperen, N. and Buunk, B. (1990), A longitudinal study of equity and satisfaction in intimate relationships. *European Journal of Social Psychology*, 20, pp.287–309.

Verdejo-García, A., Bechara, A., Recknor, E.C., and Pérez-García, M. (2007). Negative emotion-driven impulsivity predicts substance dependence problems. *Drug and Alcohol Dependence*, 91(2–3), pp.213–219.

Vogt, T.M., Mullooly, J.P., Ernst, D., Pope, C.R., and Hollis, J.F. (1992). Social networks as predictors of ischemic heart disease, cancer, stroke and hypertension: incidence, survival and mortality. *Journal of Clinical Epidemiology*, 45, pp.659–66.

Wagner, G.C., Beuving, L.J., Hutchinson, R.R. (1979). Androgen dependency of aggressive target biting and paired fighting in male mice. *Physiology and Behaviour*, 22, pp.43–46.

Walster, E. and Festinger, L. (1962). The effectiveness of 'overheard' persuasive communications. *Journal of Abnormal and Social Psychology*, 65, pp.395–402.

Walters, G.D. (1999). *The Addiction Concept: Working Hypothesis Or Self-Fulfilling Prophecy?* Englewood Cliffs, NJ: Prentice Hall.

Walters, G.D. and Gilbert, A.A. (2000). Defining addiction: Contrasting views of clients and experts. *Addiction Research*, 8(3), pp.211–220.

Ward, A., Ramsay, R., and Treasure, J. (2000). Attachment research in eating disorders. *British Journal of Medical Psychology*, 73(Pt 1), pp.35– 51.

Ward, A., Ramsay, R., Turnbull, S., Steele, M., Steele, H., and Treasure J. (2001) Attachment in anorexia nervosa: A transgenerational perspective. *British Journal of Medical Psychology*, 74(Pt 4), pp.497–505.

Warren, C. and Cooper, C.J. (1988). Psychological effects of dieting. *British Journal of Clinical Psychology*, 27, pp.269–270.

Watanabe, H., Kodama, M., Tanabe, N., Nakamura, Y., Nagai, T., Sato, M., Okabe, M., and Aizawa, Y. (2008). Impact of earthquakes on risk for pulmonary embolism. *International Journal of Cardiology*, 129 (1), pp.152–154.

Watson, J.B. (1930). *Behaviorism* (revised edition). New York: W.W. Norton and Co.

Watts, S.A., Noble, S.L., Smith, P.O., and Disco, M. (2002). First-line pharmacotherapy for tobacco use and dependence. *Journal of the American Board of Family Medicine*, 15(6), pp.489–497.

Whaley, A.L. (2004). Ethnicity/race, paranoia, and hospitalization for mental health problems among men. *American Journal of Public Health*, 94(1), pp.78–81.

Williams, J. and Best, D. (1990). Measuring sex stereotypes: A multi-nation study. In W. Stainton Rogers and R. Stainton Rogers (2001) *The Psychology of Gender and Sexuality*. Maidenhead: Open University Press.

Wills, T.A., Vaccaro, D., and McNamara, G. (1992). The role of life events, family support, and competence in adolescent substance use: a test of vulnerability and protective factors. *American Journal of Community Psychology*, 20(3), pp.349–374.

Wimmer, H. and Perner, J. (1983). Beliefs about beliefs: Representations and constraining function of wrong beliefs in young children's understanding of deception. *Cognition*, 13, pp.103–128.

Wing, L. and Gould, J. (1979). Severe impairments of social interaction and associated abnormalities in children: Epidemiology and classification, *Journal of Autism and Developmental Disorders*, 9, pp.11–29.

Wood, D. and Middleton, D. (1975). A study of assisted problem solving. *British Journal of Psychology*, 66(2), pp.181–191.

Wood, D.J., Bruner, J.S., and Ross, G. (1976). The role of tutoring in problem solving. *Journal of Child Psychology and Psychiatry*, 17(2), pp.89–100.

Woodhams, J., Hollin, C.R., and Bull, R. (2007). The psychology of linking crimes: A review of the evidence. *Legal and Criminological Psychology*, 12, pp.233–249.

Wynne, L.C. and Singer, M.T. (1963). Thought disorder and family relations of schizophrenics: I. A research strategy. *Archives of General Psychiatry*, 9, pp.191–198.

Young, K.S. (2007). Cognitive behavior therapy with Internet addicts: treatment outcomes and implications. *Cyberpsychology and Behavior: The Impact of the Internet, Multimedia and Virtual Reality on Behavior and Society*, 10(5), pp.671–679.

Young, W.C. (1964). Hormones and sexual behaviour. In T. Cooper and I. Roth (eds) *Challenging Psychological Issues*. Milton Keynes: Open University.

Zamble, E. (1992). Behavior and adaptation in long-term prison inmates' descriptive longitudinal results. *Criminal Justice and Behavior*, 19(4), pp.409–425.

Zak, P. (2011). Oxytocin: Could the trust hormone 'rebond' our troubled world? http://guardian.com/science/2011/aug/21/oxytocin-zak-neuroscience-trust-hormone

Zimbardo, P.G. (1969). The human choice: Individuation, reason, and order versus deindividuation, impulse, and chaos. In W.T. Arnold and D. Levine (eds), *Nebraska symposium on Motivation*, Vol. 17. Lincoln, NE: University of Nebraska Press.

Zimbardo, P.G. (1972). Comment: Pathology of imprisonment. *Society*, 9(6), pp.4–8.

Zimbardo, P.G., Banks, P.G., Haney, C., and Jaffe, D. (1973). Pirandellian Prison: The mind is a formidable jailor. *New York Times Magazine*, 8 April 1973, pp.38–60.

Index

Wilson, M. 407–408
Wimmer, H. 232, 233
Wing, L. 233
withdrawal symptoms/syndrome 382, 482–483
Woodruff, G. 232
working memory, and schizophrenia 269
work-life balance 373
workload, and stress 373
workplace stress 372–376

Y

Z

Acknowledgements

Cover; Alfred Pasieka/Science Photo Library

p8: Getty Images; **p41:** Editorial Image, LLC/Alamy Stock Photo; **p42:** Corbis; **p74:** Shutterstock; **p75:** Bettmann/Corbis; **p76:** Mary Evans Picture Library; **p81:** Tony Marshall / Associated Newspapers/REX/ Shutterstock; **p86:** © Chris Slane; **p93:** F1online digitale Bildagentur GmbH/Alamy; **p112:** Susan Kuklin/Science Photo Library; **p119:** Courtesy Scott Dobson-Mitchell; **p128:** svetikd/iStock; **p129:** Shutterstock; **p130:** Luis Montanya/Marta Montanya/Sciencephotolibrary; **p131:** Eky Studio/ Shutterstock; **p132:** mikeledray/Shutterstock; **p135:** Perrett, D.I., Lee, K., Penton-Voak, I., Burt, D.M., Rowland, D., Yoshikawa, S., Henzi, S.P., Castles, D. & S. Akamatsu, S. (1998) Sexual dimorphism and facial attractiveness. Nature 394, 884–886; **p140:** Broadimage/REX/Shutterstock; **p146:** Shutterstock; **p150:** Shutterstock; **p158:** Breuel/PicturePerfect/ Age Fotostock; **p170:** Paolo Bona/Shutterstock.com; **p171:** Shutterstock; **p172:** Jan Kruger/Getty Images; **p173l:** Allstar Picture Library/Alamy; **p173r:** dpa picture alliance/Alamy; **p175l:** Terrence Jennings/Retna Ltd./ Corbis; **p175r:** vortexdigital/Shutterstock.com; **p180:** Getty Images; **p181:** CTK/Alamy Stock Photo; **p182:** Yva Momatiuk & John Eastcott/ Minden Pictures/Corbis; **p187:** Nina Prommer/epa/Corbis; **p188:** keith morris / Alamy Stock Photo; **p189:** Shutterstock; **p190:** Fotosearch/Getty Images; **p196:** 2/Ocean/Corbis; **p199l:** Mary Evans Picture Library/Alamy Stock Photo; **p199r:** Private Collection / © Look and Learn / Bridgeman Images; **p204:** Shutterstock; **p208:** Sam Bloomberg-Rissman/Eddy Joaquim/Blend Images/Corbis; **p209:** Shutterstock; **p210:** © Archives Jean Piaget; **p211:** Shutterstock; **p212:** Shutterstock; **p219:** Heritage Images/Corbis; **p220:** Shutterstock; **p221:** Danita Delimont/Alamy; **p244:** Shutterstock; **p245 & p253:** slightlywarped.com; **p259:** With permission of Dr M. Picchioni; **p265:** Shutterstock; **p266:** Ellan Young/ Science Photo Library; **p273:** National Library of Medicine (NLM); **p275:** Dr P. Marazzi/Science Photo Library; **p276t:** Paul Doyle/Alamy Stock Photo; **p276b:** Aaron Haupt/Science Photo Library; **p277:** Photo Business Wire; **p280:** Bruce Ayres/Getty Images; **p294:** Getty Images; **p295:** Comstock/Getty Images; **p297:** Theo Allofs/Corbis; **p298:** Shutterstock; **p300:** Jim Brandenburg/Minden Pictures/Corbis; **p305:** Hanan Isachar/ JAI/Corbis; **p311:** © Neal Miller Estate. By permission of Professor E. Coons; **p316:** Photo Image Press/Splash News/Corbis; **p323l:** Donaldson Collection/Michael Ochs Archives/Getty Images; **p323r:** Ken McKay/ ITV/REX/Shutterstock; **p324:** Shutterstock; **p327:** Alan Davidson/FFR/ Getty Images; **p335:** Oak Ridge National Laboratory/Us Department Of Energy/Science Photo Library; **p352:** Shutterstock; **p353:** Shutterstock; **p361:** Alfred Pasieka/Science Photo Library; **p363:** Shutterstock; **p378:** Shutterstock; **p380:** s5iztok/iStock; **p396:** Shutterstock; **p397:** Oktay Cilesiz/Anadolu Agency/Getty Images; **p402:** Shutterstock; **p405:** Shutterstock; **p417:** Philippe Lissac / Godong/Godong/Corbis; **p426:** Mark Harvey/Alamy Stock Photo; **p427:** Cultura Creative (RF)/Alamy Stock Photo; **p433:** Ciaran McCrickard/REX/Shutterstock; **p434:** Archive Photos/Getty Images; **p437:** Mirrorpix/Trinity Mirror; **p439:** REX/ Shutterstock; **p447:** Mary Evans Picture Library; **p460:** The LIFE Picture Collection/Getty Images; **p465:** Ros Drinkwater/Alamy Stock Photo; **p466:** Stu Forster/Getty Images; **p478:** Ace Stock Limited/Alamy Stock Photo; **p479:** Shutterstock; **p483:** Rob Judges/Oxford University Images/ Science Photo Library; **p507:** Aj Photo/Hop Americain/Science Photo Library; **p510:** George Rose/Getty Images.

Artwork by Aptara

We are grateful to the following for permission to reproduce copyright material:

An extract on pp.78-79 from *Essays on Moral Development: The Philosophy of Moral Development,* (Volume I) by Lawrence Kohlberg, copyright © 1981 by Lawrence Kohlberg. Reproduced by permission of HarperCollins Publishers; An extract on p.82 from "Issues and New Directions in Global Consumer Psychology" by Durairaj Maheswaran and Sharon Shavitt, published in *Journal of Consumer Psychology,* Vol. 9 (2), pp.59-66, copyright © 2000, Elsevier, Inc. Reproduced by permission of Professor Durairaj Maheswaran and Professor Sharon Shavitt; Figure 1.3, p.84 'A Schematic mapping of the main philosophical positions on freedom of the will' adapted from "Neuroscientific challenges to free will and responsibility" by Adina Roskies, published in *Trends In Cognitive Sciences,* Vol. 10 (9), pp.419-423, September 2006, copyright © 2006 Elsevier Ltd. All rights reserved; An extract on p.97 from *Behaviorism,* revised edition by John B. Watson, p.104, copyright © 1924, 1925 by the People's Institute Publishing Company. Copyright © 1930 by W. W. Norton & Company, Inc., renewed 1952, 1953, © 1958 by John B. Watson. Used by permission of W. W. Norton & Company, Inc.; An extract on p.124 from 'Ethical and professional dimensions of socially sensitive research' by Joan E. Sieber and Barbara Stanley, published in *American Psychologist,* Vol. 43 (1), pp.49-55, January 1988, copyright © 1988, American Psychological Association; The Celebrity Attitude Scale on p.160 from "Extreme celebrity worship, fantasy proneness and dissociation: Developing the measurement and understanding of celebrity worship within a clinical personality context" by John Maltby, Liza Day, Lynn E. McCutcheon, James Houran and Diane Ashe published in *Personality and Individual Differences,* Vol. 40 (2), pp.273-283, January 2006, copyright © 2005 Elsevier Ltd. All rights reserved; Figure 4.5, p.233 'Asperger syndrome: the triad of impairments' www.autism.org.uk/, copyright © The National Autistic Society; Activity 5.1, p.247 An extract

From the author team:

David Cox: To my special adult children and very special grandchildren.

Kevin Silber: To my wonderful grandchildren, Zackery and Eden.

from "Listening to the Wherewho: A Lived Experience of Schizophrenia" by Molly Watson, published in *Schizophrenia Bulletin,* Vol. 41 (1), pp.6-8, January 2015, copyright © 2015, Oxford University Press; An extract on p.265 from "A cross-cultural study on expressed emotion in carers of people with dementia and schizophrenia: Japan and England" by Hiroko Nomura, Shimpei Inoue, Naoto Kamimura, Shinji Shimodera, Yoshio Mino, Lynsey Gregg and Nicholas Tarrier, published in *Social Psychiatry and Psychiatric Epidemiology,* Vol. 40 (7), pp.564-570, July 2005, copyright © 2005, Springer-Verlag; An extract on p.283 from "Cognitive therapy for people with schizophrenia spectrum disorders not taking antipsychotic drugs: a single-blind randomised controlled trial" by Anthony P. Morrison, Douglas Turkington, Melissa Pyle, Helen Spencer, Alison Brabban, Graham Dunn, Tom Christodoulides, Rob Dudley, Nicola Chapman, Pauline Callcott, Tim Grace, Victoria Lumley, Laura Drage, Sarah Tully, Kerry Irving, Anna Cummings and Rory Byrne et al, published in *The Lancet,* Vol. 383 (9926), pp.1395-1403, April 2014, copyright © 2014 Elsevier Ltd. All rights reserved; Quotation on p.315 by Dr Walter Kaye, from "Understanding the Oxytocin System and Its Relevance to Psychiatry" by Simone Shamay-Tsoory and Larrry J. Young, published in *Biological Psychiatry,* Vol. 79 (3), pp.150-152, February 2016. Reproduced by kind permission of Dr Kaye; Data on p.331 adapted from "Statistics on Obesity, Physical Activity and Diet" March 2015, Health and Social Care Information Centre. Reproduced by permission; A data sample on p.342 adapted from "Restrained and unrestrained eating" by C. Peter Herman and Deborah Mack, published in *Journal of Personality,* Vol. 43 (1), pp.647-660, December 1975, copyright © 2006, John Wiley and Sons; Figure 7.3, p.358 'General Adaptation syndrome' from *The Stress of Life* by H.S. Selye, McGraw-Hill, NY, 1956; Table 7.1, p.367 from 'The social readjustment rating scale' by Thomas H. Holmes and Richard H. Rahe, published in *Journal of Psychosomatic Research,* Vol. 11 (2), pp.213-218, August 1967, copyright © 1967 Elsevier Inc; Table 7.2, p.368 from 'Comparison of two modes of stress measurement: Daily hassles and uplifts versus major life events' by Allen D. Kanner, published in *Journal of Behavioral Medicine,* Vol. 4 (1), pp.1-39, January 1981, copyright © 1981, Plenum Publishing Corporation; Figure 7.6, p.373 from " Job Demands, Job Decision Latitude and Mental Strain: Implications for Job Redesign" by R. A. Karasek, as published in *Administrative Science Quarterly,* Vol. 24 (2) pp.285-308, 1979, copyright © 1979, SAGE Publications; Figures 9.1, 9.2 and 9.3 on pp.429, 431, 432 Police-recorded Crime from *Crime Survey for England and Wales,* http://www.ons.gov.uk, Office for National Statistics, © Crown copyright 2015. Licensed under the Open Government Licence v.3.0; Table 9.1 and Figure 9.11, pp.437, 445 from "An Experimental Evaluation on the Utility of Burglary Profiles Applied in Active Police Investigations" by Bryanna Hahn Fox and David P. Farrington, published in *Criminal Justice and Behaviour* Vol 42 (2), pp.156-175, February 2015, copyright © 2015, © SAGE Publications; Quotation on p.440 by Crawford Wilson from "Mapping the Criminal Mind" interview by Kim Rossmo, *New Scientist,* Vol. 178 (2392), pp.46-49, 26/04/2003, https://www.newscientist. com, copyright © 2003 Reed Business Information 0- UK. All rights reserved. Distributed by Tribune Content Agency; Dictionary definition on p.480, from the *Oxford English Dictionary online* http://www.oxforddictionaries. com, copyright © Oxford University Press; Figure 10.2, p.491 from "Chronic Stress, Drug Use, and Vulnerability to Addiction" by Rajita Sinha, published in *Annals of the New York Academy of Sciences,* Vol. 1141, Addiction Reviews 2008, pp.105-130, October 2008, Fig 1, copyright © 2008 New York Academy of Sciences; An extract on p.495 from The US Surgeon General concerning the definition of nicotine addiction, 2010. Source: US Department of Health and Human Services; Table 10.2, p.518 from "Medication Management of Pathological Gambling" by Jon E. Grant, J.D., M.D., M.P.H. and Suck Won Kim, M.D. published in *Minnesota Medicine,* Vol. 89 (9), pp.44-48, September 2006, copyright © 2006, Minnesota Medical Association. Reproduced with permission; Figure 10.6, p.523 "Theory of Planned Behaviour" by Icek Azjen, http://people.umass.edu/aizen/tpb.diag. html, copyright © Icek Azjen, 2006. Reproduced with permission; Table 10.3, p.530 from "Stages and processes of self-change of smoking: Toward an integrative model of change" by J. O. Prochaska and C. DiClemente, published in *Journal of Consulting and Clinical Psychology,* Vol. 51, pp.390-395, copyright © 1983, APA. Reproduced with permission; and Question and mark scheme on p.539 from *AQA A-level PSYCHOLOGY (7182/2) Paper 2 Psychology in Context Specimen Material,* Question 3, www.aqa.org.uk/. AQA examination questions are reproduced by permission of AQA.

We have made every effort to trace and contact all copyright holders before publication, but if notified of any errors or omissions, the publisher will be happy to rectify these at the earliest opportunity.